The Hebrew Bible

THE HEBREW BIBLE

A **BRIEF** SOCIO-LITERARY INTRODUCTION

Norman K. Gottwald

FORTRESS PRESS
MINNEAPOLIS

THE HEBREW BIBLE
A Brief Socio-Literary Introduction

Cover image: Darius I the Great (550–486 B.C.E.) giving audience. Detail of a relief in the treasury of the palace at Persepolis, Persia. Achaemenid Period, 491–486 B.C.E. Photo: © SEF / Art Resource, N.Y. Used by permission
Cover design: Laurie Ingram
Book design: Zan Ceeley, Trio Bookworks

Library of Congress Cataloging-in-Publication Data
Gottwald, Norman K. (Norman Karol)
 The Hebrew Bible : a brief socio-literary introduction / Norman K. Gottwald.
   p. cm.
 Includes bibliographical references (p.   ) and index.
 ISBN 978-0-8006-6308-7 (alk. paper)
 1. Bible. O.T.—Social scientific criticism—Textbooks. I. Title.
 BS1182.6.G68 2009
 221.6—dc22   2008038874

The paper used in this publication meets the minimum requirements of American National Standard for Information Sciences—Permanence of Paper for Printed Library Materials, ANSI Z329.48-1984.

Manufactured in Canada

13   12   11   10   09   1   2   3   4   5   6   7   8   9   10

To all those in whose company I have learned what I know of the Hebrew Bible

~

Family and friends
Students and colleagues
Scholars and amateurs
Believers and doubters
Activists and quietists

CONTENTS

IV: HOME RULE UNDER GREAT EMPIRES: ISRAEL'S COLONIAL RECOVERY

Conclusion: The Interplay of Text, Concept, and Setting in the Hebrew Bible   337

ILLUSTRATIONS

Figures (cont.)

Gallery (following page 232)

A   Amenhotep as scribe
B   Standard of Ur, side B
C   "High place" in Megiddo
D   Head of a prosperous Israelite woman
E   Bust of a woman with an Egyptian hairstyle
F   Clay lid of an Egyptian anthropoid coffin
G   Shrine of the Steles
H   Jebel Musa (Mount Sinai)
I   Israelites carrying the Ark of the Covenant
J   Stone pillars from a possible storehouse at Hazor
K   Goddess of the Nome (province) of Thebes with club, bow, and quiver
L   Square altar with horns from Megiddo
M   Tunnel of Siloam
N   Female figurine from Gath
O   Horses and riders
P   Tambourine girl and double pipe player
Q   Brown jasper seal with Hebrew inscription
R   Winged human-headed bull from the Northwest Palace of Ashurnasirpal II
S   Darius I the Great
T   Ishtar Gate
U   Representatives of the conquered people present a gift to Darius I
V   Shadrach, Meshach, and Abednego
W   Early portrait of Alexander the Great
X   Two bronze coins
Y   Caves of Qumran
Z   Scroll of Isaiah

AA *Judea capta* coin
BB Roman soldiers taking spoils from Temple in Jerusalem

Tables

Charts

Maps

On the Website: www.fortresspress.com/gottwald

Note, all of the above materials are available as PDFs on the Website.

In addition, the following Tables and Charts are available only on the Website.

Web Tables

A	Ancient Near Eastern Texts Related to the Hebrew Bible by Theme, Literary Genre, or Historical Connection
B	Literary Genres, Forms, or Types in the Hebrew Bible
C	Versions and Translations of the Hebrew Bible since 1952
D	Major Excavations in Biblical Palestine
E	Jewish Books among the Pseudepigrapha of the Old Testament Predating 70 C.E.
F	Important Documents among the Dead Sea Scrolls
G	Tradition Units of Genesis 11:27-50 Distributed by Sources
H	Tradition Units of Exodus, Leviticus, and Numbers Distributed by Sources
I	Comparison of Greek Amphictyony and Israelite Confederacy
J	Distribution of DH Verses to Kings of the United Monarchy in 1 and 2 Samuel and 1 Kings 1–11
K	Distribution of DH Verses to Rulers of Israel and Judah in 1 Kings 12—2 Kings 17
L	Distribution of Verses to Kings of Judah in 2 Kings 18–25
M	Refrains and Repetitions in Song of Songs
N	Jewish Apocalypses, 250 B.C.E.–150 C.E., according to Literary Criteria

Web Charts

Black Sea

Pontus Mts.

MACEDONIA

THRACE

ANATOLIA
(ASIA MINOR)

Aegean Sea

Taurus Mts.

GREECE

SYRIA

CYPRUS

PALESTINE

CRETE

Mediterranean Sea

LIBYA

LOWER
EGYPT

SINAI

Nile R.

Red Sea

UPPER
EGYPT

MAP 0.I THE ANCIENT NEAR EAST

CAUCASUS

Caspian Sea

URANTU

ARMENIA

PARTHIA

Elburz Mts.

ASSYRIA

MEDIA

Zagros Mts.

MESOPOTAMIA

BABYLONIA

Tigris R.

ELAM

Euphrates R.

SUMER

PERSIA

Approximate ancient coastline

Persian Gulf

ARABIA

Fertile Crescent

0   500 mi

0   500 km

Norman K. Gottwald's magisterial work *The Tribes of Yahweh* (1979) marked a revolutionary turning point in biblical studies—in more ways than one. Since its publication, his interpretation of the revolutionary origins of Israel in the land of Canaan has been widely discussed and widely accepted, his conclusions being described or assumed in introductory textbooks and study Bibles alike. In 1985, the publication of *The Hebrew Bible: A Socio-Literary Introduction* made those conclusions and the methodological considerations that led to them more broadly accessible in a clearly organized textbook supplemented with maps and diagrams.

Now Fortress Press is pleased to present this textbook, carefully and faithfully abridged from *The Hebrew Bible* for the college and university classroom. Here the reader will find a helpful overview of the methods of Hebrew Bible study. Here are Professor Gottwald's key insights, arguments, and conclusions regarding the formative stages in ancient Israel's history that shaped the writings of the Hebrew Bible. Here, and on a companion Web site, http://www.fortresspress.com/gottwald, are clear and informative charts, maps, and illustrations to bring that history and those writings to light.

Students and teachers will appreciate a number of features of *The Hebrew Bible: A Brief Socio-Literary Introduction*:

- **Suggested Bible readings** to accompany chapters 4–12 are prominently listed on the opening page of each chapter and can be made part of course reading assignments. If students will read major portions of the Pentateuch and Joshua through 2 Kings, they can refer to Tables 6.1, 6.2, III.1, 7.1, and 11.1 and (on the Web site) Web Tables G and H.

- **Readings from ancient Near Eastern literature** are also identified in correlation with each chapter, as indicated by Web Table A, keyed to collections by James B. Pritchard (*The Ancient Near East in Texts Related to the Old Testament*, 1969) and Walter Beyerlin (*Near Eastern Religious Texts Related to the Old Testament*, 1978).

- The **charts and diagrams** that made *The Hebrew Bible* such a valuable resource are presented here (and on the Web site) in clearer, more readable, and more colorful detail.

- **Numerous maps** have been prepared especially to orient the reader of this textbook to the world of the Bible. For more specific detail the opening pages of chapters 2 and 4–10 are keyed to the historical maps in Yohanan Aharoni et al., *The Carta Bible Atlas*, 4th ed. (Jerusalem: Carta, 2002).

- This abridged edition of *The Hebrew Bible* also contains **new bibliographical resources** that supplement and update the bibliography to the original edition. These include (1) select lists of further readings appended to each chapter, and at the end of the book, (2) a fuller chapter-by-chapter bibliography and (3) a topical bibliography treating subjects that cut across chapter divisions. These resources are also provided, along with the extensive bibliography to the 1985 edition, on the Web site.

- **The companion Web site (www.fortresspress.com/gottwald)** provides valuable resources both for teachers (a pre-made test, suggestions for one- and two-semester course syllabi, reading assignments, and a digital bank of maps, charts, and tables for classroom use) and for students (chapter summaries, study questions, and a guide to writing research papers). Teachers may obtain an electronic key to the test by writing to Pamela.Johnson@augsburgfortress.org.

- One of the great strengths of *The Hebrew Bible* is Professor Gottwald's correlation of historical, literary, social, and religious-theological spheres in ancient Israel. **Clear cross-references in the text** enable readers to pursue any of these "tracks" through the text; a key for instructors who wish to assign readings along these tracks is also available on the Web site.

We are grateful to Rebecca Kruger Gaudino and to Norman Gottwald for providing a clear and concise manuscript and to Zan Ceeley, Ann Delgehausen, and Beth Wright of Trio Bookworks for the exercise of their various talents in bringing this textbook to the light of day.

Neil Elliott
Fortress Press

This new abridged edition of my book *The Hebrew Bible: A Socio-Literary Introduction* (1985) brings the insights and perspectives of that larger book to a new audience by means of a clear and concise abridgement, made even more accessible by the addition of updated resources for students and instructors.

For more than two decades, *The Hebrew Bible* has filled an urgent need: to acquaint beginning students with the explosion of new methods of inquiry that have revolutionized biblical studies. It shows how the newer approaches supplement and enrich—rather than negate or displace—the traditional historical-critical methods and theories that have dominated the field since the rise of biblical criticism two hundred years ago. The sea change in Hebrew Bible studies that I described in *The Hebrew Bible* continues to be the dominant reality in biblical interpretation.

Although the newer literary methods and their counterparts in the social sciences have by now become fully recognized instruments in biblical studies, their full impact has yet to penetrate newly published or recently revised introductions to the Hebrew Bible. In my judgment, none has offered as sustained a use of socioliterary methods as the present work—reason enough to present this new and abridged edition in a format suited to a new generation of biblical students and scholars.

My approach in *The Hebrew Bible: A Brief Socio-Literary Introduction* is to describe how the new literary and social-scientific methods, in concert with older historical-critical methods, apply to each of the three major divisions of the Hebrew Bible and to each historical period in ancient Israel from its inception through the Hellenistic era. In the conclusion, I sum up the status of Hebrew Bible studies with the help of a comprehensive chart (also available on the companion Web site) that displays the interrelated social, literary, and theological sectors of ancient Israel's manifold corporate life as these gave rise to the Hebrew Bible.

That I have succeeded in making the new methodological situation in Hebrew Bible studies intelligible to two generations of students has been gratifyingly attested by younger scholars who have told me that, in the course of their doctoral studies, they used my text as a framework or template for plotting the range of methods they needed to take into account in preparation for their comprehensive exams. Later, as instructors in biblical studies, they found the same overview of the field useful in organizing their own courses and preparing syllabi. In a sense, they were using my work as a scholar's and teacher's handbook for orientation amid the rapidly changing discipline of biblical studies.

Of course biblical studies have not stood still since *The Hebrew Bible* was first published. Not only is there the ongoing flow of work in all the established older and newer modes of study—for instance, in ideological criticism and feminist criticism—but additional methods have arisen that further complicate the organization and advancement of biblical studies. Some of these emerge out of existing literary or social critical methods, while others have more independent origins. Examples of more recent cutting-edge methods are narrative criticism, new historicism, dialogical criticism, postcolonial criticism, deconstruction, cultural studies, and psychological criticism.

Sometimes this array of emerging methods is referred to under the blanket term "postmodernism." All have been inspired and fueled by paradigm shifts and methodological departures that have swept over the scientific disciplines within the humanities and the social sciences. Readings on these more recent methodological contenders are listed in the topical bibliography under "Methodology in Hebrew Bible Studies."

Indeed, so pervasive are the paradigm shifts in mainstream Hebrew Bible studies that long-cherished views of the formation of the biblical text have been called into radical question. Notably, the hypothesis that the Pentateuch consists of four primary sources (J, E, D, and P) composed over several centuries of time has been widely dismissed as invalid or indemonstrable. I retain these source divisions in this new abridgement for two reasons: (1) the four-source Pentateuchal hypothesis is the cornerstone of past critical study of the Hebrew Bible and the necessary point of departure for considering alternative hypotheses; (2) to date, no alternative hypothesis for explaining the composition of the Pentateuch, which nearly everyone agrees must be understood as a compilation of earlier materials, has won anything like a consensus among scholars.

Similarly, the application of newer literary-critical methods to the prophetic books has thrown into question the trustworthiness of the historical claims made within the writings attributed to the named prophets. In the extreme form of this argument, a prophet such as Amos or Isaiah may be construed as no more than a literary construct with little or no reference to an actual historical figure or to the events recited or alluded to in his writings. Granted the tempering effects of these warnings against a positivist reading of the prophets, it is my contention that new developments in historiography and in social-scientific criticism warrant a continued serious regard for a substantial historical core to these admittedly redacted writings.

In addition, a highly charged debate swirls around the scope and structure—and for some scholars, the very existence—of the united monarchy of Israel. This debate hinges on the disputed dating of archaeological evidence, on notions of state formation, and on the perceived hyperbole of the biblical accounts of the reigns of David and Solomon. While there is wide agreement that the initial stage in Israelite state formation was more rudimentary than a superficial reading of Samuel through Kings suggests, the complex issues entailed in discerning that first step to statehood remain far from resolved.

Compared to some other introductions, including my own earlier work *A Light to the Nations: An Introduction to the Old Testament* (New York: Harper & Row, 1959), this volume gives greater attention to the exilic and postexilic periods. Neglect of the later biblical era can be seen as a peculiarly Christian, even specifically Protestant, bias uncritically reflected in the work of many non-Jewish biblical scholars. The increasingly ecumenical character of biblical scholarship has helped to correct the blind spots of any single tradition and thus to sharpen the tools we can now bring collegially to bear upon these texts.

This textbook is organized in four parts. Part I sets forth contextual knowledge for approaching the Hebrew Bible: the history of its interpretation, the biblical world, and the literary history of the Hebrew Bible. Parts II–IV present the biblical literature in sequence according to its sociohistorical settings. A prologue to each of the last three parts discusses the sources of our knowledge for each period as it is examined.

A problem of organization arises when presenting biblical writings in approximate historical sequence, as in parts II–IV. Where should one place biblical books or sources that have a long tradition history and reflect a growth in stages over centuries? When treating composite or slowly evolved biblical writings, two flexible working principles are followed in this volume: (1) When there is wide agreement about a writing's sociohistorical anchor points, the work is discussed as often as necessary at each relevant stage, as, for example, with the Priestly writer (pp. 89–90; 105–7; 116–17; 120–23; 267–79) or the book of Isaiah (pp. 216–21; 284–88; 290–91). (2) When, on the other hand, the sociohistorical settings of a writing are vague or highly disputed, it is presented only at its most securely fixed historical point. Thus, the composite books of Amos and Micah, although containing much later material, are discussed only once and in their eighth-century contexts (202–4; 215–16), and Daniel, although preserving older traditions, is treated solely in its second-century milieu (pp. 331–33).

The chronology adopted for the divided monarchy is that of Edwin R. Thiele, *The Mysterious Numbers of the Hebrew Kings*, 3rd ed. (Grand Rapids: Zondervan, 1983). I chose this scheme not because it is unimpeachable, but because it seems to me as satisfactory a solution of the chronological problems as any proposed to date. Other reputable chronologies have been published by Simon J. DeVries ("Chronology of the OT," *IDB*, 1:580–99; "Chronology, OT," *IDBSup*, 161–66); John Hayes and Paul K. Hooker, *A New Chronology for the Kings of Israel and Judah and Its Implications for Biblical History and Literature* (Atlanta: John Knox, 1988); Paul K. Hooker ("Chronology of the Old Testament," *NIDB*, 1:636–43); Mordechai Cogan ("Chronology, Hebrew Bible," *ABD*, 1:1002–11); and Gershon Galil, *The Chronology of the Kings of Israel and Judah* (Studies in the History of Culture of the Ancient Near East, vol. 9; Leiden: Brill, 1996).

I have transliterated Hebrew terms approximately as they are pronounced, even though this entails some inconsistencies according to the customary systems of transliteration.

Last, I have consistently used the dating sigla of B.C.E. (before the Common Era) and C.E. (the Common Era), in preference to the more usual B.C. ("before Christ") and A.D. (*anno Domini*, "in the year of the Lord"), because I feel that it is important for all students of these texts to make a mental break between our own religious stances and the conditions and beliefs of biblical times. This is a necessary break if we are to appreciate the Bible as more than a sectarian or dogmatic document that simply mirrors our own religious ideas.

I send this abridgement on its way with special thanks to Rebecca Kruger Gaudino for the excellence of the abridgment, which I have reviewed with full approval. I am also most grateful to Neil Elliott and Michael West at Fortress Press, who first proposed this abridgement, and to Josh Messner, Tim Larson, and Paul Boenke at Fortress and to Zan Ceeley, Ann Delgehausen, and Beth Wright of Trio Bookworks, who have facilitated its production in this attractive format. I also wish again to salute the late John A. Hollar, who fanned the first sparks of my interest in writing this volume and whose advice and encouragement sustained me in the task. I am pleased to credit his direct and indirect imprint on many of the organizational and instructional features of this work. At a more technical level, close colleagues in various working groups of the American Academy of Religion and the Society of Biblical Literature have given timely support and challenge.

Within the wide network of my indebtedness to others as expressed in the dedication, I single out the curiosity and imagination of my students, who over more than five decades have helped me to deepen and clarify my understanding of the Hebrew Bible and to communicate that understanding concretely and appealingly.

THE TEXT
IN ITS CONTEXTS

I

ANGLES OF VISION ON THE HEBREW BIBLE

SUMMARY

Various methods have been used in studying the Bible

- traditional doctrinal interpretation
- historical criticism, including source and form criticism
- existential synthetic approach
- literary and social-science approaches
- structuralism

The Hebrew Bible, known to Jews as the Tanak[1] and to Christians as the Old Testament, attracts and engages readers for many reasons. Among its many literary forms are vivid compact narratives and lively image-filled poems. The story line recounts a conflict-charged political history, intertwined with more than a thousand years of ancient Near Eastern history. Its laws, stories, lists, prophetic speeches, and wisdom sayings touch on a host of social institutions and practices that change over the centuries. It presents the public words and deeds of figures, such as Moses, David, and Jeremiah, who are often seen as examples of religious faith or of communal leadership. It teems with strong expressions of Israelite/Jewish[2] belief in the God whose special name was Yahweh, leading to a wide spectrum of religious and ethical concepts and practices closely connected with the social and political experience of the people. Finally, because the Hebrew Bible is sacred scripture for Jews and Christians to this day, and has gained a significant place in Western civilization, it beckons the reader to understand and consider its notions of deity and humanity, of historical process and social order, and of ethics and the good life.

A WEALTH OF METHODS
IN BIBLICAL STUDIES

Any one of the mentioned points of engagement with the Hebrew Bible—and I have stated only the most prominent—constitutes a proper starting point for approaching the text, and necessarily carries with it distinct methods of analysis and interpretation. In earlier centuries, when the Bible was almost solely used to provide underpinning for Jewish and Christian religious communities, there were decided limits on the ways the text was studied. In recent centuries, owing to the Renaissance, the Reformation, the Enlightenment, major social changes, and the steady expansion of scientific method over most areas of human experience, the Bible has been freed from an exclusively doctrinal (confessional) and church-centered religious approach. It has now become approachable in scientific ways.

"Scientific" is here intended in the broad sense of a systematic method of study necessary for the intelligible analysis and explanation of any subject matter. Science includes not only natural, social, and psychological sciences, but also efforts at greater precision of method in the humanities, as in the study of language, literature, and history, and in the exercise of philosophy as a kind of overarching reflection on scientific methods and results as they relate to other kinds of knowledge.

It is typical of current study of the Hebrew Bible that more and more methods used in the human sciences, especially refinements in the humanities and the social sciences, have been employed in order to understand these ancient writings. As recently as 1960 or so there was a consensus among scholars about using a fairly limited number of critical methods for study of the Bible, but today the spectrum of methods employed in biblical studies has enlarged dramatically. Moreover, each of these methods is sufficiently self-contained and fundamental in its presuppositions and ways of working that the methods taken together do not suggest any single obvious picture or model (paradigm) of the nature and meaning of the Bible. How to relate these different methods of biblical inquiry logically and procedurally has become a major intellectual challenge that will require a comprehensive frame of reference not readily at hand. At present there is probably no single biblical scholar who commands an in-depth grasp of all the methods now operative in biblical studies.

It is desirable that the serious student of the Hebrew Bible have some sense of the main phases in the development of methods in biblical studies. These stages can be described in chronological order because certain methods arose earlier than others and in various combinations held dominance among biblical interpreters until other methods joined, altered, or displaced them.

There is wide recognition today that virtually all methods ever employed in biblical study have some reasonable basis for their use, so that the issue is now seldom seen as a matter of agreeing on what *one* method should replace the others but rather the question of how *various legitimate methods,* according to the purposes in view, should be joined so as to produce an overall grasp of the Hebrew Bible in its most fundamental aspects. In short, the emergence of so many methods of biblical study for various purposes has tended to relativize and qualify the status of every method.

It is easy to be impatient with discussions of method. We want to get on to the content and the meaning of the Bible, often forgetful of the fact that we have no access to the content and meaning of the Bible apart from *some* method of study. All interpreters come to the text with assumptions, dispositions, and tools of analysis that lead them to single out aspects of the text and to arrange, emphasize, and interpret those aspects in meaningful patterns. Only by an awareness of method, as actually applied to the text, will we be able to see concretely why biblical interpreters have differed in their conclusions and to give a confident account of the basis and justification for our own methods.

THE CONFESSIONAL RELIGIOUS APPROACH TO THE HEBREW BIBLE

The first stage in the study of the Hebrew Bible was basically religious in a confessional sense. Jews and Christians studied scripture to give understanding and shape to the practice of their religions. In both communities, until the eighteenth century, there was a solid consensus about the religious role of the Bible. It was believed to be the divinely revealed foundation document of their faith. Departures from the normative religious readings of the Hebrew Bible were a threat that might be tolerated, as in the case of mystics, or more often had to be expelled, as in the case of heretical sects.

It is not as though a confessional religious understanding of the Hebrew Bible has ceased in our time. It is rather that *multiple* Jewish and Christian religious interpretations have emerged, and not simply along denominational lines within each religion but also along a spectrum from more literal to more symbolic interpretations and from more conservative to more liberal or radical interpretations. Moreover, there are now thriving formulations of an understanding of the Hebrew Bible that are free-thinking—humanist and secular in orientation. These approaches acknowledge the religious content of the Bible but interpret its truth claims and meanings in ways contradictory to the main bodies of Jews and Christians.

Although the traditional confessional interpretations are no longer unchallenged, they are still powerfully advocated in many Jewish and Christian circles. It is common for faithful synagogue and church members to be surprised and shocked when they first seriously encounter other ways of viewing the Bible. The Bible has been internalized as a basic part of their religious instruction, so that when their unclouded naive grasp of the Bible confronts scientific methods of biblical study, it often becomes a mind-stretching, value-questioning, and soul-searching experience.

THE HISTORICAL-CRITICAL APPROACH TO THE HEBREW BIBLE

The second major phase in the study of the Hebrew Bible was adoption of the historical-critical method. Instead of taking the stated authorship and contents of documents at face value, this method tries to establish the actual origins of the text and to evaluate the probability that events it relates happened in the way described. Evidence for this critical inquiry derives from within the document and from a comparison with other documents from the same period or of the same type.

Based on Renaissance study of ancient writings, the secular historical-critical method was unleashed on the Bible in full measure during the Enlightenment of the eighteenth century. Initially concentrated in Germany, the historical-critical study of the Bible rapidly spread over the entire educated Western world. From the beginning this scientific way of studying the Bible made an uneasy place for itself within the very Jewish and Christian religious communities that had traditionally interpreted the Hebrew Bible solely in a confessional religious manner.

The Bible as a Human Creation

In their choice of secular method to study the Hebrew Bible, historical critics were not denying the inherent religious character of the Bible, nor did they for the most part believe that the Bible lost its religious significance when studied critically. The basic presupposition of historical critics was that the religious aspect of life is similar to all other aspects of life. Religious ideas and practices arise, gain dominance, change, combine, mutually interact, decline, and die out. As with everything human, religious phenomena have a history.

In particular, historical critics believed that a careful study of the Hebrew Bible would be able to uncover the actual origins and development of Israelite/Jewish religious ideas and practices long hidden behind the compiled form of the Hebrew Bible interpreted as a unified supernatural story. The valid religious truth or message of the Hebrew Bible could only be brought to light when seen as the religion of a particular people at a particular time and place as expressed in these particular writings.

Source Criticism and Form Criticism

Historical critics turned to the study of the Hebrew Bible as they would to the study of Homer, Thucydides, Dante, or Shakespeare, discovering as they went the peculiarities of the biblical literature. For one thing, the Bible proved to be a sizable collection of books from many hands with an inner history of development that had to be reconstructed from clues in the text and from analogies with similar types of literature. Authors of biblical books were frequently anonymous, and explicit information for dating books was often meager.

A limited aspect of literary criticism as we now understand it, namely, source criticism, was employed to identify both fragmentary and extended sources within biblical books. By the early twentieth century this source-critical project was expanded by so-called form criticism, which aimed to isolate characteristic smaller units of tradition that were felt to be oral in their origin and highly conventional in their structure and language (see pp. 63–65). These smaller and larger sources, merged or strung together in the completed books of the Bible, were placed, insofar as possible, in their respective historical or typical settings.

Furthermore, it became evident that the order in which the books were finally arranged in the Hebrew Bible was *not* the order in which the books had been written. Solutions to this chronological puzzle were made all the more complicated by the fact that single biblical books often contained materials from different time periods. An arrangement of blocks of literary materials from the Hebrew Bible according to their approximate order of composition shows a very different sequence than now appears in the traditional ordering of the books (Web Chart A). Even the traditional grouping of biblical books has varied among Jews, Catholics, and Protestants.

Authorship of Biblical Books

The authorship of biblical writings received close scrutiny by historical critics. It was argued, on the basis of ancient literary practices and in terms of internal evidence, that many of the biblical claims to authorship were traditional assignments that are not to be taken strictly in terms of modern literary authorship. The biblical world was surprisingly devoid of personal pride in authorship and knew nothing of copyright laws. When the Torah or Pentateuch is assigned to Moses, the Psalms to David, and wisdom books to Solomon, we should probably understand Moses as the prototype of lawgiver, David as the prototype of psalmist, and Solomon as the prototype of sage or wise man. On such an understanding, any or all laws, psalms, and wisdom sayings might be traditionally attributed to those figures as the true fountainheads of the tradition.

Historical critics also observed that even when the core of a biblical book is correctly attributed to the named author, such as Isaiah, additions have been made by later hands, some by second- or third-generation disciples of the master (one thinks of the problem of distinguishing Socrates from Plato in the latter's dialogues) and others by literary editors (redactors). Critical assessment of the traditions of biblical authorship, first pursued by source criticism, later by form criticism and tradition (tradition-historical) criticism, and most recently by redaction (editorial) criticism (see pp. 12, 62–65, 83–84, 172–74, 278–79) has shifted the emphasis from privately motivated and self-conscious "authors" in a

modern sense to writers in a communal context and especially to the creative processes of tradition formation in the Israelite/Jewish community. The oral and written molding and remolding of traditions is seen to be a crucible in which biblical literature was refined by abbreviating, expanding, combining, and elaborating units of tradition, often through many stages of development, until the final state of the Hebrew Bible was reached over a span of postexilic time from the sixth through the second centuries B.C.E.[3]

Biblical History and Archaeology

The process of unraveling the literary structure of the Hebrew Bible and assigning its parts to a long historical trajectory has underlined the intimate connection between the Bible as a literary collection and the history of the Israelite/Jewish people from the exodus to Maccabean times, somewhat over a thousand years in all. The biblical text itself relates a large part of that history, but does so selectively and unevenly. Also, one has to reckon with the reality that much of the biblical history is given a moralizing or theologizing twist, or is interpreted from the bias of a later standpoint in history.

Historical critics enlarged their task accordingly in order to recover as much additional information as they could, both about the history of the biblical communities and about the history of surrounding peoples with whom Israel was in frequent interaction. Historically enlightening records from Israel's neighbors, although rarely mentioning Israel, have the advantage of surviving in the form in which they were first written, without the kind of expansion and revision that biblical materials have undergone (see pp. 31–34, 58;

Web Table A). Archaeological recovery of material and intellectual culture, including an ever-growing body of inscriptions and texts, has aided greatly in the task of cultural and historical reconstruction (see pp. 34–35).

It has become possible to plot the broad outlines of the growth of the biblical literary traditions against a historical scenario with spatial and temporal axes. The *temporal axis* stretches from the Middle Bronze Age (ca. 2100–1550 B.C.E.), as the most commonly accepted period for the biblical ancestors Abraham, Isaac, and Jacob (patriarchs), down to the Maccabean age in Palestine (167–63 B.C.E.), the age of the composition of Daniel and Esther, probably the last biblical books to be written. The *spatial axis* locates Israelite Canaan/Palestine at the center, extending first to non-Israelite Palestine and Syria, then to Egypt and Mesopotamia (including Sumer, Assyria, and Babylonia), and finally to Anatolia (Asia Minor), Iran (Media, Persia), Arabia, and the eastern Mediterranean coastlands, including Greece (see pp. 21–24).

INTERACTION BETWEEN RELIGIOUS AND HISTORICAL-CRITICAL APPROACHES TO BIBLICAL STUDIES

Collision and Accommodation of Conflicting Methods

As previously noted, the historical-critical method of biblical studies early found its way into Jewish and Christian circles. For two hundred years now, two methods of biblical study have operated among Jews and Christians: the Bible approached as the revealed Word of God and the Bible approached as the human literary product of an ancient sociopolitical and religious community. To greatly simplify, one can say that historical-critical method has found readiest acceptance among educated clergy and laity and in the universities and theological faculties, and more rapidly among Protestants and Jews than among Catholics. To this day, however, large bodies of orthodox Jews and Christians are actively hostile to the method, and many rank-and-file members of religious groups supposedly accepting of the method are poorly informed about it. Relatively few synagogues and churches regard it as an intrinsic part of their task to practice the method and instruct their members in it.

Then there are those who wish to combine religious and historical-critical methods, claiming that the central religious ideas of the Bible and/or the significance of the synagogues and churches springing from biblical Israel are not invalidated by the fact that the Bible is a human document. God is viewed as having used the human processes in Israel's history to reveal religious truth and to preserve it in written records that continue to awaken faith in God even if they are not statements of a literal truth.

Some believers make peace with the historical-critical method by applying it to carefully limited aspects of the Bible. They may, for instance, accept critical literary analysis, since they find it immaterial for faith whether Moses wrote the Torah, but they may insist that theological dimensions of the Bible, especially its views on creation, sin, and redemption, must be exempted from criticism since they are absolutely and eternally true. Or they may admit critical method in the form of textual criticism that establishes the nearest possible approximation to the original Hebrew text. Or they may open the physical worldview of the Bible to criticism, which they admit to be prescientific, while insisting that on all matters of history and religion the Bible is sacrosanct.

On the whole it seems fair to say that Jews and Christians have yet to work out ways of correlating the religious and historical approaches to the Hebrew Bible that can become an intrinsic and convincing part of the daily life and thought of believers. The relativizing humanistic implications of the historical-critical method clash with the practical belief in an unchanging, transcendent God. This unresolved tension, repeatedly bursting into open conflict, is a nagging source of disquiet in many religious bodies among those who want authoritative and secure mental and spiritual maps of the world. Literalistic biblical interpretation, misconstruing both the substance and emphasis of biblical teachings, sometimes accompanies socially reactionary thinking as people fear for the stability of their social world.

The climate of public philosophy and social theory in the West during the emergence of the historical-critical method has not encouraged a new synthesis of the meaning of the Hebrew Bible that could go beyond the traditional religious interpretations, or at least offer a coherent alternative to them.

Attempts at a Synthesis: Existentialism and Biblical Theology

We shall now look at some of the specifically churchly and theological efforts to synthesize religious and historical perspectives on the Bible. Between the two world wars a revival of Protestant Reformation theology in modern form, known as neo-orthodoxy, provided an attractive way to harmonize the results of historical-critical biblical study with a high view of biblical revelation. This theological synthesis was widespread in Europe and had a major impact in the United States from 1940 to 1960. In biblical studies it took the form of a biblical theology movement that forged the category of "history" into a bridge between the critical results of biblical scholarship and a notion of biblical faith as "revelation in history" or "the acts of God in history." Somewhat similar influences were at work among Roman Catholic biblical scholars, encouraged by the liberalizing tendencies of the Vatican II Council in 1965. However, the biblical theology bridge between history and theology collapsed as it became clear that the Hebrew Bible, when viewed historically, contains several theologies and that in the end any theology or philosophy for integrating the interpretation of the whole Bible has to be provided by the modern interpreter.

Among the most influential modern schemes for reading off the meaning of the biblical text have been the existentialist philosophy of Jean-Paul Sartre and the phenomenological philosophy of Martin Heidegger. In contrast to the biblical theology movement, which emphasized the religious meanings of particular historical events (exodus, conquest, exile, restoration) as revelations of God, the existentialist reading of the Bible saw the historical revelations of the Bible as models or paradigms of the human situation faced with crisis that offers an ever-emerging possibility of new beginnings through self-understanding and self-renewal. For example, biblical critic Rudolph Bultmann insisted on the central reality of the death and resurrection of Jesus, but this core was not securely attached to probable historical events. Later existentialist biblical interpreters were often more consistent in regarding the biblical events and their interpretation as valuable but not indispensable occasions for self-understanding and self-renewal.

Breakdown of Consensus in Biblical Studies

In the late 1960s both "revelation in history" and "existential self-understanding" reached a point of diminishing returns as resources for biblical studies. Each seemed to be straining after an artificially constructed center of meaning in the Bible, or in the interpreter, which obstructed the way to an adequate examination of the multifaceted shape of the biblical text.

Newer forms of religious thought, such as process theology and political theology, have made only tentative excursions into the biblical materials but not enough to produce alternative master schemes or paradigms with the convincing power that biblical theology and existentialist interpretation expressed in their day.

By the opening of the 1970s, study of the Hebrew Bible was pervaded by a sense of dissatisfaction and disorientation. The older theological modes of confessional orthodoxy and liberalism had proven incapable of synthesizing the historical and religious meanings of the Bible, and the more recent excursions into biblical theology and existentialism had not been, in the end, any more satisfactory. Moreover, no other theological current commanded the necessary explanatory power to replace the previous inadequate formulations.

With the relative shift away from theological domination of biblical studies, the drastic paradigm crisis surrounding the limitations of the historical-critical method has come fully to light. Theology can no longer be cited as the sole obstacle to an integral understanding of the Hebrew Bible. Theology aside, the Hebrew Bible is seen now as a different sort of object to different kinds of interpreters. What characterizes the present period in biblical studies, and makes it so difficult to typify in any simple way, is the explosion of several methodologies, each claiming to grasp an important neglected or downgraded feature—even the sole essential feature—of the structure and meaning of the Hebrew Bible. So rapid has been the expansion of these methods in small-scale studies that there has been little time or occasion to think through their implications for biblical studies as a whole.

EMERGENCE OF NEW LITERARY AND SOCIAL-SCIENCE APPROACHES TO THE HEBREW BIBLE

Perceived Limits of Historical and Religious Approaches

The relation of the newer methods to the dominant methods of the past is complex and ambivalent. Most advocates of new methods seem to recognize that the confessional religious and the historical-critical methods of interpretation succeeded in identifying and clarifying important aspects of the biblical text. Misgivings and objections to the older methods center on their limitations and the tendency of their conflicting presuppositions to monopolize discussion about the meaning of the Hebrew Bible.

Clearly, the historical-critical method has been able to illuminate the collected writings of the Hebrew Bible, rooted in the history of Israel, as expressions of a religious faith unfolding in communal settings and historical sequences over more than a thousand years. By specifying in detail how the writings are shaped and colored by the sharp religious perspectives of writers and editors, this method was able to interpret what the confessional approach saw as divinely caused revelation as a richly nuanced historical development. Nonetheless, the result was that certain classic problems—such as the composition of complex books like Deuteronomy and Isaiah— were repetitiously reworked without a fresh approach or much new evidence.

Just as the older confessional religious approach lost explanatory power when it gave dogmatic answers to historical questions, so the historical-critical method exposed its limits when it could answer only some historical questions adequately. New questions about the literary shape of the Bible and the social milieu of ancient Israel were beyond its competency. In short, religious and historical-critical schemes of biblical interpretation are widely perceived to have reached their limits on their own turf and to be inappropriate to clarifying major aspects of the Hebrew Bible that excite curiosity and imagination.

Yet we must state the shift from older to newer methods carefully, so as not to miss the notes of ambivalence and tentativeness in the present methodological situation. If it is now widely believed that religion and history—at least as customarily formulated by confessional religious and historical-critical methods—are not sufficient paradigms for understanding the Hebrew Bible, the question insistently arises: What other methods are able to carry us forward to new understandings?

At least two major related sets of methods have emerged in an attempt to get around the present impasse in the study of the Hebrew Bible. One is the paradigm of the Hebrew Bible as a *literary production* that creates its own fictive world of meaning and is to be understood first and foremost, if not exclusively, as a literary medium, that is, as words that conjure up their own imaginative reality. The other is the paradigm of the Hebrew Bible as a *social document* that reflects the history of changing social structures, functions, and roles in ancient Israel over a thousand years or so, and which provides an integral context in which the literary, historical, and religious features of the Israelite/Jewish people can be viewed and interconnected.

Newer Literary Methods

Within the new literary paradigm for approaching the Hebrew Bible there is substantial agreement that the text as it stands constitutes the proper object of study in that it offers a total, self-contained, literary meaning that need not depend upon analysis of sources, historical commentary, or normative religious interpretations. Biblical literary critics vary in how they make this point. Many allow that the older methods of study have value and may helpfully give context or nuance to literary study, but they express a nearly unanimous caution against predetermining literary study of the Bible with the old questions and modes of attack. For them literature is not, in the first instance, a means to something else, such as historical or religious understandings of the writers and their everyday world. Literature is a world all its own, in and of itself, biblical literature included. Thus, "Who wrote this book, or part of a book, from what sources, in what historical setting, and with what aims?" is for literary critics in the new mode a far less productive series of questions than "What is the distinct structure and style of this writing, or segment of writing, and what meaning does it project from within its own confines as a work of art or as a system of linguistic meanings?"

The Bible as Literature and New Literary Criticism

One current in the literary paradigm derives from the so-called *new literary criticism* in secular literary studies, now some decades old. Looking at a work as a finished whole, this perspective stresses the distinctiveness of each literary product and seeks to analyze its peculiar conventions of genre, rhetorical devices, and the overall resulting unity and effects. In this sense the Bible-as-literature movement is closely related to rhetorical criticism, a spinoff from form criticism, which seeks to establish the literary individuality of texts by analyzing their arrangements of words, phrases, and images that structure firm beginnings and endings, sequences of action or argumentation, repetitions, points of emphasis, and dynamic interconnections among the parts.

The approach to the Bible as literature has affinities also with *redaction criticism*, a late development of the historical-critical method whose aim is to discern the hand of the final writer or editor (redactor) in single books, or in a series of books, by distinguishing how the final framing stage of composition has arranged earlier materials and added interpretive cues for the reader. In this way one can see how the entire composition was intended to be read, even though much of the content

derived from earlier writers with differing points of view.

Overlapping in some aspects with redaction criticism, and sharing with the Bible-as-literature movement a concern for the finished state of the text, is a method that has generally been known as *canonical criticism* (see pp. 67–70; 267–73). Advocates of this approach are interested in how the biblical text was intentionally developed and interpreted as scripture.

Careful distinctions are necessary among these various related types of criticism. Biblical literary critics of the new breed, for instance, concur with redaction and canonical critics in trying to illumine how the entire composition of a biblical writing is to be read in its integrity but leave aside what shape parts of the work may have had before the finished book was produced or arguments about the theological authority of the finished Hebrew Bible. Unlike form criticism, tradition criticism, rhetorical criticism, redaction criticism, and canonical criticism, the new literary criticism of the Bible is interested in comparing and contrasting biblical literature with other literatures on the assumption that all individual texts comprise one vast corpus of literature and share similar creative properties (see pp. 123–25).

Structural Criticism

A second current in the new literary paradigm is known as structural criticism or structural exegesis. It differs from the Bible-as-literature movement in its assumptions about structural patterns that lie not only within particular writings but also under them in what are often called "deep structures." These structures may be traced in groups or "sets" of similar texts, such as in parables or miracle narratives, and are correlated with primary functional elements in a story, such as a fixed set of roles and schematized plots. Structuralism tends to see deep structures in terms of polar categories rooted in basic mental structures that organize great ranges of human experience into such binary oppositions as good/bad, nature/culture, man/woman, life/death, secular/profane, and having/not having (see pp. 125, 147–49). A multidisciplinary methodological approach to reality, structuralism analyzes structures that range from numerical groups through organisms to literary texts and religious or philosophical concepts.

One impression accompanying the inrush of structural criticism to biblical studies is that it has no regard whatsoever for the historical and social dimensions of texts, although some biblical structuralists see many openings for the possible synthesis of literary structural and historical/social concerns. A major problem with biblical structuralism to date is that it uses technical jargon, which is particularly confusing to many because different vocabularies are used by different structuralists. Before structuralism can be fully productive in biblical studies there will need to be further progress toward clarifying and standardizing technical terms and concepts, and selecting those forms and possibilities of structuralism that offer the best payoff in analyzing biblical texts.

Social-Science Methods

Within the social-science paradigm there is broad concurrence that the biblical writings were rooted in interacting groups of people organized in social structures that controlled the chief aspects of public life, such as family, economy, government, law, war, ritual, and religious belief. Moreover, it is widely perceived that these units of

social life, taken as a total network in flux, supply an indispensable context for grounding other aspects of biblical studies, including both the older and the newer methods of inquiry. The guiding question for social-science approaches becomes, What social structures and social processes are explicit or implicit in the biblical literature, in the scattered socioeconomic data it contains, in the overtly political history

FIG. 1.1 Statue of the influential minister of Egyptian pharaoh Amenhotep III, Amenhotep son of Hapu, as a scribe. This image signified status second only to the king and gods, and so was a form used to depict the most powerful men in the land. New Kingdom, Eighteenth Dynasty, 1390–52 B.C.E. Egyptian Museum, Cairo. Photo: © Werner Forman / Art Resource, N.Y.

it recounts, and in the religious beliefs and practices it attests? Not entirely new to the study of the Hebrew Bible, the social-scientific approach has in the past largely been oriented to solving literary and historical puzzles and has at times been hampered by misconstrued or outdated anthropological and sociological methods and models.

Social Reconstruction of Early Israel

In the early 1960s, a new hypothesis about the origins of Israel was advanced with the assistance of data and methods from the social sciences. It was contended that Israel originated not as nomads invading or infiltrating from the desert, but largely as a coalition of peasants who had been resident in Palestine as subjects of the hierarchic city-states (see pp. 154–57; 160–63). At first largely dismissed as preposterous, this so-called revolt model of Israelite origins has gained credibility through more systematic examination of the internal biblical evidence and the external data from the ancient Near East. The model entails a cautious comparative method for employing studies on social forms—such as nomadism, tribalism, peasant movements and revolutions, and imperial bureaucracies—in order to theorize about the early social history of Israel in a period when the texts are too fragmentary and revised to be able by themselves to give us a whole picture of the beginnings of Israel. Whether or not this model will prove adequate in the main, it is evident that an entirely new concern with social history and social system has entered biblical studies alongside the continuing concerns with political and religious history.

Social Reconstruction of Prophecy and Apocalyptic

Sociological interest, at first concentrated on Israelite origins, has now spread to other segments of Israelite history and religion. Social-scientific tools, notably studies on millenarian sects in the Third World and within the history of Christianity, have contributed to new interpretations of the bizarre symbolic systems of intertestamental apocalyptic thought, as in the biblical book of Daniel, and to a social-psychological understanding of the advocates of such views (see pp. 328–33). More recently, biblical prophecy is being reexamined sociologically with insights from studies of spirit possession and the function of inspired holy persons in simpler societies in order to get a better comparative grasp of Israelite and non-Israelite prophecy. Social psychology has been employed to illuminate aspects of prophetic performance and the reinterpretation of failed prophetic predictions.

Varieties of Social-Scientific Criticism

Like the literary paradigm, the social-science paradigm is represented by different methodological currents. Some inquiries are focused on institutional sectors of ancient Israelite social life, treating offices or role functions and administrative structures at the points where they appear as traces or outcroppings in biblical texts, often with attention to ancient Near Eastern parallels or wider-ranging comparisons from comparative anthropology or sociology. Other approaches are broadening the field of comparison under the influence of studies in prehistory and anthropology, so that cautious analogies are proposed between ancient Israelite society and virtually any other society thought to exhibit similar features in some relevant regard, always allowing for different developmental and structural-functional contexts in the instances compared.

Some biblical social-science critics are expanding their horizons toward a comprehensive account of Israelite society under the impetus of the macrosocial (large-scale/global) theorists Karl Marx, Emile Durkheim, and Max Weber. Precisely how the methods and constructs of these social theorists are to be related in their own terms, and how they are to be applied to specific Israelite social conditions, is by no means agreed. Nonetheless, neo-evolutionary social theory is finding application to ancient Israel, allowing as it does for different rates of social change in different societies, for leaps in stages and retrograde developments, and for calculations of trends or tendencies in terms of probabilities instead of heavy-handed determinisms according to a supposed predestined inexorable march of history.

Finally, all of the above types of anthropological and sociological criticism are having a spillover effect on the task of exegesis (systematic interpretation) of texts, to the extent that one may now speak of sociological exegesis. Sociological exegesis tries to situate a biblical book or subsection in its proper social setting—taking into account the literary and historical relations between the parts and the whole. It further attempts to illuminate the text according to its explicit or implied social referents, in a manner similar to the historical-critical method's clarification of the political and religious reference points of texts. It is evident that all adequate future exegesis of biblical texts will have to entail a social-science dimension alongside the customary literary, historical, and religious dimensions.

Meanwhile, social-scientific criticism has stimulated an interest among archaeologists to examine ancient Israelite remains with more explicit cultural and social questions by means of appropriate methods and strategies. This is a shift from the typical orientation of earlier decades when interest in the Hebrew Bible among archaeologists was largely religious and historical.

Common Ground in New Literary Criticism and Social-Scientific Criticism

New literary and social-science methods of biblical study share a common frustration with the limited achievements of the religious and historical-critical paradigms. Each of the newer approaches in its own way tries to shift the object of study in biblical studies so as to provide access to overlooked dimensions of the writings considered indispensable to a full understanding of the Hebrew Bible. The literary paradigm does this by shifting attention from religious systems and historical reconstructions to the Hebrew Bible as a literary world. While initially this limits the range of what is studied, it actually enlarges the data by opening up fictive literary worlds that exist by virtue of the original composition of the biblical books and their endurance into the present. The social-science paradigm shifts attention from history and religion by concentrating on the Hebrew Bible as a residue of social worlds in which real people lived in social networks and fought out social struggles that were highly influential in the environment of the biblical writers, and attested in social data and allusions in biblical texts. This anthropological and sociological accent also seems at first to be a reduction of subject matter, but it provides a wider milieu in which to locate and interconnect other kinds of interests in ancient Israel.

But do the newer literary and social-science methods have anything more in common than a shared grievance with older methods of biblical inquiry? Indeed they do, because common to both paradigms is a central concern with *structure:* the structure of the writings of the Hebrew Bible and the structure of the Israelite/Jewish society in which the Hebrew Bible was written and handed down.

For the moment, the chief stress lies on the sharp differences between the newer paradigms and the older paradigms, rather than on the relationship of the newer paradigms to one another. Much in the stance of literary and social-scientific critics can be explained by their impatience with religious and historical monopolies on the Hebrew Bible that overlook the literary and social worlds and either grasp at a historical picture that is irretrievable or trivial, or else conjure up a religious system abstracted from the world of language and of social interaction.

How might literary structure and social structure be more exactly related? If, on the one hand, literary critics insist that social context has no bearing on texts and if, on the other hand, anthropological and sociological critics claim that texts are pure and simple projections of social life and consciousness, it is likely that points of contact between them will be minimal at best and hostile at worst. On the other hand, if language itself as the medium of literature is a social code and thus literature is a social expression, why and how is it that literature creates its own special world and does not simply directly mirror its society? Exactly how does social reality inscribe itself in language and in literary creations? To date the theoretical lines for relating the two kinds of structure in biblical studies are only in a rudimentary stage of exploration (see pp. 147–49).

CREATIVE FERMENT IN CONTEMPORARY BIBLICAL STUDIES

A Commonsense Assessment of Options

A commonsense reflection on the history of angles of vision for approaching the Hebrew Bible, and on the methods appropriate to its study, might proceed as follows. Each of the paradigms we have examined points to an undisputed dimension of the Hebrew Bible as a collection of writings that teems with religious concepts and practices, discloses segments of an involved history, reflects and presupposes social structures and processes, and is itself an artful literary work.

The paradigm of the Hebrew Bible as a *religious testimony* has the advantage of having been the controlling conception by which the collection of writings was made as an authoritative body of texts, the canon, as well as the advantage of being the chief way that millions of Jews and Christians view their Tanak or Old Testament. The disadvantage of this approach (and certain types of canonical criticism) is that it blocks out of consideration much else of interest in the Bible, on the assumption that what is explicitly or traditionally religious is always of highest concern and importance, not to mention the growing lack of religious consensus in our culture on the basis of which biblical authority could be assured. Not to be overlooked also is the question of whether "religion" meant the same thing to biblical writers as it does to moderns, or whether it was viewed as prescriptive or authoritative in the same way throughout biblical times as it is for Jews and Christians today.

The paradigm of the Hebrew Bible as a *historical witness* has the edge attained by impressive scholarly accomplishment in reconstructing the main outlines of the development of Israelite literature, history, and religion and in offering basic procedures and main conclusions that form a part of even its detractors' outlook on the Bible. The disadvantage of this approach is that it treats the literature of the Hebrew Bible as instrumental to historical and religious interests and fails to contextualize political and religious history sufficiently in its wider social history.

The paradigm of the Hebrew Bible as a *literary world* has the advantage of concentration on the accessible form of the biblical text and does so with the valuable aid of a comparative body of related or contrasted literatures. By teaching us to observe rhetorical structures and devices in the text it prepares a way to suspend judgment and enter the language world of the Hebrew Bible without the need to decide prematurely what is of significance in that world. The disadvantage of this approach is that it ignores the social and historical substrata or contexts out of which the literature arose, genre by genre, source by source, writing by writing, collection by collection, until it reached its end form.

The paradigm of the Hebrew Bible as a product and reflection of the *social world* has the advantage of establishing the public and communal character of biblical texts as intelligible creations of a people working out their social conflicts and contradictions in changing systemic contexts. The social world of ancient Israel gives us a vital integral field, larger than but inclusive of its political and religious history, and likewise linked to a literary world, since both literature and society constitute

fictions that are intimately if indirectly connected. The disadvantage of this approach is that it has to hypothesize structures and processes at points where textual information is insufficient to rule firmly for or against alternative hypotheses.

The social-science paradigm is also capable of quite as much self-defeating dogmatism as the historical-critical and religious paradigms, and can lapse into a kind of pseudotheology. It is also evident that anthropological and sociological categories deal with the typical and thus provide average descriptions and general tendencies that by themselves may miss the momentary oddities and exceptions of historical figures and happenings.

A Preview of Biblical Studies to Come

It sounds commonplace to say that the advantages and disadvantages of the various paradigms of biblical studies are largely due to a required limitation of perspective and method in order to achieve clarity and coherence of results. Yet this truism has significant implications not often considered. Once a question about the Hebrew Bible or ancient Israel is framed in a certain way, the search for an answer gravitates toward one or another of the broad methodological channels we have described.

Consider, for example, the widely different methodological plans of attack customarily adopted to deal with such questions as these: Who wrote the book of Proverbs and when? Are the stories of the patriarchs historically true? What sources were used in writing the books of Samuel? What was the relation between state and tribes during the Israelite monarchy? Was the understanding of God held by Moses theologically correct? What authority does pentateuchal law have for practicing Jews or Christians today? Quite different sorts of evidence and criteria are appropriate from question to question.

The point is that the range of questions an intelligent reader is likely to ask spill out beyond the province of any single paradigm. Moreover, we may discover that more than one paradigm is appropriate, even necessary, to answer a single question fully. By what rules, then, do we leap from one paradigm to the other? When does one paradigm have precedence over another? How are we to bring together the results from different paradigms?

More important than pressing any particular way of negotiating the paradigms, however, is the awareness that we have entered a situation in biblical studies where interaction among an enlarged number of paradigms is potentially more complex, problematic, and exciting than ever before in the long history of interpretation of the Bible. With the emergence of the new literary paradigm and the social-science paradigm, the former two-party conversation between the confessional religious and historical-critical paradigms suddenly enlarged into at least a four-party conversation. Obviously there will have to be considerably more research, discussion, and debate among all self-aware participants before the outlines of the most recent stage of biblical studies will become clear enough to know how the paradigms will shake out.

In any event, the present introduction to the Hebrew Bible will observe various ways of relating, or separating, the paradigms, along with their noteworthy methods and results to date, but no attempt will be made to provide a single higher-order covering paradigm for integrating all the paradigms into a single interpretive structure. In the conclusion of this book, however, one way of collecting and mapping some of the major results of the various paradigms in terms of trajectories will be suggested and tentatively illustrated.

NOTES

1. *TaNaK* is an acronym from the first letters of the three divisions of the Hebrew Bible: *Torah* (Law or Pentateuch), *Nevi'im* (Prophets), and *Ketuvim* (Writings). Wherever "Bible" or "biblical" are used in this book, reference is to the Hebrew Bible, unless context makes clear that the Christian Bible, including the New Testament, is intended.

2. In current biblical studies, "Israel" and "Israelite" (distinguished from "Israeli," a citizen of the modern state of Israel) refer to the people in their early history down to or through the Babylonian exile, while "Jew" and "Jewish" refer to the people after their restoration to Palestine following exile. The term "Jew" comes from the Hebrew word *yehūdī*, "Judahite" ("Judean" in later Latinized form), that is, of the tribe or land or kingdom of Judah in preexilic usage. After the exile, the word *yehūdī* referred mainly to Jews in an inclusive sense, wherever they lived, but on occasion was applied more restrictedly to Judahites/Judeans, that is, those Jews who lived in a restored Palestinian community in the land and former state of Judah. "Israel" is also used for the entire biblical period, especially in speaking of the people as a religious entity.

"Hebrews," once used extensively to refer to the early Israelites, is now out of favor. The language of the Bible, a form of Old Canaanite, is called "Hebrew." Thus by "Hebrew Bible" we mean that the Jewish Scriptures were written in the Hebrew language.

3. I use the abbreviations B.C.E. (Before the Common Era), instead of B.C., and C.E. (Common Era), instead of A.D., to identify dates in the biblical period.

FOR FURTHER READING

Barton, John. *Reading the Old Testament: Method in Biblical Study.* Rev. ed. Philadelphia: Westminster, 1996.

Bible and Culture Collective. *The Postmodern Bible.* New Haven: Yale University Press, 1995.

Kugel, James L. *How to Read the Bible: A Guide to Scripture, Then and Now.* New York: Free Press, 2007.

Yee, Gale A., ed. *Judges and Method: New Approaches in Biblical Studies.* 2nd ed. Minneapolis: Fortress Press, 2007.

QUESTIONS FOR STUDY

1. Briefly describe the historical-critical method. How does it differ from the confessional approach to interpreting the Bible?

2. How have insights from archaeology, existentialism, new literary criticism, and social-science approaches enhanced our understanding of the Hebrew Bible?

3. Of all the approaches to interpreting the biblical text and studying its social and historical contexts discussed in this chapter, which ones do you believe have the greatest potential to contribute significantly to biblical studies? Why?

2

THE WORLD OF THE
HEBREW BIBLE

SUMMARY

The ancient Near East: geology, topography,
    climate, human culture
The topography of Palestine and its four
    north-south strips
What we can know from archaeology about
    ancient Palestine
The political, cultural, and social history of
    the ancient Near East

*See additional materials at fortresspress.com/
gottwald; consult* Carta Bible Atlas *maps 1–42.*

PHYSICAL AND
ECONOMIC GEOGRAPHY

The immediate land of the Bible—known as
Canaan, Israel, or Palestine—bordered the
eastern Mediterranean Sea. It was here, in
an area not more than 150 miles from north
to south and 75 miles from west to east, that
most of the Hebrew Bible was written and
most of the events it relates took place. Geographically and historically, however, this
heartland of the Bible was merely a small part
of a vast area known today as the Middle East
and, in its early history, generally characterized as the ancient Near East. It is the whole of
this ancient Near East that forms the proper
horizons of biblical Israel.

The Ancient Near East

The region pertinent to understand biblical
geography reaches from west to east approxi-

mately two thousand miles, from Turkey to Afghanistan. From north to south a nearly similar distance is spanned from the Caucasus Mountains between the Black and Caspian seas to the tip of the Arabian Peninsula. However, the ancient Near East did not consist of a large, undifferentiated square of land. The land mass of this region was penetrated and constricted by five large bodies of water—the Red, Mediterranean, Black, and Caspian seas, and the Persian Gulf—and it was differentiated internally by mountains, plateaus, deserts, and river valleys.

Moving shields of rock created mountains that run generally west to east across the entire northern section of the region in Turkey and Iran. The great pressure that folded up these northern mountains caused the southern rock shield to crack and break, opening rifts or faults along whose lines materials either rose to form block mountains or fell to form rift valleys that would extend from Syria and Palestine through the entire length of Arabia and Egypt, including a great rift valley in which the Red Sea eventually formed. An immense desert area to the south and east of the major mountain building was relatively undisturbed geologically, extending over the territory of present-day Iraq, Syria, Jordan, Saudi Arabia, and the smaller Persian Gulf states.

By Neolithic and early historical times, the climate of the Near East had become rainfall-deficient. Rainfall was seasonal, coming during the winter in the northern sections and during the summer in the far southern sections. This rainfall was often torrential and accompanied by rapid evaporation, fast runoff, and heavy soil erosion. In the great interior region of Mesopotamia and the Arabian Peninsula, as well as northeast Africa west of the Red Sea, rainfall rapidly tapered off to amounts too slight to permit regular cultiva-

tion of the soil. All in all, the ancient Near Eastern combination of geology and climate presented precarious conditions for human life. Yet it was in the Near East that two of the great cradles of civilization were located. How did this come about?

We first observe that along the southern slopes and piedmonts of the northern mountain ranges, rainfall was fairly plentiful and climate more temperate than in the deserts or mountains. Similarly hospitable conditions prevailed along the eastern Mediterranean coast. From these areas come our earliest evidences of plant and animal domestication and settled village life.

Ancient humans observed the great rivers of the Nile, Tigris, and Euphrates that arose in the well-watered mountains and flowed across vast desert spaces, depositing rich alluvium along their course. In spite of the great summer heat of these river valleys, the rich soils were inviting. To cultivate these alluvial soils dependably, however, it was necessary to capture and control the seasonal runoffs of the rivers through canal and dike systems that coordinated the efforts of many people over great distances and spans of time. By about 3000 B.C.E. irrigation projects promoted intensive farming and a greater density of population.

In this manner "history" began along the great rivers, first in Sumer and a little later in Egypt, as people were at last able to concentrate in larger communities in the irrigation-fertile river valleys. When we speak of "the dawn of history," we mean the beginning of a written record of human events and achievements, but we also mean the emergence of a more elaborate social organization that introduced authoritative leadership and administration to oversee the taming of the rivers and the cultivation of the fields, and to enforce certain allocations of the increased wealth that the new techniques and organization made possible. This form of social organization was the state, and with its development politics in the full sense of the word came into being.

From about 3000 B.C.E. down through biblical times, a succession of states dominated social organization and wrote the majority of records in the ancient Near East. At first these states were confined to the river valleys, but in time the state form of human social organization spread to other Near Eastern regions. From time to time people from within or from outside these various Near Eastern states were able to overthrow the regimes in power and to replace them with their own forms of political organization, generally another centralized state (see pp. 35–39). It is of significance for our study that Israel first appeared on the stage of history as just such a disturber of the existing order in ancient Canaan (see pp. 84–87, 150–63).

If one traces a line from the mouth of the Tigris-Euphrates rivers northward along the course of the rivers, curving west to the Mediterranean Sea and then southward as far as the Nile Delta of Egypt, this line will appear as an arc or crescent. The land demarcated by this arc includes the largest concentrations of population, the most fertile agricultural areas, the most frequently traveled routes, the territories most fought over by armies, and the great majority of powerful states in the ancient Near East. This so-called Fertile Crescent designates the crucial zone of economic and political development in the ancient Near East. It embraces and connects the two great river valleys at either end along a route of easy access that avoids the hazards of desert and high mountain transport.

Within this great arc describing and connecting Egypt and Mesopotamia, the populace engaged in many economic activities, especially farming. Animals were raised for milk products, meat, wool, and hides as well as for transport, farmwork, and even military action. In time pastoral nomads specialized in grazing herds of sheep, goats, and eventually camels, over regions not normally cultivated, although nomads were usually in close and regular mutual relations with the more sedentary peoples.

The needs of farmers and pastoral nomads were largely met by their own labor, and bartering led to a modest division of labor in rural areas. In the great state administrative centers ruling classes supported the work of skilled artisans. Trade in valuable resources and finished products such as precious metals, building materials, and military equipment began to flourish. A system of roads fanned out over the Fertile Crescent, branching out beyond it. Maritime trade followed the Indian Ocean and the Mediterranean Sea.

Privileged corps of bureaucrats—tax administrators, diplomats, military commanders, and priests of state cults—operated the great states and their smaller counterparts. Thus alongside the centralized state in the ancient Near East there appeared social stratification. A small minority of government-favored people (from 1 to 5 percent of the total population) controlled most of the economic surplus. "Surplus" here refers to what is produced over and above the minimum required to keep the 95–99 percent of farmers, herders, and laborers alive and working. Professional soldiers formed the backbone of state armies, but for major campaigns the common people were often conscripted, with the most menial work, including the monumental building projects, often done by state slaves.

Palestine

Palestine was located along the arc between Mesopotamia and Egypt at a point where the sea on the west and the desert on the east constricted the inhabited area into a corridor ranging in width from about 35 miles in the north of the land to about 90 miles in the south. Palestine was the southern section of the Syro-Palestinian corridor that extended between the Euphrates River and Egypt, and its relief structure is generally described as a series of four longitudinal zones, which proceed in order from the sea on the west to the desert on the east:

1. The coastal plain
2. The western mountains or highlands (Cisjordan in Palestine)
3. The Rift Valley (the Jordan River and Dead Sea in Palestine)
4. The eastern mountains, highlands, or plateau (Transjordan in Palestine).

The terrain is actually far more complicated than this customary division. For one thing the four zones do not continue unbroken or with the same prominence over the whole Syro-Palestinian corridor. Furthermore, although the most obvious features of the Palestinian landscape run north and south, the underlying geological structure—which the north-south Rift Valley has obscured—is on a tilted axis from north-northeast to south-southwest.

The net effect of the complicated relief structure of Palestine is that the country consists of a fair number of markedly different subregions that did not easily communicate with one another. The trend toward local self-sufficiency in these regions made unification of the land, for whatever reason, a difficult task. The nature of the initial Israelite social movement, the division into two kingdoms, the hostility between Jews and Samaritans, as well as many other aspects of Israel's history,

can only be understood on the ground plan of the cantonal divisions of Palestine.

Like the greater part of the ancient Near East outside Egypt and Mesopotamia, Palestine lacked any great river that could be harnessed for irrigation. Its people, crops, and herds were necessarily rain-fed. Vital but variable and unpredictable rains came off the Mediterranean from about mid-October to early April, falling most abundantly in the north and on seaward slopes of the land and decreasing strikingly toward the south and on leeward slopes. The soils in Palestine also varied greatly in their suitability for cultivation. The result of this combination of relief, rainfall, and soil factors was that the reliable farming areas of Palestine amounted to less than one-half of the total land area. The reliable core farming regions of Palestine were approximately as follows:

1. The coastal plain north of Mount Carmel and between the Plain of Sharon and Gaza to the south, and including the lateral Esdraelon-Jezreel valleys
2. The Cisjordan highlands for their whole length from Galilee to a point south of Hebron in a strip averaging perhaps twenty miles in width
3. Some points in the upper Jordan Valley north of Beth-shan
4. The Transjordan highlands for their whole length from Bashan to Edom in a strip averaging perhaps ten miles in width.

Land outside the reliable agricultural heartland was used for grazing where possible, and here and there spring-fed oases interrupted otherwise arid regions.

Yet it was precisely in the securest farming lands of the Cisjordan and Transjordan highlands that the first Israelites lived as farmers

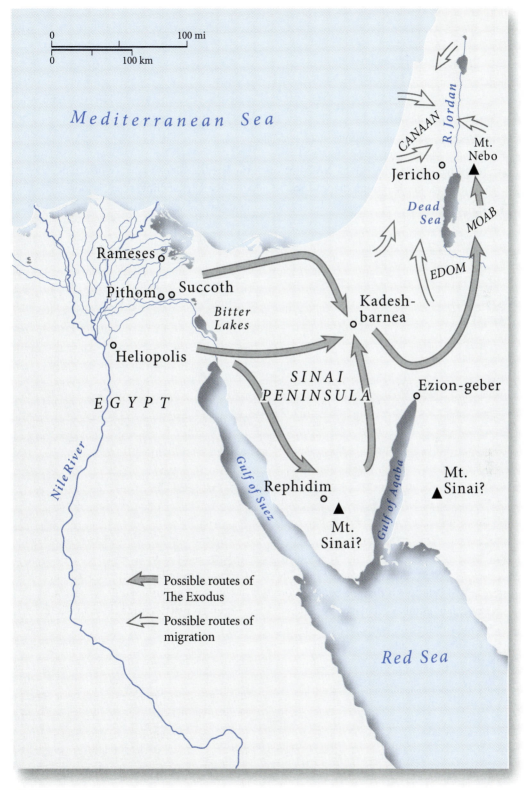

0   100 mi

0   100 km

Mediterranean Sea

CANAAN

R. Jordan

Mt.
Nebo

Jericho

*Dead
Sea*

MOAB

EDOM

Rameses

Pithom

Succoth

*Bitter
Lakes*

Kadesh-
barnea

Heliopolis

*SINAI
PENINSULA*

Ezion-geber

E G Y P T

Nile River

Gulf of Suez

Gulf of Aqaba

Rephidim

Mt.
Sinai?

Mt.
Sinai?

Possible routes of
The Exodus

Possible routes of
migration

Red Sea

MAP 2.1 THE EMERGENCE OF ISRAEL

Canaanite Sites in the Late 13th/Early 12th Century B.C.E.

○ Cities destroyed

● Cities not destroyed

■ New settlements on previously unoccupied sites

□ New settlements on long deserted sites

0   20 mi

0   20 km

Mediterranean Sea

Sea of Galiee

River Jordan

Dead Sea

Hazor ○

Dor ■

Megiddo ○

Taanach ●

Beth-shan ●

Shechem ●

Succoth ○

'Izbet Sartah ■

Shiloh □

Tell Radanna ■

Bethel ○

Ai □

Mizpah

Gibeon ■

Gibeah ■

Jerusalem ●

Gezer ●

Ashdod ○

Beth-shemesh ○

Giloh ■

Lachish ○

Bethzur □

Eglon ○

Debir/ Kiriath Sepher ○

Beersheba ■

Tell Masos □

MAP 2.2 CANAANITE SITES IN THE LATE THIRTEENTH/EARLY TWELFTH CENTURY B.C.E.

Sidon

Damascus

PHOENICIA

Tyre

Dan

Hazor

Mediterranean Sea

Acco

*Sea of
Galiee*

Jokneam

Megiddo

Ramoth-
gilead

Taanach

Ibleam

Beth-shan

Shechem

River Jordan

Qasile

Joppa

Aphek

KINGDOM
OF AMMON

Gezer

Bethel

Ekron

Rabbath-
ammon

Ashdod

Beth
Shemesh

Jerusalem

Heshbon

Ashkelon

REUBEN

Gaza

PHILISTIA

Lachish

*Dead
Sea*

Dibon

Raphia

Hebron

KINGDOM
OF MOAB

Beersheba

NEGEB

Israelite Settlement before the Monarchy

Areas of Israelite settlement
and sovereignty

*KINGDOM
OF EDOM*

| 0 | | 20 mi |
| 0 | | 20 km |

MAP 2.3 ISRAELITE SETTLEMENT BEFORE THE MONARCHY

and resident pastoralists. The territories of Judah, Benjamin, Ephraim, and Manasseh in the western highlands formed the heartland of ancient Israel. Here were located cities such as Hebron, Bethlehem, Jerusalem, Bethel, Shechem, and Samaria. Two major Israelite strongholds stood apart from this central base: Galilee to the north, separated by the Esdraelon-Jezreel valley corridor, and Gilead to the east, cut off by the deep Rift Valley. These two strongholds were always precariously held by Israel, and the regionalism of the land shows up in the suspicion and hostility often expressed back and forth among these regions. Only under David were the coastal plain, the Rift Valley, and most of Transjordan brought under Israel's control. The hill country of southern Cisjordan, and the more vulnerable offshoots in Galilee and Gilead, remained the physical and economic base and the cultural and spiritual homeland of biblical Israel.

Subregions Important to Biblical Israel

Against the backdrop of the general features of Palestinian geography, we will now pinpoint the subregions that had the most significant bearing on Israel's experience.

The Coastal Plain

For its entire length Palestine was flanked on the west by the Mediterranean Sea. Natural and political circumstances blocked Israel from settling the coastal plain or becoming a maritime power.

To begin with, the Palestine coast, with the exception of the Bay of Acco north of Mount Carmel, was unrelieved by indentation, and the development of harbors was frustrated by silting from the Nile Delta deposited all along the coast. As for settlement in the coastal plain,

the intractable marshes of the Plain of Sharon in its center and the continued Philistine presence in the broad, desirable southern part of the plain inhibited occupation. The chief Philistine cities were Gaza, Ashkelon, Ashdod, Gath, and Ekron. Along the narrow northern coastal plain in Syria and Lebanon lived the skilled exploiters of the Mediterranean, the Canaanites known as the Phoenicians. The major posts of Ugarit and Byblos were succeeded by Tyre and Sidon, whose merchants rapidly became the chief maritime power of the great inner sea (see pp. 181–82).

Despite occasional reports in the Bible of Israelite activity upon the sea, Israel remained largely landlocked. The chief significance of the coastal plain for Israel was that through it ran the trunk road from Egypt to Mesopotamia, bringing merchants, diplomats, and invading armies. North of Mount Carmel, the valleys of Esdraelon and Jezreel—through which passed two branches of the trunk road as it turned inland toward Damascus—extended the level coastal terrain into the heart of Israel. This region was a mixed blessing of fertile land, facilitated communication, and vulnerability to attack.

The Hill Country of Judah

Judah comprised the southernmost extension of the western highlands. Its center was a high, rocky plateau averaging three thousand feet in altitude, fertile to the west of the water divide with the desolate Wilderness of Judah to the east. The most important settlement in this wilderness was the oasis at En-Gedi on the Dead Sea. In the cliffs at the northwest end of the sea a sectarian community, keepers of the renowned Dead Sea Scrolls, lived in virtual isolation from roughly 150 B.C.E. to 70 C.E.

The fertile western heights of Judah were protected by the rugged lower hills of the Shephelah ("lowlands" or "foothills"). Much contested by Philistines and Judahites, these hills contained settlements like Lachish, Mareshah, and Beth-shemesh. The Judean massif dropped away into the undulating Negeb, or southland, where the territory of Simeon, with settlements like Beersheba, was early incorporated into Judah. The approaches to Judah, heavily fortified during the monarchy, were thus decidedly defensible on all sides except the north (see pp. 194, 198–200).

In the fertile highlands of Judah lay such towns as Hebron, Tekoa, Bethlehem, and Jerusalem. Throughout this area vineyards were the specialty crop, wheat and barley were grown in quantity, and sheep and goats were extensively bred.

The Hill Country of Samaria

The central bulk of the western highlands was separated from Judah by the so-called Saddle of Benjamin, where, just north of Jerusalem, the highlands dropped several hundred feet. This was a major crossroads, offering the easiest access into the highlands. The buffer zone of Benjamin, containing the settlements of Gibeah and Ramah, was often disputed by the northern and southern kingdoms of Israel and always presented a problem for the adequate defense of nearby Jerusalem.

To the north the limestone dome of Ephraim stretched across the entire highlands. Major towns included Bethel, Ophrah, and Shiloh. Still farther north lay the territory of Manasseh with the major crossroads city of Shechem situated between two mountains. The basins of this area were ideal for growing grains, and the slopes abounded in vineyards and olive groves.

The interplay between geography and politics is complex in this region. The proximity of the valleys of Esdraelon and Jezreel to the north invited Manasseh to spread out into them. It was thus mainly Manasseh that challenged the Canaanite hold on cities like Megiddo and Jezreel in the transverse valleys, but Manasseh was not itself well defended against penetration from three sides. The territories of Ephraim and Manasseh taken together (the so-called Joseph tribes) were eventually known as Samaria, but the unity of this heartland of the northern kingdom was jeopardized by its vulnerable location (see pp. 198–200).

Mount Carmel was the farthest northwest extension of a miles-long ridge that reached to the very edge of the sea. Forbiddingly steep and forested, this ridge served to split the coastal plain so that traffic was channeled through its narrow passes into the valleys of Esdraelon and Jezreel, which became the central nexus of communication in the north of Palestine.

The Hill Country of Galilee

Galilee resumed the north-south mountainous terrain, rising in two steps northward from the Esdraelon-Jezreel valleys. Lower Galilee was composed of shattered limestone and chalk hills, not exceeding two thousand feet. Here lay biblical settlements like Jabneel, amid slopes and basins well adapted to olives, vines, and grains. To the east, basalt rock extended to the Lake of Galilee in the Rift Valley, a region crossed by the trunk road from the Valley of Esdraelon to the north of the Lake of Galilee.

Upper Galilee rose to three thousand feet and higher over a large area prominently uplifted. At its foot ran a direct route from the Lake of Galilee to Acco on the coast. On the edges or within this rocky fastness lay Hazor, Kedesh, and Beth-anath. The Bible itself says very little about this region, although there is archaeological evidence that a network of small farming villages, possibly Israelite, did spread over parts of this region prior to the monarchy (see pp. 150–53).

The Rift Valley

By and large, the Rift Valley was not condu-cive to settlement except at a few oasis sites such as Jericho and Beth-shan, or where high-land streams emptied into the Jordan Valley. The water of the Jordan River itself was too sa-line for agricultural use. The Rift Valley did af-ford convenient north-south travel, although roadways had to be carefully chosen because of difficult terrain.

The Hill Country of Gilead

Located east of the Rift Valley, opposite Manasseh and Ephraim, Gilead rose in a great limestone dome that protected small village life and encouraged the typical mixed farm-ing patterns of the Israelites. Gilead was split by the east-west course of Wadi Jabbok, but similar natural conditions on both sides of the deep wadi contributed to a feeling of unity in the entire region. Ramoth-gilead, Jabesh-

gilead, and Penuel, among other settlements, were located in the highlands, while other towns were situated at the edge of the Rift Valley, where wadis issued out of the Gilead escarpment. The rocky and forested regions of Gilead were a frequent place of retreat in times of political difficulty.

Ammon, Moab, and Edom

Three plateau kingdoms in Transjordan had frequent, mostly hostile contacts with Israel. Ammon, to the southeast of Gilead, was a mixed farming and shepherding state on the very edge of the desert. Moab, directly south of Gilead, was a grain-growing and sheep-raising tableland overlooking the Dead Sea from the east. Edom rose on a long uplift over five thousand feet high, where its altitude as-sured it sufficient rainfall for limited agricul-ture along the plateau crest.

FIG. 2.1 The Jordan River, east of Jericho, where the ten tribes of Israel crossed from Moab into Canaan (and where, in the first century C.E., John the Baptist preached and baptized). Photo: Erich Lessing / Art Resource, N.Y.

The second most important route in Palestine, the King's Highway, connecting with the spice route to south Arabia, ran from the head of the Gulf of Aqabah northward through Edom, Moab, and Ammon toward Damascus. It was heavily trafficked by merchant caravans that were obliged to pay tolls whenever the plateau kingdoms were strong enough to exact them. Whenever an Israelite king aimed at dominion over Transjordan, it was imperative to gain control of the lucrative commerce along the King's Highway (see pp. 181–82, 196).

Archaeology: Material and Written Remains

Archaeology of the Ancient Near East

The previous description of relief and climate in the ancient Near East and Palestine rests heavily on geology, geography, and meteorology. At the same time, even so simplified a description calls attention to how the relief and climate influenced and shaped the lives of ancient people, which necessarily calls into play historical knowledge. Strictly speaking, this knowledge is written knowledge. It is possible, however, to acquire knowledge of human life in the past by carefully examining material remains.

Archaeology is the recovery and systematic study of the material remains of the past, from which inferences are drawn about the culture, society, and history of the people who left the remains. If we are fortunate, among the recovered objects will be occasional written materials, which may range from crudely scratched letters and words to extended literary texts. The material objects must be studied in relation to one another, both at the sites where found and in connection with other related objects and writings, in order to build up a grid of knowledge about the underlying culture, society, and history.

Fortunately we possess a growing wealth of knowledge about the ancient Near East from archaeological excavations. Ancient Near Eastern cities often developed in successive levels of occupation on strategically chosen sites that tended to be used again and again rather than abandoned, with the oldest occupations at the bottom of the mound and the most recent at the top. Excavations all over the ancient Near East, heavily concentrated in the Fertile Crescent, have uncovered ancient cities and libraries that allow us to write a political history of those times with some accuracy and detail. Most of the evidence in writing is from state or temple texts in the archives of the major powers such as Egypt, Sumer, and Assyria. Similar records survive within the Hebrew Bible and appear additionally in an array of written inscriptions, mostly fragmentary, from Israelite Palestine.

It is essential for the biblical interpreter to be aware of the astonishing range and number of ancient Near Eastern texts that have a bearing both on the history recounted or presupposed in the Hebrew Bible and on virtually the entire spectrum of biblical genres and topics. A sample of ancient Near Eastern texts is provided at fortresspress.com/gottwald in connection with appropriate biblical books (see p. 58). The texts are identified there by their linguistic and/or political provenance and are keyed to the pagination of the standard English translations for ready reference.

This linkage of biblical and nonbiblical literature is not intended to imply that there is any necessary direct literary dependence

TABLE 2.1 ARCHAEOLOGICAL PERIODS IN BIBLICAL PALESTINE

Archaeological Periods	Biblical Periods
Mesolithic (Natufian) 　　8000–6000 B.C.E.	
Pre-Pottery Neolithic 　　6000–5000 B.C.E.	
Pottery Neolithic 　　5000–4000 B.C.E.	
Chalcolithic (Copper) 　　4000–3200 B.C.E.	
Esdraelon 　　3200–3000 B.C.E.	
Early Bronze (EB) 　　3000–2800 B.C.E.	
EB I 　　3000–2800 B.C.E.	
EB II 　　2800–2600 B.C.E.	
EB III 　　2600–2300 B.C.E.	
EB IV (or IIIb) 　　2300–2100 B.C.E.	
Middle Bronze (MB) 　　2100–1550 B.C.E.	
MB I (or EB-MB) 　　2100–1900 B.C.E.	
MB IIa 　　1900–1700 B.C.E.	Possible period of the patriarchs
MB IIb 　　1700–1600 B.C.E.	Abraham, Isaac, and Jacob 　　(differently dated by various
MB IIc 　　1600–1550 B.C.E.	Scholars in EB IV, MB, or LB) 　　[see pp. 93–102]
Late Bronze (LB) 　　1550–1200 B.C.E.	
LB I 　　1550–1400 B.C.E.	
LB IIa 　　1400–1300 B.C.E.	

TABLE 2.1 ARCHAEOLOGICAL PERIODS IN BIBLICAL PALESTINE (cont.)

Archaeological Periods	Biblical Periods
Late Bronze (LB) (*continued*)	
LB IIb	
1300–1200 B.C.E.	Moses and the exodus [see pp. 107–9]
Iron I (Ir) or Early Iron (EI)	
1200–900 B.C.E.	
Ir Ia	
1200–1150 B.C.E.	Joshua
Ir Ib	
1150–1025 B.C.E.	Judges of Israel
Ir Ic	
1025–950 B.C.E.	Saul
	David
	Solomon
Ir Id	
950–900 B.C.E.	Division of the kingdom
Iron II (Ir) or Middle Iron (MI)	
900–600 B.C.E.	
Ir IIa	
900–800 B.C.E.	
Ir IIb	
800–700 B.C.E.	Fall of Israel (northern kingdom)
Ir IIc	
700–600 B.C.E.	Reformation of Josiah
Iron III, Late Iron, or Persian	
600–300 B.C.E.	Fall of Judah (southern kingdom)
	Exile to Babylonia
	Restoration of Judah
	Nehemiah and Ezra
Hellenistic	
300–63 B.C.E.	Maccabean Revolt
	Hasmonean Dynasty
Roman	
63 B.C.E.–323 C.E.	Rise of Christianity
	First Jewish Revolt
	Second Jewish Revolt
Byzantine	
323–636 C.E.	
Islamic	
636 C.E.–	

of one writing on the other or that the biblical and nonbiblical texts always correspond closely in matters of form, content, and detail. Web Table A is meant to show that not only did Israel participate in a common geographical and historical world but also in a common literary and religiocultural world.

Archaeology of Palestine

Palestinian archaeology has typically expressed a double-barreled interest in illuminating the Bible and in clarifying the relation of Israel to the surrounding cultures. Because archaeological work has at times been crude, the results of the large volume of archaeological work to date are uneven and must be evaluated critically. There are now recognized professional and publishing forums where the methods and conclusions of archaeological research are critically assessed and refined in ongoing dialogue.

Excavations in Palestine have unearthed materials from the entire range of archaeological periods, beginning with the Mesolithic Age and extending on through the most recent Islamic period. The generally accepted designations for the archaeological periods and their dating are listed in table 2.1, together with chronologically related biblical periods, either known or conjectured. The convention is to specify some periods—especially those applicable to biblical times—according to the most advanced metal in use, for example, copper (chalcolithic), bronze, or iron.

Palestine has probably been as extensively surveyed and excavated as any ancient country in the world. An enormous number of sites remain to be attended to, and additional sites keep coming to the attention of archaeologists.

Web Table D is arranged according to the geographical divisions of the land discussed in pages 25–31. Unless biblical names of locations are known with a high degree of certainty, the modern names of sites are given. A key is included to indicate remains at each site according to the archaeological periods represented (only a very few pre-Bronze sites are included; Iron I and II are treated together, and Iron III is called Persian). It is at once apparent that the coastal plain, Judah, and Samaria exhibit a larger concentration of important excavated sites during the biblical period than do Galilee, the Rift Valley, Gilead, and the kingdoms of Ammon, Moab, and Edom.

Palestinian archaeology has commonly been called biblical archaeology, which appropriately emphasizes the consuming interests of past archaeologists in the bearing of archaeology on the literature and history of ancient Israel. These interests supplemented the historical-critical aspect of biblical studies (see pp. 94–95, 150–57, 171–72, 235–37) and continue to have a vital place in the archaeology of Palestine. Paralleling the emergent methods of new literary criticism and social-scientific criticism in biblical studies, however, is a growing interest in archaeology as an important contributor to the reconstruction of ancient Israelite life in its total cultural range, including its social history (see pp. 150–57). The relation between the older and newer emphases is highlighted in the ongoing discussion as to whether the discipline should be called biblical archaeology or Palestinian archaeology.

Even during the long period when history and religion in relation to the biblical text dominated Palestinian archaeology, the process of excavating and recording inevitably produced an impressive range of information that advanced our knowledge of the physical, technological, economic, social, aesthetic, and intellectual life of the ancient inhabitants of Palestine. Nonetheless, our archaeological information, like Near Eastern archaeology as a whole, is mostly about life among the rulers and upper classes in the large administrative centers of the land. Growing sensitivity to class indicators reflected in the data and growing interest in excavation of rural sites are important to many of the classical topics of biblical studies, from the origins of Israel in a tribal social movement to the basic terms of Judah's restoration to Palestine.

POLITICAL, CULTURAL, AND SOCIAL HISTORY OF THE ANCIENT NEAR EAST

The accumulating wealth of material and written remains from the ancient Near East has made it possible to write a coherent history of that region beginning shortly after 3000 B.C.E. As expected, the focal points of that ancient history were in the Nile Valley and in the middle and lower Tigris-Euphrates valleys, although important political centers in other regions like Anatolia and Iran at times also dominated international affairs in the ancient Near East.

An attempt at schematizing these political developments is presented in chart 2.1: in their chronological order (reading horizontally) and in terms of the coexistence of states in different regions (reading vertically). The various political regimes are arranged on vertical lines representing the major geographical regions of the ancient Near East. Reading

from left to right on the chart, these lines follow the arc of the Fertile Crescent from Egypt in the west to Iran in the east. Three of these geographical regions—Anatolia, Iran, and Greece—lie outside the Fertile Crescent altogether, but from each of them came conquerors who dominated part or all of the Fertile Crescent: from Anatolia came the Hittites, from Iran the Persians, and from Greece the Macedonians.

Of all these regions, Egypt showed the firmest political continuity, doubtless due to isolation of the country by desert and sea. Yet Egypt experienced periods of decline and contending dynasties, as well as major conquests from without. The Tigris-Euphrates valleys, open to entrance on all sides, experienced more frequent political changes and domination by regimes whose ruling classes came from outside the Fertile Crescent.

The original political core of Mesopotamia was in the southern Sumerian city-states. Later the center passed to Akkad and Babylon in the middle section of the valleys. Babylon remained an important capital or administrative center through Persian times. Meanwhile, Assyrian power emerged along the northern Tigris Valley, and the Hittites and Mitannians held sway in the northern Euphrates region. The upper Euphrates adjoined Syria on the west, and over this whole area there appeared midsized kingdoms such as Mari, Ugarit, and Ebla.

The state form of political organization that facilitated irrigation agriculture spread rapidly over the whole ancient Near East. The smallest independent region usually had its king, bureaucracy, and army, although leaders or even entire regimes were periodically swept away. States facilitated trade with one another, carried on elaborate diplomacy, established alliances, and fought for supremacy.

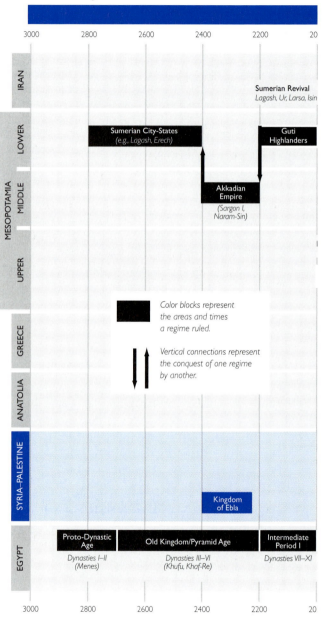

Chart 2.1

Political Regimes of the Ancient Near East, 3000-63 B.C.E.

	3000	2800	2600	2400	2200	20

IRAN

Sumerian Revival
Lagash, Ur, Larsa, Isin

MESOPOTAMIA

LOWER

Sumerian City-States
(e.g., Lagash, Erech)

Guti Highlanders

Akkadian Empire

(Sargon I, Naram-Sin)

MIDDLE

UPPER

Color blocks represent the areas and times a regime ruled.

Vertical connections represent the conquest of one regime by another.

GREECE

ANATOLIA

SYRIA–PALESTINE

Kingdom of Ebla

EGYPT

Proto-Dynastic Age	Old Kingdom/Pyramid Age	Intermediate Period I
Dynasties I–II (Menes)	*Dynasties III–VI (Khufu, Khaf-Re)*	*Dynasties VII–XI*

	3000	2800	2600	2400	2200	20

CHART 2.1 POLITICAL REGIMES OF THE ANCIENT NEAR EAST, 3000–63 B.C.E.

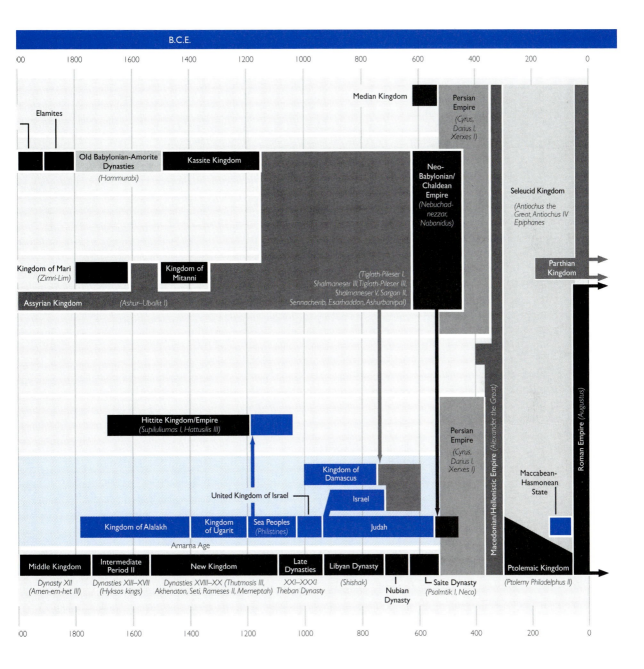

Everywhere religion served as an ideology to legitimate the existing social and political order.

Powerful states began to extend their rule far beyond their homelands, dominating larger and larger sections of the ancient Near East. Kingdoms thus became empires. The Akkadians and Old Babylonians had considerable success in imperial ventures. The Hittites of Anatolia penetrated from the north into upper Mesopotamia and Syria. Assyria eventually dominated the entire Fertile Crescent and held Egypt for a brief time. The Neo-Babylonians emulated the Assyrian success for a shorter period. The Persians, based in Iran, mastered the whole Fertile Crescent, Egypt and Anatolia included. The Macedonians, under Alexander, briefly possessed the entire Persian domain until, at their leader's death, it was divided among his generals.

These ancient Near Eastern imperial adventures were of varying magnitude, cohesion, and durability. It was customary to subordinate conquered states as vassals headed by local princes, thereby securing military and economic assets on the side of the conqueror. To secure greater control and efficiency, the Assyrians began to turn many of their conquered territories into provinces headed by Assyrian officials. This practice was continued by the Neo-Babylonians, Persians, and Macedonians. After the brief flowering of Israel as a united kingdom under David and Solomon, its weakened divided branches were drawn increasingly into imperial diplomacy and warfare (see pp. 195–200, 210–15). The northern branch, Israel, fell to the Assyrians, and the southern branch, Judah, was overthrown by the Neo-Babylonians. The return of Judahite exiles to Palestine was sponsored by the Persian Empire with the aim of securing its frontier with Egypt by means

of a strong colony of loyal subjects (see pp. 248–54).

The imperial adventures of Egypt first surfaced under the Middle Kingdom when it penetrated the Sinai Peninsula. For a time Egypt held Palestine and southern Syria (see pp. 154–57), while the Hittites controlled northern Syria. Egypt was engaged in repeated contests with Assyria and the Neo-Babylonian Empire, and the little Palestinian states of Israel and Judah were often caught in this cross fire between imperial powers.

The political history of the ancient Near East is easier to picture in chart form than are the cultural and social histories. It is generally agreed that a common core of culture runs through the history of both Egypt and Mesopotamia, with Syria-Palestine developing local features heavily influenced from the older valley centers. The shape and flavor of these cultures come to expression in the abundance of ancient Near Eastern texts, as sampled in Web Table A.

The political, cultural, and social histories of the ancient Near East, which scholars normally treat in isolation from one another, intersect when we try to visualize the actual continuities and discontinuities of daily life in relation to the clash and succession of political regimes. As noted above, the records we possess for the ancient Near East are primarily accounts written by ruling classes. In the past, changes in Mesopotamian and Syro-Palestinian regimes and cultures have usually been explained as the displacement or overrunning of populations by nomadic hordes from the desert or mountains. It is now clear that pastoral nomadism was never the major force in the ancient Near East that anthropologically uninformed scholars took it to be. Nomadism aside, there are many difficulties with an undiscriminating appeal to population displacement. A change of political regimes can occur in many ways; new regimes may differ greatly in the extent to which they use or replace old structures; and changes in language can be ambiguous, for diplomats, rulers, and subjects may all speak different languages.

The deceptively simple surface of the political history of the ancient Near East passes over a depth and complexity of cultural and social dynamics that are a matter of great significance in ascertaining the origins of the biblical Israelites. The straight story line of the Hebrew Bible may be, and often is, read like a perfectly clear political account of self-contained events. But as soon as we look attentively at the literary forms in which Israel's early life is reported, we are immediately carried into the complex cultural and social world of ancient Palestine. It is a world in which Israel appears at a date well past the midpoint in the whole course of ancient Near Eastern history. The concept of Israelite pastoral nomads sweeping in from the desert to kill off all the Canaanites makes a dramatic picture, but it accords neither with the full evidence of the Hebrew Bible nor with our growing understanding of the ancient Near East.

FOR FURTHER READING

Baly, Dennis. *The Geography of the Bible*. Rev. ed. New York: Harper & Row, 1974.

Deist, Ferdinand E. *The Material Culture of the Bible: An Introduction*. Sheffield: Sheffield Academic, 2000.

Dever, William G. *What Did the Biblical Writers Know and When Did They Know It? What Archaeology Can Tell Us about the Reality of Ancient Israel*. Grand Rapids: Eerdmans, 2001.

Hallo, William W., and William R. Simpson. *The Ancient Near East: A History*. 2nd ed. New York: Harcourt Brace Jovanovich, 1998.

Hopkins, David C. *The Highlands of Canaan: Agricultural Life in the Early Iron Age*. Decatur, Ga.: Almond, 1985.

King, Philip J., and Lawrence E. Stager. *Life in Biblical Israel*. Louisville: Westminster John Knox, 2001.

QUESTIONS FOR STUDY

1. Describe the major geographical features of biblical Israel. What were the primary agricultural and pastoral activities of the people living there? What is the strategic significance of Israel's location on the land bridge between Egypt and Mesopotamia?

2. Identify the major powers in the ancient Near East during the period 1400 to 63 B.C.E. How did each of these empires influence ancient Israel for good or for ill? (See chart 2.1, pp. 36–37.)

3. How does the social status of the authors of ancient Near Eastern writings affect our understanding of the region's history and cultural development? What other resources or material evidence exists that can contribute to our knowledge of this area?

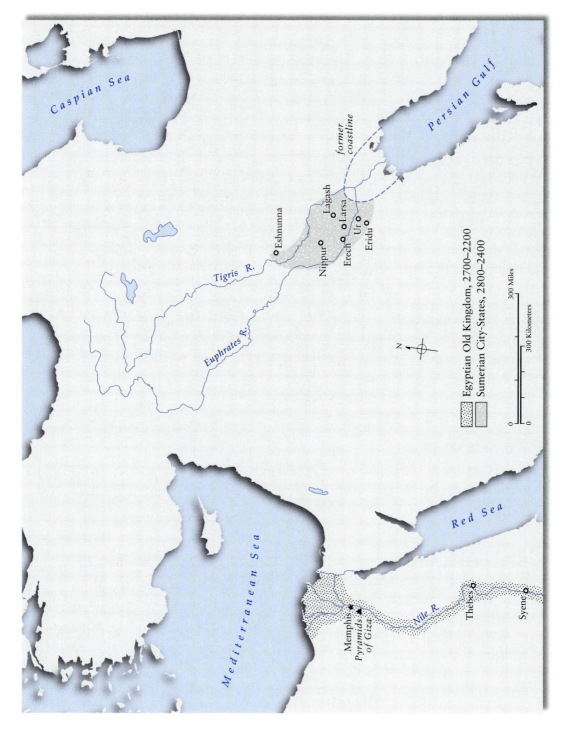

Caspian Sea

Persian Gulf

former coastline

Eshnunna

Lagash
Larsa
Nippur
Erech
Ur
Eridu

Tigris R.

Euphrates R.

Egyptian Old Kingdom, 2700–2200
Sumerian City-States, 2800–2400

N

300 Miles

300 Kilometers

Red Sea

Mediterranean Sea

Memphis
Pyramids
of Giza

Nile R.

Thebes

Syene

MAP 2.4 THE NEAR EAST IN 2600 B.C.E.

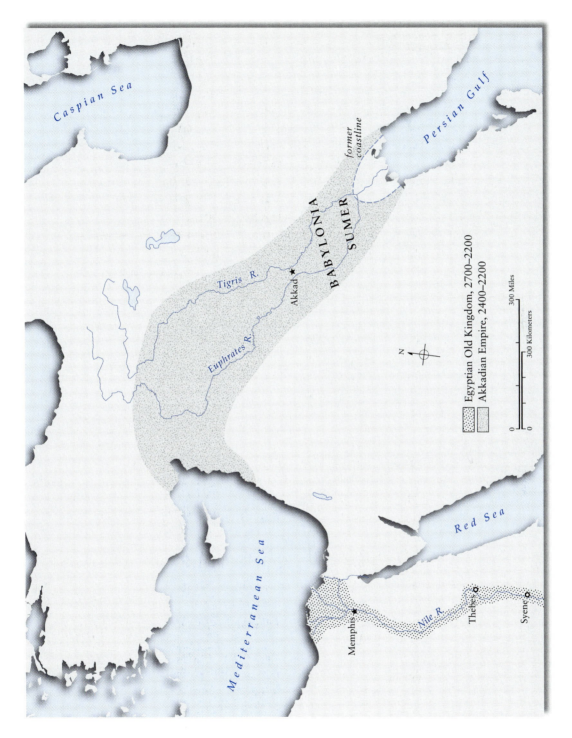

MAP 2.5 THE NEAR EAST IN 2300 B.C.E.

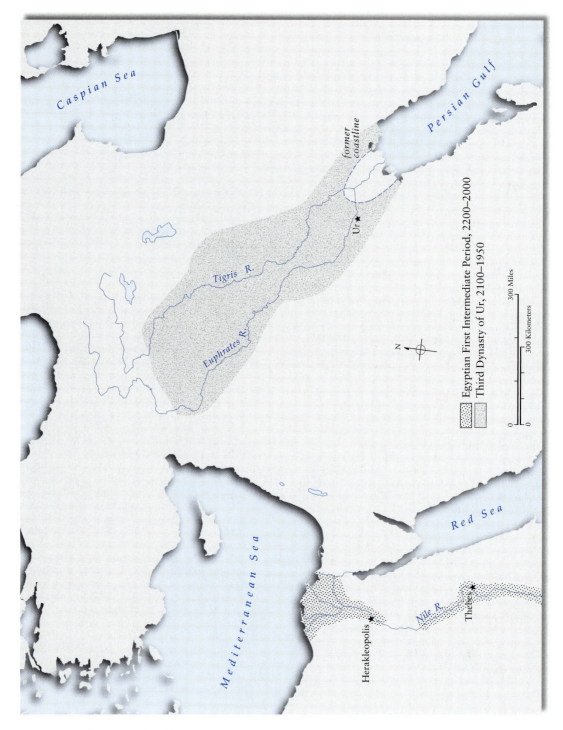

MAP 2.6 THE NEAR EAST IN 2050 B.C.E.

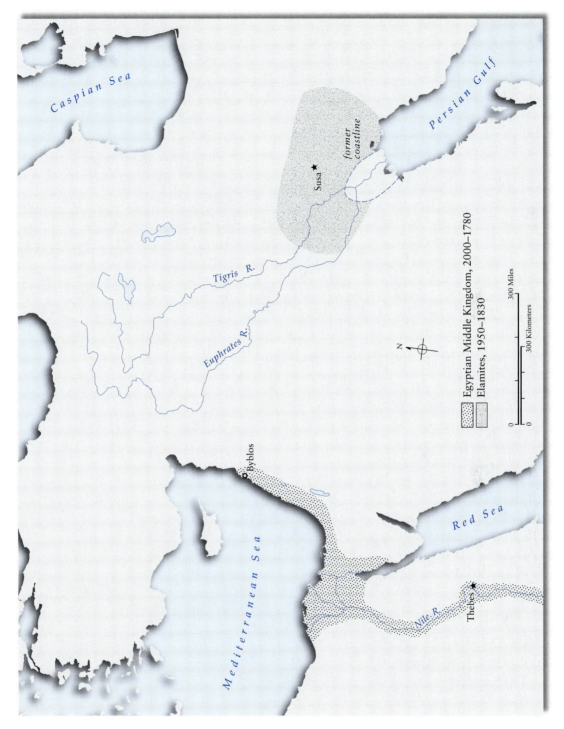

MAP 2.7 THE NEAR EAST IN 1900 B.C.E.

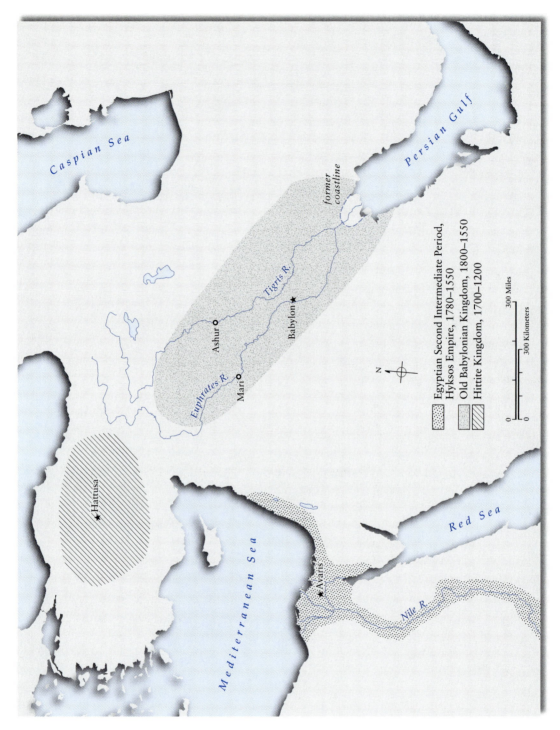

Caspian Sea

Persian Gulf

former coastline

Tigris R.

Ashur ○

Babylon ★

Euphrates R.

Mari ○

Egyptian Second Intermediate Period, Hyksos Empire, 1780–1550

Old Babylonian Kingdom, 1800–1550

Hittite Kingdom, 1700–1200

300 Miles

300 Kilometers

N

★ Hattusa

Red Sea

Mediterranean Sea

Avaris ★

Nile R.

MAP 2.8 THE NEAR EAST IN 1700 B.C.E.

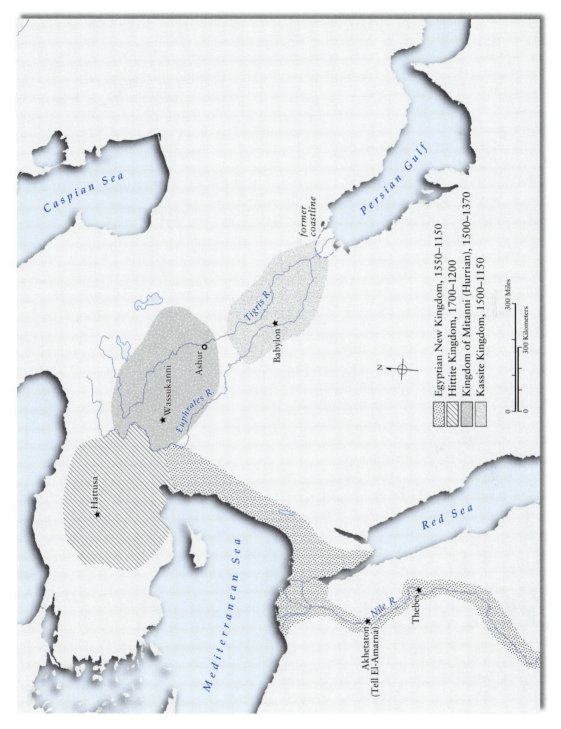

MAP 2.9 THE NEAR EAST IN 1400 B.C.E.

Caspian Sea

Persian Gulf

former
coastline

Kingdom of Mitanni (Hurrian), 1500–1370
Egyptian New Kingdom, 1550–1150
Hittite Kingdom, 1700–1200
Kassite Kingdom, 1500–1150

300 Miles

300 Kilometers

Wassukanni

Ashur

Tigris R.

Babylon

Euphrates R.

N

Hattusa

Mediterranean Sea

Red Sea

Nile R.

Akhetaton
(Tell El-Amarna)

Thebes

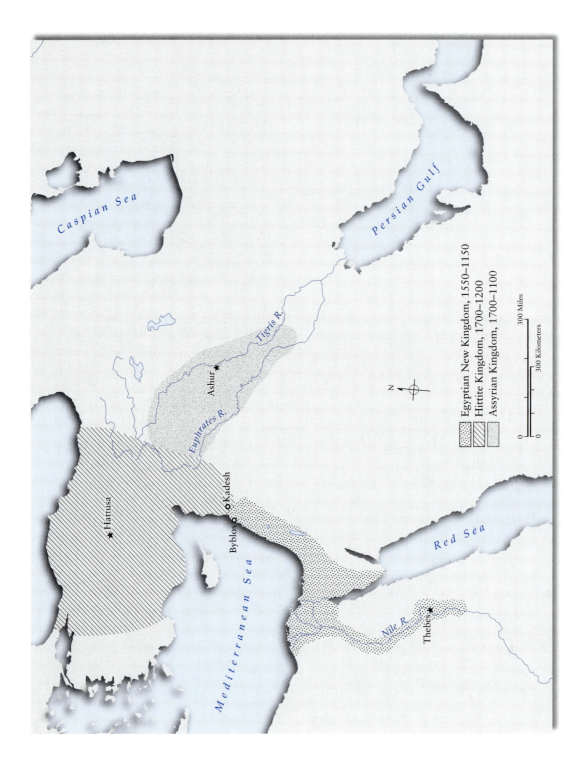

Caspian Sea

Persian Gulf

Tigris R.

Ashur

Euphrates R.

N

Egyptian New Kingdom, 1550–1150
Hittite Kingdom, 1700–1200
Assyrian Kingdom, 1700–1100

300 Miles

300 Kilometers

Hattusa

Kadesh
Byblos

Red Sea

Mediterranean Sea

Nile R.

Thebes

MAP 2.10 THE NEAR EAST IN 1225 B.C.E.

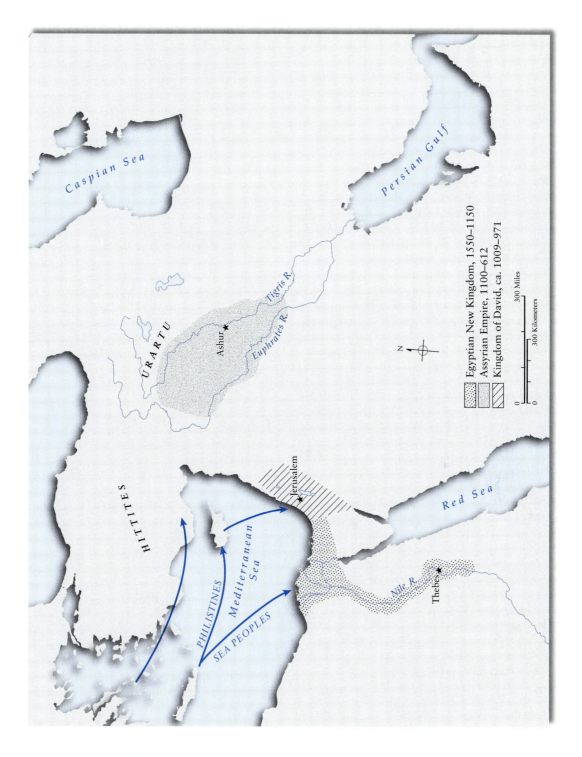

MAP 2.11 THE NEAR EAST IN 1000 B.C.E.

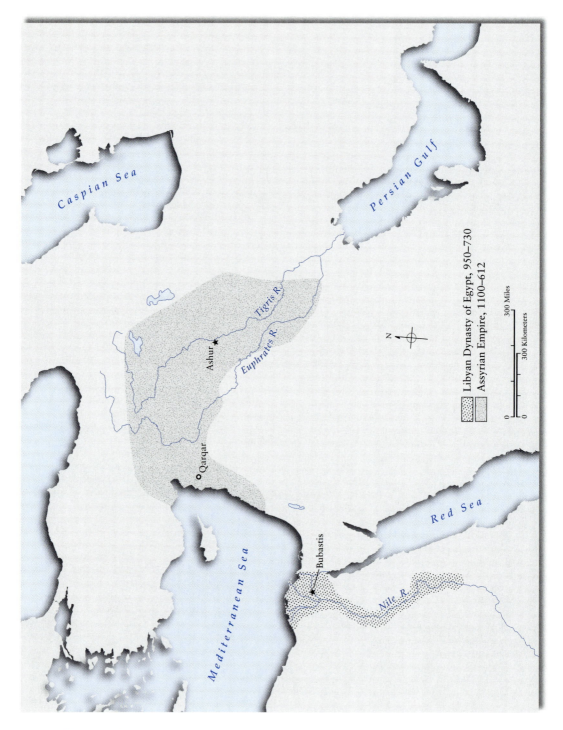

Caspian Sea

Persian Gulf

Tigris R.

Euphrates R.

★ Ashur

Qarqar

Libyan Dynasty of Egypt, 950–730
Assyrian Empire, 1100–612

N

300 Miles

300 Kilometers

Red Sea

Bubastis

Nile R.

Mediterranean Sea

MAP 2.12 THE NEAR EAST IN 800 B.C.E.

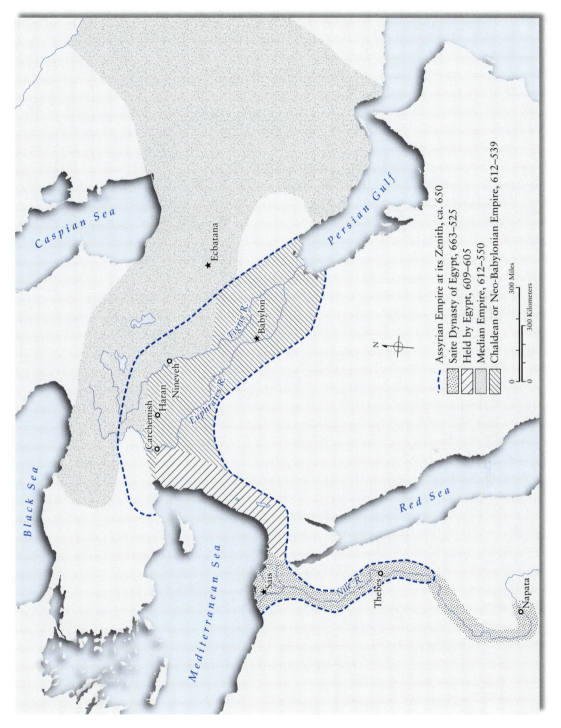

Caspian Sea

Ecbatana

Persian Gulf

Tigris R.

Babylon

Haran
Nineveh

Carchemish

Euphrates R.

Black Sea

Red Sea

Mediterranean Sea

Sais

Nile R.

Thebes

Napata

Assyrian Empire at its Zenith, ca. 650

Saite Dynasty of Egypt, 663–525

Held by Egypt, 609–605

Median Empire, 612–550

Chaldean or Neo-Babylonian Empire, 612–539

N

300 Miles

300 Kilometers

0

0

MAP 2.13 THE NEAR EAST IN 660–605 B.C.E.

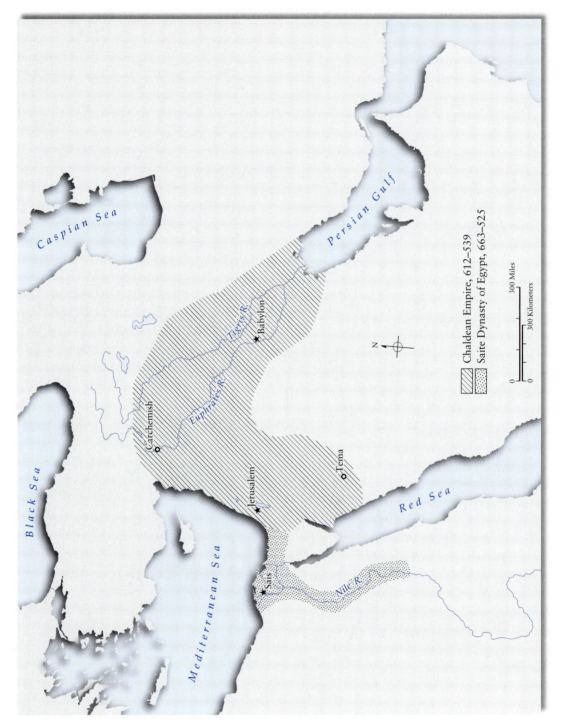

MAP 2.14 THE NEAR EAST IN 580 B.C.E.

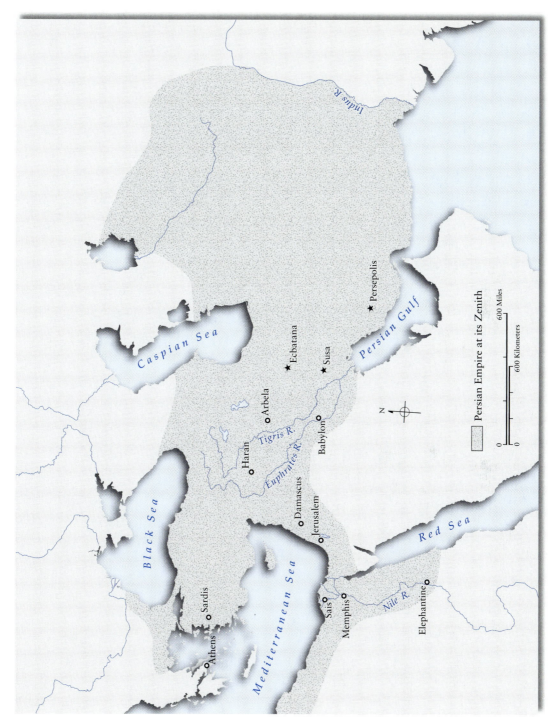

MAP 2.15 THE NEAR EAST IN 500 B.C.E.

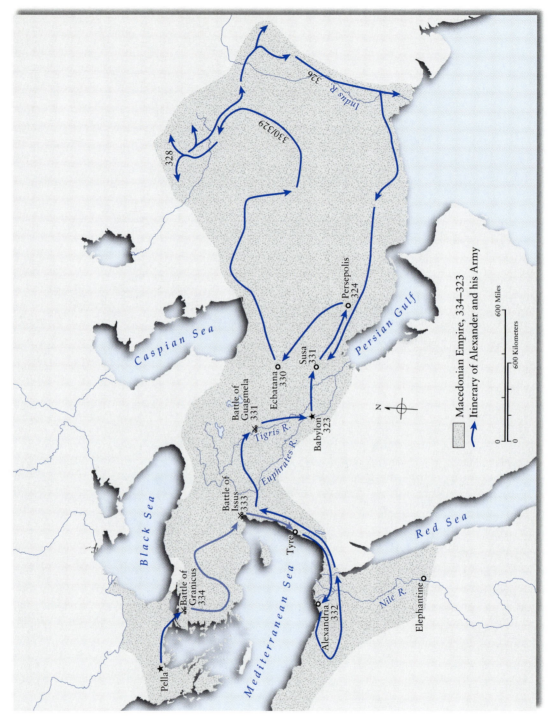

MAP 2.16 THE NEAR EAST IN 334–323 B.C.E.

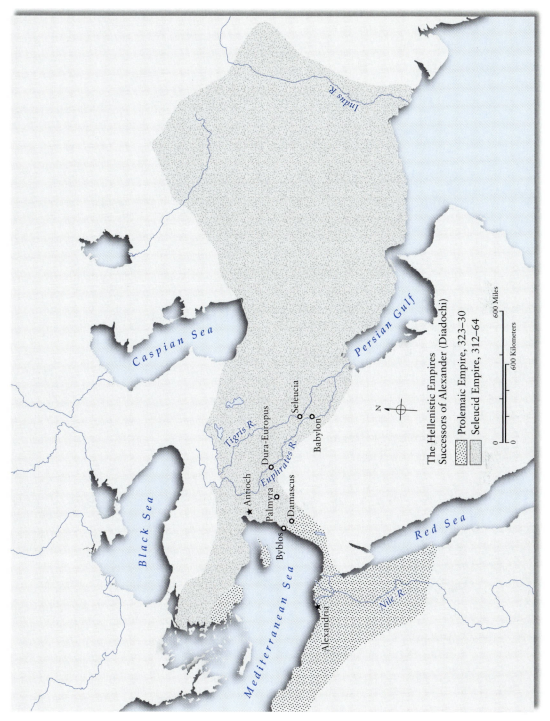

Caspian Sea

Black Sea

Mediterranean Sea

Red Sea

Persian Gulf

Indus R.

Tigris R.

Euphrates R.

Nile R.

Seleucia
Babylon
Dura-Europus
Palmyra
Antioch
Damascus
Byblos
Alexandria

N

The Hellenistic Empires
Successors of Alexander (Diadochi)

Ptolemaic Empire, 323–30
Seleucid Empire, 312–64

600 Miles

600 Kilometers

MAP 2.17 THE NEAR EAST IN 290 B.C.E.

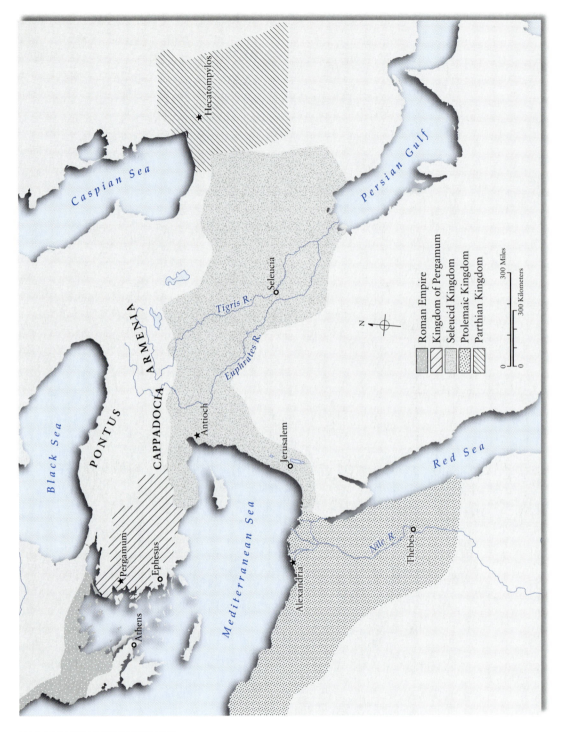

MAP 2.18 THE NEAR EAST IN 168 B.C.E.

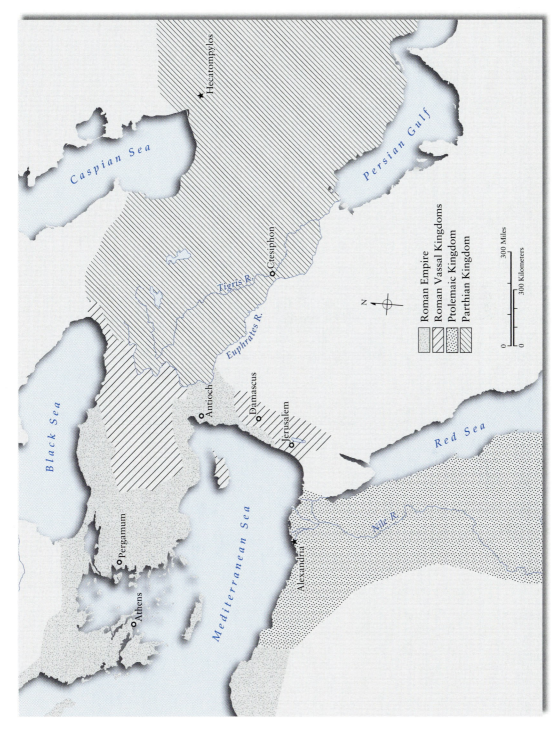

MAP 2.19 THE NEAR EAST IN 63 B.C.E.

CHART 3.1

The Relation of the Hebrew Bible to Other Ancient Literatures

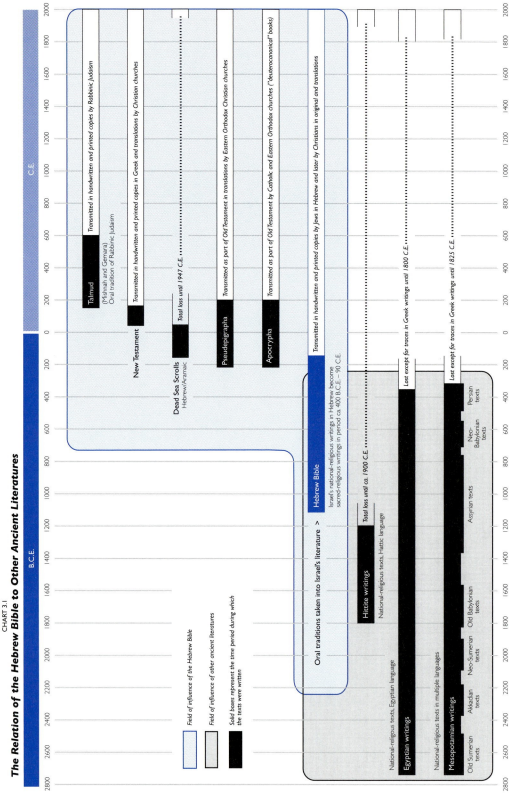

CHART 3.1 THE RELATION OF THE HEBREW BIBLE TO OTHER ANCIENT LITERATURES

THE LITERARY HISTORY
OF THE HEBREW BIBLE

3

SUMMARY

The Hebrew Bible and earlier literature of
the ancient Near East

Bodies of literature influenced by the
Hebrew Bible: the Apocrypha, the
Pseudepigrapha, the Dead Sea Scrolls, the
New Testament, the Talmud

The long process of the formation of the
books of the Hebrew Bible

The three main parts of the Hebrew Bible

The canon of the Hebrew Bible

Versions and translations of the Hebrew
Bible

*See additional materials at fortresspress.com/
gottwald.*

RELATION OF THE HEBREW BIBLE TO OTHER BODIES OF LITERATURE

An appropriate start for tracing the literary
history of the Hebrew Bible is to situate its
writings in relation to other closely related
bodies of literature in terms of their temporal sequences, their original languages, their
affinities, and their transmission and translation histories (see chart 3.1, opposite).

The Hebrew Bible itself was written between roughly 1200 and 125 B.C.E., largely in
Hebrew but with brief passages in Aramaic.
It has been continuously transmitted by religiously observant Jewish communities. From
earliest times Christians also made use of the
Hebrew Bible, but almost entirely in translation until the Renaissance and Reformation.
In recent centuries, Protestant and Catholic
scholars have devoted increasing attention to
the original text of the Hebrew Bible.

Independent National Literatures: The Ancient Near Eastern Texts

Beginning long before the first biblical writings, the peoples of the ancient Near East developed extensive literatures (see chart 3.1) written in the favored languages of the literate circles where these texts were composed: Egyptian, Sumerian, Akkadian, Old Babylonian, Assyrian, Neo-Babylonian, Persian, Aramaic, and Hattic (Hittite). Unlike the Hebrew Bible, however, these extensive writings largely disappeared with the decline of the ancient Near East, although excavations have brought these submerged literatures of antiquity to light, making them accessible in modern translations. It is obvious that the Hebrew Bible and the ancient Near Eastern texts share a broad cultural heritage. Since Israel was a relatively small and insignificant historical force in the biblical era, its literature did not noticeably influence its neighbors. The literary dependence of Israel on the writings of its neighbors, however, was immense in terms of common literary forms and themes (see Web Table B), but the direct literary dependence of biblical texts on ancient Near Eastern texts is arguable only in a comparatively few instances (see pp. 323–25).

Jewish and Christian Literatures Dependent on the Hebrew Bible

The other literatures to be surveyed all arose after the Hebrew Bible was largely completed. Since these later literatures were written by Jews, or by Gentile Christians familiar with the Jewish heritage, they are totally aware of the Hebrew Bible and either continue along its lines of development or comment and interpret it.

Apocrypha and Pseudepigrapha

The Apocrypha[1] of the Hebrew Bible (table 3.1) contains writings composed between about 200 B.C.E. and 100 C.E. Although widely used by Jews in that period, they did not become part of the accepted Jewish canon of scripture. Instead, they were venerated by the early Christians and became part of the canon of Catholic Christianity. At the Reformation, Protestants denied the Apocrypha equal status with the Hebrew Bible, while the status of the Apocrypha in the major Eastern Orthodox churches has varied over time.

The Old Testament Pseudepigrapha[2] of the Hebrew Bible (see table 3.1) derive from the same period as the Apocrypha but are more numerous and include more apocalyptic writings similar to Daniel in the Hebrew Bible. The books of the Pseudepigrapha were not part of the Jewish or Catholic canons of scripture, but they were accepted in varying combinations among certain Eastern Christian bodies such as the Coptic, Ethiopic, and Syrian churches (see Web Table E), in whose languages many of these books were preserved.

Protestant Bibles are increasingly returning to the practice of including the Apocrypha in an appendix to translations of the Hebrew Bible. Critical editions of both bodies of literature in modern translation are available, but the exact boundaries of the Pseudepigrapha are yet to be agreed upon.

Dead Sea Scrolls

The Dead Sea Scrolls (see chart 3.1), found in the library of a Jewish sectarian community, probably Essenes, include a wealth of biblical and nonbiblical documents, mostly fragmentary, the latter written between 150 B.C.E. and 70 C.E. (Web Table F). The nonbiblical texts include already-known Apocrypha and Pseudepigrapha, but there are several writings known only from this source. The discovery of the biblical texts, older by many centuries than any other extant manuscripts, is of the highest importance for reconstructing the history of the development and transmission of the text of the Hebrew Bible (see pp. 70–72).

New Testament and Talmud

These two important Christian and Jewish literary works are grouped together in this discussion because each in its own way interprets the Hebrew Bible that Christians and Jews jointly share but appropriate very differently. The early Christian community, at first a Jewish movement, had become a separate religious entity by the end of the first century C.E. Rabbinic Judaism, surviving the fall of Jerusalem in 70 C.E., rapidly standardized forms of ritual and biblical exegesis that had earlier been much more fluid and contested among Jews. While both religious communities adhered tenaciously to the Hebrew Bible, the authoritative New Testament and Talmud guaranteed that they would see the same texts through markedly different confessional lenses.

For the first Christians, who were Jews (see pp. 73–74), the Hebrew Bible was their only scripture for many decades. Only as conflicts in the church over the nature of Christian faith and identity arose in the second century C.E. did it become urgent to assert that the Hebrew Bible was indeed scripture—to be designated as the Old Testament or Old Covenant—but that, in addition, a core of early Christian writings constituted a second equally authoritative division of scripture, the New Testament or New Covenant (chart 3.1). Thereafter, the Hebrew Bible in Greek or Latin transla-tion, supplemented by the Apocrypha, was combined with the New Testament to form the Bible of Catholic Christians. The Eastern Orthodox Christians concurred, but included further books of the Pseudepigrapha.

The Talmud ("study/instruction") is the vast body of codified Oral Law that developed from about 180 C.E. to 550 C.E. (chart 3.1), on the basis of which rabbinic authorities definitively shaped the structure of Judaism after the fall of Jerusalem in 70 C.E. had effectively eliminated rival forms of Jewish religious life and thought. The essence of these oral interpretations/reinterpretations was to elicit from the biblical text exact directives for current Jewish religious and ritual conduct (halakah, "walking, guiding one's life"). Generations of interpreters, identified with the Pharisees from about 150 B.C.E., developed these oral laws, which were codified about 180 C.E. in the Mishnah ("repetition/study") and combined with commentary on the Mishnah (Gemara, "completion") around 550 C.E. to form the Talmud.

Meanwhile, pious interpretation/reinter-pretation of nonlegal biblical texts was also developing through elaboration on the biblical stories and prophecies (haggadah, "narration"). These haggadic reflections found their way into Midrash ("exposition"), consisting of many commentaries on biblical books that were written from 150 to 1300 C.E.

As a whole, the Talmud as codified Oral Law was conceived as the continuing living word of Moses, entirely consistent with the words of the Law. The Hebrew Bible received the simple descriptive name Tanak, calling attention to its threefold contents (chap. 1 n1), or it was simply called Torah, employing the name of the first division to refer to the whole.

TABLE 3.1 CANONS OF THE HEBREW BIBLE AND OLD TESTAMENT

Hebrew Bible	Protestant Old Testament	

Torah
Genesis
Exodus
Leviticus
Numbers
Deuteronomy

Prophets (Former)
Joshua
Judges
Samuel (1 and 2)
Kings (1 and 2)

Prophets (Latter)
Isaiah
Jeremiah
Ezekiel
Minor Prophets
  ("The Twelve"):
  Hosea, Joel, Amos,
  Obadiah, Jonah,
  Micah, Nahum,
  Habakkuk,
  Zephaniah, Haggai,
  Zechariah,
  Malachi

Writings
Psalms
Proverbs
Job
Song of Songs
Ruth
Lamentations
Qoheleth
  (Ecclesiastes)
Esther
Daniel
Ezra-Nehemiah
Chronicles (1 and 2)

Pentateuch
Genesis
Exodus
Leviticus
Numbers
Deuteronomy

Historical Books
Joshua
Judges
Ruth
1 Samuel
2 Samuel
1 Kings
2 Kings
1 Chronicles
2 Chronicles
Ezra
Nehemiah
Esther

Poetry/Wisdom
Job
Psalms
Proverbs
Ecclesiastes
  (Qoheleth)
Song of Solomon
  (Songs)

Prophets
Isaiah
Jeremiah
Lamentations
Ezekiel
Daniel
Hosea
Joel
Amos
Obadiah
Jonah
Micah
Nahum
Habakkuk
Zephaniah
Haggai
Zechariah
Malachi

Apocrypha
1 Esdras
2 Esdras
Tobit
Judith
Additions to Esther
Wisdom of Solomon
Ecclesiasticus
  (Wisdom of Sirach)
Baruch
Letter of Jeremiah
Prayer of Azariah
  and Song of the
  Three Young Men
Susanna
Bel and the Dragon
Prayer of Manasseh
1 Maccabees
2 Maccabees

TABLE 3.1 CANONS OF THE HEBREW BIBLE AND OLD TESTAMENT (*cont.*)

Roman Catholic Old Testament

Pentateuch	**Poetry/Wisdom**	**Prophets**
Genesis	Job	Isaiah
Exodus	Psalms (Greek and	Jeremiah
Leviticus	Russian Orthodox	Lamentations
Numbers	Bibles include	Baruch (includes
Deuteronomy	Psalm 151 and Prayer	Letter of Jeremiah)
	of Manasseh)	Ezekiel
Historical Books	Proverbs	Daniel (with
Joshua	Ecclesiastes	additions)
Judges	(Qoheleth)	Hosea
Ruth	Song of Solomon	Joel
1 Samuel	(Songs)	Amos
2 Samuel	Wisdom of Solomon	Obadiah
1 Kings	Ecclesiasticus	Jonah
2 Kings	(Wisdom of Sirach)	Micah
1 Chronicles		Nahum
2 Chronicles		Habakkuk
Ezra (Greek and		Zephaniah
Russian Orthodox		Haggai
Bibles also include		Zechariah
1 Esdras, and Russian		Malachi
Orthodox includes		
2 Esdras)		
Nehemiah		
Tobit		
Judith		
Esther (with additions)		
1 Maccabees		
2 Maccabees (Greek		
and Russian		
Orthodox Bibles		
include 3 Maccabees)		

HOW THE HEBREW BIBLE CAME TO BE

The printed copies of the Hebrew Bible used by readers today, either in the original language or in a modern translation, are the end product of a complex literary process reaching over more than three thousand years. The literary history of the Hebrew Bible is divisible into three partially overlapping phases:

1. The formation of the separate literary units, oral and written, that eventually became part of the Hebrew Bible, from about 1200 B.C.E. to 100 B.C.E.

2. The final formation of the Hebrew Bible as an authoritative collection of writing in three parts (Law, Prophets, Writings), beginning around 400 B.C.E. with the Law as the kernel, later supplemented by the Prophets, and culminating about 90 C.E. with delimitation of the boundaries of the Writings.

3. The preservation and transmission of the Hebrew Bible, both in the original tongue and in translations, which involved two phases:
   a. The period when the finalization of the contents of the Hebrew Bible was still in process, about 400 B.C.E. to 90 C.E.
   b. The period when the Hebrew Bible had reached definitive form, from 90 C.E. to the present.

Formation of the Separate Literary Units

Processes of Literary Composition

Israel did not begin as a book-oriented people, nor was its religion a book-based religion until toward the end of the biblical period. One may confidently say that, with the exception of a few final redactors (editors) responsible for writing only a relatively small amount of the text, biblical writers had no awareness or intent of contributing to a great collection of writings that would form the authoritative basis of a religion.

Israel was primarily a sociohistorical entity, possessed of a distinctive religion, that produced over the centuries a rich literature addressed to immediate situations of communal need and crisis. The Hebrew Bible grew as the result of the combination of separate literary units that were progressively grouped together and treated as sacred literature under the pressure of events and circumstances in postexilic Judah. Of course, Jews and Christians have claimed that God foresaw and designed the Hebrew Bible, but that is a value judgment made after the fact, not a description of the actual literary process as experienced by those who did most of the writing and collecting and editing.

The vast majority of biblical books give plentiful indications that they are of composite authorship, whether a single author has quoted from other sources or separate literary units have been joined together, so that it can be said that the formation of the Hebrew Bible proceeded by adding together and splicing smaller compositions to form larger entities. Frequently spanning centuries, this process varied from book to book, but often there were several stages in adding, rearranging, merging, and commenting editorially on the joined subcollections or on the supplemented core.

Precisely because the biblical books by and large had long trajectories of growth, it is necessary to view their formation not only in terms of the successive phases of single books or bodies of tradition, but also as the simultaneous development of coexisting or parallel books and bodies of traditions. For example, while the early anonymous sources of Genesis–Numbers, known as J and E, were being written in the tenth and ninth centuries, cycles of stories and state and temple records that were eventually to be part of Joshua–Kings were also taking written shape. Many hands were at work in the manifold processes of literary formation that were intimately tied to the tides and fortunes of the social, political, and religious institutions of biblical Israel.

The metaphor of a large river system may help to visualize the composition of the books of the Hebrew Bible, individually and as a whole. The waters of a great river are the confluence of rivulets, brooks, streams, tributary rivers, and branches of the main river. When we see such a river near its mouth, we are impressed by its singular irresistible sweep toward the sea, and yet we know that the waters now concentrated in one channel are actually slowly collected from scattered runoff over the vast basin that the river drains. Likewise the final unity of the Hebrew Bible arises through an additive process spread out over time and space.

Oral Tradition and Literary Genres in the Composition Process

In tracing the formation of the Hebrew Bible we must be attentive to the powerful influence of oral tradition, which contributed far more to the literary structure than we are apt to think because of our bookish orientation toward the text. In the course of trying to determine the authorship, date, and sources of biblical books, scholars gradually realized that much biblical literature had complex and deep-seated oral roots and that these could be located and described only by expanding the repertory of historical-critical methods to include form criticism. Form or genre criticism works on the widely demonstrated axiom that in the everyday culture of people there are relatively fixed forms of oral communication appropriate to particular settings in life.[3]

Oral forms may be as simple as the accepted formulas for exchanging greetings or for addressing people according to their different stations or roles in society. These oral forms ramify into all the spheres of life, particularly among preliterate peoples or in premodern societies, such as ancient Israel, where reading and writing tend to be restricted to certain groups and used for limited purposes. Among the common oral forms identified as underlying the biblical texts are the following: *narratives* of important ancestors or religious figures in an imaginative wonder-filled style that transcends everyday experience and that may serve to explain the origins of geographical features, institutions, and customs; *hymns* and *thanksgiving songs* celebrating victory in war or deliverance from famine, sickness, or oppression by attributing the turn of fortune to deity; *laments* mourning the death of important persons or bewail public catastrophes; *laws* regulating communal behavior; *priestly regulations* to guide ritual practices; *prophetic sayings* proclaiming judgment or salvation to individuals or nations; *aphorisms or artistic proverbs* that distill wisdom drawn from wide experience.

These oral forms had characteristic structures and verbal formulas, treated a customary set of topics, and were recited in specific life settings. Many of the first written texts in Israel had probably been orally composed and recited before being committed to writing. The transition from the tribal period of Israel's life to the monarchy witnessed the rise of a literary court culture alongside the old oral forms of tribal life. There was a sudden burst of literary activity as the earlier oral forms were taken up into writing and often arranged in larger compositions that had a distinctly literary character.

As long as oral forms were anchored to definite life situations, they stayed within clear boundaries and kept their typical shapes. A lament, for instance, was restricted to some immediately experienced loss or suffering, such as David's lament over the death of Saul and Jonathan in 2 Sam. 1:17-27. With their conventions of speech and conceptual structures, the forms continued to exert a powerful influence on writers who imitated but also modified them. Prophets, for example, employed laments to bewail the moral and religious state of the nation. In new literary contexts, the oral forms acquired new life settings and changed the particulars of form and content.

The relation of oral tradition and its forms to the literary composition of the Hebrew Bible is a complicated subject still being explored by biblical form critics and literary critics. Long after certain oral forms ceased to be widely used in everyday life, or were used in altered ways, a literary prophet like Isaiah of the Exile could employ an impressive array of oracles of salvation, hymns, trial speeches, and disputation speeches, plus other genres, to construct a studied work of powerful rhetorical force that was intended to be read, probably aloud, in order to inculcate specific religious attitudes and policies among the exiled Israelites (see pp. 284–88).

In sum, to sketch adequately the forma-

tion of the biblical literature it is necessary to engage in two processes. The first task is to discern the overall compositional shape of a biblical writing (what holds it together), and the second task is to isolate the intact or broken genre elements that contribute structural building blocks or rhetorical mortar to the finished text (what makes it come apart). One is looking both for instances of preexistent oral or written units taken into the larger work and also for the way genre elements have functioned as models for fresh literary compositions.

Because the analysis of literary types or genres is not familiar to most readers of the Bible, and also because the classification of biblical materials by genres is not fully agreed upon by scholars nor are the genre names standardized, it is advisable to present a fairly full list of the major literary types that have been identified in the Hebrew Bible. Fifty-nine literary genres out of more than two hundred—which one or another scholar has claimed to find in the biblical text—are listed in Web Table B. Among the listed genres, some are clearly much more pervasive than others, especially in the extent to which they generate biblical materials at the literary level.

Under each of the broad categories of writings (historical-legal, psalmic, prophetic, and wisdom), the most prominent types are listed. Although types tend to cluster in one or another category of writing, they are very movable in that they can appear in changing combinations and varying literary contexts, indicated by cross-reference numbers at the end of each major category.

Once the major literary genres of the Hebrew Bible are in view, it is possible to represent the growth of the writings from the smallest literary units to the great literary compositions. A graphic representation such as Web Chart A suggests a literary river system, with the smaller and more numerous units at the left of the chart, suggesting rivulets, brooks, and streams, flowing into the larger compositions at the right of the chart, suggesting tributary rivers and branches of the main river. More detail with reference to particular biblical books and bodies of tradition in this chart will come in later chapters. In the conclusion we will see how the literary streams of tradition, intermixed with social and theological developments, formed recognizable trajectories over long spans of biblical history.

Final Formation of the Hebrew Bible

The final formation of the biblical text entailed two developments: (1) the task of collecting and editing that rounded out the finished form of each of the three parts of the Bible, and (2) the investing of these collections with a definitive authority as the foundational documents for the community. The finished Hebrew Bible viewed as authoritative in this manner is generally called the *canon* (from a Greek word for "reed, measuring rod, standard"), and the process by which valued writings became uniquely authoritative writings is called *canonization*.

The Authoritative Collections

◆ THE LAW

The first portion of the Hebrew Bible to reach completed form as a definitive collection was the Law, encompassing Genesis through Deuteronomy. The demarcation of this unit was probably simultaneous with the decision of the postexilic Jewish community to make this

document the written foundation of its developing style of religious faith and practice. This very likely occurred about 450–400 B.C.E. during the reforming activities of Ezra and Nehemiah (see pp. 252–53). Precise circumstances and motivations attending the elevation of the Law are poorly known, but a general reconstruction of the situation is possible.

The Jews who were restored by the Persians to Palestine following the exile were in a problematic position, no longer politically independent but under the control of the Persian Empire. They were accorded freedom in cultural and religious affairs but had largely ceased to speak Hebrew in daily life. They now spoke the Aramaic language they had adopted in Babylonia.

The clearest connecting feature that postexilic Jews had in common with their ancestors was their religion, which had grown stronger in exile. In order to define and solidify the restored community, the returned Jews reaffirmed their religious past by rebuilding the temple and reestablishing its services of prayer and sacrifice, along with the festivals and rites that had helped to preserve Israelite identity during the exile. This same link with the past was affirmed literarily by carefully collecting and reading the ancestral writings that had managed to survive the exile.

By about 450 B.C.E. these ancestral writings included two major blocks of narratives that treated the history of Israel: Genesis through Numbers and Deuteronomy through Kings (see Web Chart A). These two blocks were the equivalent of national epics in that they recounted the story of Israel's past down to the exile. Among those narrative chains were instructions about worship and the daily conduct of life preserved in the form of laws given by Moses. It was on the basis of these laws that the community was reconstructed in its cultural and religious dimensions, including the revival of the temple cult. Indeed, so central was the prescriptive role of these laws that the entire collection of Genesis through Deuteronomy came to be known as the Law of Moses.

But why were Genesis through Deuteronomy chosen, rather than Genesis through Numbers (the first narrative block) or Genesis through Kings (both blocks)? Probably two factors account for the inclusion of Deuteronomy in the Law and the exclusion of Joshua through Kings. The intent in elevating the Law was to make it the undisputed foundation document that every member of the restored Jewish community had to observe to be in good standing. Deuteronomy, which introduced the long historical work extending through Kings, also contained laws attributed to Moses, so it was necessary to include at least Deuteronomy along with Genesis through Numbers.

The remaining books following Deuteronomy posed a problem, however. Recounting the conquest of Canaan through the history of the divided kingdoms, these narratives were blatantly political and military and openly at odds with Persian imperial power. It was decided to sever Deuteronomy from its position at the beginning of what is called the Deuteronomistic History (Joshua–Kings) and attach it to the end of Genesis–Numbers, thereby forming the five books of Moses, known as the Law or Torah (see pp. 267–73).

◆ THE PROPHETS

The next stage in the collection of the Hebrew Bible is difficult to discern because we have almost no historical documentation from Palestine between 400 and 200 B.C.E. During this period the prophetic writings were rounded out. Probably all of the prophetic books existed in some form by 400 B.C.E., although additions were made in most of them during the next two centuries.

The severe restriction of Jewish national life in Palestine and the increasing sense that the golden age of religious revelation was in the past contributed to the decline of fresh prophecy. Now that the highly venerated prophets were no longer alive, their writings constituted a virtually completed collection that logically supplemented the Law (see pp. 267–73) and was arranged on two principles: size and chronological order. The longer books of Isaiah, Jeremiah, and Ezekiel came first, in proper temporal order. The much shorter remaining books, forming the so-called Book of the Twelve, were also grouped in what appears to have been an approximate chronological order.

Curiously, however, the prophetic collection was not confined to gathering together the explicitly prophetic writings. The great bulk of the Deuteronomistic History, its introduction already removed to become the last book of the Law, was placed at the beginning of the prophetic collection, where it would be known as the Former Prophets, while the prophetic books proper, Isaiah through Malachi, were known as the Latter Prophets. The decision to give the Deuteronomistic History the recognition that it had missed acquiring in the fifth century as part of the Law was probably facilitated by a change in the political climate after the collapse of the Persian Empire.

Prefacing the explicitly prophetic works with Joshua through Kings was sensible in that those books also told of prophets who did not write books (e.g., Nathan, Ahijah, Elijah, and Elisha), and they further provided historical setting for the prophets who did write books. By this time there also existed a third independent narrative account in Chronicles, Ezra, and Nehemiah (see pp. 235–37, 298–301), dependent in part on Samuel–Kings, but carrying the story of Israel another 150 years beyond the Deuteronomistic History, that is, down to about 400 B.C.E. Possibly its extensive repetition of parts of Samuel–Kings as well as its post–"golden age" focus made it unacceptable to the collectors.

◆ The Writings

The remaining works that came to form the Hebrew Bible were grouped in a miscellaneous collection called "the Writings" (see ch. 12): (1) the Psalms, which had become the songbook of the restored temple; (2) the wisdom writings of Job and Proverbs, which struggled with questions of human success and adversity in the light of the promises of Israel's religion; (3) five short compositions used at festivals: the short stories of Esther and Ruth, the dirges over the fall of Jerusalem in Lamentations, the love poetry of the Song of Songs, and the skeptical wisdom of Ecclesiastes; (4) the apocalyptic book of Daniel; and (5) the just-mentioned historical works of Chronicles, Ezra, and Nehemiah.

Probably the latest compositions in the Writings were Daniel, written about 165 B.C.E. (see pp. 331–33), and the final redaction of Esther, perhaps as late as 125 B.C.E. (see p. 316). By this time there also existed a number of other Jewish books, in Hebrew, Aramaic, and Greek, which we have briefly characterized as the Apocrypha and Pseudepigrapha (see p. 58), and the Dead Sea Scrolls (see pp. 58–59). This literature continued to appear, and even to intermingle in usage and regard with Psalms, Proverbs, Job, the Festival Scrolls, Daniel, Chronicles, Ezra, and Nehemiah. Not until 90 C.E. were the fixed boundaries of the Writings agreed upon.

Beginning with the Maccabean Wars in 167 B.C.E. and ending with the war against Rome and the destruction of Jerusalem in 66–70 C.E. (see pp. 257–64), production of religious books flourished. Some of these books were the work of Dispersion Jews, especially those living in Alexandria, Egypt, where they were greatly influenced by Hellenistic society. Particularly popular in Palestine were apocalyptic writings in the manner of Daniel that attempted to read the chaotic events of the age within a symbolic framework of doomed earthly kingdoms giving way to the kingdom of God (see pp. 328–31). Historical books, wisdom compositions, and short stories also appeared.

With this sudden literary explosion, Jews might have gone on endlessly creating such authoritative collections of scripture. Why did the scripture-building process stop with the Writings? And how was it decided which books, among the many contenders, would be allowed among the Writings? The circumstances of the Jewish revolt against Rome, beginning in 66 C.E., and the resulting destruction of Jerusalem in 70 C.E. effectively eliminated the leadership and programs of all the bitterly contending Jewish tendencies and parties, except for one. The Pharisees, champions of the Oral Law, which was in time to become the Talmud (see p. 59), were left to have the final say about which books would be included among the Writings and, more importantly, how the canon of the Hebrew Bible as a whole would be interpreted and how it would function within the emerging rabbinic Jewish community.

Factors in the Canonical Closure: From Ezra to the Rabbinic Assembly at Jamnia

Public religious usage of the biblical writings has ordinarily been stressed as the key factor leading to canonization. In a way it is hard to quarrel with this view, since unused books certainly do not get canonized, but it is not evident that this notion unaided has much explanatory power. In one often-overlooked detail, however, the precise nature of the usage of biblical books is important.

What we mean by a canonical collection at that time is simply the bringing together in the synagogues and scribal schools of all the books regarded as of equal value and authority but as yet copied on separate scrolls. In this sense the role of institutional religious use of the canonical scrolls was critical. Canon was a recognized concept for ensuring the supervised preservation, transmission, and use of the books judged to be acceptable, while firmly excluding others, whatever their value in other respects.

Yet it is insufficient to talk about religious use of the biblical books in a generalized sense. The struggle to determine which of the Israelite/Jewish writings were authoritative, and in what way they were authoritative, was a struggle for power among contending groups in the community. Very rarely has the canonization process of the Hebrew Bible been studied in terms of the religious politics entailed. While our knowledge about the period 400 B.C.E.–90 C.E. is uneven, some of the basic developments in this period may help us to understand the persisting forces that moved Jews steadily toward becoming a people of a very deliberately constructed Book.

From the exile on, in spite of the successful restoration of a Judahite community in Palestine, the power of self-determination exercised by Jews decidedly declined. Much energy went into securing what autonomy they could from their political overlords, while resisting intrusions into their cultural and religious life and protecting their land from excessive economic depletion.

A large factor in this postexilic struggle was the exercise of class privilege within the Jewish community, since it was in the conquerors' interests to cultivate a local Jewish elite (see pp. 241–43), whether the leadership of the restored Judahite community, including Ezra and Nehemiah (see pp. 248–54), the hellenized Jews who collaborated with the Seleucids (see pp. 257–60), or the Hasmonean kings who over time sought to play power politics on a par with other Hellenistic kingdoms (see pp. 260–64).

Jewish elites operating under such imperial conditions were in an ambiguous position and were looked upon with ambivalence by their less-advantaged fellow Jews. Both elites and their critics tried to summon religious support for their positions and programs. Decisions about holy books were thus not only decisions about religious matters but about who had controlling power in the life of the community (see pp. 267–73).

Since the religion of Israel had always been a communal matter that tended to find expression in the whole range of national life, whatever diminished the total life options of postexilic Jews also reduced their religious options. This mood found expression in the notion that God was more remote and not as active in Israel's behalf as in ancient days, revelation having ended with Ezra about 400 B.C.E. In the deliberations in 90 C.E. that concurred on the contents of the canon, one objective criterion for judging the authority of books was the conviction that all sacred texts must have been written no later than the time of Ezra.

The splitting of Israel's religious history into a past golden age and a present age of decline and limitation was combined with a countervailing determination to make the utmost of the religious options for self-expression that were available. Thus the restored temple assumed a singular communal importance that it had not had when it was one of a number of national monarchic institutions. Since the distinctive features of Jewish identity were rooted in the Law of Moses, the faithful observance of that document as the constitution of the restored community became central. Focus on the text of the Law as a guide for the essential matters of communal life also served to stimulate interest in and influence the shaping of all the surviving literary traditions of Israel.

In this situation of restricted possibilities and determined commitments, the period from 167 B.C.E. to 70 C.E. was riddled with threats and crises for Palestinian Judaism (see pp. 257–64). The Seleucid and Roman powers impinged on Palestine more drastically than had the Persian and Ptolemaic authorities. In the Maccabean Wars the religious identity of Jews as observers of the Law was nearly expunged. Moreover, these wars exposed deep internal divisions among the Jews of Palestine over how open they should be to Hellenistic culture.

Elites rose and fell, coalitions formed and fell apart, as religion, politics, and social class intermixed in changing patterns. The collapse of the Hasmonean kingdom and the entrance of Rome into Palestine, at first under native Herodian princes and then under Roman administrators, brought heavier taxation and harder economic conditions for a depressed peasant populace. Meanwhile, Jews living outside Palestine were subject to the allurements of Hellenistic culture, and the turning of the sect of Jewish Christians into a missionary religion among Gentiles and Dispersion Jews raised the danger of major attrition in the ranks of Jews.

In short, the process of canonizing scripture came to its culmination as one aspect of a larger response of the Jewish community under virtual siege conditions, endangered by Roman oppression and by Hellenistic culture, and torn within by competing programs for survival advanced by Sadducees, Essenes, Zealots, Jewish Christians, and Pharisees. When the Jewish uprising against Rome was suppressed, the Pharisees alone survived it as an effective force in the Jewish community. By default, as it were, their program of building grassroots Jewish communities around the Law as interpreted by oral tradition stepped front and center. It was they who met for consultations at Jamnia around 90 C.E. to put the finishing touches on the shape of the Hebrew Bible to be recognized as Holy Scripture.

Those at Jamnia recognized that the Law and the Prophets and the Writings, as we now know them, carried sole scriptural authority. Reports of these deliberations in the Talmud tell of objections and reservations about Ezekiel (because of inconsistencies between his imaginary design of a new temple and the Law of Moses), Song of Songs (because of its explicit, erotic poetry), Ecclesiastes (because of its bitterly despairing outlook on life), and Esther (because it was secular and endorsed the Feast of Purim, not yet widely accepted in the Jewish community).

In the end all objections were met, at least to the satisfaction of a majority of rabbinic scholars in the assembly. Using the aims and methods of rabbinic reinterpretation and harmonizing of inconsistencies in biblical writings, Ezekiel's discrepancies were explained away, Song of Songs was given a mystical reading so that it spoke of God's love for Israel, both the Song of Songs and Ecclesiastes were accepted as the work of Solomon, and Esther was approved because it had become a symbol of Jewish survival in the face of severe persecution. Nonetheless, Jamnia did not issue a formal edict. More than anything else, it placed a seal of approval upon the books that the rabbinic movement had already been using for some time, officially confirming that books infected by Hellenistic culture or distorted by eschatological fervor had gone the way of destruction and discredit along with the Sadducean, Essene, Jewish Christian, and Zealot proponents.

If we ask how the canonizers at Jamnia viewed the authority of the Hebrew Bible they affirmed, the place to look is in the way the Talmud and the Midrash exegete scripture in order to develop a system of highly motivated and well-ordered daily religious practice. The Hebrew Bible was moving from being simply the story of a people and its God to becoming a full-orbed resource for determining the will of God in every present situation. The Hebrew Bible—at last clearly demarcated and viewed through the Oral Law—provided a discipline of religious practice in community and a strategy for coping with life in a hostile world. A book-centered piety and practice became central to the religiocultural enclave system by which late biblical Jews forged their way of life.

Preservation and Transmission of the Hebrew Bible

The process of transmitting the Hebrew Bible began with the handing down of the separate literary units, and their ingredient subunits, after they first appeared in writing. This process extended through all the stages of the growth and stabilization of the text. It continued with the passing along of the stabilized text in manuscripts written by hand and published in printed editions—all the way down to the present moment, including translation into other languages.

The Transmission Process Extending to the Stabilization of the Consonantal Text about 100 C.E.

All the original copies of the individual biblical writings, as well as their sources, have perished or eluded excavators. It is probable that they were written on scroll-form papyrus, made from the sliced stem of a fibrous Egyptian plant. As the writings gained status, they were copied on scrolls of more durable and high quality leather known as parchment or vellum. About twenty-five feet long, a scroll would accommodate one large biblical book, or two at most if the writing were very fine.

Most, if not all, of the biblical documents were written in the Old Hebrew or Phoenician script that the preexilic Israelites had shared with the Canaanites and Phoenicians. After the exile, the Aramaic script influenced the writing of Hebrew in the direction of the Square Script, which had fuller, block-shaped letters, and eventually became the standard form.

Prior to 1947, our earliest Hebrew manuscript evidence was almost entirely confined to medieval manuscripts no earlier than the late ninth century C.E., with some fragments reaching back to the fifth century C.E. A version of the Law in Old Hebrew Script of similar dating (the Samaritan Pentateuch) had been preserved by the Samaritan community that had broken away from the main body of Jews in pre-Christian times.

With the recovery of the Dead Sea Scrolls (see pp. 58–59) came a radical change in the state of our Hebrew manuscript evidence. In addition to one virtually complete copy of Isaiah (1QIsa[a]) that may date as early as 150 B.C.E., the Dead Sea Scrolls included fragments of all biblical writings except Nehemiah and Esther, some of these fragments dating to the third, possibly even the fourth, century B.C.E.

Easily the most significant textual feature of the biblical manuscript finds at Qumran is the discovery that they represent a variety of family types or redactional traditions. The official standardized text of the Hebrew Bible that reached its pinnacle of development in the medieval Jewish Tiberian school of Palestine is called the Masoretic Text (MT), and forms the basis of all modern printed editions and translations of the Hebrew Bible. Scholars found that 1QIsaᵃ, along with other manuscripts, exhibited a text that was a clear forerunner of MT, differing mainly in spelling and grammar. It was evident that the medieval Masoretes had preserved a manuscript tradition that ran back to pre-Christian times.

What greatly surprised scholars, however, was the simultaneous discovery of other bib-lical manuscripts at Qumran that did not fit a proto-Masoretic type. Some of these corresponded closely at points with the Samaritan Pentateuch readings. Others explained some of the differences between the Greek translation of the Hebrew Bible, known as the Septuagint (LXX; see pp. 73–74), and the MT.

One way of viewing the fluidity of the Hebrew text traditions in this pre-Christian period is to think of three basic families of texts: (1) a proto-Masoretic family of texts that fed into the later MT; (2) a family of texts most fully represented in the Samaritan Pentateuch; and (3) a family of texts from which at least part of the Septuagint was translated. However, some are not inclined at all to see three distinct families of texts, but recognize instead a plurality of redactional traditions. Nevertheless, all concede that the Hebrew text was still in flux prior to the end of the first century

FIG. 3.1 The caves of Qumran, where the Dead Sea Scrolls were found in 1947. Photo: © Erich Lessing / Art Resource, N.Y.

C.E., with extensive variations in spelling and grammar and moderate variations in words and phrases and even in contents and order of materials.

As we might expect, in moving to consolidate the Jewish community after 70 C.E., the rabbinic leaders stabilized both the canon and the form of the text, selecting one of the existing text types as the official text. As was the practice, this stabilized Hebrew text was written in consonants only. A tradition of proper vocalization kept alive among copyists and interpreters accompanied the text from generation to generation.

The Transmission Process Extending to the Stabilization of the Vocalic Text about 1200 C.E.

Once a consonantal text (MT) had been officially adopted, it was the task of the copyist-scholars to exercise utmost care in passing it on.[4] A critical test of accuracy in preservation of the text occurred each time a copy was made to replace a worn-out scroll with a fresh scroll. By the fourth or fifth century C.E., the codex form was adopted by Jews, except for scrolls of the Law and Esther mandated for synagogue reading. The codex form greatly facilitated the transmission of the text, since it was now possible to include the entire Hebrew Bible in one binding.

As the Talmud neared completion in the period 450–500 C.E., copyists and scholars of the text began to experiment with critical markings in manuscripts in order to indicate the proper vocalization of the text. The correct way to read a text must have come more into question the longer the vowel sounds were carried only in the oral tradition. Various graphic systems for indicating the vowels were worked out in Babylon and Palestine. The basic method was to specify vowels by placing dots and strokes called "vowel points" above or below the consonants.

Besides the introduction of vowel points and accents, the copyist-scholars made critical observations of a grammatical and statistical nature, at first orally and then on all four margins of the text and at the end of manuscripts. Included in the marginal and final Masorah was a great mass of technical information and instructions that served to alert copyists to the minutest details and peculiarities of the text so that they might be copied with unfailing accuracy.

As for the internal divisions of the MT, spaces were left to mark paragraphs, and verses were often marked but not numbered. The present numbered chapter divisions, first inserted in the Latin Vulgate in 1205, were entered in a Hebrew Bible by a rabbi in 1330 in order to facilitate references to the text in matters of controversy with Christians. The numbering of the verses was first employed in a Hebrew Bible in 1571.

FIG. 3.2 Strips from the Isaiah Scroll, found in the caves of Qumran. Archaeological Museum, Amman, Jordan. Photo: © Erich Lessing / Art Resource, N.Y.

In the centuries that the Masoretes worked, they did everything conceivable to ensure a faithfully preserved text. Given the long period of fluid textual traditions before the consonantal and vocalic texts were stabilized, however, textual errors and alterations occurred that were taken up into MT. The Masoretes noted some of these difficulties. At times this seems to be the Masoretes' way of making oral emendations where the received text seemed ungrammatical, offensive, or irreligious. In other cases these oral substitutions apparently preserve textual variants that attest to the fact that alternative readings of the biblical text had not been entirely suppressed.

The work of the Masoretes reached its apex in the Tiberian school of Palestine in the tenth century C.E. The major accomplishment in this regard is attributed to the influential ben Asher family, whose work is represented in a codex of the Prophets from 895 C.E. (Codex Cairensis); a codex of the entire Bible from 900–950 C.E., three-fourths of which has survived (Aleppo Codex); and a codex of the complete Bible from 1008 C.E. (Codex Leningradensis or MS B 19a). The heritage of this Tiberian school of Masoretes provided the basis for all printed editions of the Hebrew Bible to this day.

Printed Editions of the Hebrew Bible

Printed editions of the Hebrew Bible began to appear in 1477. The Second Rabbinic Bible, edited by Jacob ben Chayyim and published in 1524/1525 C.E., became the basic received text (Textus Receptus) among Jews and Christians, and the foundation of all printed editions down to 1936. It was employed by the translators of the chief English versions, including the King James Version (KJV). But ben Chayyim's edition involved arbitrary

decisions regarding Masoretic notes and depended on manuscripts that were inferior to those used in ben Asher's work.

With the growing understanding of the work of the Tiberian Masoretes, the weaknesses of ben Chayyim's eclectic text as a Textus Receptus have become evident. In 1936 the third edition of Rudolph Kittel's *Biblica Hebraica* (BHK) abandoned the ben Chayyim text and printed the ben Asher Codex Leningradensis, the basis of subsequent editions of Kittel's text and also of the more recent *Biblica Hebraica Stuttgartensia* (BHS).

TRANSLATIONS OF THE HEBREW BIBLE

Ancient Versions

Greek Septuagint

The first and most significant of the early translations of the Hebrew Bible was made into Greek. It was known widely as the Septuagint ("seventy," hence abbreviated LXX) because of the tradition that seventy (actually seventy-two) scholars translated it in Alexandria, Egypt (ca. 250 B.C.E.–75 B.C.E.). It is probable that the LXX owed its origin to the needs of the Greek-speaking Jewish population in Egypt (see pp. 254–57). Many writings were translated into Greek and included in the LXX that did not become part of the Jewish canon in 90 C.E. but were accepted into the early Christian canon and assigned to the Apocrypha by Protestants (table 3.1).

The Bible of the first Christians was largely this Greek version of the Hebrew Bible. In fact, LXX's extant codices are all Christian in origin. Most of the scriptural quotations in the New Testament are based on the Greek version rather than on the original Hebrew. The LXX is of great importance in textual criticism since it is the most ancient translation and, in conjunction with the Dead Sea Scrolls, affords us access to an ancient Hebrew text type that differed from the proto-MT.

Other Greek Versions and the Hexapla

In the early Christian centuries other Greek versions appeared, ranging from literal to free renderings. Around 230–240 C.E. the Christian scholar Origen compiled several of these translations, arranged in columns alongside the Hebrew text, in the Hexapla. It is one of the great losses of antiquity that, except for fragments, the Hexapla has perished.

Aramaic Targums

Palestinian, Babylonian, and Syrian Jews spoke Aramaic from the time of the exile. The Hebrew sacred books were read in synagogue services, and, in addition, an interpreter (meturgeman) gave an Aramaic translation or paraphrase (targum). What we call the Targum are the several written versions, characterized by free interpretation, into which these oral renderings were cast beginning early in the Christian era.

Old Syriac, Peshitta, and Syro-Hexapla

Syriac translations of the Hebrew Bible, influenced by Targums, may have begun as early as the mid-first century C.E., possibly by Jewish converts in the Syrian kingdom of Adiabene or somewhat later by Christians who spread to the Syriac-speaking interior of Syria. A revision of these translations was the Peshitta ("simple version"), which became the official Syriac Christian Old Testament. In the seventh century C.E. a Syrian churchman prepared a literal Syriac translation that also reproduced the LXX column of Origen's Hexapla.

Old Latin and Vulgate

Most of the earliest Christians were Greek-speaking. With the spread of the faith to the western part of the Roman Empire, Latin began to emerge as a church language. From about 200 C.E. we have evidence of the first rough translation of biblical books into Old Latin.

Commissioned to produce an official Latin version in 382 C.E., Jerome learned Hebrew and used it for his Old Testament translation. The resulting version was known as the Vulgate ("common version"). The Catholic Church asserted the sole sufficiency of the Vulgate, and all other translations of the Bible were required to be based on it until 1943, when Catholic scholars were at last permitted to work from the original languages.

English Versions and Translations

Although the terms are often loosely used interchangeably, there is a difference between a version and a translation. A *version* is a translation authorized by some ecclesiastical or governmental body and normally involving a number of translators, whereas a *translation* is an unofficial rendering that may entail many translators but more often is the work of one or two persons. There is a tendency, however, to speak of all ancient translations as versions, even though many of the early English Bibles were expressly opposed by crown and church. Accordingly, this convention will be followed for the older translations, but in discussing English Bibles in the twentieth century care will be taken to note which are versions in the technical sense.[5]

English Versions and Translations through 1952

The early English versions, from the Anglo-Saxon through Wycliffe, were all based on the Latin Vulgate. With the invention of printing and rediscovery of Greek and Hebrew occasioned by the Renaissance, William Tyndale produced the first English version to be based on the original languages, although his translation of the Hebrew Bible was confined chiefly to the Pentateuch (1529). Pressure for uniformity in a series of English translations prompted James I to summon the Hampton Court Conference in 1604. More than fifty scholars working in committees produced the Authorized Version (AV) of 1611, commonly known as the King James Version (KJV). The KJV gained its superior position only after long competition with other translations.

As changes in the English language accumulated and new manuscript and archaeological finds provided improved tools for textual criticism, it became clear that the KJV had to be updated. The Revised Version (RV) was published in England in 1885, and an American English version was issued as the American Standard Version (ASV) in 1901. Both revisions set out to give literal constructions of the text, at times to the point of obscurity.

FIG. 3.3 William Tyndale is depicted with a beard and wearing a ruff on this title page from a printed edition of his New Testament, 1534. The Gothic script is surrounded by a decorative border with cherubs. British Library, London. Photo: © HIP / Art Resource, N.Y.

In 1952 the complete Revised Standard Version (RSV) was published, having been mandated to revise the KJV-RV/ASV versions. The RSV was the work of American scholars who were able to use far more critically edited manuscripts than any of their predecessors. The RSV quickly gained a wide following both in general church use and for serious study.

All the above versions were Protestant Bibles, although by 1973 an RSV Common Bible, including Apocrypha/deuterocanonical books, was approved for use by Catholic and Orthodox churches. Earlier the needs of Roman Catholics were met by the Douay-Rheims Version of 1609, translated from the Vulgate. Taking account of earlier translations under Jewish auspices in England and the United States, as well as the Protestant English versions, the Jewish Publication Society of America published the *Holy Scriptures According to the Masoretic Text* in 1917, drawing on Jewish rabbinic and medieval interpretive traditions.

English Versions and Translations since 1952

In the latter part of the twentieth century there was an explosion of translations into English. The RSV was updated as the New Revised Standard Version (NRSV) in 1989. The New International Version (NIV) appeared in 1978, and the New Jewish Publication Society Version (NJPS) in 1982. Roman Catholic translations are the New American Bible (NAB) of 1970 and the New Jerusalem Bible (NJB) of 1985. (See Web Table C.)

These translations tend to follow one or the other of two basic philosophies of translation, although with varying degrees of rigor and consistency. *Formal correspondence* translations, sometimes misleadingly called "literal," try to preserve the technical vocabulary, sentence structure, and imagery of the original Hebrew as much as possible, even when the result is not natural English. In contrast, *dynamic equivalence* translations strive to render the meaning of the original text into the most natural and fluent English idiom.[6]

NOTES

1. *Apocrypha* means literally "hidden things or writings," referring to these books being hidden or lost to view when they were rejected from the canon by Judaism and Protestantism. Technically, however, an *apocryphon* (singular) is a book whose traditional author (e.g., an ancient such as Enoch or Moses) is said to have withheld the work from general circulation until the approaching end of time. In this sense, only 2 Esdras in the Apocrypha is an apocryphon. Catholics call the books of the Apocrypha "deuterocanonical," that is, the second set of canonical Old Testament books, since they have always been part of Catholic scripture.

2. *Pseudepigrapha* means literally "false superscriptions," that is, false claims to authorship—many ancient authors, especially apocalyptic writers, claimed that their compositions were written much earlier by honored ancestors such as Abraham, Moses, or Isaiah. In this technical sense, many of the Pseudepigrapha are indeed pseudepigrapha, but many others are not. Even though the title is inaccurate in this respect, Pseudepigrapha is firmly established in scholarly and popular usage.

3. Gerhard Lohfink (*The Bible: Now I Get It! A Form-Critical Handbook,* trans. Daniel Coogan [Garden City, N.Y.: Doubleday, 1979]) skillfully introduces the student to form criticism by citing modern fixed forms of oral and written speech, such as letter, weather report, obituary, recipe, and sermon.

4. Ernst Würthwein (*The Text of the Old Testament: An Introduction to the Biblia Hebraica*, trans. Erroll F. Rhodes [Grand Rapids: Eerdmans, 1979], 12–44) describes the main features of the MT, including the Masoretic notations, and illustrates with sample pages from manuscripts (pls. 17–25).

5. Some authorities reserve "version" for an edition of the Bible that incorporates the language and style of a previous translation or version in the same language, while using "translation" for editions that proceed directly from Hebrew or Greek. This usage partially suits earlier centuries but fails to take into account that recently sponsored "versions," such as TEV and NIV (see Web Table C), proceed directly from the original languages and are thus fresh translations.

6. The most widely used translations since 1952 are listed in Web Table C with annotations.

FOR FURTHER READING

Nickelsburg, George. *Jewish Literature between the Bible and the Mishnah: A Historical and Literary Introduction.* 2nd ed. Minneapolis: Fortress Press, 2005.

Sparks, Kenton L. *Ancient Texts for the Study of the Hebrew Bible.* Peabody, Mass.: Hendrickson, 2005.

Strack, Hermann L., and Gunter Stemberger. *Introduction to the Talmud and Midrash.* Minneapolis: Fortress Press, 1996.

Tov, Emanuel. *Textual Criticism of the Hebrew Bible.* 2nd ed. Minneapolis: Fortress Press / Assen: Van Gorcum, 2001.

Wise, Michael, Martin G. Abegg Jr., and Edward Cook. *The Dead Sea Scrolls: A New Translation.* Rev. ed. San Francisco: HarperSanFrancisco, 2005.

QUESTIONS FOR STUDY

1. What are the Apocrypha and the Pseudepigrapha? Explain their roles in the sacred literature of Judaism and Roman Catholic and Protestant Christianity.

2. List some of the literary genres found within the Hebrew Bible. What is the significance of the range of genres found in biblical literature? How do these relate to the role of the oral tradition?

3. How did the rise and fall of the Persian Empire affect the development of the Hebrew Bible?

4. Explain how the Dead Sea Scrolls discovery aided scholars in reconstructing the development of the Hebrew Bible.

5. What is the difference between a *version* of the Bible and a *translation* of the Bible?

INTERTRIBAL CONFEDERACY: ISRAEL'S REVOLUTIONARY BEGINNINGS

II

Al preliminaries being over, we are about to embark on a reading of the Hebrew Bible. The aim of the body of this book (parts II–IV) is to facilitate a reading of the Hebrew Bible by placing its literature within the full history of Israel—material, cultural, social, political, and religious—viewed in the context of all that we know about the ancient Near East at the time.

In part II we shall examine the origins of Israel in the period before it became a national kingdom under Saul and David. In chap. 4 we shall see why there is as much as a one-thousand-year disagreement about Israel's date of origin, from as early as 2200 B.C.E. to as late as 1150 B.C.E.

Our biblical starting point will be the traditions of Genesis 12–50 about the ancestors of Israel. The traditions of Genesis 1–11 will be studied later (see pp. 184–88, 273–79) because these accounts of origins are part of a broad literary and conceptual heritage that Israel shared with its ancient Near Eastern neighbors. To understand the distinctive perspective of Israel on the origins of the world it is advisable to examine first the traditions about Israel's own beginnings.

Our chief source of information about Israel's early history is the Hebrew Bible itself. Although all the biblical books were completed after the exile, they contain older sources that derive from earlier stages of Israel's history. By probing these older traditions, it is possible to discern some of the history that lies behind and beneath the literature. To undertake historical reconstruction adequately, however, it is necessary to understand the distinctive shape of the literature relevant to each period of the history. Consequently, throughout parts II–IV, we shall be asking two fundamental questions:

1. How did the oral and literary traditions of the Hebrew Bible take shape, and what is the sociohistorical understanding they provide or presuppose concerning each period in ancient Israel?
2. How does the sociohistorical picture of each period presented or implied in the Hebrew Bible enable us to comprehend Israel's place in its total ancient Near Eastern context?

Because the historical value of the biblical traditions is highly problematic, we will begin with an assessment of the literary sources.

THE GREAT TRADITIONISTS OF ANCIENT ISRAEL

Biblical data concerning Israel's earliest history are found in the Law and Former Prophets. Historical-critical study has identified four major literary hands at work in the growth of these traditions.

The Yahwist (J)

A connected story of Israel's beginnings from the creation of the world to at least the verge of Israel's entrance into Canaan was composed around 960–930 B.C.E., during the reign of Solomon, in the view of many scholars. This source can be identified, with a margin of variation, in Genesis, Exodus, and Numbers, perhaps also in Joshua and Judges (see pp. 141–45).

We do not know the name of the writer. Apparently it was someone in governmental favor in Judah, who provided a kind of national epic for the young kingdom of David and Solomon, stressing Judah's central role among the tribes. This writer had a preference for calling the God of Israel by the proper name Yahweh, who is said to have been worshiped by humans from ancient days (Gen. 4:26). Thus the unknown author is commonly called the Yahwist or J writer (J from the German spelling Jahweh/Jahwist). The symbol J refers secondarily to Judah.

The Elohist (E)

After the disruption of the united monarchy, in the period 900–850 B.C.E., another writer told the early story of Israel from the perspective of the northern kingdom, called Israel as well as Ephraim, for one of its major territories (see pp. 200–201). This story covered most of the same ground as J. This writer deliberately chose the name Elohim for Israel's God in the period before Moses because of the belief that the name Yahweh was first given to Israel by Moses. Consequently, this anonymous writer is commonly called the Elohist or E writer, although E also refers secondarily to Ephraim.

How did the Elohist compare with the Yahwist? And why was a second story over the same historical ground deemed necessary? Beginning with Abraham, E developed historical themes in literary types and with topical interests closely akin to J's. On the other hand, E frequently differed in vocabulary, style, mood, and emphasis, and a number of E's traditions have no parallel in J. The Elohist put special emphasis on early Israel as a religiously and ethically obligated community in treaty (or covenant) with Yahweh. If the nearest affinities of J were with court circles in Jerusalem, the closest connections of E appear to have been prophetic circles of the sort that venerated Elijah and Elisha. In all events, the Elohist was fairly explicit in presenting criteria for defining Israel that transcended and criticized the current kingdoms of Judah and Israel. The E document was apparently intended as a conscious corrective to the J document.

The Deuteronomistic History (DH)

Circles of traditionists in the northern kingdom, beginning perhaps as early as the E writer, began to develop a sermonic style of instruction that impressed on people the significance of obedience to the covenant with Yahweh as expressed in old laws about social justice and religious fidelity. These covenant traditions showed a definite tension, and at times outright conflict, with the power politics of the Israelite monarchies. We speak of these traditionists as Deuteronomists, or in the singular as the Deuteronomist, designated D, because their work is most clearly exhibited in the book of Deuteronomy (see pp. 221–23).

When the northern kingdom collapsed in 722 B.C.E., the Deuteronomic traditions were preserved by sympathizers in the south. A century later, in 622 B.C.E., the Deuteronomic tradition surfaced as the driving force in a major reform of the kingdom of Judah launched by King Josiah. When Josiah's reform efforts failed, Deuteronomists brought together a great mass of traditions in order to interpret the course of the monarchies in Israel from the point of view of covenant loyalty and disobedience. These traditions appear in the present books of Deuteronomy through Kings in what is called the Deuteronomistic History (DH or Dtr). During the Babylonian exile, the Deuteronomists undertook a second (Lat. *deutero-*) and final revision of their history, beginning with a second telling of the law by Moses beyond Jordan just before his death and ending in the midst of the exile. It is likely that DH reworked JE conquest traditions as part of this new composition, trying to harmonize conflicting traditions about the conquest (see pp. 136–41).

The Priestly Writer (P)

The last major contribution to the national epic in Genesis through Numbers was the work of a Priestly writer, symbolized as P, who wrote in the late exilic or early restoration period, about 550–450 B.C.E. (see pp. 273–79). Anchoring the epic in a well-ordered account of the creation, this writer was concerned with supplementing the old traditions with materials such as priestly instructions and dietary provisions that would underscore the institutional and ritual constitution of Israel as a unique religious community (see pp. 116–18, 120–23). Most of the latter half of Exodus and the whole of Leviticus, as well as the first third of Numbers, come from the P writer (see pp. 105–7).

The Redaction of JEP

In contrast to the Deuteronomistic History, which seems to have had a fairly rapid and homogeneous internal development in two editions, the combination of the separate J, E, and P documents was a slower process.

The Yahwist and Elohist versions of the national epic were firm competitors until after the destruction of the northern kingdom in 722 B.C.E., when a redactor in the southern kingdom supplemented J extensively with parts of E (between 722 and 609 B.C.E.), preserving much less of the northern version. In effect, the national political tone of J was leavened with the religious and ethical qualifications of E.

The joining of combined JE with P was accomplished either by the P writer or by an independent editor. The Priestly composition formed the framework into which JE traditions were inserted intermittently. This editing affirmed the old JE political and religious tendencies, but at the same time subordinated them to the overweening ritual concerns of the Priestly frame composition.

The Common Source of Yahwist and Elohist (G)

The far-ranging similarities of the two earliest continuous sources J and E strongly suggest that both derived from an older pool of traditions, often called G (German *Grundlage,* "foundation"). This stock of thematically grouped traditions probably took shape in the cult, that is, formal worship assemblies, before the tribes of Israel opted for kings. Some of the differences in J and E may be due to different versions of the traditions circulating in the southern and northern regions of Israel. In that event, G would not stand for a single standard version but would refer to a range of oral/written variants within broadly fixed parameters.

THE BEARING OF THE LITERARY TRADITIONS
ON THE EARLY HISTORY OF ISRAEL

We have now described the main stages in the complex growth of the literary traditions in Genesis through 2 Kings. Starting from oral units that were arranged according to leading themes in the cult of tribal Israel, these materials were later written into continuous sources that were finally revised or redacted to form the present biblical books. What are the implications of this literary growth for reconstructing the early history of Israel?

Nongovernmental and Oral Origins of the Traditions

It is clear that the traditions about premonarchic Israel derived from an essentially preliterary setting in communal life. Writing throughout the ancient Near East was chiefly a politically oriented or enabled activity, sponsored and controlled by governmental authorities and their schools of professional scribes in order to record administrative and ceremonial affairs of state (see pp. 31–34, 35–39).

The united tribes of Israel arose, however, as a disturber of Canaanite state interests and authority. Israel's first literature was low literature, both in its origin among lower-class Canaanites and in its subject matter, that is, the worth and competence of a simple people to determine their own lives without the intervention of upper-class rulers. The early oral literature recounted the deeds of the people and their special God, Yahweh (see pp. 154–57; 160–63). This literature, spoken or sung, served to validate and strengthen the intertribal movement of Israel. Only later, when Israel acquired kings, did the literary traditionists feel motivated to write connected accounts that validated Israel's own monarchy (J), or criticized the Israelite states (E and D), or sought a substitute for the lost Israelite states (P).

The preliterate people of Israel made use of precisely those literary types that belong characteristically to the prestate life of a people. The literary types from Web Table B (see also pp. 63–65) give us our primary information about Israel's early life:

Rules of conduct in categorical form (2)[1]
Legal maxims and decisions (3)
Treaties between Israel and Yahweh (4)
Blessings (7)
Sagas (20)
Legends (21)
Novellas (22)
Anecdotes (23)
Lists (24–25)
Taunts (32)
War and victory songs (34)
Hymnic songs (36)
Thanksgiving songs (38)

Designed to be instructional and celebrative and making no pretense of being carefully researched historical accounts, these literary types may be used cautiously and indirectly to reconstruct history, especially cultural and social history (see pp. 105–7, 131–45).

United Tribal Israel as the Subject of the Traditions

Within the preliterary phase of Israelite history, we must distinguish between the period when the tribes of Israel gathered as a united people in Canaan and the preceding periods of the patriarchs and Moses. Properly speaking, the patriarchs and Moses belong to the prehistory or protohistory of the united tribes of Israel. The stories of these figures speak of relatively small groups of people who were not yet part of any great intertribal Israelite movement. The process of extending these traditions from smaller groups to the whole of Israel took time and involved interplay between how these ancestors had been remembered by segments of Israel and how they came to serve as ancestral or prototypical figures for the entire people (see pp. 93, 99–102, 109–12, 126–28).

Expansion and Elaboration of the History-like Themes of the Traditions

Within these early traditions a firm distinction must be drawn between the sequence of events from the patriarchs down to the judges, on the one hand, and the actual order in which events assumed importance and received attention in the process of tradition building in the cultic assemblies of tribal Israel, on the other hand. The sequence of history-like themes preserved in the final form of the Law and the Former Prophets is as follows for the premonarchic period:

Primal History: From Creation to Abraham
Patriarchs:
    Promise to Abraham
    Promise to Isaac
    Promise to Jacob
Descent into Egypt: Joseph
Bondage and Deliverance from Egypt: Moses
Guidance in the Wilderness: Moses (from Egypt to Sinai)
Law and Covenant at Sinai/Horeb: Moses
Guidance in the Wilderness: Moses (from Sinai to Moab)
Conquest of the Land: Joshua
Consolidation of Conquest: Judges

These history-like themes, however, did not appear full-blown at the beginning of the traditioning process; instead, they snowballed over decades of time within the living cult and later in the work of the great literary traditionists.

It is probable that the original core of tradition-telling in the cultic assemblies consisted of two basic themes (ca. 1200 B.C.E.):

Bondage and Deliverance from Egypt: Moses
Conquest of the Land: Joshua

This core was expanded *externally* by prefacing it with additional history-like themes: first, about the patriarch Jacob (of the northern tribes), then about the patriarchs Abraham and Isaac (of the southern tribes), and further by an explanation of how the Israelites fell into Egyptian bondage (by ca. 1100 B.C.E.).

The original core was also expanded *internally* by the insertion of new history-like themes at its center: the theme of Guidance in the Wilderness (to account for the survival of Israel in the

Sinai, Negeb, and Transjordan on its way from Egypt to Canaan), and the theme of Law and Covenant at Sinai/Horeb (to give the long-standing, public, covenant-renewal ceremony a narrative position in the unfolding origin story of Israel). Interestingly, the Guidance in the Wilderness theme, probably of southern origin, was split open, and the Law and Covenant theme, probably of northern origin, was sandwiched into it (by ca. 1025 B.C.E.).

This multiple-stage sacred tribal history of premonarchic Israel constituted the probable structure of G, the common pool of the united tribal traditions that J and E drew upon. One major addition and one important alteration of history-like themes occurred, however, in the later literary stage of the growth of the traditions. The Yahwist (J) added traditions from the creation of the world to Abraham, and the Deuteronomistic History rearranged the confusing traditions about the settlement of Canaan into two parts—the conquest of Canaan proper under Joshua and later setbacks and consolidation under the judges.

Summary and Methodological Implications

Three major conclusions about the intent, locus, and thematic sequence of the traditions stand out as important for reconstructing Israel's early history:

1. *The intent of the traditions.* The traditions about premonarchic Israel were not documents intended to record historical information but rather sacral-oral origin or charter stories, poems, and laws intended for immediate instruction and celebration.
2. *The locus of the traditions.* The traditions come from and witness to united intertribal Israel, so that they tell us only secondarily, and at a considerable remove, about the groups and leaders of the earlier times of the patriarchs and Moses.
3. *The thematic sequence of the traditions.* The core of traditions about deliverance from Egypt and conquest of the land was expanded and embellished over decades and centuries, so that the eventual ordering and stressing of events resulted from a slow accumulation of tradition and *not* from a direct representation of events continuously reported by eyewitnesses.

Because the traditions do not yield a direct coherent history of early Israel, scholars understandably differ in the amount and type of historically relevant information they think can be derived from them. To date no nonbiblical information about the patriarchs and Moses has come to light, so that the varying scholarly interpretations of those figures have depended largely on differing estimates of the historical reliability of the traditions (see pp. 94–99, 107–12). Given the softness of our evidence about Israel's beginnings, there is as yet no single commanding version of how Israel emerged into history. At most there are a number of widely shared assumptions, differently emphasized and combined, on the basis of which scholars organize the source materials into a range of partly concurring and partly opposing versions of the premonarchic history of Israel.

NOTE

1. The numbers in parentheses are keyed to the enumerated literary genres presented in Web Table B.

Traditions about the Fathers and Mothers of Israel

SUMMARY

Traditions of Israel's ancestors in J, E, and P
The Deuteronomic History
The shape of stories in Genesis 12–50
Social history and the ancestor traditions

READ THE BIBLICAL TEXT

Genesis 12–50

See additional materials at fortresspress.com/ gottwald; consult Carta Bible Atlas *maps 43–46.*

The Shape of the Traditions in Genesis 12–50

Distribution of the Tradition Units in J, E, and P

The traditions about the ancestors of united Israel appear in Gen. 11:27—50:26 and are recounted in three extended sources that cover much the same chronological and thematic ground. The Yahwist (J) and the Elohist (E) depended on an old oral—and perhaps partly written—pool of traditions, and the Priestly writer (P) drew upon JE, together with some independently derived oral or written traditions. The distinctive vocabulary, style, tone, and religious outlook of each of these traditionists can be appreciated by reading their versions of the patriarchal traditions as listed in Web Table G. When they are read separately, it is clear that J provides the most cohesive continuous account, since E appears largely as a redacted supplement to J, whereas P, in providing the final frame for Genesis, presupposes the incorporated JE document to provide the basic plot line (see pp. 273–79).

There is generally little disagreement about the identity of the P traditions. There is more dispute about the separation of J and E, particularly in passages where they have been closely woven together and where the most distinctive criteria of each are not represented.

Analysis of the Tradition Units by Literary Genres

Form criticism indicates that by far the most frequent building block in these traditions is the literary type known as *saga*. Of the seventy-nine tradition units listed in Web Table G, sixty-nine fall in this genre. Each saga is a complete story, fairly brief (Genesis 24 is the longest example), with few characters, terse dialogue, frequent repetition, artful use of suspense, and great restraint in descriptions of scene and in analyses of the motivations and feelings of the actors.

Other literary types also appear, either independently developed alongside the sagas or as fragments or elements within a saga or other tradition unit. Two of these serve as vehicles for introducing the role of deity in the unfolding account of the ancestors: the *treaty or covenant* form (e.g., 6, 68, 19 in Web Table G) and *blessings or promises of blessings* (e.g., 41, 43). *Lists* of persons or groups also recur (e.g., 13, 5, 49), as well as a *vision report* form (e.g., 6) and the type of a *disputation speech* (e.g., 9).

Composite Unity of the Traditions

The most fascinating and challenging literary feature of the ancestor traditions, as elsewhere in Israel's early written records, is the manner in which the individual units have been grouped and edited so as to produce complex and subtle literary effects. Both traditional and more recent methods of criticism have helped to identify significant literary features.

Saga Cycles and Saga Chains

One of the most obvious larger groupings is the clustering of the traditions around prominent ancestors. Abraham and Jacob each formed magnets for the growth of cycles of traditions. Within the Abraham and Jacob cycles, there are subgroupings. The Jacob cycle is more complexly constructed than the Abraham cycle, with the Jacob-Laban saga chain, for example, bracketed within the Jacob-Esau saga chain. The Joseph novella serves the overall tradition structure admirably by accounting for the descent of Jacob and his family into Egypt and thus for the subsequent bondage of Israel in that land.

The positioning of the cycles and saga chains so that Abraham, Isaac, Jacob, and Jacob's twelve sons represent four successive generations in a single family provides the axis for the entire narrative complex. An unrelenting focus is sustained on this one biological line of descent that bears the divine blessing: Jacob's sons alone are the fathers of the twelve tribes of Israel.

Itinerary and Chronology

Another means for articulating the separate traditions is the device of the itinerary. A considerable number of settlements and regions in and around Canaan are named in the traditions. It is argued that in many instances the separate tradition units originated at the places prominently named within them. In bringing the traditions together around the ancestors, a parallel or supplementary tendency arose to relate these many scattered places as points on the itinerary of a wandering ancestor. By supplying itineraries linked closely to the divine directives and promises, the collectors of the traditions have imbued ancestors like Abraham and Jacob with a sense of restlessness and inner urging that points forward toward the later themes of bondage and deliverance from Egypt, wilderness wandering, and conquest of Canaan. At the same time, many of the sites in the itineraries are locations for a revelation of God to the ancestors or an occasion for sacrifice to God by the ancestors. In this manner sacred places like Shechem, Bethel, and Mamre-Hebron are explained as having been established in the first instance by one of the ancestors. Form critics have referred to sagas of this sort as etiologies (origin accounts) of sacred sites, or as foundation legends in that they explain the founding of important sanctuaries.

Another binding feature in the traditions is the chronology provided by the Priestly writer. The old sagas are almost totally lacking in temporal indicators, beyond occasional references to day or night. It was P, however, who supplied the total ages of the ancestors as a part of the comprehensive chronology with which he structured his work from Genesis through Numbers. Also, important events are dated by the age of an ancestor. Abraham was eighty-six at the birth of Ishmael, ninety-nine when God covenanted with him, and one hundred at the birth of Isaac. While the geographical and temporal indicators cited serve effectively to give unity to the mass of ancestor traditions, their value for situating the traditions historically is a much more problematic issue (see pp. 94–95).

Motifs of Divine Promises to the Ancestors
Motifs of divine promise and present blessing are very subtly employed at key points in the traditions to impart a sense of continuity that links saga to saga and generation to generation. Form critics have intensively studied the traditions with a view to unraveling the many types of divine blessings anticipated by promise or conferred in actuality. The most recurrent promises are of children and land. In these varied promises we can see that both the immediate situation of the ancestors and their families and the later situation of Israel as a confederation of tribes or as a monarchy have become intertwined in the great body of traditions. This use of family stories to personify group history becomes a critical factor in estimating the historical precision of such traditions (see p. 93).

Type-Scenes and Other Literary Features
Newer literary methods of biblical criticism have begun to work on the ancestor traditions from new perspectives.

Working by analogy from Homer scholarship, one literary critic[1] has characterized the stylized treatment of conventional situations in the sagas as *type-scenes,* that is, typical episodes in the life of an ancestor hero that are composed of traditional elements that any particular storyteller may elaborate and vary within limits determined by skill and audience rapport. Among the stock type-scenes are the following:

1. Birth of an ancestor hero to his barren mother:[2] 6, 7, 8, 11 (Isaac to Sarah); 23, 49, 56 (Jacob's sons to Rachel)
2. Encounter with the future betrothed at a well: 14 (Abraham's servant finds Rebekah); 22 (Jacob finds Rachel)
3. The ancestor hero pretends that his wife is his sister: 3 (Abraham and Sarah in Egypt); 44 (Abraham and Sarah at Gerar); 18 (Isaac and Rebekah at Gerar)

4. Rivalry between a barren, favored wife and a fertile co-wife or concubine: 7, 45 (Sarah and Hagar); 23, 49 (Rachel and Leah)
5. Danger in the desert and discovery of a well: 7, 45 (Hagar and Ishmael)
6. Treaty between an ancestor hero and a local king: 5 (Abraham and Melchizedek); 46 (Abraham and Abimelech); 19 (Isaac and Abimelech)
7. Testament of the dying ancestor hero: 20 (Isaac); 41, 64, 78 (Jacob)

Many of these and other type-scenes recur in the later history-like themes of Exodus, Numbers, Joshua, and Judges.

Type-scene analysis touches directly on a feature that has long been recognized by biblical critics: more or less the same story is often told about different ancestors or about the same ancestor in different settings. The most striking instance is the threefold tale of the ancestor's wife in danger (cf. no. 3 in the list of type-scenes above). While source and form critics have assumed, and then tried to reconstruct, an original form of the story at the level of oral tradition, it may be that there never was an original full story. Perhaps it was a challenge to each storyteller or writer to fill out the traditional episode and its conventions with fresh, varied content.

Source criticism in the past has tended to analyze vocabulary and style with little guidance from professional literary criticism. As a result, important rhetorical features were often missed or misunderstood. For example, one of the recognized peculiarities of the Priestly (P) style of composition (see pp. 274–75) can be analyzed as the use of "echo" from unit to unit (repetition of key words, phrases, or clauses) and "panel writing" that constructs successive scenes similar in form and content. The ped-

antry or monotony that scholars have often noted in P is interestingly paralleled structurally in children's literature, which may suggest that the style of P was intended for instruction or catechesis.[3]

Similarly, a careful stylistic analysis of the Hagar stories in J and E (see Web Table G, 7, 45) yields striking differences in the overall representations within doublets, or two closely related units. The directly told J story has the actors relating directly to one another but not to God and leaves all action in the hands of Sarai. The subtly told E story has the actors relating directly to God and not to one another and gives the decisive action to Abraham, with God interacting at the human level with miracles.[4]

Yet a further contribution of the newer literary criticism, particularly in its structuralist forms, is to focus on the effects that literary devices have on the total composition, irrespective of how it may have reached its final state. In the older criticism, literary doublets and triplets were studied either as differentiating source phenomena or as pointers backward to the underlying oral form. Rhetorical criticism and structuralism are more likely to consider how doublets or triplets function in the total composition—for example, how the threefold transformations of the type-scene "the ancestor's wife in danger" (see Web Table G, 3, 18, 44) operate in the whole of Genesis 12–50. Seen in this way, the repetitions and novelties in the reenactments of one type-scene provide a progressive amplification of the concrete conditions under which the promises to the ancestors concerning children and land will be worked out in reality.[5]

It is obvious that the newer forms of literary criticism, though for the most part not directly concerned with the growth of the traditions, nevertheless are unearthing important new understandings that have far-ranging implications for the abiding questions about how the traditions grew into their present mammoth composite structure.

Individual Family Traditions or Tribal Group Traditions?

A perplexing aspect of the ancestor traditions is the way they seem to vacillate between describing the actions of ancestors as individual family heads, on the one hand, and the actions of ancestors as symbolic heads of entire tribes, on the other hand. A person whose name, and often whose actions, represents a much larger group of people is known as an eponym ("to name after"), and sagas about individuals in this collective role are called eponymous sagas. In Genesis 12–50 the eponymous function of the sagas emerges slowly but accumulates substance and overtones as the tradition sequences unfold. Most all of the Abraham sagas can be read as events in the life of a family head, but as we reach the Jacob cycle of traditions the eponymous dimension of the traditions becomes more explicit and insistent. Esau, brother of Jacob, is also openly identified as Edom, by use of a wordplay on the color red, linking Esau's red hair and the red stew that he ate with the red sandstone that distinguishes the land of Edom (25:24-31; cf. 36:1-8). Jacob wrestles with "a man" who turns out to be "God (Elohim)" and who gives Jacob the new name of Israel (32:22-32). The capstone of the eponymous interpretation occurs with the birth of Jacob's sons (29:31—30:24; 35:16-20), whose names are identical with the later tribes of Israel.

Fixing upon these and other pronouncedly eponymous aspects of the ancestor traditions, a number of past scholars attempted to understand the entirety of the traditions as more or less veiled tribal histories. Births were read as the origins of tribes, and marriages were seen as the unions of two tribes. Aside from the difficulty that some of the names of individuals have no known identity as tribal groups (e.g., Abraham, Lot, Isaac, Laban, or even Jacob), it requires a very strained allegorical interpretation to carry through such a systematic collectivization of the traditions. It is far more likely that sagas about individuals and their families have been given direct or indirect eponymous meanings, and have in turn given rise to tradition units that are eponymous at their core.

SOCIOHISTORICAL HORIZONS OF THE ANCESTOR TRADITIONS

Based as it was on a confessional religious approach to the Bible, the traditional interpretation of the stories about Abraham, Isaac, Jacob, and Joseph viewed them as straightforward historical reports. Historical-critical method took another tack by demonstrating that these ancestor traditions were not a historical work using documentation or eyewitness testimony (see pp. 63–65). The traditions were largely chains and cycles of sagas, and the literary type of the saga was recognized as an orally based form in which past persons, events, and typical experiences were imaginatively reworked to celebrate the ancestor heroes of their sagas as exemplary founders or precursors of a new socioreligious order.

Once the historical character of the ancestors fell into fundamental doubt, many biblical critics concluded that nothing historically substantial could be determined about them, since they were fabrications of a later community. Other critics nonetheless tried to isolate valid historical elements in the traditions that could fix the approximate time and setting of the ancestors. Using extrabiblical texts and archaeological remains as external checkpoints, many scholars asserted that the ancestors of Israel could be placed from somewhere in the Middle Bronze I period (ca. 2100–1900 B.C.E.) to the early part of the Late Bronze period (1550–1200 B.C.E.). More recently this way of anchoring the ancestors in the historical world of the ancient Near East has been thrown into radical doubt.

An alternative option, still quite undeveloped, tries to correlate the literary peculiarities of the traditions with the sociohistorical conditions of emerging Israel. On this view, the traditions of Genesis 12–50 may help us to reconstruct how Israel took shape through the joining of preexisting groups that lived amid conditions and pressures of the sort attested in the sagas.

Chronology and Archaeology

The biblical text supplies a skeleton of chronological information that can be pieced together from the DH and P sources. Solomon is said to have begun construction of the temple 480 years after the exodus (1 Kgs. 6:1; DH). A date in the period 967 to 958 B.C.E. for the laying of the temple cornerstone seems assured.[6] Reckoning backward, we arrive at a fifteenth-century date for the departure from Egypt (ca. 1447–1438 B.C.E.). Exodus 12:40 (P) states that the stay in Egypt totaled 430 years (Gen. 15:13, from E, states 400 years), which would place the descent of Jacob into Egypt in the nineteenth century (ca. 1877–1868 B.C.E.).

When miscellaneous Priestly chronological notes are calculated (Gen. 47:9; 25:26; 21:5; 12:4), we reach a date of roughly 2092–2083 for Abraham's departure from Haran.

What should we make of this chronology? To begin with, it requires that we take at face value the excessively great ages of the ancestors (see pp. 90–91). Also, it is noted that the numbers given in the Samaritan Pentateuch and in the LXX frequently vary from those in the MT. More seriously, to posit a fifteenth-century exodus flies in the face of the biblical picture of political conditions in Egypt at the time and also fails to explain why Israel was so little visible in Canaan in the period 1400–1250 B.C.E. In connection with the latter objection, it cannot be shown that the 'apiru malcontents mentioned in the Amarna letters (see Web Table A, 3B) as highly active in Canaan in 1425–1350 B.C.E. are to be equated with the Israel of the books of Joshua and Judges. With respect to the ancestors, there is simply nothing specific in the biblical traditions that can connect them with known history in or around Canaan in the period between 2092 and 1868 when, according to the biblical chronology, the ancestors were supposedly in Canaan.

On the assumption that some traces of the manner of ancestral life reflected in Genesis 12–50 might appear in the material remains from Canaan, archaeology has been freely invoked to argue for one or another scheme for dating the patriarchs. Middle Bronze I (2100–1900 B.C.E.) has appealed to many scholars as the patriarchal age because of its now richly attested nonurban culture, often assumed to indicate an incursion of nomadic peoples presumably similar in lifestyle to the ancestors of Israel.

Middle Bronze II (1900–1550 B.C.E.) is the preferred patriarchal era for other biblical specialists. An open-air sanctuary at Shechem, dating to about 1800 B.C.E., is associated with patriarchal worship at that site (Gen. 33:18-20), and the manner of Abraham's residence in a satellite village of Hebron is said to be paralleled in the layout of unwalled Givat Sharett close by Beth-shemesh (Gen. 13:18). Moreover, advocates of Middle Bronze II feel that a lowering of the patriarchal era by two or more centuries brings the ancestors into more satisfactory chronological connection with the widely accepted thirteenth-century date for the exodus.

All in all, however, archaeological buttressing of one or another date for the ancestors has not proven convincing. For one thing, the evidence does not consistently support any scheme of dating. Neither of the important patriarchal sites of Beersheba and Shechem yields any sign of occupation in Middle Bronze I; indeed, Beersheba appears not to have been built until around 1200. According to the biblical texts, the location of the early Israelite holy place at Shechem was probably not within the walled city where excavators found the cultic installation. Moreover, most of the archaeological assessment has proceeded on a vast overestimation of the role of pastoral nomadism in early Israel and on very dubious assumptions about how pastoral nomadic social organization can be read as present in material remains (see pp. 157–58).

Perhaps most critically, archaeology has been made to carry more of a burden than it can possibly bear in reaching historical conclusions. Only when solid historical elements can be established in the ancestor sagas—through independent historical evidence, like inscriptional evidence, or through controlled comparative literary studies that demonstrate the historical particulars that sagas are prone to preserve—only then will archaeology be able to offer unambiguous supplementary support or clarification to those elements.

Political and Geographical Data

The relatively sparse political allusions and the more abundant geographical references in the ancestor traditions have been ransacked in a search for clues to the historical setting(s) of the ancestors. The results have been either vaguely inconclusive or blatantly contradictory. Historical contexts ranging over as much as eighteen hundred years have been seriously proposed as the periods when the ancestors lived or, if they were literary fictions, when they were created. The earliest positioning of the ancestors wants to make them contemporaries of the Ebla texts from northern Syria, around 2400–2000 B.C.E., and the latest would bring the existing textual representations of the ancestors into the sixth-century Judean exile. A brief survey of the political and geographical data shows why scholars vary so drastically in their historical situating of the ancestors, and why many scholars desist from any endeavor in that direction.

The fullest political information in these traditions appears to be found in Genesis 14, where Abraham defeats a coalition of four kings from afar, who carry out a punitive campaign against five rebellious vassal kings. The regimes of the foreign kings are apparently in Mesopotamia and Anatolia. Elam is clearly named, and the other three states are probably conceived as Assyrian, Babylonian, and Hittite. Especially dubious is the text's conception of Elam, based in southwestern Iran, exercising imperial control over part of Canaan. Moreover, there is no evidence that four kings from these distant regions ever formed a coalition against city-states in Canaan. A widely held view is that Genesis 14 is a midrash (free interpretation) intended to show that Abraham, "the father of a multitude of nations" (17:5), was a fully participating equal of great kings. Melchizedek, king of Salem (Jerusalem?), who blesses Abraham after his victory (14:17-20), is otherwise unknown. King Abimelech of Gerar, who joins Abraham and Isaac in treaties (21:27; 26:26-31), is also not known from any other source. The identification of Abimelech as "king of the Philistines" (e.g., 26:1; cf. 21:32) would not have been a historically accurate title until the Philistines colonized Canaan beginning about 1150 B.C.E. If we shift to the Jacob cycle, the historical ambiguities continue.

The pharaoh who enlists Joseph in his service is anonymous, while the Egyptian names that appear in the Joseph novella are not familiar before the tenth century from Egyptian sources. The centralized agricultural policy reported in 47:13-26 probably best accords with Egyptian economic controls under the New Kingdom, but that embraces the long period from 1570 to 1085 B.C.E.

Do the regions and settlements named in the ancestor traditions point toward a specific historical context any more persuasively than the more limited political data? The place names tend to fall into two categories: (1) references to places in the mountainous heartland or in the northern Negeb of ancient Canaan where the ancestors resided; and (2) references to outlying areas of Canaan and the wider Near East with which the ancestors were in contact.

Two sources understand that Abraham immigrated to Canaan from an area around Haran in northern Mesopotamia, called Aram-naharaim (Aram between the Rivers) by J and Paddan-aram (the Field of Aram)

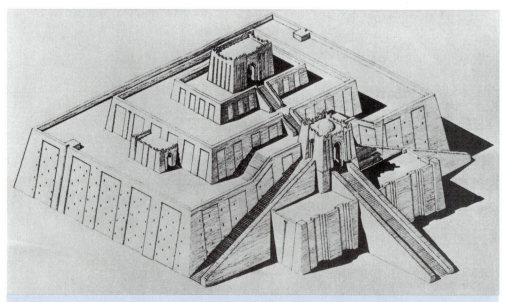

FIG. 4.1 Reconstruction of the Temple of Ur, Iraq. 2500–2000 B.C.E. Photo: © Bildarchiv Preussischer Kulturbesitz / Art Resource, N.Y.

by P. The Priestly source (and maybe J) adds that, prior to coming to Haran, Abraham had lived in southern Mesopotamia at Ur. Support for the northern Mesopotamian origin of the ancestors of Israel is often cited in that several of the relatives of Abraham possess names identical with known cities in that region: Terah, Nahor, Haran, and Serug. The specific connection of the first homeland of Abraham with places in Mesopotamia, however, belongs more to the P framework of the traditions than to the contents of the sagas.

It is striking that the E source locates the homeland of Laban not in far northern Mesopotamia, but just to the east or northeast of Transjordan. That Ur is explained as a city of the Chaldeans would not have been a way of identifying that ancient Sumerian city until at least the tenth century and more likely in the eighth century when a strong Chaldean (Neo-Babylonian) dynasty arose there. The designation of upper Mesopotamia as "Aram" depends on the rise to prominence of Aramean peoples that probably began by the fifteenth century but may not have led to the practice of naming regions as subdivisions of larger Aram (e.g., Aram-naharaim, Paddan-aram) until the eleventh century. Even the existence of northern Mesopotamian cities bearing patriarchal names is not compelling evidence for Middle Bronze II origins of the ancestors in that region, since some of these names occur also in texts from much later centuries.

In short, a tendency toward systematizing the origins of the ancestors, and their relationships to other peoples, is noticeable in the literary stages of framing the traditions. It is far less clear that we can identify the beginnings of that process in the oral phase of the traditions, for which the generality of E's reference to the ancestors' homeland in "the land of the people of the east" (Gen. 29:1) may be more typical than the citing of place names.

The Palestinian locales of the ancestor sagas are concentrated in four areas: (1) in the Samarian highlands at Bethel and Shechem; (2) in Transjordanian Gilead at Penuel and Succoth; (3) in the Judahite highlands at Mamre-Hebron; and (4) in the Negeb of Judah at Gerar and Beersheba. Jacob is primarily associated with the first two groups of sites and Abraham-Isaac with the last two groups. This concentration of the key patriarchal sites in precisely the areas where the Israelite tribes first appeared in strength at the end of the thirteenth century is significant. But to translate these geographical allusions into a prior historical setting for the individual ancestors is precarious, not only because the biblical references are not clearly related on a single historical plane but also because the highland area of Canaan seems to have been politically undeveloped during most of the Bronze Age and consequently does not yield much textual information. Since the ancestor sagas developed orally and as literature over centuries of time, it is difficult to judge when, and with what historical understanding, the various place names were introduced to the traditions.

Customs and Laws

One of the most strongly asserted links in reconstructions of the patriarchal world in a Bronze Age setting has been the remarkable find of texts treating family law from Nuzi and adjacent locations in the upper Tigris Valley. These documents date from the fifteenth and fourteenth centuries B.C.E. and come from a Hurrian society situated some distance to the east of the supposed homeland of the patriarchs in Aram-naharaim (see Web Table A, 1K).

A great range of customary legal practices evidenced in the Nuzi tablets have suggested close affinities with the marriage, family, and inheritance customs of the ancestors of Israel. Among the parallels between Nuzi and patriarchal family custom and law are the following:

1. A barren wife must provide her husband a slave girl through whom he may have children (Gen. 16:1-2; 30:9).
2. The status of the slave girl and her children is protected against the jealousy or arbitrariness of the wife or husband (21:9-14).
3. A husband could have the concurrent status of brother by adopting his wife from her natural brother (12:11-13; 20:2, 12; 26:7).
4. A person could sell a birthright to another (25:29-34).
5. A childless couple could adopt someone to provide for them who would in the end inherit their property, except that any subsequent naturally born son would automatically inherit in place of the adopted son (15:1-4).
6. The practice described in no. 5 was also applicable in cases where a son-in-law was adopted as one's son (31:1-2).
7. Possession of household gods (KJV "teraphim") was a kind of title deed to inheritable property (31:34).
8. A deathbed testament, or blessing, by the head of a family could have the force of law (27:35-37; 48:8-22).

On the strength of these parallels it was widely concluded that Hurrian family law was observed over the whole of upper Meso-potamia and thus was known to the Israelite ancestors in Aram-naharaim, whence they brought it to Canaan. Data from the Mari texts on the middle Euphrates, from about 1800 B.C.E., were also judged to support some of these conclusions.

Despite the impressiveness of the argument from Hurrian and Amorite customs and laws, the weight of the evidence has been strongly challenged and extensively undermined by further study, including the publication of additional Hurrian texts. First, it is noticed that earlier interpreters tended to supply either the Genesis sagas or the Nuzi documents with missing elements or provisions that would permit the two traditions to harmonize more closely with one another. Second, it is now believed that the Nuzi archives are by no means peculiar to upper Mesopotamia in Middle Bronze II and Late Bronze. Traces of similar laws have been detected in Old Babylonian and Assyrian laws, and the presence of the same or similar customs is cited in later centuries in the ancient Near East. The tendency, therefore, is to qualify sharply, or to deny totally, the claim that the Nuzi finds necessarily, or even probably, situate the ancestors of Israel in a Hurrian societal context in upper Mesopotamia in the period 2000–1400 B.C.E.

Another customary aspect of the Genesis traditions is the Egyptian coloration of the Joseph novella, which reflects Egyptian loanwords, court customs and titles, burial practices, and so on (see, e.g., chaps. 40–41; 47:13-26; 50:26). Many of these Egyptian elements are so general as to denote no particular historical period. Those that can be checked out against Egyptian data generally suggest that the Egyptian milieu reflected is more likely from the tenth century and later rather than from the Bronze Age. Moreover, two emphatic notices about Egyptian refusal

FIG. 4.2 A mosque covers the cave of Macpelah in Hebron in this photograph from c. 1860. Photo: © The Francis Frith Collection / Art Resource, N.Y.

to eat with Hebrews (Asiatics?) or to consort with shepherds (43:32; 46:34) find no support from Egyptian sources. It appears, then, that the most detailed Egyptian flavor in the Joseph novella is provided at the JE stage of written composition or later, and that it is not at all required that the oral storytellers or the writers of the Joseph traditions had any eyewitness knowledge of Egypt.

Social Struggles in the Ancestor Traditions

The Uncertain Socioeconomic Niche of the Ancestors

We have noted difficulties in trying to fit the ancestors of Israel into any particular historical or social setting when pursued by the cus-

tomary historical-critical methods. The fairly sparse chronological, political, and geographical data from the biblical text do not correlate and converge toward any definite setting. Nor does the external evidence from archaeological remains and from custom and law form any conclusive links with the biblical text. In short, the ancestors of Israel fit broadly into the whole sweep of Bronze and Iron Age Canaan and its environs, but without any more detailed reliable indication of date and without firm connections to political and social structures and events known from sources outside the Bible.

These obstacles to situating the ancestors of Israel have often been obscured by the assumption that references to their movements and manner of life indicate that the ancestors were pastoral nomads. However, the movements of the ancestors are largely explained as historically caused migrations for purposes of change of residence, religious pilgrimage, securing wives, escaping famine, and the like, rather than due to the regular seasonal movements of pastoral nomads. The references to the ancestors' forms of wealth include not only the flocks of sheep and goats typical of (though not exclusive to) pastoral nomads at the time, but also herds of cattle, wealth in metal, and cultivated land, which suggest either sedentary farming and animal husbandry or commercial enterprise. Some interpreters have proposed that the patriarchs were merchants who moved their goods by donkey caravans or independent transport contractors, or, with the detail of Abraham as a commander of 318 armed men (14:13-16), even military adventurers of the 'apiru type (mentioned in the Amarna letters [Web Table A, 3B].

The ancestors are shown to reside in the vicinity of major population centers in the highlands, and, insofar as they are nomadic at all, some members of their larger families/ clans/bands apparently took flocks into favorable seasonal pasturage while the rest of the group remained at home/headquarters (so-called transhumant pastoralism; see 37:12-17; 38:12-13; and possibly also 26:12-23). All in all, the socioeconomic traits of the ancestors are not delineated as clearly belonging to any one type. This may mean either that the traditions reflect different occupational statuses because they refer to different groups or that changing conceptions of the occupational status of the ancestors came into play at different points in the process of gathering and editing the traditions about them.

There is also the challenge of sorting out defensibly which representations of ancestors are references to actual individuals and which

are collective representations of tribes or of the whole people Israel. If it is judged that actual individual ancestors have been later turned into symbols of larger groups, how are the two kinds of references to be distinguished in the sagas? There is no more or less consistent method for sifting the sociohistorical indicators of individuals and their families from those of larger groups for whom the ancestors are eponyms.

Given such uncertainties, the soundest procedure for the moment is to recognize that the ancestor traditions entered the body of Israelite traditions in the tribal period. The earliest sociohistorical anchor point for them is

FIG. 4.3 Abraham is depicted as a prophet in this fresco from the Cathedral of San Marco, Venice. Photo: © Cameraphoto Arte, Venice / Art Resource, N.Y.

the confederation of Israelite tribes in Canaan before the rise of the kingdom. The traditions about ancestors become conceivable as the special legacies of different groups that joined to form Israel. It is noteworthy that the ancestors stand out as separate figures connected with different locales in Canaan. Only secondarily do they appear to have been linked by means of genealogies and itineraries.

It is plausible that Jacob was the ancestor hero of a group of northern Israelites in the regions of Ephraim and Manasseh, and that Abraham and Isaac were the ancestor heroes of groups of southern Israelites in the regions of the highlands of Judah and the northern Negeb. The communities who remembered these figures through sagas tended to view the life experiences of the ancestors as anticipations or prophecies of the later experiences of the entire groups who claimed descent from them (see p. 93). Whereas the type-scene format for developing the sagas permeated all the ancestor traditions (see pp. 91–93), the use of eponyms, for example, for the Jacob saga chain but not the Abraham saga chain, was more uneven.

Moreover, fairy tale or folklore motifs tended to be employed more frequently in connection with Jacob than with Abraham or Isaac. Jacob is portrayed in a variant on the motif of the wily trickster and the one who has the prodigious strength to wrestle all night with a preternatural figure who turns out to be God (32:22-32).

Further, Jacob was apparently the first ancestor to be securely absorbed into the traditions of the Israelite tribal league, so that he became the immediate father of the people whose very name was Israel and whose sons bore the precise names of the twelve tribes. Entering the ancestor corpus later, Abraham was nonetheless accorded the honored posi-

tion of the primal father of the people, the one who first ventured to Canaan and who became father of Isaac and grandfather of Jacob. In this way the separate experiences of ancestors dear to different segments of Israel were joined in one body of traditions that reflected the combined unity of the confederate tribes (see pp. 160–63).

Concerns about Production, Reproduction, and Self-defense

If we begin from the relatively secure sociohistorical point of united tribal Israel remembering different segments of experience contributed by various of its member groups, we can pursue one important line of inquiry: Can we determine the consuming interests and concerns of the groups who formulated and transmitted the ancestor traditions? Can we identify why it was in the interests of united Israel to combine the separate ancestor traditions in the form of all-Israelite traditions?

The concerns and interests of the ancestor traditions are primarily of two kinds: (1) the arduous struggle to secure a viable community as expressed in the need for offspring and productive land; and (2) the repeated defense of the community against outside pressures to absorb or destroy it. A majority of the type-scenes noted (see pp. 91–93) focus on the first struggle: how the ancestors are to get sons and to gain a secure hold on land. The net sociohistorical profile of the ancestor traditions shows groups of people, who, because they are reportedly newcomers to Canaan, are only marginally integrated into the economy, society, and politics of the highlands of Canaan. Scholars have naively assumed that they were also pastoral nomads. The contents of the sagas, however, tend to disclose that the ancestors were not well integrated into highland Canaan because they constituted small communities of people who did not want to integrate or submit to the prevailing social and political structures (see pp. 154–57, 160–63).

One particularly intriguing aspect of the ancestor traditions is the prominence of the women within them. For example, Sarah is a strong-willed equal of Abraham, capable of expelling her handmaid in a jealous fit (Gen. 16:1-6) and not above laughing at the promise of a son in her old age (18:9-15). Hagar is sketched as a person able to risk her life and the life of her son in the wilderness (16:7-14; 21:15-21). A frequent approach of older scholars to the initiative taken by women (e.g., in naming their children) and to the supposed signs of matrilocality (e.g., Jacob lives for some time in his wives' home) was to suppose either that the "patriarchal" society was really matriarchal or at least that it attested to survivals of an earlier Semitic matriarchal society. The evidence for this hypothesis is extremely tenuous. It is possible that this habit of presenting active feminine characterizations was one of the contributions to united Israel made by the groups that developed the ancestor traditions.

In sum, there appears to be some promise in locating the sociohistorical horizons of the ancestor sagas in the struggle for existence among small groups of people before they were able to combine into the intertribal confederation of Israel. In such a social space we should not expect to find political documentation about the ancestors. The great yearning for sons may very well reflect a situation of population decline in the Canaanite hill country, and the preoccupation with barren wives may indicate that sterility, whether because of deficient diet or disease, was a serious threat to the pre-Israelite residents of rural Canaan. The hunger for land may be the search of marginated peoples for pasturage and arable fields, but this hunger was not the unique prerogative of pastoral nomads but of anyone who dissented from the sovereignty of city-state and imperial apparatuses.

Once one recognizes that the several ancestors of Israel, and the complex traditions about them, have derived from different member groups within Israel, it may indeed be the case that they tell us indirectly—as the saga form always does—about several different socioeconomic strategies employed by the Canaanite highland populace to cope with their survival needs prior to the large-scale emergence of united Israel, whether as farmers, transhumant pastoralists, military mercenaries, or merchants.

To propose the sociohistorical horizons of the ancestor traditions in this way is only to suggest relevant boundaries and possibilities for further inquiry. This much is clear: historical-critical methods of research, coupled with archaeology, have reached an impasse in trying to contextualize the ancestors and the ancestor traditions. The presently emerging newer forms of literary criticism and of social-scientific criticism are beginning to assess the possibilities that exist for establishing a description of the social processes by which groups of Canaanite people became united in Israel and, at the same time, a description of the literary processes (including oral literature) by which those groups expressed their deepest values and aims in the course of their struggles. To establish this social-literary interplay within the ancestor sagas as the central focus of inquiry is not to abandon history, but to conceptualize history on a plane to which the documented political history and the archaeological remains of the ancient Near East do not give direct access (see pp. 34–39).

NOTES

1. Robert Alter, "Biblical Type-Scenes and the Uses of Convention," in *The Art of Biblical Narrative* (New York: Basic, 1981), 47–62.
2. The enumerated examples are keyed by number to the tradition units in Web Table G.
3. Sean E. McEvenue, *The Narrative Style of the Priestly Writer*, Analecta biblica 50 (Rome: Biblical Institute Press, 1971).
4. Sean E. McEvenue, "A Comparison of Narrative Styles in the Hagar Stories," *Semeia* 3 (1975): 64–80.
5. Robert Polzin, "'The Ancestress of Israel in Danger' in Danger," *Semeia* 3 (1975): 81–98.
6. The chronological system followed in this book (see pp. 167–68) dates the foundation of the temple to 967 B.C.E.

FOR FURTHER READING

Alter, Robert. *The Art of Biblical Narrative.* New York: Basic, 1981.

Campbell, Anthony F., and Mark A. O'Brien. *Sources of the Pentateuch: Texts, Introductions, Annotations.* Minneapolis: Fortress Press, 1993.

Delaney, Carol. *Abraham on Trial: The Social Legacy of Biblical Myth.* Princeton: Princeton University Press, 1998.

Gunkel, Hermann. *The Stories of Genesis.* Vallejo, Calif.: Bibal, 1994.

QUESTIONS FOR STUDY

1. What is type-scene analysis? How does it contribute to literary critical methods of interpreting the biblical text? How does this method differ from source and form criticism?
2. What literary and/or archaeological evidence have scholars used to support their theories about the dates for (1) Solomon's construction of the temple, (2) the exodus from Egypt, and (3) the patriarchal age?
3. What evidence has been used to support the theory that the ancestors of Israel were pastoral nomads? What evidence opposes this theory?
4. What can the biblical portrayals of Jacob and Abraham tell us about their historical and cultural roles?

TRADITIONS ABOUT MOSES

Exodus, Covenant, and Lawgiving

SUMMARY

The editing of traditions about Moses in
    Exodus, Leviticus, and Numbers
The large P component
The Egyptian context
The covenant and its "laws"
    The Decalogues
    The divine name
Folktale plot-motifs
The Moses group as pre-Israelite entity

READ THE BIBLICAL TEXT

Exodus
Leviticus
Numbers

*See additional materials at fortresspress.com/
gottwald;* consult Carta Bible Atlas *maps 47–53.*

THE SHAPE OF THE TRADITIONS IN EXODUS, LEVITICUS, AND NUMBERS

Distribution of the Tradition Units by Sources and Literary Genres

The traditions about Moses in Exodus, Leviticus, and Numbers are almost three times the length of the traditions about the patriarchs in Genesis 12–50. The greater bulk of the Moses traditions is not to be explained by an excessively complicated plot, for the main story is easily summarized, beginning with the oppression of the offspring of Jacob in Egypt to their escape from Egypt and covenanting with Yahweh, to their reaching Canaan's border. Around this basic plot is a wealth of traditions that include more or less complete subplots or type-scenes. See Web Chart H.

The sources J, E, and P, already isolated in the ancestor traditions (see pp. 89–90), continue into Exodus, Leviticus, and Numbers. There is, however, a radical shift in the relative proportions of the traditions assignable to each source. Therein lies much of the explanation for the complexity of the traditions. While J and E account for far fewer verses in Exodus than in Genesis overall, P accounts for a fifteenfold increase in verses. In addition, there is a body of theophany, covenant, and law texts that is clearly non-P but that cannot be assigned with confidence to J and E.

Corresponding to the shift in the relative sizes of the three main sources is a distinct shift in literary types. While saga is the most prevalent tradition unit in the ancestor traditions, in the Moses traditions twice as many verses in Exodus through Numbers are given to laws and lists, most of them P traditions, as are given to narratives and poems/songs.

Complex Editing of the Moses Traditions

The saga clusters that carry the plot in the Moses traditions are concentrated in Exodus 1–24, 32–34, and resume more sporadically in Numbers 10–36. In the Exodus sagas, the people move out of Egyptian bondage and come to Sinai/Horeb. In the Numbers sagas, the people move from Sinai/Horeb to Kadesh and then to the border of Canaan. The majority of the remaining traditions, including the entirety of Leviticus, are P source instructions on such matters as building the tabernacle (86–88),[1] offering sacrifices (89), as well as the so-called Holiness Code (93), and assorted other laws and lists that intermix with narratives as the people migrate from place to place. A few non-P Sinai traditions are relatively brief and compact, but drastically and complexly edited, including the so-called Ethical Decalogue (58) and the Covenant Code (60), as well as theophanies (55–57 62) and a covenant-concluding ceremony (63).

At this point in Exodus begins the vast P excursus of instructions on matters such as building the tabernacle (86–88) and offering sacrifices (89) as well as the so-called Holiness Code (93) and assorted other laws and lists that intermix with narratives as the Israelites move from Sinai to Kadesh and thence to Canaan.

A literary convention of repetition or reiteration, characteristic of folk and epic styles of narration, is especially evident in P's way of presenting the laws. A noteworthy instance occurs when the tabernacle is twice described in laborious detail—once as a set of instructions to Moses (Exodus 25–31) and a second time as the plans are executed and the tabernacle is assembled (Exodus 35–39). Between the two recitations is the story of the Israelites' worship of the golden calf and the breaking of the tablets of the law, which according to 31:18 contained the tabernacle instructions. When the tablets are reinscribed, however, they are said to contain the so-called Ritual Decalogue, having mainly to do with sacrifices and feasts and entirely oblivious of the tabernacle and of the previous Decalogue in Exod. 20:1-17 (cf. 34:1, 4, 28). This reiteration of the tabernacle laws has given an editor the opportunity to try to bind together different Sinai traditions. The need to mass the various traditions strategically at Sinai/Horeb has definitely taken precedence over any concern to present an intelligible narrative course of events.

In spite of all the effort to constellate Israel's law around the Sinai revelation, not quite all the supplemental P law managed to get—or to stay—connected to Sinai. Even after the Israelites moved on to Kadesh and thence to the

Plains of Moab, they still received legal instructions. The book of Deuteronomy, yet another recitation of the laws of Moses, understands that Moses reviewed the Sinai/Horeb laws by reciting them once again in Moab just before his death. Since the covenant texts in Exodus and Deuteronomy contain many signs of having originated in periodic covenant-renewal

FIG. 5.1 The royal family of Amenophis IV Akhnaton is depicted offering sacrifice to Aton, the sun god, in a relief from Amarna, Egypt. New Kingdom, 1350 B.C.E. Egyptian Museum, Cairo. Photo: © Erich Lessing / Art Resource, N.Y.

ceremonies, the confusing editorial practice of distributing laws not only to Sinai but also to Kadesh and Moab may be a literary attempt to assert the ever-renewed relevance of covenant and law. Though given first at Sinai/Horeb, the covenant and law journey on with Israel through time and space.

In sum, we can say that onto the narrative frame of the themes about deliverance from Egypt, wilderness wandering, as well as theophany, covenant, and lawgiving at a sacred mountain, there has been grafted a large and complicated body of laws, the majority of this body composed of sizable blocks and single units provided by P. On the strength of this profusion of laws connected primarily with Sinai, Genesis through Deuteronomy was eventually called Torah (instruction/teaching/law [see pp. 62–63]). Later Israelite covenant and law concerns overwhelmed the saga form and have made it virtually impossible for historical-critical method to penetrate the thicket of traditions to ascertain what thirteenth-century events may underlie them.

HISTORICAL-CRITICAL APPROACHES TO THE MOSES TRADITIONS

The Egyptian Context

A primary approach of historical-critical method to the Moses traditions has been to attempt to contextualize them within our considerable wealth of knowledge about ancient Egypt. Indeed, it is chiefly the weight of the Egyptian evidence that has inclined most scholars to prefer a thirteenth-century date for Israel's exodus from Egypt rather than the fifteenth-century date prescribed by the questionable biblical chronology (see pp. 94–95).

On initial examination, a fifteenth-century setting for the departure from Egypt seemed plausible, with Thutmose III (ca. 1468–1436) as the likely pharaoh of the exodus. The Eighteenth Dynasty, which had expelled the Hyksos conquerors from Egypt, presumably had a great distaste for Asiatics and thus bore down heavily on their Hebrew slaves. Moreover, references in the Amarna letters to 'apiru (= Hebrews) actively disrupting Canaanite city-states in the period around 1425–1350 were often explained as the activities of Israelites in their early attempts to conquer Canaan. Nevertheless, many scholars recognized that

the Hyksos and 'apiru data did not correlate in most respects with the biblical traditions. Joseph and his family appear neither as conquerors of Egypt nor as cultural equals or kin of the ruling-class Egyptians. Likewise, the names, distributions, and tactics of the Amarna age 'apiru do not correspond with the reports of Israelite conquest in Joshua and Judges.

Increasingly the circumstances depicted in the Moses traditions were judged to accord best with a thirteenth-century setting, with Rameses II (1290–1224) serving as the likely pharaoh of the exodus. The Israelites are shown as living and working in the vicinity of the Egyptian capital. In the fifteenth century the capital was far up the Nile at Thebes, whereas by the thirteenth century the Nineteenth Dynasty had established Avaris in the

FIG. 5.2 Fishermen on the Nile in front of the pyramids at Giza, Egypt, in this photograph from the late nineteenth or early twentieth century. Photo: © François Guenet / Art Resource, N.Y.

eastern delta, renamed Raamses, as its capital, undertaking extensive building projects to strengthen it and surrounding cities as a base for Egyptian military campaigns into Canaan and Syria. The Israelites as forced laborers in the Delta store cities of Raamses and Pithom (Exod. 1:11) fit suitably into the known circumstances of the time but not into the fifteenth century.

Although a thirteenth-century date for the exodus contradicts the literal chronology of the later pentateuchal sources, it seems to accord best with the biblical data taken as a whole. Indeed, the DH and P chronologies may rest upon an ancient scheme that reckoned one generation as forty years so that the time in the wilderness might have been very much shorter. The 480 years of 1 Kings 6:1 in that case would stand for twelve generations, which, more accurately calculated at twenty-five years per generation, would yield 300 years and thus a thirteenth-century exodus. Also, some genealogical references in the Bible tend to shorten the lapsed time between the descent into Egypt and the exodus (e.g., Num. 32:10 lists the grandson of Joseph as a contemporary of Moses) and between the exodus and the judges. Of course this evidence is qualified by a well-known tendency of genealogies to drop unimportant intervening generations.

In sum, historical-critical assessment of the Moses traditions against the backdrop of ancient Egypt has suggested a probable thirteenth-century setting for the exodus. What we are given is this useful but hypothetical formulation: if some elements of the Moses traditions are taken to be historically attached, then they best fit into the Egyptian and Canaanite milieus at this time and in this way.

Cautions about the essentially undatable character of the Egyptian milieu of the exodus are appropriately sounded from time to time. The pharaohs are unnamed in the Joseph and Moses traditions, Asiatics and even ‘apiru captives and slaves are referred to over several centuries in Egypt, Egyptian names were given to people living in Canaan, and even the store cities of Raamses and Pithom, where Israelite slaves reportedly worked, are mentioned down to as late as the fifth century. In other words, nothing in the biblical traditions points unequivocally to the thirteenth century as the time of the exodus. Some scholars go so far as to question that the Egyptian milieu of the Moses traditions is historically grounded; but if Moses and at least some Israelites were never in Egypt, why has tradition claimed that they were?

Moses: Formative Influences and Leadership Roles

Moses is presented as a deliverer of his people from bondage who also led them through the first phases of their new life of freedom. All of our information about him comes from narrative literature of a history-like quality that stops short of being actual historiography. Scholars have attempted to look within the traditions for signs of a reliable outline of his career and how he might have been concretely rooted in his time and place.

From among the history-like accounts of Moses it is possible to extract a plot line that exhibits unity of action and causal connections. For example, his life could be described in capsule form as follows: Moses was born to Israelite parents in Egyptian slavery and bore an Egyptian name, as did other Israelites in the period. After unsuccessful efforts to alleviate the affliction of his people in their slavery, he fled into Sinai/Midian, married into a priestly family, and returned to lead his people out of Egypt. In the wilderness he struggled to organize the community by means of religious covenant and law, and he led them to the verge of Canaan, where he died. This is not, however, much information for reconstructing anyone's life.

Such a sketch of the life of Moses is no more than an abstraction from the rich saga-related account of Moses as the immediate hero through whom the invisible, ultimate divine hero Yahweh works. Every attempt to discern the historical Moses struggles against the historiographic resistance of the saga form of literature. Nonetheless, historical-critical method has undertaken just such a struggle, if only to be able to say that some reconstructions of the historical Moses are more probable than others, but because of questionable methodology none has won consensus.

If we grant that an actual leader of some group that became a part of Israel is referred to in these traditions, how might he be conceived in his historical environment? Of course, even in exploring some of the most favored ways of approaching that question, we are inevitably caught in a measure of circular reasoning because the very traditions we want to assess constitute the greater part of the evidence we have to work with. But we may at least try to formulate hypotheses for which there is some possibility of external support.

One element in the traditions claims that Moses was brought up in the Egyptian court, and this may be lent some credence by the fact that his name, meaning "son," is Egyptian. His reportedly bicultural context has led some to conjecture that the monotheistic religion of Pharaoh Akhenaton (ca. 1364–1347) influenced the religious views of Moses, although no indications of Moses' dependence on Akhenaton's reforms appear in the Bible or

in Egyptian history. In terms of the content or the sociopolitical structure of the two religions, there is also no recognizable bridge between Atonism—the sole worship of the sun mediated through the pharaoh—and the Yahwism attributed to Moses.

Another proposal is that Moses learned about the religion of Yahweh from the traditions of his own people, a notion that depends on one or another fancied occurrence of the name Yahweh outside the Bible. For example, it has been proposed that the Israelites were from that larger body of Asiatics identified in Egyptian texts as Shosu, often explained as "bedouins/nomads" but more correctly understood as "plunderers." Egyptian records from the fourteenth/thirteenth centuries contain references to "the Shosu land Yahweh," which seems to have been in central Syria. This place name, however, has no demonstrated connection with a deity or with a pre-Israelite belief in Yahweh.

The most substantial notion of formative influence on Moses depends on a particular reading of the biblical evidence. It is contended that Moses derived his belief in Yahweh, along with many cultic and legal practices, from his Midianite father-in-law. Jethro is called "priest of Midian" and joins (presides at?) a feast with the Israelites as they celebrate the deliverance from Egypt (Exodus 18). Kenites/Rechabites, who appear to have been a subgroup of Midianites, lived among the Israelites in Canaan and were ardent devotees of Yahweh (Judg. 1:16; 4:11; 1 Sam. 15:6-7; 2 Kgs. 10:15-27; Jer. 35:1-11).

Support for the Midianite/Kenite origins of Yahwism has been claimed on the basis of the discovery of a shrine at copper mines in the Arabah, some distance north of the Gulf of Eilat in Midianite territory. After about 1150, when the Egyptians abandoned the site,

Egyptian cult symbols were discarded, and a tent shrine was introduced in company with a gilded copper snake image. Possibly this points to Midianites who continued a type of worship employing a tent shrine (cf. the tabernacle or tent of meeting in Exodus and Numbers) and a bronze serpent (Num. 21:8-9; 2 Kgs. 24:8), cult regalia that they had already contributed to the Israelites under Moses. Of course the opposite explanation is not impossible, namely, that Moses introduced Yahwism to the Midianites.

In turning to the leadership roles credited to Moses, it is astonishing how numerous his functions are said to have been: negotiator with Pharaoh, miracle worker, logistics expert, covenant mediator, lawgiver, military commander in chief, appointer and installer of priests, judge, and prophet—indeed more than a prophet—in the directness of his communication with God. His comprehensive authority was sometimes shared or delegated for the occasion or in perpetuity, notably in the case of priestly office.

How Moses is to exercise supreme leadership, while distributing the workload and delegating authority, is an issue that runs through the traditions both as the sine qua non of Israel's birth and survival and as the source of continual unrest and bitter power struggles. A careful reading of the traditions about priesthood throughout the Bible makes clear that rival priestly groups throughout Israel's history sought to trace their pedigrees back to a commissioning by Moses, Samuel, or David (see pp. 267–73). The exaltation of Aaron in the P traditions is underscored by the foolish endeavor of the Levite Korah to seize some of Aaron's authority (see Web Table H, 109). But in J, E, and non-P Sinai traditions, Aaron lacks the sole priestly prerogative (see Web Table H, 47 and 65).

Besides the general murmuring and complaints of the people against Moses for deepening their oppression under Pharaoh and for leading them into a hostile wilderness, there are also frequent references and allusions to factionalism and uprisings in the community as a whole. The golden calf apostasy is put down by armed Levites. Miriam, with Aaron's complicity at least, objects to Moses' behavior in monopolizing leadership. All the scouts, except Joshua and Caleb, recoil from an attack on Canaan in spite of Moses' encouragement, but a little later attempt the attack after Moses has forbidden it. Dire fates are reserved for the rebels in these instances. On the other hand, Moses accepts advice to spread the task of judging the people among a sizable staff of judges. On another occasion "the spirit of prophecy," which had rested peculiarly on Moses, was shared with seventy elders in order to help him "bear the burden of the people."

In the end, there is no consistently principled way of knowing which leadership roles, and which aspects of those roles, a real Moses actually performed, in contrast to those that have been attributed to him as a way of validating later Israelite forms of communal leadership. A tremendous overload of leadership roles is obviously heaped on Moses, and yet it is well recognized that major leaders in tribal social organization often do exercise broad and fluid leadership powers. Likewise, the pervasive theme of obstinate rebellion against Moses was a convenient way to stigmatize various kinds of dissenters against subsequent Israelite leaders who invoked Moses' authority. On the other hand, it is not at all surprising that early Israel, venturing into new forms of social organization, should have been torn repeatedly by internal strife and rival leadership. It has been suggested plausibly, although without conclusive evidence, that Moses failed to enter Canaan because he was murdered in one of the uprisings against his command.

Unity of Action in Exodus and Wandering

On the assumption that the Moses traditions record a more or less unified and continuous movement of people from Egypt to Canaan, there have been many attempts to reconstruct the route of march and particularly to identify the exact locations of the crossing of the sea and the mountain of covenant making and lawgiving. Numbers 33 presents a complete itinerary of the people from Egypt to the verge of Canaan, attributable to the P source. Only the cities of Raamses and Pithom at the start of the journey, Kadesh and Ezion-geber in the wilderness, and Moabite sites at the end

of the itinerary have been identified with any degree of certainty. The location of the critically important sea and mountain are simply unknown.

In the past the general consensus was that the crossing of the sea occurred at the northern extremity of the Red Sea in the Gulf of Suez. Taking account of the fact that the Bible speaks of the "Sea of Reeds" (not Red Sea) and that the Gulf of Suez would have been a very exposed route for escaping from the Delta region, scholars have also proposed alternative crossing sites.

According to a tradition that goes back to the fifth Christian century, Mount Sinai/Horeb has been identified as Jebel Musa in the southern Sinai Peninsula. It is an impressive upthrust of granite, the sort of place where the holy mountain ought to have been. Historians who doubt that the sacred mountain could have been as distant as Jebel Musa is from the

FIG. 5.3 Photo of Jebel Musa, traditionally identified as Mount Sinai (Mount Horeb). Ca. 1860, by Francis Frith (1822–1898). Photo: © The Francis Frith Collection / Art Resource, N.Y.

main wilderness encampment at Kadesh have argued for one or another of several less spectacular mountains, but independent verification of these various sites of the mountain is unobtainable.

As to the events at the sea, historians frequently single out a J reference to the action of Yahweh, who "drove the sea back by a strong east wind all night" (Exod. 14:21). This can be understood as a storm-driven and tide-related recession of coastal waters, allowing passage of the Israelites, followed by a sudden return of the waters that engulfed the Egyptians. P's account tells of deep waters split to form a land bridge through the heart of the sea (14:22). A third conception of what occurred at the sea infers from the poetic Song at the Sea (15:4-10) that the Egyptians pursued the Israelites in boats that capsized from a violent storm. In spite of intense efforts to reconstruct the crossing of the sea, our evidence is far too scanty to do more than guess as to how natural and historical elements were combined in the events that underlie the biblical traditions.

The dominant line of interpretation, beginning with later biblical writers, has identified the crossing of the sea as the nucleus of the exodus. However, another tradition, perhaps more ancient, speaks of the Israelites despoiling or plundering the Egyptians (Exod. 3:21-22; 11:2-3a; 12:35-36; Ps. 105:37). This tradition pictures the Israelites escaping from Egypt by stealth with spoil taken from their captors. As the text now stands, the plundering of the Egyptians is subordinated to the crossing of the sea. But the two versions may once have existed independently.

Interpreters who insist that the sea crossing must rest on some actual experience not only overlook the option of a secret flight but also take little account of the possibility that

the theme of the sea as a cosmic force of chaos and death may have been used to heighten the significance of the exodus. It has also been proposed that the experiences of more than one group of escapees from Egypt—more than one exodus—have been combined in the biblical traditions.

We have observed that the complex editing of the Moses traditions has greatly confused the unity of action that ever so tenuously holds together the immense body of traditions (see pp. 106–7). This is evident in trying to visualize the movement of the people in the wilderness and, in particular, in attempting to establish the relationship between Sinai and Kadesh. In the present form of the traditions, Israel goes from Egypt to the mountain at Sinai/Horeb and then travels far to Kadesh. But the itinerary in the wilderness is presented in a very fragmentary and discrepant manner. Indeed, the traditions contain hints that Sinai and Kadesh were close together. Particularly striking is that a series of incidents and themes first placed between Egypt and Sinai (Exodus 16–18) are repeated at Kadesh (Numbers 10–20):

1. Moses consults with Jethro (Exod. 18:13-27; Num. 10:29-32).
2. The people murmur against Yahweh and Moses (Exod. 16:1-12; 17:1-7; Num. 11:1-6; 14:1-3, 26-38; 16:41; 17:11).
3. Quails are provided for food (Exod. 16:13; Num. 11:31-35).
4. Water is provided from a rock at Meribah (Exod. 17:1-7; Num. 20:2-13).

Clearly, later Sinai traditions intentionally disrupt earlier traditions regarding Kadesh, perhaps to make it appear that Sinai was a great distance from Kadesh and to shift some of the originally Kadesh-oriented traditions to points on the route from Egypt to Sinai. In short, the great cultic and theological significance attached to covenant making and lawgiving has been expressed structurally in the final state of the Moses traditions by sharply separating Sinai geographically from the rest of the wilderness sites, making it a mysteriously remote mountain.

Kadesh is identifiable as 'Ain el-Qudeirat, a copious spring permitting limited agriculture, located approximately fifty miles southwest of Beersheba on the southern fringe of Canaan. If there is any single discernible unity of action beneath the wilderness accounts, it is that the Israelites moved directly from Egypt to Kadesh (as reported in Judg. 11:16). Any covenant making and lawgiving that occurred in the wilderness would thus have taken place at or near Kadesh. It has been suggested that the alternative name of En-mishpat ("well of judgment") for Kadesh, reported in Gen. 14:7, retains a memory of Moses' judgment of the people (Exod. 18:13-27), or possibly even of lawgiving at Kadesh rather than at a distant Sinai. The Meribah of Exod. 17:7, connected with Kadesh in Num. 20:1, 13, is more explicitly called Meribath-kadesh by Ezekiel (47:19; 48:28).

Consequently, one way of resolving the problem of the unity of action behind the Moses traditions is to suppose that all the wilderness events took place at or near Kadesh, including the covenant making and lawgiving, later transferred to far-off Sinai. An alternative way of perceiving the underlying events is to presuppose that the Kadesh traditions originally had nothing to do with Israelites who had been in Egypt but rather with a different group of Israelites. This hypothesis raises the question of how the Sinai and Kadesh groups were related to Israelites who escaped from Egypt, whether by a crossing of the sea or by secretive flight.

It is likely that such analysis and speculation will appear to many Bible readers as hairsplitting or nit-picking. The primary point is that the critical reconstructions are inconclusive and incomplete precisely because the biblical traditions are inconclusive and incomplete on the historical plane, and extrabiblical sources of information are unhelpful because they are too general. Historical inquiry must rest content with a very incomplete picture that can be filled in only if further extrabiblical evidence comes to light.

RELIGION OF MOSES AND THE EXODUS-WILDERNESS ISRAELITES

The effort to ascertain the religious concepts and practices of the actors in the Moses traditions runs up against the same problem faced by all historical-critical research into this early horizon of Israel's experience. The essential problem is to isolate the religious elements that are credible within the imperfectly known historical context of Moses from the religious elements that later traditionists have intermixed in their retelling, rewriting, and reediting of the traditions. Instead of thinking that we are delving into the original historical core of the religion of Moses and his people, we are wiser to accept that we are sketching how the religion of Moses was remembered and conveyed in traditions that arose among the intertribal Israelites in Canaan during the generations after his death.

Covenant

Israelite tradition identifies Moses as the one who first brought the whole people into covenant with Yahweh, as distinguished from the anticipatory covenants made earlier with the individual ancestors Abraham, Isaac, and Jacob. "Covenant" is an awkward and somewhat misleading term for the Hebrew word *b*e*rīth,* which refers to a formal, solemn, and binding agreement between parties in which there are obligations to do certain acts, or to refrain from doing them, and there are promises or threats of consequences that follow fulfillment or breach of the obligations.

Many biblical covenants are arrangements between two persons, between a person and a group, or between groups. Other biblical covenants are arrangements between a person or a group, notably the entire people Israel, and God. As long as we understand "covenant" in this latter instance to mean an ordered relationship between God and people that is two-sided, though not necessarily evenhanded in the involvements and obligations of both parties, it is a useful term to employ.

Interestingly, the Moses traditions themselves are not heavily charged with direct covenant references. The non-P Sinai materials speak of a covenant between Israel and Yahweh mediated by Moses, first in an anticipatory election proclamation (Exod. 19:5) and again in two tradition units that describe covenant-making incidents at the mountain (24:7-8; 34:10, 27-28). A third unit does not use directly covenantal language (24:1-2, 9-11) and is seen by some critics as simply a theophany. Indeed, some who claim a Deuteronomistic revision of the non-P Sinai units deny that there are any pre-D references to covenant in the Sinai texts, which they tend to read as theophanies throughout. Identifiable J and E traditions do not refer to the covenant, except for J's "ark of the covenant" (Num. 10:33; 14:44).

The weight of this testimony seems to put the tradition of Moses as covenant mediator into some doubt, especially given that so many biblical recitations of exodus, wandering, and entrance into the land omit any reference to covenant and law. There is, however, another way of viewing the literary evidence. If one accepts the argument that the matrix for the history-like traditions of the ancestors, exodus, wandering, and conquest of the land was the covenant-making and law-reciting assembly of Israelite tribes, it is obvious that covenant concepts and mechanisms existed in Israel not long after the reputed lifetime of Moses.

This constitutes fairly strong testimony in favor of the covenant as deriving in some way from the Mosaic period, although the narrativized form of that covenant in Exodus 19–24 and 32–34, composed of diverse and severely edited texts from ritual ceremonies, appears to have arisen in the common pool of pre-JE materials later than all the other major narrativized traditions about Moses, the exodus, and the wanderings. The P laws and regulations were arbitrarily spliced into Exodus with the apparent purpose of asserting that the P laws depended on the prior covenant.

One of the difficulties that has bedeviled a full understanding of the covenant in early Israel has been the persisting tendency to see the covenant solely in religious terms. Insofar as covenant was a way of symbolizing the ground and origin of the proper ordering of Israel's communal life, the covenant was a total religiopolitical reality. The religious covenant was a way of binding together the tribes so that they could effectively subordinate their separate interests to the common project of winning their collective freedom and security from Canaanite city-states that tried to subject them to state domination. That the covenant mechanism associated the religious sovereignty of Yahweh with the historical sovereignty of the people is clear from the prohibitions against making treaties (i.e., covenants) with the Canaanite ruling classes and adopting their religious practices (Exod. 23:32; 34:12, 15). If a historical thread does run backward from the intertribal covenant of the free tribes in Canaan to Moses as a covenant-making leader of some of the peoples who later became part of the tribal confederacy of Israel in Canaan, one of its strongest strands was probably a political affirmation of Israelite self-determination—in the face of either Egyptian control or Canaanite city-state control.

In recent decades a theory about the origin of the covenant has developed that argues both for the origin of the covenant with Moses and for its explicit political derivation and significance. The theory is that the instrument adopted by Israel to formalize its relation to the god Yahweh was the ancient Near Eastern international suzerain-vassal treaty concluded between an imperial overlord and a subject ruler. The majority of the texts of suzerain-vassal treaties are fourteenth- and thirteenth-century Hittite texts, but Aramean and Neo-Assyrian texts of similar form are known down to the seventh century (see Web Table A, 2G and 2H). The chief elements of the suzerainty treaty form, which either occur typically in the treaty texts or are inferred from references in other texts, are listed in table 5.1 along with biblical passages that have been claimed to exhibit these formal elements.

The assumption is that Israel conceived of its relation to Yahweh as that of subject peoples to a world king and that they expressed this re-lationship in the concepts and formulas of the suzerainty treaty. At issue is whether the suzerainty treaty form is evidenced in biblical texts, and particularly whether the earliest covenant texts show dependence on it. There is wide agreement that the treaty model was influential on the Deuteronomic versions of the covenant dating from the eighth/seventh centuries (see pp. 221–23), since in many respects they show familiarity with Neo-Assyrian diplomatic conventions and treaty forms. But aside from Deuteronomy, the major elements of the treaty form are not solidly represented in any single text but have to be culled from several texts.

Some maintain, however, that the Israelite formulas more closely correspond to the typical concepts and language of the suzerainty treaty form than they do to any other ancient Near Eastern forms of agreement. Moreover, the adoption by Moses of the treaty form is viewed as a highly effective way to assert that in the new community of equal families/clans (later tribes) of Israel there were to be no human overlords but simply a sovereign god who legitimated the familial/clan-based (later tribal) social organization of the covenanting people.

Covenant Stipulations: Laws

Among the various covenantal stipulations of obligation in the early biblical traditions, are any likely to have derived from the historical Moses? The stipulations or laws are of different sorts and present different problems in understanding and dating them.

Priestly Instructions and Regulations

It is overwhelmingly clear that the style and emphases of these stipulations represent a late exilic and early postexilic priestly community

---

TABLE 5.1 STRUCTURAL ELEMENTS OF THE SUZERAINTY TREATY FORM[*]

1. Preamble or title of the author/superior party to the treaty
       (Exod. 20:2a; Deut. 5:6a; Josh. 24:2a)

2. Historical prologue or antecedent history of relations between the treaty partners.
       (Exod. 20:2b; Deuteronomy 1–3, 5:6b, Josh. 24:2b-13)

3. Stipulations stating the obligations imposed upon the vassal or inferior party to the treaty.
       (Exod. 20:3-17; Deut. 5:7-21; 12–26; Josh. 24:14)

4. Provision for deposit of the treaty text in a temple and periodic public reading
       (Exod. 25:21; 40:20; Deut. 10:5; 27:2-3; 31:10-11)

5. Lists of gods (or elements of nature/people) as witnesses to the treaty
       (Josh. 24:22, 27; Isa. 1:2; Micah 6:1-2)

6. Curses and blessings invoked for disobedience/obedience to the treaty stipulations
       (Deuteronomy 27–28)

7. Oath by which the vassal pledges obedience to the treaty
       (Exod. 24:3; Josh. 24:24)

8. Solemn ceremony for formalizing the treaty
       (Exod. 24:3-8)

9. Procedure for initiating sanctions against a rebel vassal
       (Hosea 4:1-10; Isa. 3:13-15)

[*]The elements of the suzerainty treaty form and the biblical covenant citations are drawn chiefly from K. Baltzer, D. J. McCarthy, G. E. Mendenhall, and P. A. Rieman.

---

that was striving to establish the legitimacy of its leadership in a restored Judahite community (see pp. 273-79). The P stipulations of Exodus, Leviticus, and Numbers cannot have come directly from the time of Moses. For one thing, Aaron and his family are given an eminence among the priests that contradicts his more limited role in the JE traditions and that corresponds temporally with later elevation of the Aaronic priests (see pp. 280-84, 298-301). Some elements in P, however, are older than the source as a whole and may go back at least to tribal times, if not to Moses, in their nuclear form: (1) socioeconomic and ritual laws in the Holiness Code (see Web Table H, 93C and G); (2) census data that may refer to old army musters (see Web Table H, 95 and 113); (3) details concerning the tabernacle that may accurately reflect an ancient tent shrine (see Web Table H, 86E; see also pp. 120–23).

Collections of Customary Socioeconomic and Religious Laws

The so-called law codes of Exod. 20:22—23:19 and Deuteronomy 12–26 are compilations of case law precedents for specific aspects of civil and religious life. The so-called Covenant Code of Exod. 20:22—23:19 was probably compiled in its present form in ninth-century northern Israel, and the Deuteronomic Code of Deuteronomy 12–26 in seventh-century Judah (see pp. 221–23). The difficulty in connecting many of the provisions that originate before the monarchy with Moses is that they presuppose a sedentary village life and an agricultural cultus that would hardly have been operative among the Israelites in the wilderness.

Terse Lists of Prohibitions: The Ten Commandments

There are two lists of pithy prohibitions in Exod. 20:1-17 (paralleled in Deut. 5:6-21) and in Exod. 34:11-26 that occupy pivotal points in the theophany and covenant texts. The lists of Exodus 34 and Deuteronomy 5 are called "ten commandments" in the biblical text (cf. Exod. 34:27 and Deut. 4:13; 10:4), and that title, or the equivalent Latin term *Decalogue,* has traditionally been applied to the list of Exodus 20/Deuteronomy 5. Biblical scholars often distinguish the Exodus 20/Deuteronomy 5 list from the Exodus 34 list on the basis of content by referring to the former as the Ethical Decalogue and the latter as the Ritual Decalogue.

The basis for precisely ten commandments as the summation of ethical or ritual requirements was probably to facilitate memory by associating each prohibition with one of the ten fingers. Actually, Exodus 34 has twelve commandments, although the original probably comprised only ten. Characteristic of the decalogue form is that it is composed of brief negative commands or prohibitions, without any provision of punishment for violating them. Most likely the Ethical and Ritual Decalogues in their original form were negatively formulated. Also, from the Ethical Decalogue, expanded by explanations and motivations, ten brief and grammatically complete prohi-

bitions can be disentangled. These ten pithy prohibitions are widely attributed to Moses.

In judging the age of the Ethical Decalogue, we can look first at the degree of generality of this list. It is evident that the prohibitions are far from clear in specifying the exact conduct they exclude from the community (see table 5.2 for the prohibitions with some of the disputed lines of interpretation).

We must also consider the socioeconomic and religious implications of this Decalogue in judging its age. The assumption that the prohibitions presuppose the village life of Israel in Canaan is qualified considerably once the secondary expansions of the short form of the prohibitions are removed. It is possible to construe all the brief prohibitions as consistent with the conditions of Israelite life in Moses' lifetime. Whether the Decalogue goes back to Moses depends of course on the closely related issue of whether Moses mediated a covenant between Yahweh and the people. In any case, it is probable that the Decalogue belongs to a relatively early period of Israel's life, probably within the premonarchic age. Had it been constructed as a late summary or abstraction from the existing case laws, one might have expected it to be more explicit and precise about the exact meaning of the prohibitions.

The Divine Name

The plain truth is that no one knows the meaning of the divine name Yahweh. The P source explicitly says that the deity known to the ancestors as El Shaddai ("God Almighty" in many translations) became known to Moses by the name Yahweh (Exod. 6:2). The E source prior to the revelation to Moses agrees with P in consistently avoiding the use of the name Yahweh. The J source, on the contrary,

TABLE 5.2 PROHIBITIONS OF THE ETHICAL DECALOGUE

1. *Prohibition of the worship of any god other than Yahweh,* either in the sense that no other god may be worshiped at a cultic site devoted to Yahweh or in the sense that there is to be no recognition of any other god as having a claim upon Israelites (Exod. 20:3; Deut. 5:7; cf. Exod. 22:20)

2. *Prohibition of making images of gods/God,* either to represent Yahweh or to represent any other god, or in both senses (Exod. 20:4; Deut. 5:8, cf. Exod. 20:23)

3. *Prohibition of misuse of the name of Yahweh,* either in the sense of oaths undertaken lightly, unnecessarily, or dishonestly, or in the sense of magical use of the name to curse or call up evil spirits to do harm to others unjustly (Exod. 20:7; Deut. 5:11)

4. *Prohibition of work on the seventh or Sabbath day* (Exod. 20:8; Deut. 5:12)

5. *Prohibition of cursing one's parents,* either in the sense of youths who dishonor parents who still have guidance over them or in the sense of mature adults dishonoring or failing to care for their older parents (Exod. 20:12; Deut. 5:16)

6. *Prohibition of murder of another Israelite,* either homicide with malice or in the sense that the murderer or perpetrator of a capital crime may not be executed without proper judicial procedure, or both (Exod. 20:13; Deut. 5:17)

7. *Prohibition of adultery,* either embracing a variety of prohibited sexual liaisons, as in Lev. 18:6-18, or referring to sexual union with a married or affianced woman (Exod. 20:14; Deut. 5:18)

8. *Prohibition of stealing property/person(?),* either in the sense of stealing all kinds of personal possessions or in the sense of stealing, that is, kidnapping, a person, which was a common source for the slave trade in antiquity (Exod. 20:15; Deut. 5:19; cf. Exod. 21:16)

9. *Prohibition of accusing another Israelite falsely,* either as plaintiff in a suit or as a witness, or both (Exod. 20:16; Deut. 5:20)

10. *Prohibition of lusting after/seizing another Israelite's house/household members,* either in the sense of condemning the inner desire or greed to take property or persons belonging to another or in the sense of willfully seizing property to be distinguished from the seizure of persons in no. 8 (Exod. 20:17; Deut. 5:21)

declares that Yahweh was worshiped by that name in preflood antiquity (Gen. 4:26).

The Elohist and Priestly sources seem closest to historical reality in stressing that a radically fresh understanding of deity appeared with Moses, an understanding that was taken up into the intertribal confederacy of Israel in Canaan when it adopted Yahweh as its god. On the other hand, the Yahwist source, underscoring the continuity of Yahweh's work from pre-Mosaic through Mosaic times, may also indirectly preserve a historical memory about the pre-Israelite worship of Yahweh. We have seen that if a god Yahweh was known before the time of Moses, it was most likely among the Midianites (see pp. 109–12), but unfortunately we do not possess a shred of evidence as to how the Midianites might have interpreted the meaning of the divine name.

The one and only explanation of the divine name in the Hebrew Bible appears in the E source (Exod. 3:14-15), and this explanation has prompted a host of interpretations. When asked about the divine identity, Elohim says to Moses, "Say this to the Israelites, ''ehyeh has sent me to you,'" which is then enlarged so as to connect 'ehyeh (= Yahweh) with the Elohim of Israel's ancestors: "Yahweh, the Elohim of your fathers, the Elohim of Abraham, the Elohim of Isaac, and the Elohim of Jacob, has sent me to you."

Exodus 3:14 regards the divine name as formed from the Hebrew verb hyh, "to be." If this verb is understood in the simple stem, 'ehyeh means "I will be" or "I am," and Yahweh is understood to mean "he will be" or "he (always) is." The LXX translation renders 'ehyeh into "I am the one who (eternally) is." This metaphysical twist has accorded well with later Jewish and Christian theological affirmations of an absolute and unchangeable god. It is highly questionable, however, that the Elo-

hist understood the divine name in this way, or that Moses would have so understood it.

If the verb is understood in the causative stem, 'ehyeh conveys the meaning "I cause to be" or "I bring about what comes into existence." This has often been construed as implying a notion of creation, of a sort not strongly evident in Israel before the time of the monarchy. The causation implied, however, may be focused on Yahweh as the producer of novel realities, the bringer of a people out of bondage. One theory, which also attempts to explain the connection between the older divine name El/Elohim and the newer divine name Yahweh, suggests that the proper name Yahweh sprang from an original epithet for El, perhaps "El who creates (yahwī) the hosts."[2] For Israel this would have meant "hosts" in a double sense: the armed hosts of heaven (natural elements such as sun and moon, rain, hail, wind, and personifications of the divine agency such as the angel or messenger of Yahweh) and the armed hosts of earth (the citizen army of Israel). In time, according to this hypothesis, the causative verb yahwī was separated to form an independent and distinctive, even preferred, name for Israel's god. This attractive theory lacks conclusive verification.

Despite exhaustive studies and yet other proposals, there is no way to uncover precisely what the name Yahweh meant to Moses or to the circle of tradition that gave this name to the tribal deity of Israel in Canaan. More than this, Exod. 3:14 is deliberately vague and cryptic, perhaps insisting on the reticence and mystery of Israel's God.

Cultic Rites and Objects

The final redaction of the Torah, decisively influenced by the Priestly viewpoint, assumed that the worship practices of the postexilic community had been received from Moses and had continued unchanged over the centuries. Once it is recognized that the cult of ancient Israel underwent development over time, the question arises: Is it possible to determine the actual worship forms of Moses, or at least of the first Israelites who developed the Moses traditions?

The P source gives an elaborate description of sacrifices, presided over by an Aaronic priesthood with Levitical assistants, and conducted at a movable shrine (tabernacle) housing a wooden chest (ark) that stood at the center of the Israelite wilderness camp. The portable wooden chest, or ark, and the portable shrine, or tent of meeting (= tabernacle), are mentioned in the JE Moses traditions, but never together.

The ark was a wooden chest that apparently represented the presence of Yahweh in the form of the imageless deity's pedestal or throne. It is also conceived as a repository for tablets containing the Decalogue that accompanied and safeguarded the Israelites in battle. The cover of gold (the mercy seat) to which were attached winged guardian figures (the cherubim) seems to have been a P retrojection into the wilderness of adornments first given the ark in Solomon's temple.

The tent of meeting as mentioned in E, where it is a small oracle shrine in contrast to P's mini-temple for sacrifice, is congruent with a simple desert shrine in tent form. Both among pre-Islamic and Islamic Arabs such shrines, usually carried on camelback, are well attested. For example, in pre-Islamic times, the shrine, holding the tribe's stone

FIG. 5.4 *Israelites Carrying the Ark of the Covenant* from *The Gates of Paradise* (1425–1452) by Lorenzo Ghiberti (1370-1455). Bronze doors of the Cathedral baptistery, Florence, Italy. Photo: © Timothy McCarthy / Art Resource, N.Y.

idols, was carried in combat and consulted for oracles. While not directly equatable, the general functional parallels between Arab and Israelite shrines are instructive. The use of portable cultic objects of the ark/tent type is consistent with conditions of migratory life and with monotheistic religious claims.

All in all, the evidence for the ark as a Mosaic element in Yahwism is somewhat stronger than the evidence for the tent, in the sense that the ark can be traced at points in early Israelite history, while the whereabouts and existence of the desert tent after the entrance into Canaan are more obscure. Some scholars have argued that the ark and tent derived from separate groups and were never associated in the cult. On the other hand, an ark would have necessitated a shelter like a tent, and a tent shrine would have invited some symbol of deity like the ark.

The sacrificial system according to P included the following types of offerings:

1. Animal offerings entirely burnt on the altar (whole burnt offerings or holocausts)
2. Animal offerings partly burnt and partly consumed by priests and worshipers (peace or communion offerings)
3. Animal offerings to atone for sins, not consumed by the guilty parties (sin and guilt/reparation offerings)
4. Grain or cereal offerings
5. Offerings of incense or spices
6. A display of loaves of bread on a tabernacle table (showbread or bread of the Presence).

Narrated references to whole burnt offerings and peace offerings go back to earliest times in Israel. On the other hand, sin and guilt offerings are not certainly mentioned earlier than Ezekiel and P (see pp. 273–79) and, even

if older, did not have the major significance in early Israel that P attached to them. Also, the pre-P references to sacrifice show no evidence that Aaronide priests had a monopoly on sacrifice in contradistinction to the whole body of Levites. Moreover, a number of ancient biblical references indicate that laypeople were entirely competent to offer sacrifice.

When one compares Israelite sacrifice and the sacrifices of other Near Eastern peoples, it is apparent that the closest connections are between Canaanite and Israelite forms of sacrifice, especially in the prominence given to whole burnt offerings and peace offerings, although the importance assigned to the blood in certain sacrifices stands closest to Arab practices.

A much-debated issue concerns the incidence and obligatoriness of human sacrifice in ancient Canaan and within Israel proper. It is clearly stated that Jephthah sacrificed his daughter (Judg. 11:30-40) and that, in the late monarchy in national emergency, the kings Ahaz and Manasseh sacrificed their sons by fire (2 Kgs. 16:3; 21:6). Ancient cultic stipulations to give all the firstborn to Yahweh (Exod. 22:28-29), or to allow firstborn children to be ransomed while firstborn animals were to be sacrificed (Exod. 34:19-20), are construed by some interpreters to mean that human sacrifice was a mandated feature of the earliest Yahwism, later tempered by animal substitutions. In that context, the near-sacrifice of Isaac by Abraham is seen as a polemic against widely accepted human sacrifice (Gen. 22:1-14).

Evidence on human sacrifice from the immediate Canaanite environment of Israel is blurred. Archaeological recovery of the skeletal remains of children may attest to interring sacrificed children in the foundations of new buildings in order to gain divine favor (cf. 1 Kgs. 16:34). However, these skeletal remains may simply point to a high infant mortality rate. Inscriptions and historical reports from Phoenicia and its colonies in Carthage and Malta, from the seventh through the fourth centuries, speak more tellingly of child sacrifice in time of national crisis.[3]

In sum, it is unlikely that either Canaanite or Israelite religion directly mandated or normally required human sacrifice. The notion, however, that all life belonged to the deity and that even human life could be efficaciously returned to the deity in order to resolve an extreme crisis seems to have hovered in the background waiting to be activated in times of desperation.

As for the Israelite festivals, they are presented essentially as a cycle of agricultural feasts geared to the rhythms of harvest in Canaan: an early spring wheat harvest (Passover), a late spring barley harvest (Weeks, later called Pentecost), and an early fall harvest of grapes (Ingathering or Booths). The Day of Atonement in P, like the sin and guilt offerings, is not attested in early Israel. It is probable that this sequence of festivals, together with the types of sacrifice, was developed in Canaan. On the other hand, what some conjecture may be the oldest form of Israelite sacrifice, the Passover, contains not only an agricultural component (unleavened bread) but a pastoral component as well (a sacrificed lamb with blood rites). Many interpreters believe that the pastoral Passover derived from Moses and was later conflated with a wheat harvest festival at the same time of year.

The prohibition against Israel making images or idols, either of Yahweh or of other gods, appears to have been an ancient one. It is impossible to reconstruct the exact force and scope of the prohibition. It may have been meant to set up barriers against copying or borrowing from other religions or entering

alliances with their practitioners, or it may have been to stress the invisibility of Israel's God, whose presence and activity could not be contained or manipulated. If ark and tent go back to Israel's beginnings, however, it is evident that prohibition of images did not exclude all symbols of deity.

NEWER LITERARY APPROACHES TO THE MOSES TRADITIONS

Folktale Plot-motifs and Traditional Episodes

One line of literary approach to the Moses traditions has attempted to apply the categories of folktale analysis to the biblical narratives. For example, one study looks at plot-motif ("a plot element which moves the story forward a step") and traditional episode ("a series of events in the story [that] taken together forms a more or less set part of the tale").[4]

This is recognized as a precarious fledgling enterprise, since ancient Near Eastern and biblical folktale types and motifs have never been classified, largely because the materials available are very limited in comparison with European and other folk literatures. Nonetheless, it is argued that motif and episode analysis can help to clarify the plots of biblical tales and can also bring out the values and emphases peculiar to biblical tale-tellers and hearers.

Typically the plot-motifs have very different imports in their ancient Near Eastern and biblical uses. In the extrabiblical environment they often concern the escapades of the gods, sometimes cater to the whims of royalty, and occasionally have a moral application. The Israelite plot-motifs tend to focus on the political imperative of releasing the Israelites from bondage, which includes its own prophetic morality of a community-yet-to-be.

The traditional episode cited in the Moses narratives is that of "sending the savior." Three Sumero-Babylonian, one Hittite, and one Ugaritic example of "sending the savior" may be compared with Exodus 3–4 and three later formulations in the Hebrew Bible. An organically linked set of elements unfolds as a traditional pattern lying behind the many examples, no one of which contains all the elements.

An examination of the plot-motifs and traditional episodes (type-scenes? see pp. 91–93) is helpful in differentiating the stock conventions employed by biblical narrators. There are, however, such a relatively small number of biblical and extrabiblical examples in each category, and such great plasticity in the way the plot-motifs and episodes are treated, that one is not sure how sound a footing the comparative study rests on. By conceiving the sending of Moses in an episodic linkage of scenes and images of the divine council, the enemy as chaos to be overcome, the demurrer of the elected savior, the efficacy of wonders in the conduct of the mission, and so on, the stylized story elements are brought into prominence for further study.

One interesting observation flowing from this comparative folktale approach is the analyst's conclusion that, unlike the ancient Near Eastern versions, the biblical sending of a savior episode sees the established forces of order as the oppressive enemy to be overthrown, which view "might almost characterize OT

theology, with its dedication to the success of the unpromising and its hymn to upheaval (see 1 Sam. 2:1-10)."[5]

Suggestive as this folktale analytic method is, it will doubtless remain somewhat impressionistic until there is a thorough comprehensive and controlled study of all available ancient Near Eastern and biblical texts in relation to European and other folk literatures.

Biblical Comedy

Another new literary approach, applying a distinction between comedy and tragedy, compares Exodus 1–15 as comedy with Euripides' *Bacchae* as tragedy, and concludes that the two works use similar literary conventions to opposite ends.[6] Both Exodus 1–15 and *The Bacchae* tell stories of how strange and little-known gods (Yahweh/Dionysus) authenticate their claims to godhood by unleashing their divine power against proud and stubborn unbelievers (Pharaoh/Pentheus, king of Thebes). The heart of both works is a contest between deity and the unbeliever. Pharaoh and Pentheus function as examples of the *alazon*, or boaster, who claims more knowledge and power than he actually has, and Moses and Dionysus in human incognito are examples of the *eiron*, or dissembler, who pretends to know less than he actually knows in order to lead the *alazon* to destruction.

The result in Exodus 1–15 is a comedy because the hero Moses is incorporated into the new community of liberated Israelites, while the result in *The Bacchae* is a tragedy because the hero Pentheus is cut off by death from his position of leadership in Thebes. Interestingly, it has been argued that Exodus 1–15 is a legend that owes its composite dramatic form to recitation/reading in a Passover ritual where the crucial contest between Moses and Pharaoh was declaimed and perhaps enacted in "cultic glorification."[7]

This comparative study of the Greek and Israelite works does not, however, take sufficient account of their differences in literary genre and in sociohistorical setting. Coterminous with the events it creates, *The Bacchae* is a staged drama by a single playwright outside the Dionysian cult aimed at provoking reflection on the positive and negative vitalities of the Dionysian mystery religion, whereas Exodus 1–15 is an agglomeration of anonymous traditions growing out of the firmly rooted Yahweh cult and aimed at the periodic celebration of the foundations of the Israelite community in struggle. In short, genre and sociohistorical distinctions will have to be taken more adequately into account before comparative literary studies of this sweeping order can make their fullest contributions to biblical studies.

Structural Narrative Programs and Themes

David Jobling, a structural critic, has proposed a reading of Numbers 11–12.[8] The main program of the narrative is analyzed as follows: Yahweh is the "sender/giver" of the promised land as "object" to the people of Israel as "receiver." Moses is the "subject/protagonist" who facilitates the action with provisions of quail, manna, and elders conceived as "helper." Under this program, movement toward Canaan is positive, and delay in the desert is negative, but movement can occur only if certain conditions are met by the people. The rebellions of the people are counterprograms, to which Yahweh responds with blocking measures or counter-counter-programs. Meaningful themes are worked out in the text through a series of codes or systems of classification: geographical and temporal codes, political-hierarchical code, topographical codes (tent, camp, outside the camp), and alimentary (food) code.

The method is controlled and fruitful in its manner of bringing out complex structures in the narrative, although there is as yet no agreement among structural critics as to how appropriate the method is for analyzing heavily edited narrative texts in contrast to oral myths.

Concluding Assessment

The three reported instances of newer literary approaches to portions of the Moses traditions vary greatly in their methods of analysis and their precision in applying these methods—to such an extent that the results are not simply combinable nor can they be directly linked with historical-critical or social-scientific methods. Of the three studies, the structural exegesis is most explicit about its methodology, purpose, and limitations, and it is the most tightly argued. The more such precision about method can be developed in all literary studies and the more texts that can be analyzed by means of the various literary options, the sooner it should be possible to consider how the literary methods relate to one another and what compelling considerations they present for historical-critical and social-scientific methods.

SOCIOHISTORICAL HORIZONS OF THE MOSES TRADITIONS

The Moses traditions have a more compact origin than the ancestor traditions, in the sense that they point to a movement in the thirteenth century of a group (possibly groups) of state slaves from Egypt to Canaan. Through the link with the ancestor traditions and on the basis of Egyptian historical texts, the escapees from Egypt are conceivable as former residents of Canaan, probably including war captives as well as voluntary migrants. Their leader, Moses, who organized the slave uprising and flight but died before entering Canaan, bore an Egyptian name, intermarried with Midianites of the Sinai region, was of Levitical descent, and was identified as the grandfather of a priest of Dan in the time of the judges (Judg. 18:30).

The Moses Group as a Pre-Israelite Entity

The socioreligious element in the traditions most often judged to be authentic for that period is the introduction of a new deity named Yahweh and of a cult that may have included an ark and/or tent and sacrifice (see pp. 120–23). To this horizon may also belong a covenant instrument and very likely also basic provisions such as the brief Decalogue for the internal ordering of the community (see p. 118). On the other hand, it is evident that the fullest statement of the cult, laws, and regulations belong to the sociohistorical horizon of priestly practice at Jerusalem many centuries later, during the late monarchy, exile, and Judahite restoration (see pp. 273–79).

It is important to identify the differences between the Moses Israelites and the later Israelites in Canaan. For one thing, the very name Israel (with reference to the divine name El/Elohim), rather than Israyah (with reference to the divine name Yahweh), was probably first adopted by the community in Canaan. Second, the Moses group was not yet a people engaged in intensive farming on its own home ground and defending itself against adjacent city-states, as was to be the case with Israel in Canaan. Third, the Moses group, generally estimated to have been no more than a few hundred or thousand in number, were as yet not the large conglomerate of federated peoples from varied historical and cultural experiences who would form larger Israel. Whatever the diversity of their origins, once the Moses group entered Canaan and joined with other peoples to form the confederation of Israel, the earlier distinguishing traits of the group were merged with the norms and experiences pooled by the whole body of Israel, and the group's organization was restructured as a vastly expanded and elaborated social system of tribes in mutual aid.

Socioreligious Strategies Connecting the Moses Group and Later Israel

This way of viewing the relationship between the exodus-wandering forerunners of Israel and the whole people of Israel in Canaan immediately poses the question: Why was it in the interests of the confederacy of Israel to concentrate so much attention on the fortunes of what had been only one among many groups who became part of Israel?

One answer is that the key leadership in the formation of united Israel in Canaan seems to have come from the Levitical Moses group, as did also the crucial revelation and cult of Yahweh. Given the political decentralization of tribal times, it is hardly sufficient to explain the centrality of the Moses traditions as a forceful imposition of a minority heritage upon a submissive majority of Israelites. The socioreligious attraction of the Moses traditions for the confederacy of Israel, however, has to be explained with reference to lines of connection drawn between the critical problems faced by the Moses group and by later Israel, and with reference to the lines of connection between the socioreligious strategies for coping with those problems developed respectively by the earlier migratory and later sedentary communities. It is to be noted that the desert community was migratory, not pastoral nomadic, in terms of its long-standing sociocultural identity.

Among the significant lines of connection between Israel-in-embryo in the wilderness and Israel-in-florescence in the land are the following:

1. A people oppressed by kings unites to escape from bondage to the oppressor.
2. A freed people unites and experiments to create a tribal/intertribal community of mutually supported equals.
3. A people struggles to create necessary leadership in the absence of coercive state power.
4. A people in a very precarious economic situation labors to provision itself both as it migrates and as it cultivates its own land.
5. A people threatened by disease and plague, and perhaps underpopulation, struggles to reproduce and preserve itself by adequate hygienic measures.
6. A people without precedents for the public activity of women, discovering that women have been active and necessary participants in the fight against external oppression, now struggles to determine what the roles of women will be in their own society.

In each of the spheres cited, the experience of the Moses group and its legacy of Yahwism were regarded as prototypical. What happened to the Moses group in Egypt became an umbrella metaphor for what happened when other Israelites fought with Egyptians in Canaan (as recounted in the Merneptah stela [Web Table A, 2D]), or with various Canaanite city-states, or with Midianites and Moabites, or with Philistines (as the heirs of Egyptian sovereignty over Canaan). And the work of Moses in forming a desert community was analogous to what Israelites faced in the even more complicated and ambitious task of forming many tribes into a confederacy. These socioeconomic and religiopolitical themes that span the two Israels and come to expression in the Moses traditions are charter themes of the new community, paradigms of Israel's root condition as a people.

Probably the most problematic of the lines of connection cited is that of the role of women. As in the ancestor traditions (see pp. 99–103), women frequently occupy key positions as facilitators and celebrants of Israel's deliverance from oppression in the Moses traditions, for example, the Hebrew midwives who frustrate Pharaoh's genocidal plans. At the same time women are a threat, either to external apostasy or to internal leadership: Miriam is defrocked of her leadership functions when she challenges Moses' monopoly on authority. These latter involvements of women are clearly connected with the boundaries and cohesion of the community and with matters of public health, and it may be that the Miriam incident reflects a move for greater power by women within the confederacy that was suppressed. The full meaning of the place given to women in the traditions is far from clear because of our limited knowledge of the actual status of women in early Israel.

Finally, the current debate over the adequacy of the suzerainty treaty form as a model for the early Israelite covenant (see pp. 115–16) can be constructively furthered by comparing the sociopolitical organization implicit in the treaty form with the socioreligious organization of early Israel. In three respects the treaty model does *not* appear closely analogous to Israel's self-formation and self-understanding. First, Israel understood itself to be a new people without a pre-history as a people. By contrast, a suzerainty treaty was always enacted between the heads of two already-existing states but did not create the vassal state. Second, Israel understood itself as both internally and externally constituted by its covenant with Yahweh. By contrast, a suzerainty treaty controlled only the foreign policy of a vassal state, entering into its internal affairs only so far as to ensure the continuity of leadership within the vassal state. Third, Israel saw itself as the sole people in such an explicit knowing relationship with Yahweh. By contrast, the suzerainty treaty was not restricted to a single vassal state. Whatever the influence of the suzerainty treaty on Israel's covenant tradition, it will henceforth be necessary to take sociohistorical base factors into account in assessing the combination of derivation and innovation reflected in Israel's covenant practice and thought.

NOTES

1. The numbers in parentheses throughout this subsection are keyed to units or blocks of biblical traditions as enumerated in Web Table H.

2. Frank M. Cross Jr., *Canaanite Myth and Hebrew Epic* (Cambridge: Harvard University Press, 1973), 65–71.

3. Lawrence E. Stager and Samuel R. Wolff, "Child Sacrifices at Carthage—Religious Rite or Population Control?" *BARev* 10/1 (1984): 30–51.

4. Dorothy Irvin, "The Joseph and Moses Narratives [Parts 3–4]," in *IJH*, 180–209.

5. Ibid., 202.

6. David Robertson, "Comedy and Tragedy: Exodus 1–15 and the Bacchae," in *The Old Testament and the Literary Critic,* Guides to Biblical Scholarship (Philadelphia: Fortress Press, 1977), 16–32.

7. Johannes Pedersen, *Israel: Its Life and Culture,* vols. 3–4 (London: Oxford University Press, 1940), 728–37.

8. David Jobling, *The Sense of Biblical Narrative: Three Structural Analyses in the Old Testament (1 Samuel 13–31; Numbers 11–12; 1 Kings 17–18),* JSOTSup 7 (Sheffield: JSOT Press, 1978), 26–62.

FOR FURTHER READING

Assmann, Jan. *Moses the Egyptian: The Memory of Egypt in Western Monotheism*. Cambridge: Harvard University Press, 1997.

Crüsemann, Frank. *The Torah: Theology and Social History of Old Testament Law*. Minneapolis: Fortress Press, 1996.

Redford, Donald B. *Egypt, Canaan, and Israel in Ancient Times*. Princeton: Princeton University Press, 1992.

QUESTIONS FOR STUDY

1. What is the significance of the Sinai traditions in Exodus and Deuteronomy?
2. Describe the major theories about Moses' religious upbringing and relationship to the religion of Yahweh.
3. Define the biblical concept of covenant. What evidence in the biblical text supports regarding Moses as a covenant mediator? What argues against this view?
4. Describe the traditional episode of "sending the savior." How does its role in the Moses narratives differ from its role in extrabiblical ancient Near Eastern texts?

TRADITIONS ABOUT INTERTRIBAL ISRAEL'S RISE TO POWER IN CANAAN

SUMMARY

Genres and sources of Joshua and Judges

* Relation to the Deuteronomistic history

* Recent methods of interpretation

Three hypotheses about Israel's rise to power

Three hypotheses about Israel's tribal organization

READ THE BIBLICAL TEXT

Joshua
Judges

See additional materials at fortresspress.com/ gottwald; consult Carta Bible Atlas *maps 54–82.*

THE SHAPE OF THE TRADITIONS IN JOSHUA AND JUDGES

Contents and Literary Genres

Our information about the rising presence of Israel in Canaan during the period around 1200–1000 B.C.E. derives largely from the books of Joshua and Judges. The first of these books relates how Joshua, successor to Moses, led the united tribes of Israel in the conquest of sizable parts of the western hill country of Canaan and how the conquered (and yet-to-be-conquered) lands were divided among the tribes. The second of these books relates the successes and failures of individual tribes in displacing Canaanite rule, goes on to tell of the exploits of military leaders and the rule of civilian leaders (variously called "deliverers" and "judges"), and concludes with stories of the relocation of the tribe of Dan and of a civil war between Benjamin and the rest of Israel.

It is widely agreed that Joshua and Judges constitute parts of one immense composition—the Deuteronomistic History (see p. 83)—beginning with Deuteronomy and extending on through Samuel and Kings. It is furthermore recognized that a deliberate and comprehensive editorial point of view has been imposed on the diverse traditions of Joshua and Judges by the Deuteronomistic compiler/author. Any adequate understanding of these books, and of the events and processes they attest, requires attention both to the forms and contents of the separate traditions and to the editorial perspectives that shape the diverse traditions into an uneasy multifaceted unity. We shall first attend to the major divisions in the books, an outline of their contents, the primary literary types, and the major difficulties standing in the way of coherent interpretation.

Joshua 1–12

In Joshua 1–12 the dominant literary form is a chain of sagas that relate events in the Israelite occupation of Canaan. Several of the sagas seem to be etiological (origin) sagas. It was once thought that the sagas were largely created ad hoc to satisfy popular curiosity about the origins of places, objects (e.g., standing stones), people (e.g., the Gibeonites, Rahab and her family), customs, or rituals (e.g., enactment of the crossing of the Jordan River and the circling of the ruined = "captured" city of Jericho). It is now more widely proposed that etiological motifs tended to be attached secondarily to stories already in existence, more or less altering the older sagas. For example, an old saga about a treaty between Gibeon and Israel appears to have been drastically obscured by the inclusion of an etiological motif. Attempts to reconstruct the supposed pre-etiological form of the sagas have, however, lacked convincing criteria.

On analysis, it is clear that most of the sagas in Joshua 2–11, in contrast to the comprehensive DH introduction and summaries, are restricted to the locale of the tribe of Benjamin. Interestingly, nothing is said about battles in Samaria, the territories of Manasseh and Ephraim, even though Joshua is identified as an Ephraimite. Indeed, the DH image of Joshua as leader of united Israel in a total conquest of the land is thrown into radical doubt by the restricted scope of this saga collection.

Joshua 13–24

In Joshua 13–24 the primary literary form is a series of lists of the territorial holdings of the tribes of Israel containing boundary, city, and regional inventories, none of which is given in its entirety. Distributed among the allotment lists, according to their tribal connection, are annals telling briefly of battles, seizures or occupations of cities and regions, and failures to expel Canaanites (see parallels in Judges 1). The subject in each of the annals is a single tribe and not the united Israel of the sagas in Joshua 1–12.

Just as the Priestly regulations of Exodus, Leviticus, and Numbers were narrativized by events at Sinai and during the wilderness wandering, so the boundary and city inventories of Joshua 13–21 are narrativized as land grants to the tribes after the conquest of Canaan. There are internal inconsistencies in this narrativization. Joshua 14:1-5 reports that Joshua, the priest Eleazar, and the tribal heads, gathered at Gilgal, distributed land to nine and one-half tribes in Cisjordan. However, Josh. 18:1-10 reports that Joshua alone, located at Shiloh, distributed land to seven tribes in Cisjordan following a land survey required because Judah, Ephraim, and half-tribe Manasseh had monopolized the choicest

TABLE 6.1 MAJOR DIVISIONS OF JOSHUA-JUDGES

A. Joshua 1–12: Israel's Conquest of Cisjordan under Joshua's leadership

1. Preparation for conquest: 1
2. Spying out Jericho; treaty with Rahab: 2
3. Crossing of the Jordan River: 3–4
4. Israel at Gilgal: circumcision; Passover, theophany: 5
5. Conquest of Jericho; rescue of Rahab: 6
6. Achan's theft; defeat at Ai; Achan's punishment: 7
7. Conquest of Ai: 8:1-29
8. Altar and reading of the Law at Mt. Ebal and Mt. Gerizim: 8:30-35
9. Treaty with the Gibeonites: 9
10. Battle at Gibeon/Beth-horon; conquests to the south: 10
11. Battle at Merom; conquests in the north: 11:1-15
12. Summaries of conquests and list of defeated kings: 11:16—12:24

B. Joshua 13–22: Allotments of Land to Tribes and to Public Institutions by Joshua

13. Preparation for land allotments: 13:1-7
14. "Flashback" to allotments of land to Reuben, Gad, and half-Manasseh by Moses in Transjordan: 13:8-33
15. Land allotments to Caleb, Judah, Ephraim, and half-Manasseh in Cisjordan: 14–17
16. Land allotments to Benjamin, Simeon, Zebulun, Issachar, Asher, Naphtali, Dan, and to Joshua in Cisjordan: 18–19
17. Designation of six cities of refuge for legal asylum: 20
18. Designation of forty-eight cities for the priestly Levites, and brief summary of conquest-settlement: 21
19. Dispute of Transjordanian and Cisjordanian tribes over an altar built by the former at the Jordan River: 22

C. Joshua 23–24: Two Farewell Addresses of Joshua

20. Joshua warns Israel against apostasy from Yahweh and consequent annihilation/expulsion from the land: 23
21. Joshua recites saving deeds of Yahweh and brings tribes into treaty with Yahweh; Joshua's death recorded: 24

D. Judges: 1:1—2:5: Piecemeal and Incomplete Conquests of Land by Individual Tribes after Death of Joshua

22. Judah, Simeon, Othniel, Kenites, and Caleb take the southland: 1:1-20
23. Benjamin fails to take Jerusalem: 1:21
24. House of Joseph takes Bethel, but its member tribes Manasseh and Ephraim fail to drive out Canaanites: 1:22-29
25. Zebulun fails to drive out Canaanites: 1:30

Table 6.1 continues on following page

TABLE 6.1 MAJOR DIVISIONS OF JOSHUA-JUDGES (*cont.*)

D. Judges: 1:1—2:5: Piecemeal and Incomplete Conquests of Land by Individual Tribes after Death of Joshua (*cont.*)

26. Asher fails to drive out Canaanites: 1:31-32
27. Naphtali fails to drive out Canaanites: 1:33
28. Dan fails to drive out Amorites, but Ephraim conquers the Amorites: 1:34-35
29. Messenger of Yahweh announces: because of Israel's treaties with Canaanites, Yahweh will not drive out the Canaanites whose religion will "snare" Israel: 2:1-5

E. Judges 2:6—3:6: Interpretive Introduction to the Era of Judges

30. Joshua's death retold; a new generation arises who do not know Yahweh: 2:6-10
31. Theological introduction: Yahweh raises judges to deliver sinful and unrepentant Israel: 2:11-19
32. Theological introduction: Yahweh will not drive out Canaanites who will "test" Israel's obedience to Yahweh and "train" Israel in war: 2:20—3:6

F. Judges 3:7—16:31: Narratives and Annals of "Judges/Deliverers" in Military Roles (= M) or in Civil Roles (= C)

33. Othniel of Judah (M): 3:7-11
34. Ehud of Benjamin (M): 3:12-30
35. Shamgar (M): 3:31
36. Deborah of Ephraim (C and M[?]) and Barak of Naphtali (M): 4–5
37. Gideon of Manasseh (M): 6–8
38. Abimelech of Manasseh/Shechem, an illegitimate king: 9
39. Tola of Issachar (C): 10:1-2
40. Jair of Gilead (C): 10:3-5
41. Jephthah of Gilead (M): 10:6—12:6; (C): 12:7
42. Ibzan of Judah or Zebulun (C): 12:8-10
43. Elon of Zebulun (C): 12:11-12
44. Abdon of Ephraim (C): 12:13-15
45. Samson of Dan (M): 13–16

G. Judges 17–21: Two Narrative Supplements

46. Resettlement of the tribe of Dan and foundation of a sanctuary with a kidnapped Levite as its priest: 17–18
47. Crime and punishment of the tribe of Benjamin for the rape-murder of a Levite's concubine; measures to save Benjamin from annihilation: 19–21

land. Moreover, 14:5 and 19:49 imply a form of the tradition in which the allotment of the land was determined by the people at large rather than by Joshua.

Chapter 23 is a farewell address, and chap. 24 is a narrative (a narrativized liturgy?) of an assembly of tribes at Shechem over which Joshua presides. Joshua recites the saving deeds of Yahweh and calls for the gathered tribes to enter into covenant/treaty with Yahweh. After suitable solemnities, the compact with Yahweh is concluded. The final verses concern death and (re)burial accounts of Joshua, Joseph, and Eleazar.

Judges 1:1—2:5

The opening of the book of Judges is composed of a string of annals that tell of the military-political struggles of individual tribes (or at most two tribes collaborating) to gain control over the western hill country. While it recounts successes by Judah, the opening dwells heavily on the weaknesses of the northern tribes in failing to dislodge large numbers of Canaanites. The section closes with a stern announcement that because of Israel's disobedience not all the Canaanites will be expelled from the land (2:1-5).

Since annals about Israel's struggles for dominion appear in Numbers, Joshua, and again at the end of Judges, it is probable that there once existed a stock of dominion annals that recorded separate tribal victories, settlements, and necessary accommodations with Canaanites. They strongly challenge the oversimplified view of a rapid conquest by united Israel set forth in Joshua 1–12 and presupposed by division of conquered Canaan among the tribes in chaps. 13–21. It is clear, however, that this arbitrary selection of dominion annals in Judges 1 is put together in present form in order to magnify Judah, denigrate the north-

ern tribes, and justify the judgment of the author concerning the covenant disloyalty of Israel as a whole (Judg. 2:1-5).

Judges 2:6—3:6

What amounts to a second introduction to Judges is launched by a restatement of the death and burial of Joshua (Judg. 2:8-9 = Josh. 24:29-30) and the inauguration of the era of the judges as "another generation who did not know Yahweh or the work which he had done for Israel" (Judg. 2:10b). The body of the introduction is a two-stage moral and theological discourse by the DH narrator. The first section of the discourse dwells on the apostasy of Israel from Yahweh, the divine anger in giving Israel over to oppressors, and the divine mercy in raising up judges to deliver them periodically, even though the Israelites persist in deepening their apostasy (2:11-19). The second section of the discourse emphasizes that Yahweh will leave Canaanites in the land in order "to test" Israel's obedience and in order "to train" Israelites in war (2:20—3:6).

Judges 3:7—16:31

The main body of the book of Judges consists of traditions about measures of self-defense taken by various sectors of Israel against oppressors. Characteristically only a few tribes are involved in each military action, but as many as six tribes collaborated in one crucial victory over the Canaanites, while four others are condemned as violators of their religiopolitical duty (5:12-18). The saga literary form predominates with vivid narratives of military victories achieved by Ehud, Deborah and Barak, and Gideon and the exploits of the eccentric loner, Samson.

The Israelite cult is visible, either through the cultic activities of actors in the sagas or through the influence of cultic models on the literary form of the sagas. Some commentators view the story of Jephthah's rash vow that compelled him to sacrifice his daughter as an etiology for an annually observed four-day mourning by the daughters of Israel (11:37-40; probably a Canaanite festival?). The call of Gideon (6:11-24; see the traditional episode of "sending the Savior" [or "sending the messenger"], see pp. 123–24) and the announcement of the birth of Samson (13:2-25; type-scene, see pp. 91–93) are framed as *theophanies* by the messenger of Yahweh, and each entails animal sacrifice. Other literary traditions include *annotated annals* (a roster of leaders: 10:1-5; 12:7-15), *hymns* (chap. 5), *fables* (9:7-15), and *riddle* (14:14, 18), all joined together by a framework that carries through the program of moral and theological evaluation of the era already starkly announced in the introduction of 2:6—3:6.

Traditionally the Israelite leaders described in this book of diverse traditions have been called "judges." Unfortunately the term gives an erroneous impression of the Hebrew terminology employed and also a false sense of certainty as to what the functions of these leaders actually were. It is striking that only in the DH introduction (2:16-19) are these leaders called "judges." Elsewhere in the framework they are called "deliverers" (3:9, 15) or are said to have "judged Israel" (15:20; 16:31). Within the sagas themselves only Deborah is said to have been "judging Israel," referring to her making "judgment" in cases brought to her as she sat under a palm tree (4:4-5). The Israelite leaders told about in the sagas, however, are overwhelmingly military deliverers. On the other hand, the leaders cited in the annotated annals are consistently said to have "judged" Israel, although they are never called "judges."

The source of the difficulty seems to be that DH tried to standardize terminology for the leaders of Israel in the premonarchic era and, in doing so, misconstrued the slim evidence available. Noticing that the old annotated annals stated that the leaders named "judged Israel," DH assumed that they bore the title of "judges," and then, through the reference in the annals to Jephthah the military leader as judge, regarded all the military leaders in this era as "judges" (2:16-19).

Judges 17–21

Two lengthy sagas flesh out the book of Judges. Compositionally they lack the customary DH framework concerning judges, but they are flagged by editorial notes as belonging to the general period (18:1; 19:1; 21:25). While there is no foreign oppressor in sight and thus no Israelite military deliverer, the sagas treat the fortunes of two tribes, Dan and Benjamin, in conflict with fellow Israelites; feature Levitical priests as central figures; and allude to important sanctuaries.

Joshua–Judges and the Deuteronomistic History

The Deuteronomistic Historian conceives the history of Israel from Moses to the exile as encompassing four phases: the era of Moses and lawgiving (Deuteronomy), the era of Joshua and the conquest (Joshua), the era of the judges and Israelite apostasy and oppression (Judges—1 Samuel 7), and the era of the monarchy from Saul to the fall of Judah (1 Samuel 8—2 Kings). Representations and evaluations of these eras are formulated in relation to how the Law given to Israel through Moses (Deuteronomy 12–26) was implemented or violated in the course of the history. Deuteronomy serves as the programmatic pacesetter for what follows in Joshua through Kings.

It is characteristic of the DH author-compiler to supply the major historical periods with interpretive passages in the form of introductory and summary surveys, speeches, and prayers, often placed in the mouths of principal characters. These interpretive inserts link the four historical periods according to the moral-theological program established in Deuteronomy.

The structure and motifs of DH for the first three eras (we shall examine the fourth period, the monarchy, in part III) may be grasped by a careful reading of the programmatic texts presented in table 6.2 (see pages 138–39).

The relations among the three eras treated in Deuteronomy through 1 Samuel 7 may be summarized as follows:

1. The *era of Moses* constituted the people of Israel in a covenant relationship with Yahweh that was to be lived out by obedience to the Law and to the revelations given through Moses, the covenant-law interpreter. The disobedience of the people prevented them from an immediate entrance into the land and condemned them to a forty-year wandering in the wilderness.

2. The *era of Joshua* represented the completion of the program to conquer the land that had been frustrated by the sins of the people and of Moses. Joshua is the bona fide successor to Moses as the covenant-law interpreter and as the military commander. Joshua and his generation are largely faithful to the commands of Yahweh, since all actual or potential infractions of the Law are punished or avoided before the whole people is endangered.

3. The *era of the judges* is stamped by a turning of Israel to wholesale apostasy, for which Israel is repeatedly given into the hands of oppressing nations. When Israel cries out

to Yahweh, he repeatedly raises "judges" to deliver the people, who nonetheless persist in apostasy and even deepen their waywardness. Although Yahweh continues to deliver his people in their extremities, he also resolves not to drive out the remaining nations, for they will now serve to test Israel's fidelity to the Law and to teach them the bitter lessons of warfare brought on by apostasy.

The implication of the DH discourse in Judg. 2:6—3:6 is that both the seductive "other gods" and the enemy "plunderers" of Israel are from the ranks of the remaining nations. Two interpretive passages give another impression, however: that the seductive foreign gods are the gods of the Canaanites/Amorites among whom Israel dwells and who have therefore not been totally annihilated or expelled (Judg. 2:1-5; 6:7-10). Even the concluding verses of the DH introductory discourse (3:5-6) state that Israel was thus condemned to live among local pagans whom Deut. 7:1-5 had targeted for destruction immediately upon entering Canaan.

These tensions within the highly moral-theological perspective of DH, revolving around fidelity/infidelity to the Law, raise the question of the place of national guilt and repentance in the prosecution of the conquest. All the frames of DH, whether or not they concede foreign influences and enemies within the already-conquered territories, jointly pay service to the view that Israel's success or failure in taking and keeping the land depends ultimately on Israel's adherence to or deviation from the Law. What is striking, however, is that this condition for Israel's success is not at all apparent in the old, pre-DH stories of the judges. The angelic judgment speech of 2:1-5 assumes that the Israelites refused to conquer all the Canaanites because of compromise. But the old materials of Judges 1

TABLE 6.2 PROGRAMMATIC TEXTS IN DH: DEUTERONOMY–1 SAMUEL

I. Era of Moses and Lawgiving

A. *Introductory Speech of Moses (Deut. 1:1—4:40)*
Summary of events from Horeb to Plains of Moab
Joshua will lead Israel in conquest (1:34-40; 3:18-19)
Obedience to the Law sanctioned positively by long life in the land and disobedience to the Law sanctioned negatively by expulsion from the land

B. *Summary Speech of Moses (Deut. 31:1-29; 32:44-47)*
Moses announces his impending death
Joshua summoned and commissioned to lead Israel into the land
Moses gives the Law and a song of reproach to the people as "witnesses" against their anticipated apostasy
Obedience and disobedience to the Law sanctioned positively and negatively

II. Era of Joshua and Conquest

A. *Speech of Yahweh to Joshua (Josh. 1:1-9) and Introductory Speech of Joshua (Josh. 1:10-18)*
Joshua commanded to lead the people decisively and courageously into the land
Yahweh will be with Joshua as he was with Moses
Obedience to the Law sanctioned with promises of success in taking the land
All Israel will find "rest" in the land after the Transjordanian tribes help the Cisjordanian tribes to complete the conquest
The people promise to obey Joshua, the living interpreter of Yahweh's commands, just as they obeyed Moses

B. *Summary Speech of Joshua (Joshua 23)*
Joshua announces his impending death
Yahweh has fought for Israel and provided secure allotments of land in Canaan
Obedience to the Law by not mixing with the remaining nations (through intermarriage or adopting their religions) is sanctioned positively with a promise to drive out the remaining nations
Disobedience to the Law by mixing with the nations is sanctioned negatively with a threat of Israel's expulsion from the land

C. *Other DH Interpretive Passages*
Josh. 8:30-35: At Mts. Ebal/Gerizim (Shechem) Joshua builds an altar, writes the Law on standing stones, and reads the Law to the people in fulfillment of Moses' command in Deut. 27:1-8
Josh. 11:15-23: Summary of Joshua's conquests in carrying out the command of Yahweh through Moses, extending to the vicinity of Mt. Hermon (far short of the Euphrates River specified by Moses in Deut. 1:7)

TABLE 6.2 PROGRAMMATIC TEXTS IN DH (*cont.*)

Josh. 13:1-7: Joshua instructed to allot the conquered land to the Cisjordan tribes, and is promised that the remaining land will be possessed as far as the "entrance of Hamath" (farther north than Mt. Hermon but not as far as the Euphrates River)

Josh. 21:43—22:6: Summary of Yahweh's gift of the land to the people who, having overcome all enemies, find "rest" in the fulfillment of all the promises of Yahweh. Joshua returns the Transjordan tribes to their lands with an injunction to observe the Law

III. Era of the Judges: Apostasy and Oppression

A. *Introductory Discourse on the Judges (2:6—3:6)*
    A new generation does not known Yahweh or his work for Israel (repeats elements of Josh. 24:29-31)
    Apostasy of Israel brings enemy oppression, which Yahweh mercifully alleviates from time to time by raising up "judges" who deliver Israel; even though the people deepen their apostasy, Yahweh refuses to drive out the remaining nations, leaving them in order "to test" Israel's obedience to the Law and "to teach" them the hard lessons of war

B. *Summary Speech of Samuel (1 Samuel 12)*
    Recapitulation of foreign oppression in the ear of the Judges and of the confession and repentance of Israel issuing in deliverance by Jerubbaal = Gideon, Bedan (perhaps a mistake for Barak), Jephthah, and Samuel (cf. 1 Sam. 7:15—8:3 for Samuel as the last "judge")
    Israel confesses the further sin of asking for a king
    If people and king obey the Law, Israel will continue as God's people, but if they disobey, they will be "swept away"

C. *Other DH Interpretive Passages*
    Judges 2:1-5: An angelic judgment speech condemns Israel to live henceforth with the Canaanites as "adversaries" and their gods as "a snare" since Israel has "made treaty" with them, for which the people lament and sacrifice
    Judges 6:7-10: A prophetic judgment speech indicts Israel for worshiping Amorite = Canaanite gods in spite of Yahweh's deliverance of the people and his express command to avoid pagan worship
    Judges 10:6-16: A divine judgment speech rejects an initial confession of apostasy by Israel; only when the people match confession with a renunciation of foreign gods does Yahweh (reluctantly?) take up their cause

presuppose that Israelites were militarily incapable of dislodging all the Canaanites and had to accept temporary enforced accommodations with them.

Uneasiness about how closely Israel's settlement in Canaan was conditioned by law observance extends into the DH frames themselves. There is much less reference in these frames to Israelite repentance than has often been assumed. The introductory discourse pointedly maintains that the Israelites "did not listen to their judges; . . . they soon turned aside from the way in which their fathers walked, . . . whenever the judge died, they turned back and behaved worse than their fathers" (Judg. 2:17, 19). But what presupposes at least a formal adherence to Yahwism at times during the leadership of the judges appears to be no more than grudging compliance, and then only briefly after Yahweh has dramatically granted them deliverance through each new judge. Several of the story frames observe that "Israel cried to Yahweh" for deliverance, but this resort in crisis is very dubiously interpreted as containing implicit repentance.

Only in the expanded frame preceding the Jephthah story is the people's cry a confession of sin (10:10). In this instance Yahweh's judgment speech does not accept the validity of their superficial confession until the foreign gods are actually set aside (10:16), although

even here Yahweh's response may be irritable impatience (see pp. 147–49).

Some interpreters distribute the frames lacking or containing repentance to different editions of DH, or to pre-DH or post-DH editors, but the literary and conceptual criteria for this solution are not convincing. DH contains a built-in ambivalence and ambiguity about how law observance, and attendant guilt and repentance, affected the course of history under the judges and, by implication, under Joshua as well (see pp. 147–49). All in all, DH perceives the contrition and repentance of Israel with respect to its violation of covenant law as either nonexistent or, when expressed, woefully superficial, belated, and ephemeral.

A final consideration in the DH framing of Joshua and Judges is the relation between the

FIG. 6.1 The "high place" at Shechem, Israel, near modern Nablus. According to the Bible, Abraham built an altar at Shechem, Jacob bought a piece of land here, and Joseph's body was brought here from Egypt for burial. Joshua also renewed the covenant with God in Shechem. Photo: © Erich Lessing / Art Resource, N.Y.

all-Israelite perspective of DH and the actual, more limited subjects of the tradition units compiled by DH. The conquest sagas within Joshua 1–12 assume the form of stories about the whole of Israel conquering the land. The land conquered, however, is chiefly in Benjamin, with thrusts into Judah and Galilee. The boundary, city, and regional inventories of Joshua 13–19, on the other hand, are formally constructed as lists of individual tribal holdings that necessarily have to be described singularly, but that when combined treat all the tribes as part of the intertribal system.

The assembly at Shechem in Joshua 24 is pictured as a gathering of all the tribes where the people reaffirm their covenant with Yahweh. The structure of the assembly, however, strongly suggests that this text is a transformed account of negotiations between a core Yahwistic group and previously non-Yahwistic groups who for the first time become Yahwists and join the Israelite movement, given the "free" religious choice by Joshua's "house" (house of Joseph, i.e., Ephraim and possibly Manasseh).

The annals concentrated in Judges 1, and paralleled in Joshua, are accounts of the military-political struggles of individual tribes to gain control of regions of Canaan. The individual stories of Judg. 3:7—21:25, however, display a complicated texture with respect to the unity and diversity of Israel. All the stories with military judges are localized in particular regions and identify the tribal origins of the military leaders or other chief actors, as well as those tribes that joined with them to do battle. Only in the concluding story of the crime and punishment of Benjamin is all Israel massed for action. In its concept of united Israel, Judges 19–21 is the one story in the book on a plane with the stories of Joshua. Nonetheless, by means of numerous allusions, all the judges stories presuppose that

the discrete tribes named are functional parts of a larger religiopolitical and cultural whole known as Israel.

The brief notations about minor judges in Judg. 10:1-5 and 12:7-15 report that they "judged Israel," but in each instance their locales are restricted to a single tribe, or at most two tribes.

Pre-Deuteronomistic Sources in Joshua–Judges

We have seen that DH had available a number of bodies of tradition for the shaping of Joshua–Judges. Having characterized the shape of the tradition complexes (see pp. 131–33), and having observed the main tendencies and emphases of DH (see pp. 136–41), we will now indicate leading theories about the growth of the pre-DH traditions and the possible stages of their inclusion in DH.

The sagas about a united conquest under Joshua (Joshua 1–12) are grounded in localized accounts of the occupation of its territory by the tribe of Benjamin, early recounted in a cultic ceremony of the procession of the ark across the Jordan and around Jericho. This Benjaminite account became the skeleton for developing narratives that fleshed out the last of the old history-like themes of Israel's early traditions (see pp. 86–87). The centralized cult that shaped this narrative sequence was north Israelite, and its original content was exclusively that of the Joseph tribes in central Canaan.

This core sequence of conquests in the south-central highlands has been expanded by accounts of conquests in Judah (10:16-43) and Galilee (11:1-14), most likely to include references to later Judahite and Galilean converts to united Israel and to lend greater credence to the claim of a united conquest under

FIG. 6.2 The biblical narrative describes the dramatic military conquest of Canaan, including the ritual siege and miraculous destruction of Jericho, depicted here in *The Seven Trumpets of Jericho* (ca. 1896–1902) by James Jacques Joseph Tissot (gift of the heirs of Jacob Schiff, x1952-216); photo by John Parnell. © The Jewish Museum, N.Y. / Art Resource, N.Y.

FIG. 6.3 Archaeological excavation of Jericho—one of the oldest known inhabited settlements, if not the oldest—has revealed that the moat, tower, and fortification wall shown here date from the Neolithic Age; the site was not fortified—if it was inhabited at all—in the thirteenth century. Tel-el-Sultan, Jericho. Photo: © Erich Lessing / Art Resource, N.Y.

MAP 6.1 TRIBES OF ISRAEL BEFORE THE MONARCHY

Moses' successor, Joshua, an Ephraimite leader introduced as the leader of all Israel. Because the notion of all Israel in conquest is so decisive in these sagas, it is probable that this stamp of unity was put upon the sagas in the premonarchic cult and that the sagas formed a part of the basic pool of old materials available to J and E.

The localized settlement or dominion annals (Judges 1 and parallels in Joshua), apparently part of a larger body of annals (see p. 135), were summaries of individual tribal occupations of land derived from the divergent subhistories of the several member groups of Israel. Whether they were gathered together in premonarchic times as a total counterprogram to the united conquest scenario of Joshua 1–12 is uncertain. Since the lists of tribal holdings in Joshua 13–19 are probably from administrative dockets of David's kingdom, it is plausible to look also to sociopolitical conditions in the time of David as the occasion for the first definite collection of the dominion annals.

By describing how each of the tribes had acquired territory and slowly gained political ascendency over Canaanites who resisted them, the combined annals formed a memorial, or set of public minutes, concerning the contributions of the individual tribes to the formation of the confederacy and the monarchy. As such they were a reminder of the historical-territorial reality on the basis of which the tribal elders negotiated a treaty with David as the king of all Israel (2 Sam. 5:1-5).

The present form of Judges 1, however, is far from being such a complete statement of accounts. It is a highly slanted condensation that throws the successful conquests of Judah into sharp contrast with the circumscribed achievements of the northern tribes. It may be that an earlier form of Judges 1 presented the J writer's version of the conquest, as many scholars have contended. The J substratum of Judges 1 may have reached a DH reviser who undertook to edit it with the bias of the angelic judgment speech, more or less in line with the other judgment speeches in the framework of Judges (see 6:7-10; 10:6-16).

In an attempt to identify the life settings of the poorly preserved tribal allotment lists (Joshua 13–19), scholars have noted a basic distinction between the boundary inventories and the city inventories. The city lists are taken to be administrative in intent and monarchic in date and variously placed from the reign of David to the reign of Josiah. The boundary delineations, by contrast, are widely thought to reflect the actual divisions of the tribes in the intertribal covenant community prior to the monarchy. It is more probable, however, that the originals of both were part of the archives of internal administration of the late Davidic–early Solomonic kingdom.

It is problematic whether the inventories have deeper roots in the premonarchic confederacy. City inventories may have roots in clan rosters of the intertribal militia that, insofar as clans were identified with villages, laid the foundation for administrative city lists under David. A firm beginning for the boundary inventories, as for the city inventories, is best assigned to the rise of the monarchy, when the tribal regions that formed the socioeconomic components of premonarchic Israel were transformed into administrative districts in David's kingdom, particularly for purposes of taxation and the muster of manpower for public labor projects and military service.

We can best account for the lamentable condition of the allotment descriptions on the theory that once they were no longer administratively employed after Solomon's reorganization of the kingdom, they fell into disuse. Only later did learned collectors gather them with an eye to including them in the traditions about the original division of the land among the united tribes under Joshua.

As for the traditions in Judges, it is now widely hypothesized that 3:12—9:55 was composed as a collection of deliverer stories that told of Ehud, Deborah and Barak, and Gideon, and ended with the figure of Abimelech as an anti-deliverer, joined to the sequence by a secondary identification of his father, Jerubbaal, with Gideon. The northern locales of the stories, the polemic against kings, and the elevation of the prophetess Deborah suggest an origin in northern prophetic circles, perhaps in the late ninth century. In general terms, an initial DH revision set forth the full form of the moral-theological framework. A further DH reworking provided the introductory survey over the whole period of judges, the annotated annals about leaders who judged Israel, and the schema of the judges as military figures through Eli and Samuel to the brink of the monarchy.

NEWER LITERARY APPROACHES TO JOSHUA AND JUDGES

New Literary Studies of Deborah and Samson Traditions

The Song of Deborah has long been recognized as an artful specimen of ancient Israelite poetry (see pp. 301–2). Older literary studies of Hebrew poetics focused on scanning meter and characterizing the ways in which Hebrew

poetic lines formed two parallel members that echoed, contrasted, or advanced the imagery and thought. Newer literary criticism attends to a wider range of poetic features within an overall structure and has benefited by the recovery of extensive examples of old Canaanite poetry.

Recent literary studies of the Song of Deborah look for the wider rhythms within the poem, encompassing imagery and metaphors, means of emphasis, and so forth. One study emphasizes a general compositional style known as parataxis, which involves words, clauses, images, and scenes placed side by side without connectives to coordinate the parts.[1] This creates a subtle, implicit, indirect unity below the surface.

Parataxis is seen as especially suited to the presentation of action. The song's staccato motifs of the cosmic power of Yahweh, the watery chaos unleashed on the enemy, the hammering hooves of the fleeing Canaanite horses, the desperate flight of Sisera on foot, and the sharply contrasted women ("daring Jael" and "self-deluding Canaanite ladies") produce a multilayeredness of characters, events, and scenes whose meanings and relations must be synthesized in the mind of the audience. Such studies have increased respect for the received biblical text, since apparent irregularities may be an aspect of the literary art.

Interestingly, the battle celebrated in the Song of Deborah is also treated in a prose narrative, which permits us two different literary outlooks on the same event. An analysis of the narrative structure and technique of Judg. 4:4-22 has uncovered a story developed in four episodes whose varied elements build tension and excitement toward the brief and stunning culmination of the story.[2] Although the surface of the story concerns the victory of Deborah and Barak over Sisera, the underlying structure concerns the culturally unexpected power of the women Deborah and Jael over against the culturally presumed power of the men Barak and Sisera.

Two conclusions follow from this close study of Judges 4. It appears that not only the poetic account of the battle but also the prose account are shaped by interests very different from historical reportage. The fundamental interest of the story is to dramatize how Yahweh has given Israel power over Canaanite warriors through women rather than through men. In that event, the story cannot be trusted to throw direct light on the actual circumstances of the battle viewed as a whole. For example, the apparent, but probably ahistorical, proximity of Jael's tent to Sisera's headquarters tightens the action and maximizes the ironic ineffectuality of both Sisera and Barak. The

FIG. 6.4 Jael and Sisera. *Mirror of Human Salvation*. France. Fifteenth century C.E. Ms.139, fol.32 recto. Musée Condé, Chantilly, France. Photo: © Réunion des Musées Nationaux / Art Resource, N.Y.

presence in both the story and the song of the feminist irony of Jael's role raises the issue of the connection between the two compositions and their place in the design of DH. Why has the feminist irony been deepened in the story and why the interest of DH in such a story, whatever its source?

Rhetorical-critical study of the Samson stories has similarly focused on narrative structure and technique of great intricacy.[3] For example, Judges 13 is a ring composition concerning Samson's birth, framed by promise and fulfillment. It skillfully stresses the importance of his mother by redirecting attention away from the father and showing her to be more perceptive about Samson's divine destiny than is her husband. The birth story of Judges 13 balances the death story of Judges 16, both chapters being constructed around a fourfold asking and answering discourse. Thematic symmetry is traceable in the two clusters of Samson adventure stories in chaps. 14–15 and 16. In each of these cycles Samson sees a woman, is persuaded by a woman to reveal a secret, is bound and given captive to the Philistines as a result of his liaison with a woman, and in extremity calls on Yahweh and is answered.

The recognition of literary artistry in these stories raises the question of how such authorial design intersects, if at all, with historical interests in disclosing the course of border warfare between Israelites and Philistines. Furthermore, the relation of this literary design to the various stages of the composition of Judges is sharply posed. Are such patterns to be connected with the old sagas, with an intermediary stage of collecting and editing, or with DH? Even though the Samson stories contain no distinctively Deuteronomistic vocabulary or style, is it possible that their internal literary shaping is after all DH's work? In any case, how do the Samson literary patterns fit into the larger DH structure?

Structuralist Studies

Two structuralist studies, one on Numbers 32 and Joshua 22 and the other on Joshua and Judges within DH, offer tantalizing possibilities for relating new literary analyses to source critical and sociohistorical concerns.

David Jobling's shorter study starts off from the structural similarities between A. J. Greimas's literary analyses of the structures of narratives and anthropological and social-scientific analyses of the structures of early Israelite society as practiced by N. K. Gottwald.[4] To explore the grounds for a meeting between biblical literary and social-scientific structuralists, Jobling selects a central sociohistorical question about Israelite origins that might be testable through a structuralist textual study: Did Israel originate through the immigration of groups of outsiders or through a revolt of indigenous Canaanites (see pp. 153–57)? Since the immigration theory assumes major movement of Israelites from Transjordan into Cisjordan, he decides to study two texts, Numbers 32 and Joshua 22, that show how the early narratives of Israel viewed the idea of Israelites living east of the Jordan.

One aspect of this structuralist analysis is to examine the stories in terms of three major semantic themes: (1) the unity of Israel, (2) Israel's land, and (3) women and children and the coming generation(s). Jobling concludes that Transjordan is viewed as ambiguous and problematic Israelite territory that poses a sense of danger, and the relationship of the main body of Israelites to the Transjordanians is precarious, although the bearing of these structuralist findings on the central

FIG. 6.5 "Shrine of the Steles" from a Canaanite temple, Hazor. Basalt. Israel Museum (IDAM), Jerusalem. Photo: © Erich Lessing / Art Resource, N.Y.

question of immigration versus revolt models is felt to be "obscure."

One sociological connection probed by this study involves theories about daughters, local women, and concubines appearing in genealogies who serve as eponyms of dependent, peripheral, foreign, inferior, or indigenous population elements. These theories suggest that, in the stories, insecurity over how to deal with the Transjordanian women is an expression of sociopolitical tension and conflict. Indeed, at a deep level Cisjordan and Transjordan may be coded "male" and "female," thus delivering the message that Transjordan by its peripheral status and its devious fighting style is a troublesome threat to the dominance of the Israelites west of the Jordan, from whose perspective the stories are told.

While this study about Transjordan is modest in its results, it is still promising for its programmatic formulation of possible collaboration between literary and social-scientific structuralist approaches and offers some suggestive first steps toward a method of correlation.

The larger-scale structuralist study by Robert Polzin sets out ambitiously to grasp the literary composition of the entirety of DH by a structuralist/formalist analysis of voices orchestrated by an "implied author."[5] The voices are of two kinds: mixtures of reported speech (addresses of God, Moses, prophets, etc.) and reporting speech (DH's direct utterances as a narrator), both on the expression plane of the text and on the ideological plane of the text. The ideological perspective of the implied author, in this case the final author-compiler (DH), shows up in the way the utterances of narrator and characters in the text are interwoven so that the contending ideological voices are finally "resolved" by the dominance of one voice over another.

In Deuteronomy the discourse is largely the reported speech of Moses within a terse framework of reporting speech by the narrator. In Joshua through Kings the ratio of the two kinds of speech is dramatically reversed: reported speech is carried within a very much larger body of reporting narratives. On the expression plane of the text, the voice of Moses is at first distinguishable from the voice of God, then the speech of Moses merges with the speech of God, and, after the death of Moses, the words of Moses merge with the words of the DH narrator. On the ideological plane, two primary voices are heard: the voice of *authoritarian dogmatism*, which claims finality and completeness for the Mosaic law of Deuteronomy, and the voice of *critical traditionalism*, which, by transferring the authority of God and Moses to DH, insists on the necessity and validity of interpreting, applying, and even modifying the Mosaic law according to new circumstances. Standing in dialectical tension are the unconditionality of covenant and the insistence of retributive justice should the covenant be violated. Divine justice and mercy operate in an exceedingly complex combination, so that the history of Israel goes forward but not according to the strict constructions of the Mosaic law posited by authoritarian dogmatism.

The voices set forth in Deuteronomy also come to expression in Joshua and Judges. Joshua is composed of narratives that show how both God and Joshua critically interpret the Mosaic law, along with fresh commands of God and outbursts of divine wrath, in keeping with unfolding circumstances that entail modifications of the Law unacceptable to authoritarian dogmatism. By counterposing speech about how the Canaanites must be and were destroyed against speech about how

Canaanites remained in the land and were even accepted into Israel, DH weaves an ironic exposition on the problem of carrying out God's commands.

It is noteworthy that throughout Joshua special attention is devoted to "exceptional outsiders," that is, groups of Canaanites and Israelites who do not belong to the primary core of "authentic" Israel: Rahab, Gibeonites, women, children, resident aliens, Levites, Transjordanian tribes, Caleb, daughters of Zelophehad, and even the exempted animals of Ai. The result is that not only are many Canaanites unconquered, so that the full extent of the promised land is not taken, but numbers of weak and alien people are taken into Israel and given protective status.

The book of Judges carries forward the ideological impulse of DH by assembling stories in a framework that exposes Israel's desertion of God through religious apostasy and intermarriage with Canaanites. The debasement of Israel is so extreme that the whole people, according to the authoritarian dogmatism of one voice in Deuteronomy, ought to have been cast off by God. Yet God in mercy continually delivers Israel even though there is no repentance. In this manner the stories of Judges are assembled and framed not only to undermine authoritarian dogmatism but also to throw into question the handy applicability of critical traditionalism to history, since the religious and moral stances of the chief actors have so little to do with whether they prosper or fail. A pall of ignorance and ambiguity falls over the text, purposely conjured by DH in order to show how difficult it is to interpret Israel's history by any strict univocal reading of the divine law.

This structuralist analysis of Joshua and Judges teems with insights and imperatives for further inquiry. It also suggests live possibilities for relating literary structural exegesis to other forms of biblical criticism.

The sophisticated display of literary structure in Joshua and Judges prompts immediate dialogue with long-standing issues of literary history. If the contending ideological voices of DH are approximately as described, the role of DH might be further investigated by identifying how far the ideological voices penetrate into particular tradition units (where they once were thought to appear only in the frames). The result might be either to reveal that DH was a much more original author than usually supposed, or that the pre-DH sources were more ironically ideological than previously recognized, or both may prove to be the case.

Striking in this structural rendering is that DH comes off not as a clumsy editor who stupidly, or perhaps bound by tradition, selected stories of partial conquest that badly undermined his expressed belief in total conquest. Instead, DH appears more like an astute author-compiler who deliberately mixed a profusion of data and interpretations about partial and total conquests in order to show the ambiguous success of Israel in the land as a combination of mixed peoples, including "exceptional outsiders," many of whom did not fit the profile of later nationalistic orthodoxy. Indeed, the inclusion of the "scandalous" annals and stories of Judges 1 and 17–21 may well be a supreme instance of the DH ideology of suspicion toward too-neat historical interpretations. In any case, the current rethinking of Joshua and Judges as sources for the reconstruction of the origins of Israel (see pp. 150–63) is clearly facilitated from a literary angle by this trenchant structural analysis.

SOCIOHISTORICAL HORIZONS OF JOSHUA AND JUDGES

Hypotheses about Israel's Rise to Power

The fundamental question of the origins of Israel may be posed in the following manner: How did Israel come into control of Canaan? Three primary explanatory models, accented in various ways, have been proposed:[6] unified military conquest, immigration, and social revolution.

The Conquest Model

The model of an Israelite military conquest of Canaan derives from the scenario of a united twelve-tribe invasion and seizure of the land under the direction of Joshua as reported in Joshua 1–12.[7] A straightforward reading of the biblical text envisions a series of lightning attacks that defeat armies, overthrow cities, and annihilate or expel the Canaanite populace en masse. The attackers are a people, escaped from slavery in Egypt, who have crossed the Sinai wilderness, traveled north through Transjordan, and launched their assault across the Jordan River from east to west. The sharp demarcation between Israelites and Canaanites as mortal antagonists seems to accord with this conception of two national and religious entities struggling over control of territory.

Archaeology has been enlisted to support the conquest model. Two types of evidence are cited: (1) widespread destruction of Canaanite cities in the approximate period when Israel is believed to have entered the land (ca. 1230–1175 B.C.E.); (2) a new and uniform type of oc-

cupation at some of the destroyed cities that is most logically associated with Israelites.

A series of excavated mounds, identified as particular biblical sites with a high degree of probability, show evidence of having been extensively or totally destroyed during the late thirteenth and early twelfth centuries. Five of the nine destroyed cities are reported to have been taken by Joshua or the house of Joseph. Moreover, some cities omitted from the accounts of the conquest—or specifically said not to have been conquered by Joshua—have, on excavation, shown no signs of destruction in this period.

Another kind of archaeological evidence, less dramatic and slower in accumulating, is given increasing credence. That is the evidence of the type and distribution of occupation in the layers following the late-thirteenth- and early-twelfth-century destructions. In four instances, following virtually complete destruction, unfortified and architecturally simple, even crude, settlements appear. Assuming the new residents to have been the destroyers of the Late Bronze cities on whose ruins they settled, one is tempted to see them as the technically impoverished seminomadic Israelites. Also, the pottery at settlements on previously unoccupied sites or at places where there had been long breaks in occupation shows continuity with the pottery from the simple encampments and crude buildings at the settlements on destroyed sites.

When the biblical and archaeological data are examined, however, the case for the conquest model of Israelite origins in Canaan is sharply reduced if not undermined beyond repair. The stories of Joshua 1–12 tell about military action in no more than three tribal areas: Benjamin, Judah, and Naphtali. A list of thirty-one defeated kings who ruled over cities throughout the land shows only that all these kings were defeated, not necessarily that their cities were captured or destroyed (Josh. 12:7-24). Perhaps because the negative or limited conquest reports have been placed outside the Joshua conquest narratives proper and included either in tribal boundary and city lists (Joshua 13–19 or Judges 1), interpreters have been able to avoid the contradictions or to rationalize that Joshua did conquer all or most of the land, but that after his death Canaanites staged a comeback, and various tribes had to reconquer lost territories.

Given all the equivocations in the biblical data, most contemporary proponents of the conquest model have developed sharply modified versions of the hypothesis. What they now tend to say is that Joshua led a group of tribes (probably not all twelve of them) in a concerted attack that broke the resistance of the Canaanites in three swift campaigns: one in the center of the land at Jericho-Ai-Gibeon, a second into Judah, and a third into Galilee. These attacks left the Israelites free to consolidate and extend their holdings without serious opposition.

Many proponents of the conquest model also concede that the absence of reports about military blows in the central regions of Ephraim and Manasseh, coupled with the assembly summoned by Joshua at Shechem (Joshua 24), probably show that the center of the land was linked to Israel by peaceful entente (perhaps similar to the Gibeonite treaty) or by an amalgamation of the entering tribes with ethnically related peoples ('apiru?).

Curtailing the scope of the conquest model made its essential features strained and dubious. Joshua is not sharply characterized, appearing rather as an editorially introduced bridge figure to join the disparate narratives under the impression of a massive initial Israelite conquest. It is frequently contended that

the assembly of tribes he gathered at Shechem was more truly Joshua's historical work than the various battles claimed for him, especially since no specifically Ephraimite or Manassite conquests are recorded under his leadership.

How is one to evaluate the archaeological evidence for total conquest? It turns out that there is as much—and maybe more—to be said against using the archaeological results to

FIG. 6.6 Grey granite double-sided stele called the "Israel Stele" or "the Victory Stele of Merneptah" inscribed with a list of defeated peoples, including the first mention of Israel, erected by Merneptah 1213–1204 B.C.E. Photo: © The Art Archive / Egyptian Museum, Cairo / Dagli Orti.

support the conquest model as there is in its favor. To begin with, there is the gaping hole in the Joshua accounts created by the negative archaeological results from Jericho, Ai, and Gibeon. If Jericho stood at all in the late thirteenth century, it was no more than a small unwalled settlement, or at most a fort. Ai was not occupied at the time and had not been for centuries. No Late Bronze remains have been located at Gibeon (other than some tomb pottery from the fourteenth and possibly early thirteenth centuries), raising questions about Israel's purported treaty with the Gibeonites.

Such difficulties point up the necessity of cross-examining the archaeological data amassed to support the conquest model. Three questions are pertinent:

1. Do we really know that it was the Israelites who conquered all the cities found destroyed in the late thirteenth and early twelfth centuries? The conquerors of the Canaanite cities did not leave any written or material record of their identities, so there is no evidence to tell us outright who they were. The Egyptians are probable candidates for at least some of the destructions.

The pharaohs of the Nineteenth Dynasty sought to reassert dominion over Syria-Palestine after a century of decline in their Asiatic empire. Although the itineraries of cities conquered by Seti I, Rameses II, and Merneptah tend to concentrate on the coastal regions and in the valleys, it is probable that Merneptah (or an earlier pharaoh) had a garrison near Jerusalem, and Merneptah claims to have conquered Gezer and to have "destroyed Israel" (ca. 1230–1220 B.C.E. [Web Table A, 2D]). With the exception of Bethel and Debir, the destroyed cities in question were either in the valleys or in the lowlands on the edge of the highlands, within easy reach of Egyptian forces operating along the coastal road.

Similar openness must be maintained to the possibility of destruction caused by intercity strife or by open revolt within cities. The Amarna letters show that Canaanite cities were attacking one another in the fourteenth century, and the response of Jerusalem and its allies to Gibeon's treaty with Israel (Josh. 10:1-5) indicates that the same was true in the late thirteenth century. Judges 9:26-49 reports what terrible destruction could be inflicted on a city such as Shechem torn by civil strife, a reality earlier alluded to in some of the Amarna letters (see Web Table A, 3B). Indeed, the proposal that Canaanites may have destroyed one another's cities, or that the cities may have been ruined in civil wars and revolts, appears entirely consonant with the archaeological evidence.

2. How do these late-thirteenth- and early-twelfth-century destructions and new settlements compare in number, quality, and distribution with destructions and resettlements of the same or similar cities in earlier and later periods? Archaeologists have tended to address specific historical questions arising from the biblical text. They have been less interested in making a refined inventory of the frequency and types of destruction and settlement over regions of Canaan during long spans of time.

Apparently the period in question did not see any marked technological changes in siege warfare between the arrival of the Hyksos in the eighteenth century and the penetration of the west by Assyrians in the ninth century. By contrast, a more refined archaeological interpretation of the modes of settlement, urban and rural, seems nearer attainment, especially with area surveys and studies of unwalled rural settlements. The results so far, however, do not register unequivocally in favor of conquest as the means by which Israel took Canaan.

3. If it was Israelites who destroyed some or all of these cities, what is there in the material evidence to show that they were destroyed in a coordinated campaign by united Yahwist Israelites? Nothing whatsoever shows that the cities were conquered in a coordinated campaign or series of campaigns by a particular group of people(s). On the other hand, it is demonstrable that a culturally distinct network of settlements spread over mountainous Cisjordan from the late thirteenth century onward. Since it can hardly have been Philistine, and since it clearly was not Egyptian, it is entirely plausible to regard these settlements as broadly "Israelite." The decisive rub comes in giving specificity to this materially observed culture in terms that correlate with the biblical text. There simply is no one-to-one correspondence between "Israelite" as understood from the material cultural evidence and "Israelite" as projected by the centralized biblical scheme of united Israel under Joshua.

"Israelite" in the material cultural sense does not mean twelve-tribe Israel taking Canaan by storm. It does not even imply that the material cultural remains belonged in all cases to groups who were at the time members of a Yahwistic league of tribes. "Israelite" in the material cultural sense supported by archaeology might well allow that its bearers were still proto-Israelites, or some combination of rebellious Canaanite peoples and incoming Yahwists from which "Israel" in its centralized biblical sense was only beginning to take form. The archaeological typology of the period creates significant preliminary cultural material parameters that prove to be as complex and ambiguous as the biblical parameters themselves.

The Immigration Model

Another view of how Israel entered Canaan began to gain advocacy as critical study of

the Hebrew Bible succeeded in identifying and exposing the fragmented and contradictory character of the tradition units within the range of "conquest" traditions.[8] The immigration model theorized a long, complicated process of peaceful infiltration, uneven amalgamation with local peoples, and a final military-political triumph achieved only by Israel in the time of David. The DH vision of a total conquest by united Israel is judged to be a retrospective idealizing view developed after this protracted struggle for Canaan was won under the monarchy. By contrast, amid the older separate tradition units enclosed by DH can be seen traces of an originally peaceful occupation of the land, and even of outright intermarriage and treaty making with the Canaanite inhabitants.

The cultural and religious separation between Canaanites and Israelites was construed as initially a difference between resident peoples and pastoral nomads and, in some cases, the difference between politically established people and social drifters described in the Amarna letters as 'apiru, a term that is cognate with the biblical word "Hebrew(s)." Only slowly did these tensions push the parties into total ethnic and religious opposition.

On the one hand, stress is laid on the normalcy of bedouin penetration into settled areas. Many conceive the earliest Israelites as seasonal nomads or seminomads entering empty space and only slowly becoming numerous and coordinated enough to threaten the Canaanites. Other theorists see more contact and treaty relations, even measurable intermixing of the two populations, as the Israelites more and more abandoned pastoral nomadic life and took up farming.

On the other hand, continuity is often underlined between at least some Israelites and the 'apiru peoples who appear as social outcasts and outlaws throughout the ancient Near East, and whose presence in Canaan is documented from the late fifteenth century through the early thirteenth century. The prominence of Shechem, as a city that collaborated with 'apiru in the Amarna age and served as an assembly point for early Israel, is frequently construed in terms of 'apiru-Israelite collaboration. Unrecognized inconsistencies in the sociological analysis of early Israel often arise at this juncture when pastoral nomadic and 'apiru data are uncritically harmonized.

One of the cardinal features of the immigration model has been its stress on uncoordinated movements of Israelites (or potential Israelites) into Canaan from different directions and at different times. An early wave is generally assigned to the central western highlands. It is argued that, if the exodus from Egypt is historical—immigrationists are inclined to be skeptical on this point—only a fraction of the eventual roster of Israelite tribes was involved in it. The penetration of the tribes of Benjamin, Ephraim, and Manasseh across the Jordan in the vicinity of Jericho-Gilgal later became the nucleus of the Joshua 1–12 stories of total conquest. Yet other infiltrations followed.

When the immigration model first arose, it was assumed that the twelve-tribe system in Israel was a late development during the monarchy. It was subsequently argued that the twelve-tribe system was the early socioreligious framework by which the otherwise disparate tribes organized themselves in Canaan. On this view, the religion of Yahweh was the official cult of a new tribal league called Israel. The adequacy of this theory will be examined (see pp. 158–60).

The traditions were analyzed as an amalgam of premonarchic materials drawn from the several members of the tribal league and worked up in cultic recitations as enlargements of a series of basic history-like themes that give the foundation story of united Israel as the object of Yahweh's saving acts (see pp. 86–87). The present form of Joshua and Judges lends the stories a façade of national unity.

Advocates of the immigration model have tended either to ignore or to discount the historical value of archaeological evidence for illuminating the specifics of Israelite origins. They believe that it was methodologically mistaken in the first place to think that, given the sparseness of solid historical records, archaeology could underpin the historicity of traditional biblical accounts that are so clearly partial, disconnected, and schematic.

The Social Revolution Model

In the last two decades, a revolt model has emerged with the controversial proposal that we can adequately account for what the Bible tells us of Israel's emergence in Canaan on the theory that Israel was composed in large part of native Canaanites who revolted against their overlords and joined forces with a nuclear group of invaders and/or infiltrators from the desert (the exodus Israelites). This model draws on key elements from the conquest and immigration models, rearranging and nuancing them to form a fundamentally new conception of Israel's rise to power.[9]

In common with the conquest model, revolt theorists acknowledge an important dimension of armed conflict in Israel's emergence from the start, and they are inclined to see the exodus Israelites, with their faith in the militant delivering God Yahweh, as the final catalyst that clinched a long-brewing social revolution among depressed and marginated Canaanites. In keeping with the immigration model, revolt theorists urge that the formation of Israel was a coalition of many groups with separate prehistories and cultural backgrounds who contributed to the potpourri of traditions underlying the surface unity both in Genesis–Numbers and in Deuteronomy–Judges.

For some centuries Canaan had been dominated by city-states with hierarchies of aristocratic warriors and bureaucrats who took over the agricultural surplus of the villages where the majority of the populace lived and primary production was based. This tributary mode of production (often called the Asiatic mode of production) laid on the mass of peasants and herdsmen heavy burdens of taxation in kind, forced labor, and military service. Indebted peasants, deprived of independent means of subsistence, were recruited as cultivators of large estates or reduced to the status of tenant farmers. A large percentage of the communal productive energy and resources went into warfare and the luxuried life of the ruling classes, which included lavish religious displays. Local Canaanite kings and elites passed on some of this communal product in tribute to the Egyptian imperial overlords when compelled to do so.

Various sectors of the Canaanite populace struggled against this social burden in different ways. During the fourteenth and thirteenth centuries, as warfare among the city-states increased and as population apparently declined (for reasons unknown at present), restive peasants, pastoral nomads, 'apiru, and other disaffected elements were drawn toward closer cooperation, even alliances, in order to fend off the control of the city-states. In time, probably with the arrival of the exodus Israelites, the religion of Yahweh became the socioreligious ideology and organizational framework that won over these rebellious peoples and helped to forge them into an effective revolutionary movement that expelled the tributary mode of production from the highlands and substituted a system of free peasant agriculture within a loose tribal design.

Early theories tended to overstate the polarization of the total Canaanite populace for or against revolution and also to conceive the revolution as sudden, cataclysmic, and conclusive. Subsequent elaborations of the model have stressed that rebellious and potentially revolutionary forces had been at work in Canaan for decades, at first divided from one another by city-state and regional boundaries and by socioeconomic types (separate strategies by peasants, pastoral nomads, 'apiru, and other less clearly differentiated sectors such as the Shosu mentioned in Egyptian texts, ca. 1500–1150 B.C.E.). Slowly coalescing, first in an El-worshiping union, they finally became a greatly expanded Yahweh-worshiping coalition.

The Israelite revolution could succeed only by struggle on many fronts: by undermining the peasant base of the city-states, by countering the city-state religiopolitical propaganda with superior egalitarian Yahwist propaganda, and by driving a wedge into the loyalty of the governing apparatus. The social revolution of early Israel was arduous and did not culminate until the early rule of David, by which time hierarchic tendencies were resurgent within Israel.

As normally happens in a social revolution, the Canaanite populace responded to the uprising with varying degrees and kinds of support or opposition. There are instances of the formation of Israel out of Canaanite converts, for example, Rahab and her group at Jericho (Joshua 2; 6:22-25). There are other cases of Canaanite neutrals who observed nonintervention in the internal affairs of Israel and noncooperation in hostile actions against Israel initiated by other Canaanites, for example, Shechem and other cities in Manasseh (Gen. 48:22; Joshua 24; Judges 9). Lastly, there are examples of Canaanite allies under the protection of Israel who gave support to Israel while maintaining a separate status within the Israelite movement, for example, Gibeon and the other Hurrian cities in Benjamin (Joshua 9–10; 2 Sam. 4:1-3; 21:1-14). These shifting and nuanced alignments are typical of revolutionary situations that involve vacillating middle forces who only reluctantly are driven toward one side or the other in the conflict.

Moreover, whole Israelite tribes give evidence of having been composites of local Canaanites, and possibly even of Philistines. The assembly at Shechem (Joshua 24) makes sense as a ritual incorporation of part of the Canaanite populace, purged of their oppressing kings, newly tribalized, who throw off the Baal religion and accept Yahweh of the Israelites, who has helped them in their victories.

Moreover, Issachar, described as one who "bowed his shoulder to bear, and became a slave at forced labor" (Gen. 49:15), may well refer to the vulnerable position of underclasses in the Valley of Jezreel and their forced subservience as estate laborers to nearby city-states, until these Canaanite serfs grew strong enough to throw off their oppressors and join free tribes near them. It has also been proposed that the tribe of Dan derived from the Sea Peoples known from Greek and Egyptian sources as the Denen or Danuna, who settled first on the Palestinian coast north of the Philistines before their conversion to Yahwism and eventual migration to the headwaters of the Jordan.

Thus the stock opposition of Israelite versus Canaanite can be seen to have undergone a conceptual shift over time. The term "Canaanite" came to refer to city-state hierarchical structure, with its concomitant religious ideology of Baalism, that continued in the cities of the plains and tended to creep back into Israel as revolutionary fervor abated. In time, as Israel gained primary identity as a national state with its own distinctive cult, "Canaanite" and "Israelite" were used as labels for two fixed national domains and peoples who presumably had always had entirely separate histories, with religious differences especially emphasized as the chief criterion of separation between them.

As for archaeological evidence, the revolt model deals more flexibly with material evidence of destruction levels in Canaanite cities than the immigration and conquest models have tended to do, although so far it is not apparent how archaeology might validate or invalidate the revolutionary hypothesis. Destruction of cities by any of several agencies could easily fit within the theory.

Moreover, the typological evidence for a distinctive early Iron Age culture in highland Canaan seems to accord well with the hypothesis of a tribalizing confederacy of collaborative lower-class Canaanites and exodus refugees who took over the name Israel that had been adopted by an earlier El-worshiping union. That new kiln techniques appear with Iron I may suggest that potters who served the elites were killed off or driven out with their overlords, so that the exodus and native rebels had to develop their own means of pottery making with new forms and color preferences. The markedly lower incidence of imported wares reflects no doubt the decline in luxury trade accompanying the radical shift from the Canaanite tributary system to the Israelite egalitarian social system. Likewise, discrepancies and gaps between archaeological and biblical data, as in the cases of Jericho and

Ai, are no difficulty for the revolt model on principle since it shares with the immigration model the belief that the traditions of early Israel were frequently compressed, inflated, transposed, and conflated in the process of slow accumulation toward their finished status as a literary etiology of united Israel.

Hypotheses about Israel's Tribal Social Organization

The debate over models of Israel's rise to power in Canaan is in reality a much larger conflict over the proper understanding of Israel as a social system. This conflict has not fully surfaced in biblical studies because of biblical scholarship's backwardness in adopting a sociological approach to early Israel. The need for methodological clarity on the issue of Israel's social constitution is by now so urgent that further significant progress even on the historical front is impeded by the anemic state of social inquiry. For the issue at stake is not simply the territorial-historical problem of how Israel took its land but also the complementary questions that lurk behind this concern: What was this formation of people called Israel that took control over the hill country and whose social system took form as it came to power? What were the shared goals and bonding structures of Israel's social system in comparison with those of other social systems from which it emerged and against which it was counterposed? Up to now biblical studies have grappled with models of the settlement in Canaan and of the development of literary traditions, but there has been no larger analytic model of the social system operative simultaneously in the twin processes of land taking and tradition making.

The Pastoral Nomadic Model

Efforts by both conquest and immigration theorists to understand the origins of Israel have been saddled with naïve, hopelessly exaggerated, and outmoded assumptions about Israelites as pastoral nomads who invaded or infiltrated Canaan from the desert. These presuppositions must be radically reassessed.[10]

Pastoral nomadism is a socioeconomic mode of life based on intensive domestication of livestock that requires movement in a seasonal cycle dictated by the need for pasturage and water. Data from prehistory and anthropology have clarified the secondary and limited development of pastoral nomadism out of a prior mixture of agriculture and animal husbandry in settled areas. Humans first entered the river valleys of Mesopotamia not from the Arabian Desert but from the Anatolian and Iranian hills and grasslands (see pp. 21–24). Under specific economic and political conditions, goats, sheep, and asses (already domesticated in farming communities) were grazed in large herds on the marginal desert steppes. In modern times no more than 10 percent of the total Middle East populace has been composed of pastoral nomads, and there appear to be no ecological or technological factors that would have enlarged that percentage in biblical times. Indeed, before the advent of camel and horse nomadism, permitting deeper penetration of the Arabian Desert (from the twelfth century on), the number of nomads was probably far fewer.

The degree of self-sufficiency and isolation of pastoral nomads varies markedly and has usually been grossly exaggerated by biblical exegetes and historians. Historical reconstructions of the ancient Near East, and of Israel in particular, have been distorted by a pan-nomadic hypothesis that posits the Arabian Desert as an inexhaustible source of population influxes, military conquests, dynastic changes, cultural departures, and religious innovations. Migrations due to uprooting by natural and historical circumstances have been repeatedly equated unjustifiably with nomadism as regular movement in the exercise of a socioeconomic mode of life.

In socioeconomic terms, typical elements of rural life and key features of tribal organization have been gratuitously identified as exclusively pastoral nomadic traits. Asses were used as favorite riding animals and reliable beasts of burden throughout the settled zone, and sheep and goats were kept regularly by settled peoples. Tents were used by merchants, armies, and royal hunting parties, and by farmers for guarding and harvesting distant fields or where building materials were scarce. On the other hand, nomads often lived not in tents but in grass or wood huts, mud houses, or caves.

There is likewise a regular litany of tribal social practices in Israel that are indiscriminately attributed to democratic or egalitarian pastoral nomadic origins, for example, blood revenge and hospitality. These traits can be found throughout a range of tribal, and even statist, social organizations in which not a single pastoral nomad is present.

Nonetheless, a careful reading of the biblical texts suggests that a component of pastoral nomadism did exist in early Israel alongside the more dominant socioeconomic modes of life. Two forms of transhumant pastoral nomadism were practiced by members of settled communities in early Israel: (1) winter treks into the steppes of Canaan, and (2) spring/summer treks into the better-watered uplands of Canaan. Owing to the close proximity of steppe and cultivated zone in Canaan, agricultural and pastoral nomadic modes of life were closely juxtaposed and interwoven.

Many pastoral nomads were part-time or seasonal, and there were farmers who took to pastoral nomadism and returned to farming as economic and political circumstances prompted.

Migration is not ipso facto pastoral nomadism, a distinction regularly overlooked by those who automatically assume that the biblical patriarchs were pastoral nomads (see pp. 99–102). A similar judgment is normally made concerning the exodus Israelites in the wilderness. The movement of Israelites out of Egypt and across the wilderness, however, fails to satisfy the appropriate criteria of the pastoral nomadic trek. The departure from Egypt was flight, expulsion, or armed escape—not a seasonal herding trek.

Did land-hungry Israelite pastoral nomads conquer Canaan? Once the assertion of the pastoral nomadic identity of patriarchs and exodus Israelites is set aside as counterindicated, the remaining evidence is precarious in the extreme. The tribalism of early Israel is in no way a phenomenon restricted to pastoral nomads, nor is the repeatedly cited practice of holy war, which is actually more extensive among state-organized peoples. The logical move, following the exposure of the pastoral nomadic mirage, is to look for the origins of Israel in the land of Canaan itself, for even those who came out of Egypt are represented as once having lived in the land of Canaan.

The Religious League Model (Amphictyony)

Common to both conquest and immigration theorists, as well as some revolt theorists, has been the notion of early Israel as a twelve-tribe religious league. The assumptions and applications of this hypothesis, while by no means entirely baseless, have been almost as damaging for achieving a holistic view of

Israelite social organization as has been the pastoral nomadic hypothesis.[11]

In this interpretation, Israel was a confederacy of exactly twelve tribes organized around the cult of Yahweh celebrated at a central shrine in analogy with the sacral leagues of Greek, Old Latin, and Etruscan city-states. This classical religiopolitical institution, best attested by the Apollo league at Delphi, was known to the Greeks as an amphictyony, generally derived from a term meaning "inhabitants of the neighboring district" or "dwellers around [a common sanctuary]." The Israelite religious confederacy construed as an amphictyony was believed to have possessed a central shrine, a council with tribal delegates and law-proclaiming officials, and to have consisted of twelve members—on the still-undemonstrated assumption that each tribe cared for the upkeep of the central sanctuary for one month of the year. The central shrine in Israel was located at Shechem at the beginning and at Shiloh by the late eleventh century; in between it seems to have been at Bethel and Gilgal, and perhaps at Gibeon.

The most prevalent reconstruction of the growth of the amphictyony posited an original six-member amphictyony in northern Israel expanded to twelve members after the entrance of the exodus tribes. Within a short time Levi became a priestly tribe and was dropped from the tribal enumeration, but the roster of twelve members was maintained by dividing Joseph into the two tribes of Ephraim and Manasseh. It was also supposed that Judah was itself formed out of an older six-member amphictyony at Hebron composed of Judahites, Simeonites, Othnielites, Calebites, Jerahmeelites, and Kenites.

The religious league model recognized that the amphictyonic tribal lists do not quite correspond to any specific historical situation in premonarchic Israel but reflect rather a historical process that made adjustments in the membership of the league to retain archaic features and to accommodate new tribal developments.

In spite of the ingenuities of this theory, it is much more likely that Israel did not become a precisely twelve-member confederacy until the verge of the monarchy and that the tribal roster omitting Levi and including Ephraim and Manasseh is a list of the tribal entities used by David as administrative divisions of his kingdom (cf. pp. 132–35), while the tribal roster including Levi and Joseph is a later programmatic all-Israelite statement formulated after Solomon reorganized the kingdom and ceased to use David's system of administration by tribal divisions.

This amphictyonic theory, which did much to explain the function of covenant and law within a basically prestate form of social organization, has been criticized both in its detailed reconstruction and in its adequacy for explaining the total scope of Israelite society. The theory begins from a fact: the undoubted association of Israelite tribes in a common religious institutional and ideological framework in premonarchic times. Finding a broadly analogous situation in ancient Greece and Italy, the model makes doubtful interpretations of the Greek and Italian amphictyonies and gleans the biblical texts far too arbitrarily to recover the Israelite amphictyony.

The comparable and singular traits of the two institutions may be represented as in Web Table I. Surveying this trait typology, it is clear that the comparability of the two associational forms holds good on only two very general points: the formal likeness of associated autonomous political units and the formal likeness of primary definition of the association in terms of a common religious cult. But the Israelite confederacy comprehended the whole of society, whereas the Greek amphictyony was only one of several circumscribed league arrangements within a much larger society. Moreover, the Israelite confederacy was a consciously contrived substitute state opposed to surrounding city-state organization, indeed a veritable anti-state, whereas the Greek amphictyony was a limited arm of autonomous city-states to achieve certain purposes.

The model also drastically overstates the role of religion in Israelite society, in this sense confirming the old confessional religious approach to the Hebrew Bible, so that Israel as an amphictyony is seen to be solely or largely a religious creation centered on faith in and worship of Yahweh. In the process, the reality of Israel's material cultural and sociopolitical life is ignored, downplayed, or treated as an ideal spinoff from the religious foundation.

However we conceive the early religious confederacy of Israel, it must be understood as the religious dimension of a fundamental program of communal self-determination in all aspects of the common life. Unfortunately, most critiques of the amphictyonic design have concluded that no intertribal league whatsoever existed in premonarchic Israel, only discrete tribal groupings with a more or less common form of religious affiliation who only randomly cooperated. On the contrary, the amphictyonic theory is mistaken not because it claimed an all-Israelite confederacy but because it misconceived its inner structure, modes of operation, and social scope. Only on the theory of far-ranging affiliation and cooperation among the tribes is it possible to understand how they mounted and sustained their successful social and religious revolutionary movement.

The Socioreligious Retribalization Model

Prevailing models of Israel as an invading or immigrating seminomadic and/or 'apiru people of a distinct ethnic type who formed a league almost exclusively devoted to religious matters have fundamentally failed to provide a plausible account of Israelite beginnings (see pp. 150–54). More convincing is the hypothesis that Israel burst into history as an ethnically and socioeconomically mixed coalition composed of a majority of tribally organized peasants (80 percent or more of the populace), along with lesser numbers of pastoral nomads, mercenaries, and others. These sectors of the indigenous populace joined in a combined sociopolitical and religious revolution against the imperial and hierarchic tribute-imposing structures of Egyptian-dominated Canaan (see pp. 154–57).[12]

Early Israelites were primarily engaged in intensive rain- and spring-irrigated agriculture, supplemented by stockbreeding and simple handcrafts. Within the momentum of the Israelite movement, diverse segments of the Canaanite underclasses, previously divided and at odds in their struggles, gathered in the hill country and united in free agriculture. They possessed small herds, a fraction of which were tended by seasonal movements into the steppes or uplands.

Therefore, Israelite tribal organization must be accounted for not by the imaginary extension of pastoral nomadism into Canaan, but by the organized resurgence of suppressed rural and village independence against the drafting and taxing powers of the tributary state system exercised by the Egyptian Empire, Canaanite city-states, Midianites who attempted a commercial empire in eleventh-century Transjordan, the nascent national states of Ammon, Moab, and Edom, and the Philistine military oligarchy. Family and village networks of self-help and mutual aid were revived and extended to larger social groupings, gaining strength and experience in proportion as the military and political dominion of the city-states was expelled from the hill country.

The egalitarian project of early Israel was a risky venture in retribalization. Its success was facilitated by a timely conjuncture of technological developments exploited by the peasant movement: introduction of metal farming tools, waterproof cisterns and small-scale irrigation systems, and rock terracing on the steep slopes and in wadi bottoms. In order to establish themselves securely, the renegade Israelites needed to gather enough people, well-enough fed and housed and skilled enough in the new methods of upland agriculture, to be able to extend mutual aid to one another, to absorb and encourage newcomers, and finally to defend themselves collectively against efforts of the politically declining city-states to reestablish and secure their control.

The socioeconomic relations of Israelites were egalitarian in the sense that the entire populace was assured of approximately equal access to resources by means of their organization into extended families, protective associations of families (sometimes called "clans," but not to be construed as clans that mandate marriage outside the group), and tribes, federated as an intertribal community called "Israel," "Israelites," or "the tribes/people of Israel/Yahweh." The vertical residential groups arranged regionally as largely self-contained productive units were cross-cut and bonded by horizontal associations among which were the mutual aid supplied in protective associations, the citizen army, the ritual congregation, the Levite priests (landless and distributed among the tribes as instructional cadres), and probably also the Kenites/Rechabites (understood as itinerant metalworkers).

The basic unit of material production and reproduction was the extended family, which consumed or bartered what it produced. The larger groupings of protective associations, tribes, and intertribal confederacy operated in various ways to provide mutual aid, external defense, and a religious ideology of covenanted or treaty-linked equals. Tribal leadership was heavily male-oriented, although women as a whole—relative to Canaanite class society—benefited from their participation as members of the tribal production and defense systems. We have noted how surprisingly large and positive a place women occupied in the early traditions of Israel (see pp. 99–102, 126–28).

The defining feature of politics in old Israel was that political functions were diffused throughout the social structure or focused in temporary, ad hoc role assignments. Primary leadership fell to tribal functionaries. Elders applied customary laws to cases requiring adjudication and made consensus decisions for war and peace. Priests taught the instructions of the deity as they related to societal norms and priorities as well as to the narrower sphere of ritual. Military leaders emerged to command forces from one or more of the tribes in defense of Israel's free zone of settlement. There may have been a priestly or lay figure who played the mediator role of Moses in the covenant-renewal ceremonies, a kind of prototype of the later DH law interpreter (see pp. 109–12). There were regular means of consultation among the tribes, possibly by a council of the confederacy.

We have seen how confusing a spectrum of leadership functions is depicted in Judges, complicated by the DH habit of viewing disparate roles as the work of judges (see pp. 135–36). No interpretation of the office(s) of judge in early Israel has convincingly unraveled the textual difficulties. Some think that the minor judges of the annotated reports were all-Israelite officials of the confederacy. Others see them as local figures. The sharp line between civilian and military judges is denied by others, who point out that Jephthah was a military leader who gained the top post of leadership in Gilead. Max Weber's delineation of the judges as classic "charismatic" types, inspired leaders in crisis who are self-authenticating, has obscured the extent to which they appear within the fabric of traditional leadership roles, somewhat in the manner of "the big man" role in observed tribal societies.

Some of the supposedly freewheeling charismatic judges begin their judging either on the basis of a traditionally sanctioned office they already hold (Ehud as head of a delegation carrying tribute to Moab, Deborah as a prophetess to whom Israelites come "for judgment") or on the basis of a direct charge by those occupying traditionally sanctioned offices (Barak is summoned by Deborah; Jephthah is appointed by the elders of Gilead after shrewd negotiations). In all events, the multiple leadership functions in early Israel lay outside the realm of state power and bureaucratic credentials. Where powerful local leaders mustered wealth and influence in a move toward chiefdom or petty kingship (Gideon and Abimelech), they were fiercely resisted. Power lay widely distributed in the hands of many groups so that a leveling process worked against ambitious power seekers.

In the socioeconomic spheres similar efforts were made to ensure the self-sustaining integrity of the household productive units. Many laws and stories allude to or describe some of these measures. Land was to be held continuously within extended families and never sold for speculation. It was obligatory

to extend aid to other Israelites in need, and no interest was permitted on such emergency loans. Strict limits were placed on contract servitude. Special provisions for the socially vulnerable (widows, orphans, strangers) were insisted on. An evenhanded judicial system was highly prized.

The retribalization model of early Israel's social system as a correlate of the revolt model of Israel's rise to power supplies a connecting link between the religious thrust of Yahwism and the socioeconomic and political realities of Canaan, a link that neither the pastoral nomadic nor the amphictyonic models—either in their conquest or immigration forms—could offer, other than in the most abstract ways. It proposes a combined social and religious revolution as the key to explaining the phenomenal rise of Yahwism that addresses the life circumstances of underclass or marginal Canaanites, its indigenous roots and power to adapt, its cultural pervasiveness, and its astonishing growth and integrating inclusiveness.

The revolutionary retribalization hypothesis also furnishes a plausible sociopolitical matrix for the snowballing proliferation of Israelite literary traditions. In overthrowing or escaping their rulers, the Canaanite insiders had, like the outsiders from Egypt, overthrown their pharaoh and had been delivered in their own exodus (see pp. 154–57). Converted Canaanite peoples contributed their experiences in literary form to lend support to the sovereign unity of Israel and to praise their covenant overlord Yahweh.

Israel entered history as a people fully active in creating and sustaining their lives in all respects. The name "Israel" referred not merely to a religious community but to a sovereign retribalizing society concerned with fundamental issues of survival and the good life. The covenant linkage on the religious plane was at the same moment a set of covenant linkages on the socioeconomic, political, and cultural planes (see pp. 115–16). The literary traditions of this covenanted people show continuities of theme running from the patriarchs through Moses and on to the conquest of the land that reflect critical problems in revolting and the constant search for strategies to deepen and secure the revolution (see pp. 99–102, 126–28). The insistence on Israel's part that it was a new people without a customary prehistory, that it was first constituted from within as a covenant people of Yahweh, and that it was the sole people in its environment to have such an explicit knowing relationship with Yahweh (see pp. 126–28) is an understandable symbolic assertiveness rooted in the eruptive distinctiveness of this revolutionary retribalizing movement of Canaanites-become-Israelites.

NOTES

1. Alan J. Hauser, "Judges 5: Parataxis in Hebrew Poetry," *JBL* 99 (1980): 23–41.

2. D. F. Murray, "Narrative Structure and Technique in the Deborah and Barak Story," in *Studies in the Historical Books of the Old Testament,* ed. J. A. Emerton, Vetus Testamentum Supplement 30 (Leiden: Brill, 1979), 155–89.

3. J. Cheryl Exum, "Promise and Fulfillment: Narrative Art in Judges 13," *JBL* 99 (1980): 43–59, and "Aspects of Symmetry and Balance in the Samson Saga," *JSOT* 19 (1981): 3–29.

4. David Jobling, "'The Jordan a Boundary': A Reading of Numbers 32 and Joshua 22," *SBLSP* 19 (1980): 183–207.

5. Robert Polzin, *Moses and the Deuteronomist: A Literary Study of the Deuteronomic History* (New York: Seabury, 1980).

6. For a concise review, see George W. Ramsey, *The Quest for the Historical Israel* (Atlanta: John Knox, 1981), 65–98. The work of Marvin L. Chaney, "Ancient Palestinian Peasant Movements and the Formation of Premonarchic Israel," in *Palestine in Transition: The Emergence of Ancient Israel,* ed. David N. Freedman and David F. Graf, Social World of Biblical Antiquity Series 2 (Sheffield: Almond, 1983), 39–90, while opting for one model, subjects all of them to a careful critique.

7. G. Ernest Wright, *Biblical Archaeology,* rev. ed. (Philadelphia: Westminster, 1962), 69–85; idem, "Introduction to Joshua," in *Joshua* by Robert G. Boling, AB 6 (Garden City, N.Y.: Doubleday, 1982), 1–88 (written in 1973 and published posthumously).

8. Martin Noth, *The History of Israel,* trans. Stanley Godman, rev. ed. (New York: Harper & Bros., 1960), 68–84; Manfred Weippert, "Canaan, Conquest and Settlement of," in *IDBSup,* 125–30.

9. George E. Mendenhall, *The Tenth Generation: The Origins of the Biblical Tradition* (Baltimore: Johns Hopkins University Press, 1973); Norman K. Gottwald, *The Tribes of Yahweh: A Sociology of the Religion of Liberated Israel, 1250–1050 B.C.E.* (Maryknoll, N.Y.: Orbis, 1979); Chaney, "Ancient Palestinian Peasant Movements."

10. Manfred Weippert (*The Settlement of the Israelite Tribes in Palestine,* trans. James D. Martin, SBT 2/21 [London: SCM, 1971], 102–26) reaffirms pastoral nomadic origins for Israel; Gottwald (*Tribes of Yahweh,* 435–63) rejects the nomadic hypothesis; see also Chaney, "Ancient Palestinian Peasant Movements," 41–44.

11. For a concise presentation of the amphictyonic hypothesis, see Noth, *History of Israel*, 85–109. For rebuttals of the hypothesis that still recognize a social organizational unity to premonarchic Israel, see C. H. J. de Geus, *The Tribes of Israel* (Amsterdam: Van Gorcum, 1976); and Gottwald, *Tribes of Yahweh*, 345–86.

12. George E. Mendenhall, "Social Organization in Early Israel," in *Magnalia Dei, the Mighty Acts of God: Essays on the Bible and Archaeology in Memory of G. Ernest Wright*, ed. Frank Moore Cross, Werner E. Lemke, and Patrick D. Miller Jr. (Garden City, N.Y.: Doubleday, 1976), 132–51; Gottwald, *Tribes of Yahweh*, 464–587, 650–63; Chaney, "Ancient Palestinian Peasant Movements," 48–83.

FOR FURTHER READING

Boer, Roland, ed. *Tracking "The Tribes of Yahweh": On the Trail of a Classic.* Sheffield: Sheffield Academic, 2002.

Dever, William G. *Who Were the Israelites and Where Did They Come From?* Grand Rapids: Eerdmans, 2003.

Gottwald, Norman K. *The Tribes of Yahweh: A Sociology of the Religion of Liberated Israel, 1250–1050 B.C.E.* Twentieth anniversary edition with new preface. Sheffield: Sheffield Academic, 1999.

———. "Israel, Origins of." *NIDB* 3 (2008): 132–38.

Lemche, Niels P. *Early Israel: Anthropological and Historical Studies on Israelite Society before the Monarchy.* Leiden: E. J. Brill, 1985.

Smith, Mark S. *The Early History of God: Yahweh and the Other Deities of Ancient Israel.* 2nd ed. Grand Rapids: Eerdmans / Dearborn, Mich.: Dove, 2002.

QUESTIONS FOR STUDY

1. Describe how the term *judges* is used in the Deuteronomistic History (DH).

2. Describe how the Deuteronomistic themes of adherence to the Law, guilt and repentance, and conquest of the land are interconnected in Joshua and Judges.

3. How are women portrayed in the Song of Deborah, Judges 4:4-22, and the Samson stories? What questions arise based on these portrayals?

4. What sociological and historical themes arise in the structuralist studies of Numbers 32 and Joshua 22 (see pp. 147–48)?

5. Describe the social revolution model of Israel's rise to power. How does it relate to the older immigration and conquest models?

MONARCHY:
ISRAEL'S
COUNTERREVOLUTIONARY
ESTABLISHMENT

III

The monarchy of ancient Israel spanned four centuries, twice the length of the intertribal era. The first three kings of Israel ruled over a united kingdom that lasted, at most, about one century, beginning around 1020 B.C.E., and possibly for a much shorter period. With the death of Solomon the monarchy was fatally ruptured. The dynasty of David continued to control Judah and a fluctuating area of Benjamin. All the other tribes withdrew to form their own monarchy, which carried the comprehensive national name "Israel" in contrast to the retention of the tribal name "Judah" for the southern kingdom. The two kingdoms ran parallel until the fall of Israel to Assyria in 722 B.C.E., followed eventually by the fall of Judah to the Neo-Babylonian Empire in 586 B.C.E.

In what follows, I will first treat the united monarchy (chap. 7) and then follow the northern kingdom through its history, with reference also to the southern kingdom during the same span of time (chap. 8), before tracing the history of the southern kingdom during the time it stood alone (chap. 9). Important biblical writings that derive at core or in whole from the monarchic age will be discussed in their sociohistorical contexts.

After discussion of the vexed chronology of the divided kingdoms, I shall provide orientation to the direct historical sources for the monarchy contained in the DH books of Samuel and Kings and in the separate work of Chronicles. I shall also take note of archaeological information on the period and briefly examine the nature of the literary forms in the prophetic books.

CHRONOLOGY OF THE DIVIDED KINGDOMS

The dating of the rulers of the divided kingdoms is under dispute. Dates in pre-Roman times were expressed in terms of the years of the reigns of kings or by designating each year with the name of a high official or a memorable event or even the reigns of kings in different countries. This third option was the procedure followed by DH in reporting on the kings of Israel and Judah.

Each of the northern kings (Israel) is introduced with a notice of the date of accession expressed as the year of the contemporary southern king, a statement of length of reign, and a judgment on the king passed according to DH standards. For the southern kings (Judah), these details are supplemented by the age of the monarch at accession and the name of the queen mother. During the period when the two kingdoms ran parallel, the accounts are interwoven by switching back and forth so that events are not always described in strict chronological order.

The reigns of biblical kings can be correlated to the reigns of Assyrian and Neo-Babylonian kings, who in turn can be dated absolutely by astronomical observations. The biblical numbers themselves are problematic. Based on differing assumptions, scholars reach conclusions that vary by as much as ten years at the beginning of the divided kingdoms and narrow to a difference of one or two years toward the end of Judahite rule. The chronology of the divided kingdoms followed in this book succeeds in adhering closely to the numbers in MT by arguing that various systems of reckoning were used at different times in the two kingdoms according to discernible patterns.[1]

DH AS A SOURCE FOR MONARCHIC HISTORY

In Samuel and Kings, DH goes on to tell the story of the monarchy over its entire course, giving us by far our fullest source on the biblical monarchies (table III.1). The presence of the DH hand in Samuel–Kings stands out at once in the persistence of anticipatory and summary surveys, speeches, and prayers of the sort displayed in Deuteronomy through Judges (see table 6.2). These passages divide the monarchy into critical phases and highlight the explanations that DH advances for the ups and downs of Israel's experiments with kingship.

Within the framework of these pivotal interpretive passages, DH has enclosed materials of great historical value from many sources and stamped them with DH's strongly biased interpretation:

1. Independent cycles of traditions about Samuel, Saul, David, and Solomon
2. Administrative documents from the united monarchy
3. Excerpts from the royal archives ("chronicles") of the divided kingdoms
4. Excerpts from the Jerusalem temple archives
5. Cycles of prophetic tales.

In addition to the interpretive link passages cited above, DH used two compositional devices that further bind together the disparate traditions: (1) a synchronization of the rulers of the divided kingdoms (see pp. 167–68), with varying opening and concluding formulas surrounding

TABLE III.I PROGRAMMATIC TEXTS IN DH: SAMUEL–KINGS

1. Speech of Samuel (1 Samuel 12): The fateful choice of monarchy

Recapitulation of oppression, repentance, and deliverance under the judges
Israel confesses the sin of asking for a king
If people and king obey the Law, Israel will continue as Yahweh's people; if they disobey the Law, they will be "swept away"

2. Speech of Nathan and prayer of David (2 Samuel 7): The promise of a "house" for David and a "house" for Yahweh

Yahweh gives David "rest" from all his enemies, and Israel has peace and security unknown under the judges
Yahweh will build a "house" (dynasty) for David, and David's son will build a "house" (temple) for Yahweh
The dynasty of David will last forever, although a particular wicked king in the dynasty may be chastised

3. Blessing and prayer of Solomon (1 Kings 8:14-6): The temple ("house") dedicated as a lasting focus for Law observance

Solomon has fulfilled the promise of Yahweh that David's son will build the temple
Solomon prays for fulfillment of Yahweh's promise that David's dynasty shall last forever
Whenever individual Israelites or the whole people sin, they will turn to the temple, repent, and pray for deliverance, including preservation in any possible future exile from the land
All the promises of Yahweh to Moses have been fulfilled; Israel has "rest" and is urged to continue to observe the Law

4. Discourse (2 Kings 17:17-23): Rationale for the fall of the northern kingdom (Israel)

Jeroboam, first king of Israel, sinned and set a pattern habitually followed by later kings of the north
Israel has fallen and its people exiled because they turned to the religious aspotasies of other nations and their own wicked kings
In spite of repeated warnings by prophets, Israel stubbornly adhered to its apostasies
Judah also began to practice the same apostasies as Israel

5. Discourse and speech of prophets (2 Kings 21:2-16): Rationale for the fall of the southern kingdom (Judah)

Manasseh, king of Judah, introduced idolatry to Jerusalem and seduced Judah into more evil than the Canaanites had committed
Manasseh also "shed very much innocent blood"
Prophets announce that Judah, like Israel, is soon to be "measured" and "cast off" in judgment

reports about the kings; and (2) a schema of prediction and fulfillment, often in the speeches of prophets, for specifying how the words of Yahweh shaped events.

We have ample reason to believe that DH appeared in two editions, the first during the late reign of Josiah, the reforming king of Judah (622–609 B.C.E.), and the second in the exile after 561 B.C.E. (the date of the last incident in 2 Kings). The most compelling argument for two editions lies in the tension in DH between threatened national doom and anticipated national survival or restoration, which is most reasonably explained if DH was a work first addressed to a declining but reforming Judahite state and only secondarily to groups of stateless Jews after the fall of Judah.

The main thrust of DH is to show how the monarchy, united and divided, stands under the obligation of obedience to the Law of Moses. Since that Law was repeatedly violated, the northern kingdom perished and the southern kingdom now faces the same dire judgment (first edition).

In contrast to the sin of idolatry of the founder of the northern kingdom, Jeroboam, stood the promise of Yahweh to his faithful servant David that holds out the prospect that Judah will be spared the terrible fate of Israel. "For the sake of David" the sins of southern kings are viewed as less fatal than the sins of northern kings. More than this, the southern kings Hezekiah and Josiah are reported to have carried out major cultic reforms that correspond closely to the program of DH urged in Deuteronomy (2 Kgs. 18:3-7; cf. 2 Chronicles 30; 2 Kgs. 22:8—23:25).

It is likely that the bulk of DH was composed as a propaganda work for Josiah's reformation of the cult and his political program to restore the empire of David in the wake of Assyria's sudden decline and retreat from northern Israel. In DH's mind, the fall of the north had been richly deserved. The south could escape the same fate only by backing Josiah's reform.

As events turned out, the reform did not stick; Judah collapsed at the hands of a major new world power, the Neo-Babylonians; and its leadership was taken into captivity. With this catastrophic turn of events, DH was expanded to recount the sorry end of Judah (2 Kgs. 23:26—25:30), and significant ideological revisions were made to explain why Josiah's reformation had failed (second edition). Tragically, it was concluded that the gross sins of Manasseh had outweighed all the good efforts of Josiah (2 Kgs. 21:2-15; 22:15-20; 23:25b-27).

Was all hope in the promises of Yahweh and the future of Israel now lost? Far from it. The updating of events into the exile indicates that the DH revision meant to explain the fall of both kingdoms so as to prepare the stateless Judahites for continuing adherence to their religio-cultural identity. It was Yahweh who had brought about this abysmal state of affairs because Israel and Judah alike had failed to observe the Law of Moses. But Israelites survived who, like the DH reviser, still believed in Yahweh.

To round out DH as a document serviceable for conquered and dispersed Jews, forewarnings of the exile were introduced into many parts of the original DH composition (e.g., Deut. 30:1-10; 1 Kgs. 9:6-9; 2 Kgs. 17:19).

The positing of two settings for the present DH—one a reformed state context and the other a forlorn stateless context—brings considerable intelligibility to the mixed messages of doom and hope that sound throughout the work. It is interesting to speculate on the possible connection of this view of DH's literary history to the structuralist analysis of DH so far carried through Judges (see pp. 147–49). The two structurally identified voices of authoritarian dogmatism and critical traditionalism appear to be at play differently in the DH Josianic and exilic contexts. In the DH exilic revision, dogmatic authoritarianism, straining to explain the exile by overweighing Josiah's faithfulness with Manasseh's sins, is itself outweighed by the stark reality of surviving Judahites who still listen to the words of Yahweh through the authoritative interpreter DH. This chastened audience will be given another chance as a recognizable people of God, protected, even favored, by their captors (1 Kgs. 8:46-53; 25:27-30), and maybe eventually reempowered in their land (Deut. 30:1-10).

Finally, the books of Chronicles provide limited additional information on the monarchy (see pp. 298–301). Written between 525 and 375 B.C.E.—depending on whether the books of Ezra and Nehemiah belong to the same work—Chronicles repeat large parts of Samuel and Kings to which they add some fresh information and much additional interpretation. Chronicles cite many sources on the kings and prophets, but the outcome is a religiously edifying work that must be used cautiously for reconstructing history, although some reliable details of genealogies, topography, and political administration flesh out the skeletal information in Samuel–Kings.

Certain psalms (see pp. 302–10) and older sections of Proverbs (see pp. 323–25) are evidently preexilic in setting, although both finished books are manifestly of postexilic date. There is some value in the indirect picture of the monarchic cult shown in these early psalms and also in the reflections of life among mid-level echelons of government bureaucrats indicated as the context for many of the oldest proverbs.

ARCHAEOLOGY AS A SOURCE FOR MONARCHIC HISTORY

In recent decades archaeological information on the monarchic period has measurably enlarged, with some corrections of earlier interpretations of architectural remains. Solomonic casemate walls (double walls with intervening rooms) and monumental city gates have appeared at Megiddo, Hazor, and Gezer (1 Kgs. 9:15-17) and also a ceremonial palace at Megiddo. Nothing of Solomon's lavish building program in Jerusalem has been certainly identified because of later severe disturbances and rebuildings.

The northern kingdom is well represented by Jeroboam I's city gate and sanctuary at Dan, the Omri-Ahab capital city splendidly laid out on a hill at Samaria, and Omri-Ahab structures at Megiddo. Water tunnels for assuring the city supply during siege have been found at Megiddo and Hazor.

The southern kingdom has yielded ample evidence of Sennacherib's destruction of Lachish at the end of the eighth century. Our understanding of Judahite military defenses and political administration is enhanced by the excavation of well-fortified sites at Beersheba and Arad in the Negeb, and under Hezekiah Jerusalem's walls were extended. Weights and measures indicate a growth and standardization in trade and probably a more systematically planned national economy administered from Jerusalem. Although the interpretation is tentative, archaeological comparisons of ninth/eighth-century Israel and eighth/seventh-century Judah seem to suggest that greater prosperity was distributed throughout the countryside in Judah than in Israel.

In addition to the sanctuary at Dan, Yahwistic sanctuaries at Lachish and Arad have been uncovered, and Beersheba may have had a sanctuary, judging by a horned altar found there, similar to one at Dan (1 Kgs. 1:50). Archaeological demonstration of Judahite Yahwist sanctuaries outside Jerusalem in monarchic times corroborates the historical-critical view that the Deuteronomic confinement of worship to Jerusalem did not take place until at least the time of Hezekiah and probably not with full effect until Josiah.

Of particular value for illuminating monarchic history are inscriptions and texts from the period (see Web Table A, 4). Pharaoh Shishak (ca. 940–915) relates his military campaign into Palestine against Judah and Israel. Also valuable are the annals of Assyrian kings, from Shalmaneser III (858–824) through Ashurbanipal (668–633), which recount military and administrative encounters with the western part of the empire, including Israel and Judah (see Web Table A, 4J). The Neo-Babylonian Chronicles from the reign of Nebuchadnezzar (605–562) help to clarify the last years of independent Judah (see Web Table A, 4K). The sum total of material and written remains accumulates impressively, although the lapsed time among archaeologists in publishing, interpreting, and synthesizing the finds—and among biblical scholars in appropriating them—appears to be as much as a decade or more.

FORMS AND SETTINGS OF PROPHETIC SPEECH

Several prophetic books provide significant, broadly historical information on the monarchy, especially on socioeconomic life: chiefly Amos and Hosea for the northern kingdom, and Micah, Isaiah, and Jeremiah for the southern kingdom. The nature and value of that information can be appreciated only by grasping the peculiar literary character of prophetic books.

There is abundant evidence that all the preexilic prophets were first speakers of relatively short, usually poetic messages, which they and their followers later committed to writing (on oral forms, see pp. 63–65). These speeches drew upon and modified or broke conventional fixed forms for special effects or to expand the range and subtlety of prophetic messages (on literary types in the prophets, see Web Table B, also 41–50). Prophetic books also contain narrative sections that include, for example, time and place indicators for particular prophetic words, reports of commissioning to a prophetic vocation, and incidents of acceptance or rejection of prophetic words.

Some scholars have located the origin of prophetic speech in the cultic oracle, a divine communication solicited by devotees of the cult and delivered by authorized cult personnel. That many prophetic speeches represent Yahweh speaking in the first person, with the phrases "says Yahweh" or "oracle of Yahweh" attached, broadly accords with this understanding. Evidence is also cited that some, many, or all prophets served regularly—or had formerly served—in the official cult connected with shrines. On the other hand, many prophetic speeches are not direct words of God, their oracles were for the most part not asked for, and the content of their messages often directly challenged the presuppositions and typical messages of the official cult.

Another approach to the roots of prophetic speech and ideology starts off from the formulations of lawsuits brought by Yahweh against Israel or the nations that appear in prophetic books. The prophets are seen as messengers of Yahweh the divine judge, delivering his verdict of guilt and sentence of punishment on a wayward covenant people. But there was simply no jurisdictional body competent to try a legal charge brought by Yahweh against the whole people or its collective leadership.

It is likely that interpreters make a mistake in trying to move so directly from given speech forms to particular institutional contexts. The great variety of prophetic forms of speech suggests a deliberate drawing on traditions and practices from many spheres of institutional life—including religious cult, law courts, military practice, political administration, and scribal procedures—without any necessary implication that particular prophets served in these institutions.

By the time of Amos at any rate, whose word launched the first complete prophetic book, prophecy seems to have been well on the way to creating its own institutional matrix. It was achieving formalization and broad public recognition as a kind of regularized criticism of the established order, drawing extensively on a wide range of preexisting speech to establish rapport and authority with audiences, while simultaneously transforming speech forms in order to deliver arresting messages. This prophetic movement most likely took its rise from within cultic institutions, but it soon achieved enough institutional and ideological independence to stand on its own.

The literary history of prophetic books is an unavoidable but complicated issue for biblical interpretation. Speeches and narrative reports from a named prophet formed the nucleus of the book bearing the prophet's name. In time, the words of other prophets or of commentators in the tradition of the original prophet were added to the nucleus. The grouping of the prophetic traditions according to various organizing principles—whether by original prophet, later followers, or final editor (redactor)—has become a subject of much inquiry by redaction critics.

Finally, there is a set of sociopolitical questions about how the prophets were located in their social matrix and what stance they took toward other social actors and the social system itself. These issues are closely related to the authority of the prophets and the sources of prophetic inspiration and revelation. Former social interpretations of prophecy tended to be psychosocial and to maximize the role of prophets as lone critics of society or as "isolated intellectuals who feel left out of public decisions." A broader application of social-scientific methods to prophecy suggests that the prophets were intimately a part of their society even as their stances toward its current directions were highly oppositional.[2]

Studies of shamanism and spirit possession among holy men/women have noted innumerable forms of inspiration and authority variously connected to traditional social institutions and roles. A basic question is whether these prophets are part of the central socially empowered establishment or part of peripheral socially devalued and marginated groups. In many respects Israelite prophets appear to have been mixtures of central and peripheral types, the great prophets of later tradition being largely peripheral during the monarchy but surprisingly central in the exile once their interpretations of events were accepted as vindicated.

Studies of nativist, revitalization, and millennial movements have stressed the role of religious leaders or prophets in protest movements of broad social import, spurred by a sense of strategic social deprivation. The overtly religious motives and language of the prophetic leaders are entangled with social aims that may or may not have been recognized by them and their followers. The explicit involvement of Israelite prophets in the social and political conflicts of the monarchy are rather obvious on the surface of the biblical text, but the detailed social dynamics require reconstruction. This process of social class and conflict analysis in prophecy, as throughout the Hebrew Bible, has been obstructed and sidetracked by biblical scholars who lack a sense of the forms and complexities of class struggle.

For reconstructing the sociohistorical horizons of monarchy, the implications of the origin and shape of prophetic writings and of the sociopolitical matrix of prophetic functions may be summed up as follows:

1. The prophetic writings usually supply brief vignettes or slices of public life that lack directly noted connections with other prophetic passages or with sociohistorical conditions. These writings, like much of Hebrew poetry, are often formed by parataxis (see pp. 145–47), presenting a succession of unintegrated vivid details and strong judgments that must be mulled over and interconnected by reader and historian in order to relate them to a whole fabric of sociohistorical circumstance.

2. Since the original prophet's words are fused together with additional words from later prophets and commentators, the materials in any particular prophetic book are likely to reflect sociohistorical settings widely separated over time.

3. The prophetic references to broader contemporary groups in sociopolitical conflict—and the place of prophets in those conflicts—are fragmentary and indirect. Nonetheless, it is no longer permissible in biblical studies to neglect the immersion of prophets in sociopolitical conflict on the basis of arguments that we lack such information or that prophets were so totally religious that they had no determinable secular intentions, functions, or meanings.

NOTES

1. The chronological system adopted is that of Edwin R. Thiele, *The Mysterious Numbers of the Hebrew Kings,* 3rd ed. (Grand Rapids: Eerdmans, 1983), and followed by Simon J. DeVries, "Chronology of the OT," in *IDB* 1:580–99; idem, "Chronology, OT," in *IDBSup,* 161–66. For a condensed account of Thiele's chronology, see E. R. Thiele, *A Chronology of the Hebrew Kings* (Grand Rapids: Zondervan, 1977). The other chronological system widely employed among North American biblical scholars is that of William F. Albright ("The Chronology of the Divided Monarchy of Israel," *BASOR* 100 [1945]: 16–22), followed by John Bright, *A History of Israel,* 3rd ed. (Philadelphia: Westminster, 1981).
2. Burke O. Long, "Prophetic Authority as Social Reality," in *Canon and Authority: Essays in Old Testament Religion and Theology,* ed. George W. Coats and Burke O. Long (Philadelphia: Fortress Press, 1977), 3–20; Robert R. Wilson, *Prophecy and Society in Ancient Israel* (Philadelphia: Fortress Press, 1980); David L. Petersen, *The Roles of Israel's Prophets,* JSOTSup 17 (Sheffield: JSOT Press, 1981).

TRADITIONS ABOUT THE UNITED KINGDOM

See additional materials at fortresspress.com/ gottwald; consult Carta Bible Atlas *maps 83–117.*

THE SHAPE OF THE TRADITIONS IN 1 AND 2 SAMUEL AND 1 KINGS 1–11

Source Statistics

The status of our sources for a knowledgeable reconstruction of the united monarchy of Israel can be formulated statistically in terms of the amount and kind of coverage devoted to its three rulers and to Samuel, who prepares Israel for the transition to monarchy. Using biblical verses as the unit of computation, one can divide the materials in DH between two kinds of traditions (see Web Table J): (1) *annalistic political-historical documentation,* the kind of hard data on political administration, military affairs, foreign policy, building operations, and religious measures that form the skeleton of historical writing; and (2) *miscellaneous literary traditions* in the form of sagas or legends, prophetic narratives, and poems, the kind of soft literary productions that touch political history less directly.

The division between these two types of material is not hard and fast. Still, the basic differences are clear, and an approximate distribution of the DH materials on this basis serves to point up some of the problems in writing a history of monarchic Israel.

The figures in Web Table J are a rough reflection of the relative scarcity of direct sources on the monarchy, and, in particular, they register the extreme difficulty historians have in gaining a properly detailed and proportioned picture of the roles of Samuel and Saul in the rise of the monarchy.

Older Literary-Critical Studies

In discerning and assessing the sources for the early monarchy, historical critics were impressed by the concentration and relative fullness of materials with respect to a few basic themes: (1) how Saul came to be the first king; (2) how kingship was transferred from Saul to David; (3) how Solomon, among David's several sons, succeeded his father to the throne; (4) how the temple was built; and (5) how Solomon attained and displayed his wisdom. An intense focus on the personal relationships among the leading figures in the history was, however, not accompanied by substantial clarification of the wider sociopolitical and religiocultural factors that prompted and shaped the monarchy.

Early on it was seen that the accounts fell into thematic blocks with varying degrees of internal cohesion and problematic connections.

1. One tightly composed block, dubbed the "Court History" or "Succession Narrative," treated a cluster of family and public affairs in the court of King David (2 Samuel 9–20; 1 Kings 1–2).
2. A segment relating the rise to power of David, in tandem with the decline of Saul (1 Samuel 16—2 Samuel 5), was judged to contain more disparate units and doublets.
3. A section describing how Saul was elected and then rejected as king (1 Samuel 8–15) was seen to divide into two sources, one promonarchic (1 Sam. 9:1—10:16; 11:1-11; 13:1—14:46) and the other antimonarchic (1 Samuel 8; 10:17-27; 12; 15).

Several shorter blocks of tradition were identified in Samuel.

1. The Samuel birth and "call" stories (1 Samuel 1–3; 2:27–36; cf. 2 Sam. 15:24–37; 20:25; 1 Kgs. 1:22–39; 2:26–27)
2. The story of the fortunes of the ark (1 Sam. 4:1–7:2; 2 Samuel 6)
3. An inset of material showing Samuel in various guises as a military and civil "judge" (7:3–17)
4. An appendix of miscellaneous David traditions (2 Samuel 21–24).

The account of the reign of Solomon (1 Kings 3-11) was assessed as an eclectic mix of detailed description of the temple, administrative lists, reports of diplomatic relations, legends about the wise king, and heavy doses of DH ideology. It was observed that 1 Kings 3–11 was organized so that Solomon's external political difficulties and his internal conflicts were placed at the end of his otherwise halcyon reign and blamed on religious corruption owing to the influence of his foreign wives (1 Kgs. 11:1-13).

As was noted in citing key interpretive passages in Samuel and 1 Kings (see table III.1), DH intruded strongly ideological passages here and there in the text. Because these DH interventions were confined to a few obvious points, scholars turned to other options to explain the continuity of the materials prior to the work of DH. Starting off from signs of parallel sources, as in 1 Samuel 8–15, and of twice-told incidents, efforts were made to trace the pentateuchal sources J and E from Joshua and Judges into Samuel and Kings. Based as they were on meager evidence and differing in criteria and results, these source analyses have won few adherents. In the meantime literary analysis has turned in other directions.

Newer Literary-Critical Studies

The impact of new forms of biblical literary criticism has been felt in fresh assessments of the separate literary blocks in terms of their literary genres, frequently illuminated by similar ancient Near Eastern traditions. In addition, there is a strong move toward identifying a basic pre-DH ordering of the shorter blocks that does not depend on the dubious analysis into J and E sources. This new wave of work on the recognized segments within Samuel and their interconnections carries sizable implications for historical uses of these sources in studying the early monarchy.

The *ark narrative* has been treated as an instance of an ancient Near Eastern genre: a report of the capture in battle and the subsequent return of a people's god(s).[1] Victors sometimes displayed captured gods in their temples as trophies and signs of the impotence of the defeated nation. The genre shaping Israel's ark narrative is cast from the perspective of the defeated people, who locate the reason for their defeat and for the capture of the god(s) in some national sin that has greatly displeased the deity. In time, however, the still-powerful captured god bests his captors and forces them to release the image(s), which are returned home in triumph. Moral: the angry deity has caused and controlled the humiliating events in order to teach his people a lesson. Given the applicability of the genre, the temporal location of the story would have been prior to David's sound defeat of the Philistines, for after that turn of events such a story was no longer needed to bolster Israel's morale.

Frequently *an old cycle of Saul stories* is posited in which Samuel played little or no part and in which ideological contention over the merits and demerits of kingship was not involved.[2] A cycle of this sort implies affinities with cycles about military deliverers in Judges. One study notes that the often observed "tragic" characterization of Saul, unbiblical in tone but recognizably Greek, may be related to the foreign motifs of the dead as effective beings, heroic suicide, mutilation of a fallen enemy, and honorable burial by cremation (in 1 Samuel 28; 31). These features suggest that the author of the Saul cycle was someone familiar with practices and literary traditions of Greeks and Hittites, plausible enough when one recalls that Philistines and Hittites were part of the Jerusalem court in David's time.

The *story of David's rise to power* has been compared with a special genre of Hittite historiography, best represented in the thirteenth-century *Apology of Hattusilis III*.[3] The Hittite apology is composed to defend or justify a king who has usurped the throne. It shares with David's apology several themes, for example, early military successes as a trusted commander of his royal predecessor, popularity among the people, blamelessness in all his dealings with his predecessor, and the favor of deity as the reason for his rise to the throne.

It is noted that David's apology responds defensively and effectively to charges that David tried to advance himself at Saul's expense, even collaborating against his own people and finally being implicated in Saul's death. This older defense of David's legitimacy as king does not show a developed royal theology of the dynastic type (unlike 2 Samuel 7). The document was probably written in Jerusalem and addressed to northerners during David's reign or thereafter, when the Davidic right to rule over the north was in question (2 Sam. 16:4-14; 20:1-22; see p. 195).

The search for an intermediate link between these separate tradition blocks and the final DH has led some critics to postulate a "Prophetic History" that brought together all the segments of tradition in 1 Samuel 1 through 2 Samuel 5, so that DH needed only to introduce a few interpretive passages and expansions to link the work to the preceding judges and to the following kings.[4] The pervasive tendency of this pre-DH book of Samuel was to elevate prophetic leadership over royal leadership. Kings are viewed with suspicion but tolerated as long as they remain subject to the election and guidance of prophets like Samuel, the prophetic kingmaker. The old cycle of stories about Saul, the ark, and David were reworked and reordered to fit this pre-DH view.

The posited date for this Prophetic History was during or shortly after the fall of Israel in 722 B.C.E., and its presumed setting was within a northern prophetic circle critical of the monarchy in the manner of Hosea.

The sympathy expressed for the Davidic dynasty means that the writer of the Prophetic History looked to the continuing kingdom of Judah as a context where the monarchic abuses of the annihilated northern kingdom could be corrected by subordinating kingship to prophecy. Since traditions lying behind Deuteronomy are believed to have originated in the north and to have passed into Judah after the debacle of 722 B.C.E., it is appropriate to speak of the Prophetic History as "proto-Deuteronomic."

For a long time the estimation of *the Court History of David* as a wonderfully constructed historical writing by an eyewitness to the events provided the linchpin for understanding the reign of David.[5] Three major new interpretations have been offered following from weaknesses exposed in the work's credibility as history.

One new line of interpretation envisions the document as political propaganda.[6] The dominant form of the theory sees an attempt in it to justify and legitimate Solomon's succession to the throne of David, although an opposing position finds the propaganda to be anti-Davidic and anti-Solomonic.

A second hypothesis categorizes the Court History as narrative wisdom writing, in particular as a royal novel from Solomonic scribal circles, where Egyptian state administrative practices and wisdom writings inculcating virtues like friendship and loyalty influenced court tastes.[7]

Yet a third approach to the Court History points out that it contains many alerting indicators that the intended audience was not familiar with circumstances and customs in Davidic-Solomonic times. The document is rather best typified as a work of art and serious entertainment.[8] The story's humanizing and universalizing treatment of the main characters is developed by the theme of David's giving and grasping in the interplay and conflict of family and political interests and forces. A wealth of traditional motifs and stock story episodes suggests that the stories originated in or were influenced by oral tradition. Historical matters may be related in this David story, but they are clearly incidental to the function of entertainment.

Implications of Literary Analysis for Historical Use of the Sources

The bearing of recent literary analysis on the historical use of early monarchic sources introduces sober caution, if not outright warning. Our examination of the sources according to recent literary analyses bears out the initial impression of the statistical survey: the political-historical core of textual data on the early monarchy gives us a narrow historiographic base, although around that core swirls a considerable body of literature, formed from a number of once-independent blocks, that gives us fascinating selective readings of limited aspects of the history of the times filtered by the lenses of genre and ideology.

THE RISE AND TRIUMPH OF MONARCHY IN ISRAEL

External and Internal Factors

The most commonly recognized factor in the rise of kingship in Israel has been the military threat of the Philistines, who gained a solid hold on the southern coastal plain after 1150 B.C.E. and by 1050 B.C.E. were posing a serious threat to the mountainous heartland of Israel. The Philistines had the advantage of oligarchic leadership, unlike the divisive Canaanite city-states, and their iron weaponry and mobile strike force made them effective fighters in the hill country.

Israel's intertribal movement toward social equality was incomplete at the dawn of the monarchy, frustrated largely by a failure in socioeconomic leveling and sharing. There are reports of priestly abuses (1 Sam. 2:12-17) and of bribery and perversion of justice (1 Sam. 8:1-3). That David could gather several hundred distressed and indebted followers during his period of social banditry (1 Sam. 22:1-2) suggests imbalances in wealth and lapses in the tribal mutual aid system. The struggles between the houses of Saul and David probably embodied efforts to monopolize leadership by coalitions of prosperous families and priesthoods in the two strongest areas of Israel.

Saul

The only certain functions of Saul as the first king of Israel were military, although he doubtless also had a role in cultic activities. Saul's major achievement was to drive back the Philistines for a season from the central hill country. In the end, he died in a crushing defeat by the Philistines, during a time when Israelite energies were badly divided in a dispute between Saul and one of his underlings, David.

During the Philistine emergency, Saul operated with a corps of seasoned Benjaminite warriors, to which the levies of other tribes were added as needed. He had a headquarters rather than a capital in the usual sense. There is no sign that he set up a state apparatus. In what appear to be the most ancient segments of the Saul traditions he is called *nāgîd*, "prince/commander," rather than *melek*, "king." The actual powers exercised make him appear more an intertribal military chieftain than a king in the usual ancient Near Eastern sense. On the other hand, it was early assumed that one of his sons should succeed him in office, a useful vehicle for powerful northern forces to insist on keeping the chieftainship/kingship in their hands rather than relinquish it to a southerner.

David

David emerged in the service of Saul, fled from the king when a split opened up between them, and, after Saul's death, returned to Judah to become its *nāgîd*. David prevailed when the tribal elders of the north, without a worthy son of Saul to rally around, joined the Judahites in a treaty with David as king of all Israel. Interpreters differ as to whether David was king over a single political entity Israel, or whether he joined the kingdoms of Israel and Judah in a personal union, mediated by his rule from the independently captured Canaanite city-state of Jerusalem.

David decisively defeated the Philistines and moved to establish a state apparatus with its administrative center at Jerusalem. He assured a Yahwistic significance for Jerusalem by bringing the ark of the confederacy to a tent shrine at the capital city (see pp. 120–23) and by appointing Abiathar and Zadok as state priests, who may have represented respectively the old Israelite and new Canaanite components of the state of Israel.

David is properly called "king" in several regards. He ruled over a territorial state that embraced Canaanites who had not been a part of the old intertribal confederacy. In a time when no sizable outside powers were contesting for control of the Syro-Palestinian corridor, he took the initiative in fighting offensive wars that extended Israelite domination over Transjordanian and Syrian states. He assembled the basic elements of a state administration. In all these respects he was fully a king. It appears, however, that he conducted a modest building program, raised his military levies by tribal mechanisms, and found it unnecessary to tax his Israelite-Canaanite subjects, since the state revenues required were drawn from foreign tribute.

FIG. 7.1 Head of King David. Limestone. Ca. 1150. Harris Brisbane Dick Fund, 1938 (38.18); The Metropolitan Museum of Art, New York. Photo: © The Metropolitan Museum of Art / Art Resource, N.Y.

FIG. 7.2 Walls and tower remains of the City of David. Photo: © Richard T. Nowitz/CORBIS.

Solomon

Solomon became successor to David after a bitter dynastic fight in which he had to forcibly suppress a powerful faction that backed his rival brother Adonijah. Opening his reign with an iron fist may have helped to stabilize his control in Judah and emboldened him to launch an ambitious program of political economy calculated to increase the wealth of his kingdom dramatically. His basic resources were the agricultural surpluses of peasants, which he supplemented by income from trade through tolls on caravans in transit and through shrewd commercial deals such as arms sales of Anatolian horses and Egyptian chariots to other states.

In order to secure his booming economic empire, he reached for military superiority by building massive fortifications, often with subjects forced into corvée labor gangs, and equipping large chariot forces. With his new-found wealth he built lavishly in Jerusalem, including a temple constructed on Phoenician lines[9] and a palace for himself that exceeded the temple in size. Before long, Solomon re-districted his kingdom and appointed officials in each of the new districts, thereby centralizing the command structure. By this new system he lavishly provisioned his court and also hoped to control or neutralize the dangerously powerful northern tribes.

Clearly Solomon was successful in securing a luxuried and privileged life for a small upper class in government and trade, but only with mutually contradictory policies that reduced agricultural production, as laborers were pulled off the land to serve in the army or to build fortifications. Economic advantage to the common people was marginal at best. Over the years whatever improvements in productivity occurred were vulnerable to siphoning off for the benefit of the already-bloated rich. Insofar as this familiar model of the hierarchic city-state was totally contrary to the simplicities of previous Israelite social organization, it fueled intense resentment and grievance, and eroded the morale of the people. The overextended and unevenly modernized Solomonic economy left the gaudy empire vulnerable to the rebellion of his own subjects.

Major Enduring Structural Effects of the Monarchy

The combined work of David and Solomon moved Israel a long distance from chieftainship to hierarchic kingship along a trajectory that catapulted Israel into the forefront of ancient Near Eastern states, facilitated by the lack of any major contender for international dominance at the time. The Solomonic bubble burst at his death when the empire split into two weaker core states after losing most of its extra-Palestinian territories. Nonetheless, the forms of state rule launched by David and maximized by Solomon set patterns that were continued in both kingdoms. Four structural changes had enduring interlocking consequences.

1. *Political centralization.* Israel had now become a state (and later would become two states) with taxing and conscripting powers and a monopoly of force over and above its people. These powers reached into the fields and villages to take crops and to conscript peasants for purposes decided by a small

FIG. 7.3. The ruins of the Roman city of Scythopolis, destroyed by an earthquake, lie in the foreground; the Stone Age Beth-Shean and Tel Beth-Shean, where Saul was slain, lie behind. Photo: © Erich Lessing / Art Resource, N.Y.

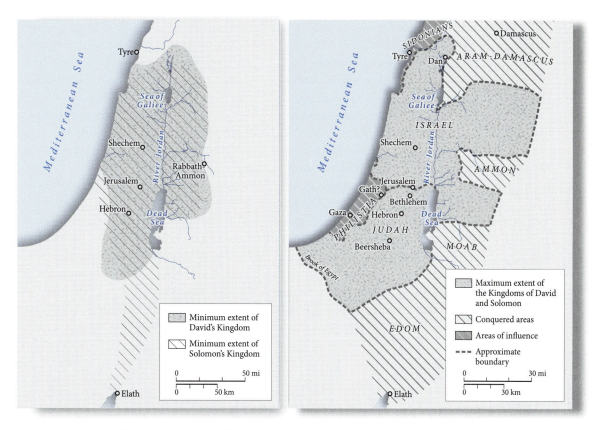

MAP 7.1. THE KINGDOMS OF DAVID AND SOLOMON

minority in the royal court rather than by tribal elders sifting the mind of the people for a consensus.

2. *Social stratification.* The monopoly of power in the new state was the monopoly of particular social groups. The state policy of deliberately transferring wealth from the mass of productive people to a parasitic nonproductive class spawned not only a stratum of government officials but also strata of enterprising merchants and landlords who gained affluence and status. These social divisions put severe strains upon the old economic and legal structures of Israel.

3. *Shifts in land tenure.* In the intertribal confederacy land had been held in perpetuity by extended families and could not be sold out of the family (see pp. 160–63). As entrepreneurial wealth accumulated, the upper class looked for investment opportunities, most likely in purchases of land and extensions of loans at interest within the administrative urban centers and among the Canaanite regions of Israel unpracticed in old Israelite law. In time, however, the acquisitive drive began to encroach on tribal institutions and ways of life. Gradually loans at interest were extended to needy Israelites and their property mortgaged; many of them ended up as tenant farmers, debt servants, or landless wage laborers. Tribal economic security and tribal religious identity were undermined, and the

social unity and political trust of the people put in radical doubt.

4. *Domestic repercussions of foreign trade, diplomacy, and war.* To be a state in the Syro-Palestinian corridor meant to be caught up in an international web of trade, diplomacy, and war. Under David and Solomon, Israel was at first amazingly successful in that political-military game. For brief periods during the divided monarchies similar successes fell to Israel and Judah. When one of the Israelite states grew aggressive or a foreign power intruded on them, however, the contradictory real interests of people came to the fore and the lengthening social divisions among them were aggravated by what amounted to a war of attrition against ordinary Israelites, who bore the brunt of their leaders' vaulting ambitions.

LITERARY CULTURE, RELIGIOUS CULT, AND IDEOLOGY

The Yahwist (J)

We have briefly characterized the J source of the Pentateuch (see p. 82) and listed its contents in Genesis 12–50 (see Web Table G) and in Exodus–Numbers (see Web Table H) as well as noted the possibility that J survives in conquest traditions such as Judges 1 (see pp. 141–45). For a full picture of the hypothetical Yahwist document one must include the appropriate passages in Genesis 2–11 (table 7.1).

The Yahwist fashioned a work of epic proportions that combines simplicity and grandeur. Single traditions and clusters of traditions, vividly shaped at an oral stage of composition, are joined in a great literary sweep of artfully arranged units and thematic emphases. Economy of expression and emotional restraint hold the story line in taut relief and mounting suspense. The Yahwist theologizes less by formal religious statement than by the linking of the stories and by the more or less direct way that the deity participates in or influences the action.

The J writer has an ample distinctive vocabulary: for example, "to know" as a euphemism for sexual intercourse; "to call upon the name of Yahweh" for worship of the deity; "to bless" as the beneficent action of deity toward humans and other creatures; "Canaanites" for the inhabitants of Palestine ("Amorites" in E); "Sinai" for the holy mountain (as in P, but "Horeb" in E); "Israel" for the third patriarch ("Jacob" in E).

The Yahwist also displays a wide-ranging interest in etiologies, especially reveling in popular etymologies of the names of persons and places, often cast in the form of puns: for example, Eve, "the mother of all living" (ḥawwāh, "Eve," resembles ḥay, "living," Gen. 3:20); Babel, where the tongues were confused (Babylonian babel/bab'ilu, "gate of God," resembles Hebrew bālal, "to confuse," Gen. 11:9). These fanciful associations of similar sounds and condensed word pictures are unreliable as actual etymologies, but they are wonderfully evocative of popular play with language.

Compared to later pentateuchal sources, which are more restrictedly religious in their concerns, J shows a far-ranging interest in the wider sociocultural and political situation of Israel, connecting the stories of the ancestors of Israel with traditions about the earliest pre-Israelites, reaching as far back as the traditional original human pair. The Yahwist relates the deeds of the ancestors of Israel with gusto, even when their behavior is question-

TABLE 7.1 YAHWIST (J) TRADITIONS IN GENESIS 2–11	
Creation of earth and the first human pair	2:4b—3:24
Cain and Abel	4:1-16
Genealogy of Cain (Kenites)	4:17-26
Genealogical fragment of Noah	5:29
Divine beings copulate with women to produce giants on earth	6:1-4
Destruction of Earth by flood	
Introduction: Devine decision to destroy	6:5-8
Body: Execution of the flood	7:1-5, 7-10, 12, 16b-17, 22-23 8:2b-3a, 6-7a, 8-12, 13b
Conclusion: Divine renunciation of ecological destruction	8:20-22
Noah's curse of Canaan (Ham?) and blessing on Shem and Japheth	9:18-27
Table of nations	10:8-19, 21, 24-30
Tower of Babel	11:1-9
Genealogy of Terah	11:28-30

able or blatantly reprehensible. For example, there is no flinching at the lie of Abraham (Gen. 12:10-20) or at Moses' rashness in killing the Egyptian overseer (Exod. 2:11-15). P seldom reveals such weaknesses in Israelite leaders, while E typically rationalizes or tones down these human blemishes.

The Yahwist stratum in the Pentateuch projects an intensely realistic conception or dramatization of God, shot through with descriptions of deity in terms of human physical features (anthropomorphisms) and feelings (anthropopathisms). Without abashment, the Yahwist pictures God strolling in the garden in the cool of the day (Gen. 3:8) and sealing the door of Noah's ark (7:15c). Also, Yahweh is evidently not all-knowing, but shows an experimental openness toward creation, abandoning one line of action for another as advisable, at times taxed to find new methods for coping with humans.

On the other hand, the Yahwist does not seem to make literalistic univocal assertions about deity. The Yahwist may be playfully ringing changes on an older, robust, even touchingly comic portrait of God as a forceful folk expression of divine presence and agency in the world. Yahweh is high god, not confused with nature spirits, but an overarching root metaphor of a living reality pictured necessarily in human imagery.

The Yahwist thus became the first Israelite writer to give extended graphic literary expression to a personal and transcendent mode of conceiving deity that has prevailed in popular Judaism and Christianity ever since.[10] On the whole, Yahweh is experienced as personal but not as mere creature, as the parent of all creatures without being sentimental, as respectful of human freedom without being impotent, as moral without being moralistic, and as strong-purposed without being dictatorial. Nonetheless, one must be extremely cautious in giving a profile of J's doctrine of God, since the stories vary markedly in the words, actions, and attributes assigned to deity and contain virtually no direct theological reflection.

The J story of creation treats questions of human powers and limits in a form intelligible to the simplest mind, yet tantalizing to the wisest. The sociocultural viewpoint is that of a Palestinian peasant, for ʾādām, "the human being," shaped from the dust as "a living being," a body-spirit totality, is none other than the cultivator of the ʾadāmāh, "the ground/soil." Life depends on the fickle dews and rains rather than on the irrigation waters of the great river valleys. Chaos is waterless waste.

The story does not permit any simplistic equation of work or sexuality with sin and its punishment. The human being already works before disobeying Yahweh, and the man and woman share bodily union before their defiance of Yahweh. Indeed, the story has little technical theological language: "fall," "sin," "disobedience," "punishment," "freedom" are not words that occur in it at all. With respect to the relation of the sexes, the narrative strongly implies that prior to 2:21 Adam is asexual (or intersexual?), that is, the inclusive human being, who only becomes specifically "man" when "woman" is simultaneously created through dividing this single hermaphroditic human into its respective sexual halves.

Coequality of man and woman is expressed, and in many respects the woman is shown as more intelligent and resourceful than the man. The imposition of man's "rule" over woman (3:16) is presented as a reprehensible lapsed condition that might be overcome through a restored relation of the human pair with Yahweh. Nevertheless, later Jewish and Christian exegesis has tended to read the story through male chauvinist eyes that blame woman disproportionately for the disobedience, even associating eating the fruit with sexuality itself and playing on the misogynist theme of woman as temptress.

This elusive fall story may have been more combed for meaning than any other passage in the Hebrew Bible. Surprisingly, however, the exegetical and theological tradition that has labored over its meaning was very slow in developing. The first speculation occurs in postbiblical Judaism (2 Esdras) and in early Christianity (Paul), tracing a connection between the sin of the first human pair and the subsequent sin of all humans, and Christian orthodoxy later developed a metaphor into the ironclad doctrine of original sin.

What the discourse of the story means in its own terms remains elusive. For instance, the import of the tree of the knowledge of good and evil has been endlessly discussed. The Yahwist was probably not thinking mainly of moral judgment but of the secrets of divine knowledge and power, which humans cannot possess but can and will strive after and tap into both creatively and destructively. The agency of discord between Yahweh and the humans and between the man and the woman is personified in the serpent, who is not diabolical and malicious so much as shrewd and crafty, sowing doubt about received judgments and arousing thirst for knowledge and control. He is certainly not equated with Satan, a much later figure in Israelite thought (see pp. 325–26).

The main tenor of the story has been perceived as the legitimation of Yahweh's behavior and the guilt of the human rebels. The story, however, has a strong undercurrent that at least tacitly commends the human pair for gaining knowledge, without which history outside the garden could never have begun.

The unresolved inner divisions of the story have been exposed in a recent structuralist analysis following Greimas's actantial model (see p. 125).[11] Yahweh is shown to be functioning in the deep structure of the story in such a way as to occupy three roles that are expressly conflicted: sender, helper, and opponent. This reading gives a narrativized parallel to the theological enigmas that have built up around the story. Yahweh's conflicted roles are ways of alluding to the unresolved problems about divine justice and power and about human freedom that are posed by the prohibition and the punishment for its violation. One can say that we have a theological puzzle because we have a narrative program in which Yahweh appears to have put himself and the human pair in a no-win situation hedged by a double bind. Message one reads: "Don't eat the fruit! Stay here in the garden! But of course then you will not 'know,' and human life in the real world will never begin!" Message two reads: "Do eat the fruit! Gain knowledge and start living in the historical world! But of course then you will live a frustrated and limited life lacking the social harmony and physical abundance of the garden!"

Beginning with the analysis of the Yahwist by Gerhard von Rad,[12] scholars have greatly stressed the architectural design of the traditions as arranged and linked by this inventive compiler-author. In the case of Genesis 1–11, the effect is to underscore the step-by-step deterioration of the human situation. There is an increase of sin and suffering that parallels the increase of human knowledge and skill in the episodic movement from the garden, through the Cain and Abel and flood stories, to the Tower of Babel. The inventiveness of humans does not gain unalloyed blessing but leads to social discord and violence, and Yahweh punishes these early humans.

At the same time another line of development is interwoven with the first. Yahweh mitigates each punitive intervention with mercy in the sense that Yahweh assures that human life will go forward toward new opportunities and possibilities, for example, clothing the first human pair or sparing Noah from death in the flood.

The spread of human sin issues in a catastrophic flood that nearly undoes creation altogether. Here the Yahwist is explicitly dependent on Mesopotamian traditions: (1) a Sumerian version where the counterpart of Noah is Ziusudra (see Web Table A, 1G); (2) an older Babylonian version with the hero Atrahasis (see Web Table A, 1I); and (3) a somewhat later Babylonian version contained in the longer Gilgamesh Epic in which Utnapishtim survives the flood (see Web Table A, 1H). Most likely, J was familiar with the third version of the flood and possibly also with the second (P's acquaintance with the Atrahasis version is more explicit [see pp. 273–79]). As for attempts to demonstrate an ancient universal flood lying behind these traditions, there is simply no geological evidence that the entire Tigris-Euphrates region, much less the inhabited world, was ever inundated at once.[13] It is possible that flood in these myths is a metaphor for military invasion and political collapse.[14] Nor is there any basis for crediting claims to have recovered remains of the ark on Mount Ararat.[15] Many of the same formal elements appear in the Mesopotamian and biblical flood stories, although the differing J and P flood accounts express the divine action in much more reflective moral and theological categories by underscoring human sin and divine judgment and mercy. Nonetheless, the seed features of the Israelite flood traditions are all present in the older prototypes.

Early phases of historical-critical study stressed the work of J as a collector and editor of old stories and poems, whose small units and oral tradition roots were subsequently studied intensively by form criticism (see pp. 63–65, 90). Around the mid-twentieth century, the position gained currency that the Yahwist was an original writer who shaped the ancient materials to stress the judging and saving activity of Israel's God over the span of time from creation to the conquest of Canaan. The Yahwist is now widely dated to the Solomonic enlightenment, more or less contemporary with the Court History of David, and expressive of a robust confidence that providence rules in the sometimes clouded acts and motives of human beings.

There is merit in viewing J as an etiology of the Davidic monarchy toward which the promises to the patriarchs are said to point (e.g., Gen. 15:17-19), and sometimes as a measured warning to the Davidic dynasty: beware of excessive human, even kingly, pride! If the early monarchy provided the cultural and technical literary conditions for writing the J document, the extent of its intended reference to the monarchy is much more difficult to ascertain.

While various counterproposals to this dating for J have yet to be taken into account fully, the political geography of J appears to fit most appropriately into the tenth-to-ninth-century horizon. On the other hand, a supposed programmatic theological unity in the Yahwist has probably been overstated, and one should also recognize that some elements in J may derive from the eighth or seventh century, or possibly even later.

Psalms and Wisdom

The present book of Psalms (see pp. 302–10) and the wisdom writings (see pp. 319–28) are manifestly postexilic in their existing shapes. It is evident, however, that songs and wisdom writings were very ancient literary types in the Israelite milieu. The centralized cultic and court institutions introduced by David and Solomon provided opportune settings for psalmic and wisdom literature to be cultivated by royal officials. This royal sponsorship of psalmody and wisdom was expressed in the traditions of David as psalmist and Solomon as sage. The headings to the psalms claiming Davidic authorship are late and unreliable, as are also the attribution of wisdom books, such as Proverbs, Ecclesiastes, and Song of Songs, to Solomon. Certain psalms (such as the royal psalms, e.g., 2; 18; 20–21; 45) and some proverbs (among the collections in Prov. 10:1—31:31), however, reveal preexilic monarchic references and codes of conduct typical of high court officials. These royal-oriented texts are very instructive about the general ethos and culture of the upper-class circles, among whom the wise mixed the symbolic concreteness of Yahwism with more aesthetic and cosmopolitan concerns.

David and Zion Traditions

We have called attention to a key DH interpretive passage in 2 Samuel 7 that grants the promise of an "everlasting" dynasty to David (table III.1, 2). The language and concepts of this Davidic promise are far older than DH (and in tension with DH's overall outlook), as is evident in older psalms (e.g., Psalms 89; 132) and in eighth-century prophecies (Isa. 9:6-7; 11:1-5; Mic. 5:2-5).

It is now common to distinguish a Davidic covenant of a *promissory type* from a Mosaic covenant of an *obligatory type* (see pp. 115–16), each as it were contesting the same ideological-institutional ground: either the national life is unequivocally assured by Yahweh (Davidic covenant), or it is problematically conditional on proven loyalty to Yahweh (Mosaic covenant). Others view the two concepts as operative in different spheres, either harmonistically (*if* the nation is faithful and endures, *this* is the dynasty that will rule in it) or formally unrelated (*granted* that the nation exists in which there are various possible candidates and claimants for royal office, *this* dynasty alone will rule because of entitlement by divine promise). The promise to David has been shown to resemble the ancient Near Eastern genre of a royal grant by a king to a faithful servant, as in the decree of Hattusilis, the Hittite monarch, to his chief scribe, Mittannamuwa.[16] The motif of disciplining the grantee, or his successors, as wayward sons is consistent with the irrevocable grant. A similar unconditional premise in promises to the patriarchs has often been underscored, and the covenant with Abraham (Genesis 15) is frequently viewed as a typological foreshadowing of the covenant with David.

Other interpreters believe that the pervasiveness of a Davidic covenant notion has been overstated; in fact, the term "covenant" is rather infrequent in these promissory royal texts. They claim that the dynastic promise was only one of a number of motifs of royal theology, which included traditions about Zion (= Jerusalem) as the unshakable earthly abode of Yahweh. By means of David's choice of Jerusalem as his capital, these motifs mingled in complex ways within the royal cult and the literature of psalms and prophets. The nature of the monarchic cult in Jerusalem, how it conceived and celebrated kingship, has been much debated in relation to similarities and differences between Israelite and Canaanite/ancient Near Eastern concepts of the king vis-à-vis deity.

Whatever the exact delineations of genres and motifs concerning kingship at Jerusalem, it is clear that various positive religious evaluations of the office within Judah were developed, no doubt beginning with Davidic-Solomonic times. In one way or another the Judahite kings were judged to be (1) in a distinctive filial relation to Yahweh; (2) intermediaries between Yahweh and the people; (3) exemplars of piety and obedience to Yahweh; and (4) executors of Yahweh's justice domestically and among the nations. From these roots sprang the later messianism associated with the Davidic dynasty.

David and Zion traditions were henceforth to retain a crucial place in Israelite self-reflection. For some, they were unequivocal supports for resting unqualified hopes of security in the triumphal Israelite state or Jewish restored community. For others, they were ambiguous symbols of hope that required tempering in the larger context of Mosaic and prophetic sociotheological judgment. Many of the social organizational, cultic, and ideological conflicts that we will trace in following chapters were focused on how the disputants read the promises of Yahweh about David and Zion.

NOTES

1. Patrick D. Miller Jr. and J. J. M. Roberts, *The Hand of the Lord: A Reassessment of the 'Ark Narrative' of 1 Samuel,* Johns Hopkins Near Eastern Studies (Baltimore: Johns Hopkins University Press, 1977).

2. J. Maxwell Miller, "Saul's Rise to Power: Some Observations concerning 1 Sam. 9:1–10:16; 10:26–11:15 and 13:2–14:46," *CBQ* 36 (1974): 157–74; W. Lee Humphreys, "The Rise and Fall of King Saul: A Study of an Ancient Stratum in 1 Samuel," *JSOT* 18 (1980): 74–90.

3. P. Kyle McCarter Jr., "The History of David's Rise," in *I Samuel,* AB 8 (Garden City, N.Y.: Doubleday, 1980), 27–30.

4. Bruce C. Birch, *The Rise of the Israelite Monarchy: The Growth and Development of 1 Samuel 7–15,* SBLDS 27 (Missoula, Mont.: Scholars Press, 1976); McCarter, *I Samuel,* 18–23.

5. Gerhard von Rad, "The Beginnings of Historical Writing in Ancient Israel," in *The Problem of the Hexateuch and Other Essays,* trans. E. W. Trueman Dicken (Edinburgh: Oliver & Boyd, 1966), 166–204 (originally published 1944).

6. R. N. Whybray, *The Succession Narrative,* SBT 2/9 (London: SCM, 1968), 50–55.

7. Ibid., 56–116.

8. David M. Gunn, *The Story of King David: Genre and Interpretation*, JSOTSup 6 (Sheffield: JSOT Press, 1978), chap. 3.

9. W. F. Stinespring ("Temple, Jerusalem," in *IDB* 4:534–60) includes illustrated ground plans, drawings, and models, all of which are necessarily hypothetical reconstructions; for an update on comparative archaeological data see Jean Ouellette, "Temple of Solomon," in *IDBSup,* 872–74. Carol L. Meyers ("The Elusive Temple," *BA* 5 [1982]: 33–41) emphasizes considerable changes over time in the structure and furnishings of the Solomonic temple due to economic, political, and religious factors.

10. Dale Patrick (*The Rendering of God in the Old Testament,* OBT 10 [Philadelphia: Fortress Press, 1981]) develops the biblical depiction of deity as a dramatis persona and notes of Genesis 1–11 that "here at the beginning . . . the style and tone of biblical God-language is set" (15).

11. David Jobling, "The Myth Semantics of Genesis 2:4b–3:24," *Semeia* 18 (1980): 41–49.

12. Gerhard von Rad, *Genesis: A Commentary,* trans. John H. Marks, OTL (Philadelphia: Westminster, 1961), 23–30, and *Old Testament Theology,* trans. D. M. G. Stalker, 2 vols. (New York: Harper & Row, 1962–1965), 1:48–56, 136–65.

13. André Parrot, *The Flood and Noah's Ark* (London: SCM, 1955).

14. Thorkild Jacobsen, "The Eridu Genesis," *JBL* 100 (1981): 526–27.

15. Lloyd R. Bailey, *Where Is Noah's Ark?* (Nashville: Abingdon, 1978).

16. Moshe Weinfeld, "Covenant, Davidic," in *IDBSup,* 190.

FOR FURTHER READING

Finkelstein, Israel, and Neil Asher Silberman. *David and Solomon: In Search of the Bible's Sacred Kings and the Roots of the Western Tradition.* New York: Free Press, 2006.

Halpern, Baruch. *David's Secret Demons: Messiah, Murderer, Traitor, King.* Grand Rapids: Eerdmans, 2001.

Handy, Lowell K., ed. *The Age of Solomon: Scholarship at the Turn of the Millennium.* Leiden: Brill, 1997.

Kille, D. Andrew. "Exploring Genesis" and "A Myth of Human Maturation: Developmental Readings." In *Psychological Biblical Criticism*, 39–55, 109–24. Guides to Biblical Scholarship. Minneapolis: Fortress Press, 2001.

McKenzie, Steven L. *King David: A Biography.* Oxford: Oxford University Press, 2000.

QUESTIONS FOR STUDY

1. What is the Prophetic History? Explain its connection to 1 and 2 Samuel and the DH.
2. How did David and Solomon contribute to the political development of the kingdom of Israel?
3. Describe the Yahwist's portrayal of the character of Yahweh. What aspects of Yahweh are emphasized? Why is it problematic to draw conclusions about the Yahwist's theological views?

TRADITIONS ABOUT THE NORTHERN KINGDOM

SUMMARY

The shape of the traditions in
  1 Kings 12—2 Kings 17
Sources, including prophetic narratives
The history of the northern kingdom
Its major dynasties
Its relations with Judah
Literary culture and prophetic critique:
  Elijah, Amos, Hosea

READ THE BIBLICAL TEXT

1 Kings 12—2 Kings 17
Amos
Hosea

*See additional materials at fortresspress.com/
gottwald;* consult Carta Bible Atlas *maps 118–51.*

THE SHAPE OF THE TRADITIONS IN 1 KINGS 12—2 KINGS 17

Source Statistics

Our DH sources on the independent northern kingdom of Israel and the parallel kings (and one queen) of southern Judah, extending over 209 years, are composed of the two kinds of traditions identified for the united monarchy (see Web Table K): annalistic political-historical documentation and miscellaneous literary traditions (see pp. 175–76).

As with the united monarchy, we encounter sparseness of sources and unequal distributions of verses by types of sources. Annalistic political-historical documentation from DH for the total of thirty-one rulers in both kingdoms over two hundred years (140 verses) is less than the same sort of documentation for Solomon (162 verses), who ruled a maximum of forty years.

Especially striking are the meager data on kings otherwise judged to have been of major political importance: Jeroboam I (10 verses), Omri (5 verses), Ahab (4 verses), Jehu (2 verses), and Jeroboam II (2 verses) in Israel; and Jehoshaphat (4 verses DH; 10 verses Chronicles) and Uzziah (3 verses DH; 10 verses Chronicles) in Judah. Constant mention is made of the chronicles of the kings of Israel and Judah, evidently the source for the annalistic comments of DH, but these official records of the two kingdoms were patchily and arbitrarily excerpted by DH.

Prophetic Narratives

The accounts of the northern kings are expanded by miscellaneous literary traditions, the great majority being stories about prophets, which selectively illuminate aspects of the reigns of certain kings: for example, *Ahijah of Shiloh* in the reign of Jeroboam I (1 Kgs. 11:26-40; 14:1-17); *Elijah the Tishbite* in the reigns of Ahab and Ahaziah (1 Kings 17—2 Kgs. 2:12); and *Elisha ben Shaphat* in the reigns of Jehoram, Jehu, Jehoahaz, and Jehoash (1 Kgs. 19:19-21; 2 Kings 2–10; 13:14-21).

Many of the prophetic stories carry overt military-political content that focuses on changes of dynasty, battles, and confrontations between kings and prophets. The account of Jehu's purge of the Omri dynasty, triggered by Elisha, is full and vivid, but concerning Jehu's twenty-eight-year rule over Israel we have not a shred of biblical information identified as such (see pp. 196–98). Since many of the kings in these prophetic stories are not named, the royal subjects cannot be taken for granted in all cases merely on the strength of the DH placement of the stories. Many interpreters are of the view that some or all of the prophetic traditions assigned to the reign of Jehoram, last ruler of the Omri dynasty, and even some assigned to Ahab, actually belong to the following Jehu dynasty.

The prophetic narratives as a whole disclose varying supportive and critical stances of prophets toward kings, and vice versa, but it is not always clear how to transpose the moral-theological judgments of the prophetic stories and messages into the terms of military and political policies in the conduct of state. The excerpted chronicles of the two kingdoms and the prophetic narratives move on two different levels of narration and interpretation that often fail to meet at a point of common discourse.

The form and style of the prophetic stories show affinities with the sagas of Genesis through Numbers (Web Table B, also 20–21; see pp. 90, 105–6), and some of them are legends in the technical sense of celebrating the wonderful powers of a prophet. The stories appear to have been shaped and passed on (written down?) in circles or schools of prophets.

Other Sources: Prophetic Books and the Elohist

All of the prophets discussed above are presented by DH in narratives told *about* them, within which some of their brief messages are enclosed. The first books actually written *by* prophets are those of Amos and Hosea in the mid-eighth century. In these books the relation of narrative and speech is reversed: collections of prophetic words enclose brief narrative passages. The information that can be gleaned from Amos and Hosea concerning the specific history of Israel in its last decades is minimal. But both writings, even though strongly colored by their critical outlooks, are of high value in disclosing aspects of the socioeconomic, political, and religious life firsthand.

Finally, it is to this period in Israel's history that the Elohist is assigned (see pp. 200–201), presenting a northern version of the traditions that the Yahwist rendered in a southern version. The E source shows many affinities with the Elijah-Elisha traditions and with the prophet Hosea (see pp. 205–6). It is most likely to be dated in the late Omri or early Jehu dynasties.

History of the Northern Kingdom and Its Relations with Judah (931–722 b.c.e.)

The Schism (931 b.c.e.)

The immediate cause of the breakup of the united kingdom was the oppressive economic and political policies of Solomon (see pp. 181–82). Revolt broke out among the labor battalions of Ephraim led by Jeroboam, who became the first king of the north. The larger background of this political split was the long rivalry between Judah and Ephraim-Manasseh-Benjamin as the two major power centers in the old confederacy.

Jeroboam and Baasha Dynasties (931–884 b.c.e.)

The basic structures of dynastic kingship seem to have been adopted over time in the new northern kingdom. There were difficulties in settling on a suitable capital. The main data on Jeroboam I concern his replacement of the Jerusalem temple cult with sanctuaries at Dan and Bethel, where he introduced golden calf worship. The calves, however, were probably symbolic throne supports for Yahweh and no more idolatrous than the cosmic imagery in Solomon's temple. Jeroboam installed his own priests with a new schedule of festivals. These measures were intended to give his kingdom independence from Judah.

Details concerning the internal administration of Israel are lacking. Jeroboam would have required at least modest taxes, but a limited building program may have forestalled the need to reintroduce corvée. Since the first monarch of the north inherited Solomon's military and administrative structures in his territory, the extent to which they were revised or dropped will have depended greatly on the disaffection of the peasants, whom Jeroboam rode to power.

In the fifth year of Jeroboam and Rehoboam, a destructive military campaign by Pharaoh Shishak of Egypt seriously depleted both kingdoms and further prevented a clear military victory of either Israel or Judah over the other. Another struggle, this one between Israel and the now-independent Arameans of Damascus, began during Baasha's rule and went on intermittently throughout the ninth century.

To the south, Judah's most urgent immediate problem, after the withdrawal of the northern tribes, was to secure its position defensively. Rehoboam constructed a chain of fortresses to protect his kingdom. Because Jerusalem was so close to the northern border, Judah under Asa succeeded in pushing the border about nine miles north of Jerusalem to provide a buffer zone for defense of the Judean capital.

Omri Dynasty (880–841 B.C.E.)

Omri was the product of a military coup, but to gain the throne he had to prevail in a civil war against "half of the people," who followed Tibni (1 Kgs. 16:21). It is possible that the Tibni faction pressed for a limited monarchy, while the Omri faction favored a more centralized monarchy. On becoming king, Omri launched an ambitious Davidic-Solomonic type of reign by establishing an opulent new capital at Samaria and developing military and trade alliances with Phoenicia, Damascus, and Judah. He and his son Ahab were eminently successful in raising Israel's status in international politics.

During Omri's dynasty the first sustained prophetic opposition to Israel's kings is reported. Elijah and Elisha mounted criticisms that focused on the penetration of Baal worship into Ahab's court by way of the king's marriage to a Phoenician princess, Jezebel (see pp. 201–2). How far this worship penetrated among the masses of Israelites is problematic, but the very espousal of Baal and Yahweh worship side by side in the royal court was in itself abhorrent to these exclusive Yahwists. Also, we begin to hear of socioeconomic abuses that included the expropriation of free Israelites' property.

The burgeoning Omrides made peace with Judah, sealed by the marriage of the Judahite Jehoram to the daughter (or sister) of Ahab, Athaliah. Another Judahite ruler, Jehoshaphat, is said to have reorganized the administration of justice in Judah with a new court system centralized from Jerusalem.

Jehu Dynasty (841–752 B.C.E.)

Jehu came to power in a military coup sparked by the prophetic support of Elisha. He stamped out the practices of Baal religion in court circles and ruthlessly killed all representatives and influential supporters of the Omri dynasty, including Phoenician and Judahite royalty. But early in his reign he submitted to the Assyrian king Shalmaneser III and paid heavy tribute. Wars with Damascus went badly for Israel until reasserted Assyrian pressure on Damascus freed Israel for a revival of power in the first half of the eighth century.

If the prophetic program of Elijah-Elisha was to restore exclusive Yahweh worship, to avoid all foreign alliances because they entailed recognition of foreign gods, and to maintain old practices and institutions of socioeconomic equality, the prophetic forces must have been disappointed in Jehu. He did extirpate Baal worship in Israel and broke off Omride foreign ties, but he immediately submitted to Assyria, which meant the formal acknowledgment of Assyrian gods, and there is no evidence that he improved the socioeconomic conditions of the common people.

Jehu's coup also had repercussions to the south, when the purge of the Omrides also swept away the Judahite king Ahaziah. At this point Ahaziah's mother Athaliah took the throne and allegedly attempted to extirpate the entire line of David. It is more likely, however, that Athaliah was serving as guardian and royal stand-in for her underage grandson Jehoash.

With Damascus and Assyria both weakened in the first half of the eighth century, first Jehoash and then Jeroboam II were able to reign over a peaceful and increasingly prosperous Israel, while a period of similar accomplishment was enjoyed by Judah under Amaziah and Uzziah. From the book of Amos we learn, however, that the prosperity and national confidence were experienced chiefly at

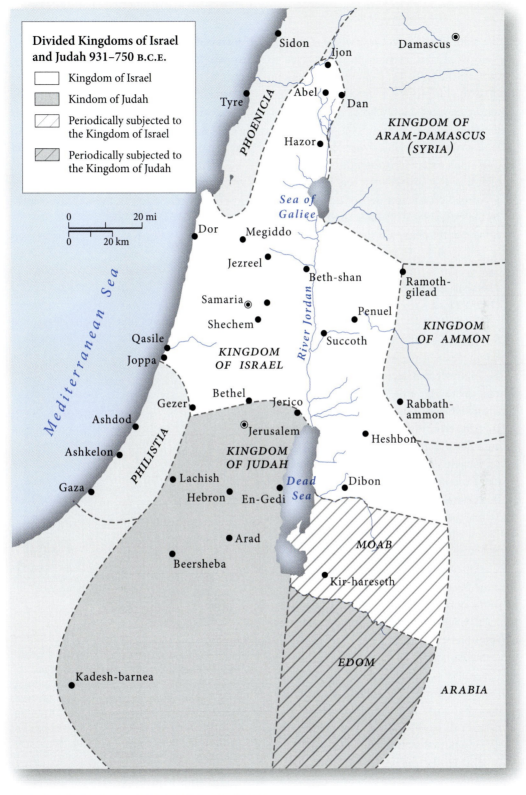

MAP 8.1 DIVIDED KINGDOMS OF ISRAEL AND JUDAH

the summit of the society, whereas the majority of peasants were in dire straits (see pp. 202–4). The particular focus of Amos is on the massive shift in land tenure from traditionally guaranteed family holdings to privately amassed estates taken over by debt foreclosures on impoverished farmers. In short, as in Solomon's united kingdom, the "wonders" of eighth-century Israel were concentrated in a privileged class who rose to their advantages by the systematic deprivation and disempowerment of the peasant majority.

Collapse of the Northern Kingdom (752–722 B.C.E.)

Solomon's nemesis had been internal revolt; the nemesis of the northern state proved to be a renascent Assyria that launched attacks into Syria-Palestine. The assassination of Zechariah ended the Jehu dynasty. Menahem tried to secure his place on the throne with an enormous payment to Assyria, raised by a tax on Israelite landholders, a tax that probably helped to spur an anti-Assyrian reaction led by Pekah with Rezon of Damascus. Israel and Damascus pressured Ahaz of Judah to join them, which provoked the so-called Syro-Ephraimite War between Israel and Judah.

Ahaz appealed to Assyria, and Assyria attacked Damascus and Israel, and turned most of the northern kingdom into Assyrian provinces, leaving a greatly reduced Israelite state. A final rebellion against Assyria by Hoshea led to the capture of Samaria, deportation of its upper classes, and an end to the independent kingdom of Israel. The climate of desperation and civil strife that pervaded the last three decades of Israel's independence is forcefully communicated in the embittered words of the prophet Hosea (see pp. 205–6).

Patterns of Development in the Two Kingdoms

Generalizations about the course of development in the two kingdoms are hampered by sketchy and uneven sources. To all outward appearances, Judah was a far more stable kingdom than Israel. During the two hundred years of the kingdom of Israel, there were twelve Davidic rulers in the south (excepting

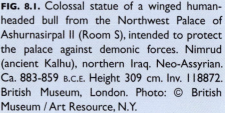
FIG. 8.1. Colossal statue of a winged human-headed bull from the Northwest Palace of Ashurnasirpal II (Room S), intended to protect the palace against demonic forces. Nimrud (ancient Kalhu), northern Iraq. Neo-Assyrian. Ca. 883-859 B.C.E. Height 309 cm. Inv. 118872. British Museum, London. Photo: © British Museum / Art Resource, N.Y.

FIG. 8.2. A tower in the fortifications of Samaria (Shomron), capital of the northern kingdom of Israel after King Omri abandoned his former capital Tirza. Omri's son Ahab and Jezebel, his wife, built a temple for Baal in Samaria (I Kings 22:39). Photo: Erich Lessing / Art Resource, N.Y.

Athaliah) and nineteen northern rulers distributed through five dynasties (counting Menahem-Pekahiah as a dynasty). The acid test, of course, was that Judah survived, whereas Israel came to an end.

The relative strength of the two kingdoms has been estimated and accounted for in various ways. One explanation is that Judah adhered to a dynastic principle of leadership, whereas Israel tried to operate with the old charismatic principle of leadership. Thus each change of rule offered the potential for turbulence. While the Prophetic History in 1 Samuel 8–15 seems to imply such a charismatic program (see pp. 177–79), it is not likely that it was ever undertaken as a recognized scheme of government, as everywhere in our sources

it seems assumed that an able king will found a dynasty.[1]

A more probable explanation of northern turbulence is geopolitical. Judah was a geographically compact area, separated from other regions and nations. By contrast, the northern tribes were sprawled over a larger territory, more difficult for centralized rule, but more open and inviting to foreign powers, who eyed its strategic communication routes and its rich grain crops. For a king to succeed in Israel, given Israel's exposure to other powers as well as its severe regional factionalism, he probably had to satisfy a far-wider range of vested interests than any southern king. The practical result was that the more homogeneous leading families in Judah could close ranks in support of one royal lineage more readily than the diversified leading families of the north, who tended to fight out their different interests politically.

One should also not overlook that Judah retained a tremendous asset by being the home ground of the illustrious dynasty of David and Solomon, with whom any alternative claimant for leadership would face comparison. By contrast, the northern kingdom had to start from scratch in its more difficult geopolitical context. As for Judah's survival after Israel's collapse, if anything spared Judah, it was Ahaz's decision to cooperate with Assyria and not join the Israelite-Damascus rebels.

An even more concrete political organizational factor seems to have worked very much to Judah's advantage. From the time of Asa, Judahite monarchs began the practice of forming coregencies. An incumbent king would designate his successor and involve him in practical affairs of state as coruler. This both assured the exact line of succession and trained the next king for his eventual sole exercise of office. In contrast, there seems to have been only one coregency in Israel.

LITERARY CULTURE, RELIGION, AND PROPHETIC CRITIQUE

The Elohist (E)

The E source has been briefly characterized (see pp. 82–83), its contents listed in Genesis 12–50 (Web Table G) and in Exodus–Numbers (Web Table H). It has also been observed that E probably survives in conquest traditions such as Joshua 1–12 (see pp. 141–45). It remains to elaborate E's literary features, leading motifs, basic perspective, and setting in life.

The vocabulary of E is set off clearly from J and P at many points of variance: for example, "Amorites" for the inhabitants of the land ("Canaanites" in J); "Jacob" for the third patriarch ("Israel" in J); "Horeb" for the holy mountain ("Sinai" in J and P); and the temporal use of "after these things" in narration (in J, "after this manner"). "The River" designates the Euphrates, and *ba'al* is used of a man as "master" or "husband." Stylistically the Elohist has a fondness for repetitions, especially in direct address: "Abraham, Abraham!" (Gen. 22:11) and "Moses, Moses!" (Exod. 3:4). "Here I am!" is a favored expression on the lips of one replying to a divine or human superior.

The Elohist's moral and religious consciousness is given explicit articulation in a series of emphases that distinguish his work from the Yahwist. The moral imperfections of the ancestors of Israel, which J did not hesitate to tell straight out, are glossed over or explained as appropriate in context. Abraham's lie is mitigated by the notation that Sarah was after all his half sister, thus presumably a permissible marriage partner, or at the very least Abraham was technically truthful (Gen. 20:12).

The ritual interest is more pronounced in E than in J. In the latter, the various altars raised at open-air sanctuaries are memorial in nature and never described as places of sacrifice, while in E these altars are explicitly used for offerings. Among the abundant instances of ritual practice are the call of Abraham to sacrifice his son (22:1-2) and Jacob's pouring oil on the stone pillar at Bethel (28:18).

Over all, the Elohist tends to draw moral conclusions and to admonish readers more freely than the Yahwist. There is more explicit teaching, but it is often skillfully introduced on the lips of chief participants in the story. Joseph, for example, warmly attests to the providential purposes of God when he consoles his brothers (Gen. 45:7; 50:20), while the deity elusively explains the new divine name Yahweh in answer to Moses' puzzlement (Exod. 3:13-15).

The Elohist emphasizes the status of Israel as a religious community in the sense that the total national life of Israel is grounded in faithful adherence to Yahweh through a purified cult and obedience to the fundamental laws traditionally connected with Moses. It is widely thought that the earliest form of the laws, the so-called Covenant Code (Exod. 20:22—23:19), was preserved in the E source (see pp. 117–18). In some respects E retains more aspects of the premonarchic pool of tradition than does J (see p. 84) and reflects the origins of Yahwism in northern Israel among the Joseph tribes. In E there is simply not the same focus on land and state that there is in J. The impetus to return to the deepest foundations of community, and thus not to be restricted or misled by hierarchic state structures, is strongly articulated in E by means of a confidence in the whole people as recipients of Yahweh's judgment and grace.

The style and motifs of E have a preaching flavor. The danger of apostasy is frequently sounded in company with a call to repentance and obedience. There is a stress on the proper fearful approach to God in observing correct cult forms and in noting the various ways that Yahweh communicates with humans in rituals, dreams, and visions and through divinely sent messengers. The aim of all this cultic theology is changed public life. In spite of the majesty and wrath of Yahweh, the God of Israel is incredibly patient, constantly inviting the people to turn and renew itself.

How, then, did E enter the larger traditions

that would become the Hebrew Bible? The joining of J and E occurred in Judah after the fall of Israel in 722 B.C.E. in a milieu where other bodies of north Israelite traditions (Elijah-Elisha stories, Prophetic History of the origins of the monarchy, and core materials in Deuteronomy) were salvaged from the political ruin of the north and entered into the stream of southern literary and religious culture. Because the JE redaction project was controlled by southerners, J was employed as the ground plan of the redaction, and E materials were severely reduced and used to supplement J.

The date and life setting of E are difficult to determine. E presupposes a dire situation of religious apostasy so great as to threaten the continuation of the nation. The Omri dynasty would satisfy that situation admirably, but hardly exclusively, considering that the stories of Elijah-Elisha and the words of Amos suggest that the Jehu dynasty failed to live up to its initial prospect.

Because E keeps its distance from state structures, it is not likely that it was written in court circles as often hypothesized for its southern counterpart J. The prophetic circles responsible for Elijah-Elisha stories and the book of Hosea (probably also for the Prophetic History) approximate the motifs and language of E. It may also have originated in covenant-renewal contexts, among Yahwistically committed landed families and priests or Levites preserving old covenant and law traditions behind Deuteronomy.[2]

Elijah and Elisha

The Elijah-Elisha stories are a rich reservoir of popular stories about conflicts over military and political policies between prophets and kings, and also of marvel or problem-resolution stories that tell how prophets met the basic life needs of common folk who were suffering under government abuse and famine. The bearers of these stories must have been active propagators of Yahweh allegiance and consistent opponents of Baal, who suffered from famine, sickness, poverty, and expropriation of their land, and who doubted the capacity of the Omri (and Jehu?) dynasty to reliably initiate the necessary cult and social praxis.

The Elisha stories have to do with scarcity of food, shelter, and tools, both among prophetic communities and the rural populace at large. The elaborated legend of 2 Kgs. 4:11-37 and 8:1-6 implies that the prophetic miracles were performed on behalf of weak and endangered members of prophetic groups and their supporters in cases with no relief from king or law courts. The Elijah-Elisha stories may even be stories intended to advocate the cause of Yahwists wronged by Israelite officials, victims repeatedly brought to the attention of the established leadership by prophetic intervention.

From this angle the bearers of the Elijah-Elisha stories look like religious formations at the lower fringes of society that functioned as rescue stations and advocacy groups. The underside of Israelite life was filling up with more and more people pushed out of the old protective tribal structures by political centralization and social stratification.

Amos

The nine chapters of the book of Amos present a stunning array of literary traditions. The work divides into clearly distinguishable sections. Oracles against various nations form a closely constructed series, each introduced by a set formula (chaps. 1–2). A collection of judgment speeches against the northern kingdom is punctuated by the formula "Hear this word!" (chaps. 3–6). A sequence of vision reports about impending judgment is interrupted both by a narrative report and by further judgment speeches (7:1—9:6). The book concludes with a threat of total destruction, softened by assurance to righteous individuals and expanded into a promise of national restoration (9:7-15).

There is a sharp distinction in the book between speech of God in the first person, framed by the formulas "thus Yahweh has said" and "utterance of Yahweh," and speech of the prophet in the third person. There has been extensive inquiry into the life settings of the forms of speech used by the prophet and much speculation as to whether the sources of the speech identify the institutional setting and role of the prophet.

There is considerable evidence that the round of foreign oracles in chaps. 1–2 was modeled on a liturgy of curses against enemy nations and domestic sinners, attested in the Egyptian Execration Texts (see Web Table A, 3A).[3] It may well be that such a liturgy was practiced in the Israelite cult and that Amos drew upon it to structure his oracle format. That this also argues for Amos himself having been a cultic prophet is more doubtful. It has also been argued that Amos began as a cult prophet who was radicalized to the point that he broke with the cult and called down destruction on the very institution he had formerly served.

The hymnic language of the doxologies (4:13; 5:8-9; 9:5-6) is likewise cited as evidence that Amos was a cult prophet. Now that we are aware of the pervasiveness of hymnic speech outside the cult, even in wisdom literature, this is a weak argument. The main point in employing the doxologies is to turn this cult-originated hymnic language against the cult in affirming Yahweh's cosmic transcendence.[4]

On the other hand, several features of the prophet's speech have been connected with wisdom tradition, such as the graded numerical saying ("for three transgressions, . . . and for four"). The wisdom indebtedness of Amos in this instance is probably not to the wisdom cultivated in the royal court but to the so-called clan wisdom of the older residual tribal organization of Israel in its village matrix (see pp. 160–63). To have been a sage in that context would have meant being a local leader practiced in giving counsel and in passing judgment in the trial of peers. The reported activity of Amos as a shepherd and part-time agricultural worker from Tekoa provided him a milieu to imbibe deeply of the old tribal ways.[5] It is striking that for the most part his speech about God's judgment on Israel is in the language of struggle against a harsh natural environment that he knew firsthand as herder-farmer from one of the marginal cultivated zones of Judah.

The status of Amos in relation to other prophets has been hotly debated without much profit. When Amos makes his famous disclaimer in 7:14, does he mean that he had not been a prophet or member of a prophetic group *until* Yahweh called him, or that he is not a prophet *even now* that Yahweh has called him to speak? And what is to be made of Amos's denial that he is a "prophet" (*nābî*) following Amaziah's rebuke of Amos as a "seer" (*ḥōzeh*)? It is by no means evident that this exchange of barbs tells us anything about the relation of Amos to other prophets in his day, for his remark seems focused on making clear to Amaziah that he has a direct call to speak for Yahweh despite any conventional understandings of prophets and seers that the

priest may have: "I am not like those 'prophets' who will say or do whatever they are paid or threatened to say and do!"

Redaction criticism has rendered a more complicated picture of the growth of the book than was once imagined. Source criticism (old-style literary criticism) has usually attributed the great bulk of the book to Amos, excepting only the oracles against Tyre, Edom, and Judah, the promises of salvation in 9:8b-15, and sometimes the doxologies. More recent redaction-critical studies assign as much as half or more of the work to later reworkings and supplements, for example, during the hopeful time of Josiah's reforms (see pp. 212–14).

While these studies differ in their details, the prophet whose work lies at the core of this redacted book attacked the patriotic and pious conservative reaction that had gained currency among the upper classes during the prosperous reign of Jeroboam II (see pp. 196–98). The upper classes, with governmental and juridical connivance, were systematically expropriating the land of commoners so that they could heap up wealth and display it gaudily in a lavish, conspicuous consumption economy. Hatred of other

FIG. 8.3. Seal of Jeroboam, king of Israel. Copy of lost original. Israelite. Tenth century B.C.E. Reuben & Edith Hecht Collection, Haifa University. Photo: © Erich Lessing / Art Resource, N.Y.

nations, military swaggering, and religious rhetoric were generously employed to persuade people to accept their miserable lot because it was, after all, the best of all possible societies.

Much of the monopolized wealth was poured into spectacles of worship at splendid sanctuaries. Amos savagely attacked the overheated religious fervor as a fraudulent and despicable mask for the leaders' gross selfishness and practical atheism. Or, as one commentator remarks, "It may cause surprise that the people, according to Amos' judgment, are doing too much rather than too little for Yahweh."[6] Amos announced that the kingdom of Israel would be overthrown by an enemy power, probably Assyria, and its leaders deported, which would be "the end" (see 8:1-3) of an arrogant, misplaced confidence in Yahweh as the deliverer of his people.

From what sources did Amos draw the moral and intellectual energy single-handedly to proclaim the total rejection of Israel by Yahweh? First and foremost must have been his overwhelming encounter with God that left him completely confident in his commission by God. Yet precisely this calling was grounded in the wholeness of his personhood in a particular community and tradition. Which elements of that tradition were ignited by the call of God? There is no single certain answer to that question.

It has been proposed that Amos drew upon a conditional covenant tradition of the sort articulated in Deuteronomy, but he does not even refer to Israel's covenant with Yahweh. The exodus is referred to in 2:10 and 9:7, and probably also in 3:2, where the unique "knowing" of Israel by God seems to be a kind of special election tradition, from which the prophet concludes a special responsibility on Israel. The particulars of Israel's responsibility are nowhere given, as would have been the case had Amos cited the infraction of particular laws as the basis for judgment.

If we pay heed to the crushing of the poor as the central sin Amos condemns and to the way he pictures divine activity through rhetorical questions and figures of speech from the natural and social world of rural Palestine, we can make an informed estimate of what weighed most in his thinking. He knew firsthand about the murderous oppression of the poor. He also knew that it was diametrically opposed to Yahweh's will as declared in the traditions in narrative and law shaped by the old tribal life of Israel and presently enshrined in the practice of mutual help and discharge of justice in local courts (see pp. 160–63). The substance of the socioethical laws of Israel was known to him, even if he had never seen written laws (see pp. 117–18). These laws were more or less faithfully practiced before his eyes in villages like Tekoa, as they were grotesquely ignored and overridden in the governing circles of Israel by the very people who were loudest in their praise of Yahweh. Thus the living integrity of village life based on traditional Yahwism and an astounding immediate experience of God provided both the structure of his critical analysis and the ground of his undeterred passion.

The immediate consequences of such forthright criticism are hinted at: probable expulsion of Amos from Israel (7:10-17) and then the collapse of the Jehu dynasty, followed by Israel's downward slide to political oblivion. The impressed followers of Amos preserved his words—and reshaped and added to them as new situations dictated. More than this, Amos stirred other voices with the result that a virile tradition of critical prophecy breaks forth and continues unbroken for three hundred years.

Hosea

The prophet Hosea was active in the northern kingdom in the final decades of the decline of Israel following the death of Jeroboam II. Hosea encounters a generation of leaders bent on protecting their own narrow interests by seizing every advantage at the expense of others. Yahweh has become for them the guarantor of personal advantages. The line between Yahwism and Baalism has worn thin.

The book of Hosea divides into two unequal parts: (1) chaps. 1–3, narratives and sayings about the prophet's marriage and offspring; (2) chaps. 4–14, judgment and tempered salvation speeches, which berate the sins of Israel and hold forth the hope of renewal only after national destruction and purgation. The text of these passionate reports and speeches is in a poor state, the meaning of many words, phrases, and whole lines hanging in doubt and the delimitation of the literary units difficult to determine.[7] Most of the work seems to have been written down by the prophet or at his dictation, or by gathered recollections in a circle of followers within a generation or so of the prophet's death, but it is possible that the turmoil at the fall of the northern kingdom damaged the original text before it could be transferred to safekeeping in Judah.

One reconstruction of the composition of the book sees it as the result of combining three collections more or less simultaneously developed:[8] (1) Hosea's own text in 2:2-15 and 3:1-5, supplemented with a narrative about Hosea's marriage and the birth of his children; (2) transcripts of the public preaching of Hosea and of private communications to his followers in 4:1—11:11; (3) mixed public and private communications with several stylistic peculiarities in 11:12—14:9. All three complexes move from accusation and judgment to promise of salvation, and all three show marked linguistic and conceptual affinities with Deuteronomic thought (see pp. 221–23).

In these collections, the prophet worked up a marriage metaphor for the relation between Yahweh and Israel (chaps. 1–3), as well as a father-son metaphor (11:1-7). These are but two of the more prominent specimens of a rich stock of metaphors and similes: for example, Yahweh as a fowler, a lion, a bereaved she-bear, a luxuriant tree; and Israel as a flighty dove, a grapevine and grapes, a woman in labor, and a slack bow.

The tradition complex in chaps. 1–3 tells of the prophet's marriage by divine command to Gomer, a woman who proved unfaithful but whom he is in the process of winning back. Yahweh is attempting a like reespousal with faithless Israel. Whether this was an actual marriage experience in Hosea's life (in contrast to an allegory) or indeed if the woman in chap. 3 is Gomer or another is much disputed by interpreters.[9] It is possible, some believe probable, that the woman named was a cult prostitute and in that case the image bore a double punch, inasmuch as the prophet was a searing critic of Baal worship, which had undermined Yahwism from within to the point that Yahweh was worshiped as though he were a Baal figure who could be magically manipulated.

Recovered from a shrine of the ninth/eighth century, inscriptions and drawings from northern Sinai seem to show that Yahweh was worshiped there either as Baal, or in tandem with Baal, and that Yahweh had a consort called "his Asherah."[10] Thus, in spite of Jehu's supposed extirpation of Baalism in the north a century before (see pp. 196–98), it appears that a thoroughgoing syncretism had so fused the elements of Yahwism and Baalism that Hosea could describe the resulting cultic and sociopolitical situation as one of "no knowledge" (4:1-3; 5:3-4; 8:1-3). The prophet lays responsibility for this betrayal of old Yahwism at the door of short-sighted and self-serving leaders, especially priests, prophets, kings, and officials (4:4-6; 5:1-2; 8:4-5). Over against the confusion of the times Hosea sets the justice of God as an offended struggling love, both poignant and terrible.

Some say that Hosea did not condemn the socioeconomic wrongs that aroused Amos's ire. This is not the case. There are enough allusions to make plain that Hosea also knew and opposed the internal maldistribution of wealth and depression of the lower classes. For example, the crimes listed in 4:1—false swearing, stealing, and murder—were all involved in the debt foreclosures, land-grabbing, and court corruption pinpointed by Amos. Especially striking is the use of Genesis traditions about Jacob as a sharpster who cheated his brother in order to epitomize the northern kingdom as a land of economic greed and plunder (12:8-9). Finally, the climactic true confession of Israel in 14:1-3 states that "in you [Yahweh] the orphan finds mercy," a code phrase for the socioeconomic program of tribal Israel for protecting the weak.

It is the political situation of Israel that is particularly assessed by Hosea. Internecine strife among political factions (7:5-7) and between Israel and Judah (5:8-12) has rent the land, as well as the incorporation by Assyria of more than two-thirds of Israel (see p. 198). Alliances with Egypt and Assyria are futile, since Yahweh will neutralize the strength of the ally or allow it to turn on Israel. In the meantime, the heavy drain in tribute (10:6) and in exports to allies (12:1) will deplete the economy and even the land itself.

With Amos, Hosea foresees military conquest and deportation of the leadership. He goes beyond Amos in talking about the conditions of the exile as a return to the typological wilderness in which the integrity of the people as a community will be retained in spite of terrible suffering. Drawing on the salvation traditions of the exodus, wilderness wanderings, and conquest, Hosea views the future "wilderness state" in a twofold way: as a time of punishment or enforced sociopolitical and religious regression and as a period of probation in which a renewal of national life can begin.[11]

Earlier interpreters were inclined to assume that Hosea, like Amos, held out no hope for Israel whatsoever and that all promissory passages in the book must be from later hands. There is, however, reason for believing that it was in keeping with the prophet's outlook to anticipate that after the total political destruction of Israel—and only after—repentance and renewal of genuine faith in Yahweh would lead to a new communal life. Because Hosea saw Yahweh as grieving husband and father, he understood that God was in a struggle to win the people by a love that would not forgo justice.

In short, the kind of modestly hopeful eschatological thinking that we meet in Hosea, the belief that necessary destruction of false structures will release new possibilities of communal life, began to emerge in the prophetic communities from Hosea's time onward as a way to learn from history and to be ready for making new kinds of history instead of surrendering oneself to traditionless despair and unsocial self-aggrandizement.

NOTES

1. The interpretation here follows Giorgio Buccellati, *Cities and Nations of Ancient Syria: An Essay on Political Institutions with Special Reference to the Israelite Kingdoms,* Studi Semitici 26 (Rome: Instituto di Studi del Vicino Oriente, 1967); and Baruch Halpern, *The Constitution of the Monarchy in Israel,* Harvard Semitic Monograph 25 (Chico, Calif.: Scholars, 1981); against Albrecht Alt, "The Monarchy in the Kingdoms of Israel and Judah," in *Essays on Old Testament History and Religion*, trans. R. A. Wilson (Garden City, N.Y.: Doubleday, 1968), 313–35.

2. Alan W. Jenks, *The Elohist and North Israelite Traditions,* Society of Biblical Literature Monograph Series 22 (Missoula, Mont.: Scholars, 1977), chaps. 3–4.

3. Aage Bentzen, "The Ritual Background of Amos 1:2—2:16," *Oudtestamentische Studiën* 8 (1950): 85–99.

4. James L. Crenshaw, *Hymnic Affirmations of Divine Justice: The Doxologies of Amos and Related Texts in the Old Testament,* SBLDS 24 (Missoula, Mont.: Scholars, 1975), 39–46.

5. Hans Walter Wolff, *Amos the Prophet: The Man and His Background,* trans. Foster R. McCurley (Philadelphia: Fortress Press, 1973).

6. Hans Walter Wolff, *Joel and Amos,* trans. Waldemar Janzen et al., Hermeneia (Philadelphia: Fortress Press, 1977), 104.

7. Francis I. Andersen and David N. Freedman (*Hosea,* AB 24 [Garden City, N.Y.: Doubleday, 1980], 57–76) analyze the peculiar textual and literary qualities of the book with sensitivity and acumen.

8. Hans Walter Wolff, *Hosea,* trans. Gary Stansell, Hermeneia (Philadelphia: Fortress Press, 1974), xxix–xxxii.

9. Andersen and Freedman (*Hosea,* 115–309) explore at length the possible connections between the marriage metaphor, literarily and conceptually, and its roots in the prophet's family life.

10. Preliminary reports of the Kuntillet ʿAjrud finds in northern Sinai appear in Zeev Meshel and Carol Meyers, "The Name of God in the Wilderness of Zin," *BA* 39 (1976): 6–10; and Zeev Meshel, "Did Yahweh Have a Consort?" *BARev* 5/2 (1979): 24–35.

11. Gottwald, *AKE,* 132–35.

FOR FURTHER READING

Brueggemann, Walter. *Testimony to Otherwise: The Witness of Elijah and Elisha.* St. Louis: Chalice, 2001.

Carroll, M. Daniel R. *Contexts for Amos: Prophetic Poetics in Latin American Perspective.* Sheffield: JSOT Press, 1992.

Cook, Stephen L. *The Social Roots of Biblical Yahwism.* Chaps. 6 and 8. Atlanta: Society of Biblical Literature, 2004.

Coote, Robert B., ed. *Elijah and Elisha in Socioliterary Perspective.* Atlanta: Scholars, 1992.

———. *Amos among the Prophets: Composition and Theology.* Philadelphia: Fortress Press, 1981.

Moeller, Karl. *A Prophet in Debate: The Rhetoric of Persuasion in the Book of Amos.* Sheffield: Sheffield Academic, 2003.

Weems, Renita J. *Battered Love: Marriage, Sex, and Violence in the Hebrew Prophets.* Overtures to Biblical Theology. Minneapolis: Fortress Press, 1995.

QUESTIONS FOR STUDY

1. Describe some of the theories about why the kingdom of Judah outlasted the kingdom of Israel.
2. Describe the missions of Ezra and Nehemiah as agents of the Persian Empire, and explain their influence on religious developments.
3. Based on the literary themes of the book, what were Amos's primary concerns? Did Hosea have similar emphases? Explain.

TRADITIONS ABOUT THE SOUTHERN KINGDOM

SUMMARY

The shape of the traditions in 1 Kings 18–25
Sources
The history of the southern kingdom and its
  major kings
The end of Judah
Literary culture and prophetic critique:
  Micah, Isaiah, Deuteronomy, Jeremiah

READ THE BIBLICAL TEXT

2 Kings 18–25
Micah
Isaiah 1–39
Deuteronomy
Nahum
Zephaniah
Habakkuk
Jeremiah

*See additional materials at fortresspress.com/
gottwald; consult* Carta Bible Atlas *maps 152–164*

THE SHAPE OF THE
TRADITIONS IN 2 KINGS 18–25

Source Statistics

The last segment of the history of Judah as an independent state continues to depend upon the DH sources, supplemented by Chronicles, once again broadly separable into sources that yield political-historical data excerpted from the royal archives and literary traditions in the form of prophetic narratives (Web Table L).

The final 136 years of the kingdom of Judah are reported in 96 annalistic verses, DH and Chronicles combined, with 130 verses of miscellaneous literary traditions. Nonetheless, the data are concentrated in such a way, and enough other kinds of sources are available, to give a much fuller comprehension of the period than appears from the text of 2 Kings.

The Spectrum of Sources

The annals cover religious measures of several kings as well as political and military activities that culminate in the Neo-Babylonian deportations of leaders of Judah and the destruction of Jerusalem. Prophetic narratives featuring Isaiah appear in 2 Kgs. 18:17—20:21 and are found practically verbatim in Isaiah 36–39, believed to have been derived from prophetic circles and then taken up by DH. Huldah, a prophetess, appears in the narrative of Josiah's reforms, but her presence is integral to a temple narrative, since she seems to be a member of the temple staff.

The description of the last years of Judah in 2 Kings 24–25 has been drawn into Jeremiah 52 as an appendix to the prophet's words. On the other hand, Jer. 52:28-30 provides data on the Judahite deportees not in DH, and Jer. 40:7-41:18 is a fuller version of Gedaliah's administration summarized in 2 Kgs. 25:22-26.

Our understanding of the reign of Hezekiah is enhanced by speeches and one report in the book of Isaiah (see pp. 216–21), and the reigns of Jehoiakim, Jehoiachin, and Zedekiah are illuminated by words of Jeremiah and sizable prophetic narratives about Jeremiah (see pp. 225–30). There are, in addition, the annals of the Assyrian kings (Web Table A, 4J; see *ANET*, 286–88) and the Neo-Babylonian Chronicles (Web Table A, 4K; see *ANET*, 303–5, 563–64), which fill out aspects of the suzerain-vassal diplomatic and military connections with Judah. Archaeological data on the last years of Judah are relatively full, including military letters from Lachish and Arad (Web Table A, 4I, 4L).

In short, several categories of evidence converge to provide a fuller clarification of the history of Judah in this period than we possess for any other period of the divided kingdoms. The most serious gap involves the long, little-covered reign of Manasseh.

HISTORY OF THE SOUTHERN KINGDOM (722–586 B.C.E.)

Ahaz and Hezekiah (722–686 B.C.E.)

Having courted Assyria's favor to escape the menacing alliance between Israel and Damascus, Ahaz continued as a compliant vassal of Assyria. In an about-face, Hezekiah ascended the throne with hopes and plans for escaping Assyrian domination. In 705 B.C.E. Hezekiah wholeheartedly joined in a coordinated revolt, but it unraveled, and he suffered the decimation of the Judahite countryside before he submitted and paid tribute, and was thereafter allowed by the Assyrians to remain vassal king. This much the Assyrian annals and the biblical text agree on (Web Table A, 4J; see *ANET*, 287–88).

Why the siege of Jerusalem reported in the prophetic narrative (Isaiah 37) was in force if Hezekiah had indeed paid the tribute is unclear, unless Sennacherib demanded an increase in tribute that Hezekiah balked at. In order to make sense of the discrepancies between the biblical and Assyrian accounts, some favor a two-invasion hypothesis: (1) an invasion of 701 B.C.E. in which Hezekiah was forced to submit and pay tribute, and (2) an otherwise unknown second invasion by Sennacherib, probably about 688 B.C.E., in which the Assyrians failed to take Jerusalem. The accounts of the two invasions are claimed to have been confusedly interwoven in 2 Kings.

It is far more likely, however, that the miraculous delivery elements in Isaiah 36–39 (see pp. 216–21) are due to an ex post facto effort to understand what was a logical Assyrian policy of keeping a rebellious but now chastened local vassal on the throne after demilitarizing and looting his land.

The religious measures of Hezekiah were an aspect of his nationalistic anti-Assyrian

FIG. 9.1. The tunnel of Siloam brought water from the spring of Gihon to the Pool of Siloam inside the city of Jerusalem, constructed under King Hezekiah, 700 B.C.E., to ensure the water supply of the city during a siege. Photo: © Erich Lessing / Art Resource, N.Y.

program. He purified the temple cult of Assyrian and local non-Yahwist elements and probably attempted to close down the centers of popular worship outside Jerusalem (the so-called high places). His summons of northern Israelites to observe Passover in Jerusalem, using the northern calendar, was a practical embodiment of his wish to be regarded as the legitimate ruler of all Israelites, now that the northern kingdom was demolished.

Manasseh (687/686–643/642 B.C.E.)

Manasseh's reign of fifty-five years (counting his ten-year coregency with Hezekiah) was the longest of any monarch in either kingdom, but it is poorly documented. The DH exilic revision attributes the fall of Judah to this king's apostasies and to his spilling of "very much innocent blood" (2 Kgs. 21:16). It looks as though Manasseh ruled as a loyal, even ardent, Assyrian vassal, at least for much of his time in office. Recent studies of Assyrian imperial policy reveal that the Assyrians did not force their religious cults upon subjects as once supposed. In that event, Manasseh may have been an enthusiastic vassal for whom collaboration with Assyria represented a cultural cosmopolitanism perhaps welcomed by a sizable group of upper-class Judahites. Civil strife may have broken out, with repression and murder of Yahweh partisans, perhaps driving prophets into hiding or silence.

The claim that Manasseh was carried captive to Babylon, and then returned to power by his Assyrian overlord, is difficult to evaluate (2 Chron. 33:10-13). Because of his pro-Assyrian stance and the silence of the Assyrian records regarding any captivity, a majority of scholars view the Chronicler's report as a fanciful concoction to show that Manasseh was after all punished for his evil ways and to foreshadow the later Babylonian exile.

Josiah (641/640-609 B.C.E.)

Josiah's reign coincided with the decline and demise of the Assyrian Empire. He was able to further the program of national purification and expansion that Hezekiah had tentatively begun. DH connects the king's reforms with the discovery of the law book in the temple, undoubtedly some form of the laws in Deuteronomy. Chronicles, on the other hand, pictures the reforms as having begun prior to the finding of the law book. It is widely thought that DH has telescoped several stages in the reform efforts: (1) purification of the Jerusalem temple, (2) purification of outlying Judean holy places, (3) discovery/public presentation of the law book and a decision to centralize all worship at Jerusalem by closing outlying shrines, and (4) extension of purification and centralization to all the newly controlled territories, as Assyrian rule disintegrated.[1]

The Deuteronomistic History concentrates almost exclusively on the religious reforms, whereas the law book of Deuteronomy prescribes a range of socioeconomic and political administrative measures integral to the reform movement (see pp. 221–23). We do not know if, or how, these noncultic aspects of

FIG. 9.2. The walls of the important Israelite fortress at Lachish, which guarded the road from the coast to Jerusalem. Lachish was destroyed by Assyrian King Sennacherib in 701 B.C.E. and again destroyed by Nebuchadnezzar II, king of Babylon, in 598 B.C.E. Lachish, Israel. Photo: © Erich Lessing / Art Resource, N.Y.

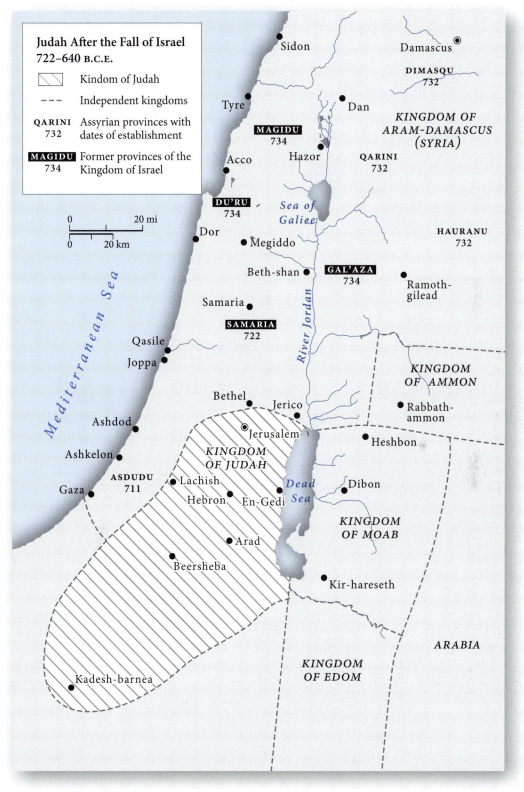

Judah After the Fall of Israel
722–640 B.C.E.

▨   Kindom of Judah

- - -   Independent kingdoms

QARINI
732   Assyrian provinces with dates of establishment

MAGIDU
734   Former provinces of the Kingdom of Israel

0   20 mi
0   20 km

Mediterranean Sea

Sidon

Damascus ◉

DIMASQU
732

Tyre

Dan

MAGIDU
734

KINGDOM OF
ARAM-DAMASCUS
(SYRIA)

Acco

Hazor

QARINI
732

DU'RU
734

Sea of
Galiee

Dor

HAURANU
732

Megiddo

Beth-shan

GAL'AZA
734

Ramoth-
gilead

Samaria

River Jordan

SAMARIA
722

Qasile

Joppa

KINGDOM
OF AMMON

Bethel

Jerico

Rabbath-
ammon

Ashdod

◉ Jerusalem

KINGDOM
OF JUDAH

Heshbon

Ashkelon

ASDUDU
711

Lachish

En-Gedi

Dead
Sea

Dibon

Gaza

Hebron

Arad

KINGDOM
OF MOAB

Beersheba

Kir-hareseth

ARABIA

Kadesh-barnea

KINGDOM
OF EDOM

MAP 9.1 JUDAH AFTER THE FALL OF ISRAEL

the reform were implemented, other than the testimony of Jeremiah that Josiah's record for social justice was far better than that of his successor Jehoiakim (Jer. 22:13-19). In any event, in 609 B.C.E, just as Josiah was about to reap the full harvest of his program, he challenged, and lost his life to, Egyptian forces under Pharaoh Neco, campaigning through Canaan in order to bolster the remnants of the Assyrian army and to secure eventual Egyptian sovereignty over the international corridor against the Neo-Babylonians.

Jehoiakim, Jehoiachin, and Zedekiah (609–586 B.C.E.)

Egypt immediately claimed Judah as a dependency and put Jehoiakim on the throne as vassal. Subsequently, when the Neo-Babylonian Empire drove Egypt out of Canaan, Jehoiakim shifted his allegiance to Nebuchadnezzar II, but then revolted at the first opportunity. In a retaliatory campaign, Nebuchadnezzar captured Jerusalem and deported Jehoiakim's son Jehoiachin, along with a sizable group of government officials. Zedekiah was installed as a vassal regent. After another revolt, Judah was crushed—this time with the baleful result of the destruction of Jerusalem and its temple, further deportations of leaders, and the cessation of the independent kingdom of Judah.

The Neo-Babylonians chose a Judahite official, Gedaliah, to serve as governor of the province of Judah, residing at Mizpah, some eight miles north of the ruins of Jerusalem. Shortly, however, Gedaliah and many of his staff were murdered by an aspirant to the Judahite throne, and many of those who had joined in Gedaliah's regime fled to Egypt out of fear of Neo-Babylonian reprisals.

The End of Israelite Efforts at Political Independence

The account of the history of Judah from Hezekiah to Zedekiah has attained an iconic, even canonical, form, interpreted and embellished by DH and the prophets. It appears as the fatal consequence of religious apostasy and an oppressive social order. It is difficult to assess the events in terms of the options open to the people and leaders of Judah and the factors at work in one direction or another. Self-assertion, entailing revolt against foreign imperialists, invited reprisal and destruction, and the danger of political extinction. On the other hand, acquiescence led to the diminution of the distinctive national culture and religion, if not because of foreign demand, through the fascination of the ways of a superior power in the eyes of aspiring Israelite and Judahite elites.

If the continuation of Israelite identity and national self-determination was the goal, then it is difficult to say that any other course of *state* foreign policy would have led to securer results, especially given Judah's position in the strategic corridor between Assyria / Neo-Babylonia and Egypt. We can perhaps say that Judah did as well, perhaps much better, than other small hierarchic states at the time.

The reality was, however, that in their historic pasts Israel and Judah had known—and had moved away from—another kind of social organizational experience: that of a *tribally organized confederacy* with approximate equality for all its members (see pp. 160–63). That confederacy had neither the power nor the will to enter into international politics in the way that rival states did.

Only in terms of that tribal social organizational base, however, can E, DH, and the prophets, together with the social constituencies they represented, be at all understood. In their indirect religious symbolic way, these critical traditionalists were reminding Israel that the charter of Israel's existence had been social equality and that, by endangering social equality in the process of becoming a state, the basis of Israelite strength and its difference from other ancient Near Eastern peoples were jeopardized.

Especially in the radical prophets we encounter an implicit political theory that tended to pose the thorny problematic of being both a *state* and a *community* capable of serving the vital interests of all the Israelite people. Social equality and sociopolitical hierarchy did not readily mix, and it was the former that steadily lost ground to the latter. The human costs of waging war and engaging in hierarchic politics were so enormous that Israel as winner, or merely as survivor, stood to be an overall loser in all those vital social interests that had brought it into existence in the first place. Stated starkly, some prophets concluded that it would be just as well, and possibly more fruitful in the long run, for Israel and Judah to be subject to foreign oppressors than for the Israelite people to be crushed and disheartened by native Israelite oppressors.

Whatever security Israel could attain, and that would be worth attaining, would lie in the realization of its fundamental need and mandate for social equality. Accordingly, it would be better to hew to a program of national social equality, against the tide of ancient Near Eastern political organization, and trust to Yahweh's future than to go forward under the cause of national security that systematically eviscerated the very social equality that was the substance and raison d'être of Israelite national culture.

When, like Israel before it, Judah fell, the debacle could be read in either of two ways:

we did not elevate national security to a high enough priority, or we did not ensure the social equality that would have truly united and strengthened us. But of course what had happened under the monarchy could never again be replayed. There could only be another time or times when similar variables might come into play and new decisions would have to be made—provided of course that a self-conscious, tradition-bearing group survived.

LITERARY CULTURE, RELIGION, AND PROPHETIC CRITIQUE

Micah

For so small a work, the complexly edited book of Micah contains an amazing range of literary genres and varied concepts. Only the materials in chaps. 1–3 can be confidently connected with the prophet Micah of Moresheth (1:1; see 1:14), a contemporary of Isaiah active in the approximate period 725–701. Like Amos, he came from a small town in Judah but spoke his indictments of socioeconomic injustice to the national leaders. The prophet knew firsthand about the expulsion of small landholders from their traditional means of livelihood, dishonest business practices, venal priests and prophets, and a royal regime that connived in the oppression of the poor.

Starting off with an attack on the urban centers of Samaria and Jerusalem as the institutional nerve centers for the robbery and murder of defenseless small-town people (1:2-7), Micah moves on to attack the political and religious leaders responsible for the deterioration of the old tribal order of communal equity. His descriptions of the violations of the person and property of vulnerable Judahites by the rich and powerful culminate in the announcement that the city of Jerusalem and its temple will be flattened, never to be built again (3:12).

A close look at the redactional scheme of the book discloses alternating panels of judgment oracles (chaps. 1–3; 6:1—7:7) and salvation oracles (chaps. 4–5; 7:8-20). Although he was a prophet dead set against urban Zion, Micah ironically becomes the lodestone for attracting blocks of salvation oracles that point toward the redemption of the holy city as the center for a purified people of Israel and as an assembly point for the nations. This means that the words of a prophet whose firm rootage was in tribal Yahwism are now in the sharpest contradiction to Zion and Davidic traditions that fill out his book (see pp. 188–89, 310–12). In addition to the oracles about the rebuilt and glorified Zion being fundamentally out of step with Micah's outlook in chaps. 1–3, it is reported that the memory of Micah's prophecy of the destruction of Jerusalem was happily recollected by elders in the time of Jeremiah who were able to cite it as a precedent in defense of Jeremiah's similar audacious prophecies (Jer. 26:16-19). This almost certainly means that as late as the end of the seventh century there were no salvation oracles as yet connected with the Micah tradition, for if there had been, the appeal to Micah as a vindication of Jeremiah would have been greatly weakened if not entirely invalidated.

The panels of salvation and further judgment oracles that follow after Micah's prophecies in chaps. 1–3 are very intricately redacted. These panels include some familiar oracles, for example, the "swords to plowshares" oracle of 4:1-4, identical with Isa. 2:1-4 and generally nowadays attributed to a third source from which the redactors of Isaiah and Micah have separately drawn; the prophecy of a ruler to come forth from Bethlehem Ephrathah (5:2-4); and the torah on acceptable worship that reflects the design of priestly and especially wisdom instruction and that concludes with the celebrated epitome of prophetic religion:

> He has showed you, O man, what is good;
> and what does Yahweh require of you
> but to do justice, and to love mercy
> and to walk humbly with your God? (6:8)

The final chapter is a collection of characteristically nonprophetic genres joined as a liturgy, perhaps used in exilic and postexilic contexts, to extol the salvation of Zion and its redeemed people.

Isaiah of Jerusalem

A contemporary of Micah and Hosea, Isaiah was a Judahite prophet active at several crisis points between 740/739 and 701. He was called to prophesy by a stunning vision of Yahweh (chap. 6). Isaiah's commission was to announce the unmitigated destruction of both Israel and Judah. He lived to see the fall of the northern kingdom to Assyria in 722 and the supine vassalage of the southern kingdom to the same world power.

The basis of the announced total destruction of the twin kingdoms was their rulers' rampant violation of the rights of the common people and their headlong rush to amass wealth and political power at any cost (1:12-17; 3:13-15; 5:1-7, 8-10). These leaders carried "bloodguilt" for their crimes (1:15; 5:7). Gross disregard of the fundamental requirements of Yahweh as known in the received traditions of Israel made both states vulnerable to annihilation by Assyria, their *external* fate being directly linked with their *internal* abandonment of the Yahwistic charter of social justice and equality.

Isaiah is often credited with belief in a saving remnant that would survive the debacle and form a new community. Indeed, he may have struck such a note, but always ambiguously, hinting at a modest contingent hope at best. As with Hosea (see pp. 205–6), he insisted that any hopeful future could be realized only after the total collapse of the existing perverse national structures.

Precise determination of the theological perspectives and political judgments of the prophet is complicated by the way his book has been edited so that everywhere his own words are mixed with later prophetic words that grew up as a carryover of his influential outlook into later generations. These expansions and additions in an Isaianic stream of tradition are often credited to disciples who formed self-perpetuating groups, somewhat loosely called "schools." In general, a minimal note of hope—contingent on repentance—was picked up and developed by interpreters in following centuries, and the core of the prophet's collected works was supplemented by extensive traditions of salvation appropriate to later sociohistorical settings. The most notable of these is chaps. 40–66, which come from sixth-century exilic and postexilic prophets (see pp. 284–88, 290–94).

Isaiah's resources in Israel's traditions are eccentric compared to Amos and Hosea. He did not appeal to Mosaic or Sinai traditions, although his understanding of what constituted proper Israelite norms of behavior was broadly congruent with those dominant traditions. Instead, Isaiah cited images and norms concerning Zion as a city of righteousness and Davidic rulers as executors of peace and justice in the community.

Although still much disputed, it is likely that Isaiah penned 9:2-7 as an imitation of a coronation psalm that celebrates the righteous deeds of a Davidic king, a text probably directed to Hezekiah at his accession to the throne.[2] Like so many of Isaiah's words, it was a deliberately ambivalent statement, both announcing the claim and possibility of royal righteousness and ironically exposing the frustration of its realization in contemporary Judahite monarchs. In short, to Isaiah's way of thinking the Davidic traditions contained all the ethical and theological standards and

FIG. 9.3. A column from the Scroll of Isaiah discovered among the Dead Sea Scrolls. Israel Museum (IDAM), Jerusalem. Photo: © Snark / Art Resource, N.Y.

political orientations necessary for the leaders of Judah to pull back from their willful plunge toward destruction—but they would not believe! It was virtually inevitable that later traditionists, seeing the positive portrait of kingship in 9:2-7 but missing Isaiah's subtle irony, would read and elaborate it as an unequivocal promise.

Toward the beginning of his prophetic project, Isaiah had to deal with Ahaz, who wished to submit to Assyria (see pp. 210–11). Isaiah insisted on Judahite noninvolvement in international politics: neither to submit to Assyria nor to join in a Syro-Israelite attack on Assyria. Neither narrowly religious nor wildly utopian, the prophet appears to have believed that what was religiously requisite was also politically practical. His conception of action in the world has been called "theopolitical."[3] Since Yahweh is lord of the world of nations, what is right for Judah to do will also be in the best national interests and will lead to the total welfare of the people. Isaiah understood "what is right" for Judah to consist of a vigorous pursuit of domestic social justice coupled with neutrality in foreign affairs.

The irony of the prophet in pointing to the radically different courses of events that would be set in motion depending on the king's choice is starkly underscored by the double-edged meanings carried by the symbolic names of each of his children.[4] Shearjashub ("A Remnant Shall Return," 7:3) may mean that no one but a few survivors will be left if Ahaz pursues his alliance politics, or it may mean that a faithful remnant will rebuild Judah if the king is wise enough to believe in Yahweh and stay politically neutral. Immanuel ("God with Us," 7:14) may mean that God is with us to destroy us if we invite Assyria into southern Palestine, or it may mean that God is with us to save us if we avoid getting mixed up

with Assyria or with Israel and Syria. Mahershalal-hashbaz ("Speeds the Spoil, Hastens the Prey," 8:1) may mean that if Judah joins Israel and Syria against Assyria the superior power will hurry on to destroy Judah after it has easily disposed of the other allies, or it may mean that a neutral Judah will be delivered of any threat from Israel and Syria because their rebellion against Assyria will utterly fail.

The ironic and subtle play of Isaiah's mind is everywhere at work with cunning wordplay that exposes the way the leaders of Israel and Judah become entrapped and boxed in by their own clever plans that repeatedly backfire because they are insubstantial and run straight against the grain of Yahweh's way of working in the world.

Because Ahaz was impervious to Isaiah's counsel, the prophet appears to have withdrawn for a time from public life and to have committed the incidents of that period to writing in what has been called his Memoirs or Testimony, or Book of Signs (6:1—8:18). In this way, Isaiah, although rebuffed, was fully on record. With the coming of Hezekiah (see pp. 210–11) to the throne in 716/715, Isaiah may have had a somewhat more favorable hearing, at least for a period, and influenced Hezekiah toward reforms. The Deuteronomistic History speaks of these measures as cultic reforms (2 Kgs. 18:4), but whether Hezekiah also paid heed to the call of proto-Deuteronomy and of Isaiah for needed social justice in the land is not known (Isa. 1:12-17; 22:12-14; 29:13-14).

By 705, with the death of the Assyrian king Sargon, Hezekiah became a ringleader in a major revolt of Syro-Palestinian states against Assyria that was backed by Egypt and that ended in greatly reduced territory and heavier tribute. One strand of thought in the book of Isaiah shows the prophet holding unswervingly to an announcement of doom throughout the revolt of Hezekiah and the decimation of Judah until only Jerusalem was left unmolested and Hezekiah had to surrender (22:1-4; 29:1-4; 30:1-5; 31:1-3). Another strand, both in narratives (chaps. 36–39, derived from 2 Kings 18–20) and in speeches of salvation (e.g., Isa. 10:16-19; 14:24-27; 31:5 + 8-9), pictures Isaiah declaring a reprieve and imminent deliverance of Jerusalem coupled with the destruction of Assyria (see pp. 210–11).

This contradiction has been explained in different ways. One view is that Isaiah simply changed his mind as the siege of Jerusalem wore on and switched from a message of doom to one of salvation. Others, who favor the two-invasion hypothesis, see Isaiah as a staunch prophet of doom in the 701 invasion, but, concluding that it was time for Assyria to be punished, he changed into a prophet of Jerusalem's salvation by the time of the supposed second invasion. Since the book of Isaiah is a compilation and redaction of material over a long tradition history, it is far more plausible to attribute the salvation relapse connected with 701 to postdeliverance Isaianic traditionists who were impressed by the historical fact that Jerusalem proper had not been destroyed and who retrojected this marvel into the prophecies of the master.[5]

It is obvious that later Isaianic traditionists played upon the many facets of Isaiah's fertile mind and modes of expression. The many-sidedness of Isaiah was a function of his dialectical way of thinking. Motives, confidences, plans, expectations, and beliefs alike turn into their unexpected opposites.[6] On the one hand, the nations were used by Yahweh as punitive instruments against Israel and Judah ("Ah, Assyria, the rod of my anger, the staff of my fury!" 10:5). On the other hand, as free agents the nations exceed their assigned or permit-

ted role as chastisers of others and engage in prideful excesses that Yahweh will in turn recompense ("Shall the ax vaunt itself over him who hews with it?" 10:15). If, as seems certain, his announcements of judgment on nations (e.g., 10:5-15) were dialectically and consistently thought through, then it would have made no sense for him to anticipate the breaking of Yahweh's rod Assyria *before* Judah had received the thorough thrashing that constituted the central political content of the prophet's message.

The collection and arrangement of the prophet's words together with expansions and supplements from other hands was an exceedingly complex redaction process that we are just beginning to understand. The book of Isaiah divides as follows:

1. *Isaiah 1–12.* Grouped around the centrally positioned Memoirs (6:1—8:18) are early oracles of judgment from Isaiah against Israel and Judah (chaps. 2–5; 8:19—10:33), among and after which are sprinkled later additions. The whole is introduced by a summation of the prophet's message in chap. 1.

2. *Isaiah 13–27.* A collection of prophecies against named foreign nations (chaps. 13–23), a majority of which may be from Isaiah himself, leads to the announcement and celebration of a general judgment on the nations en masse and the promise of a final deliverance for Jerusalem/Judah = Israel/Jacob (chaps. 24–27).

3. *Isaiah 28–35.* Oracles of judgment from Isaiah against Judah, and one against Israel that heads the collection, derive largely from the later career of the prophet in 705–701 (chaps. 28–31). Prophecies about the coming righteous king (chaps. 32–33) and a celebration of judgment on the nations and deliverance for Zion (chaps. 34–35) are stylistically linked to chaps. 40–66.

4. *Isaiah 36–39.* A narrative about the crisis of Sennacherib's dire threat to Jerusalem in 701 has been excerpted from 2 Kings 18–19 with the intent of documenting the prophet's promise of divine protection as a factor in the survival of the city and as a way of bridging the gap between Isaiah 1–35 and 40–66 (see p. 210).

5. *Isaiah 40–66.* Oracles of redemption for the Judahite exiles have been composed in a rhetorically vibrant and elevated style. On the basis of content and historical background, this section is usually subdivided into chaps. 40–55 (see pp. 284–88) presupposing the last years of exile (ca. 550–539) and chaps. 56–66 (see pp. 290–94) presupposing a return to Judah and a difficult struggle to reconstitute the Palestinian Jewish community (ca. 538–500).

The first three major divisions of the book start off with judgment and rise to a crescendo of salvation. By contrast, chaps. 40–66 project salvation as their dominant message and tone, within which reminders of former judgment and of impending judgment are incorporated. The entirety of chaps. 40–66 has been linked to 1–39 by the common focus on Zion / Jerusalem as the center of a sociopolitically righteous and culturally faithful community that Israel's God works to perfect against the backdrop of other nations, whom he likewise controls. In terms of historical settings, the book spans more than two centuries: the context of chaps. 1–39 is basically judgment on Israel and Judah by means of Assyria (eighth-seventh centuries [see pp. 198–200, 210–11]), while the context of chaps. 40–66 is basically redemption for Judah by means of the Persians after decades of punishing subjection at the hands of the Neo-Babylonians (sixth century [see pp. 243–48]).

While early analyses of Isaiah concluded that the book was rather arbitrarily redacted, recent studies of the growth and redaction of traditions within the book suggest a more purposeful process. The redactional maneuvers within the book of Isaiah are complex, versatile, and pervasive. Chapters 40–66, for example, have been joined to 1–35 by the narrative seam of 36–39 in which Hezekiah's negotiations with a precursor of the later imperialist Neo-Babylonians sets up the Babylonian exile as the proper context for 40–66. There are words and motifs that recur, functioning adroitly as clamps to hold together the once-separate subdivisions and as signals that encourage a back-and-forth and part-to-whole reading of the completed work.

Zion and Babylon are two such recurrent redactional binders. Zion, punished and/or redeemed, appears prominently in each of the major subdivisions, notably in the openings and conclusions. Babylon is cited at the beginning and end of the oracles against foreign nations (14:3-20; 23:13). The diverse salvation prophecies and hymns that culminate the first three subdivisions (in chaps. 11–12, 24–27, and 34–35) show marked stylistic and thematic connections with chaps. 40–66, thereby anticipating the ecstatic tone and expectation that pervade 40–66. Chapter 1 (with its own superscription; see 1:1; 2:1) is both a compendium of the message of eighth-century Isaiah and a foretaste of the purgative redemption of Jerusalem spelled out over the course of the whole book. There are striking links in vocabulary and motifs between chaps. 1 and 65–66, strongly pointing to a redactional *inclusio* for the finished book.

In some cases, the same subunits in the book of Isaiah have been analyzed both by redaction-critical and also by rhetorical-critical methods. Isaiah 28 is one such subunit.[7] Broadly speaking, the combined effect of redactional and rhetorical studies on the same subunit in the book of Isaiah is to expose an intricate texture of Isaianic speech that has grown by an inner-textual layering process. The surface structure of brilliant tangled imagery, juxtaposed and interlocking motifs, speech units constructed out of key words from widely scattered contexts, and chiastic arrangements that nest inside one another—all this seems to have been built up in a process over time, like geological layering.

Isaiah of Jerusalem seems to have worked with a range of complex historical and theological topics that he attacked in a dialectical style, rich in multivalent language, which tended to set the tone for those who elaborated on his work. The recognized wisdom elements in this prophet accord with his aim of forcing his contemporaries to think long and hard, to look at what was happening around them in a comprehensive way, and to act at a level that cut through superficial appearances. To call Isaiah "aristocratic" in a social class sense, as has sometimes been done, is to infer more than we know, but if we mean by that term noble or elevated in thought and style of expression, it is a permissible characterization of his penchant to put every concrete situation into a large and principled context and to expose the deep logic beneath the surface surprises of events and to do so in colorful and memorable speech.

Deuteronomy

We have so far considered Deuteronomy mainly as the programmatic preface to the Deuteronomistic History (see pp. 82–83, 136–41). Prior to its final bookish function, however, Deuteronomy was shaped by a long organic growth of its traditions out of covenant-renewal ceremonies and recitations of the law, and some form of its laws, contained in chaps. 12–26 and 28, eventually emerged as the platform for Josiah's reformation (see pp. 212–14).

The prose of Deuteronomy is written in a highly rhetorical style marked by long verbose sentences built from stereotyped phrases and linked by subordinate clauses (unlike the usual paratactic syntax of Hebrew; see pp. 145–47). This peculiar style communicates a distinctive cluster of concepts that gives the book an obvious unity. On analysis, however, Deuteronomy shows abundant signs of a long process of growth, both in the processes of cultic recitation and of redaction as Deuteronomy was prefaced to DH.

The structure of the materials in Deuteronomy is the structure of a covenant-making or covenant-renewing ceremony, corresponding to the basic arrangement of the Sinai traditions in Exodus 19–24 (Web Table H, sec. C). The stages in the growth of the traditions, cultic or didactic, are not easily determined.[8] In Deuteronomy the covenant sequence is apparent in a historical résumé of the Sinai events (chaps. 1–11), a recital of the laws (12:1—26:15), a proclamation of the establishment of covenant (26:16-19), and a recital of blessings and curses (chaps. 27–28), with appended exhortations, poems, and narratives that adapt the document to introduce Joshua—2 Kings (chaps. 29–34). It has been suggested that the arrangement of the laws follows the divisions of the Decalogue (Deut. 5:6-21 [see p. 118]) in that the laws of chaps. 12–18 refer to "the privileges of Yahweh" analogous to 5:6-15, while the laws of chaps. 19–26 concern murder, family, neighbors, and court procedure in correspondence with 5:16-21.

The Deuteronomistic Historian reports that Josiah followed the instructions of a law book when he enforced centralization of worship at Jerusalem and celebrated Passover at the temple rather than in private homes, as also when he prohibited forms of astral worship, sacred poles and pillars, cult prostitution, immolation of children, magic, and divination (2 Kgs. 23:4-14, 21-24). All of these reforms are explicitly legislated in Deuteronomy. Moreover, when it is said that the Levites from the banned centers of worship were not admitted into the Jerusalem temple service (2 Kgs. 23:9), it reads like an apology for the failure to carry out the incorporation of the country Levites at Jerusalem as directed by Deut. 18:6-8. In fact, Deuteronomy itself legislates triennial tithes to support Levites who are socially deprived now that the country sanctuaries are closed (14:28-29).

In Deuteronomy "priests" and "Levites" are interchangeable terms and all Levitical priests possess legitimacy of office; however, they may practice henceforth only at the Jerusalem temple. Since the central sanctuary in Deuteronomy is explicitly connected with Shechem in blessings/curses passages (11:26-32; chap. 27), it is probable that the old cultic materials of Deuteronomy first developed in the north before the fall of Israel and, carried over into Judah, were subsequently transposed into a validation of sole worship at Jerusalem. Since the *Levitical priests* occupy so prominent a place in Deuteronomy, it is logical to assume that, as leaders in the covenant-renewal and law-recitation ceremonies, it was also they who were the bearers of the traditions and the shapers of the final form of Deuteronomy.[9] More recently, however, the occurrence of wisdom language and legal constructs that relate to Neo-Assyrian diplomacy and treaty texts (Web Table A, 2H) has prompted the notion that the Deuteronomic traditionists were court officials, probably scribes.[10] Correspondences between the socioeconomic provisions of the laws and the prophetic critique have also favored an origin of Deuteronomy in prophetic circles.

It is possible to formulate a conception of Deuteronomy's development that takes the various influences into account. The cultic covenant-law provenance of Deuteronomy is the necessary foundation for any hypothesis. It was, however, only as this covenant-law stream of tradition entered into the royal establishments of Hezekiah and Josiah that it became a visible and effective part of national religious life in Judah. In that context, the Levitical priests at Jerusalem, familiar with teaching, and the court officials, familiar with wisdom and treaty language (see 2 Kgs. 22:3-4, 8-14), were no doubt collaborators in effecting reforms and in shaping the text of Deuteronomy. Simultaneously, the preaching of the eighth-century prophets had sensitized priests and government officials to the urgencies of socioeconomic justice.

It is obvious that the reform program had far-reaching sociopolitical impact. In terms of the old north-south divisions, by adapting traditional northern covenant-law practices and concepts, the Davidic dynasty of Josiah was able to present itself as the true guarantor of Israelite interests north and south. Josiah's recovery of northern territories abandoned by the Assyrians was ideologically legitimated by Deuteronomy. Likewise, the intensification of Jerusalem's control over the countryside of Judah was enabled by reforming fiscal affairs so that the flow of revenues no longer passed through rural priests and elders but came directly to Jerusalem.[11]

It is disputed whether the old northern Deuteronomic tradition ever mandated exclusive worship at one site, such as Shechem (see pp. 158–60). In any case, by making centralization of worship at Jerusalem the cornerstone of the reforms, Josiah masterfully strengthened the administrative and religious power of Jerusalem. What price Josiah paid in accepting constitutional limits on the monarchy (e.g., Deut. 17:14-20) is far from clear, since we do not know the extent to which he implemented the noncultic aspects of Deuteronomic law.

Deuteronomy as preface to DH is concerned with land-getting, land-keeping, and land-recovering. The laws within the book provide the fundamental conditions for Israel's *retention* of the land (seen from the viewpoint of Josiah and the first edition of DH) and, failing that, for Israel's eventual *recovery* of the land (seen from the viewpoint of stateless Jews and the DH exilic revision). The sonorous, almost mesmerizing, liturgical style of Deuteronomy and DH interpretive passages sets forth a solemn coherent message about the indivisible unity of *one God* for *one people* in *one land* observing *one cult*.

Prophets of the International Power Shift

Apart from the abundantly documented work of Jeremiah, three other prophets from the last half of the seventh century are known to us from books credited to them: Zephaniah, Nahum, and Habakkuk. They responded to the decline and fall of Assyria and the rise of the Neo-Babylonian Empire in terms of Yahwistic theology and with reference to the people of Judah.

Zephaniah is given an extended genealogy (1:1), which may intend to show either that he was a great-great-grandson of King Hezekiah or that his father Cushi ("Egyptian/Ethiopian"?) was after all a full Israelite and not a foreigner. Dated in the reign of Josiah, Zephaniah's sharp criticism of religious irregularities and foreign attire strongly implies that he preached in Judah prior to the Deuteronomic reform. Concerning Nahum, the text tells us only that he was from Elkosh, an unknown place. He is situated between 663 and 612 because he refers to the Assyrian destruction of Thebes in the former year and anticipates (or perhaps celebrates) the fall of Nineveh in the latter year. The book of Habakkuk tells nothing about the prophet, but he is to be dated in conjunction with the rise of the Neo-Babylonians ("Chaldeans" of 1:6), who gained hegemony over Palestine by defeating the Egyptians at Carchemish in 605.

The divine governance of the world in the face of cruel imperial powers and in the light of extensive unfaithfulness in Judah forms the conceptual matrix of the prophetic books of Zephaniah, Nahum, and Habakkuk. The problematic of the justice of God is worked out in these books in a way that makes clear that the issue of divine justice in the unjust world of the ancient Near East continued to perplex and demoralize Jews far beyond the lifetimes of these prophets. Around the core of the original words of the three prophets, larger literary structures were built that extended and prolonged their reflections in a way that made them useful and compelling for later generations who continued to face foreign domination, domestic injustice, and religious disloyalty.

Nahum

The construction of the book of Nahum is relatively straightforward. Two vivid prophecies of the destruction of Nineveh in chaps. 2 and 3 are prefaced by a psalmic introduction concerning divine power in creation and justice in history. Underlying the psalm in vv. 1-8 was an acrostic in which each line began with a successive letter of the Hebrew alphabet. As it stands, the acrostic has been disordered and broken off. The emphatic echo of the rhetoric of Isaiah of the Exile in v. 15 points to at least late exilic times as the date of redaction.

While earlier biblical critics depreciated Nahum as a nationalistic or even a false prophet because he does not summon Judah to repentance and merely condemns Assyria out of hatred and vengeance, the terse allusion to "the bloody city, all full of lies and booty" (3:1), and the concluding rhetorical question, "For upon whom has not come your unceasing evil?" (3:19), constitute clear evidence of a moral judgment on the Assyrians. Crucial to an understanding of Nahum is a grasp of the logic of prophetic criticism of foreign nations, attested already in Amos and Isaiah. The basic point was that nations stood under the judgment of Yahweh irrespective of the attitude or conduct of other nations.

As for whether Nahum derived any warning for Judah from the fall of Assyria, we cannot say because only the triumph songs of chaps. 2–3 are the work of Nahum. The good news of Judah's deliverance is expressed in the terms of Isaiah of the Exile (cf. 1:15 with Isa. 40:9; 52:7), for whom the deliverance of Israel occurs in full awareness of its former sinfulness, which has been paid for, and its present sinfulness, which must be constantly fought and overcome (see pp. 284–88). Interpreters who have advanced an amoral chauvinist reading of Nahum were moralizing in defiance of the history of prophetic literary forms and prophetic theology about the nations.[12]

Zephaniah

The articulation of the book of Zephaniah is in the classic pattern of oracles against Judah (1:1—2:3), oracles against the nations (2:4—3:8), and oracles of salvation to Judah (3:9—20). While the first section shows evidence of redaction, a distinctive note is struck by the imperative that culminates the opening section of judgment oracles and is addressed to "all you humble of the land, who do his commands" (2:3). This body of "the humble" who take steps to reform themselves morally and religiously will be the historical vehicle for the renewal of Judah after the terrible judgment of the day of Yahweh. This appears to have been the kernel of the work of the prophet named Zephaniah.

In the second section, toward the close of customary oracles against foreign nations, comes the introduction of judgment on Jerusalem in 3:1-5. Perhaps influenced by Amos 1–2 (see pp. 202–4), this section seems to make the point that Judah along with all nations stands under judgment. The distinctive twists of Zeph. 3:6-10 are that judgment of other nations ought to serve Judah as a basis for self-correction, as well as to create new opportunities for the chastised nations to repent and worship Yahweh.

The book closes with an ecstatic paean of deliverance in the manner of Isaiah of the Exile in which the accent is on the defeat of oppressors and the ingathering of the exiles (3:14-20). Zephaniah's day of Yahweh has been universalized to all the earth, and while this is to be a thoroughgoing judgment on all nations, it also contains the possibility (certainty?) of the conversion of the nations. The proud and impenitent in Judah and among the nations will be destroyed, and the humble and lowly in Judah and among the nations will be saved. Like Isaiah of the Exile, this final redaction seems to picture purged nations worshiping Yahweh and returning the Jewish exiles to Palestine. A single dominant nation, such as Persia, is not pictured, however; we see rather a struggling community of humble and lowly Jewish exiles or returnees to Palestine.

Habakkuk

The book of Habakkuk is eccentrically constructed for a prophetic book, although the divisions are clear enough. The prophet opens with a complaint about injustice in Judah (1:1-4), to which a divine response assures him that the Neo-Babylonians are arising, presumably to bring punishment on Judah (1:5-11). When the prophet complains that the Neo-Babylonians are merciless predators (1:12-17), Yahweh's response is a "vision" consisting of words that the prophet is to placard for all to read: "Behold, the one who is not upright in his very being shall fail [or "be puffed up"], but the righteous shall live by his faithfulness" (2:4). The Neo-Babylonian king is apparently the one who is "not upright in his very being" and whose greed will destroy him and his empire. The composition closes with a psalm (chap. 3) about the power and justice of God.

Alternative identifications of the wicked nation (some interpreters prefer Assyria or Macedonia under Alexander the Great) point to the force of the redactional framework of the book, which pulls the specific instance of the Neo-Babylonians in the direction of a general paradigm about wicked oppressing nations. No doubt "Chaldea"/"Babylon" became a cipher for ruthless conquerors and overlords in later times.

The impressive combination of prophetic and psalmic forms in the book of Habakkuk has stimulated much speculation about both the prophet's and the completed book's relation to the cult. Although clearly borrowing, as many prophetic writings do, from forms of speech shaped in the cult (see pp. 172–74), the resultant shape of Habakkuk 1–2 lacks conclusive liturgical signs. The appended psalm may imply a later cultic usage for the book, but even this is not certain, since the psalm may simply be a rhetorical embellishment to reinforce confidence in the prophet by appeal to cultic traditions.

Habakkuk shared with Zephaniah a sense of faithful waiting upon Yahweh in the face of prevailing arrogance and disillusionment. A difference is that Habakkuk internalizes the problem of abiding faithfulness by speaking in the first person (2:1; 3:1, 16-19). Yet this autobiographical confidence in Yahweh is not solipsistic, for it speaks against the backdrop of the whole people's plight (1:1-4) and looks to the vindication of faithfulness in a future salvation of the community (chap. 3). Habakkuk would have been recognizable among the humble and lowly bearers of the faith of whom Zephaniah spoke.

Jeremiah

Jeremiah is said to have prophesied from 626 to a time some few months or years following the destruction of Jerusalem in 586. Since the prophet's book contains no oracles concretely linked to Josiah's reign or to the Deuteronomic reformation, either the prophet experienced a long and implausible silent period (626–609), or else the date in the superscription should be interpreted to refer to the date of his birth. This interpretation makes a measure of sense given the prophet's consciousness of having been predestined at birth to a prophetic task (1:4).[13] In any case, as far as the record goes, the public activity of Jeremiah began in 609 in connection with Josiah's death, which precipitated a wrenching change in political leadership in Judah.

Jeremiah's work presupposes the failure of the Deuteronomic reformation and the shift of power in the ancient Near East from

Assyria to the Neo-Babylonian Empire. The burden of Jeremiah's message was that Judah's internal order was so corrupt that it would be swept away by the Neo-Babylonian Empire, unless the leadership repented and practiced social justice, so long violated. In his view, the covenant traditions and the cult of Jerusalem provided no basis for security in the absence of social justice, nor did reliance on Egypt to spare Judah from the Neo-Babylonia Empire provide an external way of escape.

By the time Jehoiakim and, later, Zedekiah rebelled, and as the Neo-Babylonian Empire moved to crush the second rebellion as it had the first, Jeremiah perceived that there was no more breathing space for internal reform. He took the next logical step of calling on Zedekiah to surrender to the besiegers. Jeremiah was convinced that the ensuing stage of the people's life would have to be lived without king or temple cult. That Jeremiah fully intended such a reduced and altered program for his people is shown by his decision to stay in Judah and to participate in the Neo-Babylonian regime of reconstruction (see pp. 243–48) established at Mizpah under the direction of Gedaliah, the native governor appointed by the conquerors and an erstwhile supporter of the prophet (40:1-6).

Jeremiah thus not only drew the radical conclusion that his people's future was detachable from institutions of monarchy and cult, but he lived to take part in one brief political venture, when nationalists who aspired to revive a Judahite state assassinated Gedaliah and many of his associates (40:13—41:18) and fled to Egypt to escape the expected Neo-Babylonian reprisals, carrying Jeremiah with them against his will (42:1—43:7). The last we hear of the prophet is a threat against Egypt and the fugitive Judahites who trusted in Egypt for asylum (43:8-13).

The exact balance and interaction of judgment threats and calls to repentance in the message of Jeremiah must be assessed in terms of the way his book came into existence. Earlier scholarship stressed the role of Jeremiah in writing down or dictating his own oracles and the role of his secretary Baruch in penning narrative passages about the career of the prophet, to which were added sermons with marked affinities to DH prose.[14]

Nowadays there is much more emphasis upon a Jeremianic stream of tradition that included the prophet's own poetry, narratives about how his words were received by his contemporaries, together with prose reactualizations of words and themes from the prophet developed as preaching and teaching materials to apply to the situation of exiles or of politically deprived Palestinian Jews.[15] No doubt we meet the authentic Jeremiah within his book, but all the materials were preserved and put together by survivors of Jerusalem's fall who were constantly reading, assessing, and elaborating the prophet's words and deeds to instruct them in their present, wholly altered conditions of life (see pp. 243–48).

Jeremiah 36 tells how in 604/603 the prophet, debarred from the temple because of his critical preaching, dictated his words of judgment to Baruch, who prepared a scroll that was publicly read by the secretary to a temple audience. When it was contemptuously destroyed by Jehoiakim, Jeremiah instructed Baruch to rewrite the scroll—but with further words added (36:32). Scholars have generally sought the contents of the original scroll in the poetic oracles of chaps. 1–25. Many of these oracles, however, are just as likely to have been formulated after 604 as before, so that conflicting opinions on the contents of the scroll have been advanced without consensus.

Theories of the composition of Jeremiah were long dominated by the assumption that the three types of material (poetic oracles, narratives, and prose sermons) were separately originated and then combined in stages to form the completed book. Some scholars have subsequently developed a strong preference for the view that all three types of material developed side by side in a number of tradition complexes generally identified as follows:

1. Jeremiah's words of judgment against Judah and Jerusalem (chaps. 1–24)
2. Jeremiah's words of judgment against the nations (chaps. 25, 46–51)
3. Narratives about the reception of Jeremiah's words by those in authority (chaps. 26–35, [36])
4. A relatively cohesive extended narrative about Jeremiah and the last years of Judah's independence ([35], 36–45).

All these tradition complexes were probably developed and preserved in Deuteronomistic circles and eventually were assembled as a book by joining the complexes in a final redaction.

The previous assumption that Baruch was Jeremiah's biographer in the narratives of chaps. 26–45 is no longer evident. For one thing, Baruch was carried into Egypt along with Jeremiah (43:5-7), and an Egyptian setting for the compilation of the book of Jeremiah is less likely than a Palestinian or Babylonian setting. More significant is the lack of true biography in the book of Jeremiah, since the narratives do not give us a proportioned "life of the prophet" so much as they clarify the character of the domestic opposition to his preaching and validate the fulfillment of his words of doom.

The narratives in the complexes of chaps. 26–36 and 37–45 have likely been clustered for the purpose of showing how the word of Yahweh through Jeremiah overcame enormous resistance and misunderstanding to bring about a judgment on Judah that was fully explained in advance by Jeremiah and thus avoidable, had the leadership of Judah heeded him.

The insertion of chap. 52 (see 39:1-10) produces the effect that both DH (in 2 Kings) and Jeremiah close with the same incident: the release of Jehoiachin from prison and his reception at the table of the king, thus giving him the status of most favored royal prisoner. Some interpreters, however, claim to see in the addition of "until the day of his [Jehoiachin's] death" a corroboration of Jeremiah's prediction in 22:26 and thus a denial or dampening of hope in a monarchic restitution in Judah.

The tradition complex of Jeremiah 26–35, as well as the earlier chap. 24, contains several expressions of chastened hope concerning Yahweh's future for his people beyond destruction.

1. *The Exiles of 597 as "Good Figs."* In a visionary report dated sometime after the deportation of 597, Jeremiah likens Jehoiachin and the deportees of that year to a basket of good figs and Zedekiah and the deportees of 586 to a basket of bad figs (chap. 24). Only the first group will be restored—repentant—from exile. The Jeremianic core of the passage was probably a severe warning to the Zedekiah faction that their hopes of rebellion were as untimely as spoiled fruit. By comparison, those already in captivity stood to learn obedience to Yahweh and could rightfully expect to return to Palestine.

2. *Letter to the Exiles of 597.* Apparently in 594, in the face of news about plots of rebellion, Jeremiah sent a letter to the exiles of 597

counseling them to settle into a normal life in Babylonia in anticipation of a long exile (29:1-14). Here and elsewhere in the book he speaks of a seventy-year dominion of the Neo-Babylonian Empire before the exiles can expect release. Apparently the prophet intended to project a long period of time for Judah's subjection and exile, perhaps the typical full life span (Ps. 90:10), and the seventy years may have carried overtones of a fixed world period as implied in a text of the Assyrian king Esarhaddon, who remarked that his predecessor Sennacherib's destruction of Babylon was to last seventy years according to the god Marduk.[16]

3. *Redemption of Family Property.* During the final siege of Jerusalem, Jeremiah exercised his "right of redemption" by purchasing a field located in his hometown of Anathoth (chap. 32). The prophet interpreted the purchase as a sign of the future renewal of socioeconomic life in Judah: "Houses and fields and vineyards shall again be bought in this land!" (32:15). Although 32:36-41 embellishes the action with reference to a return of exiles, the central reference of the purchase appears to have been to renewed life in Judah among those who would stay in the land under a Neo-Babylonian regime of reconstruction.

4. *"The Little Book of Comfort" and the New Covenant.* Collected in chaps. 30–31 are prophecies of salvation to follow disaster in what has been called "the little book of comfort." Most likely they are a potpourri of promissory pieces from the exilic Jeremianic traditionists who reworked units from Jeremiah and developed more encouraging words of their own.

This collection contains the famous "new covenant" passage, which foresees a fresh relationship between Israel/Judah and Yahweh that is internally grounded and motivated, no longer requiring external admonition and teaching, yet thoroughly communal. Christian readings of this passage as an anticipation of the new covenant in Jesus Christ (cf. Luke 22:20; 1 Cor. 11:25; Heb. 8:8-13; 10:16) have frequently distorted it into a highly individualized and spiritualized expectation. While the promise may very well presuppose the end of cult, it nonetheless envisions the realization of the old laws in a corporate body continuous with old Israel. It reads like the work of an exilic Jeremianic preacher who has pulled together aspects of the prophet's thought into a bold formulation of radical renewal.

Jeremiah also produced a number of individual laments in which he speaks in the first person about his mission, his opponents, his frustrations, and his self-doubts, sometimes cast in the form of dialogue between himself and deity (e.g., 11:18-23; 12:1-6; 15:10-12). Although some scholars have fastened on these so-called Confessions as disclosures about the man's personal thoughts and feelings concerning his task,[17] form critics and tradition-historical critics have countered that the "I" of the prophet functions as the spokesman for the desolation and alienation of his people.

There is much value in these reminders about the corporate context of Jeremiah's words and deeds.[18] Nonetheless, aspects of individual torment cannot be expunged from the laments and vividly highlight the human struggle Jeremiah waged to sustain his work in the face of opposition so great that at times he had to reassess the grounds, motives, and resources of his calling. We learn of his voluntary desistance from marriage, his withdrawal from feasts and funerals, the scoffing and plots on his life from friends and relatives, his accusations of desertion and deception against Yahweh, his conclusion to speak the truth he knew in spite of consequences, and the fortification of resolve that he received from his religious commitment. The cultic interpretation of the Confessions does contain the valid proviso that all these sufferings of the prophet were experienced as a fate with and on behalf of his people.

Particularly striking is Jeremiah's head-on confrontation with prophets like Hananiah who first promised the invulnerability of Jerusalem and, after 597, the speedy return of the king and deported leaders (chap. 28). Jeremiah accuses these prophets of following visions of their own making and of stealing one another's words: they are glib triflers with the welfare of Judah who simply do not have a word from Yahweh (23:9-40).

It is evident, however, that this was not simply a narrow religious issue over who had the best foresight into coming events. Considerable sociopolitical information in the book of Jeremiah reveals two opposed political alignments of prophets, priests, and political leaders in the period 609–586.[19] The kings and a majority of bureaucrats, priests, and prophets formed an autonomy party that sought independence from Babylon with the aid of Egypt. A smaller group of court officials, Jeremiah and perhaps other prophets and some priests, formed a coexistence party that favored continued submission to Babylonia or, once revolt had broken out, capitulation to the besieging enemy. There are also discernible differences in the domestic assessments and policies of these two parties. The anti-Babylonian autonomists equated national survival with the full independence of Judah under its present leadership, whereas the pro-Babylonian coexisters equated national survival with the socioeconomic and religiocultural preservation of the people of Judah.

In short, autonomists saw the main clash or contradiction in the situation to be an interstate conflict between Judah and Babylon, whereas coexisters saw the main clash or contradiction to be an interclass conflict between the opposed interests of the ruling class and the majority populace of Judah. For autonomists it was the will of Yahweh, expressed through his prophets (e.g., Hananiah), to preserve Judah under its present regime and prevailing policies. For coexisters it was the will of Yahweh, expressed through his prophets (e.g., Jeremiah), to preserve the people of Judah by sweeping away the present leadership and policies through a purging Neo-Babylonian military and political action.

In all probability both parties were headed by socially prominent and powerful persons. There was a division in the ruling class, one segment seeing internal socioeconomic and cultural oppression as central to the determination of foreign policy, whereas the other segment either did not recognize oppression within Judah or merely dismissed it as exaggerated or trumped up and, in any case, inconsequential in comparison to the threat of foreign domination.

In terms of anthropological and sociological perspectives on prophecy, Jeremiah and his allies occupied the dangerous position of peripheral irritants who sought to become central influencers of those in power. Jeremiah and allies were outsiders in the sense that the public policies they fought for lost out at the time, but insiders in the sense that their point of view was vigorously represented within the establishment before it was finally vanquished and its advocates neutralized.

We do not know the extent to which the disputing coalitions were directly linked to a base in the general populace. It is known from contemporary military correspondence, the

Lachish letters (Web Table A, 4L), that opposition to the revolt against Babylon was a serious issue within the Jerusalem court and the army ranks. Jeremiah's opponents certainly believed that he had great power to sway people to his treasonous views and thus to undercut national unity in the war effort.

It is sensible to expect that many of the long-suffering peasants of Judah sympathized with popular preaching that implied or advocated policies that would lighten their burdens and spare them more war and hardship. Nevertheless, neither mob actions nor organizing activities among them are reported. Also, as far as we can judge, Jeremiah and the other coexisters did not attempt a coup or uprising against Jerusalem leadership but depended on the impending intervention of Babylon to overturn a status quo they viewed as prejudicial to the real interests of the people and inimical to the known will of Yahweh (see pp. 214–15).

NOTES

1. Stages and aspects of the reformation are discussed by Bustenay Oded, "Josiah and the Deuteronomic Reformation," in *IJH*, 458–69.

2. R. B. Y. Scott, "Isaiah," in *IB* 5:231–32.

3. Martin Buber, *The Prophetic Faith* (New York: Macmillan, 1949), 67, 135.

4. The first and third of Isaiah's sons were unmistakably Isaiah's children, and the context strongly argues that the second, Immanuel, was also the prophet's child. See Norman K. Gottwald, "Immanuel as the Prophet's Son," *VT* 8 (1958): 36–47.

5. Roland E. Clements, *Isaiah and the Deliverance of Jerusalem,* JSOTSup 13 (Sheffield: JSOT Press, 1980).

6. For an analysis of the Isaianic dialectic between what people intend and hope, especially in politics, and what they actually achieve, see Gottwald, *AKE*, 147–208.

7. See David L. Petersen, "Isaiah 28, A Redaction Critical Study," *SBLSP* 17 (1979): 2:101–22; and J. Cheryl Exum, "Isaiah 28–32: A Literary Approach," *SBLSP* 17 (1979): 2:123–51 = "'Whom Will He Teach Knowledge?': A Literary Approach to Isaiah 28, " in *Art and Meaning: Rhetoric in Biblical Literature,* ed. D. J. A. Clines et al., JSOTSup 19 (Sheffield: JSOT Press, 1982), 108–39.

8. Norbert Lohfink, "Deuteronomy," in *IDBSup,* 229–32.

9. Gerhard von Rad, *Studies in Deuteronomy,* trans. David Stalker, SBT 1/9 (London: SCM, 1953), 60–69.

10. Moshe Weinfeld, *Deuteronomy and the Deuteronomic School* (Oxford: Clarendon, 1972).

11. W. Eugene Claburn, "The Fiscal Basis of Josiah's Reform," *JBL* 92 (1973): 11–22; Shigeyuki Nakanose, *Josiah's Passover* (Maryknoll, N.Y.: Orbis, 1993), 1–112.

12. Childs, "Nahum," in *IOTS*, 441–46.

13. J. Philip Hyatt, "The Beginning of Jeremiah's Prophecy," *ZAW* 78 (1966): 204–14.

14. J. Philip Hyatt, "Jeremiah," in *IB* 5:788; John Bright, *Jeremiah,* AB 24 (Garden City, N.Y.: Doubleday, 1965), e.g., lv–lxxxv.

15. E. W. Nicholson, *Preaching to the Exiles: A Study of the Prose Traditions in the Book of Jeremiah* (New York: Schocken, 1971); Robert P. Carroll, *From Chaos to Covenant: Prophecy in the Book of Jeremiah* (New York: Crossroad, 1981).

16. Gottwald, *AKE*, 265–66; Carroll, *From Chaos to Covenant,* 203–4.

17. John Skinner, *Prophecy and Religion: Studies in the Life of Jeremiah* (Cambridge: Cambridge University Press, 1922), 201–30.

18. Carroll, *From Chaos to Covenant*, 107–30.

19. Burke O. Long, "Social Dimensions of Prophetic Conflict," *Semeia* 21 (1981): 31–53, with response by Gottwald, 107–9. Carroll (*From Chaos to Covenant,* 136–97) collects and comments, often astutely, on texts that treat Jeremiah's conflicts with kings and prophets, but generally from the perspective of exilic redactors rather than in the direct terms of sociopolitical organization and conflict in the late kingdom of Judah.

FOR FURTHER READING

Cook, Stephen L. *The Social Roots of Biblical Yahwism.* Chaps. 5 and 7. Atlanta: Society of Biblical Literature, 2004.

Hayes, John H. and Stuart A. Irvine. *Isaiah: The Eighth Century Prophet.* Nashville: Abingdon, 1987.

House, Paul R. *Zephaniah: A Prophetic Drama.* Sheffield: Almond, 1987.

Kim, Uriah Y. *Decolonizing Josiah: Toward a Postcolonial Reading of the Deuteronomic History.* Sheffield: Sheffield Phoenix, 2006.

Mosala, Itumeleng J. *Biblical Hermeneutics and Black Theology in South Africa.* Grand Rapids: Eerdmans, 1989.

Rubenstein, Richard E. *Thus Saith the Lord: The Revolutionary Moral Vision of Isaiah and Jeremiah.* Orlando: Harcourt, 2006.

Sharp, Carolyn J. *Prophecy and Ideology in Jeremiah: Struggles for Authority in the Deutero-Jeremianic Prose.* London: T & T Clark, 2003.

QUESTIONS FOR STUDY

1. What do the reigns of Ahaz, Hezekiah, and Manasseh tell us about the Assyrian Empire?

2. What lessons do the Elohist, the DH, and the prophets appear to emphasize in the rise and fall of Israel and Judah?

3. Explain what is meant by the "theopolitical" advocacy of Isaiah. What contradictory positions did the prophet hold in relation to the revolt against Assyria?

4. Who were the Levites? What does Deuteronomy tell us about them? How does one theory connect them and court officials to the text of Deuteronomy?

5. What do the details of Jeremiah's biography tell us about the role of the prophet in ancient Israel?

Fig. A. Statue of the influential minister of Egyptian pharaoh Amenhotep III, Amenhotep son of Hapu, as a scribe. This image signified status second only to the king and gods, and so was a form used to depict the most powerful men in the land. New Kingdom, Eighteenth Dynasty, 1390–1352 B.C.E. Egyptian Museum, Cairo. Photo: © Werner Forman / Art Resource, N.Y.

Fig. B. Detail from the so-called *Standard of Ur*, side B. This panel shows, in the top register, men of leisure seated at a banquet, perhaps after a victory; in the second register, men driving cattle and sheep. In a lower register (not shown), slaves bear heavy burdens on their backs. Wood, lapis lazuli, and shell. Ca. 2500 B.C.E. Photo: © Werner Forman / Art Resource, N.Y.

Fig. C. The "high place" in Megiddo, Israel. Megiddo is the legendary Armageddon, the site of the ultimate battle described in Revelation. The settlement dates back some six thousand years. During Solomon's kingdom, it was a fortified chariot city (according to I Kings 9:15). Photo: © Erich Lessing / Art Resource, N.Y.

Fig. D. Head of a prosperous Israelite woman with diadem of pearls, two long curls falling on her shoulders, and two rows of pearls around her neck, from the Hebron district, Israel. Ivory. Late Iron Age II. Height 5.3 cm. Reuben & Edith Hecht Collection, Haifa University. Photo: © Erich Lessing / Art Resource, N.Y.

Fig. E. Bust of a woman with an Egyptian hairstyle, from Gaza. Stone. 1550–1200 B.C.E. (Late Bronze/Early Iron Age). Reuben & Edith Hecht Collection, Haifa University. Photo: © Erich Lessing / Art Resource, N.Y.

Fig. F. Clay lid of an Egyptian anthropoid coffin from the cemetery of Deir el-Ballah. Israel Museum (IDAM), Jerusalem. Photo: © Erich Lessing / Art Resource, N.Y.

Fig. G. "Shrine of the Steles," from a Canaanite temple at Hazor. Basalt. Israel Museum (IDAM), Jerusalem. Photo: © Erich Lessing / Art Resource, N.Y.

Fig. H. Photo of Jebel Musa, traditionally identified as Mount Sinai (Mount Horeb). Ca. 1860, by Francis Frith (1822–1898). Photo: © The Francis Frith Collection / Art Resource, N.Y.

Fig. I. *Israelites Carrying the Ark of the Covenant* from *The Gates of Paradise* (1425–1452) by Lorenzo Ghiberti (1370–1455). Bronze doors of the Cathedral baptistery, Florence, Italy. Photo: © Timothy McCarthy / Art Resource, N.Y.

Fig. J. Stone pillars from a possible storehouse at Hazor, Israel. Use of this type of structure is still debated: was it a stable, a storehouse, or a bazaar? Hazor was one of the royal cities and supply posts in Solomon's kingdom. Photo: © Erich Lessing / Art Resource, N.Y.

Fig. K. The goddess of the Nome (province) of Thebes with club, bow, and quiver leads rows of Palestinian prisoners. Are they Philistines, Canaanites, or Israelites? Relief in memory of the victory of Sheshonk I, Pharaoh Shishak of the Bible. Bas relief, south wall, Amon Temple, Karnak, Thebes. 930 B.C.E. (Tanite Period). Photo: © Erich Lessing / Art Resource, N.Y.

Fig. L. Square altar with horns on the four top corners, from Megiddo. Limestone. Israelite. 1000–586 B.C.E. (Iron Age). Israel Museum (IDAM), Jerusalem. Photo: © Erich Lessing / Art Resource, N.Y.

Fig. M. The Tunnel of Siloam brought water from the spring of Gihon to the Pool of Siloam inside the city of Jerusalem, constructed under King Hezekiah, 700 B.C.E., to ensure the water supply of the city during a siege. Photo: © Erich Lessing / Art Resource, N.Y.

Fig. N. Female figurine from Gath, associated with the cult of fertility. Eighth–seventh century B.C.E. Photo: Foliet © Snark / Art Resource, N.Y.

Fig. O. Two models of horses and riders. Clay figurines from Judah. Tenth–sixth century B.C.E. (Late Iron Age). Israel Museum (IDAM), Jerusalem. Photo: © Erich Lessing / Art Resource, N.Y.

Fig. P. Tambourine girl and double pipe player. Clay figurines. Ca. 800 B.C.E. Israel Museum (IDAM), Jerusalem. Photo: © Erich Lessing / Art Resource, N.Y.

Fig. Q. Brown jasper seal with Hebrew inscription: "Lidnihu son of Nadnihu." Found near Jerusalem. 1.8 x 1.2 x 2.1 cm. 800–700 B.C.E. Reuben & Edith Hecht Collection, Haifa University. Photo: © Erich Lessing / Art Resource, N.Y.

Fig. R. Colossal statue of a winged human-headed bull from the Northwest Palace of Ashurnasirpal II (Room S), intended to protect the palace against demonic forces. Nimrud (ancient Kalhu), northern Iraq. Neo-Assyrian. Ca. 883–859 B.C.E. Height 309 cm. Inv. 118872. British Museum, London. Photo: © British Museum / Art Resource, N.Y.

Fig. S. Darius I the Great (550–486 B.C.E.) giving audience. Detail of a relief in the treasury of the palace at Persepolis, Persia. Achaemenid Period, 491–486 B.C.E. Persepolis, Iran. Photo: © SEF / Art Resource, N.Y.

Fig. T. The Ishtar Gate, built during the reign of Nebuchadnezzar II (605–562 B.C.E.). Babylon. Sixth century B.C.E. Color-glazed terra-cotta tiles, 14.73 x 15.70 x 4.36 m. Inv. VAMF 94. Vorderasiatisches Museum, Staatliche Museen zu Berlin. Photo: © Bildarchiv Preussischer Kulturbesitz / Art Resource, N.Y.

Fig. U. Representatives of a conquered people present a gift to Darius I. Detail relief from the palace of Darius I. Persepolis, Iran. Photo: © SEF / Art Resource, N.Y.

Fig. V. Shadrach, Meshach, and Abednego, the "three youths" in the "fiery furnace" of Nebuchadnezzar (Daniel 3). Catacomb of Priscilla, Rome. Photo: © Erich Lessing / Art Resource, N.Y.

Fig. W. One of the earliest known portraits of Alexander the Great. Silver tetradrachm of Lysimachus. Greek. 305–281 B.C.E. From the Mint of Lampsakos (modern Lâpseki, Turkey). On the reverse is a seated figure of the goddess Athena, and a Greek legend that translates "Of King Lysimachus." 30 mm diameter. CM 1919,0820.1. British Museum, London. Photo: © British Museum / Art Resource, N.Y.

Fig. X. Two bronze coins. Left: Coin of Antigonus, last Hasmonean king of Israel, shows a menorah. 40–37 B.C.E. Right, inscription in the wreath: "Period of John Hyrcanus II" (High Priest, 67–40 B.C.E.). 1.5 cm diameter. Reifenberg Collection. Israel Museum (IDAM), Jerusalem. Photo: © Erich Lessing / Art Resource, N.Y.

Fig. Y. The caves of Qumran, where the Dead Sea Scrolls were found in 1947. Qumran, Israel. Photo: © Erich Lessing / Art Resource, N.Y.

Fig. Z. A column from the Scroll of Isaiah discovered among the Dead Sea Scrolls. Israel Museum (IDAM), Jerusalem. Photo: © Snark / Art Resource, N.Y.

Fig. AA. Left, portrait of the emperor Vespasian (69–79 C.E.). Right, *Judea capta* (Judea is vanquished), Latin inscription accompanying the image of a disconsolate woman beneath a palm tree. Israel Museum (IDAM), Jerusalem. Photo: © Erich Lessing / Art Resource, N.Y.

Fig. BB. Roman soldiers taking the spoils from the Temple in Jerusalem. Full-size cast of the bas-relief on the Arch of Titus in the Roman Forum. The original arch was built after 81 C.E. to celebrate the capture of Jerusalem in 70 C.E. Museo della Civilta Romana, Rome. Photo: © Vanni / Art Resource, N.Y.

HOME RULE
UNDER GREAT EMPIRES:
ISRAEL'S COLONIAL RECOVERY

IV

DEMARCATION OF THE HISTORICAL PERIOD

We have accounted for the oldest parts of the Hebrew Bible as the writings of a politically independent people who lived near the southernmost end of the Syro-Palestinian corridor joining Mesopotamia and Egypt. Beginning with the sixth century, however, the geographic and socio-historical frameworks of ancient Israel shifted radically.

The people of Israel were increasingly scattered into foreign lands, no longer ruling themselves but subjects of successive great imperial powers: Neo-Babylonia, Persia, Macedonia, Ptolemaic Egypt, and Seleucid Syria. These new conditions posed far-reaching challenges to the self-identity, ideology, and organizational life of the self-conscious descendants of old Israel.

The segment of this later history that we shall trace extends from the destruction of Jerusalem in 586 B.C.E. to Pompey's imposition of Roman rule on Palestine in 63 B.C.E. The choice of the introduction of Roman dominion as a terminal date is shaped by the fact that this was the first major political breaking point following the completion of all the writings that were to be included in the Hebrew Bible, although a full accounting of the canon also involves the triumph of the Pharisees as the shapers of Judaism following the unsuccessful war against Rome in 66–70 C.E. (see pp. 67–70).

BIBLICAL AND EXTRABIBLICAL SOURCES

There are major problems in reconstructing the exilic and postexilic history of the Jews, owing to meager biblical records that depend for their interpretation on meager extrabiblical information.

Many key questions in this later biblical history must be answered by inference and conjecture. This does not mean that the later period was literarily inactive; indeed, the contrary was true. All three parts of the Hebrew Bible were edited in this period (see pp. 65–67). Moreover, new writings eventually found their way into the Law, the Prophets, and the Writings (see p. 238). The difficulty is that hard historical data are scant except for the Maccabean-Hasmonean era. Some of this slack is taken up by Greco-Roman historians, by documents from the great empires under which the Jews lived, and by the archaeology of the Persian and Hellenistic periods in Palestine.

For exilic and postexilic history there is nothing to equal the fullness and continuity of the historical and history-like materials of earlier Israel. The last great history-like compilation within the Hebrew Bible is 1 and 2 Chronicles, Ezra, and Nehemiah (see pp. 298–301). Chronicles, however, tells us nothing about the exile other than that Cyrus ended it, while Ezra and Nehemiah clarify aspects of the reconstruction of Judah and give scattered clues to Jewish life in Babylonia and Persia, beginning in 538 B.C.E. and ending in the period around 432–398 B.C.E. (depending on the date given to Ezra). Within this span of time, the period from 515 to about 458–445 B.C.E. (again depending on the Ezra date) is unreported.

The next great block of Jewish historiography is 1 and 2 Maccabees (in the Apocrypha), which treat the Maccabean revolt and the early Hasmonean dynasty from 186 to 135 B.C.E. Josephus, writing at the end of the first century C.E., recounts the whole history from 586 to 63 B.C.E. in his *Jewish Antiquities* and is our sole connected source for more than two hundred years (from 432–398 B.C.E. to 186 B.C.E.). His recital of Jewish life under the late Persian kings, Alexander the Great, and the Ptolemaic rulers, however, is sketchy and, at points, confused.

Prophetic writings of Ezekiel and Isaiah of the Exile (Isaiah 40–55) obliquely provide valuable limited historical data on the Babylonian exile, as does Lamentations for exilic conditions in Palestine. The prophetic books of Haggai and Zechariah 1–8 are important for documenting the rebuilding of the temple in 520–516 B.C.E., and Isaiah 56–66, Malachi, and Joel among the late prophetic writings throw light on communal conditions in restored Israel within the broad period 538–450 B.C.E. Daniel's propaganda piece for Jewish resistance dates from the Maccabean War against the Seleucids, 167–164 B.C.E., but may include older traditions of some historical value.

The remainder of the canonical writings are in literary genres that do not use historical modes of expression or attach obviously to particular historical milieus. They consist of cult lyrics (Psalms, Lamentations), love songs (Song of Songs), short stories (Ruth, Jonah, Esther), didactic wisdom (Proverbs, Job, Ecclesiastes), and symbolic prophecies with obscure references to historical events (Isaiah 24–27; Zechariah 9–14).

Since the biblical books and sections of books written after 586 B.C.E. are so meager in historical reference, it is difficult to construct a history or social location of the literature in other than very general terms (chart 13.2; also, see the conclusion).

Fortunately, extrabiblical Jewish writings in the Apocrypha and Pseudepigrapha (see p. 58; table 2.1 and Web Table E) illuminate the cultural conditions of Jews in the Hellenistic Dispersion, especially in Egypt. The same sources, along with the Dead Sea Scrolls (see pp. 58–59; Web Table F) and early rabbinic traditions (see p. 59), helpfully clarify the proliferation of traditions and parties in Palestine from 200 B.C.E. onward.

The recovery of occasional contemporary documents has enriched our knowledge of particular points in exilic and postexilic history: (1) the ration system of the Neo-Babylonians for royal captives (Weidner tablets [Web Table A, 5A]); (2) economic activities among Babylonian Jews in the fifth century (Murashu texts);[1] (3) cultic institutions among Egyptian Jews at the end of the fifth century (Elephantine papyri [Web Table A, 5D]); (4) political events in Samaria under Alexander the Great (Samaria or Wadi Dâliyeh papyri);[2] and (5) the political and economic administration of Ptolemaic Palestine (Zenon papyri).[3] A wealth of archaeological data on the earliest synagogues, all from Greco-Roman times, has yielded nothing to favor the long-popular view that the synagogue originated as early as the Babylonian exile. The earliest appearance of the synagogue seems to have been about 250 B.C.E.

DECLINE OF LATE BIBLICAL HISTORIOGRAPHY

Why do the later writings of the Hebrew Bible reflect such a diminished interest in large historical frameworks? The answer lies in a complex of factors, all of which have to do with the profound shock that Israelites underwent in the transition from political independence to colonial servitude and in the limiting of their ability to determine their own destiny.

No historical or history-like overview of the entire span of Jewish colonial experience was attempted after the exile. The Israelite sense of making history was attenuated. In just this climate, the Law, and then the Prophets, stood out as collections of witnesses to a great past that was no longer matched in contemporary Jewish experience.

In Seleucid and Roman times, when major revolts shook Jewish Palestine—and when for about a century Jews were again politically independent—there was an outburst of historiography best surviving in 1 and 2 Maccabees and in Josephus, but the former did not enter the canon because they were written in Greek and celebrated political solutions that had become dubious to the rabbinic leaders rounding out the Hebrew Bible.

The phasing out of late biblical interest in historiography prior to and even after 1 and 2 Maccabees seems to be a corollary of the move toward authoritative traditions about a more distant past whose interpretation set the norms for a community that felt marginalized from the decisive currents of contemporary history. The diminishment of prophecy as a movement of critical interpreters of present history was also a facet of this sense of history being made over the heads of the Jews. Religiously, this sense of powerlessness was expressed in terms of faithful preservation of the glorious history of God's past deeds in Israel during a period of marking time and making do with cult, wisdom, and apocalyptic (see pp. 74–76, 328–33).

ORGANIZING THE PRESENTATION OF LATE BIBLICAL LITERATURE

All in all, the paucity of historical sources in comparison with the fullness of chronologically free-floating religious writings in colonial Israel makes it difficult to organize the presentation of the later parts of the Hebrew Bible along the historical lines compatible to the preexilic traditions. Sometimes syntheses of the period have been organized around central and peripheral institutions and bodies of tradition, characteristically placing law and temple cult at the center and treating wisdom and apocalyptic as eccentric departures from the norm. But this approach tends to overstate the primacy of the core features, as though they were exclusive monopolies on religious interest and expression.

The wisest procedure is to characterize the sociohistorical developments as precisely as possible and then to examine the late literature of the Hebrew Bible, distinguishing between those exilic and postexilic writings that went into the completion of the first two segments of the Hebrew Bible (the Law and the Prophets), and those exilic and postexilic writings that eventually fell into a third collection (the Writings). The miscellaneous Writings developed partly because some of these other books were written after the Law and Prophets were completed as collections and partly because many of them exhibited literary genres and ideological outlooks that were either altogether absent from Law and Prophets or constituted minor aspects of the older narrative and prophetic writings.

In choosing this literary-canonical principle of division for treatment of the later biblical literature, we must be on our guard against an overly restrictive literary approach that neglects the literature as an expression of social reality and also against an overly rigid canonical outlook that retrojects the later decisions about canon (e.g., that the canon will be composed of three parts or of so many books) into the earlier periods.

The whole of the Hebrew Bible grew by parts and in stages, and determinations of what was or was not authoritative were related to existing interests and conflicts in the community. Only at the end of the first century C.E. was the canon of the Hebrew Bible rounded out as a whole, since prior to that time it had not seemed critical for Jews to fix the boundaries of authoritative writings more exactly.

Accordingly, chap. 10 will set forth the known history of late biblical times, with pertinent late biblical literary traditions commented on in context, plus writings of the Apocrypha, Pseudepigrapha, and Dead Sea Scrolls. In chap. 11 biblical traditions that completed the Law and the Prophets as collections will be considered in their own right, with rough chronological ordering of the later prophetic writings (table IV.1). In chap. 12 we shall examine biblical traditions that extended beyond the Law and the Prophets to become the canonical Writings, not clearly delineated until the Roman period. We shall group these traditions according to literary genres, discussing both the separate books and the sociohistorical settings of the genres (table IV.2). We shall take occasional comparative note of extrabiblical Jewish writings that throw light on the late biblical works.

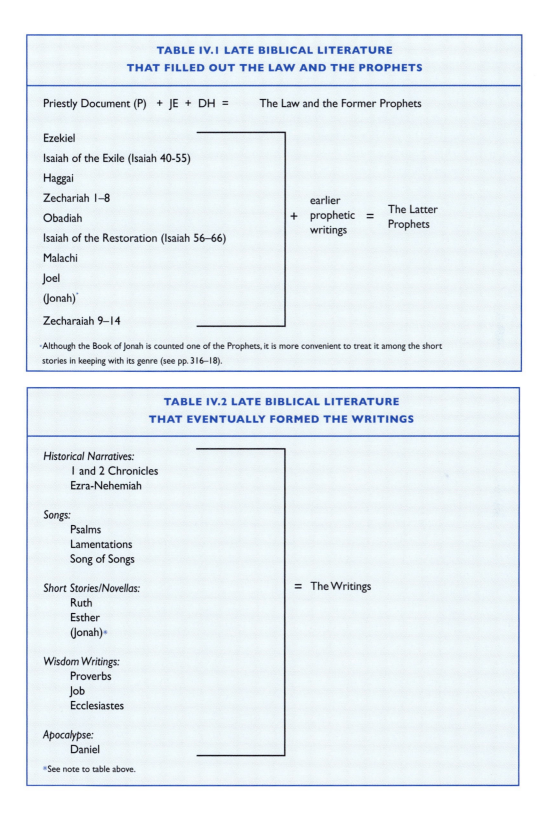

TABLE IV.I LATE BIBLICAL LITERATURE
THAT FILLED OUT THE LAW AND THE PROPHETS

Priestly Document (P) + JE + DH =   The Law and the Former Prophets

Ezekiel

Isaiah of the Exile (Isaiah 40-55)

Haggai

Zechariah 1–8

Obadiah   +   earlier prophetic writings   =   The Latter Prophets

Isaiah of the Restoration (Isaiah 56–66)

Malachi

Joel

(Jonah)*

Zecharaiah 9–14

*Although the Book of Jonah is counted one of the Prophets, it is more convenient to treat it among the short stories in keeping with its genre (see pp. 316–18).

TABLE IV.2 LATE BIBLICAL LITERATURE
THAT EVENTUALLY FORMED THE WRITINGS

Historical Narratives:
    1 and 2 Chronicles
    Ezra-Nehemiah

Songs:
    Psalms
    Lamentations
    Song of Songs

Short Stories/Novellas: = The Writings
    Ruth
    Esther
    (Jonah)*

Wisdom Writings:
    Proverbs
    Job
    Ecclesiastes

Apocalypse:
    Daniel

*See note to table above.

NOTES

1. On the Murashu tablets see D. Winton Thomas, ed., *Documents from Old Testament Times* (London: Nelson, 1958), 95–96.
2. On the Samaria or Dâliyeh papyri see Paul W. Lapp and Nancy Lapp, eds., *Discoveries in the Wâdī ed-Dâliyeh,* AASOR 41 (Cambridge: American Schools of Oriental Research, 1974).
3. On the Zeno(n) papyri see Victor A. Tcherikover and A. Fuks, *Corpus Papyrorum Judaicarum* (Cambridge: Harvard University Press, 1957), 1:1–47.

Sociohistorical Horizons of Colonial Israel

SUMMARY

Sources for the dispersion and restoration

Jewish responses to Neo-Babylonian domination

Jewish responses to Persian domination: Sheshbazzar, Zerubbabel, Nehemiah, Ezra

Jewish responses to Macedonian and Ptolemaic domination

Alexander

Jewish responses to Seleucid domination: The Maccabees

The rise and fall of the Hasmonean state

READ THE BIBLICAL TEXT

Ezra-Nehemiah

I and 2 Maccabees

See additional materials at fortresspress.com/ gottwald; consult Carta Bible Atlas *maps 165–217*

FROM INDEPENDENT ISRAELITES TO COLONIZED JEWS

The customary way to periodize the history of late biblical Israel is to speak of the exilic and postexilic ages. This division focuses on the deportation of upper-class Judahites to Babylon and their extended captivity there until they were freed by the Persians to repopulate a Jewish province under the Persian Empire. The well-worn exilic/postexilic categories, however, slide over important aspects of the period and break apart the fundamental unity of the dispersion/reconstruction process.

For one thing, it is evident that only a fraction of the populace of the state of Judah was exiled to Babylonia. Moreover, many of those who were driven away or fled the land went to other nearer foreign lands. For many, probably a majority of Jews who continued to live in Palestine, there never was an exile in the sense of a deportation or expulsion from the land. Correspondingly, the return of thousands of Jews to Palestine in the century following Cyrus's edict to reconstruct Judah was not a return of all or even a majority of Jews from abroad.

"Exile," as commonly understood, suggests a temporary compulsory removal from the land, whereas increasingly self-confirmed "dispersion" became the reality for large numbers of Jews due to the uncertainties or inequities of life in Palestine. Beginning as early as the Assyrian destruction of northern Israel in 722 B.C.E., this larger dispersion accelerated dramatically during the Persian and Hellenistic periods.

In time, the reconstructed community of Judah gave a vital impulse to the survival of Israel, as well as a critical institutional-ideological center and focus for Jewish communities elsewhere, but it could only do so by being in communication with the whole body of Dispersion Jews, a numerical majority spread widely over the Persian and Greco-Roman worlds. It is clear, therefore, that while the terminology of "exile" and "postexile" aptly characterizes the experiences of Jews carried to Babylon who returned under Persian aegis, it does not accurately describe the experience of multitudes of Jews who did not participate in that set of events.

In other words, at all times from 586 to 63 B.C.E. there was a Jewish community in Palestine organizing some aspects of its own life, although its renewal by groups of returned exiles gave it new directions. At the same time, parallel communities of Jews widely spread abroad grew in size due to the push of socioeconomic and political pressures in Palestine and the pull of socioeconomic attractions in the wider world.

Given the dialectical unity of this Jewish dispersion/restoration process within the great empires of the time, it is appropriate to typify the condition and process of Israel's life in this period as "Jewish colonialism" in a twofold sense:

1. *Jewish colonialism as extensive settlement or colonization of Jews in foreign lands.* The old heirs of the tribal system and former subjects of the states of Israel and Judah were scattered by force or voluntarily emigrated to form settlements in other lands. There they constituted minorities that nonetheless remained linked by tradition and sentiment to Jerusalem, and perhaps also to Samaria in some cases. After the reconstruction program of Nehemiah and Ezra, these foreign colonies increasingly looked to Jerusalem as the religiocultural center for shaping the essential forms of Jewish religious life while allowing for secondary adaptations dictated by foreign environments.

2. *Jewish colonialism as subservience of all Jews to the political dominion of great empires.* All Jews, whether restored to Judah or colonized abroad, were subject to the sovereign power of the great empires that successively ruled them, except for the period of the Jewish Hasmonean dynasty in Palestine from 140 to 63 B.C.E. The Jewish colonies abroad were dependent on the toleration of cultural and religious diversity for Jewish survival. The very revival and reconstitution of Judah proper was enabled by the sponsorship of the Persian government. The home rule of Jews in Palestine, divided into political and religious jurisdictions, was a colonial form of rule over which the empire held ultimate veto power.

In sum, "Jewish colonialism" meant that Jews were subject to imperial rule both at the Palestinian center and in the peripheral colonies. This produced a complex structure of double loyalties and jurisdictions that tended to run at cross-purposes: whereas for Jews Judah was the metropolis and Jewish settlements abroad were the colonies, for the ancient political world as a whole the regnant great empire was the metropolis while Judah was one among a number of semiautonomous homelands and the dispersed Jewish settlements were minority religiocultural communities among others in the polyglot populace of the empire.

It is consistent with the epochal shift from Israelite autonomy to Israelite colonialism that we should henceforth speak of the Israelite people as Jews. Until 586 B.C.E., the name *yᵉhūdīm* had the restricted meaning of "Judahites" (or "Judeans" in later Latinized form) referring either to members of the tribe of Judah or later to citizens of the state of Judah. This usage continued into the age of dispersion and restoration, but now with reference to the province of Judah as a political subdivision of the great empires or to the region of Judah as the restored homeland and center of Jewish life. In time, *yᵉhūdīm* was also used in a wider sense to refer to all those who stood in the heritage of old Israel and the religion of Yahweh, defined more and more by the restored community in Judah.

This broadened sense of *yᵉhūdīm* as "Jews" marked the people primarily with a religiocultural identity that on the one hand linked them to Palestine and its traditions, but on the other hand permitted a fully Israelite and Yahwistic identity in any land where the people happened to live.

JEWISH RESPONSE TO NEO-BABYLONIAN DOMINION (586–539 B.C.E.)

The destruction of Jerusalem and the infrastructure of the state of Judah in 586 B.C.E. signaled the decisive shift from Israelite autonomy to Jewish colonialism. The monarchic state of Judah ceased to exist, and the normal operation of the cult of Yahweh centered at the Jerusalem temple was disrupted. The leadership of the state and of the cult were killed or deported to Babylonia, except for a relatively small number assigned to the administration of the region as a part of the Neo-Babylonian Empire.

This political and religious institutional rupture was enormously consequential. A religious and cultural restoration did take place slowly and by increments, but only by means of a fundamental alteration of former arrangements. After 586 B.C.E. Jewish history proceeds on a tension-filled double track among Palestinian Jews and Dispersion Jews.

The Continuing Community in Palestine

Neo-Babylonian policies profoundly affected how Jewish life developed both in Palestine and abroad. One source reports that forty-six hundred leading citizens of Judah were deported in three waves (in 597, 586, and 582 B.C.E.; Jer. 52:28-30). An alternative claim that ten thousand were deported in 597 alone (2 Kgs. 25:14-17; no figures for the later dates) may include the families of the exiles, not just the captive officials. This left a sizable Jewish

Sidon

SIDON

Damascus

DAMASCUS

Tyre

TYRE

Mediterranean Sea

ACHZIB

Hazor

Acco

KARNAIM

Sea of Galiee

Karnaim

HAURAN

ACCO

GALILEE

Dor

Beth-shan

Pella

GILEAD

DOR

Samaria

River Jordan

SAMARIA

Joppa

? Ono

AMMON

? Lod

Bethel

Rabbath-ammon

Mizpah

?

Gezer

Jericho

Ashdod

Jerusalem

Heshbon

ASHDOD

JUDAH

Kellah

Bethzur

Ashkelon

Dead Sea

Gaza

Lachish

Hebron

En-Gedi

MOAB

IDUMEA (EDOMITES)

Raphia

Beersheba

NABATEAN ARABS

Judah as a Province of the Persian Empire 445–333 B.C.E.

Province of Judah

MOAB Persian provinces in the satrapy "beyond the river"

NABATEAN ARABS

0 — 20 mi

0 — 20 km

MAP 10.1. JUDAH AS A PROVINCE OF THE PERSIAN EMPIRE

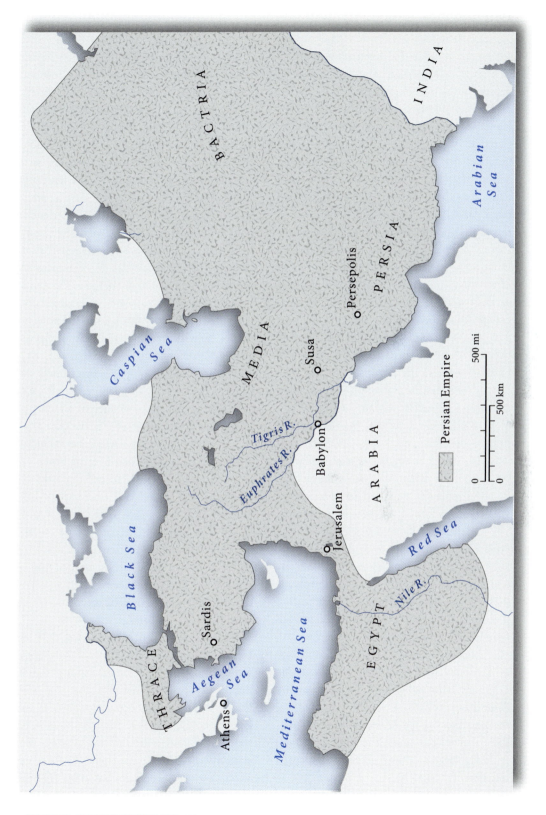

MAP 10.2. PERSIAN EMPIRE 500 B.C.E.

settlement in Judah that, even when shorn of its high-level leadership, consisted of 90 to 95 percent of the total populace.

A group of leaders who had been pro-Babylonian opponents of Judah's revolt, headed by Gedaliah, were installed in Mizpah as functionaries in a new unit of Neo-Babylonian administration over Judah. With the assassination of Gedaliah, many fled to Egypt and other lands, fearing Neo-Babylonian reprisals. The deportations and continuing political and military chaos led to a decided drop in the population of Judah. The infrastructure of the surviving Palestinian community was severely strained and had to rebuild its leadership from the ground up. Lamentations (see pp. 310–12), a series of public laments over the destruction of Jerusalem, provides brief vignettes of the disruption due to war-damaged agriculture and requisitions of crops and labor imposed by the conquerors.

It is not clear how the Neo-Babylonian Empire administered Judah after the collapse of Gedaliah's regime, though some aspects contrast with Assyrian policies that involved replacing deported Israelite leaders with colonists from other parts of the empire. The leadership of Judah deported in 597 was replaced with a second team, and, when the latter was deported in 586, yet another attempt was made to form a native administration under Gedaliah. There is no indication that Nebuchadnezzar ever introduced foreign populations into Judah. On the other hand, neighboring people were enabled to encroach on the territory of Judah, most strikingly the Edomites, who settled northward into Judah. Samaritans probably pressed into Judah from the north to occupy deserted estates. Nonetheless, there remained a reduced heartland in Judah largely untouched by a residential infusion of foreigners.

Circumstances of life for the surviving Jewish populace must have been arduous. Neo-Babylonian authorities would have kept a close eye on taxable surpluses. In the DH accounts, the Jews who stayed in Palestine are called "the poor people of the land" (2 Kgs. 24:14; 25:12). Although they struggled in a scarcity economy and were inexperienced in state politics, these poor of the land tapped a wealth of local custom and were experienced participants and leaders in village cooperative networks. Thus the ancient village tribalism (see pp. 160–63), overlaid for centuries by monarchy, was able to reemerge as the dominant force in organizing and preserving Palestinian Jewish identity throughout the exile, no matter how much hampered by the imposition of Neo-Babylonian dominion.

Forms of cult continued. The ruined site of the old temple, with its large sacred rock, served as a place of worship, to which pilgrims came from as far as Samaria (Jer. 41:4-8). This worship may well have included animal sacrifices presided over by lower orders of priests who had escaped deportation. Compositions such as Lamentations and Psalms 79 and 105–106 were publicly proclaimed on fast days (Zech. 7:2-7; 8:18-19). A strong if inconclusive case can be made for Palestine as the locale for the final edition of the DH history, and it seems likely that Jeremianic and other prophetic traditions circulated there.

The prevailing assumption that most of the creative religious initiatives of this period arose among the Babylonian exiles is highly dubious, especially because the deported leaders of Judah had been antipathetic to the Deuteronomic reform circles and like-minded prophets. It is advisable, however, not to overstate the separate developments in Palestine and in the Dispersion, for we know that the two communities of Jews communicated with and influenced one another.

The Communities in Dispersion

The conditions in which the deported ex-officials of Judah were detained are practically undocumented. From brief biblical notations (Ezra 2:59; 3:13) it has been judged that they were kept together in compact groups settled on deserted agricultural sites in Babylonia. As time went by and prospects of a return of the deportees to Palestine faded, a fair number may have been enlisted in Neo-Babylonian governmental service. Whether the detention camps were dissolved before Cyrus's capture of Babylon, allowing all the captives to find their own way in open society, we do not know, although the poetry of Isaiah of the Exile may imply that many Jews at least by then were part of the cosmopolitan populace of Babylon.

Improvised forms of religion doubtless flourished among Babylonian Jews who remained Yahwists just as they did among Palestinian Jews, perhaps including animal sacrifice. Prayer and song were certainly practiced.

Two influential prophets worked among the Babylonian exiles, Ezekiel (see pp. 280–84) at the beginning of the exile and Isaiah of the Exile (see pp. 284–88) toward its end. Both sought to internalize in their audiences the lessons of national apostasy from Yahweh and to prepare them for the uprooting experiences of their forced transplantation. Ezekiel aimed at a consciousness and practice of moral and ceremonial law that would keep alive the tribes' connection with their ancestral culture. Isaiah of the Exile tried to alert the exiles to Cyrus the Persian's conquest of the Neo-Babylonian Empire that might unleash opportunities for a restored Jewish community in Palestine and for Yahwism to become the professed religion of the dawning Persian Empire.

The Priestly document is often assigned an origin among the Babylonian Jews, mainly on the strength of its Babylonian orientation toward the creation and the flood and its equation with the Law of God that Ezra, a Babylonian Jew, brought with him to Palestine in the fifth century (see pp. 273–79). However, the Priestly writing may show no more Babylonian influence than appears in biblical traditions from Palestine, and it is far from certain that Ezra's law was the Priestly document. It is possible that P traditions had been gathered among priests outside of Jerusalem, or out of power in Jerusalem during the Deuteronomic reform, who were able to compile and expand their traditions in sixth-century Palestine.

Consequently, except for the localization of Ezekiel and Isaiah of the Exile in Babylonia and of Lamentations in Palestine, it is problematic how other writings of this period should be assigned geographically. Since DH, Jeremiah, and P represent collections with preexilic Judean roots, it is likely that some form of all these bodies of traditions would have been known before long among both Palestinian and Babylonian Jews.

Earlier scholarship was often confident in tracing the origin of the synagogue to the Babylonian exile. The sudden cessation of the temple cult seemed a plausible milieu for elevating the written traditions in circles of study and prayer. In reality there is no documentary or archaeological evidence for the synagogue until centuries after the exile. There was as yet no canonical text. At most the conventicles of prayerful and studious Jews in exile, or in Palestine, were the protean forerunners of an institution whose preconditions of a canonical Law and an interpretive tradition practiced at a restored Jerusalem were not yet in force.

This sketch of Jewish life in its Palestinian and Babylonian forms has focused on the communities we know best and presupposes a continuity of Jewish self-identity. In fact, numbers of Jews now lived elsewhere, in Egypt and in Syro-Phoenicia for example, but of whom we know nothing in detail in the sixth century. It is also evident that many Judahites turned to other religions and ceased to be Yahwists, they and their descendants becoming indistinguishable from the peoples among whom they lived.

Even among those who remained Yahwists there was no single authority to decide or interpret what their identity consisted of precisely. The recognized forms of Jewishness were variable from community to community. Even the centrality of the old homeland became questionable. Many Jews did not wish to return to Palestine when they were once

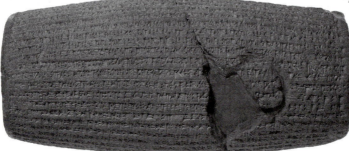

FIG. 10.1. The so-called Cyrus Cylinder, from Babylon (southern Iraq). Ca. 539–4530 B.C.E. This clay cylinder is inscribed in Babylonian cuneiform with a declaration of good kingship and an account by Cyrus, king of Persia (559–530 B.C.E), of his conquest of Babylon (in 539 B.C.E) and his capture of Nabonidus, the last Babylonian king. British Museum, London. Photo: © British Museum / Art Resource, N.Y.

again free to do so. It was not until the reforms of Nehemiah and Ezra in the last half of the fifth century that the outlines of a system of religious authority arose that could replace the shattered emblems and structures of the old religiopolitical unity of the states of Israel and Judah.

JEWISH RESPONSE TO PERSIAN DOMINION (539–332 B.C.E.)

The Neo-Babylonian Empire declined rapidly under the internally divisive rule of its last king, Nabonidus (555–539; Web Table A, 5B), just as a fresh military power from the Iranian highlands was rising meteorically. In 550 B.C.E. Cyrus of Anshan, a petty prince of the Medes, seized the throne of Media and speedily became master of the whole region north and east of Babylonia. By 539 B.C.E. this new empire, known as Persia, had captured Babylon. The Persians suddenly ruled over a territory more than twice the size of any previous empire in the region, from the border of India to the Aegean Sea opposite Greece and southward through Egypt.

Cyrus inaugurated a Persian program of extending to certain subject peoples considerable local autonomy and respect for their indigenous cultural and religious life. Combined with an improved communication system and a tight espionage and police apparatus, he sought to integrate the vast empire into a viable political whole.[1] The edict of Cyrus to return Jewish exiles to Judah and to rebuild their temple could be pictured by Jews as a partisan Yahwist affirmation (1 Chron. 36:22-23; Ezra 1:1-4 [Web Table A, 5C]), but from the Persian viewpoint it was merely one instance of a wider policy of restoring colonial subjects when it seemed politically judicious, as evidenced in the more neutral Aramaic version of the edict drawn from state archives (Ezra 6:1-5).

The fundamental features of Persian colonial restoration policy are known. Whether as a separate province from the start, or under the authority of the province of Samaria, Judah fell within the satrapy "Beyond the River" (i.e., Trans-Euphrates), which included the whole of Syria and Palestine. The leadership within the restored Jewish community was split into civil and religious spheres of responsibility, respectively delegated to a governor and a chief priest.

Because of poor sources with imprecise political terminology, it is uncertain whether the chief civil officer in Judah prior to the appointment of Nehemiah was in fact a full governor or whether Judah was independent from Samaria within the Persian imperial administration.[2] The attempts of Samaritan authorities to intervene in the rebuilding of the Jerusalem temple may be construed either as the exercise of their legitimate authority or as extralegal meddling.

It is evident that the colonial restoration of Judah proceeded slowly and by increments. Although the Persians provided overall military security and physical resources in some quantity, it took a long while to rebuild the

FIG. 10.2. The Mausoleum of Cyrus the Great of Persia, Pasargadae. Achaemenid Period. Iran. Photo: © SEF / Art Resource, N.Y.

weakened socioeconomic fabric of Judah. The Jewish restoration required a reconciliation of the interests of Palestinian Jews and Jews repatriated from Babylon. Moreover, among the Palestinian Jews were those who gave their allegiance to the Samaritan form of Jewish religion that had developed among the descendants of the former northern kingdom of Israel. The competing religiocultural alternatives of Samaritan and Judahite Yahwism were in turn intertwined with socioeconomic and political rivalries.

The restoration of colonial Judah is described as occurring in four stages, each connected with a Jewish leader from the exile sent to Judah under Persian authority. The historical status and sequence of these reformers, and the scope of the measures they allegedly enacted, are matters of dispute since the confused sources permit various interpretations.

Mission of Sheshbazzar in 538 B.C.E.

Shortly after the decree of Cyrus, a delegation of exilic Jews was sent by the Persian court to lay the groundwork for reestablishing the Judahite community (Ezra 1:5-11; 5:13-15). The head of the mission was Sheshbazzar, said to be a Judahite prince (Davidic? 1 Chron. 3:17-18). The size of this attempted resettlement of exilic Jews in Judah is unreported, and there is considerable doubt whether the rebuilding of the temple was part of the mission's assignment. Sheshbazzar may not have been sent as governor of a fully projected province but as head of an investigative team to gather information, possibly with limited charges to begin purification of the cult. No mention is made, however, of a chief priest sharing in Sheshbazzar's mission.

Mission of Zerubbabel and Joshua in 520 B.C.E.

With the death of Cyrus's successor Cambyses, a major uprising shook the Persian Empire. As part of an effort to pacify the empire, Darius decided to launch a more serious drive to recolonize Judah as a strategic military and political salient on the frontier with troublesome Egypt. In 520 B.C.E. Zerubbabel was made civil commissioner and Joshua high priest at the head of a large immigration of exilic Jews to Judah (Ezra 2:2b-70//Neh. 7:7b-73).

The returnees are detailed in subgroups verified as true descendants of the first exiles. They are pictured as resettling their former towns, while the provincial officials and primary temple personnel among them were placed in Jerusalem and vicinity, lesser temple attendants being assigned towns of their own.

A key focus of these returnees was the temple, rebuilt under Zerubbabel and Joshua in the period 520–515 B.C.E. (Ezra 5:1-2; Hag. 1:1—2:9; Zech. 4:9). After investigation of Samaritan charges of a Judahite insurrection proved groundless (Ezra 4), the Persians permitted the completion of the temple (Ezra 5–6). The unexplained disappearance of the civil head of the mission, Zerubbabel, identified as of Davidic lineage (Ezra 3:2, 8; 5:2; Hag. 1:1) and referred to in an openly messianic vein (Hag. 2:20-23; Zech. 3:8; 4:6-7; 6:12), has been taken to point to a failed Judahite bid for independence. The notion of "Zerubbabel's revolt" remains conjectural. The same is true of claims for Judahite participation in uprisings against Persia. Archaeology indicates considerable destruction to Palestinian cities in the fifth and fourth centuries, but no documents indicate Judah's participation in any of these revolts. Indeed, the Palestinian destruction that has been unearthed lies almost entirely outside the province of Judah.[3]

The periodic disturbances in the western part of the empire help to account for Persian commitment to strengthening reforms in Judah so as to secure the province as a bastion on the western frontier facing Egypt. By the same token, the reforming forces in Judah came to rely on Persian support against their Samaritan and internal Judahite opposition. No doubt there were periodic Judahite calculations of the feasibility of revolt, but the Judahite leadership had every reason to adhere closely to an imperial overlord whose support was crucial in implanting and enforcing the cult reformation they wanted.

Mission of Nehemiah in 445–430 B.C.E.

Whatever may have been the status of Jewish civil officials previously, Nehemiah was clearly sent to Judah as governor of the province with full powers to fortify Jerusalem and to reorganize the settlement patterns and provincial administration. Although the temple had been rebuilt, Jerusalem was unfortified and thinly populated. There were signs of slackness or abuse in political administration, cultic observances, and socioeconomic policies (on Isaiah 56–66 and Malachi, see pp. 290–92).

From the Persian viewpoint this meant a weak point of defense in the west, and from the exilic Jewish point of view it meant a Judahite community not yet adequately reformed in religious practice. In 445 B.C.E. Nehemiah, a Jewish official in the Persian court, was sent to carry through a firm-handed reconstruction of the province. In 433 Nehemiah returned to Persia, only to come back to Judah for a further indeterminate period.

At the heart of Nehemiah's measures was a form of synoecism ("binding together"), sometimes compared to the uniting of Attica under the central government of Athens but more closely paralleled by the forced resettlement of people for political purposes practiced by Greek tyrants. To appreciate the full impact of Nehemiah's alteration of power relations in Judah, we must view his celebrated refortification of Jerusalem together with his repopulation of the city with one-tenth of the Judahite populace selected by lot. A fortified and repopulated Jerusalem enhanced imperial administration and trade. The hand of Judah was thereby greatly strengthened against powers around the province who separately or in alliance threatened the political status of Judah and the religious reform party in Judah that contested the legitimacy of the Samaritan Jewish cult.

As an advocate of the form of Jewish religion that had developed in the Babylonian and Persian exile, Nehemiah opposed agricultural and commercial violations of the day of rest and the marriage of Judahites to women from other lands, Samaritans included.

A serious threat to stable rule in Judah sprang from the class division between the wealthy, largely returned exiles with Persian-backed privileges, and small landholders sliding into debt and losing their properties. Nehemiah moved firmly against these practices by arousing public opinion against the harsh creditors (Neh. 5:1-13) and implementing a one-time cancellation of debts. Realistically, however, since the wealth of the abusive upper class was not confiscated, the combination of landed and commercial wealth probably worked toward the eventual undermining of Nehemiah's reforms.

Nehemiah's program provided that the impoverished Levites were henceforth to receive a portion of offerings to subsidize their livelihood. Moreover, setting an example, Nehemiah waived his own right to a food allowance in support of his entourage and official guests (Neh. 5:14-19), suggesting Nehemiah's wealth or the wealth of friends.

It has been plausibly argued that Nehemiah fits the model of the tyrants in contemporary Greek politics who rode to power on waves of popular socioeconomic discontent,[4] especially over the issue of land. The measures of Nehemiah correspond to the policies of tyrants and probably had the overall intent of strengthening Persian-Jewish exilic reform control in Judah by tempering its hardships on the general populace. By appealing to the restiveness of the people at large, Nehemiah gained leverage to force policies and structural changes on the local elite that they resisted in the short run but that aided them in consolidating their hold on Judah in the long run.

Mission of Ezra in 458 B.C.E. or Later

The chronological order of the missions of Nehemiah and Ezra, and the interconnection of their work, is a baffling historical problem. A straightforward reading of the biblical text places the arrival of Ezra and five thousand returning exiles in 458 B.C.E. Ezra is called both a "priest" (a Jewish title) and a "scribe" (probably understood as a secretary in Persian governmental service). The scope and powers of his commission are pertinent to determining his relationship to the mission of Nehemiah: to investigate conditions in Judah in order to determine how they corresponded to the religious law that Ezra and his exilic Jewish community regarded as authoritative; to give donations to the temple cult and to call on supplementary Persian funds as necessary;

and to appoint judges who would enforce the observance of the law, assuming that the religious law brought by Ezra was decreed by the Persians as civil law of the province of Judah.

According to the biblical account, Ezra thus preceded Nehemiah but was presumably still present in Judah at the time of Nehemiah's mission. It is striking, however, that neither man operates with any evident awareness of the work of the other. The Ezra and Nehemiah traditions are clearly two entirely separate literary blocks fused together secondarily, with only the most superficial linkage of the two leaders.

It has been widely doubted that two Persian appointees would have been assigned closely related responsibilities in the same time period, or if they did have some overlapping jurisdictions, that they could have worked in such ignorance or disregard of one another. There are, moreover, indications that Ezra followed Nehemiah. In reviewing the populace of Judah, Nehemiah cites the repatriates under Zerubbabel but makes no mention of those who returned with Ezra. Nehemiah finds Jerusalem's defenses laid waste and the city sparsely populated, whereas Ezra discovers Jerusalem thriving within its walls. Nehemiah is the contemporary of the high priest Eliashib, while Ezra lives in the time of his grandson Jehohanan.

The most frequent resolution of this historical puzzle has been to conjecture that "the seventh year of Artaxerxes" for the date of Ezra's arrival in Judah refers to the reign of Artaxerxes II (404–358 B.C.E.), which would date Ezra's appearance in Judah in 398–397. By placing Ezra's mission after Nehemiah's mission, the work of Ezra in the religious sphere gains coherence as an accomplishment within the framework of the political consolidation achieved by Nehemiah.

Ezra's introduction of a law book as the basis for civil and religious jurisprudence in Judah was an important moment in the movement toward canonization of the Law, the first section of the Hebrew Bible (see pp. 65–70, 267–73). The law book was read (in part or in whole) at a public assembly that subscribed to it as the law of the land (Nehemiah 8). Unfortunately, it is impossible to determine the exact identity of Ezra's law book from the account of the public reading, beyond the apparent fact that it was composed of materials now found in Genesis through Deuteronomy. What is clear is that at some point between 458 and 398 or shortly thereafter, the combined political authority of the Persians and the religious authority of the exilic Jewish reformers succeeded in establishing a body of traditional legal materials as the binding law of the province of Judah.

From the side of the reforming Jews the Law assured a well-defined and purified community, and from the side of the Persians the Law guaranteed orderly and reliable colonial rule at the least cost to themselves. Persian policy in this regard is indicated by the Persian understanding of law as a continuum of religious and civil regulations with no sharp distinctions. Moreover, it was the Persian imperial habit, displayed for instance in Egypt, to encourage indigenous religious leaders to codify existing laws and customs and make them the basis of colonial law backed by Persian authority.[5] One can therefore reasonably assert that the crucial initial move toward canonization of Jewish writings was a political act imposed upon the Palestinian Jewish community by the collaboration of Persian imperial authorities and a Jewish colonial elite imported from the exile to Judah.

Developments among Dispersion Jews

A striking feature of the protracted restoration of Judah throughout this period was the repeated initiative for rebuilding and reshaping the Palestinian Jewish community that came from Jews of the Dispersion in Babylonia and Persia. It is obvious that by the fifth century these Jewish communities in the eastern Dispersion had become securely and respectably lodged in their new environments. Composed originally of the highest leadership of the destroyed kingdom of Judah, they came to provide officials in the Persian government, including Nehemiah who was "cupbearer" and Ezra who was "secretary." It was these circles who eventually called the tune in the colonial province of Judah and who provided the intellectual and religious energy for redefining Israelite-Jewish identity. That they were economically advantaged is shown by the donations they were able to send to the Jerusalem temple and also perhaps by the records of a Babylonian business firm headed by the Murashu family in the era of Nehemiah and Ezra that reveal that several clients of the firm were Jewish.

The western Jewish Dispersion is attested in the Persian period by the Elephantine papyri (Web Table A, 5D), which tell of a colony of Jewish mercenaries, perhaps totaling 350 people, who served as part of the Persian forces occupying Egypt. Intermarriage with Egyptians seems to have been practiced. A form of Passover was observed, and a temple of Yahu (Yahweh) had been built, although conflict over animal sacrifice led to its destruction by the local populace in 410 B.C.E. Shortly after 400 B.C.E., the Elephantine colony was conquered in a general uprising of Egypt against Persia, at which point the Jewish mercenaries may have shifted their allegiance to Egyptian authorities. Although we have no evidence, other groups of Jews may have settled in Lower Egypt since it was in this region that Jewish colonization of Egypt experienced rapid growth in the Hellenistic period.

JEWISH RESPONSE TO MACEDONIAN AND PTOLEMAIC DOMINIONS (332–198 B.C.E.)

Impact of Alexander: The Meeting of Hellenism and Judaism

When Alexander the Great crossed from Greece into Asia and launched his conquests that toppled the Persian Empire, he opened a new epoch in the interaction of the ancient Near East and Hellenism. Alexander was committed to a multiethnic cosmopolitan culture undergirded by the achievements and perspectives of Greek civilization. Faced with an assertive Gentile universalism, Judaism was challenged with the prospect of cultural assimilation and religious syncretism or eclipse. The tide of Hellenism had the eventual effect of confirming Judaism in its main features, but in the process it provoked heated internal Jewish conflict and shaped new developments.

Hellenism came to the ancient Near East in the form of intrusive military and political power.[6] In basic respects Jews faced the same realities of foreign domination that they had experienced under Assyrians, Neo-Babylonians, and Persians, and with a heightened measure of cultural and intellectual imperialism. When Jews struggled with the allure of Hellenism, they were making personal choices about lifestyles and mental outlooks as well as taking an inevitable stance toward political powers.

FIG. 10.3. One of the earliest known portraits of Alexander the Great. Silver tetradrachm of Lysimachus. Greek. 305–281 B.C.E. From the Mint of Lampsakos (modern Lâpseki, Turkey). On the reverse was a seated figure of the goddess Athena, and a Greek legend that translates "Of King Lysimachus." 30 mm. diameter. CM 1919, 0820.1. British Museum, London. Photo: © British Museum / Art Resource, N.Y

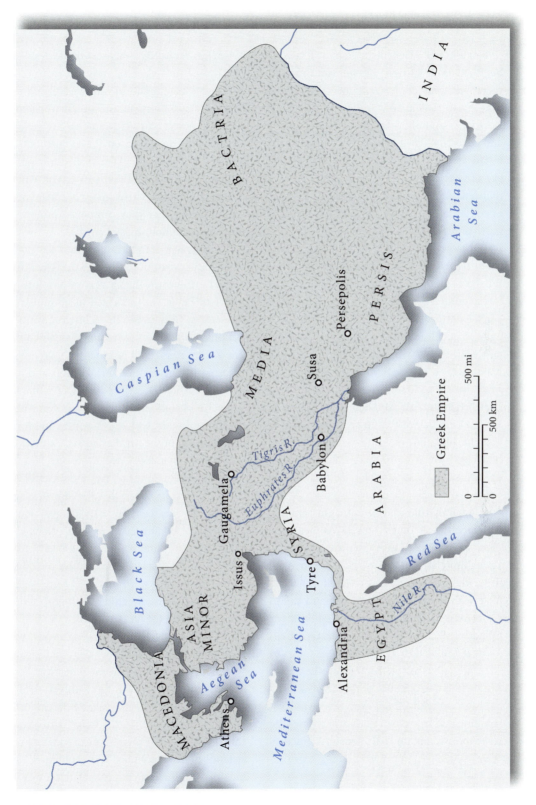

MAP 10.3. THE GREEK EMPIRE, 334–323 B.C.E.

Nor should "Hellenism versus Judaism" be posed as an outright antagonism in which there were only two clear choices. Jews were exposed to Hellenism in different forms and situations, and they found various dangers and attractions in it. The core of uncompromised Jewishness and the permitted periphery of Greek adornment and articulation of that Jewishness were worked out differently, often bitterly, in Jewish communities according to time and place.[7] Hellenism, for example, served to precipitate critical Jewish decisions about the canon of sacred writings and about the specification of authoritative leadership in interpreting and applying the old traditions.

In Palestine, as elsewhere, Alexander recognized local autonomy wherever possible, partly out of conviction and partly out of sheer inability of several thousand Macedonians to administer a suddenly acquired empire that stretched from Asia Minor to the borders of India. Occupied with military reconnaissance and consolidation of empire, Alexander had little opportunity to do more than accept the operative local forms of rule as long as they conceded Macedonian sovereignty. Where occasional rebellion broke out, as in Samaria, Alexander took quick repressive measures. Although unable to introduce any new overall administrative framework, Alexander did begin the establishment of Greek cities, replete with architectural, cultural, and political forms of Hellenism, and peopled by Greek military and commercial colonists. Other cities were founded or granted special status by Alexander's successors, especially the Seleucids. While the influence of these Greek cities has been exaggerated at times, their wide distribution and key role in trade and politics did serve to disseminate Hellenism as a practical force in Asia.

Egyptian Hellenism Controls Palestine

Alexander's premature death in 323, without effective heir, triggered more than twenty years of power struggles among his generals that led to carving up the empire into a number of still-sizable Hellenistic kingdoms. Ptolemy established himself in Egypt, while Seleucus gained control in Syria and Mesopotamia. Together they opposed Antigonus, drawing Judah into these struggles.

Judah was thereafter pulled into the Ptolemaic imperial orbit until 198 B.C.E. The Ptolemies took over the theory of royal absolutism native to Egypt and reformed its administrative system to improve the economic contributions of the colonies to the Nile heartland. The Zenon papyri tell of the tour in 260–258 B.C.E. of an Egyptian financial officer and his delegation through large parts of Palestine to inspect and tighten up the financial administration of taxes and leases and to improve management of the royal estates in Palestine.

On the other hand, the Ptolemies had to work with preexisting cultural and sociopolitical structures. Provided that the flow of taxes and goods was assured, considerable local autonomy was allowed. The high priest was titular head of Judah, but a civil officer (*prostasia*) was the official representative of Judah to the Egyptian government and responsible for keeping a close watch on the high-priestly management of the lucrative temple economy.

The tribute and tax burden on Judah was apparently measurably heavier under the Ptolemies than it had been under the Persians, who had been willing to absorb deficit spending in Judah for the sake of the military security investment. In the latter part of the third century, there were signs of Judahite resistance to the Ptolemies. When Onias II, the high priest, refused to pay the regular imperial

FIG. 10.4. Tetradrachm of Antiochus IV Epiphanes (175–63 B.C.E.), Seleucid king of Syria, who by his imposition of Greek law and customs in Judea provoked the Maccabean Revolt (167–64 B.C.E.). Israel Museum (IDAM), Jerusalem. Photo: © Erich Lessing / Art Resource, N.Y.

tribute to Egypt, a Jewish landed family, the Tobiads, installed by the Ptolemies as the head of a military colony and assigned to guard the desert frontier, intervened and compelled the high priest to pay the tribute. A Tobiad was then made general leaseholder of taxes for all of Palestine and Phoenicia.

The general intensity and rigor of Ptolemaic exploitation of Palestine, coupled with the maneuvers of a Jewish elite to prosper from farming out taxes and state trade monopolies on products such as wine and oil, sharpened the social differences that Nehemiah had tried to lessen by his reforms two centuries earlier.

Emigration to Egypt quickened as agricultural monopolies and population growth created pressures in Judah and the opportunities for mercenary service and work in the burgeoning trade centers such as Alexandria provided a foreign lure. Other parts of Palestine, particularly the coastal cities, received a share of these mobile Judahites.

Through its immersion in the life of Alexandria, the Dispersion Jewish community there soon became the chief center of Jews outside Palestine, eclipsing Babylonia in this respect. As the primary center of Greek learning and culture in this era, Alexandria stimulated the Jewish residents to translate the sacred writings into Greek (cf. pp. 73–74) and to produce further an extensive religious literature in Greek that served both to make Israelite/Jewish faith intelligible to Hellenistic Jews and to argue its intrinsic merits to the Greek world. Many of these writings have been preserved only because they found their way into Christian collections of the Apocrypha and Pseudepigrapha after they were renounced by rabbinic Judaism (table 2.1 and Web Table E). It is clear that this Alexandrian literary, intellectual, and religious culture was at the forefront of Jewish-Greek contact.

JEWISH RESPONSE TO SELEUCID DOMINION: THE MACCABEES (198–140 B.C.E.)

Syrian Hellenism Controls Palestine

When dominion over Palestine passed from the Ptolemies to the Seleucids, there was widespread rejoicing among Judahites. Antiochus III had cultivated Jewish and other ethnic minority displeasures with the Ptolemies, and, on taking Jerusalem, he decreed a general waiver of taxes for three years and permanently exempted priests and temple from taxation.

Within a very few years, however, there was a radical shift in Seleucid fortunes. The Romans defeated Antiochus III at Magnesia in 190 B.C.E. and later blocked his plan to conquer Egypt. The Seleucid Empire lost Asia Minor, and its eastern holdings were drastically reduced. A severe fiscal crisis struck the Seleucid government, which thereupon resorted to plundering temples to replenish state resources.

Enforced Hellenism and Civil War

The plans of Antiochus IV Epiphanes to consolidate his empire coincided well with the interests of hellenizing Jewish leaders in Jerusalem. These leaders viewed rapprochement with Greek forces as a way to enhance Judahite prosperity and to liberalize Jewish religion. They were attracted to the Seleucid program of equating Zeus Olympius with the Syro-Palestinian high god and specifically with the Jewish deity, Yahweh.

To meet the critical shortage of state funds, Antiochus began to sell the office of Jewish high priest to the highest bidder among these hellenizing Jews, first to Jason in 174 and then to Menelaus in 171. During their terms of office, steps were taken to create a Greek city-state, or polis, its citizens to be known as "Antiochians of Jerusalem."

Meanwhile, Antiochus reached his acme of success by conquering all of Egypt outside Alexandria. Returning from Egypt in 169, he plundered the Jerusalem temple and appointed a governor to facilitate the Jewish hellenizing reform policies. But the decision to discard the Jewish Law as the political constitution of Judah met with such resistance that Antiochus sent a force to Jerusalem that killed and looted widely, pulled down the walls of the city, and established a citadel (Acra) garrisoned with Seleucid troops and settled with a mixed Gentile-Jewish populace loyal to the hellenization program.

With this aid, the Jewish hellenizers pushed through their radical religious reform measures, which required the suppression of the traditional rites and the sacred literature of Judaism, and of temple sacrifices, Sabbath observance, and circumcision. The temple was turned into a syncretistic Syro-Hellenic shrine, with an altar to Zeus and garden precincts harking back to Syro-Palestinian nature worship.

Open rebellion broke out in the countryside, led by the priest Mattathias and his hardy sons, who came to be known as the Maccabees (after Judas, nicknamed Maccabee, "the hammerer"). Those loyal to the Law, called Hasidim, rallied to the defense of the endangered ancestral religion against Seleucid troops and Jewish Hellenists. A religious and political civil war split the country.[8] By 164 Judas was able to recapture all of Jerusalem except for the Acra strong point. At this juncture, the Seleucids rescinded their proscriptive decrees, permitting Judas to cleanse and rededicate the temple for proper Jewish worship.

The Move from Religious Independence to Political Independence

Peace was not restored, however. Judas chose to continue the movement of resistance with the goal of political independence from the Seleucids, even entering into a treaty of defense with Rome. Stronger Syrian armies were committed to pacification, but the Seleucids were unable to suppress the resistance movement and secure for their Jewish hellenizing sympathizers a firm political hold on Judah.

Sidon

SELEUCID EMPIRE

Damascus

Tyre

Cadasa
(Kedesh)

Paneas

GAULANITIS

Hazor

*Sea of
Galiee*

Ptolemais
(Acco)

GALILEE

Arbela

Gamala

Raphon

ACCO

Sepphoris

Hippos

Carnaim

Bosor

Gabae

Philoteria

Abila

Dion

Dor

Gadara

*NABATEAN
ARABS*

Strato's
Tower

Scythopolis
(Beth-shan)

Narbata

Pella

GAL'AADITIS

SAMARIA

Samaria

Amathus

Gerasa

Apollonia

Pharathon

Sichem

Ragaba

Antipatris

Joppa

Alexandrium

TOBIADS

Lydda

Gophna

Bethel

Philadelphia
Rabbath-ammon

Modein

Michmash

Tyrus

Gazara
(Gezer)

Elasa

Jerico

Azotus
(Ashdod)

Emmaus

JUDAH
Jerusalem

Qumran

Medeba

Ashkelon
(Free City-State)

Beth-zachariah

Machaerus

Gaza

Marisa
(Mareshah)

Bethzur

*Dead
Sea*

PHILISTIA

Hebron

En-Gedi

IDUMEA

Masada

*NABATEAN
ARABS*

Raphia

Beersheba

Zoara

Mediterranean Sea

River Jordan

0   20 mi

0   20 km

Maccabean–Hasmonean Palestine 166–76 B.C.E.

- Boundary of Judah before Maccabean revolt 76 B.C.E.
- Conquests of Jonathan 160–142 B.C.E.
- Conquests of Simon 142–134 B.C.E.
- Conquests of John Hyrcanus 134–104 B.C.E.
- Conquests of Aristobulus I 104–103 B.C.E.
- Conquests of Alexander Jannaeus 103–76 B.C.E.
- – – Hasmonean Kingdom at its maximum extent

MAP 10.4. MACCABEAN AND HASMONEAN PALESTINE

Jonathan took up leadership from his fallen brother Judas and extended control over Judah. Rival contenders for the Seleucid crown found themselves vying for support from Jonathan, who managed thereby to parlay his appointment as high priest and civil and military commander of Judah in 152–150.

It is probable that Jonathan's acceptance of the office of high priest so offended sectors of pious Jews that a number of them withdrew into the countryside to form strict ascetic communities where they could practice the Law without compromise. These sectarians came to be known as Essenes. Apparently the expelled high priest led a small group (perhaps fifty or so sectarians) to found the Qumran community, which over the next two hundred years wrote some, and collected the rest, of the voluminous Dead Sea Scrolls (see pp. 58–59; Web Table F). The Qumran scrolls refer to Jonathan (or possibly to Simon, his successor) as the Wicked Priest and to the unknown high priest he ousted as the Righteous Teacher.

A JEWISH STATE RISES AND FALLS: THE HASMONEANS (140–63 B.C.E.)

Triumph and Hellenization of the Jewish State

When Jonathan was murdered in 142, his brother Simon stepped into leadership, and within three years Judah had gained virtually full sovereignty over a considerable region. The hated Acra in Jerusalem was captured.

Simon was granted full hereditary rights to the highest priestly, military, and civil offices by an assembly more or less representative of the Jewish elite, a bold action agreed to by the weakened Seleucids. The Hasmonean dynasty had begun, so named after Hashmon, an ancestor of Mattathias of the Maccabee family.

The succeeding Hasmonean rulers, John Hyrcanus (135–104), Aristobulus I (104–103), and Alexander Jannaeus (103–76), despite momentary setbacks, expanded Jewish conquests until the Hasmonean kingdom approached the extent of the Davidic empire. The expansive Hasmoneans shrewdly maintained treaty connections with Rome in order to keep the Seleucids in check. They forcibly converted conquered peoples to the Jewish religion, and it was in this way that Idumea (Latinized "Edom") and Galilee became Judaized. In 128 B.C.E. Hyrcanus leveled the city of Samaria and destroyed the Samaritan temple on Mount Gerizim, suppressing the heterodox Jewish cult long practiced there in open defiance of the majority Jewish devotion to Jerusalem.

Increasingly, the administration of the Jewish state developed along Hellenistic political and military lines. John Hyrcanus gave his sons Greek names, and he began the practice of hiring Greek mercenaries to enhance his military strength and secure a power base independent of domestic support. Under his rule, an internal conflict broke out between the ruling regime and devout Judahites, successors of the Hasidim who had backed the Maccabees so long as it was a question of religious freedom. These Hasidim were taking on the features of the later Pharisees, although we cannot be certain that they bore that name as yet. These opponents of the late Hasmoneans were troubled by Jewish rulers who so openly played the part of Hellenistic princes and demanded that Hyrcanus give up the high priesthood. Hyrcanus countered by drawing closer to a group whom Josephus identifies as Sadducees, who at this time were probably largely composed of the newly enriched nobility spawned by the Hasmonean conquests.

During the reign of Alexander Jannaeus, the conflict flared into civil war. In a turnabout from his forebear Judas, Alexander Jannaeus led a small but powerful group of royal supporters in a desperate battle against a majority of countrymen who saw him as an embodiment of Hellenistic corruption and oppression. Although the Pharisees and the popular majority had victory in their grasp, the prospect of a Seleucid king once again taking control of Jerusalem prompted some of the people to switch their loyalty back to Alexander Jannaeus. Returned to power, the king took his revenge by crucifying eight hundred of the rebel Pharisees and slaughtering their wives and children. One outcome of this traumatic rift was the flight of eight thousand rebels, a number of them to Qumran.

Rivalry over the Hasmonean crown set up Rome's entrée into Palestine when Pompey captured Jerusalem, appointed the people's choice of ruler as high priest (not king), and stripped Judah of most of its Greek territories. Rome had come to stay. After yet further final spasms of Hasmonean power, Rome commissioned Herod as dependent king of Judah.

Factions and Parties in Hasmonean State and Society

The factions, parties, or sects called Sadducees, Pharisees, and Essenes originated in the Maccabean-Hasmonean period. Exactly when the Sadducees, Pharisees, and Essenes emerged in the second century and under what precise circumstances remain clouded issues. Nor is it certain how much their organizational and ideological features changed between Hasmonean times and the first Christian century, when they are more fully documented. The social classes or interests represented by these parties must mostly be inferred. Similarly, the degree to which party members were occupants of public offices is disputed, as is the extent of their active involvement in politics. Moreover, the appropriateness of the term "sect" for these factions is questionable, since "sect" usually refers to an isolated self-enclosed group that does not seek or achieve wider power or influence. Only the Essenes among these three groups might suitably be called a sect in this sense, for the Sadducees and Pharisees contested and wielded public power.[9]

The national situation that generated these factions was the major realignment of socioeconomic, political, and religious forces set in motion by the attempt to hellenize Judaism radically and by the reactive emergence of an independent Jewish state that ironically took on a decisive Hellenistic character. The radical minority coup to displace traditional Judaism failed totally. Thereafter, all sections of the populace stood firmly for maintenance of a Jewish religion based on the Law. However, there was a very wide latitude of understanding as to how the Law was to be practiced and exactly what fidelity to the Law implied. With Hellenistic religious syncretism excluded by an overwhelming Jewish consensus, the key question now had to do with whether and how Jewish society and state should appropriate the internationally operative Hellenistic socioeconomic and political structures and assumptions. Practically speaking, what did it mean to live out a fully embodied Judaism in the Hellenistic world?

In going beyond the battle for religious freedom in order to reach for political independence and then for imperial expansion, the Maccabees and Hasmoneans increasingly adopted Hellenistic technology, political and military organization, and cultural styles. The Hasidim were reserved or hostile toward Hasmonean political and cultural ambitions. It was probably the Maccabean ecclesial power grab under Jonathan that prompted some of the Hasidim to form disciplined associations of loyalists to the Law, forerunners of the Pharisees. These associations stressed the equality of Jews before the Law, and they took a more and more active role in trying to limit the power and impact of the Hasmonean rulers on Jewish life. At about the same time disciplined groups of a similar but even stricter view, later known as the Essenes, decided to pull away from the corrupt society into rural communes where they could live out their religion uncompromisingly.

The new opportunities for power and wealth in this era led to deepened social cleavages in Judah. The old aristocracy had been heavily concentrated around the upper levels of the hereditary priesthood who controlled the lucrative temple economy. This aristocracy was soon preempted at the top by the Hasmonean assumption of high priestly office. At the same time the wars of expansion offered vast new commercial opportunities for Jewish entrepreneurs attached to the Hasmoneans.

The rising commercial sectors formed an aristocracy of new wealth that openly vied with old-wealth aristocrats for political and economic power, for instance, for control of seats on the national governing council or for control of the temple economy. This new aristocracy came to be known as the Sadducees, stemming largely at first from lay circles. By Herodian times it appears that old and new aristocracies reached an accommodation based in large part on their common need to block and counterbalance the rising influence of the populist Pharisees.

Governmental power in the now-independent Jewish state was vested primarily in the king and his officials, alongside which existed an assembly of representatives of the people with extensive consultative, legislative, and juridical powers. Permitted since Persian times as the means for Jews to exercise some local autonomy, this representative body was known as the Gerousia before the Maccabean age, and as the Sanhedrin afterward. The Hasmonean dynasty, followed by the Romans, honored this same basic arrangement, dealing with the Sanhedrin as "the voice of the people."

Sadducean and Pharisaic factions fought for control of the Sanhedrin. The Sadducees promoted hellenization shorn of any attempts at religious syncretism. The Pharisees resisted the hellenization process adopted by the native princes. Broadly speaking, the Sadducees were aristocratic and the Pharisees populist.

Because Sadducees and Pharisees appear prominently in Josephus, the New Testament, and rabbinic writings, there is a tendency to exaggerate their numbers and to picture them as operative in a religious vacuum apart from social context. Relatively small in number, both parties spoke and acted for and in collaboration with other sectors of the populace. In this period, Sadducees spoke for the interests of the Hasmonean political establishment, upper-order priests, and the expansionist commercial and land-owning classes, while the Pharisees were in touch with the grievances and aspirations of a wider peasant populace, lower-order priests, and small shopkeepers and artisans. The Sadducean point of view, extravagant in praise of the Hasmonean dynasty, is apparent in 1 Maccabees, while Pharisaic acclaim for Judas Maccabee shows up in 2 Maccabees. Judith, *1 Enoch 92–105*, and *Psalms of Solomon* may also emanate from pro-Pharisaic circles.

The religious disputes between the parties were closely intertwined with socioeconomic and political issues of high moment. The Sadducees favored a narrow interpretation of the Law with the purity laws applicable primarily to priests when on duty in the temple. Their exclusion of all writings except the Law from authoritative status, combined with their double standards of purity for priest and laity, defined a narrow sphere of life as properly religious and allowed them great leeway in hellenized power politics, culture, and personal conduct. By contrast, the Pharisees offered the innovation of "the twofold Law," an oral law interpreting the written Law. This position both mandated and enabled a flexible fulfillment of purity laws by all Jews over a wide range of life. Pharisaic inclusion of the Prophets and some of the later Writings in their sacred literature paralleled their dim view of hellenized politics and culture.

Essenes shared much of the basic Pharisaic outlook on religion and politics, although they were considerably stricter in their application of the Law, accusing the Pharisees of selling out to social and political evil. Viewing themselves as the only true Israelites, the Essene community at Qumran is best known from sectarian writings that describe the history and organization of the group: *Damascus Document* (CD), *Rule of the Community* (1QS), and commentaries on prophetic books, especially on Nahum (4QpNah). (See the fuller list of Qumran books in Web Table F.)

It has been customary to equate Sadducees with priests and Pharisees with scribes,

but this is an erroneous simplification. While the upper orders of priests became largely Sadducean, not all priests were Sadducees, and many Sadducees—in the period we are studying, probably a majority—were lay. At least since the reform of Nehemiah and Ezra, interpretation and application to present practice of the text of the Law had been largely monopolized by priests, but as confidence in the priesthood was shaken and popular forces were unleashed by the tumultuous Maccabean-Hasmonean age, priestly monopoly of the interpretation of the Law was sharply contested in pious lay circles.

Sadducean and Pharisaic schemes of interpretation contended fiercely for control of the scribal office and tradition, with the Pharisaic ideology gaining the ascendancy. Pharisees proper were communities of believers, priest or lay, educated or not, mutually pledged to strict observance of purity laws and tithing. The scribe, whether Sadducee or Pharisee or neither, occupied a professional office distinguished by special education and recognized experience in rendering the old regulations of the Law into relevant and authoritative directions for contemporary daily conduct and for supplying the framework of a juridical system.

In sum, the Pharisee was a member of a religious party who took on himself strictly "the yoke of the Law." The Pharisaic orientation and influence spread out from the core group to permeate and link wider circles of Jews on varying religious and political issues. The Sadducee was a person of privilege in the priesthood or in the lay nobility who combined pro-Hasmonean sympathies with an elitist religious outlook. The Sadducean orientation and influence, like the Pharisaic, spread out from the commanding centers of Sadducean power closely allied with and buttressed by state authority. Owing to their elitism, however, the Sadducees failed to gain the loyalty and sympathy of the general populace with anything like the success of the Pharisaic faction.[10]

Modern-day evaluations of the Maccabean-Hasmonean course of events have tended to be simplistically polarized, closely affected by assumptions either that any form of independent Jewish politics was justified by the divine promise of the land at the foundation of Jewish religion, or that secular politics was tabooed by the covenantal-prophetic brand of Jewish religion that restricted the use of human power.

These same issues also tormented and divided Jewish society in the ideological struggle of Maccabean-Hasmonean times. The king, the new aristocracy, the higher order of priests—in short, the Sadducean faction or tendency—understood their traditional religion to mandate messianic political action in terms of the prevailing blunt and cruel forms of international power politics. Small farmers, day laborers, shopkeepers, artisans, lower-order priests, many scribes and members of Pharisaic associations, even the withdrawn Essenes—in short, the Pharisaic faction or

tendency—understood their traditional religion to mandate messianic loyalty to domestic social equality and justice and to popular religious practice, while eschewing the conceits and excesses of power politics, even to the point of endangering political independence as long as religious purity and freedom of practice were assured.

A crucial factor in how Jews of that age aligned themselves on these religio-political issues lay in their social class positions and perceived self-interests. It mattered greatly whether they were among those who prospered and wielded power in the Hasmonean revival of Jewish statehood or among those who suffered loss and decline of influence at the expense of the expansion of royalty and the newly enriched.

When we look at the balance of gains and losses in Hasmonean adventurism, how we assess Jewish statehood and social order in the second century B.C.E. will be greatly influenced by our own class interests and religious affiliations, as will also our views of international politics today, including the claims and policies of Israeli Zionism and of Palestinian and Arab nationalism.

NOTES

1. A caution against overstating Persian tolerance and sponsorship of indigenous cultures and religions of the empire is expressed in Amélie Kuhrt, "The Cyrus Cylinder and the Achaemenid Imperial Policy," *JSOT* 25 (1983): 83–97.

2. Sean E. McEvenue, "The Political Structure in Judah from Cyrus to Nehemiah," *CBQ* 44 (1981): 353–64.

3. Geo Widengren, "The Persian Period," in *IJH*, 500–503.

4. Morton Smith, *Palestinian Parties and Politics That Shaped the Old Testament* (New York: Columbia University Press, 1971), 136–47.

5. Widengren, "Persian Period," in *IJH*, 515; this point has also been urged and developed at some length in unpublished lectures by S. Dean McBride of Union Theological Seminary, Richmond, Virginia.

6. Mikhail I. Rostovtzeff (*The Social and Economic History of the Hellenistic World,* 3 vols. [New York: Oxford University Press, 1941]), details the brutish and vicious character of much Hellenistic politics with particular forcefulness; Samuel K. Eddy (*The King Is Dead: Studies in the Near Eastern Resistance to Hel-

lenism, 334–331 B.C. [Lincoln: University of Nebraska Press, 1961]), shows that philosophy and religion were the ideological counterpart of a fierce political contest between Near Eastern native rule and Hellenistic imperialism.

7. Saul Lieberman, *Hellenism in Jewish Palestine* (New York: Jewish Theological Seminary of America, 1950); Martin Hengel, *Judaism and Hellenism: Studies in Their Encounter in Palestine During the Early Hellenistic Period,* trans. John Bowden, 2 vols. (Philadelphia: Fortress Press, 1974).

8. Elias Bickerman (*From Ezra to the Last of the Maccabees: Foundations of Post-Biblical Judaism* [New York: Schocken, 1962], 54–135) gives a colorful account of the Maccabean struggle in terms of a Jewish civil war; Peter Schäfer ("The Hellenistic and Maccabaean Periods," in *IJH,* 562–64) nuances Bickerman's original thesis in the light of later research and hypothesis.

9. Ellis Rivkin (*A Hidden Revolution* [Nashville: Abingdon, 1978], 316–18) sorts out some of the connotations of terms such as "sect," "school of thought," and "philosophy" used to describe what we here call "factions" and "parties" in late Hellenistic Judaism.

10. This reconstruction of the parties is indebted to Shmuel Safrai, "Jewish Self-Government," in *The Jewish People in the First Century: Historical Geography, Political History, Social, Cultural and Religious Life and Institutions,* ed. S. Safrai and M. Stern, CRINT 1/1 (Assen: Van Gorcum, 1974), 377–419; Menaham Stern, "Aspects of Jewish Society: The Priesthood and Other Classes," in *Jewish People in the First Century,* ed. Safrai and Stern, CRINT 1/2 (Assen: Van Gorcum, 1976), 561–630; and Rivkin, *Hidden Revolution.*

FOR FURTHER READING

Barstad, Hans M. *The Myth of the Empty Land: A Study in the History and Archaeology of Judah during the "Exilic" Period.* Oslo: Scandinavian University Press, 1996.

Carter, Charles. *The Emergence of Yehud in the Persian Period: A Social and Demographic Study.* Sheffield: Sheffield Academic, 1999.

Davies, Philip R., ed. *Second Temple Studies 1: Persian Period.* Sheffield: Sheffield Academic, 1991.

Davies, Philip R., and John H. Halligan, eds. *Second Temple Studies 3: Studies in Politics, Class and Material Culture.* Sheffield: Sheffield Academic, 2002.

Eskenazi, Tamara C., and Kent H. Richards, eds. *Second Temple Studies 2: Temple and Community in the Persian Period.* Sheffield: Sheffield University Press, 1994.

Harrington, Daniel J. *The Maccabean Revolt: Anatomy of a Biblical Revolution.* Wilmington: M. Glazier, 1988.

Levine, Lee I. *Judaism and Hellenism in Antiquity.* Seattle: University of Washington Press, 1998.

QUESTIONS FOR STUDY

1. What are the weaknesses of dividing the history of late biblical Israel into the exilic and postexilic ages? How does the concept of *Jewish colonialism* address the problem?

2. Explain the problem of the chronology involving Ezra and Nehemiah. How have scholars attempted to resolve it?

3. What are some of the major ways that Hellenism influenced the development of Judaism?

4. Identify the major differences between Essenes, Pharisees, and Sadducees.

TRADITIONS OF COLONIAL ISRAEL

Completing the Law and the Prophets

SUMMARY

The interaction within Israel's institutional
life of the Law and the Prophets

Rounding out the Law

Antecedents of P as the charter of postexilic
Judaism

Rounding out the Prophets: Ezekiel,
Deutero-Isaiah

Prophets of the rebuilt temple: Haggai and
Zechariah

Other prophets: Third Isaiah and Malachi

READ THE BIBLICAL TEXT

Genesis 1
Ezekiel
Isaiah 40–55
Haggai
Zechariah 1–8
Isaiah 56–66
Malachi
Obadiah
Joel

*See additional materials at fortresspress.com/
gottwald.*

HERMENEUTICAL POLITICS:
THE INTERPLAY OF LAW
AND PROPHETS

Traditions of Law and Prophecy
Develop in Dialogue

Law and Prophets were to become the
first and second divisions of the three-part
Hebrew Bible. Despite their firm delimitation,
it is evident that these two sets of traditions
interacted within the institutional life of Israel
from about 1050 to 250 B.C.E.

The history-like narratives and the covenantal and legal texts of the Law were solidly
rooted in the premonarchic era in the old materials underlying J and E, and even in D and
P. From the time of Samuel onward, as centralized monarchic structures came into tension with the older tribal socioeconomic and
religiocultural priorities, prophets appeared

as supporters or critics of public institutions, policies, and leaders.

Throughout the monarchy, extensive blocks of narratives and legal texts were committed to writing by J, E, D, DH, and the forerunners of P. During the entire time when these primal traditions were being successively written, prophets were likewise active in Israel. For example, J was probably written in the time of Nathan and Gad, and E in the age of Elijah and Elisha. The traditions of P are difficult to localize prior to Ezekiel, but at least the Holiness Code of Leviticus 17–26 was probably written at a time contemporary with the late-seventh-century prophets. The history of Israel and its social organizational forms presupposed in the traditions of J, E, D, DH, and P were part of the working environment of the prophets as of all other Israelite leaders. The precise familiarity of particular prophets with specific traditions of the Pentateuch is, however, difficult to determine.

For the most part, the preexilic and exilic prophets demonstrate a broadly shared consensus with the pentateuchal traditions, alluding to foundation events in early Israelite history and presuming a structured mutual relationship between Yahweh and the people of Israel. On the other hand, prophets did not in the main quote Law traditions, while the points of possible contact with Law traditions varied among prophets. Some prophets are more concerned with the Davidic-Zion traditions than with the pentateuchal exodus and conquest. The special relationship of Yahweh and people is not seen by most preexilic prophets as specifically covenantal but more often as a divine election or calling. The prophets do not cite legal texts but allude to infractions of the divine will in the public realm that seem to rest ultimately on laws of the general type gathered in the Pentateuch, but also on a general sense of what is humanly right, virtually in the manner of "natural law."[1]

In the other direction, the criticism of monarchy and stratified society introduced by prophecy had an impact on the Pentateuch. Possibly J, and certainly E, were affected by the prophetic critique of centralized government in offering their versions of the old traditions as a caution to forms of royal politics and societal oppression that endangered tribal society and religion. Deuteronomy even more obviously imbibed the prophetic judgments on society and proposed a program of reformation. DH gave prominent place to a series of prophets throughout the monarchy who persistently sought national conversion and lasting reformation.

The traditions that eventually became the Law and the oracles that eventually became the Prophets, together with the bearers of those traditions, thus interacted and responded to one another over centuries before final fixation of the traditions in two separate collections. With respect to the Law, we have seen that its authoritative form was reached after a major break in the production of history-like traditions occasioned by the exile (see p. 237), and that the formal commitment of the Jewish community to the Law as a fixed collection was a key element in the Jewish restoration program in Palestine. Regarding the Prophets, we indicated the overall process by which the individual oral and written messages were gathered and edited, especially as their critical messages at last won a more favorable hearing once the course of events seemed to validate the prophets.

A Consensus Canon Elevates Law Tempered by Prophecy

The dominant scholarly view of the literary process by which the Law was given final form is that *Genesis–Numbers* (Tetrateuch, "four scrolls"), composed of J, E, and P materials, was joined to *Deuteronomy,* transferred from its place at the beginning of DH, to form Genesis–Deuteronomy (Pentateuch, "five scrolls").

That Deuteronomy was unnaturally separated from its sequel in Joshua–Kings was probably to play down the military and political features of Israel's history as a tribal confederation and state(s) so as not offend Persian sensibilities (see pp. 65–67). This arbitrary isolation of Genesis–Deuteronomy as a literary corpus was acceptable to the Jewish restoration leadership behind the formal publication of the Law because the Pentateuch contained all the basic religiously oriented regulations necessary for constituting Judah as a semiautonomous colonial sector of the Persian Empire.

A further factor in the delimitation of the Law underscores how Law and Prophets as authoritative collections continued to influence one another. Studies of the literary and theological streams of tradition advocated by different categories of leaders in the restored Jewish community strongly imply that the way in which Law and Prophets were put together and officially endorsed represents a *compromise among rival groups* who had to collaborate if efforts to pull the community together were to receive general consent among the Jewish populace and firm support from the Persians.[2] In order for there to be a functioning Jewish community in Palestine, there had to be civil order and legitimate cult. It was the *Law,* supplemented by *Persian imperial administration,* that provided the former, and it was the *sacrificial and ritual holiness system* centered on the temple and expounded in the Law that provided the latter.

Whoever succeeded in controlling the temple establishment in the restored Jewish community exercised significant political, economic, and ideological power. So many disturbances in the continuity of priestly leadership had occurred that there was no consensus as to which of the priestly factions had the right to be custodians of the renewed cult. The Deuteronomic reform had cancelled the exercise of priesthood in Judah outside Jerusalem, but it did not integrate the non-Jerusalemite priests into the newly centralized sanctuary. Most, if not all, of the Jerusalem priests in power were killed, deported, or scattered in 597 and 586 B.C.E. The reduced cult that continued on the site of the destroyed temple was officiated over by other priests, perhaps including Samaritans. As descendants of the various priestly groups that had presided over the cult returned to Judah, they contended for leadership in the rebuilt temple.

One group won out decisively over all the others, but at least some of the losers were given secondary positions in cult administration. Nevertheless, the victors were in need of a plausible ecclesial ideology that would certify them as true successors of the ancient priesthood. In this regard the new priesthood was amazingly resourceful in validating its claims.

The dominant view of the priesthood in early Israel is that nearly all priests were Levites and all Levites were equally legitimate priests. In restricting worship to the one temple at Jerusalem, the Deuteronomic reform created an oversupply of priests. The decisive change after the exile was to secure a victory for one group of claimants by distinguishing between higher and lower orders of cultic personnel, a change validated by tracing the greatly narrowed legitimate priestly line back to Aaron, the brother of Moses. All other priestly claimants were lumped together as Levites, henceforth attendants of the priests. The Aaronide priests, firmly in control, granted limited recognition to rival priestly groups whose support activities could be closely monitored. The older office of chief priest was elevated in status and power owing in large part to the absence of Jewish political sovereignty that had formerly accorded the king great power of appointment and administration in cultic matters.

The postexilic political and religious lines of power are reflected in the arrangement of the Law and Prophets and in their ongoing interaction. The Aaronide priests stood behind the P document (see pp. 278–79), and their decisive shaping of the Pentateuch showed forth in the rocklike stability of the cult revealed to Moses and set in the single largest sweep of materials in the Pentateuch. The demoted, less unified Levitical attendants of the priests likely shared with other nonelite groups of the Judahite populace in a more dynamic historical and moral view of the meaning and function of the cult, as expressed, for example, in Deuteronomy and DH. In accepting Deuteronomy into the collection of the Law and conceding a subordinate role for Levitical interests, the Aaronides gambled on taming their opponents through co-optation. The result was to combine, both within communal life and within the newly published Law, two rather different ways of looking upon law and cult and, at the same time, to set the stage for the eventual inclusion of prophecy as an authoritative voice of the community alongside law and cult.

The Aaronide establishment outlook, shared by a majority of the lay elite who had to cooperate with the Persians, viewed the cult as a virtually self-sufficient program for being a good Jew who at the same time had to be compliant with Persian authority. The P cult practice, and most of the P laws, were concerned with countering natural evils and contaminations (what has been called a "pollution system" [see pp. 275–78]).[3] The view of history and social order in P and Chronicles largely lacks a sense of the contingency and ambiguity of events and institutions that evokes flexibility and humility of mind and calls for continuous critical assessment of oppressive or outmoded power. History was a pageant that unfolded God's unshakable institutional endowment "once and for all" to changeless Israel.

The Levitical critical outlook tended to see the cult as deeply dependent on repentance and moral commitment, and on a finely tuned understanding of Israel's history, in order to live appropriately in each new set of altered conditions. Law and cult were fundamentally involved in countering human evils and inequities both in individual deeds and in impersonal power structures (see pp. 221–23).[4] Diverse as these protesters against the postexilic establishment were, we hear their many voices in late prophetic writings, in psalms of lament and thanksgiving, and in the bitter comments of skeptical wisdom literature. This very diversity meant that they probably formed no continuing organization or political party, but were scattered in various institutional niches.

In the final form of the Law, P assured that the structures of the cult and law stood out as the central pillars of the collection, but at the same time, through the inclusion of JE and Deuteronomy, these structures were conceded to be mediated through Israel's history and in connection with Israel's social ethical priorities as a formerly tribal people. Prophecy left its mark upon the Law insofar as E and Deuteronomy, in particular, had been leavened by the impact of the prophets. More specifically, the Law referred to Moses as a prophet and more than a prophet and even made an effort to evaluate prophecy as a fresh voice from God, to the point of acknowledging the possible emergence of "a prophet like Moses" (probably meaning a succession of prophets).

Although they saw rather different meanings in law and cult, all parties to the Judahite restoration did concur that the finished Law set forth essential foundational traditions for Israel. Yet the immense variety and somewhat arbitrary juxtaposition of traditions in the Law, together with the different interests and priorities of Judahite groups, meant that a very lively ongoing process of interpretation was urgent in order to determine how these traditions from centuries past should be applied to present conditions. In one direction, this slippage between the Law and ever-changing present circumstances of life led eventually to rabbinic Oral Law. In another direction, it forced the question of what other written traditions were necessary to guide the restored and dispersed communities of Jews.

An Expanded Canon Incorporates Prophecy Accommodated to Law

The steps in collecting and editing the Prophets have not been as fully studied as the steps in forming the Law. It has been conjectured that at the time DH was last revised, shortly after 561 B.C.E., an accompanying collection of prophetic books was made under Deuteronomistic auspices.[5]

If this conjecture is correct, then DH and prophetic writings traveled together in the same tradition circles. Once Deuteronomy was joined with Genesis–Numbers to constitute the authoritative Law, it was a logical extension to regard Joshua–Kings (Former Prophets) plus an expansion of the exilic DH collection of prophets (Latter Prophets) as two parts of a second authoritative block of writings.

More than one principle of organization was apparently followed in the collection of the Prophets. Size of the books determined that Isaiah, Jeremiah, and Ezekiel should be first, whereas all the other, much shorter works were joined together in a single Book of the Twelve (in Christian tradition, the Minor Prophets). Within the Book of the Twelve, a rough chronological grouping is observed: (1) the period of Assyrian supremacy (Hosea, Joel, Amos, Obadiah, Jonah, and Micah); (2) the period of Assyrian downfall (Nahum, Habakkuk, Zephaniah); and (3) the period of Persian domination (Haggai, Zechariah, Malachi). That there are twelve shorter prophetic books suggests an allusion to the twelve tribes of Israel.

Within the prophetic books certain broadly similar redactional conventions are at work. They are supplied with superscriptions or introductory notations that constitute a title together with information about the prophet, the book, and/or the date. There is a pronounced tendency to organize the contents of the prophecies in a threefold pattern: (1) words of judgment against Israel/Judah, (2) words of judgment against foreign nations, (3) words of salvation for Israel/Judah. The book of Amos artfully breaks with the customary pattern by opening with foreign oracles. This redactional exception scores a stunning point by leading up to similarly patterned oracles against Judah and Israel who, in their apostasy from Yahweh, are in effect stigmatized as foreigners.

The obviously diverse and complicated redactions of the separate prophetic books, extending over generations, means that any given prophetic book is apt to refer to and comment on a whole series of turbulent events, from the collapse of the northern kingdom to the restoration of Judah. Increasingly after the exile, the past critical events and the prophetic reflections on them were read and redacted as pointers to exile and restoration. This trend toward reading the Prophets for warning and consolation in the restoration era thematized the whole prophetic corpus as a message of judgment followed by salvation.[6] This consciousness of a common prophetic message ending with an upbeat hope looked toward an open future in which more blessing was expected than had so far been realized in the modest restoration program after the exile.

This larger literary context for reading individual prophetic books as parts of a collected whole that refers pointedly to the contemporary community entailed ambiguity. For example, self-confident and proud secular and priestly leaders of the restoration probably understood the prophetic judgments as referring to the past, so that only salvation lay in the future. To the contrary, when read with the DH Joshua–Kings as the preface, the individual prophecies hinted at, or openly affirmed, possibilities of judgment still hanging over the community. Indeed, more recent prophets, such as Trito-Isaiah, Malachi, and Joel, were claiming old evils to be rampant in the supposedly purified postexilic community. It was certainly in this latter way that the Prophets were appropriated, especially among protesting Levites, prophets, and lay leaders who opposed the policies of the establishment Judahite elite.

Inevitably, as the Prophets collection expanded and took on more authority, it was read in the light of the already authoritative Law. Within prophetic books, often among the speeches of the earliest prophets, there are references to *torah,* "law," in various senses such as "instruction," "prescription," or "custom" (e.g., Isa. 1:10; 2:3; Jer. 2:8). Once the collection of the Law (Torah) was given authoritative status, these varied citations of *torah* within the prophets were likely to be perceived increasingly as references to the now officially recognized *Torah.* In this way, prophets who had in fact seriously criticized aspects of law observance among their contemporaries were seen to be model preachers of fidelity to the book of the Law. *Reading between the Law and Prophets* could operate either in the direction of self-critical Levitical interpretations or in the direction of triumphalist Aaronide interpretations.

The opening and closing books of the Twelve have redactional conclusions that also highlight this harmonizing and thematizing process by which all the parts of the Law and Prophets tended to be read as congruent with the religious allegiance and practice incumbent on the restoration community. Hosea 14:9 declares that all who are "wise" can profit from reading "these things" as prototypes of present moral and religious options. Malachi 4:4 urges the critical centrality of law observance, while a further notation in 4:5-6 announces the return of Elijah as the restorer of peace through justice to the strife-torn Judahite community.

This anticipated return of Elijah, strategically placed at the close of the Latter Prophets, stands in thematic connection and open tension with the close of the Law, where it is said that no prophet like Moses has since risen (Deut. 34:10). On the one hand, the Mosaic office and law are uniquely authoritative; on the other hand, the Deuteronomic imprint on the Law has left open the probability that new prophetic revelations will occur, in which case they will not contradict the foundation laid by Moses. When Law and Prophets are placed together, these Deuteronomistic allusions to prophets yet to come serve as a signal to readers that the collection of Prophets was prophetically foreseen by Moses the Lawgiver. But as the prophet yet to come in Mal. 4:4-5 is actually one of the old prophets returned, namely Elijah, the limits of the prophetic genre have been reached, and we are close to the threshold of apocalyptic.

Thus, in countless literary and conceptual details, which redaction criticism has only barely begun to grasp, the process of collecting, redacting, and authorizing Law and Prophets contributed to a sense of the unity of message in the two works and to their jointly reinforcing effects on exegetical tradition. By this juncture, within the time span 450–250 B.C.E., the Jewish people had taken decisive steps toward becoming a people of the Book whose self-understanding and self-organization were inextricably bound up in a complex and sophisticated literary tradition that demanded constant exegesis and application to the concrete circumstances of life.

ROUNDING OUT THE LAW: THE PRIESTLY WRITER (P)

We have earlier introduced the P source of the Pentateuch (see p. 83) and listed its contents in Genesis 12–50 (Web Table G, sec. C) and in Exodus–Numbers (Web Table H, sec. D). To complete the contents of the P document it is necessary to include passages in Genesis 1–11 (table 11.1).

TABLE 11.1 PRIESTLY (P) TRADITIONS IN GENESIS 1–11	
Creation of the Cosmos and of Humans	1:1—2:4a
Genealogy of Seth (From Adam to Noah)	5:1-28, 30-32
Destruction by Flood	
Preparation for Flood	6:9-22
Execution of Flood	7:6, 11, 13-16a, 18-21, 24; 8:1-2a, 3b-5, 7b, 13a, 14-19
Covenant with Noah	9:1-17, 28-29
Table of Nations	10:1-7, 20, 22-23, 31-32
Genealogy of Shem (From Noah to Abram)	11:10-27

Vocabulary, Style, and Structure

There is a wealth of distinctive vocabulary in P: "to be fruitful and multiply," "according to their families" (in enumerations), "throughout your generations," "to be gathered to one's people" (euphemism for death), "establish a covenant" (rather than "cut a covenant" as in JE), "eternal covenant," "this is the thing that Yahweh commanded," "congregation of the Israelites" (instead of "assembly" or "people" in JE), *nephesh* in the sense of "person" (rather than "life force" or "soul" in JE).

In cultic terms, P speaks of "the unauthorized encroacher or usurper (of priestly office)" and employs 'avōdāh strictly for "manual labor" (rather than for temple cultic service as in other pentateuchal sources). There is a considerable set of terms—perhaps legally defined—for property.

The measured style of the Priestly writer is stamped by a large number of fixed, repeated formulas, notable at the beginning and conclusion of units. Each subject tends to be developed by full description and stereotyped reiteration. The methodical and precise P style is evident in a preponderance of instructions and regulations (encompassing 1,745 verses) and in a sizable number of tribal and topographical lists (amounting to another 333 verses). Even its narratives are set forth in a measured, stately form (approximately 517 verses) intended for instruction (see pp. 91–93). Since P can produce marvelous effects with this style, as in the rhythmic unfolding of the creation story, the drabness felt by many readers probably has less to do with style than with P's preoccupation with ritual and its rather colorless and contrived theological reading of history.

In a work so stereotyped in language and style, we expect, and at times find, a clearly marked structure, although the extent of secondary expansions in P and the process of combining it with JE have disturbed what may once have been a much greater symmetry. We note first of all that the formula "these are the generations of X" has been used to mark off eleven phases in the history that runs from creation to the era of Moses: the heavens and the earth (Gen. 2:4a); Adam (5:1a); Noah (6:9a); Shem, Ham, and Japheth (10:1a); Shem (11:10a); Terah (11:27a); Ishmael (25:12); Isaac (25:19); Esau (36:1, 9); Jacob (37:2); and Aaron and Moses (Num. 3:1).

In addition, P sets forth *three perpetual covenants* that sharply periodize the sacred history:

1. A covenant with *Noah* in Gen. 9:1-17, sealed by a rainbow, promising that the earth will never again be destroyed, and permitting the eating of meat as long as the blood has been drained (prior to this, humans were vegetarian; see Gen. 1:29-30)
2. A covenant with *Abraham* in Genesis 17, sealed by the rite of circumcision, and promising his descendants national and royal greatness, possession of the land, and the abiding divine presence
3. A covenant with the *people of Israel* in Exod. 31:12-18, mediated by the revelation of law to Moses, and sealed by Sabbath observance, which overtly echoes the theme of God resting on the seventh day after creating the world (Exod. 31:17; see Gen. 2:2-3).

P also provides a "covenant of perpetual priesthood" with *Phinehas* (an etiology to anchor the Aaronide line) in connection with his zealous suppression of the cult of Baal of Peor (Num. 25:10-13). As the framework of the Pentateuch, P embraces the covenant traditions in Exodus 19–24, but without comment, apparently because the most important aspect of the revelation at Sinai for P was the tabernacle cult, which assured the continuing presence of God within Israel's collective life.

Another way of viewing the structure of P is to single out two kinds of formulas that flag the completion of stages in history on the one hand and the fulfillment of God's commands on the other hand.[7] A *conclusion* or *completion formula* demarcates three important moments:

1. *Creation of the world* (Gen. 2:1-2): "Thus the heavens and the earth were finished and all the host of them . . . so God finished his work which he had done."
2. *Construction of the tabernacle* in the wilderness (Exod. 39:32; 40:33): "Thus all the work of the tabernacle of the tent of meeting was finished . . . so Moses finished the work."
3. *Division of the land* after setting up the tabernacle at Shiloh (Josh. 18:1; 19:51): "So they finished dividing the land."

A more frequent *executionary formula,* occurring forty-one times in P, runs as follows: "X did according to all that Yahweh [God] commanded him [or commanded Moses]," underscoring mandated actions by which the divine plan was implemented in the movement from creation to Israel's occupation of the land.

Everything in Its Place: A Stable Cult in a Stable Cosmos

An analysis of P by means of these completion and execution formulas brings out a definite structural correspondence between creation of the world and construction of the tabernacle and its successful establishment in the land. There is likewise a structural correspondence between the ark of Noah and the tabernacle.[8] Some interpreters detect schematizing midrashic tendencies in P toward pushing back the origins of the Israelite cult into the very intention of God in creation (God rested on the archetypal Sabbath day!) and toward viewing the Law of Moses as having made explicit what was implicit in a prior covenant with all peoples. For example, the Noachian covenant ambivalently permitted bloodless meat eating but did not yet mandate sacrifice, nor did it provide civil justice for punishing murder, which it forbade.

The drift toward *midrash* in P combines with an old Mesopotamian priestly scribal interest in fusing *myth and cult* by recounting how sanctuaries and their cults and priesthoods derive from creation itself (see Exod. 25:9, 40). Just as God overcame chaos in creating the world, he again conquered chaos with Noah's ark, and finally decisively defeated the disorder and sin of the world by means of the tabernacle with its divinely ordained cult that would secure the perpetual purity and fidelity of Israel to Yahweh.

The mythically generated fascination with cosmos and chaos should be read as a stabilizing strategy in the struggle to preserve Jewish community in the midst of disorienting exilic and restoration conditions. Similarly, the passion to differentiate Israel as a distinct people with its own peculiar marks of circumcision, Sabbath, food laws, festivals, and sacrifices is a comprehensive effort to fashion a self-perpetuating and self-correcting community that would not be eroded by internal division and uncertainty or by external oppression and persuasion.

The connection of Genesis 1 to the rest of P is better clarified by the conclusion and execution formulas. Strictly speaking, there is no execution formula in Genesis 1, since there is no higher power than God to direct the deity. On the other hand, the description of creation in six days interweaves two ways of depicting the accomplishment of creation: God *speaking* the world into being (fiat and realization formulas) and God *crafting* the world into being (work formula). On the one hand, the coupling of the fiat formula ("And God said . . .") with the realization formula ("And it was so") parallels the execution of command formula that runs throughout the remainder of P, while the work formula ("God created/made/divided . . .") parallels the completion-of-work formula that occurs in the three key moments listed above. Moreover, the distribution of creative acts over six days shows a symmetry between the acts of days 1–3 and days 4–6 and the fusion of fiat/realization and work formulas in Genesis 1 (chart 11.1).

The world picture of P that stands behind this creation story is that of a flat disk earth topped by a solid and transparent semicircular firmament, with threatening but controlled waters beneath the earth and above the firmament (fig. 11.1). This cosmos is an orderly rule-governed environment for humans, which anticipates the ark of Noah and the tabernacle in the wilderness as further God-given safe environments to protect humankind, and eventually Israel, against natural and historical chaos, as long as the rule-governed cult for the worship of God is observed faithfully.

A fusion of cosmic myth and cultic scrupulosity in these priestly scribal traditions, stretched upon a frame of stylized history, contributes to a highly differentiated world of thought and practice in which every object, person, and activity has its meaningful place and its proper function that dare not be disre-

---

Chart 11.1 "Fiat," "Realization," and "Work" Formulas in Genesis 1

(1st Day)	Light and Darkness ⟷	(4th Day)	Heavenly Bodies
	F, R, W		F, R, W
(2d Day)	Firmament and Waters ⟷	(5th Day)	Birds and Fishes
	F, W, R		F, W
(3d Day)	Land ⟷	(6th Day)	Land Animals
	F, R		F, R, W
	Vegetation ⟷		Humans
	F, R, W		F, W, R

Key:
F: Fiat Formula: "And God said . . ."
R: Realization Formula: "And it was so"
W: Work Formula: "God created/made/divided . . ."

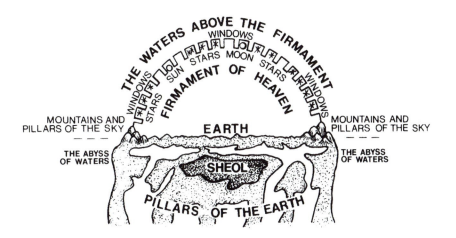

FIG. 11.1. The Cosmos of Genesis 1

garded nor mixed with other created things, lest the order of the world be undone.

The greater part of P is devoted to clarifying the *cuts,* that is, the distinctions and differentiations, appropriate to each stage of the primal history from creation to Moses: (1) the first humans are to make a cut between animals and plants, eating only the latter; (2) Noah is to make a cut between animal flesh and blood, eating only the former; (3) Abraham and his progeny are to be cut through circumcision, so that they will be separate from those uncircumcised; (4) Moses and his people are to make a complicated series of cuts between legitimate and illegitimate priests, sanctuaries, foods, kinship ties, sexual relationships, and dispositions of property. The created world and the land of Canaan belong to the deity, who sets the terms of distinction and differentiation for a prospering and enduring Israelite community.[9]

Arbitrary laws about clean and unclean foods—which in some details probably preserve hygienic origins—can be grasped as the outworking of the Priestly conviction about *orders of creation* that must be scrupulously respected by Israelites in their diet. P assumes three orders of living creatures: (1) *creatures of the earth* that walk on legs and are covered with skin; (2) *creatures of the air* that fly on wings and are covered with feathers; (3) *creatures of the water* that swim with fins and are covered with scales. Any food seen to fall within these proper categories was considered clean and edible, while all of the numerous foods that violate the divinely decreed distinctions were forbidden, for example, sea creatures that lack fins or have legs.

Similarly, sexual practices must follow a strict heterosexual order according to permitted sexual unions that do not mix parents and children (incest), humans and animals (bestiality), and do not reverse or confuse sexual identities (homosexuality). In this connection, other possible explanations may contain important elements of truth. In anthropological studies, prohibition of incest has sometimes been explained as a way of forcing human groups regularly into wider, peace-building community through out-group marriages. Biblical scholars have been inclined to think that homosexuality was stigmatized in ancient Israel because of its practice in Canaanite fertility religion; recently, however, doubts have been raised about whether cult prostitution was practiced as widely in Israel's environment as once thought. There is also the real possibility that male homosexuality (lesbianism is not mentioned in the Hebrew Bible) was abhorred in ancient Israel because it seemed to involve a prodigal waste of male seed, to be used properly in fathering the large families that were the cultural norm for the agricultural Israelites.

All in all, the Priestly conceptual and cultic world is highly rationalized and orderly, yet precarious. At any moment one may breach the balanced classificatory scheme and be plunged into the disorder of uncleanness and impending death. Thus every significant detail of life must be regulated according to the gracious revelation of the Priestly law through Moses.

Antecedents of P as the Charter of Postexilic Judaism

Older scholarship was emphatic in placing the P document in the exilic or postexilic periods, largely because its cultic provisions and its thought world do not show up in any of the preexilic literature, such as JE and D. It is only with Ezekiel during the exile and with Ezra and the Chronicler after the exile that close affinities with P appear. More recent scholarship has made clear that the date and locus of P are no simple matter to determine. Old material in P may go back to premonarchic social and military organizational data and even to some form of migratory cult shrine.

It was also seen that there are sections of P that once existed in independent form. Strik-

ing in this regard is the so-called Holiness Code of Leviticus 17–26, which is marked by the refrain, "You [Israel] shall be holy as I [Yahweh] am holy." The content of the Holiness Code includes generous sections of social legislation like that in the older codes, Exodus 20–23 and Deuteronomy 12–26. There is wide assent to the notion that the Holiness Code derives in written form from the late monarchy.

We seem to confront apparently conflicting evidence about the age and locale of P.[10] On the one hand, it is highly probable that P did not emerge in its present form until well into the exile at the earliest and that it was precisely the postexilic rebuilding of the temple that put such a high premium on P's hierarchic validation of the Aaronic priesthood and on P's passion for the cult as the distinguishing mark of Jewishness. It was this postexilic cultic coup that made P a suitable charter for the reestablished temple, won it an honored position as the framework for the final edition of the Law, and offered it as ideological justification for the power play of the Aaronic priests.

On the other hand, P's multiple traditions reached back at certain points to ancient features of Israel's institutional life that were maintained and reshaped in accord with the practice of some relatively powerless priestly community in monarchic times. That a law code like Leviticus 17–26 could be affected by these priestly traditions suggests that P-type traditions were known in monarchic times. These traditions probably existed only in small collections and did not yet possess an extended narrative framework. They accompanied a voluntary priestly observance and a self-cultivated guild ethic that was not in a position to impose itself on the whole community, as eventually became possible in the postexilic Priestly editing of the Law and in the reforms of Ezra.

It was probably the fall of Judah and the publication of DH that precipitated a P-based narrativized and utopian reading of the history from creation to Moses (or Joshua). This P history of Israelite beginnings both underlined the primacy of cult as the true anchor of Israel and in its treatment of ancient crises made veiled reference to the exilic disconti-nuities that would only be overcome through faithful adherence to the traditions published in P. It was probably in connection with the postexilic restoration of the cult that the rit-ualistic sections of P were expanded to give directives on the specifics of cultic service. Yet even here it should be noted that the old historicized utopian form of P prevailed in that all the cultic instructions were attached to the wilderness tabernacle rather than to the Solomonic temple, which would have been a more immediate and appropriate model for the rebuilt temple.

P as the Framework for the Law

The argument over whether P was an inde-pendent author or a traditionist redactor is not easy to formulate, much less decide. We have P only as the redactional framework of the Pentateuch that encompasses J, E, and D. On the other hand, the chronologies, genealo-gies, itineraries, organizational lists, and cultic minutiae of P have placed a decisive and siz-able stamp on the entire Pentateuch such that JE and D tend to be read within P's control-ling structures and assumptions. In turn, the redaction has somewhat blunted the mono-lithic message of P and, particularly at the end of Exodus and in Numbers, has contributed to insertions, combinations, and rearrange-ments of materials that are highly confusing to the reader (see pp. 106–7, 115–16). The final edition of the Pentateuch has apparently con-tributed to the fragmentation of P at points, for example, the awkward separation in the narrative between the anticipation of Moses' death in Num. 27:12-14 and its realization in Deuteronomy 34, and the redactional dump-ing ground at the end of Numbers with its mélange of P and J traditions.

By means of its P-dominated redaction, the Law was brought to its definitive form probably in the fifth century. If it was the P-redacted Law that Ezra brought with him from the Persian Diaspora, it is likely that the redaction was done among Persian Jews. It is possible—and perhaps more in keeping with the politics of the redactional process—that Ezra brought a version of the P document that was prepared abroad and, in negotia-tion with Palestinian traditionists, among whom the Deuteronomistic circles were of special importance, facilitated a redaction that put the P-oriented version in the lead-ing interpretive position but incorporated JE and gave the last word to the forceful admo-nitions and laws of Deuteronomy. The result was an amalgam of the debt system of the Deuteronomists with the pollution system of the Priestly partisans: the former stresses the *moral and historical precariousness* of Israel's status and future in a *socially unjust situation,* while the latter emphasizes the *orderliness of the world* as mediated by the *stabilizing mechanisms of the cult.* These two accents in the foundational Law, with all their affini-ties and contradictions intact, passed on to postexilic Jewish social actors and tradition-ists who went on to generate further defini-tive collections of the Scripture known as the Prophets and the Writings.

Rounding Out the Prophets

Ezekiel

The first prophet to speak out of Israel's exile reveals what a conceptually and emotionally wrenching experience removal from Palestine proved to be. The book of Ezekiel is difficult and forbidding in large part because it throws us into the maelstrom of deep consternation and radical reorientation that the collapse of Judah forced upon one highly creative person who, despite his striking individuality, was a faithful barometer of the social world of Jewish exiles at large.

Ezekiel was a priest-prophet carried off to Babylonia in the deportation of 597 who preached the deserved final doom of Judah until its demise in 586. Afterward, however, he turned quickly to the task of laying a theoretical and pastoral basis for exiled Jews to assimilate the practical meanings of catastrophe and thus prepare themselves for the future rebuilding of Palestinian Jewry based upon a total conversion to Yahweh's will both in spirit and in practice. In this task the prophet labored until at least 570.

On the surface, Ezekiel presents the austere messages of a transcendent deity who had forthrightly abandoned his temple in Jerusalem but who would return there in good time with a people purified by shame, guilt, repentance, and radical reform. Behind the almost unfeeling exterior of the harsh imperious words of Yahweh, we encounter a prophet who is traumatized by events, struggles to a total identification with his message, ranges in vivid imagination over the symbols and themes of judgment and salvation, and bodily experiences the terror and shock of transforming cruel events into modes of thought and action that can save the exiles, not merely as physical survivors, but as a viable community with their traditional roots intact.

The book of Ezekiel appears so unified that doubts about the cohesion of the work were slow to arise among historical-critical scholars. When traditional assumptions were at last questioned, contradictory aspects of this prophet streamed forth in a virtual torrent. How could a prophet with a moral and social vision also be a priest with ritual scruples and designs for a rebuilt temple? How could a prophet so soon after Jeremiah turn to wild and bewildering visions and even develop concepts of world calamity and of an earth-renewing temple, thus venturing to the threshold of apocalyptic thought in a single leap? How could a prophet called to preach judgment on Jerusalem do so when far removed in Babylonia?

In an effort to resolve these contradictions, it was necessary to examine the book for signs of its origin and process of composition. The initial tendency was to minimize or eliminate the inconsistencies in the portrait of the prophet. Ezekiel remained soberly anchored as a prophetic moralist by attributing apocalyptic elements to someone after the exile. He could also be given a proper audience for his message of judgment before 586 by assigning him an actual ministry in Judah for all or part of his career. The prophet appeared less crazy when his weird visions and odd behavior were judged largely or entirely to be the additions of a later writer or editor.

Various attempts to reconstruct a credible Ezekiel within a radically reduced core of the book were not satisfactory either because they were arbitrary or because they could not account for how such a trimmed-down prophet could have given rise to a multifaceted and contradictory stream of tradition. The key to the book and to the prophet lies somewhere between the simplistic notion of the book's unity and a splintering dissection that bypasses the nature of the traditions and the subtleties of Ezekiel's synthesis of judgment and salvation.[11]

The arrangement of the contents of the book of Ezekiel shows a clear plan. Following a vividly detailed account of a theophany of Yahweh leading to a cataclysmic call to prophesy (chaps. 1–3), the book divides into oracles of judgment against Judah/Jerusalem (4–24), oracles against foreign nations (25–32), and oracles of salvation directed to the exiles (33–48). Chronological and visionary schemes interconnect these subdivisions.

Placed throughout the work is a series of dates by year, month, and day reckoned from the first deportation in 597 (e.g., 1:1-2; 8:1; 20:1). The initial date places Ezekiel's vision and call in 592, and the others proceed almost entirely in chronological order down to 570. These dates are important clues to the work of the prophet and the formation of the book, with the proviso that they apply only with some certainty to the immediate subunit they preface. There is considerable concurrence that these dates reflect the prophet's own work in putting at least some of his words in written form.

Three of the dates attach to the awesome and fantastic vision of Yahweh's glory, as it first broke upon the prophet at his call (1:1), as it recurred a year later when it transported him to Jerusalem to observe Yahweh's judgment on the city and then returned him to Babylonia with fateful news (8:1), and as it recurred twenty years after his call to transport the prophet once again to Jerusalem for a tour

of the restored temple to which the glory of Yahweh could now appropriately return (40:1; cf. 43:3-5). The mechanism of the vision of God's glory suggests that Yahweh, unlimited by his temple or worshipers, has deserted the holy place so that it will be destroyed, hovers over his people in exile—threateningly for sinners and protectively for the righteous—and will at the proper time of purification inhabit a rebuilt temple on the same site. This schematization reflects the jolt and leap in consciousness called forth in a priest who is able to conceive God's complete freedom to reject his own place of worship until his corrupt worshipers are punished and purified.

A further linking of subdivisions in the book is accomplished by skillful employment of a historical-theological thematization of the fall of Jerusalem. The entire book of Ezekiel pivots on the destruction of Jerusalem, anticipated and realized during the course of a full reading of the text, thereby setting the stage for the eventual reconstruction of the city. The oracles against Jerusalem and Judah open with symbolic actions in which the prophet, for example, pictures the siege of Jerusalem with clay models and an iron plate (4:1-3) and lies immobile on his side to picture a lengthy exile (4:4-6).

In further symbolic actions, the prophet digs through a wall with baggage on his back to mime the flight of defenders during siege (12:1-7) and eats bread and water, the rations of prisoners of war (12:17-20). The oracles of judgment against Jerusalem end with the revelation that the siege of Jerusalem has begun on 15 January 588, and that the prophet will be dumb until a fugitive shall arrive to announce the city's fall (24:25-27). On that note of suspense the oracles against the nations introduce a long digression. Only in the prologue to the concluding oracles of salvation are we informed of the fugitive's arrival with bad tidings on 8 January 585, and immediately Ezekiel's mouth is opened (33:21-22). The ending of chaps. 1–24 and the beginning of 33–48 are thus directly linked by anticipation and confirmation of Jerusalem's fall, while the two subdivisions are consciously linked by various motif repetitions: for example, the mountains of Israel, the prophet's dumbness, and his appointment as a watchman over the exiles.

The watchman role of the prophet, fully developed in 33:1-20 (cf. 3:17-22) has generally been construed by interpreters as possible only after 586 because of its hope for the repentant. Yet Ezekiel's closely intertwined watchman warnings to "wicked" *and* "righteous" were probably aspects of his mission throughout (see 2:5). After the destruction of Jerusalem, the prophet worked as a pastoral moralist to guide responsive exiles beyond arrogance or despair to recognition of their shame and guilt, and finally to repentance, all the while instructing them in the content of Yahweh's teaching about the morally just and ritually proper life.[12]

In a speech form cast as a disputation about Yahweh's justice or injustice and drawing on an instructional legal style from priestly traditions, Ezekiel summoned to repentance and advised practical changes of conduct (3:17-21; 14:1-11; 18:1-32; 22:1-16; 33:1-9). The alleged major shift of Ezekiel from collective retribution to individual retribution is a misunderstanding. The new teaching role of the prophet was precisely to rebuild the collective identity and accountability of Israel by converting and disciplining exiles, one by one, as trustworthy members of a new community. While old Jerusalem's sin had grown so massive that righteous individuals could not avert its punishment, the new Jerusalem would be composed of those who took their loyalty to

Yahweh completely to heart and thus would never again contribute sins that could undermine the foundations of the community.

Beginning with the majestic vision of Yahweh that draws on old traditions of Yahweh's cultic and cosmic enthronement, as well as on iconic details of Assyro-Babylonian myth and ritual, Ezekiel asserts the holiness and honor of Israel's God that require him to destroy the political and religious establishment of Judah but also impel him to vindicate his real presence in history by purifying and restoring a Judahite community. Again and again the final aim of Yahweh's doings with Israel is declared to be "that you/they [Israel/the nations] may know that I am Yahweh."

Ezekiel recites the history of Israel, either straightforwardly (chap. 20) or figuratively (chaps. 16; 23), so as to underscore the waywardness of the people from their very origins. Not only in the wilderness, which Hosea and Jeremiah had at least thought of as a honeymoon period between Yahweh and Israel, but even during the bondage in Egypt, Israel clung to idols (20:4-9). The metaphorical recitals concerning Yahweh's orphan wife, Jerusalem (chap. 16), and his sister wives Samaria, and Jerusalem (chap. 23), are intricately constructed explorations of the husband-wife imagery that Hosea and Jeremiah had used for Yahweh and his people. Ironically, the prophet uses a feminine personification of Israel's male leadership fraught with misogynist stereotypes of wayward and willfully adulterous women.

Apparently one of the effects of the exile was to press Ezekiel to reflect on earlier prophetic traditions to the point of embracing elements of various prophetic traditions. Ezekiel shows many signs of creative dependence on Jeremiah, Isaiah, Hosea, and Amos, as also on the Elijah-Elisha traditions. Nevertheless, he transmutes all that he touches into his own exotic twists and combinations of thought and into his own pedantic modes of exposition. As with the P writer, this often plodding means of expression can attain a sparse and awesome grandeur, as in his vision of the valley of dry bones (37:1-14).

That there has been addition to and expansion of the words of Ezekiel is abundantly clear. Like Isaiah, Ezekiel gave rise to, perhaps deliberately founded, a faithful and literate following. The literary labor of the prophet's followers shows up frequently. In chap. 10 an attempt has been made to clarify aspects of the eccentric vision in chap. 1: the "wheels within wheels" are given more eyes and said to be "whirling," and the four-faced living creatures are equated with cherubim, the ox face of each replaced with a cherub face. To the vision of the restored temple shaped by Ezekiel (probably chaps. 40–43) later traditionists have added descriptions of the cultic personnel and rituals, layouts of the tribes in the land, and a description of the fructifying wilderness of Judah. Ezekiel viewed the nations in their historical particularity (see chaps. 25–32), but in chaps. 38–39 a certain Gog of Magog (identity unknown) leads a host of nations in an attack on Judah. It has been noted that 39:25-29 forms an appropriate summary after the vision of the valley of dry bones, the symbolic joining of staffs to represent the reunion of Ephraim and Judah, and the installation of David as king in chap. 37. It is probable that an early edition of the prophet's writings closed in this way, minus Gog of Magog and the restored temple.

If we look beyond redactions to the personality of the prophet himself, what can be said of the supranormal powers of perception and the bizarre modes of behavior that the book attributes to the prophet? Ezekiel has been dubbed ecstatic, visionary, mystical, neurotic,

psychotic, schizophrenic, and more—terms that label his unusualness without providing any certain understanding of it. Attempts to diagnose his symptoms or read his garish symbolism in a psychoanalytic framework have not been very productive. Explorations of mystical and parapsychic phenomena have broadened our options for understanding the prophet but struggle to decode the extraordinary or pathological behavior of the prophet in terms of its sociocultural grounding. Recent progress in the literary analysis of the vision form discounts the common interpretation that Ezekiel claimed physical transport from Babylonia to Jerusalem and back (8:1-3; 11:24-25) and that he alleged clairvoyance about the death of Pelatiah (11:1, 13).[13]

It is possible that an existentialist psychological reading comes closest to interpreting Ezekiel's psychophysical symptoms.[14] Catatonic schizophrenia may roughly characterize the paralysis of will, and thus of body, that threatens a prophet who does not wish to carry so severe a message and yet cannot refuse to stand forth and try to speak. Depending on how his dumbness is to be dated, it is possible that at times Ezekiel, preacher of unmitigated disaster, found it difficult to assume his role. It is only after 586, when circumstances give him an audience more amenable to his message, that his tongue is dependably and fully loosened.

Seen in this manner, the reluctance of Ezekiel to perform publicly is not merely a private quirk but a vivid expression of the difficulty many exiles—once the upper class of Judahite society—had in reconciling their pride of tradition and lost privilege of office with the traumatic shift in personal fortunes and communal conditions of life forced on them willynilly.[15] In the prophet's wildness of demeanor and thought we may thus see a compressed distillation of that agony of renunciation and rebirth through which the deported Judahites passed—necessarily one by one even though in mutual support—in order to reach social stability and religious confidence.

The impression given by the form of the book that Ezekiel evoked a continuing interest in preserving, collecting, commenting on, and adding to his oracles is complemented by indications that the exiled elders consulted and dialogued with him (8:1; 14:1; 20:1). Assuming that, in the absence of normal political leadership, elders who were the acting heads of the exilic community came to speak with Ezekiel, this implies their recognition of the authoritative calling of the prophet. Ezekiel is abrupt and impatient with their inquiry because it seems to deny the impending fall of Jerusalem. All of the explicit consultations with the prophet seem to precede the fall of Jerusalem. That the prophet speaks to the complaints of the people (e.g., 18:2, 19, 25) suggests that he received a renewed, possibly more serious, hearing once the gravity of a prolonged colonial fate was fully confirmed.

Ezekiel's oddity of personality and fantastic imagination apparently did not cut him off from the people, who struggled with him over the temporariness or finality of exile, over the meaning to be placed upon their circumscribed life conditions, and over a communal strategy for living through and beyond those conditions. For this reason alone it is myopic to place too much emphasis on the prophet's "mental illness," since that only obscures the social weight he carried as a person to be reckoned with even when his interpretations and recommendations were disputed and rejected as often as they were affirmed and embraced.

Isaiah of the Exile (Deutero-Isaiah)

Chapters 40–66 of Isaiah are composed in a high, formal style in which traditional psalmic and polemical speech forms are fused and transformed into a vehicle of excited proclamation and urgent summons. Presupposed throughout is the impact of the sixth-century exile as a decisive rupture in the life of Israel. Characteristic of chaps. 40–55 is a relative tightness of thematic presentation and an anticipation of imminent release from captivity and return to Palestine. By contrast, chaps. 56–66 appear to be composed of originally disconnected literary blocks that largely reflect the conditions of Jews in Palestine after the return from exile (see pp. 290–91).

On the assumption that each of these segments forms a unity, the author of chaps. 40–55 has been called Deutero-Isaiah (Second Isaiah), while the author of 56–66 has been dubbed Trito-Isaiah (Third Isaiah). The relationship between these two is often conceived as master and disciple. The unmistakable continuities of style and theme between the two sections imply that the originating mind behind this emotive and elevated way of speaking about exile and return initiated a school or stream of tradition responsible for the shaping of chaps. 40–66.

Between fifty and seventy-five literary units are customarily identified in chaps. 40–55. Form-critical analysis has been moderately successful in showing many of these units to be recognizable specimens of fixed forms of speech that emerged out of traditional life situations in monarchic Israel.

The *oracle of salvation* (41:8-13, 14-16; 43:1-7; 44:1-5; 54:4-6) addresses Israel in a personified singular, silences fear, and promises deliverance in general terms of comfort, welfare, prosperity, and victory (for Assyrian parallels, see Web Table A, 6C). The *proclamation of salvation* (e.g., 41:17-20; 43:16-21; 55:1-5), in contrast, for the most part addresses Israelites in the plural and promises deliverance in somewhat greater sociopolitical specificity: release from exile, return to Palestine, rebuilding of the temple, material abundance. The *hymn of praise* (e.g., 42:10-13; 48:20-21; 52:7-10) calls on Israel, the peoples of the earth, and all nature to praise Yahweh, who is about to deliver Israel from exile.

Alongside these affirmative speech forms stand two negating or polemical genres. The *trial speech* in its most complete form is addressed to the nations and their gods (41:1-5, 21-29; 43:8-13; 44:6-8) within a juridical scenario that exposes the ineffectuality of all gods except Yahweh God. In some cases the trial speech is turned against Israel (42:18-25; 43:22-28; 50:1-3). The *disputation* or *controversy* form is a rebuking and admonitory rebuttal of Israel's allegations of divine injustice.

The precise bearing of the diverse formal origins of the literary types employed in chaps. 40–55 on the particular shape and setting of the chapters as a whole is as yet unresolved. Many form critics insist that 40–55 are merely the aggregation of separate literary specimens strung together arbitrarily, often by catchwords. Others insist that the separate pieces have been carefully ordered with a larger plan in mind. Yet others argue that a conscious whole was constructed from the start by a skillful juxtaposing and interweaving of genre structure and idiom. On the other hand, the limits to the development and overt linkage of themes set by the strictures of traditional genre speech account for the difficulty in identifying what the shape and order of 40–55 actually consists of.[16]

Germane to the discernment of diversity and unity in Isaiah 40–55 is the problem of identifying the setting in which these chapters were spoken or written. Unlike earlier prophetic writings, Isaiah 40–55 preserves no narrative information about the prophet's work, even lacking a superscription. It is generally assumed that the exiles gathered for worship and discussion of community issues, and it is often posited that the prophet delivered his message to these gatherings, either orally or in writing. The prophet who formulated the argumentation and rhetoric of 40–55 managed to concentrate a remarkable number of themes and imaginative figures within a brief compass, to combine and recombine them, to space and accent them variously, and to build and relax tension so that a satisfying forward movement and resolution of the whole is felt.

The enormous amount of study invested in Isaiah 40–55, however, has been relatively narrow and atomized, revolving around questions that tend to miss the distinctive qualities of the work: Does Deutero-Isaiah give the first biblical statement of monotheism? Does the prophet anticipate the conversion of the nations to Jewish faith? Has he been influenced by Zoroastrianism or by the Babylonian New Year Festival? Who is the servant of Yahweh? Neither pointless nor unimportant, these questions are nonetheless often pursued in relative isolation from one another and out of context.

Damaging above all to a grasp of the work as a whole has been the hypothesis that the four extended reflections on the servant figure, known as the Servant Songs (42:1-6; 49:1-6; 50:4-9; 52:13-53:12), are independent compositions secondarily inserted into their present contexts, so that the Servant of the songs and the *servant* of the remainder of the work have two different identities that a redactor unsuccessfully tried to harmonize. The elaborated descriptions of the servant do set up an inner tension and ambiguity of meaning, but this is only the strongest epitomization of a number of enigmas and ambiguities that the work artfully stages and plays upon: Cyrus, who does not know Yahweh, will know him; the nations will be conquered and saved; a blind and deaf servant will lead forth a blind and deaf people; the same God who has been wearied by his people's sins will deliver them from their deserved bondage; and a deliverance from exile should be celebrated before it has occurred! These are but some of the astonishing breaks in logic with which the prophet regales his hearers.

The most promising heuristic question about the servant is probably not *Who* is the servant? but rather, *What* does the servant do in relation to all that is to occur in the deliverance of Israel? or *How* does the servant function in relation to the other imaginatively developed figures?[17] When the problem of the servant is approached in this manner, it becomes clear that the servant is one of a number of ways of speaking of Israel, as typified by representatives from the past and also now by someone at work in the present, probably the prophet himself.

In the first half of the work (chaps. 40–45), the prophet sets forth a wealth of historical entities and actors in individualized and personified dress: Zion/Jerusalem, the nations and their gods, Jacob/Israel, Cyrus, the servant of Yahweh, and Babylon/Chaldea. The interaction among and the destinies of these protagonists are emphatically grounded in Yahweh as creator and lord of history.

The Jewish people, alternatively viewed as Zion/Jerusalem and Jacob/Israel, are to be delivered and restored to Palestine. Yahweh will disempower the nations, who wrongly trusted in their gods, by equipping Cyrus to overthrow Babylon and to assume world empire. In this world-turning crisis, the servant of Yahweh, rising from weakness to strength, will bring the justice of Yahweh to all the nations.

In chaps. 46–47, after all the chief actors have been presented and the basic scenario outlined, the tempo of presentation slackens as the downfall of the Babylonian gods (46) and of the Babylonian Empire (47) is celebrated. In the last third of the composition (49–55), the dramatis personae of the earlier chapters are sharply reduced. Cyrus gives way before Yahweh as the ultimate source of deliverance. Jacob/Israel ceases as a designation for the people of God, and, in its place, the male figure of the servant and the female figure of Zion/Jerusalem come to the center. The images of the oppressed servant, finally victorious as a multiplier of righteousness to "many," and the bereft mother and wife Zion/Jerusalem, abandoned but shortly to be delivered and consoled, are alternately developed toward an ecstatic climax amid declarations of the enduring character of Yahweh's accomplishment.

A close structuralist analysis of the work might well reveal the fundamental binary oppositions. Apparent strength and success in history collapse into weakness and failure; apparent powerlessness and wasted effort issue in productivity that turns the course of ancient Near Eastern history. At this deep level of the ironic reversal of apparent strength and weakness into their actual opposites, there is a decided affinity between the structure of thought in Isaiah of Jerusalem and the structure of thought in Isaiah of the Exile, notwithstanding their different vocabularies and thematic arsenals.

Because the servant figure is Israel in the remaking, it is a slow and painful process of reeducation and transformation, and the figure ranges in its reference between the collective destiny of Israel and the greater commitment and teachability of some Israelites. The portraiture draws on servant features of Moses, of prophets such as Jeremiah, and even of the ideology of righteous kingship. The confessing, lamenting, and thanksgiving language of 49:1-6 and 50:4-9, in which the servant speaks, and of 52:13—53:12, in which the servant is spoken of both by Yahweh and by deeply affected onlookers, draws liberally on traditional speech of the thanksgiving and lament genres, including the latter's expression of confidence in which the sufferer affirms with certainty that Yahweh will hear and vindicate. In any event, the oppression and vindication of the servant are described in 53:8-9 and 12 with such compressed emotion and deliberate understatement that actual firsthand experience seems to inform the imagery.

In large part on the form-critical grounds that 53:1-12 is best understood as a straightforward third-person thanksgiving song, some have argued that the servant figure is the prophet himself, arrested and imprisoned by the Babylonians with the help of Jewish informers, and rescued on the verge of death, possibly by the Persian conquerors or by a pro-Persian party of Babylonians prior to the conquest of the city.[18] Because chaps. 40–55 trade in a compressed and allusive image-filled style, one must move cautiously in translating the servant figure directly into the terms of inner-communal Jewish response to the shift of power from Babylon to Persia as precipitated by this most outspoken prophet. Nonetheless, a strong odor of political conflict surrounds the acclamation of Cyrus and the hostile treatment of the servant. Given the individual thanksgiving form of chap. 53, there is good reason to hypothesize that the actual imprisonment, persecution, and deliverance of a historical contemporary, most likely the prophet himself, have been employed as a microcosm of the macrocosm of Israel's fate insofar as the people's suffering has exceeded its deserved punishment. That some of this suffering was inflicted on Jews by fellow Jews is not at all surprising in context.

In betraying the prophet to Babylonian authorities, his opponents would have thought they were sparing the Jewish community still greater suffering. Furthermore, it is highly likely that some prominent members of the exilic community had been taken into the very Babylonian government that Isaiah of the Exile declared would be shortly destroyed. In moving to neutralize the prophet, these privileged Jews would have been fighting for their own stake in the survival of the Babylonian regime.

A rich array of covenant, law, and justice/ righteousness language is used to assure Israel of its security in the hands of Yahweh amid the catastrophic events of transfer of imperial power in the ancient Near East (51:7-8; 54:9-17). Of further moment is the striking way that these very themes of assurance to Israel are set within *inclusios* that extend the operations and effects of covenant, law, and justice/ righteousness among all the nations (42:1-7; 49:5-6; 51:4-5; 55:3-5). Recent scholarship has been right to deflate the imagined missionary program of the prophet, as though he called on Israel to convert foreigners.[19] The anticipated conversion of the nations is set alongside contradictory images of the destruction and subjugation of the nations. When the nations do eventually come to their senses and confess Yahweh, it will be mainly through their own enlightenment about the efficacy of Yahweh's work in and through Israel.

Some of the confusion in this cluster of images about the nations may be reduced if we assume that the prophet envisions Cyrus as the destroyer and subjugator of the nations and Israel as the future "priestly prophetic enclave."[20] While we cannot be certain how the prophet structured all the elements of his understanding of Israel as the enigmatic "peoples' covenant" (42:6; 49:8) and "nations' light" (42:6; 49:6; 51:4), it is interesting that his later disciples speak of "foreigners" who "joined themselves" to the restored Jewish community in Palestine, worshiping at the rebuilt temple as "a house of prayer of all peoples" (56:3, 6-8). Later prophecy also envisions whole nations who "join themselves" to Yahweh (Zech. 2:10-12), and the survivors of "the families of the earth," including Egypt,

who will be obligated "to go up to Jerusalem to keep the feast of booths" (Zech. 14:16-19).

The overall fabric and tenor of the work have fared poorly at the hands of interpreters insufficiently sensitive to the work as literature and as an adroitly mediated aesthetic expression of the conflicting attitudes and responses among the Babylonian exiles to the new sociohistorical situation opening up in the years leading up to Babylon's fall. Fresh literary and sociohistorical inquiries, informing one another and not neglecting the great contributions of earlier methods of study, promise to increase our comprehension of this energetic document, which arrests and taxes us with its emotional intensity and its intellectual breadth.

FIG. 11.2 The Ishtar Gate, built during the reign of Nebuchadnezzar II (605–562 B.C.E.). Babylon. Sixth century B.C.E. Color-glazed. terra-cotta tiles, 14.73 x 15.70 x 4.36 m. Inv. VAMF 94. Vorderasiatisches Museum, Staatliche Museen zu Berlin. Photo: © Bildarchiv Preussischer Kulturbesitz / Art Resource, N.Y.

Prophets of the Rebuilt Temple

Haggai and Zechariah were the last prophets connected with known historical events, as they were also the first prophets whose immediate aims were carried out by communal leaders. They summoned Zerubbabel and Joshua to make haste in rebuilding the temple that still lay in ruins eighteen years after the edict of Cyrus authorizing the reconstruction of Judah (see p. 250). From dates formulated in the pattern of Ezekiel's chronological notations, we learn that Haggai prophesied during August–December 520 (e.g., Hag. 1:1, 15a; 1:15b—2:1) and that Zechariah prophesied from November 520 to as late as December 518 (Zech. 1:1, 7; 7:1).

Haggai

The present book of Haggai is divided between words of the prophet urging rebuilding of the temple (1:2-11) and words of the prophet urging endurance in that enterprise (2:2-9, 11-19). These oracles are separated by a report on the beginning of reconstruction in September 520 (1:12-15a), and they culminate in a promise that Zerubbabel will become the neo-Davidic ruler of an independent Judah (2:20-23). The prophet remonstrates that only as the temple is rebuilt will prosperity spring forth from the land of Palestine and from the largesse of the nations who will be drawn to the splendor of Yahweh's worship in Jerusalem. Using a highly disputatious style, Haggai comes to grips with the doubts and evasions of the community by calling them to consider the meager fortunes of the people to date and motivating them to risk the cost of temple reconstruction as the one and only course of action that will secure Yahweh's blessing.

The structure of the literary units and the prophet's line of argument, particularly in 2:10-19, are difficult to follow. On the assumption that the book is a collection of originally separate oracles serially arranged by date, there appear to be disorders and non sequiturs in argument. Rather than a collection of separate oracles, however, the book of Haggai may be more productively viewed as a redaction of prophetic speeches and chronological notes and a report of temple rebuilding cast in the third person. This redaction has taken once-separate oracles and worked them together into longer speeches in 1:2-11 and 2:11-19.[21] The fused oracles emphasize the hesitancy and reluctance of the Jews to start the rebuilding and, once begun, to continue with it, both because the structure did not seem as glorious as Solomon's temple and because the expected economic improvement had not occurred as speedily as they had hoped.

Haggai boldly insists that the risky and courageous act of rebuilding the temple will evoke the cooperation of the nations in provisioning the cult (2:6-9) and likewise trigger the political decline of the nations so that Zerubbabel can advance from his present role as a Persian-appointed petty official to the restored office of Davidic king (2:20-23). The Judahite community must do its part in readying the cult, while Yahweh does his part in blessing the ground and "shaking heavens and earth."

Zechariah 1–8

Zechariah 1–8 is organized around two foci: a set of eight nocturnal visions in chaps. 1–6 and answers to an inquiry in chaps. 7–8 as to whether fast days commemorating the fall of Jerusalem in 586 should be observed now that the temple is rising anew.

The visions are rife with bizarre imagery explained by an interpreting messenger in the manner of Ezekiel's visions. The visions are grouped in a loose thematic ring or chiastic structure that situates the work of Joshua and Zerubbabel at the center (visions 4 [3:1-7] and 5 [4:1-5, 10b-14]) surrounded by a frame of Jerusalem/Judah defended from the nations (visions 2 [1:18-21] and 3 [2:1-5]) and purged of evil (visions 6 [5:1-4] and 7 [5:5-11]) and encompassed further by the outside frame of patrolling horsemen/chariots (visions 1 [1:7-15] and 8 [6:1-8]).

The vision sequence is prefaced by a call to repentance motivated by a reflection on Israel's stubbornness toward Yahweh in the past (1:2-6) and concluded by an oracle commanding the crowning of Zerubbabel as king and Joshua as high priest (6:9-15). The passages indicate that it is Zerubbabel who will build the temple (4:7-9; 6:12-13) and who, as king of Judah, will collaborate harmoniously with Joshua, the high priest. The great confusion in these Zerubbabel-Joshua texts is probably due to the fact that the exuberant confidence of Zechariah about the reestablishment of the Davidic line did not come to fruition. The Persian Empire held firm, and Zerubbabel disappeared from the scene without leaving a revived Davidic dynasty (see p. 250).

When men from Bethel inquire of priests and prophets as to whether they should continue the fast days in memory of Jerusalem's downfall (7:1-3), Zechariah's reply becomes a long speech that weaves together the socially ethical rigor of prophecy with the obligation to build up the cult. At long last the petitioners' pointed question is directly answered: No, the fast days are no longer to be observed; instead, they are to become feast days and occasions to live justly (8:18-19). A closing oracle celebrates an insistent, even clamorous, turning of the nations to Yahweh at Jerusalem (8:20-23).

Zechariah 1–8 is an intricately redacted work that skillfully plays on the events of 520–

518 in a wider paradigm of Jewish faithfulness and expectation that would serve later post-exilic generations well. The temporal standpoint within the redaction shifts between exile and restoration. The references and appeals to Israel's experience over the preceding century are not only citations of past events but depictions of processes of exile, repentance, restoration, doing justice, and conversion of nations that are far from having run their course. Thus even the failure of the prophecy about Zerubbabel as Davidic ruler, which seems only halfheartedly concealed, is seen as one of the many twists and turns through which Judah must go in its struggle to become ever-anew Yahweh's people.[22]

Prophets of Conflicted Restoration

The last prophetic writings to be composed fell within the Persian period, following the rebuilding of the temple, possibly all appearing prior to the reforms of Ezra and Nehemiah in the latter half of the fifth century. Excluded from treatment here are the short story about the prophet Jonah, which I treat later with other short stories (see pp. 316–18), and Isaiah 24–27 and Zechariah 9–14, which exhibit a more developed apocalyptic eschatology (see pp. 330–31).

Isaiah 56–66 (Trito-Isaiah)
There is no mistaking the stylistic and conceptual influence of Isaiah of the Exile on these chapters, but it is equally evident that Isaiah 56–66 presupposes the return to Palestine and the rebuilding of the temple.

If we speak at all of a "Third Isaiah," the term should apply to the author of the central poems in chaps. 60–62, which are closest to the style and thought of chaps. 40–55 in setting forth an ecstatic announcement of the pending redemption of Zion when more exiles are to be gathered, the nations will contribute to the cult of Yahweh, and peace and righteousness will flourish without limit. The servant figure in 63:1-3 may speak of the mission of this prophet to serve his community (see 57:14-20; 65:17-25; and 66:10-14). Sharply at variance with the words of salvation are laments and indictments concerning tensions and splits within Judah attributable to those who monopolize and abuse power.

Attempts to discern a literary, topical, or chronological arrangement in chaps. 56–66 have not been convincing. It is likely that our best clue to the articulation of the contents is the central placement of the visionary restoration scenario of chaps. 60–62 around which are balanced roughly matching panels in chiastic arrangement (Web Chart C), although many details and idiosyncrasies in the matching panels do not correspond. By opening and closing chaps. 56–66 with words of salvation and by awarding the fullest scope to salvation at the center, the redactor clearly gives priority to the authorial voice of salvation. In the middle panels of this ring arrangement, however, indictments and laments underscore the dire impediments to communal salvation that call for the severest judgment.

What struggles within the restored community are referred to under these colorful, sometimes lurid, outbursts? The consistent viewpoint of the laments and indictments in Isaiah 56–66 is that those who control the temple establishment, and who are most ardent in observing cultic practices, are guilty of socioeconomic oppression and outright bloodshed, while they exercise a stranglehold on the cult that marginates and finally excludes others from leadership and participation. As we have

noted (see pp. 269–71), the composition of the postexilic priesthood was up for grabs. It is likely then that the prophetic/priestly voices speaking in Isaiah 56–66 are proponents of a more widely shared (or alternative?) exercise of priestly office by ethically upright and communally accountable religious leaders backed by the same caliber of political leaders.

The impression given by these chapters is that some group (Aaronides?) has consolidated its hold on priestly office and has pushed other claimants (Levites?) and their prophetic partisans out of the cult altogether.[23] Ironically, a prophetic critic anticipates that among the Gentile survivors who will propagandize for Yahweh throughout the nations there will be some whom Yahweh "will take for priests and for Levites" (66:21), an action that will circumvent Aaronide—or indeed any Israelite—attempt to dictate Yahweh's priesthood.

It is impossible to know over what period of time the conflict raged and with what results. It may well be that Darius's authorization of work to start (or resume?) the temple reconstruction carried with it certification of the Aaronides as sole legitimate priests, so that from 520 onward the priestly leadership narrowed, monopolizing power and corrupting itself to a point of irreconcilable conflict with other Judahite groups. This may have been the background of the reforms of Nehemiah, who took steps to redress imbalances of ecclesial and socioeconomic power through a program of limited democratization (see pp. 252–53).

Malachi
The book of Malachi throws further light on severe tensions within the postexilic community over the laxity of leadership. The work is constructed of six oracles in the form of disputations with priests and people, and what

is said of the latter implies that the socio-economic and political elite are in view. The prophet establishes the following points:

1. Yahweh loves Israel, in contrast to Edom, which he has destroyed and will not restore (1:1-5).
2. Yahweh detests the inferior animals that priests and people are offering in a betrayal of the "covenant with Levi," which mandates a faithful priesthood (1:6—2:9).
3. Yahweh rebukes Jewish husbands who break covenant with their wives by divorcing them in order to take foreign wives (2:10-16).
4. Yahweh promises to send soon his "covenant messenger" to purify the faithless priests, after which Yahweh will judge the socially unjust laity as well (2:17—3:5).
5. Yahweh condemns widespread withholding of tithes and offerings that has brought on bad harvests (3:6-12).
6. Yahweh assures that he remembers the nucleus of righteous Jews and will soon come to vindicate them against the wicked Jews (3:13—4:3).

The disputation form is well marked with an opening statement of a principle or norm by the prophet, followed by a protest from priests or people, and concluding with substantiation of the original statement accompanied by rebuke and threat of judgment.[24] The prophet faced a communal leadership suffering deep doubts about Yahweh's commitment to Judah and Yahweh's readiness to enforce justice. The social injustice condemned (3:5) has its systemic counterpart in laxity of cult and abuses of marriage and divorce. To further their economic position, well-provided worshipers were cutting corners by withholding offerings or bringing inferior offerings. The taking of foreign wives by Jewish leaders and social climbers was a ploy to enhance their status by giving them protective and entrepreneurial connections with leading families in surrounding territories.

The horizons of Malachi fit well with the fifth century prior to the reforms of Nehemiah and Ezra. Disillusionment with ecclesial and sociopolitical establishments so tartly expressed in Isaiah 56–66 suffuses Malachi as well and points toward grave confrontations between factions in the community. Malachi shows affinities with the Deuteronomic traditions, but whether the reference to Yahweh's covenant with Levi (2:4) is an explicit counter to Aaronide claims is not certain. Nonetheless, it is evident that the prophet regards the incumbent priesthood as totally corrupt and soon to be replaced or radically reformed.

Obadiah and Joel

The books of Obadiah and Joel use occasions in the historical experience of Edom and Judah to introduce and enlarge on the coming day of Yahweh when the nations will be judged.

Obadiah 1–15 is an oracle of judgment against Edom because of its failure to aid Judah against the Neo-Babylonians in 586 and its actual participation in looting the land and seizing fugitive Judahites. Whether the closely parallel Jer. 49:7-22 is the source of Obad. 1–15, or vice versa, or whether both depend on a third source, is indeterminable. It appears that Obad. 1–15 could have been written at any time after 586. The core oracle has been expanded in two stages: vv. 16–18, addressed to Israelites, promise the destruction of Edom and the elevation of Zion, while vv. 19–21 affirm Mount Zion's coming vindication through its possession of Mount Esau and belongs to restoration times.

Joel has long been a puzzling work because it presents contradictory facets that look back toward preexilic prophecy and forward toward postexilic prophecy.[25] It begins with a call to fasting and repentance in response to a devastating locust plague and drought (or is an invading army portrayed as locusts?). There then follows a series of eschatological oracles about the last days. The promise of a pouring out of Yahweh's spirit on the community (or does "all flesh" mean the whole earth?) does not link concretely to anything in the preceding lament, but at the same time it differs from the judgment of the nations that close Joel. The unifying motif throughout the book is the day of Yahweh (1:15; 2:1, 11, 29; 3:1, 14, 18).

There is as yet no generally recognized explanation for the dual character of the book of Joel. Some argue that a preexilic lament over locusts was expanded in postexilic times, perhaps in reference to the second symbolic locust plague, a foreign army. This upgrading of the eschatological dimension in the lament

FIG. 11.3. Darius I the Great (550–486 B.C.E.) giving audience. Detail of a relief in the treasury of the palace at Persepolis, Persia. Achaemenid Period, 491–486 B.C.E. Photo: © SEF / Art Resource, N.Y.

prepares for the final judgment on the nations. Others have thought to explain peculiarities of form and content by assuming the book to be a liturgy that went through stages of growth over time, at first restricted to fasting over locusts and then broadened and redirected to a celebration of coming judgment on the nations. A liturgical origin for chaps. 1–2 does help to account for the remarkable cohesion and movement of the lament and its textual preservation without major disturbance. Yet another approach is to see all the locust references as symbolic of an invading enemy, which is variously understood as Assyria, Neo-Babylonia, or Macedonia.

NOTES

1. John Barton, "Natural Law and Poetic Justice in the Old Testament," *Journal of Theological Studies* n.s. 30 (1979): 1–14, with application to Amos, Isaiah, and Ezekiel.

2. On "consensus canon" see Gerald T. Sheppard, "Canonization: Hearing the Voice of the Same God through Historically Dissimilar Traditions," *Int* 37 (1982): 25–26.

3. Fernando Belo, "The Symbolic Order of Ancient Israel," in *A Materialist Reading of the Gospel of Mark,* trans. Matthew J. O'Connell (Maryknoll, N.Y.: Orbis, 1981), 37–59; and see n. 9 below.

4. Ibid.

5. Joseph Blenkinsopp, *Prophecy and Canon: A Contribution to the Study of Jewish Origins* (Notre Dame, Ind.: University of Notre Dame Press, 1977), 101–2.

6. Roland E. Clements, *Old Testament Theology: A Fresh Approach* (Atlanta: John Knox, 1978), 131–54.

7. Joseph Blenkinsopp, "The Structure of P," *CBQ* 38 (1976): 275–92.

8. Ibid., 280–86.

9. Jean Soler, "The Dietary Prohibitions of the Hebrews," *New York Review of Books* (June 14, 1979): 24–30; see also Mary Douglas, *Purity and Danger: An Analysis of Concepts of Pollution and Taboo* (Baltimore: Penguin, 1970), 54–72; and n. 3 above.

10. Menahem Haran, "Behind the Scenes of History: Determining the Date of the Priestly Source," *JBL* 100 (1981): 321–33.

11. Childs, "Ezekiel," in *IOTS*, 355–72.

12. Moshe Greenberg, *Ezekiel 1–20,* AB (Garden City, N.Y.: Doubleday, 1983).

13. Greenberg, *Ezekiel 1–20,* 192ff.; Keith Carley, *Ezekiel Among the Prophets,* SBT 2/31 (London: SCM, 1975), e.g., 6ff.

14. Thomas Alan Parry, "Crisis in Responsibility: Existential Psychology and the Prophet Ezekiel," B.D. thesis, University of Alberta, 1964.

15. The devastating conceptual, ethical, and emotional shock of exile to people *and* prophet is analyzed with acute insight by Thomas M. Raitt, *A Theology of Exile: Judgment/Deliverance in Jeremiah and Ezekiel* (Philadelphia: Fortress Press, 1977).

16. Carroll Stuhlmueller, "Deutero-Isaiah: Major Transitions in the Prophet's Theology and in Contemporary Scholarship," *CBQ* 42 (1980): 1–29.

17. Claus Westermann, *Isaiah 40–66,* trans. David M. G. Stalker, OTL (Philadelphia: Westminster, 1969), 93. For a literary reading of the elusiveness of the servant figure, see David J. A. Clines, *I, He, We and They: A Literary Approach to Isaiah 53,* JSOTSup 1 (Sheffield: JSOT Press, 1976).

18. R. N. Whybray, *Thanksgiving for a Liberated Prophet: An Interpretation of Isaiah Chapter 53,* JSOTSup 4 (Sheffield: JSOT Press, 1978).

19. D. E. Hollenberg, "Nationalism and 'the Nations' in Isaiah XL–LV," *VT* 19 (1969): 23–36.

20. Gottwald, *AKE,* 341–46.

21. Childs, *IOTS,* 476–79.

22. Ibid.

23. Paul D. Hanson, *The Dawn of Apocalyptic: The Historical and Sociological Roots of Jewish Apocalyptic Eschatology,* 2nd ed. (Philadelphia: Fortress Press, 1979), 32–208, 380–401.

24. Georg Fohrer, *Introduction to the Old Testament,* trans. David E. Green (Nashville: Abingdon, 1968), 469–70; James A. Fischer, "Notes on the Literary Form and Message of Malachi," *CBQ* 34 (1972): 315–20.

25. Childs, *IOTS,* 386–93.

FOR FURTHER READING

Barrera, Julio C. "The Origins of the Tripartite Old Testament Canon." In *The Canon Debate,* ed. Lee Martin McDonald and James A. Sanders, 128–45. Peabody, Mass.: Hendrickson, 2002.

Clifford, Richard J. *Fair Spoken and Persuading: An Interpretation of Second Isaiah.* New York: Paulist, 1984.

Clines, David J. A. *I, He, We, and They: A Literary Approach to Isaiah 53.* Sheffield: JSOT Press, 1973.

Coote, Robert C., and David Robert Ord. *In the Beginning: Creation and the Priestly History.* Minneapolis: Fortress Press, 1991.

Mein, Andrew. *Ezekiel and the Ethics of Exile.* New York: Oxford University Press, 2001.

Smith, Paul A. *Rhetoric and Redaction in Trito-Isaiah: The Structure, Growth, and Authorship of Isaiah 56-66.* Leiden: Brill, 1995.

Tollington, Janet E. *Tradition and Innovation in Haggai and Zechariah 1-8.* Sheffield: JSOT Press, 1993.

QUESTIONS FOR STUDY

1. Explain the relationship between the Aronide and the Levitical priests. How did it influence the development of the canon?

2. Describe how themes of salvation and judgment in the Prophets could be interpreted differently by various Judahite audiences.

3. How do P's completion and executionary formulas create a correspondence between the creation of the world and the construction of the tabernacle?

4. Characterize the servant in the Servant Songs in Isaiah. Why have some scholars posited two different servant figures? Explain how the complex servant figure is used to enrich Deutero-Isaiah's message about the restoration of Israel.

TRADITIONS OF COLONIAL ISRAEL

The Writings

SUMMARY

Components of the Writings
History: Chronicles, Ezra, Nehemiah
Restored Jerusalem
Songs: Psalms, Lamentations, Song of Songs
Biblical poetry, genres
Short stories: Ruth, Jonah, Esther
Wisdom writings: Proverbs, Job, Ecclesiastes
Apocalyptic writings: Daniel
Genre and mind-set

READ THE BIBLICAL TEXT

1 and 2 Chronicles	Ecclesiastes
Psalms	Isaiah 24–27
Lamentations	Zechariah 9–14
Song of Songs	Daniel
Ruth	
Jonah	
Esther	
Proverbs	
Job	

See additional materials at fortresspress.com/ gottwald.

The Writings, as its vagueness of title hints, is less cohesive than either the Law or the Prophets. Yet the variety of the Writings is no mere miscellany nor are its contents totally unrelated to the Law and the Prophets. The third division of the Hebrew Bible contains blocks of historical writings, songs, short stories, wisdom writings, and apocalyptic writings, which we shall examine in that order. Each of these types of literature, together with their subgenres, has analogues or forerunners in the first two divisions of the Hebrew Bible. It is also evident at a number of points that these works demonstrate knowledge of the older divisions of the Hebrew Bible. The Hagiographa (Greek: "sacred writings") as a title for the third division of the Hebrew Bible has been widely used among Roman Catholics and some Protestants.

LATE HISTORICAL WORKS: 1 AND 2 CHRONICLES, EZRA, AND NEHEMIAH

The final redacted history of Israel, composed of 1 and 2 Chronicles, Ezra, and Nehemiah, forms the conclusion to the Writings or third division of the Hebrew Bible.

Relation between 1 and 2 Chronicles, Ezra, and Nehemiah

Oddly, Ezra and Nehemiah *precede* 1 and 2 Chronicles in the Hebrew Bible, in plain violation of the historical order of their contents. A conjectured rationale for this jarring transposition is that Ezra and Nehemiah were first accorded canonical status, since they covered new historical ground, whereas Chronicles was initially viewed as a mere supplement to Samuel–Kings and was only later tacked on to the end of the Writings.

The contents of this late historical work retrace, often cursorily, the entire history of Israel treated in J, E, P, and DH combined, that is, from creation to the exile, and go on to extend the story into postexilic times as far as the work of Ezra and Nehemiah (table 12.1). Proportioned as it is, it could be said to be a history of David, Solomon, the kings of Judah, Ezra, and Nehemiah or, more topically, *a history of the temple and cult community of Jerusalem*. Other political figures and affairs acquire meaning only insofar as they contribute to the founding, upbuilding, and rebuilding of the cult community centered on temple and law.

Scholarly convention speaks of the author

of 1 and 2 Chronicles, Ezra, and Nehemiah as the Chronicler and of his work as the Chronicler's History (CH). Considerable differences in style and viewpoint separate Chronicles from Ezra–Nehemiah, to the extent that many critics judge them to have been written by different authors in different streams of tradition. Characteristic thematic interests of Chronicles, such as the faithful house of David, the dual assignment of prophetic functions to familiar public figures of the past and to cult singers of the present, are absent or meager in Ezra and Nehemiah.

Defenders of the unity of Chronicles, Ezra, and Nehemiah are now more likely to recognize a Chronicler's school, to allow for secondary insertions (e.g., genealogies in 1 Chronicles 1–9; lists of David's officials in 1 Chronicles 23–27), and possibly for two or more editions of the whole. The conceptual incongruities in the two parts of CH may be explained by the diversity of sources and by shifts in the sociohistorical circumstances from the sixth to the fifth century. The Chronicler, for instance, in giving relatively free rein to the Ezra and Nehemiah reports, showed how an earlier liberality toward Samaritans lost ground amid struggles climaxing in the reforms of Ezra and Nehemiah. In any event, the more that differences of emphasis and outright tensions and contradictions between Chronicles and Ezra–Nehemiah have been highlighted, the more customary it has become to recognize two or more editions of the Chronicler's work.

Restored Jerusalem as True Successor to David's Kingdom

Assessment of CH has tended to revolve around the issue of how good or bad its history is. Omission of the darker aspects of David, complete neglect of the northern kings, insertion of liturgical and homiletical materials to the neglect of political and military data—all such features of the Chronicler have been read as marks of dogmatic distortion of history.

It is now clear, however, that CH used a version of Samuel-Kings more closely aligned to the Hebrew text underlying the Septuagint than to the proto-Masoretic Text (see pp. 70–72).[1] Many of CH's presumed alterations of Samuel–Kings are apparently faithful renderings of the Hebrew text at hand. Furthermore, at a number of points the Chronicler provides fresh information about Judah's monarchic history that may be reliable on balance,

---

TABLE 12.1 DIVISIONS AND SOURCES IN CHRONICLES AND EZRA–NEHEMIAH

1 Chronicles 1–9:   *Adam to Saul*

Here the "story" is told exclusively by means of extended genealogies, in part drawn from Torah and Prophets and in part independently supplied by the author.

---

1 Chronicles 10–29:   *David Prepares for Building and Staffing the Temple*

2 Chronicles 1–9:   *Solomon Builds the Temple*

2 Chronicles 10–36:   *Kings of Judah from Rehoboam to Zedekiah*

In these three sections the account is an interweaving of narratives from Samuel-Kings with new materials supplied by the author, who cites as many as five historical works and twelve prophetic writings, some or all of which may in fact be merely ornate ways of referring to the extant books of Samuel-Kings.

Ezra 1–6:   *Return of the Exiles and Rebuilding of Temple*

Ezra 7–10:   *Ezra's Reforms*

Nehemiah 1–7:   *Nehemiah's Reforms*

Nehemiah 8–9:   *Ezra's Reforms Continued*

Nehemiah 10–13:   *Nehemiah's Reforms Continued*

In these five sections there are sizable accounts of the work of Ezra and Nehemiah, each shifting between first-person (so-called Ezra Memoirs and Nehemiah Memoirs) and third-person reporting. These once-independent accounts of the two reformers have been rearranged so that their careers are told in a "dischronologized" or "staggered" pattern. In addition, there are lists and documents, some in Aramaic, the diplomatic language of the Persian Empire (Ezra 4:6—6:18), including a list of the returnees from exile (Ezra 2, and repeated in Nehemiah 7).

supplementing or even on occasion correcting Samuel–Kings.

The reign of Josiah is illustrative. Whereas Kings knows only of Josiah's reformation, beginning with the discovery of the law scroll in the temple in 622 (2 Kgs. 22:3-10), Chronicles refers to earlier reform activities in 632 and 628 (2 Chron. 34:3-7). Also, whereas Kings speaks cryptically of Josiah being killed by Pharaoh Neco when the Judean king "went to meet him" (2 Kgs. 23:29), Chronicles states outright that Josiah "went out against him [Neco] . . . to fight with him" (2 Chron. 35:20-22). While the Chronicler had ample biases for misconstruing or fabricating evidence, historians do take CH's potential contributions with cautious respect.

Recent study of CH has focused on the purpose in preparing a work that deliberately chose to go over historical ground long since surveyed by J, E, P, and especially DH. There is little doubt that the Chronicler was fully aware that the older histories were established as recognized versions of Israel's past. So why did CH retell the story of the southern monarchy? The basic intention was to make clear that the postexilic community devoted to Law and temple was the true continuator of the Davidic monarchy. Whether or not Chronicles anticipates a revived Davidic monarchy, it does insist that the lasting contribution of David and his successors was to bequeath a temple and priestly establishment to Judah, so that when the temple and its cult were reconstituted after the exile *all* the essential elements of monarchic life were recovered.[2] The books of Ezra and Nehemiah are set up as the history of this reconstitution.

Looked at in terms of the major streams of traditions that were shaping the restored community, CH reflects and advances the historic compromise in which the Priestly and Deuteronomic traditions and practices were blended, under the hegemony of the former but with generous inclusions of the latter. DH is prominent because of CH's decision to excerpt extensively from Samuel–Kings. With so-called Levitical sermons urging appeal to faith and obedience placed in the mouths of kings and prophets[3] (e.g., 1 Chron. 28:2-10; 2 Chron. 15:2-7) and psalms sung by Levitical singers conceived as prophets and seers (e.g., 1 Chron. 16:4-36; 2 Chron. 5:11-14; 29:25-30), all the major categories of leadership tend to run together in the conduct of a cult whose effects spill out of the temple and into political and military affairs. DH elements are also frequent in Ezra and Nehemiah, where Deuteronomistic sanctions and provisions undergird the debt, marriage, and cult reforms.

If the Chronicler was an establishment supporter of the Aaronide priestly leadership, as is generally thought, he at any rate leaned a long way to incorporate Deuteronomistic viewpoints and to see to it that the lower orders of Levitical priests were both honored and provisioned in their posts.

Redactional Disorder in the Books of Ezra and Nehemiah

We have reviewed the difficulties in establishing the order of appearance of Ezra and Nehemiah in Jerusalem and the relationship between their reforms (see pp. 251–53). On balance, the hypothesis that Nehemiah preceded Ezra, and that they worked separately, Nehemiah having returned to the Persian court before Ezra arrived, makes the most satisfactory reconstruction of a situation muddled by the way the sources have been redacted.

What literary and sociohistorical sense can we make out of the Ezra-Nehemiah traditions? The Ezra materials are found in Ezra 7–10 and Neh. 7:73b—9:37, and the Nehemiah materials in Neh. 1:1—7:73a and 9:38—13:31. Within both strands, the earlier portions are the most coherent and contain sustained "I" passages that suggest the presence of a Nehemiah Memoir and possibly an Ezra Memoir. The Nehemiah Memoir is clearly visible in Neh. 1:1—7:73a; 12:31-43; 13:4-31. The first-person Ezra Memoir is in Ezra 7:27—9:15. "Memoir" as a genre name for Nehemiah's document is a misnomer, since in it the reformer is offering political self-justification against his enemies and commends himself to God that he should be "remembered."

To get a near approximation of the course of events in the reforms, for the work of Nehemiah one should read in order Neh. 1:1—7:73a; 11:1—13:27; 9:38—10:39; and 13:28-31; and for the work of Ezra one should read in order Ezra 7–10; Neh. 9:1-37; 7:73b—8:18 (deleting the redactional references to Ezra in Neh. 12:26, 36, and to Nehemiah in Neh. 8:9). If the redacted blending of the two reformers' activities correctly retained a historical reminiscence, as some scholars think, then it depended entirely on other evidence than is preserved in the present literary records.

By drawing so straight and unerring a line from Moses through David to the restored and reformed postexilic community, CH validates a vigorous recovery of national traditions and communal practices that was both a form of accommodation to the colonial status under Persia and also an act of national resistance by marking off a religiocultural identity for Jews that was drawn so tightly that in the end it excluded fellow Jews, such as the Samaritans, who did not fully succumb to the reform leadership in Judah.

SONGS

What Is Biblical Poetry?

We have noted the presence of verse structure in many parts of the Hebrew Bible and briefly discussed some of its features in connection with the Song of Deborah in Judges 5 (see pp. 145–47). Hebrew songs are composed of sentences or lines that divide into two or three members or clauses. The clauses are separated by a slight pause, and the sentence concludes with a full pause, forming the pattern

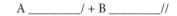

A _____/ + B _____//

or, on occasion,

A _____/ + B _____/ + C _____//

Often the component clauses of the song sentence have a correspondence described as "parallelism of members/clauses." This poetic sentence may be schematically illustrated by Ps. 24:1-3:

v. 1 A The earth is Yahweh's and the fullness thereof /
   B the world and those who dwell therein //
v. 2 A For he has founded it upon the seas /
   B and established it upon the rivers //
v. 3 A Who shall ascend the hill of Yahweh? /
   B and who shall stand in his holy place? //

Psalm 24:1-3 thus exhibits close parallelism, but there are practically as many lines in

Hebrew verse where the correspondence between clauses is slight or absent altogether:

A The angel of Yahweh encamps around those
  who fear him /
B and he delivers them //
                    (Ps. 34:7)

A Blessed be Yahweh /
B who has not given us as prey to their teeth //
                    (Ps. 124:6)

A Mark this, then, you who forget God /
B lest I rend, and there be none to deliver //
                    (Ps. 50:22)

In Hebrew verse, lines with correspondence and lines without correspondence typically intermix, as in Ps. 2:1-6:

v. 1 A Why do the nations conspire? /
     B and the peoples plot in vain? //

v. 2 A The kings of the earth set themselves /
     B and the rulers take counsel together /
     C against Yahweh and his anointed //

v. 3 A Saying, "Let us burst their bonds asunder /
     B and cast their cords from us" //

v. 4 A He who sits in the heavens laughs /
     B Yahweh holds them in derision //

v. 5 A Then he will speak to them in his wrath /
     B and terrify them in his fury //

v. 6 A Saying, "I have set my king /
     B on Zion, my holy hill" //

It is obvious that the close correspondence between clauses in vv. 1, 3, 4, and 5 in Psalm 2 is not present in vv. 2 and 6. In standard descriptions of parallel clauses it is customary to refer to such departures from strict correspondence as "synthetic" or "formal" parallelism.

More elusive has been the quest for poetic meter. On the basis of syllable counts and conjectured accenting schemes, it has been usual to identify lines with 3 + 3, 3 + 2, and 2 + 2 meters, as well as other less frequent patterns, and to assume a single meter in a composition. But there are so many exceptions and our ignorance of how the spoken language was stressed so vast that no convincing metrical analysis has yet been offered.

Our understanding of biblical poetics has been vastly enriched on the one side by the recovery of examples of ancient Near Eastern poetry, particularly Canaanite, that clarify the many ways of constructing sentences of parallel clauses and of employing rhetorical devices that Israel shared with its neighbors. On the other side more sophisticated attempts have been made to formulate precisely what it is that gives Hebrew poetry its specific character. The challenge is substantial, since meter has not been demonstrable and the paralleling of clauses has not been formulated with enough precision to cover the great variety of forms it takes.

Psalms

The canonical book of Psalms is an anthology of 150 poetic prayers composed in paired A + B (or A + B + C) clauses. The psalms are by and large addressed to Israel's God. The speech conventions of these prayers were shaped within the framework of Israel's cult, centered on the temple at Jerusalem. The subject matter of these psalms is overwhelmingly the distress and deliverance of the people of Israel as a whole and of individual Israelites.

While the speech forms presuppose stated occasions of worship, the present grouping of the psalms and the assorted titles attached to 115 of them do not fully reflect the actual occasions of worship or the exact manner in which they were used. The time line of these prayers extends in fact over centuries of cultic history, beginning with the First Temple, built by Solomon, and including its forerunners and competing shrines, continuing through the templeless exilic period, and reaching on into the era of the Second Temple, built by Zerubbabel. The book of Psalms is often called "the Hymnbook of the Second Temple," and this is apt in the sense that during the Second Temple era the compilation and redaction of the psalms were completed, perhaps around 325–250 B.C.E.

The move from live cultic performance of psalms to their collection as literature was a major one, in which much of the actual cultic functioning of the psalms has been lost or obscured. It is evident that factors other than stated worship have had a part in the shaping of the book of Psalms. In a measure, they reflect a tendency toward private devotional or study use apart from, or in between, times of temple worship. Originally separately composed, the psalms were gathered in lesser collections that were finally combined to produce the present book.

One entire category of psalms, called wisdom or didactic psalms, focuses proper prayer and worship on adherence to the divine law (probably already the canonical Law). Psalms 1 and 2, an introduction to the whole collection, epitomize this manner of praying and pondering the texts. The Davidic monarch heralded in Psalm 2, and elsewhere throughout the Psalms, was remembered and anticipated as the executor of justice in Judahite society. Indeed, the division of the book of Psalms into five parts marked by summary refrains seems to have been intended to parallel the psalms with the five books of Torah:

Book I	Psalms 1–41; see 41:13
Book II	Psalms 42–72; see 72:18-20
Book III	Psalms 73–89; see 89:52
Book IV	Psalms 90–106; see 106:48
Book V	Psalms 107–150; see 150

Modern study of the Psalms has evolved through several stages in clarifying psalmic literature and in narrowing still-unresolved questions. Breaking through the traditional religious assumption that David and singers of his generation wrote the psalms, nineteenth-century scholars emphasized the postexilic origin of the anthology, many psalms from as late as Maccabean times. Nowadays it is judged that many of the psalms, while scarcely written by David, are preexilic, and that, among the many postexilic psalms, probably all of them were composed before Maccabean times.

Literary Genres

In the early twentieth century, Hermann Gunkel began to crack the code of psalm idiom, formal structure, and function. In addition to the five predominant types of hymns, individual laments, individual thanksgiving songs, communal laments, and royal psalms, Gunkel isolated several less common or more formally elusive types: communal thanksgiving songs, songs of pilgrimage, blessings and curses, wisdom poetry, liturgies (different literary types deliberately joined in a single unit for worship), and mixed types.[4]

The main lines of Gunkel's form-critical analysis have held up remarkably well in the century since he proposed them, despite some modifications. The genres may be grouped under four types or modes of speech:

I.   Lamenting and Entreating Genres
II.   Praising and Thanking Genres
III. Performing and Enacting Genres
IV.   Instructing and Meditating Genres

I. Lamenting and Entreating Genres

A. Anonymous Individual Laments. An unnamed person in distress (excluding the data in the titles) describes suffering in harsh terms, sometimes protests innocence or confesses sin, pleads with Yahweh to remove the distress, and often passes over into an affirmation of certainty that the cry for help will be heard and deliverance is forthcoming. Subdivisions of this genre include: prayers of the falsely accused, penitential psalms, and protective psalms. The line between individual and communal laments is not agreed upon in all cases, since the "I" in some psalms may be a speaker for the community. Forty-four psalms fit in this category: 3, 5, 6, 7, 9–10, 13, 17, 22, 25, 26, 28, 31, 35, 36, 38, 39, 40, 42–43, 51, 54, 55, 56, 57, 59, 61, 63, 64, 69, 70, 71, 77, 86, 88, 94, 102, 109, 120, 130, 140, 141, 142, 143.

B. Anonymous Individual Psalms of Confidence. The section of the lament that Gunkel called "the certainty of a hearing" on occasion becomes the content of an entire psalm, with only the merest reference to the psalmist's difficulty. The anticipated deliverance from Yahweh is declared with utter confidence. There are eight of these psalms: 4, 11, 16, 23, 27, 62, 121, 131.

C. Royal Individual Laments. No entire psalm is given over to the lament of a king, but royal lamenting speech is contained in at least three psalms, one to be classified as a royal thanksgiving song (18:4-6) and the others as communal laments (89:46-51; 144:1-11).

D. Communal Laments. Afflicted by famine, plague, socioeconomic oppression, or military disaster, the community gathers to fast, lament, and sacrifice. The communal lament ("we") follows the same basic structure as the individual lament, although it is at times more explicit about the calamity referred to. These sixteen psalms are: 12, 44, 58, 60, 74, 79, 80, 83, 85, 89, 90, 108, 123, 126, 137, 144.

E. Communal Psalms of Confidence. Three psalms are the communal counterparts of the individual psalms of confidence: 115, 125, 129.

II. Praising and Thanking Genres

A. Hymns or Descriptive Praises. Praises of God, or hymns, begin and end with calls to laud or bless the divine majesty. The body of the hymn is a description of Yahweh's attributes or deeds in nature and in the history of Israel. Hymns have much in common with thanksgiving songs, except that they cite general and long-standing aspects of God's goodness and power, whereas the thanksgiving songs speak of recent deliverances from specific distress. Other subclasses, besides those below, are *victory hymns, pilgrimage songs,* and *festival songs.* The total of these psalms is twenty: 8; 19:1-6; 29; 33; 95:1-7c; 98; 100; 103; 104; 111; 113; 114; 117; 135; 145; 146; 147; 148; 149; 150.

1. Hymns of Zion: Certain hymns picture Yahweh as dwelling at Jerusalem on invincible Mount Zion, threatened by enemies whom Yahweh overpowers. Gunkel took these to be eschatological references to a future day of salvation. Sigmund Mowinckel understood that in the cultic drama Yahweh's present resecuring of the foundations of the community was affirmed.

Both scholars recognized that these hymns of Zion drew on old Canaanite mythology about an impregnable holy mountain as the seat of deity. There are six of these psalms: 46, 48, 76, 84, 87, 122.

2. Hymns Celebrating the Kingship of Yahweh. A handful of hymns assert Yahweh's rule over the nations and contain the cultic exclamation, "Yahweh has become king!" Gunkel saw in them a noncultic hope influenced by prophets and projected into the future, while Mowinckel asserted that this "hope" was cultically enacted at the annual New Year's Festival. These hymns are Psalms 47, 93, 96, 97, 99.

B. Anonymous Individual Thanksgiving Songs or Declarative Praises. The structure of this genre includes a call to give thanks, an account of past distress, declaration that Yahweh has delivered the sufferer, and sometimes announcements of a sacrifice in payment of vows, and it may contain blessings and hymnic praise. Nine psalms fall into this category: 30, 32, 34, 41, 52, 66, 92, 116, 138.

C. Royal Thanksgiving Song or Declarative Praise. In one psalm (Psalm 18 = 2 Samuel 22) the king gives thanks for deliverance from an anonymous military foe. In one communal thanksgiving song the king gives individual thanks (118:5-21).

D. Communal Thanksgiving Songs or Declarative Praises. When the communal distress was lifted, a public thanksgiving day was observed, on which occasion communal thanksgiving songs were recited, very likely in company with the thanksgiving songs of individuals as a fitting aspect of national celebration. These six psalms are: 65, 67, 107, 118, 124, 136.

III. Performing and Enacting Genres

A number of Gunkel's minor genres and some of his royal psalms can be grouped under the category of genres that describe or give the contents of cultic acts.

A. Royal Ceremonial Songs. Several of these psalms are connected with either the coronation of the king or the annual celebration of his accession. It is characteristic of them that the people (or their representative) and deity speak of the king in the third person. Psalm 45 is a royal *marriage song*, and Psalm 101 is a *royal promise*, perhaps a pledge on taking office. There are eight of these psalms: 2; 20; 21; 45; 72; 101; 110; 132:11-18.

B. Entrance and Processional Liturgies. Psalms 15 and 24 contain queries and responses concerning who is entitled to enter Yahweh's temple, probably spoken antiphonally between worshipers approaching the temple and priests replying from the temple precincts. Four of these psalms presuppose or allude to processions. A total of five psalms are in this category: 15, 24, 68, 118, 132.

C. Prophetic Oracles of Judgment or Admonition. In several psalms prominent place is given to condemnation or chiding that takes on the structure and idiom of prophetic speech. Gunkel assumed that they were noncultic texts influenced by prophetic ideals, whereas Mowinckel regarded them as *liturgies* in which cultic prophets spoke directly to the congregation as a stated part of the ceremony. These seven psalms are: 14; 50; 53; 75; 81; 82; 95:7d-11.

D. Blessings. Blessings sometimes appear in hymns and thanksgiving songs. In addition, there are three psalms that consist entirely of blessing: 128, 133, 134.

IV. Instructing and Meditating Genres

A. Wisdom and Law Psalms. A considerable number of psalms do not show any significant marks of the above genres but rather display familiar features of wisdom writings: (1) key words such as "wisdom," "fear of Yahweh," addressees as "sons"; (2) rhetorical devices such as question and answer techniques, numerical sayings, beatitudes ("happy the one who . . ."); (3) a pronounced tone of teaching and warning; (4) preoccupation with unjust suffering, the wicked rich, divine guidance and protection of the pious, and the two ways of life and death. The mood of all these psalms is reflective and didactic, and the *law psalms* in particular presuppose concentrated study and meditation on texts. Ten psalms are wisdom and law psalms: 1; 19:7-14; 37; 49; 73; 91; 112; 119; 127; 139.

B. Historical Psalms. Three long psalms review aspects of Israel's early history for purposes of reassurance, admonition, and legitimation of God's present dealings with Judah to the exclusion of the northern kingdom. Psalm 78 is introduced as a wisdom instruction, while the other two instances of the historical psalm form are hymns (105, 106).

Life Settings

With respect to the life setting and function of the psalm genres, Gunkel stressed a threefold development:

1. All the primary *psalm genres* had their origin in the *preexilic cult,* but only a small number of the extant psalms derive from the corporate worship of the First Temple.

2. Under the influence of the prophetic critique of the cult, psalm forms of speech were increasingly detached from the cult and used to express a more *private and spiritual type of piety,* and to point to a *deferred ideal future* for the nation.

3. When the Second Temple was built after the exile, older cultic and noncultic psalms were joined with new psalms to provide a *temple hymnbook* shaped by the interests of temple musicians and of law interpreters.[5]

Mowinckel, star pupil of Gunkel, constructed a very different scenario:

1. Not only did all the primary psalm genres originate in the preexilic cult, but also the great majority of *extant psalms.*

2. The *individualized spirituality* of many psalms is not a sign of withdrawal from the cult, but an integral aspect of Israelite worship. Cultic prophecy also belonged to the preexilic temple worship. The unifying festival that lay behind the main psalm genres was a fall *New Year Festival* in which Yahweh's lordship was mythically reconfirmed.

3. When Israel's institutions for affirming Yahweh's kingship collapsed, the frustrated cultic-mythological hope of Israel was projected toward the future and *eschatology* was born. Learned collectors, informed by law and wisdom, shaped the present book of Psalms for study and reflection.[6]

The merits of these two reconstructions of the origins and uses of the psalms are still vigorously debated. Gunkel's sharp split between spirituality and cult sunders the specific uses of psalms from cultic activity. His proper insistence on an important dimension of individual spirituality can be accommodated by recognizing that the First Temple cult made room for concrete expressions of personal faith and actually generated them.

On the other hand, Mowinckel's grasp of the living cult as the matrix for the experience of the immediate presence of Yahweh accords with what we know of ritual from anthropological studies and is critical for appreciating the psalm types. He is almost certainly correct in believing that a First Temple festival celebrating the reactualization of Yahweh's kingship over nature and history lies behind the Hymns Celebrating Yahweh's Kingship.

Rituals for the renewal of divine and human kingship in Israel, broadly indebted to ancient Near Eastern culture, are by no means inconsistent with Israel's strong covenantal and historical traditions. It is likely that the sphere of myth in the cultic drama was a bone of interpretive contention between status quo establishmentarians and restive critics of preexilic society and government. But efforts to deny or minimize mythic and natural aspects of divine kingship before the exile by redefining the central preexilic festival as a covenant festival or as a covenant-renewal festival turned into a Zion festival in Judah to celebrate Yahweh's election of Jerusalem and David seem unnecessarily restrictive. On the other hand, Mowinckel and other advocates of cult drama have asserted knowledge of a central festival program that remains a hypothetical reconstruction.

Redaction of the Book

Past scholarship emphasized the unprincipled, even random, manner in which the book of Psalms was formed. It was observed that the psalms are not consistently grouped by theme, literary type, apparent date, or according to authorship/dedication or musical directions provided in the headings. Nevertheless, redaction critics have lately taken a renewed interest in the long-neglected question of the formation of the Psalter. While no theory of compilation and redaction yet accounts for all the curious complexities of the subcollections within the complete anthology, certain regularities little attended to in the past are now drawing attention.[7]

There are, for example, some gross patterns in the distribution of psalm genres. Individual genres are concentrated in the first half of the anthology by a ratio of about 3 to 1, so that more than half of the texts in Psalms 1–75 are devoted to individual genres, with laments predominating. In sharp contrast, communal genres are concentrated in the last half of the book by a ratio of about 3 to 1, so that more than half of the texts in Psalms 76–150 are communal genres, with Hymns and Thanksgiving Songs predominating. In terms of the tone these distribution patterns give to the whole collection, there is a dramatic shift from the lamenting individual to the praising community, and this shift is leavened or stabilized by the common denominators of royalty, prophecy, law, wisdom, and history distributed evenhandedly in the book.

Examination of the five divisions of Psalms provides considerable, if not completely convergent, evidence of the process of compilation. Book I (Psalms 1–41) stands apart as a collection assigned to David and making overwhelming use of the divine name Yahweh (as do also books IV–V). Books II (42–72) and III (73–89) stand together in two respects: (1) Psalms 42–83 overwhelmingly prefer the divine name Elohim, and (2) authorship or dedicatory headings are arranged so that the Davidic psalms are surrounded by psalms connected with temple musicians, notably Korah and Asaph, forming something of a chiastic arrangement.

It is likely that book I and books II–III were combined to produce a first edition of the book of Psalms. By contrast, the large number of psalms in books IV–V that are untitled altogether, or lack a notation of authorship or dedication, suggests that they were more miscellaneous in origin and were grouped as addenda to books I–III.

Similarities in redactional method are detectable throughout the anthology. There are runs of individual laments (e.g., Psalms 3–7, 61–64), and of hymns (e.g., Psalms 46–48, 145–150). Psalms 120–134 are all titled "songs of ascents" and may have been associated in pilgrim rites. The close of book V shows several redactional features aimed at a grand finale to the entire book. Eight Davidic psalms are joined in Psalms 138–145: the first two strike the note of trust, the next five lament, and the last breaks into hymnic praise that introduces the five concluding *Hallelu-jah* ("Praise Yahweh!") hymns to climax the work.

Sociohistorical Horizons of the Psalms

Who are the sufferers and the oppressors that so richly populate the psalms? How did the psalms function within the social transactions and power relations of the community? One way of stating the functions of these psalms groups them into the categories of: (1) *psalms of orientation,* celebrating creation, wisdom, retribution, and blessing; (2) *psalms of disorientation or dislocation,* pouring out laments and appeals of sufferers for whom the orderly world has fallen apart; and (3) *psalms of reorientation or relocation,* in which thanksgiving and praise affirm a reconstructed order that is no longer taken for granted because it has been won in pain and struggle and must be constantly rewon. The psalms of orientation may be said to testify to secure meaning; the psalms of disorientation, to radically doubted meaning; and the psalms of reorientation, to a new level and depth of meaning that does not forget the doubt.[8]

Conceptualizing the psalm functions in terms of a dynamic passage through moments of orientation, disorientation, and reorientation has been developed more in its psychological facets than in its societal dimensions. It is evident, however, that the disorientation expressed in the psalms is not a matter of individual physical or psychic breakdown in a neutral social situation. Tensions, crises, and ruptures in the social order, while coming to very sharp expression in the lives of individuals, wrack the whole community. For example, although historical notes attached to several psalms connect the psalms to particular incidents in the life of David (e.g., Psalms 3, 7, 18, 34, 51), David stood for the righteous leader of the community. The righteousness of David and the psalmists is presented in the psalms less as a personal achievement than as a resource and power that undergirds community or, when lacking, undermines community.

The exact identity of the sufferers and their oppressors has been, nonetheless, difficult to agree upon, in large part because of the conventionality of the psalm language, often extravagant and pluriform. The sufferer sinks down into the cosmic waters or is set upon by wild beasts, for example. Even allowing for hyperbole and the indirectness of cultic speech, the corpus of language about sufferers and oppressors is bluntly evocative of a world of *socioeconomic* oppression. The accused and beleaguered sufferer has been charged with crimes and cruelly slandered in order to deprive him of rights, means of subsistence, good standing in the community, and even of health and freedom of movement. (All the psalm sufferers seem to be men. Did women not have the same access to cultic protection? Did they have cultic procedures ignored in compiling Psalms?) The oppressors spill innocent blood in their greed for gain, bribe judges shamelessly, all the while trusting and boasting in their wealth and virtue. Oppression and fraud dominate the marketplace; the innocent are brought to trial with evil schemes; creditors seize property. When this wealth of language about socioeconomic conflict is illuminated by speeches of the prophets and proverbs of the wise, there can be little doubt that an enormous part of the suffering that psalmists protest is the pauperization of the populace through the manipulation of debt and confiscation procedures so that even the traditional courts of Israel can be used to amass wealth in defiance of the explicit laws of the community.

If indeed there was such a large-scale psalmic protest against the evils of the political economy, we may well wonder what social power the priesthood and cultic institutions actually had to alleviate the long slide of pre-exilic Israel and Judah into the impoverishment of the majority through land expropriation. First, the law codes of Israel contained measures that, had they been strictly observed, would have prevented the loss of freeholdings among the Israelite peasants. These provisions are attested in the cultic and priestly layers of laws as well as in more ostensibly secular layers. The Deuteronomic reform tried to couple a renewal of the cult with a renewal of land and debt laws, which would at least have arrested the pauperization process. The priests in Jerusalem were in a difficult spot to champion the cause of the plundered freeholders because they served at the pleasure of the royal establishment that permitted, if it did not actively advance, abusive domination.

Nonetheless, insofar as the royal ideology asserted social justice as its obligation, priests had some elbow room to ameliorate abuses. Although the socially powerful had a big stake in the cult, it is likely that they could not totally repress accepted cultic procedures. That there are individual thanksgiving songs implies that sometimes the actions of oppressors were blocked and frustrated. One consequence of this reading of the psalms is to warn against drawing too sharp a line between prophets and priests and assuming that the priesthood did nothing to resist socioeconomic imbalances.

We have seen then that the rhythms of orientation, disorientation, and reorientation, which the psalms express on a psychic level, have their close inner connections with like patterns of *orientation to a just social order* (traditional tribalism and benevolent monarchy), *disorientation and destabilization of community through mass injustice* (state-empowered entrepreneurs crush the independent tribal order, and foreign conquerors smash the state and dislocate its people), and *reorientation of community through new efforts at justice* (reform efforts under the monarchy, survival in and return from exile, restored colonial Judahite community). Even the occurrences of physical illness lamented in the psalms are not to be dissociated from societal structures, since it is well known that the incidence of some diseases is closely related to poor diet, harsh working conditions, ecological abuse, social belittlement and disempowerment, and demoralization in the face of unrelenting injustice.

All in all, to interpret the settings and functions of psalms one must consider the cultic traditions and institutions of ancient Israel as they intersected with major social and psychic dislocations in the lives of the people precipitated by conflicts and ruptures in the political economy over the long course of Israel's tribal-monarchic, exilic, and restoration history.

Lamentations

Lamentations consists of five verse compositions, alphabetically structured. The first four are acrostics, that is, the twenty-two letters of the Hebrew alphabet appear in succession at the beginning of each two- or three-line strophe or at the beginning of each line. The fifth lament has the same number of lines as letters in the Hebrew alphabet. The combined conceptual-aesthetic intent on making a complete statement in sharply controlled form is the most likely motive behind this acrostic structure in Lamentations.[9]

Similarities of form and content in the first four poems suggest a single author or writers of similar mind and tradition. Since each acrostic section is a complete acrostic covering similar subject matter from varying angles and genres, it is likely that they were collected around the common theme and the public occasion of lamentation over the fall of Jerusalem. There is evidence that lamentation at the site of the destroyed temple began soon after the city's destruction (Jer. 41:5) and that fast days were observed throughout the exile and at least until the rebuilding of the temple (Zech. 7:1-7; 8:19).

The compilation of the five laments follows a chiastic principle. Chapters 1 and 5 are generalizing summaries that show a greater psychic distance from events than the grim and pitiable scenes of death and destruction that are vividly drawn in chaps. 2 and 4. With its intensified acrostic form (three *aleph* lines, three *beth* lines, etc.), chap. 3 complexly splices the lamenting voices of a number of "I" speakers alongside the national "we," in order to build a subtle but powerful theological statement about the need for Israel to wait patiently on God's eventual mercy. A communal lament, chap. 5 provides a more cohesive picture of life in Palestine under ongoing Babylonian rule in contrast to the episodic glimpses of Jerusalem's downfall presented in chaps. 2 and 4.

The dominant genre speech conventions are laments, both individual and communal, but the individual funeral dirge is applied here to a sociopolitical entity. The afflicted city is personified and given voice as the woman "Fair Zion" ("daughter of Zion"), said to be "like a widow" (1:1, although her "husband" Yahweh is not dead!), but more often lamented and lamenting as a bereaved mother whose children (the populace and leadership of the city) have been killed, starved, driven away, or humiliated. The first four compositions, drawing skillfully on varied genres, were deliberately constructed as complex liturgies of lament, aimed for public recitation, with shifting speakers.

There have been inconclusive proposals about the ideological components and institutional setting of these laments.[10] By drawing out the conceptual matrix of the poems we may be able to identify the streams of traditions and institutions where the laments were anchored.

First, the destruction of Jerusalem is seen as a horrible but deserved punishment because of Israel's enormous sins (e.g., 1:5; 3:42; 4:5). In one revealing detail it is charged that the prophets envisioned only what was false and joined the priests in spilling "the blood of the righteous" (2:14; 4:13)—a critique shared by prophets such as Jeremiah and Ezekiel.

Even so, the emotional shock at loss of state and temple and at the carnage and destruction was so severe that the initiator of these laments aims to lead the people from grief to guilt to modest hope. He finds, however, that there are blockages to moving forward. He cites notions about the world significance and impregnability of Zion that imply that many of the mourners—in keeping with the Zion traditions of Psalms 46, 48, and 76—had believed that Yahweh would miraculously protect his holy city (Lam. 2:15c; 4:12). Likewise, the people lament over the capture of King Zedekiah, who was to protect them against enemy attack (4:20). Given these shattered expectations, the writer of the laments underscores the reality that the sins of Judah had decisively overridden any apparently unconditional promises in the Zion and royal Davidic traditions.

Yet another complication emerges. The excesses of enemies in punishing Israel are felt to have been so enormous that grave injustice has been done to Judah. This makes the people reluctant to admit their own sins and provokes serious doubt about Yahweh's justice and love. Agreeing that the enemy has overdone it, the poet has the people call for punishment on the enemies and even delivers a promise of salvation. It should be noted, however, that the words about judgment on enemies/deliverance for Zion are preceded in each poem by full acknowledgment of Zion's own sins.

Since the situation, as viewed by the poet, includes adversity that is both deserved and undeserved, its very complexity poses a delicate pastoral and theological problem. With what attitude should Judah view this situation while awaiting deliverance? Chapter 3 makes a special effort to communicate an appropriate communal attitudinal shift beyond either self-righteousness or despair. The sins of sufferers are held in tension with their valid rights to vindication (sufferers may both sin and be sinned against).

The suffering "man" of chap. 3 is reflected on as a paragon of the wise and patient individual or group sufferer who confidently trusts and hopes in Yahweh, bearing adversity without complaint or despair because he knows that God "does not afflict from his heart" (v. 33) and that the deity's sovereign movements among the peoples will eventually vindicate everyone who "waits" on and "hopes" in him (see 3:21, 24-26, 29).

Lamentations thus reflects a broadly prophetic and Deuteronomistic grasp of Judah's sins against Yahweh as the primary category for understanding the catastrophe, and this starting point inexorably sets aside the illusory protection of the Zion and royal Davidic traditions taken in isolation. Also in prophetic manner (and implicitly in DH as well), the compilation of laments anticipates an ongoing punishment of nations that have overdone their attacks, together with a recovery of fortune for Judah once it has confessed its sins. The proper attitude in the interim between punishment and restoration, inculcated with wisdomlike didacticism, is to wait patiently for Yahweh. In the poet's view, this patient waiting is perfectly consistent with agonized cries for help!

As for its ideological setting, Lamentations belongs to a pluriform exilic neo-prophetic and neo-Deuteronomistic outlook of chastened hope. All that we can say about the institutional setting is that these laments were written and compiled by one or more people who had access to and interest in the cult that managed to carry on in attenuated form on the site of the destroyed temple. The writer(s) could have been a prophet, a priest, or a governmental or private lay figure. In any case this writer developed an amalgam of prophetic, Deuteronomistic, and wisdom notions that radically subordinated and neutralized the Zion and royal Davidic promises, and found a liturgical-pastoral way of expressing them in the cult. We may take this book's deft eclecticism of traditions, interconnecting a range of concepts with verve and originality, as an indication of how Jewish religious thinking in the populace of postdestruction Palestine adapted traditions in order to cope with the intellectual and cultural dislocations of the national catastrophe.

Song of Songs

This eloquent love verse is variously understood either as a loose collection of individual poems or as a unified composition consisting of perhaps five to eight longer poems that show thematic integrity or some degree of unity of action. A unitary intent is often seen in the considerable refrains and repetitions (see Web Table M). But a closer look at links, primarily between chaps. 1–2 and 8, reveals that the repeated features are distributed erratically and diffused by other elements. If indeed chaps. 1–2 and 8 have been placed as a kind of *inclusio* to the work, it is not evident that the bonded structure points any more conclusively to a unified composition than to an artfully redacted anthology.

Form criticism has differentiated the love poetry of the Song into several freely mixed genres on the basis of similar Egyptian poems (Web Table A, 11A). Among the now commonly recognized genres are songs of yearning, admiration songs, boasts, teases, descriptions of a love experience, and descriptive songs (*wasfs*) depicting the physical charms of the loved one. There are also so-called travesties, in which the lover is portrayed in a role deliberately outside his social class or occupational status (e.g., the roles of king, shepherd, servant, etc.).

For many centuries the Song was understood allegorically in the Jewish and Christian communities. For Jews the lovers represented God and Israel, while for Christians they stood for God or Christ and the church or soul of the believer, or even the Virgin Mary. Nothing in the Song itself or in the extrabiblical counterparts supports this line of interpretation. Some scholars have argued for a cultic-mythological interpretation in which the lovers originally described were male and female deities joined in sacred marriage, for example, the divine pair Tammuz and Ishtar. The presumed expurgation and revision required to make the poem safe for Jews is difficult to imagine and indeed unnecessary to account for possible traces of cultic idiom in the Song. Over the centuries, the erotic language of human love and of the cults of divine marriage mutually influenced one another, so that Jewish erotic language could readily have picked up the resonances of cult-derived speech (see Web Table M).

As for the setting of the Song, it is widely held that these are marriage songs accompanying elaborate ceremonies in which bride and groom were feted in the fanciful roles of king and queen, shepherd and shepherdess, and the like. Only 3:6-11 mentions marriage, with reference to a Solomon travesty, however, and the many comparable songs from Egypt, and a lesser number from Mesopotamia, are not connected with marriage. The imagery and sensibilities of the Song simply do not treat the social structures of marriage and family; nothing is said about children or the duties of the man and woman toward one another or their families of origin. Instead, the lovers speak of longing and passion—all with a clear destination of physical togetherness and sexual union. Sexual consummation is adroitly described through double entendres that work metaphorically with physical features, flora, and fauna. Significantly, the man and woman are toe to toe in their acts and words, a sexual equality that might equally bespeak the comradeship of peasant lovers not yet encumbered by children or the companionship of upper-class lovers whose affluence and education encourage feminist consciousness. Indeed, the parallels from Egypt suggest an aristocratic milieu of leisure and cultivated erotic self-consciousness. However, the travesty genre deliberately contrives class roles and social contexts that may be entirely imaginary.[11]

The Song of Songs is said to be Solomon's (1:1). This seems to have been taken as an attribution of authorship. Earlier, however, it could very well have meant a song of the sort that Solomon wrote (1 Kgs. 4:32) or a song "to/concerning" Solomon in the sense that the lovers were cast in fictive roles of Solomon and one of his maidens (1 Kgs. 11:3; Ps. 45:6-17; see Song 3:11; 6:8). It is likely, however, that the strongest reason for the Solomonic claim was the publishing of the collection within a wisdom circle with the intention of illustrating what one saying calls "the way of a man with a maiden" (Prov. 30:19).

If that is the case, the poems would probably have been read by the wisdom collectors as affirming a monogamous relationship issuing in an enduring marriage (Prov. 5:15-23; cf. "the wife of your youth"). Of course Solomon

FIG. 12.1. A detail of the gilt shrine of Tutankhamun, which originally contained statuettes of the royal couple. The scene depicts a ritual hunting scene in which Queen Ankhesenamun helps her husband. Eighteenth Dynasty, ca. 1357–1349 B.C.E. From Thebes, Valley of the Kings. Egyptian Museum, Cairo. Photo: © Werner Forman / Art Resource, N.Y.

himself was far from monogamous (1 Kgs. 11:1-13). The wise may have felt that their patron figure had been appropriately rebuffed for his follies. Indeed, it is possible that Song 8:6-8 is the signature of the wise collector of the Song, forming a moral for the reader to carry away:

> Set me as a seal on your heart,
>   as a seal on your arm;
>   for love is strong as death,
>   passion as relentless as the grave.
> Its flashes are flashes of fire,
>   a most vehement flame.
> Many waters cannot quench love,
>   neither can floods drown it.
> If a man offered for love
>   all the wealth of his house,
>   it would be utterly scorned.

The Egyptian Papyrus Harris 500 also juxtaposes love and death, interrupting love songs with a dour meditation on death in the face of which one should "follow your heart as long as you live. . . . Moral: Make celebration!" (Web Table A, 11A).

It is altogether likely that the trajectory of this poetry has moved through more than one social-class location, from among the peasantry who fantasize themselves highborn, through court sophisticates who fantasize themselves bucolic primitives, to the learned and moralizing circles of the wise who harness both the low and the high aesthetics to monogamous counsel in praise of love that cannot be bought. Allegorical readings were eventually given it, both to counter its secularity and to serve the cause of religious devotion.

SHORT STORIES

The Biblical Short Story: A New Literary Genre?

The three biblical short stories that form independent books in the Hebrew Bible must be viewed in the wider context of many other instances of the same genre. Some short stories are incorporated into larger biblical books (e.g., Gen. 24; 38; 37 + 39–50; Judg. 3:12-30; 4:1-24; episodes in 2 Samuel 9–20 and 1 Kings 1–2; Job 1–2; 42:7-17; Daniel 1–6). Others appear in the Apocrypha (Tobit; Judith; The Three Guardsmen in 1 Esd. 3:1—4:42) or in the LXX (Additions to Daniel, known as Susanna and Bel and the Dragon).

This frequent biblical genre, also called novella (novelette) or romance, features multiple episodes, an elevated style, and skillful literary techniques for shaping full-bodied character in a suspenseful plot that communicates lifelikeness in important respects, even when the story exaggerates or caricatures to make its points.[12] Typically the short story combines fairytale, legendary, heroic, or mythic elements with a history-like orientation to daily affairs in some recognizable sphere of life within a smaller community or in high politics. Historical vagueness, symmetries and extremities of plot, and stark reversals of fortune for the characters attest that the genre is not documentary history but believable fiction with general sociocultural lifelikeness.

The historical settings of the short stories are problematic: Ruth in the time of the judges, Jonah in the Assyrian period, and Esther in the Persian age. While traditions from the assigned age may be retained in the story, and in some cases an older version of the story may underlie the present text, the choice of an archaic setting for the story is also clearly a literary convention that aims to give its message a venerable, classical aura. The tendency at present is to view Ruth as preexilic, possibly as early as the tenth/ninth century, to locate Jonah in the sixth/fifth century, and to assign Esther to the fourth to second century.

While scholars once tended to assert that the short stories were intended to rebut the nationalist reforms and mind-set of Ezra and Nehemiah, it is nowadays claimed that combined purposes are at work in the short story: entertainment, moral instruction and formation, inspiration, and even a low-key theologizing that stresses the work of an unobtrusive God within the mundane activities of humans. The subdued religiosity in some, but not all, of the stories has been connected with the Solomonic enlightenment, which purportedly opened up a secular world to human scrutiny and adventure.

Since many instances of the short story are premonarchic in milieu and perspective, it is probable that the short story was a new form introduced by the Yahwistic revolution at the beginning of Israel's intertribal egalitarian social and religious movement. The new purpose of the Israelite short story seems to have been to stress the active participation of people in the common life as precisely the sphere where Yahweh works without restriction to the realm of formal religious practices. The new agenda of these stories concerns the making of marriages, the birthing of children, the procurement of food, the securing of stable and just self-rule, the repelling of dangerous military threats, and the long-term survival of the new people of Yahweh amid the nations.[13]

With the monarchy and later experiences of dispersion and restoration, new themes and variations on older themes develop in the short story repertory. Already evident in the preexilic Joseph story, the imperial-colonial theme of Jews in foreign service was of concern to Jews in Palestine, as in the Dispersion, since the lives of all were significantly affected by what their political overlords did. The absorption of many stories with foreigners also includes how foreigners join Israel (Ruth); how an Israelite might, even unwillingly, convert foreigners (Jonah); and how dispersed Jews can cultivate a full and rich religious life amid a foreign culture (Tobit).

It is further striking that many of these stories feature women who combine cunning and boldness to achieve ends of importance to the community: for example, Deborah arouses Israel to victory over Canaanites; Jael slays a Canaanite general. It is probable that one of the lifelike features of the otherwise fictitious Judith and Esther is that they celebrate the active part that some women took in the Maccabean-Hasmonean conflicts.

Is it possible to identify the narrators and life settings of this versatile Israelite short story genre? So artful are the tales that it is logical to believe that a class of storytellers specialized in them, perhaps performing at religious festivals but also wherever people gathered publicly, at town gate, market, or watering place. It has been proposed that the early Levites, distributed among the tribes as ardent devotees of Yahweh, formed a storytelling cadre as part of their teaching function, and that possibly wise women also engaged in storytelling.[14] Among the Megilloth (scrolls for reading at Jewish festivals), Ruth found its place for reading at the Feast of Weeks, and Esther was specifically composed for, or adapted to, recitation at the Feast of Purim.

Ruth

Ruth is easily the most charming and exquisite of the three independent biblical short stories, sharing as it does with the much later and apocryphal book of Tobit a poignant evocation of family feelings and mores. It tells how two widows, Naomi and Ruth, the one a Judahite from Bethlehem and the other her Moabite daughter-in-law, cleverly worked out their survival and happiness and at the same time secured the perpetuation of the family name of the dead. To crown it all, it turns out that these women, acting on their own behalf, have contributed to the family line of none other than King David (4:17-21). The story in final form need be no later than the united monarchy, although it likely had a precursor that lacked the Davidic genealogy.

The "little whole" of Ruth is a thoroughly credible folktale.[15] Ruth has been much analyzed by new literary critics and structuralists to the enhancement of our understanding of why the story works so effectively.[16] The plot moves through six episodes (Web Chart D) in which the first two (Flight to Moab; On the road back to Bethlehem) balance the last two (At the city gate of Bethlehem; A son is born to restore Naomi). A deep structure of emptiness in the opening scenes shifts to a deep structure of fullness in the closing scenes. The two inner episodes (In the field of Boaz; On the threshing floor of Boaz) describe the activation and execution of the means for transforming emptiness into fullness for Naomi and Ruth, also enriching Boaz's life.

The assertive deeds of Naomi and Ruth are the driving force of the story.[17] Indeed, throughout the story the women operate out of their own culture with their own values in mind. The dominant male value expressed is to perpetuate the family name. The male institution of levirate marriage, by which the relative of a dead man marries his widow, becomes the instrument of salvation for Naomi and Ruth. Yet the women do not simply identify with the male values. By the close of the story, the male elders celebrate Boaz's good fortune in finding Ruth because she will give him children, while the village women who gather around Naomi at the birth of Ruth's child rejoice in the boy who will bring consolation and pleasure to the aging grandmother. It is precisely the happy coincidence of the story that the women are able to find joyful fulfillment within the male-headed social structures in such a way that both sexes profit. It is not difficult to imagine that this story was framed by a woman confidently at home in her social world.

God appears in the story largely in conventional idioms of speech, as when Boaz says to Ruth, "Yahweh recompense you for what you have done, and a full reward be given you by Yahweh, the God of Israel, under whose wings you have come to take refuge!" (2:12). But only at two points in the narrative is deity noted as a direct participant in the story: once at the beginning, when Naomi in Moab learns "that Yahweh had visited his people and given them food" (1:6), and again at the end, when "Yahweh gave her [Ruth] conception, and she bore a son" (4:14). The parenthetical placement of these references to Yahweh's doings that set the story in motion and bring it to climax is presumably the narrator's adaptation of the folktale form with its recital of the commonplace to the encompassing faith of Israel in the providence of Yahweh.

Jonah

The book of Jonah is placed among the Prophets because of its formal topic but, unlike all the other writings in that collection, it is entirely composed of a short story about a prophet. Jonah tries to escape his calling and, when compelled to fulfill it, resents and protests against the results. Its antihero is identified as Jonah ben Amittai, who announced the territorial expansion of the kingdom of Jeroboam II (2 Kgs. 14:25). Memory of an actual mission by that prophet to Assyria is highly doubtful, for the story is filled with improbabilities and is of obvious didactic tenor in its stylization.

The plot (Web Chart E) is set forth in two parts that treat Jonah's failed flight from his call to preach doom on Nineveh (chaps. 1–2) and his shocked anger when, finally forced to deliver the message, the city unexpectedly repents and is spared (chaps. 3–4). That Jonah remains the reluctant and uncomprehending prophet quickly emerges when he responds with embitterment and personal pique to the mercy of Yahweh toward repentant Nineveh.

He cares passionately about a shade plant that brings him comfort and is outraged when it withers, while he yearns for the death of more than one hundred thousand Ninevites—indeed, Jonah would rather die himself than see those Assyrians live!

The book closes by accenting the ironic disproportion between Jonah's pity for the plant, really for himself, and Yahweh's pity for the people of Nineveh. The storyteller breaks off without telling us if Jonah ever got the point of Yahweh's dispute with him. The abrupt ending on the rhetorical question, "And should not I [Yahweh] pity Nineveh?" forces questions on the reader: Am I (or is my group) like Jonah? If so, what do I (or we) make of Yahweh's rebuke?

The story adroitly opposes the straightforward heathens to the devious Jonah. The piety of the Gentile mariners saves them from the storm, whereas Jonah has to go into the sea and to the gates of death before he is ready

FIG. 12.2. Jonah thrown to the whale. Early Christian fresco, mid-third century C.E. Catacomb of SS. Marcellino e Pietro, Rome. Photo: © Scala / Art Resource, N.Y.

to do his duty. The people of Nineveh (their animals included!) repent and are delivered, whereas Jonah wraps himself in anger and resentment toward Nineveh and toward Yahweh until he loathes his own life. The book is a satirical short story with parabolic force. Since there are no firm grounds for dating the book more precisely than the sixth or fifth century, or even somewhat later, it is idle to speculate about which groups or situations prompted the author to write his devastating lampoon.

The choice of Assyria as the classic criminal nation that repented, at least for a period of time, presupposes that the Assyrian Empire has fallen. Readers would understand at once that the story was scaffolding for a reflection on prophetic mission and prophetic self-understanding. Whoever has a call from Yahweh to warn of evil must do it obediently and with an understanding of Yahweh's intent to save all who will hear and repent (see Jer. 18:7-8). There is no indication that the book enjoins a mission to convert foreign nations or that it addresses the issue of whether proselytes should be incorporated in Israel if they come voluntarily. Nonetheless, because those who make the unexpectedly positive response to Yahweh are foreigners, the force of the book is to caution against prejudging and stereotyping Gentiles.

Esther

The book of Esther locates the origin of the Feast of Purim in a spectacular last-minute deliverance of all the Jews within the Persian Empire from a plot to annihilate them. The plot is hatched in high government circles, and it is Jews serving in those very circles who become the agents of Jewish salvation. Esther,

the Jewish queen of Ahasuerus (Xerxes; 486–465 B.C.E.), helped by her cousin and one-time guardian Mordecai, frustrates the designs of Haman to kill Mordecai and then to slaughter the entire Jewish populace. Instead, in perfect poetic justice, Haman is hanged on the gallows he prepared for Mordecai, and the enemies of the Jews who would have killed them are themselves killed by the Jews. The plot is replete with dramatic reversals.

The action is framed by court banquet scenes and audiences with the king. The driving tension in the plot is whether the anti-Jewish or the pro-Jewish forces in the court will receive the blessing of the king. The turning point in the story is debated. Is it when Esther resolves to use her influence to save her people (4:16), or when the king is troubled by sleeplessness that prompts him to investigate whether Mordecai has been properly rewarded for warning him of a plot on his life (6:1), or when Haman unknowingly counsels the king to reward Mordecai handsomely (6:7-9)?

The archaic placement of the story in the Persian court is accomplished with considerable knowledge of its inner workings and customs, but there are so many historical inaccuracies and improbabilities that the work cannot be taken at face value. The setting of the narrator is most likely in the Maccabean-Hasmonean era, given the intensity and bitterness of the Jewish-Gentile conflicts in the book, the lack of external references to the book until late Hellenistic times, and the very late appearance of Purim as a recognized Jewish festival.

Purim is first mentioned in the period 100–50 B.C.E. in 2 Macc. 15:36, where it is called "Mordecai's Day" (14 Adar) and associated with "Nicanor's Day" (13 Adar), when Jews celebrated a Maccabean victory over the Syrians. The colophon to the book of Esther in the LXX claims that a translation of Esther arrived in Egypt in 114–113 or 78–77 B.C.E., depending on which Egyptian ruler is referred to in the text. These references point to 150–100 B.C.E. as the likely date of composition for Esther. It was in this period that relations between Jews and Hellenistic Gentiles were especially strained and the Hasmonean rulers fought strenuous wars against surrounding Gentile nations (see pp. 260–61).[18] Similar bitterness in Jewish-Gentile relations and extremities of attack and defense emerge in the apocryphal book of Judith, which was written around 150 B.C.E.

Noteworthy is Esther's studied avoidance of the name of God or of specific religious motivations. The deliberation of this reticence about religion is clear from the use of "place" as a circumlocution for God ("relief and deliverance will rise for the Jews from another place [quarter]," 4:14). This refusal to speak of God and piety may have been dictated by the revelries at Purim, or it may have been a literary device to accent the importance of the Jews acting in their own behalf in order to secure divine deliverance.

In spite of the secular conception of Judaism in the book, giving it a very different tone from the explicit law piety of the otherwise related book of Judith, Esther does specify the distinctiveness of the Jews as follows: "their laws are different from those of every other people" (3:8). The alacrity and ease with which Esther and Mordecai fit into the Persian court and advance the royal interests, however, give a ringing answer to the charge that Jewish laws contravene good citizenship or service in foreign empires. Stated in the extreme, one can be both a good Persian queen and a good Jew.

WISDOM WRITINGS

What Is Wisdom?

The clearest beginning point for defining wisdom in biblical tradition is to say that it consists of those literary genres and themes found in the canonical books of Proverbs, Job, and Ecclesiastes, and in the apocryphal books of Ben Sira (Sirach) and Wisdom of Solomon. The dominant literary forms are the proverb and the admonition, and the overriding theme is how to accommodate one's life to the fundamental orderliness of the world, or what to do when the anticipated order fails. In this literature the traditional pursuit of wisdom is traced back to Solomon, the archetypal wise king and author. Similar ideas and forms of expression in related documents from Egypt and Mesopotamia happily provide a wealth of comparative data and open the way to an understanding of wisdom.

In practice, however, the characterization of wisdom has turned out to be complicated and vexed. There are a considerable number of genres in the wisdom writings (table 12.2). Wisdom themes such as creation, reward and punishment, and innocent suffering likewise appear in nonwisdom books, often dressed out in the literary features of wisdom writings. It has become a scholarly fashion to pursue this elusive wisdom influence throughout large parts of the Hebrew Bible, but it has proven difficult to know exactly what kind of influence was operative. A major difficulty is that the wisdom writings are not easy to date, and the setting(s) for their production is highly disputed.

Literary Genres and Mind-set

Each of the canonical wisdom books has its own peculiar mix of genres (table 12.2).[19] In Proverbs the basic building materials are the artistic proverbs and the admonitions, often clustered by form or topic. In Job proverbs and admonitions in some quantity are employed in subordination to the dialogue structure of a disputation in which there are prominent lament, hymn, and lawsuit features held together in an edifying narrative frame. In Ecclesiastes strings of proverbs and admonitions form almost half of the book but are embedded in a form whose reading as prose or poetry is much disputed. The overall structures of Job and Ecclesiastes are so uniquely developed that they do not conveniently fit into known genre categories.

The plentiful ancient Near Eastern wisdom literature offers many illuminative contact points. Proverbs, admonitions, instructions, and name lists are amply attested from Egypt and Mesopotamia (Web Table A, 8). The hymn personifying wisdom is probably derived from an Egyptian prototype. Job and Ecclesiastes are paralleled from abroad in their thematic preoccupations with injustice, undeserved suffering, and death (Web Table A, 9). The author of Prov. 22:17—24:22 has made free use of the Egyptian Instruction of Amen-em-opet in writing his "thirty sayings" (Web Table A, 8B).

What exactly is wisdom thought? "Wisdom" typifies a way of viewing the world based on observation and reflection in an effort to discern the substantial harmony and order that is sensed to be constitutive of it. The characteristic wisdom goal is to develop life strategies that will integrate the individual's existence with the perceived order of the world. Wisdom aims for a practical and comprehensive ethic and behavioral style.

For wisdom the sphere of the world is as broad as everything that may be encountered, and wisdom's center is the teachable human observer and social actor. Religion is looked at as one of the many areas and resources of life, its value to the wisdom outlook learned through experience. Religion is nonrevelatory, and for this reason wisdom's approach to religion appears somewhat relaxed and optional, running against the grain of other religious domains in Israel that start off from confidence in Yahweh as the authoritative revealer.

It is not that Israel's wise were antireligious, or even nonreligious, in any programmatic way. From all that we can tell they participated in the cult. Rather, the religion of Yahweh was something whose value and meaning for life had to be tested and determined and integrated with all the rest of knowledge and truth. While early including "the fear of Yahweh" in their wisdom schemes, the sages gave their allegiance to Yahweh, for the most part, not as a bowing to divine revelation so much as an assenting to truth they had established through human reflection. As Torah gained ascendancy during and after the exile, the wisdom affirmation of an orderly world that undergirded right practice was focused on Torah as the signal accessible source of wisdom.

When wisdom is defined in this descriptive manner, it is easy to see that, while distinct at its core, its interests and perspectives shaded off into many, possibly all, the other aspects of Israel's life. If, for example, we leave aside explicitly literary criteria and simply think of wisdom as a nonrevelatory mode of thought that focuses on individual consciousness of truth and right conduct, displaying a humanistic orientation and a didactic drive to pass on its understandings to others, it is easy to see "wisdom" almost everywhere in the Hebrew Bible where there is no direct speech of God.

TABLE 12.2 GENRES IN WISDOM LITERATURE

I. *Saying* or *Proverb,* a pithy aphorism distilling human experience in an apt and memorable form

    A. *Folk Proverb,* generally in prose form (e.g., I Sam. 24:14; I Kings 20:11; Jer. 23:28)

    B. *Artistic Proverb,* structured in the A_____ / B_____ // pattern of Hebrew verse

        1. *Observational* or *Experiential Proverb,* noting a feature of life without evaluation (e.g., Prov. 11:24; 17:27-28; 18:16)

        2. *Didactic* or *Learned Proverb,* inculcating values or liens of conduct (e.g., Prov. 10:7; 14:31; 15:33)

II. *Admonition,* generally structured in the A_____ / B_____ // verse form, either appearing in isolation among proverbs or grouped as an *instruction* delivered by an authoritative teacher to a learner (e.g., Proverbs 1–9; 22:17—24:22)

    A. *Command* (e.g., Prov. 8:33; 16:3; 31:6-9)

    B. *Prohibition* (e.g., Prov. 22:22-23; 30:10)

III. *Riddle,* a "tricky" question whose answer or solution is ambiguous (the only complete biblical example, Judges 4:10-18; referred to in Prov. 1:6; Ps. 49:4; etc.)

IV. *Fable,* a short story with plants or animals as characters (Judges 9:8-15; 2 Kings 14:9)

V. *Allegory,* an extended metaphor (Prov. 5:15-23, wife as "cistern"; Eccl. 12:1-6, aging person as a "falling house")

VI. *Hymn,* a praise of personified wisdom (Job 28; Prov. 1:20-33; 8; Sir. 24:1-22; Wisd. Of Sol. 6:12-20; 7:22-8:21)

VII. *Controversy Speech* or *Disputation,* characteristic of the dialogue of Job with his friends, mixed with lament and lawsuit genres (Job 4—31)

VIII. *Example Story,* concrete illustration of point made by sage (Prov. 7:6-23; 24:30-34; Eccl. 4:13-16)

IX. *Confession, Autobiographical Narrative,* or *Reflection,* in which a sage shares his rich experience with pupils or readers (Prov. 4:3-9; Eccl. 1:12—2:26; Sir. 33:16-18)

X. *Name List* or *Onomasticon* of geographical, cosmological, meteorological phenomena (Job 28; 36:27-37; 38:4—39:30; 40:15—41:34; Ben Sira 43; Wisd. of Sol. 7:17-20, 22-23; 14:25-26)

Sociohistorical Horizons of Wisdom

The main search, however, has been to find the base from which all this wisdom influence emanated. Who were the generators and propagators of wisdom teaching and its genres? Where were they situated historically and socially within the body of ancient Israel?[20] Three primary proposals about the identity and setting of the wise have been advanced. On one view the wise were parents in families or elders and counselors in clans and tribes. On a second view they were government officials, scribes, and possibly priests. On a third view they were nonpriestly authorities in the collected and venerated Law of Moses. In which of these institutional matrices (see Web Chart F) was wisdom generated and propagated during which periods?

Family and tribe were certainly spheres for the passing on of collective wisdom by parents and elders, not only before there was a state, but through all later periods. But is the wisdom of Proverbs, Job, and Ecclesiastes familial and tribal wisdom? Only, it seems, in the sense that some details of form (e.g., "father/son" metaphor for "teacher/pupil" relationship) and certain major topical interests reflect familial/tribal concerns.

State scribalism, as the biblical tradition clearly reports, began with Solomon (1 Kgs. 4:29-34) and continued to the exile (see Prov. 25:1). This was the scribalism of educated state officials who kept public records, advised kings, and taught scribal skills and political craft to their successors and colleagues. A royal court provenance for wisdom does not, of course, give us the whole story, if only because Proverbs, Job, and Ecclesiastes apparently came to completion after the government scribalism of Judah had collapsed and before the new Torah scribalism was fully developed (see Web Chart F).

Torah religion did not emerge in Israel in any sense that would have required scholars of legal texts prior to the Deuteronomic reformation. Before that time *torah* was "instruction" that included laws to be interpreted and applied by wise elders and probably by state-appointed judges, although nothing in the wisdom writings shows the sages to have been such elders or judges. The full Torah religion developed only during and after the exile. Nevertheless, the presupposed concern of the wise for an orderly society implies their interest in the upholding of legal traditions, leading to an eventual equation of Wisdom with Torah (Sirach 24).

Discerning the course that wisdom took in this later period is difficult. Among the exiles to Babylonia were numbers of Israelite government scribes and Deuteronomists. Thus we have no problem seeing how the wisdom traditions survived the exile. More problematic is how the institutional matrix for wisdom was reconstituted after the exile. We can posit on principle that a Judean province of the Persian Empire would have had Jewish scribal officials, and proverbial and admonitory sayings and skeptical reflections may have been preserved/composed in these scribal circles. The Deuteronomistic wing of the DH/P entente that produced the finished Torah was sympathetic to wisdom and was probably a factor in encouraging the shift to taming wisdom by equating it with Torah, eventually transferring most of the wisdom activities from the political scribal context to the religious scribal-legal context.

Surveying the whole course of wisdom traditioning in Israel, we can see a firm anchorage of wisdom in the royal court. Some of the wisdom literature for this reason has a very limited topical range, focused, for example, on obedience to superiors and proper court manners. On the other hand, the wise officials had family and tribal ties, as well as wider socioreligious concerns, and their literature also reflects a pronounced concern to preserve the integrity of rural communities against predatory wealth and suborned legal institutions. Family and tribe are represented in the wisdom traditions.

The much-discussed *wisdom influence* was thus not merely literary and intellectual but also ethical-social. The Deuteronomic reformation almost certainly brought together a coalition of interested Israelite functionaries from various institutions: prophets, priests, elders. This scenario explains both the narrow specificity of wisdom's institutional base and the broad range of its interests and of the influences that flowed from it and into it.

Proverbs

This anthology of several hundred proverbs and admonitions was composed out of at least six subcollections (see headings in 1:1; 10:1; 22:17; 25:1; 30:1; 31:1). Further subdivisions by form or content are also evident (e.g., chaps. 10–15; 16:1-22:16; chaps. 25–27; 28–29).

It is generally thought that the second, third, and fourth subcollections derive largely from preexilic times, since they allude regularly to kingship and an operative state structure. The first, fifth, and sixth subcollections have more often been regarded as postexilic. While chaps. 1–9 were once thought postexilic, the elaboration of admonitions into an instruction genre has been identified as an ancient Egyptian literary practice, as has the sacralizing and personifying of Lady Wisdom as a goddess. The acrostic praise of a good wife in 31:10-31 might aptly apply to an upper-class woman of either preexilic or postexilic times.

An anthologizing fascination with the words of the wise has brought the whole collection together under an introduction that connects a lavish wisdom vocabulary with Yahweh piety (1:1-7). The redactional structure of the book, probably to be dated 450–350 B.C.E., is very deliberate in its refinements. One theory has it that the book is put together as "a house of wisdom" (see 9:1; 14:1), analogous to the tripartite Solomonic temple: the front is chaps. 1–9; the nave is 10:1—22:16; the inner sanctuary is 22:17—31:31.[21] The "seven pillars" (9:1) are found in seven columns of text of twenty-two or twenty-three lines each (an alphabetizing practice) constituting chaps. 2–7. Few scholars have endorsed this scheme in toto, but it advances a productive heuristic position in the current redactional inquiry.

It has been common to stress the strictly limited prudential character of the teaching in Proverbs, even its superficiality and opportunism, as a manual for survival in royal politics. There is no doubt that such is the horizon of parts of the book. It is interesting, however, that a much larger portion of the content is devoted to familial and economic affairs. It is likewise commonplace to assume for the outlook of Proverbs a rigid dogma of reward for virtue and punishment for vice, virtually correspondent to a like Deuteronomistic dogmatism of reward and punishment. On this view, the survivalist mentality of the recommended court etiquette and mores is somewhat of an embarrassment. Generally this sensed misfit of theory and application is explained thus: those who by definition were now "wise" and "righteous" in their inner beings would be blameless when they adopted chameleonlike conduct required by royal establishments, their opportunism being justified by their preestablished status as "wise."

It becomes increasingly clear, however, that Proverbs, like DH, is not monolithic in its ideology. There were among the wise, as among the Deuteronomists, critical traditionalists as well as authoritarian dogmatists (see pp. 147–49). Much of the proverbial and instructional discourse of Proverbs stays close to actual life conditions and tries to discern the best choices in ambiguous situations where the basic order of things is not completely obvious and must be searched out. The attitudes and directives, for example, with respect to production, distribution, exchange, and consumption of goods illustrate a variety of viewpoints, which may at times represent side-by-side competing outlooks and at other times the changing emphases of differing historical settings.

The truism about wisdom's dogmatic reading of virtue and vice and their consequences construes Proverbs to be teaching that the righteous will be wealthy and the wicked will be poor (see 8:15-21). It is evident, however, that much of the commentary in the book is on the prevailing imperfect conditions that the sages are observing. When it comes to assessing the causes or occasions of wealth and poverty and to passing ethical judgment on the wealthy and the poor, there are varied angles of approach and, in the end, a dissonance in emphasis and explanatory frameworks.

It is something of a surprise that, generously reckoned, no more than one-third of the evaluative proverbs and admonitions about wealth and poverty support the alleged wisdom dogma that the rich and the poor deserve their fortunes. The largest single category of socioeconomic appraisals attributes existing wealth and poverty to the oppression and dishonesty by which riches are in effect stolen from the poor through exorbitant interest on loans, movement of boundary markers of fields, judicial perjury and bribery, violent confiscations, and killings of rightful owners. A very similar bill of particulars about riches as the product of plunder and murder on a societywide basis is given in Job and Ecclesiastes.

What practical advice follows? Corresponding to the assumption that poverty and wealth are distributed according to what people morally deserve, some texts warn against standing surety on loans to debtors, since one is likely to lose his pledge. There is also counsel to harbor rather than squander one's wealth. On the other hand, many texts emphasize God's immediacy to the poor in creation and in potential redemption, and there are repeated injunctions for the wise to show kindness by giving to the poor. It is difficult to determine the extent to which these counsels call for shoring up the solidarity system of mutual help among families, associations, and tribes, or for practicing charity to individuals now that the solidarity system is in collapse.

In short, the *bearers of wisdom are caught in class contradiction*. They enjoy a measure of class privilege through their vocational status and education. On the one hand, their class advantage and tendency to universalize their privileged position prompt them to endorse the operative socioeconomic order as an instance of wise cosmic order. On the other hand, their acute observations of how the life of the rich and the poor violates cosmic order inclines them to preach reformation of such gross "disorder" = "folly" = "injustice" = "sin against Yahweh." Precisely these sages, torn by contrary interests and perceptions, were in the thick of the great debates that took place in governmental circles over what policies Judah should adopt.

Even though many voices speak in Proverbs, the one that grew loudest over time was the authoritarian voice of *contextless wisdom dogmatism* that ripped wisdom out of its sociohistorical contexts and robbed it of its observational and inquiring mode of reasoning. It was tempting to convert the search for wisdom and righteousness into an assertion of automatic possession of wisdom and righteousness as evidenced by one's prosperity and success. We know that this dogmatic voice was loud and insistent, because two sages wrote works that openly challenged and rebutted the easy self-confidence that it voiced: Job and Ecclesiastes.

Job

Sometime during the exile or within a century or so after the first return to Palestine, a sage wrote the book of Job in order to break the grip of a moralism and dogmatism that were reducing wisdom to canards and formulas about the surface appearances of human life. Job was a provocative tour de force. Those who search in the book for a clear explanation of innocent suffering have trouble finding it. The author is content to establish that there really is *innocent* suffering. For the writer "innocent" does not mean that the sufferer is sinless but simply that suffering happens again and again for which we cannot assign any formulaic reason. A meaning to that suffering may or may not emerge in time. It is vital to our integrity as humans and to our belief in God that we not parrot conventional meanings about particular sufferings and successes.

As the springboard for his argument, the writer has used an old popular tale about a righteous man who widely benefited his community and who patiently suffered extreme adversity. This tradition takes the form of a sagalike story, reminiscent of patriarchal times. It is also a quasi-mythological story insofar as it entails a member of the divine court, an accuser (*satan* is not yet a proper name), who tests out the piety of believers in Yahweh. It looks as though the author of Job chose this contrived situation to give readers a necessary viewpoint above the awareness of Job and his friends, none of whom ever learns the real reason for Job's suffering. The author was probably not troubled by this potentially demonic view of deity but wanted to make only one point: sometimes there is suffering beyond our ability to understand, and we should spare ourselves and others the stupidity and cruelty of imposing meanings that will not fit.

The old folk story was used as an *inclusio* around a long verse composition that included: (1) an opening complaint of Job, (2) three rounds of speeches with three of his friends, (3) a summary demand from Job for God to speak, and (4) a culminating speech of Yahweh to Job. A poem on wisdom (chap. 28) underscores the superficiality of the friends' explanations of Job's plight by showing how difficult it is to come by true wisdom. The speeches of a fourth friend, Elihu (chaps. 32–39), add little to the argument, but his angry intrusion into the conversation and his self-confident academicism deliciously illustrate the flaws of his formulaic and sloganeering dogmatism.

The genre ingredients in the book of Job are numerous and artfully employed to bring several streams of Israelite tradition to bear upon the problem posed.[22] The individual lament form is common as the vehicle for Job to pour out his distress and to appeal for deliverance, but Job widens his citations of human suffering. The same speeches are fraught with legal language that picks up from the charge of the friends that God must be justly punishing Job for something he will not admit. Job turns the lawsuit around, charging God with injustice in tormenting him and including an oath of innocence.

The most apt encompassing genre description for the dialogue between Job and friends is *disputation speech*, in the course of which Job not only disputes with friends but with deity. When Yahweh finally breaks the silence in which wisdom genres customarily enshroud deity, his answer to Job has the character of a disputation speech intended to overwhelm an opponent. A reasonably close analogue has been found in an Egyptian satirical letter in which a master scribe berates his pupils for their naive presumption to knowledge (Web Table A, 9E).

The structure of the speeches in Job is normally alphabetizing (twenty-two or twenty-three lines per speech), with the replies of Job to his friends tending to be always a few lines longer than their statements. The divine reply in turn exceeds the length of Job's speech to deity in the same ratio as Job's speeches exceed his friends' speeches. The elaborate argument suggests self-conscious compositional techniques used to drive home the scribal author's stunning challenge to complacent orthodoxy.[23]

Is there not, after all, some answer or message in the book concerning theories of suffering? Job at first tries to counter Yahweh's disputation speech, but then he relents from trying to argue with God. Job does not repent of what he has earlier argued, for in that respect Yahweh confirms Job (42:7, 9). It might be said that Yahweh accepts the content of Job's rebuttal of dogmatism but reprimands Job for toying with a dogmatism of his own, that is, that any one person, even a righteous Job, can explain everything. The book may be saying that only God, the all-wise, is entitled to be a dogmatist, but that God is *not* a dogmatist can be plainly seen by looking at the irony, ludicrousness, and absurdity of what God has created. Behind the sharp satire of Yahweh's speech there seems to lurk the idea that God does not have evil and suffering totally under control and thus God also suffers.

The only explanation for what has happened to Job is further happenings: Job relents from arguing, intercedes with God for his friends' folly, and finds his fortunes restored. Rather than end the book with a theological interpretation or speech, the author chooses to tell the rest of the traditional story. As new literary critics have observed, this happy ending makes even of the tormented book of Job not a tragedy but a comedy, since the central figure is brought back into community with other humans and with God after extreme isolation and alienation (see pp. 124–25).[24]

The book of Job is so eccentric and intensely psychological in its probing of the impact of suffering that it is difficult to know what consequences the author intended. Some have taken it to be a kind of treatment in microcosm of the macrocosm of Israel's suffering in exile. Job, however, does not parabolically represent or model the whole people. The author would probably have been satisfied if his whistle blowing on moralism and dogmatism managed to alert the custodians of wisdom to the perils of cheapening and betraying its critical powers of observation and reflection.

Ecclesiastes (Qohelet)

This last and bleakest of the canonical wisdom books is a unique fusion of genre elements in an extended reflection by a sage who speaks in the first person throughout, until in 12:9-14 a third party comments on the author's wisdom activities and sums up the import of his teaching. This reflection has the thematic discursive character of an essay or treatise, although genre elements incorporated are experiential and didactic sayings, comparative sayings (often in the form "better is x than y"), observations ("I applied myself to know, . . . I saw . . ."), self-discourses ("I said in my heart"), admonitions, parables, allegory, and an extended piece of royal fiction in which the sage strikes the pose of Solomon (1:12—2:11). There is disagreement as to whether the total work can be scanned as poetry.

The varied genre elements, including strings of sayings, taken together with the explicit editorial notation of 12:9-10, make clear that the writer gathered diverse materials for his sustained and penetrating reflections. At the same time, similarity of language, recurrence of themes, and the use of numbers give to the work a pronounced unity of thought,[25] although attempts to describe a progressive development of thought have not been convincing. Likewise, the assumption of literary strata, some laid down by pious commentators on the book, does not convincingly restore an original kernel to the book and has glaringly failed to take adequate account of the curious dialectic of the author's mind.

The book begins and ends with exclamations that everything in human life is *hevel,* "vanity" in the older English translations, but better understood as "emptiness, senselessness, futility" (1:2; 12:8, plus thirty times throughout). The sage works with polar thought structures of life and death and the gains and losses in all areas of life. In each case he comes down heavily on the negative pole, but without totally surrendering a continuing tension with the positive pole.[26]

In each of the realms of human experience there are proximate values, but none of these confers an absolute gain that cannot be snatched away in this life. The result is an uneasy amalgam of contentions: there is a God; we do not know God's ways; all of our experiences may have some relative profit; we should live the uncertain relativities of our life joyously without any confidence in punishment or reward. Wisdom is plainly better than folly, but true wisdom enlightens best by showing us that wisdom confers only modest insight into and power over a world that eludes rational or moral mastery.

How are we to understand the socioreligious setting of this astonishingly blunt writer? There is a solid consensus among scholars that Ecclesiastes belongs to the third century B.C.E., that is, to Ptolemaic Palestine. The author uses the royal fiction of Solomon early on in his book, but later so speaks that he obviously distinguishes himself from kings. The Solomonic attribution of the book belongs to a later stage (1:1). In the text the writer is simply identified as *qōheleth,* usually rendered inappropriately as "the Preacher." The term rather means "the Assembler or Gatherer," and the postscript tells of his studious efforts at "weighing, studying, and arranging [or composing?] sayings."

The use of the Solomonic royal fiction, the parables drawn from political life, and the counsel about obeying kings suggests that, like preexilic wise men, this sage was in government service, although the redactional comment that he "also taught the people knowledge" implies that his instruction extended outside the limited sphere of officialdom. The remarks about injustice, agriculture, and high officialdom in 5:8-9 correspond well with what we know of the Ptolemaic administration in Palestine, however.

> If you see oppression of the poor and denial of justice in the state, don't be surprised at the situation.
> The high one [official?] is watched by a higher, and there are yet higher ones over them.
> But the gain of a country in such circumstances would be a king who serves fields [agriculture].

The Ptolemies introduced layers of colonial administration into Judah, with attending rivalry and corruption, and the intensification of agriculture that resulted was chiefly for export products such as wine and oil rather than for grain and vegetable production for the native populace (see pp. 250–51). Qohelet sympathizes deeply with the oppressed poor (cf. 4:1-3), but, given his privileged position, he only obliquely condemns crimes against them—to speak more openly would put him in conflict with his warning to obey kings, who have absolute power (8:2-9).

The socioreligious situation of this astute sage is a setting where God and government are distanced from the people. Both the divine and the secular authorities work in unfathomable ways that cannot be contested. This personal powerlessness, over against a God who is remote and a colonial apparatus of domination that milks the province of Judah for Egypt's gain and for the profit of Jewish elites, has its counterpart in the sage's strategy for keeping his own sanity by doing his work well, enjoying his family, observing the cult correctly, and spreading to all who can appreciate it his caution that life is by no means as rational or moral as inherited wisdom would have it.

APOCALYPTIC WRITINGS

What Is Apocalyptic?

The term "apocalypse," from a Greek term for "revelation," "disclosure," or "unveiling," is conventionally used for a type of revelatory literature of which there are scores of Jewish, Christian, Gnostic, Greco-Roman, and Persian examples from the period 200 B.C.E.–300 C.E. The only full-fledged apocalypse to be accepted into the Hebrew Bible was the book of Daniel, although a number of biblical prophetic texts display sufficient anticipatory marks of the genre to give us a sense of how apocalyptic arose in Jewish circles. "Apocalyptic" may refer to *apocalyptic literature, apocalyptic thought,* or the *apocalyptic movement.* Discussions of this phenomenon have often failed to distinguish adequately among the literary, ideological, and sociological aspects of the inquiry.

Literary Genre and Mind-set

Since our solidest evidence is textual, a literary clarification of apocalyptic is the place to begin. Form-critical analysis identifies elements in both the form and the content of revelation that are constitutive of the apocalyptic genre.[27] The revelation may be delivered by sight (vision) or by a spoken statement (audition), or by both together, and may be additionally contained in a written document. The vision may expand into an otherworldly journey. In all cases an otherworldly mediator either delivers, explains, or guides the revelation. The human recipient of the revelation is usually a venerable figure from the past, in

Jewish apocalypses, from the primeval period (e.g., Enoch) and especially from the era of exile and early restoration (e.g., Daniel).

The content of revelation runs along either a temporal or a spatial axis. The *temporal revelation* discloses an impending crisis of persecution and world upheavals that will lead rapidly to the end of the present world order in judgment and salvation. This end may involve world transformation, but always includes personal salvation for the faithful believer in some form of afterlife, often bodily resurrection. In order to set the stage for the end time, there is often a revelation about past history in the form of prophecy-after-the-event (e.g., "Daniel" from his claimed vantage point in the exile is shown the course of events as far as 165 B.C.E., when the book of Daniel was most likely written).

The *spatial revelation* introduces the human recipient of the revelation to the geography and demography of heaven and hell, usually in a guided journey through cosmic regions. Some apocalypses have only a temporal revelation and some only a spatial revelation, while others include both. For apocalyptic Jews, history moves toward an end time under the pressure of a sovereign heavenly realm that calls the shots about what happens *in* and *to* history.

An apocalypse customarily rounds out with instructions to the recipient to "stand fast" or "await the end," and frequently to conceal the revelation until the end time. Given the pseudonymous form, this instruction had the effect of a command to publish, since, for example, the alleged Daniel of the exile was to hide his book *until 165 B.C.E.*

This kind of close literary formulation of apocalyptic does not require any particular way of picturing the end of history but also does not include all kinds of revelations in the category, such as those that do not have any end of history or personal afterlife. It also means that an apocalypse may be part of a larger composition composed of other genres.

On the basis of the above literary characterization of apocalyptic we may say that the apocalyptic genre is *a type of revelatory literature with a narrative framework in which a revelation about end-time judgment and salvation and/or about the heavenly realms is given to a human being by an otherworldly messenger.* With these criteria for defining apocalyptic literature, one may designate approximately fourteen Jewish apocalypses up to the second century C.E. (Web Table N).

In spite of the neatness of the preceding typology, there is no clear consensus about an appropriate definition of apocalyptic and the exact scope of the apocalyptic corpus. A phenomenological description, however, identifies the heart of apocalyptic thought as a radically new *summing up and evaluation of history as having run its course.* The one remaining value of historical time is that in it individual believers prepare themselves for salvation in the dawning kingdom of God that negates degenerate history. Radical pessimism about the meaning of history fuses with radical optimism that history is about to pass away before the divine kingdom.[28]

In the light of this radically disjunctive conceptual definition of apocalyptic, the list of apocalyptic writings comprises Daniel, *1 Enoch,* 2 Esdras (= *4 Ezra*), and *2 Baruch,* and adds portions of the *Sibylline Oracles* and the *Testament* or *Assumption of Moses.* The influence of apocalyptic, however, is acknowledged over a wide front, as its motifs and idioms are employed in other kinds of literature.

Sociohistorical Horizons of Apocalyptic

Lastly, various attempts have been made to work backward from the apocalyptic literature to the several communities or larger movement that produced them (Web Table N).[29] This inquiry, while soundly based in principle, is handicapped by the limited historical and social data at our disposal. One form of this inquiry works from the apparent continuities and transformations of ideas from postexilic prophecy into full-blown apocalyptic, with attention to transitional expressions of proto-apocalyptic in works such as Isaiah 56–66, Isaiah 24–27, and Zechariah 9–14. These writings from postexilic prophetic circles show the growth of assumptions and themes fundamental in later apocalyptic: the increasing conflict between good and evil, the transformation of cosmos and history, and so on. In stressing these texts, the contribution of prophecy to apocalyptic is seen to be mainly *eschatological*, that is, with respect to notions of the end time. Another group of late prophetic writings (e.g., Ezekiel and Zechariah 1–8) seem to contribute the aspect of revelation by vision to apocalyptic.

In all instances prior to Daniel, these patently apocalyptic elements fail to congeal into the integrated literary-conceptual pattern outlined above. Thus scattered proto-apocalyptic forms and contents stemming from prophecy seem to have had a life of some four centuries within Israel before fusing in the critical mass of radical end-time revelations.

The facets of sociohistorical experience that precipitated apocalyptic communities in Hellenistic times had to do with the contact, interchange, and conflict between Jews and Gentiles over a broad cultural, political, and religious front. Jews lived widely in the Gentile world, often shared its culture, and in instances rose to power and influence in Persian and Hellenistic regimes. At the same time, Jews were subject to foreign rule even in Palestine, and the Hellenistic culture penetrated the elites of Judah so extensively that by Maccabean times the entire construct of Jewish religion was open to question.

In the Maccabean and Hasmonean struggles, the Jewish-Gentile bifurcation was projected as civil strife among Jews as to how Jewish or how Hellenistic their politics, culture, and religion should be. In the apocalyptic movement these conflicts came to expression as a radical option for the Jewish God and his righteous rule in which all the universal and individualistic impulses of the time were negated by and transformed into the kingdom of God as the end point of history.

Who were these apocalyptists? By assuming a one-to-one correlation between the tradition elements in apocalyptic, they may be seen as alienated prophets or as disillusioned wise men. By noting the prominence of apocalyptic thought in the Dead Sea community, they may be seen as priests disaffected from the Jerusalem cult.

The producers of the book of Daniel are frequently said to have been the Hasidic party that backed the Maccabean wars as long as they were struggles for religious survival. While we know very little about the origins of the Hasidim, in their Maccabean form they were probably a coalition of anti-Hellenistic traditionalists with many points of view represented, among them the apocalyptic. The book of Daniel shows affinities with wisdom tradition in that it begins with stories about Jews in foreign government service and identifies the righteous as "the wise."

Possibly the flash point for end-time thinking arose among those who once had favorable experiences with foreign governments but who now experienced the Seleucid regime joining with Jewish hellenizing elites to destroy the Jewish cult and tradition. In this situation, all human government was thrown into fundamental question, and God alone was seen to provide a way out of the terrible impasse. The resignation of the sage in Ecclesiastes was a way to respond to a precarious world as long as a Jewish survival space remained intact within it. But to the apocalyptists, the end of the Jewish world space meant the end of history.

Drawing on limited comparisons made from anthropological studies of cults, we may form some reasonable conclusions about the Jewish apocalyptic communities. We should expect that there were *various apocalyptic communities*, even if the Maccabean Hasidic context provided the first identifiable instance. We should also expect that the membership of apocalyptic groups would be *diverse in class and status*. The frequent assumption that only very impoverished people would be apocalyptists is undercut by the clear evidence from relative deprivation theory. People suffering any kind of serious disadvantage, such as Jewish courtiers in foreign governments or in Judean government who were expelled from office, might be ready candidates for membership in an apocalyptic group.

Daniel

We can solidly conclude that the present form of the book of Daniel was composed in the year 165 B.C.E. because of "the final events" announced as revelations to the seer Daniel. The author knows of the profanation of the temple by cessation of daily sacrifices and setting up of an image of Zeus Olympius in 167 ("the abomination that desolates," 11:31; 12:11), of the severe proscriptions against the practice of Judaism (7:25; 11:28, 30), and of the deaths of many righteous in the war of defense led by Judas Maccabee (11:33-35). The career of the Seleucid emperor Antiochus Epiphanes is sketched more or less accurately down to the beginning of 165. The author, however, expects a third—this time totally victorious— Seleucid invasion of Egypt, and this did *not* occur (11:42-43). He is also unaware of Antiochus's campaign in the east during which the ruler died. Also, the profaned temple still awaits rededication.

The apocalyptic structure of the book is achieved by combining a series of stories about Daniel and his companions in Babylonian-Median government service with a series of visions reviewing ancient Near Eastern history from the exile to 165 B.C.E. The stories provide a narrative setting in royal courts some four centuries earlier than Maccabean times, where the Jewish exile Daniel functioned as a wise interpreter of dreams and is the recipient of the visions that culminate the book.

The interplay between stories and visions is intricate. For example, the dream of the

FIG. 12.3. Shadrach, Meshach, and Abednego, the "three youths" in the "fiery furnace" of Nebuchadnezzar (Daniel 3). Catacomb of Priscilla, Rome. Photo: © Erich Lessing / Art Resource, N.Y.

grotesque statue representing four kingdoms (chap. 2) prefigures the first vision in which the four kingdoms are personified as four beasts (chap. 7). The effect of the association of the stories and the visions is to create a series of interchanges between ancient foreign rulers and faithful Jews that operate as foils and foreshadowings of the contemporary hostile relations between the Seleucids and pious Jews that have brought world events swiftly toward their end.

Why Daniel should have been chosen as the recipient of this revelation of the end in 165 B.C.E. and how the nonapocalyptic stories could have been included in the book have been much discussed. Apparently the stories had an extensive prehistory. From Ezek. 14:14 we learn of a righteous Daniel, named alongside Noah and Job, who may have become the prototype of Jews in foreign service (cf. Genesis 37–50; Esther). Babylon as the archetypal world power that threw Judah into a form of permanent exile may have come to stand negatively for political oppression at large and positively for cultural and vocational opportunity open to wise Jews in the Dispersion (Dan. 1:1-7).

The visions of the end in Daniel are four in number (7; 8; 9; 10:1—12:4), although the third is more accurately a spoken revelation concerning a prophecy of Jeremiah. The *vision of the four beasts* (chap. 7) giving way to the kingdom of the saints (persecuted faithful Jews) also equates the saints with "one like a son of man" who descends from the heavens. The precise force of this equation is far from clear. It may be a collective individualization of the community of saints as "human" (vs. "animalistic") in its bearing. It may also be that "one like a son of man" is an angelic messenger who serves as the guardian or head of the community of saints. The *Similitudes of Enoch*

(*1 Enoch* 37–71), written perhaps more than a century later, pictures Enoch as one who will return at the end time as "son of man" to establish God's rule on earth. Whether this is at all the sense of Daniel 7 is questionable, since no name is given to the cryptic Danielic "son of man."

The *vision of the ram and he-goat* (chap. 8) focuses on Alexander and his successors, particularly "the little horn" Antiochus Epiphanes, and looks toward the imminent reconsecration of the profaned Jerusalem temple. In chap. 9 Daniel's query about Jeremiah's prophecy of seventy years of exile is reinterpreted by Gabriel as seventy weeks of years (= 490 years), thereby accounting for the several-century time span between the exile and the Maccabean War.

In the final vision (10:1—12:4), an unnamed messenger encourages Daniel by informing him that the earthly battles between nations and with the faithful are accompanied—and ultimately determined—by *battles between heavenly beings*. The relations of the Ptolemies and Seleucids—their diplomacy, wars, and intermarriages—are then recited prophetically in a veiled manner down to the beginning of 165 B.C.E.

The end of history is described tersely and obliquely in terms of the agency of Michael, who will see that "your people" (the faithful Jews) are delivered. Deliverance here includes bodily resurrection of "many" (not all), including the righteous (martyred sectarians?) and the wicked (apostate hellenizing Jews?). This compressed scenario, however, leaves much unanswered about "the appointed end." Since the heavenly realms are only indirectly treated in the book, there is no reference to cosmic transformation. Since an aspect of the book's expectation is that the temple will be reconsecrated (8:13-14; 12:11-13), the author's understanding may be that the redeemed saints will enjoy a purified and unhindered cult at Jerusalem, an end—not to history as such—to countless injustices and frustrations in Israel's previous history.

Like other apocalyptists who have been studied in terms of social-psychological cognitive dissonance theory, the devotees of Daniel probably reinterpreted events and carried on the struggle. After all, the book does not name Antiochus Epiphanes as the last world oppressor and could be reread with a new hermeneutic of the prolongation of the times, as in fact early Christians and rabbinic Jews read it. Interestingly, however, the Danielic group did not redact the book to explain the delay of the end, nor did anyone else so redact it. The seemingly discredited work was taken into the canon of rabbinic Judaism untouched because it spoke so powerfully of God's rule over history amid the memorable Maccabean struggle to keep open the Jewish world space.

NOTES

1. Werner E. Lemke, "The Synoptic Problem in the Chronicler's History," *Harvard Theological Review* 58 (1968): 350–63.
2. Peter R. Ackroyd, "History and Theology in the Writings of the Chronicler," *Concordia Theological Monthly* 38 (1967): 501–15.
3. Gerhard von Rad, "The Levitical Sermons in I and II Chronicles," in *The Problem of the Hexateuch and Other Essays,* trans. E. W. Trueman Dicken (Edinburgh: Oliver & Boyd, 1966), 267–80.
4. Hermann Gunkel, *The Psalms: A Form-Critical Introduction,* trans. Thomas M. Horner, Facet Books 19 (Philadelphia: Fortress Press, 1967).
5. Ibid.
6. Sigmund Mowinckel, *The Psalms in Israel's Worship,* trans. D. R. Ap-Thomas, 2 vols. (New York: Abingdon, 1962), 1:1–41.
7. Childs, *IOTS*, 508–23.
8. Walter Brueggemann, "Psalms and the Life of Faith: A Suggested Typology of Function," *JSOT* 17 (1980): 3–32, and *Praying the Psalms* (Winona, Minn.: Saint Mary's Press, 1982).
9. Norman K. Gottwald, *Studies in the Book of Lamentations,* rev. ed., SBT 1/14 (London: SCM, 1962), 23–32.
10. Ibid., 47–62; Bertil Albrektson, *Studies in the Text and Theology of the Book of Lamentations,* Studia Theologica Ludensia 21 (Lund: Gleerup, 1963), 214–39; Delbert R. Hillers, *Lamentations,* AB 7A (Garden City, N.Y.: Doubleday, 1972), xxiii, 22–23, 105; and see reviews by Gottwald of Albrektson in *JBL* 83 (1964): 204–7, and of Hillers in *Journal of the American Academy of Religion* 43/2, Book Review Supplement (1975): 311–13.
11. Roland E. Murphy, "Canticles (Songs of Songs)," in *The Wisdom Literature: Job, Proverbs, Ruth, Canticles, Ecclesiastes, and Esther,* FOTL 13 (Grand Rapids: Eerdmans, 1981), 101–3.
12. Edward F. Campbell, Jr., *Ruth,* AB 7 (Garden City, N.Y.: Doubleday, 1975), 5–6, 9–10.
13. Ibid., 8–9.
14. Ibid., 18–23.

15. Jack M. Sasson, *Ruth: A New Translation with a Philological Commentary and a Formalist-Folklorist Interpretation* (Baltimore: Johns Hopkins University Press, 1979), esp. 196–252.

16. Stephen Bertram, "Symmetrical Design in the Book of Ruth," *JBL* 84 (1965): 165–68; D. F. Rauber, "Literary Values in the Bible: The Book of Ruth," *JBL* 89 (1970): 27–37; Phyllis Trible, "A Human Comedy," in *God and the Rhetoric of Sexuality*, OBT (Philadelphia: Fortress Press, 1978), 166–99; Harold Fisch, "Ruth and the Structure of Covenant History," *VT* 32 (1982): 425–37.

17. Trible, "Human Comedy."

18. Robert H. Pfeiffer, *Introduction to the Old Testament* (New York: Harper & Bros., 1941), 740–47.

19. Murphy, *Wisdom Literature,* 3–6, 9–12, 172–85.

20. Ibid., 6–9; Robert Gordis, "The Social Background of Wisdom Literature," *HUCA* 18 (1943/44): 77–118.

21. Patrick W. Skehan, *Studies in Israelite Poetry and Wisdom*, CBQMS 1 (Washington, D.C.: Catholic Biblical Association of America, 1971), 9–45.

22. Murphy, *Wisdom Literature,* 15–20.

23. Skehan, *Studies in Israelite Poetry*, 96–123.

24. J. William Whedbee, "The Comedy of Job," *Semeia* 7 (1977): 1–39; Robert M. Polzin, *Biblical Structuralism: Method and Subjectivity in the Study of Ancient Texts,* Semeia Studies (Philadelphia: Fortress Press; Missoula, Mont.: Scholars, 1977), 54–125.

25. Murphy, *Wisdom Literature,* 127–31; Addison G. Wright, "The Riddle of the Sphinx: The Structure of the Book of Qoheleth," in *Studies in Ancient Israelite Wisdom*, ed. James L. Crenshaw (New York: Ktav, 1976), 245–66; idem, "The Riddle of the Sphinx Revisited: Numerical Patterns in the Book of Qoheleth," *CBQ* 42 (1980): 38–51.

26. John A. Loader, *Polar Structures in the Book of Qoheleth,* BZAW 152 (Berlin: de Gruyter, 1979).

27. John J. Collins, ed., *Apocalyptic: The Morphology of a Genre,* Semeia 14 (1979).

28. Walter Schmithals, *The Apocalyptic Movement: Introduction and Interpretation,* trans. John E. Steely (Nashville: Abingdon, 1975).

29. Robert R. Wilson, "From Prophecy to Apocalyptic: Reflections on the Shape of Israelite Religion," *Semeia* 21 (1981): 79–95, with response by N. K. Gottwald, 109–11.

FOR FURTHER READING

Alter, Robert. *The Art of Biblical Poetry.* New York: Basic, 1985.

Ceresko, Anthony R. *Introduction to Old Testament Wisdom: A Spirituality for Liberation.* Maryknoll, N.Y.: Orbis, 1999.

Collins, John J. *The Apocalyptic Imagination: An Introduction to Jewish Apocalyptic Literature.* 2nd ed. Grand Rapids: Eerdmans, 1998.

Gunkel, Hermann. *An Introduction to the Psalms: The Genres of the Religious Lyric of Israel.* Macon, Ga.: Mercer University Press, 1998.

Kalimi, Isaac. *An Ancient Israelite Historian: Studies in the Chronicler, His Time, Place and Writing.* Assen: Van Gorcum, 2005.

Linafelt, Tod. *Surviving Lamentations: Catastrophe, Lament, and Protest in the Afterlife of a Biblical Book.* Chicago: University of Chicago Press, 2000.

Newsom, Carol A. *The Book of Job: A Contest of Moral Imaginations.* Oxford: Oxford University Press, 2003.

Sherwood, Yvonne. *A Biblical Text and Its Afterlives: The Survival of Jonah in Western Culture.* Cambridge: Cambridge University Press, 2000.

Walsh, Carey Ellen. *Exquisite Desire: Religion, the Erotic, and the Song of Songs.* Minneapolis: Fortress Press, 2000.

QUESTIONS FOR STUDY

1. Describe the relationship of the Chronicler's History to the Priestly and Deuteronomistic traditions.
2. Compare Gunkel's theory of the life setting and function of the psalm genres to that of Mowinckel. What are the strengths and weaknesses of each?
3. How does social class fit into a socioliterary interpretation of Psalms, Song of Songs, and Proverbs?
4. Why are the wisdom writings so named? What genres and major themes do they encompass?
5. What overall themes connect the four visions in Daniel? What appears to be the book's vision of the "end time"?

CONCLUSION

The Interplay of Text, Concept,
and Setting in the Hebrew Bible

A common complaint about critical study of the Bible is that it dissects and analyzes the Bible without resynthesizing it. Can the Hebrew Bible be put back together as a living whole? It certainly cannot be reunified precritically by setting aside the methods of inquiry we have studied. Alternatively, are there ways to reconceive the Bible postcritically that will ensure its integrity and active contribution to the cultural, intellectual, and religious life of today? There are strong indications that the Hebrew Bible, critically understood, can and will be revisioned as a complex unity of enduring significance and relevance.

Study of the Hebrew Bible is first and foremost study of a text. The biblical text, however, is not an isolated datum. Precisely as literature, each text in the Hebrew Bible expresses a point of view and reflects a social setting. By focusing now on the text, then on its conceptual world, and further on its social placement, different methods in biblical studies have contributed valuable understandings to the interpretation of the text as a whole. These literary, conceptual, and social understandings, which at first glance appear discrete, press toward convergence and mutual interaction.

Text, concept, and setting display distinctive features, each with its own network of connections and its own history. The history of the literary growth of the Hebrew Bible is matched by a history of the development of biblical concepts (whether seen as theology or ideology), and further paralleled by a history of biblical social contexts that include political and religious settings. A mushrooming growth of literary genres and compositions, of concepts and patterns of thought, and of sociopolitical structures and processes produces a cumulative snowballing effect through the course of biblical history.

More and more literary, conceptual, and sociopolitical options, few of which drop completely from sight, offer ever more complex ways of combining texts, concepts, and settings. We have observed that virtually all of the literary genres developed in the earlier literature reappear in the later writings. We have also noted that concepts from before, during, and after the monarchy compete or associate with one another in varying ways in the restored postexilic community. Likewise, we have seen that the social dynamics of tribalism, state rule, colonial dispersion, and subordination to great powers flow one into the other, overlap in part, and create institutional settings where new literature and concepts are generated and where old literature and concepts thrive with modifications in function and meaning.

In spite of difficulties in dating many parts of the Hebrew Bible, it is now widely recognized that the literature and concepts of ancient Israel and early Judaism developed in families or clusters of genres and composite tradition complexes stamped with distinctive theological perspectives. These firmly centered groupings of texts and concepts, elaborated and intertwined over centuries and yet open to influence on one another, have been called "streams of tradition" or "trajectories."[1]

Corresponding to these literary-conceptual groupings are sets of sociopolitical events, structures, and processes. These social groupings, treated under "sociohistorical horizons" in the foregoing chapters, generated texts and concepts and are directly or indirectly reflected in these texts and concepts. It is important to illuminate these social settings because the biblical writers were also actors in concrete social formations under particular modes of production and political regimes. This general consideration applies all the more forcefully to ancient Israel because of the explicit orientation of much of its literature and thought toward sociopolitical life sectors. By topic and stance, the literature of the Hebrew Bible is highly historical and communal in the sense that it is concerned with human life in community under concrete conditions subject to change.

The task of conceiving and fruitfully studying the correlations and interplay among texts, concepts, and sociohistorical settings is both exciting and tricky to carry out satisfactorily. Our everyday or commonsense way of thinking tends to treat these sectors separately. Granted that one-sector-at-a-time procedures will always be necessary in biblical studies, we are now at a point where regular and disciplined correlation or interreading of the literary, conceptual, and sociohistorical sectors is possible and urgent in order to make the fullest sense of the knowledge we already have. It is time to rethink the field of biblical studies and to restructure our approaches to the Hebrew Bible to encourage systemic study of the literary, conceptual, and sociohistorical sectors as integral elements of ancient Israelite / Jewish life. This is to recognize that these sectors are internally related in such a way that to know any one of them adequately we must also know as much as possible about the others.

We can make a start on rethinking and restructuring biblical studies by trying to identify the basic components of a unified socioliterary-theological grid of the Hebrew Bible. This requires that we consciously bring together all the major elements of each sector that we have uncovered in the preceding study. While our knowledge is rudimentary in certain regards, enough is known that we can sketch a grid of key components arranged along domain, sectoral, and geographical axes.

1. The *domain axis* corresponds to the historical experience of Israel that we have followed through its successive stages of socioeconomic, political, and religious organization and ideology. In this instance we are identifying the broadest determinative level of social and political organization operative in each temporal phase. The following sociopolitical domains are distinguished as of primary significance for literary and theological production:

   a. The socioreligious revolution of confederated Yahweh-worshiping tribes in Canaan
   b. The sociopolitical counterrevolution of united Israel under monarchic state rule
   c. The internal division of the united monarchy into the two weaker states of Judah and Israel
   d. The destruction of both states by imperial conquest and the subjection of their populaces to deportation and colonial rule

   e. The restoration of Judah to colonial home-rule status subject to a long succession of foreign powers, broken by eighty years of Jewish independence under the Hasmonean state.

2. The *sectoral axis* links to the domain axis by assessing within each of the above sociopolitical frames how specific social contexts produced particular literary forms with their distinctive theological expressions. We may unpack the internally related sectors by proceeding in this way:

   a. Identify and characterize the relevant *sociopolitical domain* (one of the five listed above).
   b. Identify and characterize the specific *sociopolitical sectors* that generate texts and concepts. What social institutions, offices, or roles singularly or in combination produce what texts and concepts?
   c. Identify and characterize the genres, tradition complexes, sources, and books that constitute the *literary sector*. What is the repertory of single and associated literary genres? How are the genres built into larger tradition complexes that form biblical books in part or whole, and how do they function at successive stages?
   d. Identify and characterize the concepts and patterns of thought that constitute the *theological or ideological sector*. As theology, these concepts are "talk about God," "talk to God," or "talk from God." As ideology, the religious ideas are connected to the larger sociopolitical domain, which tends to be legitimated or criticized by these concepts and their bearers. Care must be taken to distinguish concepts closely connected

with particular literary genres and tradition complexes and concepts that cross over or cross-fertilize traditions as social groups interact.

3. A *geographical axis* is involved chiefly at two points:

  a. During the divided monarchy, developments in the northern and southern kingdoms are to be distinguished.
  b. During the exile, the literary, social-organizational, and theological situations of Palestinian Jews and deported Jews likewise require separate considerations.

These intersecting domain, sectoral, and geographical axes, or categories of analysis, have been traced in some detail throughout the Hebrew Bible in the preceding chapters of this book. It remains here to sum them up in chart form. Two charts will be presented: one on the operative social and political organizational domains in historical succession (chart 13.1), and another on the literary and conceptual developments as they unfold within the framework of the sociopolitical domains (chart 13.2). A word is in order concerning certain graphic features of the charts.

1. The *sociopolitical organizational domains* (chart 13.1) condenses the history presented in this text, distinguishing the periods of Israelite *political independence* or *dependence*—the periods of *tribal* or *state dominance* and the *succession of foreign empires* to which Jews were subject throughout the later biblical era.

  a. The transparent area running horizontally from the united monarchy onward represents the endurance of tribal social organization and culture in northern and southern Israel that, although

diminishing overall in their vitality and scope, continued to shape the thought and practice of Israelites and Jews both politically and religiously throughout the biblical era. This area is transparent to emphasize that state and tribal spheres interpenetrated, often involving the same people in different roles or functions and the same or related institutions in cooperation or conflict (e.g., tribal draftees in a state army professionally staffed).
  b. Shading from darker to lighter marks the direction of political dominance. In the periods of Israelite political independence, blue shading moves *outward* to symbolize the boundary maintenance asserted by sovereign tribes or sovereign states. In the periods of Israelite political dependence from the exile onward, gray shading moves *into* Israel *from without* to symbolize that Israel has been subjected to the colonial rule of empires. These gradients pass over the transparent area of tribal organization because they represent the claims and acts of sovereign states to whom tribalism is strictly a cultural or internal administrative matter.

2. The chart of *socioliterary-theological sectors* (chart 13.2) is much more complex because it is both multidimensional and intersectoral. In it I attempt to show the *integral relations* between the literary and the theological sectors of the Hebrew Bible and the immediate social sites that generated them, given the overarching domains of general social and political organization.

  a. The clusters, families, streams of traditions, or trajectories of the literary sector, together with their respective social and theological sectors, are placed in more or less synchronized chronological order within horizontal rows.

b. Arrows indicate three forms of movement within and between the tradition sectors: (1) appropriation of north Israelite lines of tradition by Judahite circles after the fall of Israel in 722 B.C.E.; (2) introduction of tradition elements from the exile into the restored Judahite community; and (3) lateral appropriation of literary materials from one socioliterary-theological complex by another (e.g., when the royalist J epic takes over and elaborates tribal traditions).

c. The originative tribal social revolution of Israel apparently spawned a considerable unifying interlock of traditions that was fractured by the subsequent impact of monarchic and imperial-colonial structures and processes. Large brackets on the chart indicate two later sociohistorical moments when several socioliterary-theological sectors converged to support major restructuring of the total communal life that attempted to recover the vitality and integrity of the originative era: the Deuteronomic reformation and the restoration of the Judahite community following exile. Each of these catalytic moments, particularly the postexilic restoration around temple and Law, contributed enduring features to ongoing Jewish life. *Who* was to hold power in the community and *how* the texts were to be interpreted, however, remained disputed points throughout biblical times.

This initial attempt to show the coexistence and correlation of traditions and theologies in their social contexts over time is limited to components discussed in the body of this text and further limited by the intent to avoid visual overload on the chart. It should serve, however, to encourage students and scholars in the habits and skills of interreading texts, theologies, and social settings.

A final word is appropriate about how the socioliterary pluriformity of the Hebrew Bible compels Jews and Christians to rethink all forms of confession of faith and of reflective theology that base themselves on these writings as scripture.[2] It is abundantly clear that the Hebrew Bible, far from presenting a body of fixed religious ideas or doctrines, gives us theological reflections embedded in historically changing social situations and articulated in concrete literary genres and genre complexes. The theology of the Hebrew Bible is thus both "theology of social struggle" and "theology of literary imagination."[3] There is no "message" of the Hebrew Bible that can simply be lifted out of its social contexts and literary forms without irreparable loss both of its original meaning and of its potency to speak meaningfully to us.

Likewise it is evident that the theological expressions of the Hebrew Bible do not speak into a present vacuum of pure faith. We Jews and Christians experience God in our own historically evolving social situations through concrete forms of speech and imaging that are not simply repetitions of biblical speech but are the complex product of postbiblical religious and secular culture as these realities are presently embodied in ourselves. In employing the Hebrew Bible as a *mediator* of religious faith and theological reflection, we must at one and the same time interpret both the social situations and the literary idioms of the *biblical texts* and the social situations and literary idioms of *ourselves as interpreters/actors*. This is the multidimensioned interpretive task now widely called either the hermeneutical "fusion of horizons" (the horizon of the text *and* the horizon of the interpreter)[4] or "the hermeneutical circle" (the process of interpreting a text by a repeated back-and-forth movement between the parts and the whole and between the setting of the text and the contest of the interpreters).[5] As Jews and Christians, when we exegete the Bible we are also exegeting ourselves in our own socioliterary worlds.

Certain strands of Jewish and Christian orthodoxy try to circumvent the radical sociohistorical process of contemporary believing. They attempt to protect God and the Bible by raising them above and beyond qualification by historical circumstances or reduction to the psychosocial sphere of writers and readers. This defensive ploy fails, even when adopted by oppressed peoples who have good reason to seek a fixed point of reference amid their historical experience of injustice and dehumanization. It fails because it disembowels the Hebrew Bible of its socioliterary specificity and lobotomizes its religious bite and thrust. This spiritualizing and abstracting theology is in itself the most destructive form of reductionism, for it flattens the powerful individualities of style and content that play throughout the rich texture of the Hebrew Bible.

Every method of knowing involves a reduction of what is studied to regularities in phenomena and to abstractions about relationships among the phenomena. The Hebrew Bible may be looked at entirely as historical, entirely as literary, entirely as social, entirely as theological, but in such a way that none of these ways of looking is able to exclude the others. Thus an adequate theology will take into account that it has no monopoly on the Bible and that, indeed, it has in itself no capacity to reflect faithfully and intelligibly on the Bible without the assistance of historical, literary, and social-scientific methods of biblical inquiry.

The mandate of theology is continually to reexamine its status and ground in relation both to faith and to all the data it alleges to explain. Theology is an inevitable trafficker in reductionist currencies, since it must take into account whatever is plausibly validated by other ways of knowing. It wrongly reduces only when it ignores relevant results from other disciplines or when it seeks to establish historical, literary, or societal truths at its own dictate. This is of supreme import when theology is referring to data that form part of its own prime evidence, as in the case of biblical traditions. We have seen one such significant prime datum to be the growing disclosure that ancient Israel's religion—and thus the beginning of our own as Jews and Christians—was an integral aspect of a long conflictual social history that had revolutionary origins and for which it provided a wealth of symbols and ritual practices.

Insofar as theology is an arm of synagogue and church, Jewish and Christian communities are called upon to grapple with the conflictual social origins and content of their own Bible and to ponder deeply what all this means for their placement amid contemporary social conflict and for their social mission within an arena of conflict that cannot be escaped.

NOTES

1. Odil H. Steck, "Theological Streams of Tradition," in *Tradition and Theology in the Old Testament,* ed. Douglas A. Knight (Philadelphia: Fortress Press, 1977), 183–214; Walter Brueggemann, "Trajectories in Old Testament Literature and the Sociology of Ancient Israel," in *The Bible and Liberation: Political and Social Hermeneutics*, ed. Norman K. Gottwald, rev. ed. (Maryknoll, N.Y.: Orbis, 1983), 307–33.

2. Norman K. Gottwald, "The Theological Task after *The Tribes of Yahweh*," in *Bible and Liberation*, 190–200.

3. John Dominic Crossan, "Waking the Bible: Biblical Hermeneutic and Literary Imagination," *Int* 32 (1978): 281–83.

4. Hans-Georg Gadamer, *Truth and Method,* trans. ed. Barrett Barden and John Cumming (New York: Seabury, 1975), esp. 258, 333–41.

5. Juan Luis Segundo, *The Liberation of Theology,* trans. John Drury (Maryknoll, N.Y.: Orbis, 1976), where the term is treated throughout (see p. 8 for definition).

FOR FURTHER READING

Bach, Alice. *Women in the Hebrew Bible: A Reader.* New York: Routledge, 1999.

Boer, Roland. *Marxist Criticism of the Bible.* London: T & T Clark, 2003.

Brueggemann, Walter. *Theology of the Old Testament: Testimony, Dispute, Advocacy.* Minneapolis: Fortress Press, 1997.

Clines, David J. A. *Interested Parties: The Ideology of Writers and Readers of the Hebrew Bible.* Sheffield: Sheffield Academic, 1995.

Cosgrove, Charles H. *Appealing to Scripture in Moral Discourse: Five Hermeneutical Rules.* Grand Rapids: Eerdmans, 2002.

Gnuse, Robert K. *The Old Testament and Process Theology.* St. Louis: Chalice, 2000.

Kelsey, David H. *Proving Doctrine: The Uses of Scripture in Modern Theology.* Rpt. with new preface. Harrisburg, Pa.: Trinity Press International, 1999.

Levenson, Jon D. *The Hebrew Bible, the Old Testament, and Historical Criticism: Jews and Christians in Biblical Studies.* Louisville: Westminster John Knox, 1993.

Patte, Daniel. *Ethics of Biblical Interpretation: A Reevaluation.* Louisville: Westminster John Knox, 1995.

Penchansky, David. *What Rough Beast? Images of God in the Hebrew Bible.* Louisville: Westminster John Knox, 1999.

Young, Jeremy. *The Violence of God and the War on Terror.* New York: Seabury, 2008.

QUESTIONS FOR STUDY

1. Describe the purpose and value of the author's socioliterary-theological grid for interpreting the Hebrew Bible.

2. How do hermeneutical "fusion of horizons" and "hermeneutical circle" define the interpretive task?

3. What are the problems in unhistorically "spiritualizing" and "dogmatizing" the Hebrew Bible?

4. "The mandate of theology is continually to reexamine its status and ground in relation both to faith and to all the data it alleges to explain" (p. 342). What does this statement mean to you, particularly in relation to the study of the Hebrew Bible?

CHART 13.1

Sociopolitical Organizational Domains in Biblical Israel

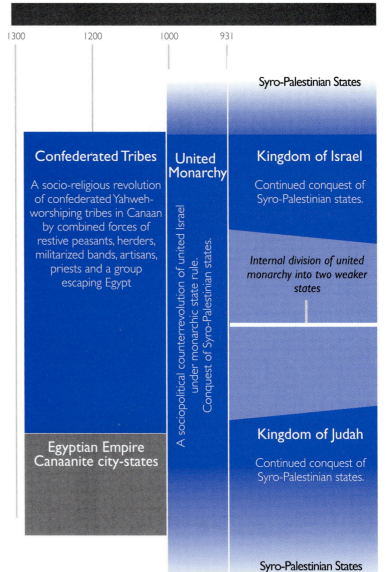

1300	1200	1000	931

Syro-Palestinian States

Confederated Tribes

A socio-religious revolution of confederated Yahweh-worshiping tribes in Canaan by combined forces of restive peasants, herders, militarized bands, artisans, priests and a group escaping Egypt

United Monarchy

A sociopolitical counterrevolution of united Israel under monarchic state rule. Conquest of Syro-Palestinian states.

Kingdom of Israel

Continued conquest of Syro-Palestinian states.

Internal division of united monarchy into two weaker states

Egyptian Empire Canaanite city-states

Kingdom of Judah

Continued conquest of Syro-Palestinian states.

Syro-Palestinian States

CHART 13.1 SOCIOPOLITICAL ORGANIZATION IN BIBLICAL ISRAEL

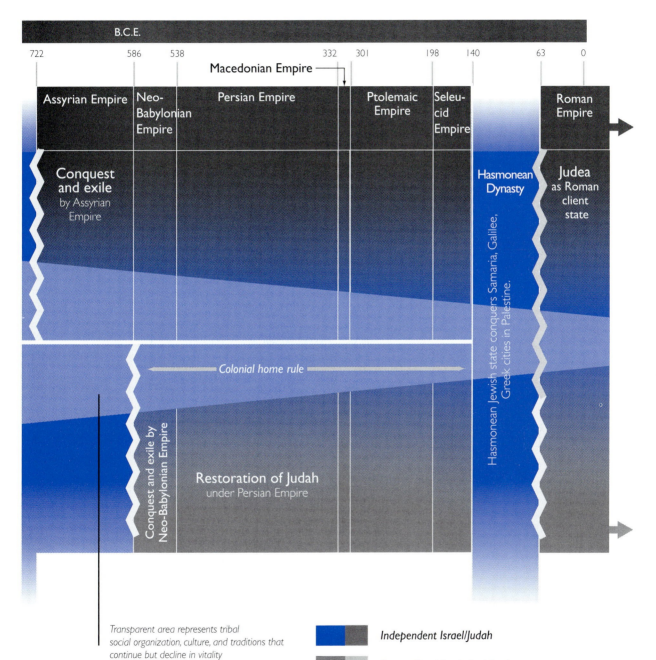

B.C.E.

722 586 538 332 301 198 140 63 0

Macedonian Empire

| Assyrian Empire | Neo-Babylonian Empire | Persian Empire | Ptolemaic Empire | Seleu-cid Empire | | Roman Empire |

Conquest and exile by Assyrian Empire

Hasmonean Dynasty

Judea as Roman client state

Hasmonean Jewish state conquers Samaria, Galilee, Greek cities in Palestine.

Colonial home rule

Conquest and exile by Neo-Babylonian Empire

Restoration of Judah under Persian Empire

Transparent area represents tribal social organization, culture, and traditions that continue but decline in vitality and scope over time.

Independent Israel/Judah

External empires/colonial rule

CHART 13.2

Social, Literary, and Theological Sectors in Biblical Israel's History

GENERAL SOCIO-POLITICAL SECTOR	1250–1000 B.C.E. *A socioreligious revolution of confederated Yahweh-worshiping tribes in Canaan*		1250–1000 B.C.E.	GENERAL SOCIO-POLITICAL SECTOR
SOCIAL	Tribal assemblies/festivals: covenant inclusions of new groups/covenant renewals	Village/tribal courts of justice	Family/village/tribal formal and informal instructional activities	SOCIAL
LITERARY	Narratives of deliverance Theophanies Covenants = treaties Categorical laws Songs of deliverance	Case laws	Wisdom sayings and admonitions	LITERARY
THEOLOGICAL	Yahweh as Deliverer from political oppression and want, Founder and Guarantor of Israel's communal order as tribes of Yahweh Yahweh as Covenant Maker/Keeper	Yahweh as Sanctioner of concrete breaches of communal order God of justice and righteousness	Yahweh as Giver and Backer of a "rational," humanly supportive, natural-cultural social-ethical-religious world order	THEOLOGICAL

GENERAL SOCIO-POLITICAL SECTOR	1000–930 B.C.E. *A sociopolitical counterrevolution of united Israel under monarchic state rule*			1000–930 B.C.E.	GENERAL SOCIO-POLITICAL SECTOR
SOCIAL	Continuing tribal cult, courts of justice, teaching functions	Jerusalem royal cult	Jerusalem royal "historian-scribes"	Jerusalem royal "wisdom-scribes"	SOCIAL
LITERARY	Songs →	Songs: Laments, Hymns, Thanksgiving songs, Songs of Zion (limited use of tribal songs)			LITERARY
	Narratives, Theophanies, Songs →	→	J Epic (major use of tribal cult traditions)		
		Priestly laws (?)			
	Wisdom sayings, Admonitions →	→	→	Artistic wisdom sayings, admonitions, instructions, hymns (limited use of tribal instructional traditions)	
			Apology of David (1Samuel 16—2 Samuel 5) Court History of David (2 Samuel 9—1 Kings 2)		
THEOLOGICAL	Continuing tribal theological conceptions	Yahweh as Creator with Jerusalem as center of world order, secure under Davidic dynasty	Yahweh as Creator and guiding Lord of Israel—at first as tribes, now as pre-eminent monarchic state	God as Creator Wisdom as norm of personal and social ethics Professional ethics of royal bureaucracy	THEOLOGICAL

CHART 13.2 SOCIAL, LITERARY, AND THEOLOGICAL SECTORS IN BIBLICAL ISRAEL'S HISTORY

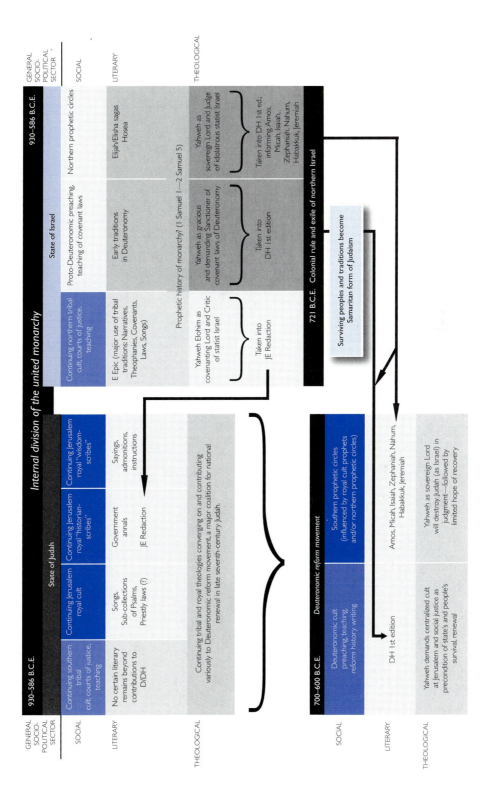

Destruction of Judah: subjection to colonial rule and exile

586–538 B.C.E.

Exile, Dispersion of Judeans in Babylonia, Persia, Egypt, etc. | Colonial rule in Judah

GENERAL SOCIO-POLITICAL SECTOR	Wisdom circles	Priestly circles (probably beginning in seventh-century Judah)	Prophetic circles	Prophetic circles	Deuteronomistic circles	Surviving Jerusalem cult on temple ruins
SOCIAL	Wisdom circles	Priestly circles	Prophetic circles	Prophetic circles	Deuteronomistic circles	Surviving Jerusalem cult on temple ruins
LITERARY	Sayings, admonitions, instructions	Holiness Code / Early edition of P (?)	Ezekiel / Isaiah of the Exile	Further collections and editions by prophets' disciples and sympathizers	DH 2nd edition / D edition of Jeremiah (other prophets?)	Lamentations / Some psalms: Laments
THEOLOGICAL	Yahweh's goodness as Creator and Governor of life thrown into question by excessive suffering and despair	Yahweh's demands for moral/ritual purity met by scrupulous observance of P laws	Yahweh, the righteous but gracious Judge of Israel, will restore Judah and Jerusalem	A future Jewish king appears in some versions of the new age	Yahweh has brought deserved end but there is modest hope for repentant survivors	Hope in Yahweh as righteous Lord of judgment who will eventually be merciful

> Majority of Jews abroad remain in Dispersion by choice. Diaspora community will continue to look to restored Palestinian center and finished literary works, Torah and prophetic writings (Prophets), for religious direction.

Restoration of Judah: colonial home rule subject to imperial dominion

538–167 B.C.E.

Restoration of community and cult, based on Temple and Law, headed by returned exiles who bring literary and theological traditions from exile; supported by coalitions of Palestinian socioreligious groups—but with reservations and ongoing criticisms and conflicts only partly moderated by reforms of Ezra and Nehemiah. | Colonial rule in Judah

GENERAL SOCIO-POLITICAL SECTOR	Wisdom circles	Prophetic circles	Deuteronomistic circles (Levites)	Restored temple cult, scribes of Law of Moses, Aaronic priests
SOCIAL	Wisdom circles	Prophetic circles	Deuteronomistic circles (Levites)	Restored temple cult, scribes of Law of Moses, Aaronic priests
LITERARY	*Proverbs, Job, Ecclesiastes*, Ben Sira	*Haggai, Zech 1–8, Isa 56–66, Malachi, Joel, Isa 24–27, Zech 9–14, plus earlier prophetic writings = "Latter Prophets"*	*Deut joined to JEP = Torah (Law of Moses)* / *Josh–Kings (DH 2nd edition) = "Former Prophets"*	P writing / JEP Redaction / *Chronicles, Ezra-Nehemiah* / Songs: redaction of *Psalms*
THEOLOGICAL	Critique of complacent moralistic wisdom; Yahweh, Creator and Governor, is beyond all human knowledge; Wisdom = Law	Yahweh accepts or rejects cult and community leaders/policies (varying from prophet to prophet); Heightened hope in eschatological judgment/salvation	Failed history of preexilic Israel/Judah is dire warning to keep Yahweh's Law with a cautious and critical eye on "cultic triumphalism"	Yahweh approves restored cult and promises life to his people as they keep Mosaic Law, Zion-David traditions applied to colonial Jerusalem in "realized eschatology"

CHART 13.2 SOCIAL, LITERARY, AND THEOLOGICAL SECTORS IN BIBLICAL ISRAEL'S HISTORY (cont.)

Ca. 167 B.C.E.–90 C.E.

Extreme sociopolitical/religious crises under the Seleucid, then Roman Empires

Ca. 167 B.C.E.–90 C.E.

GENERAL SOCIO-POLITICAL SECTOR

SOCIAL

Increasingly Hellenized nationalism after 167 in Hasmonean Jewish state. Under Roman patronage after 63 B.C.E., and especially under Herod, Temple flourishes as center of national life. Dissident groups withdraw (Qumran); the displaced support social banditry or "messianic" movements, literary remains of which are fragmentary.

LITERARY

After 200 B.C.E.: Apocalyptic circles, possibly including alienated elements from priestly, prophetic, and wisdom circles

Daniel; I Enoch (in part);
Testament of Moses (in part)

THEOLOGICAL

End of human kingdoms, in which there is no longer a space for Jewish survival, in earthly or cosmic rule of God

SOCIAL

70–90 C.E.:
Roman destruction of Jerusalem and the Temple leaves Pharisees alone in a position to consolidate Jewish community as "people of a Book."

LITERARY

Final determination of the limits of the "Writings" (including Psalms, Job, Proverbs, Ruth, the Song of Solomon, Ecclesiastes, Lamentations, Esther, Daniel, Ezra-Nehemiah, and Chronicles) alongside Torah and Prophets.

Preservation of the Oral Law which will, in time, become the Mishnah, and, later, the Palestinian and Babylonian Talmuds.

THEOLOGICAL

A more distant Yahweh is less active in Israel's behalf in an age of decline and limitation; faithful observance of Law of Moses, as constitution of the surviving community, becomes central.

AASOR	Annual of the American Schools of Oriental Research
AB	The Anchor Bible
ABD	*The Anchor Bible Dictionary*
AKE	Norman K. Gottwald. *All the Kingdoms of the Earth: Israelite Prophecy and International Relations in the Ancient Near East*. Rpt. with new preface. Minneapolis: Fortress Press, 2007.
AMB	The Amplified Bible
ANET	James B. Pritchard, ed. *Ancient Near Eastern Texts Relating to the Old Testament*. 3rd ed. Princeton, N.J.: Princeton University Press, 1969.
ASV	American Standard Version
AV	Authorized Version (= King James Version)
BA	*Biblical Archaeologist*
BARev	*Biblical Archaeology Review*
BASOR	*Bulletin of the American Schools of Oriental Research*
BHK	*Biblica Hebraica*, ed. R. Kittel. 3rd ed. Stuttgart: Württembergische Bibelanstalt, 1937.
BHS	*Biblica Hebraica Stuttgartensia*, ed. K. Elliger and W. Rudolph. Stuttgart: Deutsche Bibelstiftung, 1966–1977.
BZAW	Beihefte zur *ZAW*
CBQ	*Catholic Biblical Quarterly*
CBQMS	*CBQ* Monograph Series
CH	The Chronicler's History
CRINT	Compendia rerum iudaicarum ad Novum Testamentum
D	Deuteronomy, Deuteronomic writer(s), or Deuteronomist
DH	Deuteronomistic History (Joshua through Kings) or Deuteronomistic Historian(s)
E	Elohist
FOTL	The Forms of the Old Testament Literature
G	The common pool of united tribal traditions that J and E drew upon (from the German *Grundlage*, "foundation")

HUCA	*Hebrew Union College Annual*
IB	*Interpreter's Bible,* ed. George A. Buttrick. 12 vols. New York: Abingdon, 1951–1957.
IDB	*Interpreter's Dictionary of the Bible,* ed. George A. Buttrick. 4 vols. Nashville: Abingdon, 1962.
IDBSup	*IDB Supplementary Volume,* ed. Keith Crim. Nashville: Abingdon, 1976.
IJH	John H. Hayes and J. Maxwell Miller, eds. *Israelite and Judaean History.* 2nd ed. OTL. Louisville: Westminster John Knox, 2006.
Int	*Interpretation*
IOTS	Brevard S. Childs. *Introduction to the Old Testament as Scripture.* Philadelphia: Fortress Press, 1979.
J	Yahwist
JB	Jerusalem Bible
JBL	*Journal of Biblical Literature*
JSOT	*Journal for the Study of the Old Testament*
JSOTSup	*JSOT* Supplement Series
KJV	King James Version (= Authorized Version)
LBP	Living Bible Paraphrased
LXX	Septuagint
MLB	Modern Language Bible
MT	Masoretic Text of the Hebrew Bible
NAB	New American Bible
NASB	New American Standard Bible
NEB	New English Bible
NIB	*The New Interpreter's Bible*
NIDB	*The New Interpreter's Dictionary of the Bible*
NIV	New International Version
NJB	New Jerusalem Bible
NJPS	New Jewish Publication Society Version
NKJV	New King James Version
n.s.	new series
OBT	Overtures to Biblical Theology
OTL	Old Testament Library
P	Priestly writing or Priestly writer(s)
RSV	Revised Standard Version
RV	Revised Version
SBLDS	Society of Biblical Literature Dissertation Series
SBLSP	*Society of Biblical Literature Seminar Papers*
SBT	Studies in Biblical Theology
TEV	Today's English Version (Good News Bible)
VT	*Vetus Testamentum*
ZAW	*Zeitschrift für die alttestamentliche Wissenschaft*

Note: For abbreviations of the Dead Sea Scrolls, see Web Table F at fortresspress.com/gottwald.

Chapter 1: Angles of Vision on the Hebrew Bible

Barton, John. *Reading the Old Testament: Method in Biblical Study.* Rev. ed. Philadelphia: Westminster, 1996.

Bible and Culture Collective. *The Postmodern Bible.* New Haven: Yale University Press, 1955.

Kugel, James L. *How to Read the Bible: A Guide to Scripture, Then and Now.* New York: Free Press, 2007.

Yee, Gale A., ed. *Judges and Method: New Approaches in Biblical Studies.* 2nd ed. Minneapolis: Fortress Press, 2007.

Chapter 2: The World of the Hebrew Bible
Geography and Economy

Baly, Denis. *The Geography of the Bible.* Rev. ed. New York: Harper & Row, 1974.

Deist, Ferdinand E. *The Material Culture of the Bible: An Introduction.* Sheffield: Sheffield Academic, 2000.

Hopkins, David C. "Life in Ancient Palestine." *NIB* 1:213–27.

King, Philip J., and Lawrence E. Stager. *Life in Biblical Israel.* Louisville: Westminster John Knox, 2001.

Monson, J., et al. *Student Map Manual: Historical Geography of the Bible Lands.* Jerusalem: Pictorial Archive (Near Eastern History), 1979.

Pritchard, James B., ed. *The Harper Atlas of the Bible.* New York: Harper & Row, 1987.

Rainey, Anson F., and R. Steven Notley. *The Sacred Bridge: Carta's Atlas of the Biblical World.* Jerusalem: Carta, 2006.

Raphael, C. Nicholas. "Geography and the Bible (Palestine)." *ABD* 2:964–77.

Rogerson, John. *Atlas of the Bible.* New York: Facts on File, 1985.

Archaeology

Dever, William G. *What Did the Biblical Writers Know and When Did They Know It? What Archaeology Can Tell Us about the Reality of Ancient Israel.* Grand Rapids: Eerdmans, 2001.

Lance, Darrell. *The Old Testament and the Archeologist.* Philadelphia: Fortress Press, 1981.

Laughlin, Maxwell J. "Archaeology." *NIDB* 1:232–47.

Levy, Thomas E., ed. *The Archaeology of Society in the Holy Land.* New York: Facts on File, 1995.

The Ancient Near East

Baines, John, and Jaromir Málek. *Atlas of Ancient Egypt*. New York: Facts on File, 1980.

Hallo, William W., and William R. Simpson. *The Ancient Near East: A History*. 2nd ed. New York: Harcourt Brace Jovanovich, 1998.

Kuhrt, Amélie. *The Ancient Near East ca. 3000-333 B.C.* 2 vols. London: Routledge, 1995.

Roaf, Michael. *Cultural Atlas of Mesopotamia and the Ancient Near East*. New York: Facts on File, 1990.

Snell, Daniel C. *Life in the Ancient Near East, 3100-332 B.C.* New Haven: Yale University Press, 1997.

Chapter 3: The Literary History of the Hebrew Bible
Ancient Near Eastern Texts

Hallo, William W., and K. Lawson Younger Jr., eds. *The Context of Scripture: Canonical Compositions from the Biblical World*. 3 vols. New York: Brill, 1997–2000.

Long, Burke O., and Simon B. Parker, eds. *Society of Biblical Literature Writings from the Ancient World*. Atlanta: Scholars, 1990–.

Pritchard, James B., ed. *Ancient Near Eastern Texts Relating to the Old Testament*. 3rd ed. Princeton: Princeton University Press, 1969.

Sparks, Kenton L. *Ancient Texts for the Study of the Hebrew Bible*. Peabody, Mass.: Hendrickson, 2005.

Ancient Texts Dependent on the Hebrew Bible

Charlesworth, James H., ed. *The Old Testament Pseudepigrapha*. 2 vols. Garden City, N.Y.: Doubleday, 1983, 1985.

DeSilva, David A. "Apocrypha, Deuterocanonical." *NIDB* 1:195–200.

———. *Introducing the Apocrypha: Context, Message and Significance*. Grand Rapids: Baker, 2002.

Nickelsburg, George. *Jewish Literature between the Bible and the Mishnah: A Historical and Literary Introduction*. 2nd ed. Minneapolis: Fortress Press, 2005.

Dead Sea Scrolls

Brooke, George J.. "Dead Sea Scrolls." *NIDB* 2:52–63.

Cross, Frank M. *The Ancient Library of Qumran*. 3rd ed. Sheffield: Sheffield Academic, 1995.

Schiffman, Lawrence H., and James C. Vanderkam, eds. *Encyclopedia of the Dead Sea Scrolls*. 2 vols. New York: Oxford University Press, 2000.

Wise, Michael, Martin G. Abegg Jr., and Edward Cook. *The Dead Sea Scrolls: A New Translation*. Rev. ed. San Francisco: HarperSanFrancisco, 2005.

New Testament and Talmud

Duling, Dennis, and Norman Perrin. *The New Testament: Proclamation, Parenesis, Myth and History*. 3rd ed. New York: Harcourt Brace Jovanovich, 1994.

Koester, Helmut. *Introduction to the New Testament, History and Literature of Early Christianity*. 2 vols. 2nd ed. New York: de Gruyter, 1995.

Neusner, Jacob. *The Oral Torah: The Sacred Books in Judaism*. Atlanta: Scholars, 1991.

Strack, Hermann L., and Gunter Stemberger. *Introduction to the Talmud and Midrash*. Minneapolis: Fortress Press, 1996.

How the Hebrew Bible Came to Be

Niditch, Susan. *Oral World and Written Word: Ancient Israelite Literature.* Louisville: Westminster John Knox, 1996.

Rast, Walter. *Tradition History of the Old Testament.* Philadelphia: Fortress Press, 1972.

Schniedewind, William M. *How the Bible Became a Book: The Textualization of Ancient Israel.* New York: Cambridge University Press, 2004.

Tov, Emanuel. *Textual Criticism of the Hebrew Bible.* 2nd ed. Minneapolis: Fortress Press / Assen: Van Gorcum, 2001.

Treboille, Julio. "Canon of the Old Testament." *NIDB* 1:548–63.

Translations of the Hebrew Bible

Crim, Keith R. "Modern English Versions of the Bible." *NIB* 1:22–32.

DeRegt, L. J. "Bible Translation Theory." *NIDB* 1:452–53.

Sanderson, Judith E. "Ancient Texts and Versions of the Old Testament." *NIB* 1:292–304.

Prologue to Part II: On the Sources for Israel's Premonarchic History

Campbell, Anthony F., and Mark A. O'Brien. *Sources of the Pentateuch: Texts, Introductions, Annotations.* Minneapolis: Fortress Press, 1993.

———. *Unfolding the Deuteronomistic History: Origins, Upgrades, Present Text.* Minneapolis: Fortress Press, 2000.

Coote, Robert B., and David Robert Ord. *The Bible's First History.* Philadelphia: Fortress Press, 1989.

Friedman, Richard Elliott. "Torah (Pentateuch)." *ABD* 6:605–22.

Gottwald, Norman K. *The Tribes of Yahweh. A Sociology of the Religion of Liberated Israel.* Twentieth anniversary edition with new preface. Sheffield: Sheffield Academic, 1999.

McKenzie, Steven L. "Deuteronomistic History." *ABD* 5:160–68.

Pury, Albert de. "Yahwist ("I") Source." *ABD* 6:1012–20.

Whybray, R. Norman. *Introduction to the Pentateuch.* Grand Rapids: Eerdmans, 1995.

Chapter 4: The Fathers and Mothers of Israel

Alter, Robert. *The Art of Biblical Narrative.* New York: Basic, 1981.

Delaney, Carol. *Abraham on Trial: The Social Legacy of Biblical Myth.* Princeton: Princeton University Press, 1998.

Gunkel, Hermann. *The Stories of Genesis.* Vallejo, Calif.: Bibal, 1994.

Hendel, Ronald. "Genesis, Book of." *ABD* 2:933–41.

Westermann, Claus. *Genesis 12-36: A Commentary,* 23–131. Minneapolis: Augsburg Publishing House, 1985.

Chapter 5: Traditions about Moses: Exodus, Covenant, Lawgiving

Alt, Albrecht. "The Origins of Israelite Law." *Essays on Old Testament History and Religion.* Oxford: Basil Blackwell, 1966.

Assmann, Jan. *Moses the Egyptian: The Memory of Egypt in Western Monotheism.* Cambridge: Harvard University Press, 1997.

Coats, George W. *Moses: Heroic Man, Man of God.* Sheffield: Sheffield Academic, 1988.

Crüsemann, Frank. *The Torah: Theology and Social History of Old Testament Law.* Minneapolis: Fortress Press, 1996.

Dykstra, Laurel A. *Set Them Free: The Other Side of Exodus.* Maryknoll: Orbis, 2002.

Hillers, Delbert R. *Covenant: The History of a Biblical Idea.* Baltimore: Johns Hopkins University Press, 1973.

Larsson, Göran. *Bound for Freedom: The Book of Exodus in Jewish and Christian Traditions.* Peabody, Ma.: Hendrickson, 1999.

Redford, Donald B. *Egypt, Canaan, and Israel in Ancient Times.* Princeton: Princeton University Press, 1992.

Walzer, Michael. *Exodus and Revolution.* New York: Basic, 1984.

Yerushalmi, Yosef Hayim. *Freud's Moses: Judaism Terminable and Interminable.* New Haven: Yale University Press, 1991.

Chapter 6: Traditions about Intertribal Israel's Rise to Power in Canaan

Boer, Roland, ed. *Tracking "The Tribes of Yahweh": On the Trail of a Classic.* Sheffield: Sheffield Academic, 2002.

Chaney, Marvin L. "Ancient Palestinian Peasant Movements and the Formation of Premonarchic Israel." *Palestine in Transition: The Emergence of Ancient Israel*, ed. D. N. Freedman and D. F. Graf, 39–90. Sheffield: Almond, 1983.

Dever, William G. *Who Were the Israelites and Where Did They Come From?* Grand Rapids: Eerdmans, 2003.

Gottwald, Norman K. "Israel, Origins of." *NIDB* 3:132–38.

———. *The Tribes of Yahweh. A Sociology of the Religion of Liberated Israel, 1250-1050 B.C.E.* Twentieth anniversary edition with new preface. Sheffield: Sheffield Academic, 1999.

Lemche, Niels P. *Early Israel: Anthropological and Historical Studies on Israelite Society before the Monarchy.* Leiden: E. J. Brill, 1985.

McDermott, John J. *What They Are Saying about the Formation of Israel.* Mahwah, N.J.: Paulist, 1998.

Smith, Mark S. *The Early History of God: Yahweh and the Other Deities of Ancient Israel.* 2nd ed. Grand Rapids: Eerdmans / Dearborn, Mich.: Dove, 2002.

Yee, Gale A., ed. *Judges and Method: New Approaches in Biblical Studies.* 2nd ed. Minneapolis: Fortress Press, 2007.

Prologue to Part III: On the Sources for Israel's Monarchic History
Chronology

Cogan, Mordechai. "Chronology, Hebrew Bible." *ABD* 1:1002–11.

Hooker, Paul K. "Chronology of the Old Testament." *NIDB* 1:636–43.

Thiele, Edwin R. *The Mysterious Numbers of the Hebrew Kings.* 3rd ed. Grand Rapids: Zondervan, 1983.

The Deuteronomistic History

Cross, Frank M. *Canaanite Myth and Hebrew Epic: Essays in the History of the Religion of Israel*, 272–89. Cambridge: Harvard University Press, 1973.

Knoppers, Gary N. *Two Nations Under God: The Deuteronomistic History of Solomon and the Dual Monarchies.* 2 vols. Atlanta: Scholars, 1993–94.

Lasine, Stuart. *Knowing Kings: Knowledge, Power, and Narcissism in the Hebrew Bible.* Atlanta: Scholars, 2001.

McKenzie, Steven L. *The Trouble with Kings: The Composition of the Book of Kings in the Deuteronomistic History.* Leiden: Brill, 1991.

Noth, Martin. *The Deuteronomistic History.* Sheffield: JSOT Press, 1981.

Archaeology of the Monarchy

Dever, William G. *What Did the Biblical Writers Know and When Did They Know It? What Archaeology Can Tell Us about the Reality of Ancient Israel.* Grand Rapids: Eerdmans, 2001.

Finkelstein, Israel, and Amihai Mazar. *The Quest for the Historical Israel: Debating Archaeology and the History of Early Israel,* ed. Brian B. Schmidt, chapters 4–6. Atlanta: Society of Biblical Literature, 2007.

Finkelstein, Israel, and Neil Asher Silberman. *The Bible Unearthed: Archaeology's New Vision of Ancient Israel and the Origin of Its Sacred Texts.* New York: Free Press, 2001.

King, Philip J. *Amos, Hosea, Micah: An Archaeological Commentary.* Louisville: Westminster John Knox, 1988.

——— . *Jeremiah: An Archaeological Commentary.* Louisville: Westminster John Knox, 1993.

Levy, Thomas E., ed. *The Archaeology of Society in the Holy Land*, chapter 22 by John S. Holladay Jr. and chapter 24 by William G. Dever. New York: Facts on File, 1995.

Forms and Settings of Prophetic Speech

Ben-Zvi, Ehud. and Michael H. Floyd, eds. *Writings and Speech in Israelite and Ancient Near Eastern Prophecy.* Atlanta: Society of Biblical Literature, 2000.

Blenkinsopp, Joseph. *A History of Prophecy in Israel.* Rev. ed. Louisville: Westminster John Knox, 1996.

Gitay, Jehoshua, ed. *Prophecy and Prophets: The Diversity of Contemporary Issues in Scholarship.* Atlanta: Scholars, 1997.

Koch, Klaus. *The Prophets.* 2 vols. Philadelphia: Fortress Press, 1983–84.

Nissinen, Martin, ed. *Prophecy in Its Ancient Near Eastern Context: Mesopotamian, Biblical, and Arabian Perspectives.* Atlanta: Society of Biblical Literature, 2000.

Overholt, Thomas W. *Channels of Prophecy: The Social Dynamic of Prophetic Activity.* Minneapolis: Fortress Press, 1989.

Petersen, David L. *The Roles of Israel's Prophets.* Sheffield: JSOT Press, 1981.

Westermann, Claus. *Basic Forms of Prophetic Speech.* Philadelphia: Fortress Press, 1967.

——— . *Prophetic Oracles of Salvation in the Old Testament.* Louisville: Westminster John Knox, 1991.

Wilson, Robert R. *Prophecy and Society in Ancient Israel.* Philadelphia: Fortress Press, 1980.

Chapter 7: Traditions about the United Kingdom

Alt, Albrecht. "The Formation of the Israelite State in Palestine." *Essays on Old Testament History and Religion*, 171–237. Oxford: Basil Blackwell, 1966.

Finkelstein, Israel, and Neil Asher Silberman. *David and Solomon: In Search of the Bible's Sacred Kings and the Roots of the Western Tradition.* New York: Free Press, 2006.

Flanagan, James. *David's Social Drama: A Hologram of Israel's Early Iron Age.* Sheffield: Almond, 1988.

Frick, Frank S. "Social Science Methods and Theories of Significance for the Study of the Israelite Monarchy." *Semeia* 37 (1986): 9–52.

Halpern, Baruch. *David's Secret Demons: Messiah, Murderer, Traitor, King.* Grand Rapids: Eerdmans, 2001.

Handy, Lowell K., ed. *The Age of Solomon: Scholarship at the Turn of the Millennium.* Leiden: Brill, 1997.

McKenzie, Steven L. *King David: A Biography.* Oxford: Oxford University Press, 2000.

Schniedewind, William M. *Society and the Promise to David: The Reception History of 2 Samuel 7:1-17.* New York/Oxford: Oxford University Press, 1999.

Enduring Structural Effects of the Monarchy

Chaney, Marvin L. "Systemic Study of the Israelite Monarchy." *Semeia* 37 (1986): 53–76.

Coote, Robert B. "Israel, Social and Economic Development of." *NIDB* 3:138–43.

Gottwald, Norman K. "Government, OT." *NIBD* 2:644–54.

———. *The Politics of Ancient Israel.* Louisville: Westminster John Knox, 2001.

Holladay, John S., Jr. "The Kingdoms of Israel and Judah: Political and Economic Centralization in the Iron IIA-B (ca. 1000-750 B.C.E)." In *The Archaeology of Society in the Holy Land,* ed. Thomas E. Levy, 368–98. New York: Facts on File, 1995.

Lenski, Gerhard E. *Power and Privilege: A Theory of Social Stratification.* Chapel Hill: University of North Carolina Press, 1984.

Lowery, Richard H. *The Reforming Kings: Cults and Society in First Temple Judah.* Sheffield: JSOT Press, 1991.

The Yahwist (see also Prologue to Part II)

Jobling, David. "The Myth Semantics of Genesis 2:4b–3:24." *Semeia* 18 (1980): 41–49.

Kille, D. Andrew. "Exploring Genesis" and "A Myth of Human Maturation: Developmental Readings." In *Psychological Biblical Criticism,* 39–55, 109–24. Guides to Biblical Scholarship. Minneapolis: Fortress Press, 2001.

L'Heureux, Conrad E. *In and Out of Paradise: The Book of Genesis from Adam and Eve to the Tower of Babel.* Mahwah, N.J.: Paulist, 1983.

Van Seters, John. *Prologue to History: The Yahwist as Historian in Genesis.* Louisville: Westminster John Knox, 1992.

David and Zion Traditions

Batto, Bernard F., and Kathryn L. Roberts, eds. *David and Zion: Biblical Studies in Honor of J. J. M. Roberts.* Winona Lake, Ind.: Eisenbrauns, 2004.

Levenson, Jon D. "Zion Traditions." *ABD* 6:1098–102.

Roberts, J. J. M. "Kingship and Messiah." In *The Bible and the Ancient Near East,* 313–89. Winona Lake, Ind.: Eisenbrauns, 2002.

Chapter 8: Traditions about the Northern Kingdom

Alt, Albrecht. "The Monarchy in Israel and Judah." In *Essays on Old Testament History and Religion,* 239–59. Oxford: Blackwell, 1966.

Boer, Roland. *Jameson and Jeroboam*. Atlanta: Scholars, 1996.

Buccellati, Giorgio. *Cities and Nations of Ancient Syria: An Essay on Political Institutions with Special Reference to the Israelite Kingdoms*. Rome: Istituto di Studi del Vicino Oriente, 1967.

Coote, Robert B. *In Defense of Revolution: The Elohist History*. Minneapolis: Fortress Press, 1981.

Cross, Frank M. *Caananite Myth and Hebrew Epic*, 219–29. Cambridge: Harvard University Press, 1973.

Hayes, John H., and J. Maxwell Miller. *A History of Ancient Israel and Judah*, 218–339. 2nd ed. Philadelphia: Westminster, 2006.

Toews, Wesley I. *Monarchy and Religious Institution in Israel under Jeroboam I*. Atlanta: Scholars, 1993.

Elijah and Elisha

Bergen, Wesley. *Elisha and the End of Prophetism*. Sheffield: Sheffield Academic, 1999.

Brodie, Thomas L. *The Crucial Bridge: The Elijah-Elisha Narrative as an Interpretive Synthesis of Genesis-Kings and a Literary Model of the Gospels*. Collegeville, Minn.: Liturgical, 2000.

Brueggemann, Walter. *Testimony to Otherwise: The Witness of Elijah and Elisha*. St. Louis: Chalice, 2001.

Coote, Robert B., ed. *Elijah and Elisha in Socioliterary Perspective*. Atlanta: Scholars, 1992.

Gottwald, Norman K. "The Plot Structure of Marvel or Problem Resolution Stories in the Elijah-Elisha Narratives and Some Musings on *Sitz im Leben*." In *The Hebrew Bible in Its Social World and in Ours*, 119–30. Atlanta: Scholars, 1993.

Rofé, Alexander. *The Prophetical Stories*. Jerusalem: Magnes, 1988.

White, Marsha. *The Elisha Legends and Jehu's Coup*. Atlanta: Scholars, 1997.

Amos

Carroll, M. Daniel R. *Contexts for Amos: Prophetic Poetics in Latin American Perspective*. Sheffield: JSOT Press, 1992.

Coote, Robert B. *Amos among the Prophets: Composition and Theology*. Philadelphia: Fortress Press, 1981.

Moeller, Karl. *A Prophet in Debate: The Rhetoric of Persuasion in the Book of Amos*. Sheffield: Sheffield Academic, 2003.

Premnath, Devadasan N. "Amos, Book of." *NIDB* 1:135–41.

———. *Eighth Century Prophets: A Social Analysis*. St. Louis: Chalice, 2003.

Wolff, Hans Walter. *Amos the Prophet: The Man and His Background*. Philadelphia: Fortress Press, 1973.

Hosea

Burch, Bruce C. "Hosea, Book of." *NIDB* 2:894–900.

Cook, Stephen L. *The Social Roots of Biblical Yahwism*. Atlanta: Society of Biblical Literature, 2004, chaps. 6 and 8.

Sherwood, Yvonne. *The Prostitute and the Prophet: Hosea's Marriage in Literary-Theoretical Perspective*. Sheffield: Sheffield Academic, 1996.

Weems, Renita J. *Battered Love: Marriage, Sex, and Violence in the Hebrew Prophets*. Overtures to Biblical Theology. Minneapolis: Fortress Press, 1995.

Yee, Gale A. *Composition and Tradition in the Book of Hosea: A Redaction-Critical Investigation*. Atlanta: Scholars, 1987.

Chapter 9: Traditions about the Southern Kingdom

Cogan, Mordechai. "Judah under Assyrian Hegemony: A Reexamination of Imperialism and Religion." *Journal of Biblical Literature* 112 (1993): 403–14.

Grabbe, Lester L., ed., *"Like a Bird in a Cage": The Invasion of Sennarcherib in 701 B.C.E.* Sheffield: Sheffield Academic, 2003.

Hayes, John H., and J. Maxwell Miller, *A History of Ancient Israel and Judah*, 340–415. 2nd ed. Louisville: Westminster John Knox, 2006.

Kim, Uriah Y. *Decolonizing Josiah: Toward a Postcolonial Reading of the Deuteronomic History.* Sheffield: Sheffield Phoenix, 2006.

Kuan, Jeffrey Kah-Jin. "Hezekiah." *NIDB* 2:818–21.

Nakanose, Shigeyuki. *Josiah's Passover: Sociology and the Liberating Bible.* Maryknoll, N.Y.: Orbis, 1993.

Sweeney, Marvin. *King Josiah of Judah: The Lost Messiah of Israel.* New York: Oxford University Press, 2001.

Micah

Cook, Stephen L. *The Social Roots of Biblical Yahwism.* Atlanta: Society of Biblical Literature, 2004, chaps. 5 and 7.

Mosala, Itumeleng J. *Biblical Hermeneutics and Black Theology in South Africa.* Grand Rapids: Eerdmans, 1989.

Wolff, Hans Walter. *Micah the Prophet.* Philadelphia: Fortress Press, 1981.

Isaiah

Blank, Sheldon, *Prophetic Faith in Isaiah.* New York: Harper & Brothers, 1958.

Childs, Brevard S. *Isaiah and the Assyrian Crisis.* Naperville, Ill.: Alec R. Allenson, 1967.

Gottwald, Norman K. *All the Kingdoms of the Earth: Israelite Prophecy and International Relations in the Ancient Near East*, 147–208. Reprint. Minneapolis: Fortress Press, 2007 [1964].

Hayes, John H. and Stuart A. Irvine. *Isaiah: The Eighth Century Prophet.* Nashville: Abingdon, 1987.

Rubenstein, Richard E. *Thus Saith the Lord: The Revolutionary Moral Vision of Isaiah and Jeremiah.* Orlando: Harcourt, 2006.

Seitz, Christopher. "Isaiah, Book of (First Isaiah)." *ABD* 13:472–88.

———. *Zion's Final Destiny: The Development of the Book of Isaiah: A Reassessment of Isaiah 36–39.* Minneapolis: Fortress Press, 1991.

Sheppard, Gerald T. "The Anti-Assyrian Redaction and the Canonical Context of Isaiah 1-39." *Journal of Biblical Literature* 104 (1985): 193–216.

Deuteronomy

Berman, Joshua. *Biblical Revolutions: The Transformation of Social and Political Thought in the Ancient Near East.* New York: Oxford University Press, 2008.

Levinson, Bernard M. *Deuteronomy and the Hermeneutics of Legal Innovation.* New York: Oxford University Press, 1997.

McBride, S. Dean. "Deuteronomy, Book of." *NIDB* 2:108–17.

Polzin, Robert. *Moses and the Deuteronomist.* New York: Seabury, 1980.

Weinfeld, Moshe. *Deuteronomy and the Deuteronomic School.* Oxford: Clarendon, 1972.

Nahum, Zephaniah, Habakkuk

Cathcart, Kevin J. "Nahum, Book of." *ABD* 4:998–1000.

Gowan, Donald E. "Habakkuk, Book of." *NIDB* 2:705–9.

———. *The Triumph of Faith in Habakkuk*. Atlanta: John Knox, 1976.

House, Paul R. *Zephaniah: A Prophetic Drama*. Sheffield: Almond, 1987.

Kselman, John S. "Zephaniah, Book of." *ABD* 6:1077–80.

Sweeney, Marvin A. "Habakkuk, Book of." *ABD* 3:1–6.

Jeremiah

Carroll, Robert P. *From Chaos to Covenant: Prophecy in the Book of Jeremiah*. New York: Crossroad, 1981.

———. *Jeremiah: A Commentary*. Philadelphia: Westminster, 1986.

Gottwald, Norman K. *All the Kingdoms of the Earth: Israelite Prophecy and International Relations in the Ancient Near East*, 239–302. Reprint. Minneapolis: Fortress Press, 2007 [1964].

Holladay, William L. *Jeremiah: A Fresh Reading*. New York: Pilgrim, 1990.

———. *Jeremiah: Spokesman Out of Time*. Philadelphia: United Church Press, 1974.

Lundbom, Jack R. "Jeremiah, Book of." *ABD* 3:706–21.

O'Connor, Kathleen M. *The Confessions of Jeremiah: Their Interpretation and Role in Chapters 1–25*. Atlanta: Scholars, 1987.

Perdue, Leo G., and Brian W. Kovacs, eds. *A Prophet to the Nations: Essays in Jeremiah Studies*. Winona Lake, Ind.: Eisenbrauns, 1984.

Rubenstein, Richard E. *Thus Saith the Lord: The Revolutionary Moral Vision of Isaiah and Jeremiah*. Orlando: Harcourt, 2006.

Sharp, Carolyn J. *Prophecy and Ideology in Jeremiah: Struggles for Authority in the Deutero-Jeremianic Prose*. London: T & T Clark, 2003.

Stulman, Louis, "Jeremiah, Book of." *NIDB* 3:220–35.

Prologue to Part IV: On the Sources for Israel's Colonial History in Dispersion and Restoration

Avi-Yonah, *The Holy Land from the Persian to the Arab Conquests (536 B.C. to A.D. 640)*. Grand Rapids: Baker, 1977.

Cross, Frank M., "A Reconstruction of the Judaean Restoration." In *From Epic to Canon: History and Literature in Ancient Israel*, 151–72. Baltimore: Johns Hopkins University Press, 1998.

———. "Samaria and Jerusalem in the Era of the Restoration." In *From Epic to Canon: History and Literature in Ancient Israel*, 173–202. Baltimore: Johns Hopkins University Press, 1998.

Stern, Ephraim. *Archaeology of the Land of the Bible*. Vol. 2: *The Assyrian, Babylonian, and Persian Periods, 732-332 B.C.E.* New York: Doubleday, 2001.

———. *Material Culture of the Land of the Bible in the Persian Period, 538-332 B.C.* Warminster, Wiltshire, U.K.: Aris & Phillips, 1982.

Chapter 10: Sociohistorical Horizons of Colonial Israel
Neo-Babylonian Dominion

Ackroyd, Peter R. *Exile and Restoration: A Study of Hebrew Thought of the Sixth Century B.C.* Philadelphia: Westminster, 1968.

Barstad, Hans M. *The Myth of the Empty Land: A Study in the History and Archaeology of Judah during the "Exilic" Period.* Oslo: Scandinavian University Press, 1996.

Grayson, A. Kirk. "Mesopotamia, History of (Babylonia)." *ABD* 1:756–77.

Hayes, John H., and J. Maxwell Miller. *A History of Ancient Israel and Judah*, 416–36. 2nd ed. Louisville: Westminster John Knox, 2006.

Klein, Ralph W. "Exile." *NIDB* 2:367–70.

———. *Israel in Exile: A Theological Interpretation.* 2nd ed. Minneapolis: Fortress Press, 2002.

Lipschits, Oded. *The Fall and Rise of Jerusalem.* Winona Lake, Ind.: Eisenbrauns, 2005.

Lipschits, Oded, and Joseph Blenkinsopp, eds. *Judah and the Judeans in the Neo-Babylonian Period.* Winona Lake, Ind.: Eisenbrauns, 2003.

Smith-Christopher, Daniel L. *A Biblical Theology of Exile.* Overtures to Biblical Theology. Minneapolis: Fortress Press, 2002.

———.*The Religion of the Landless: A Sociology of the Babylonian Exile.* Bloomington, Ind.: Meyer-Stone Books, 1989.

Persian Dominion

Berquist, John L. *Judaism in Persia's Shadow: A Social and Historical Approach.* Minneapolis: Fortress Press, 1995.

Briant, Pierre. "Persian Empire." *ABD* 5:236–44.

Carter, Charles. *The Emergence of Yehud in the Persian Period: A Social and Demographic Study.* Sheffield: Sheffield Academic, 1999.

Davies, Philip R., ed. *Second Temple Studies 1: Persian Period.* Sheffield: Sheffield Academic, 1991.

Eskenazi, Tamara C., and Kent H. Richards, eds. *Second Temple Studies 2: Temple and Community in the Persian Period.* Sheffield: Sheffield University Press, 1994.

Hayes, John H., and J. Maxwell Miller. *A History of Ancient Israel and Judah*, 437–75. 2nd ed. Louisville: Westminster John Knox, 2006.

Lipschits, Oded, and Manfred Oeming, eds. *Judah and the Judeans in the Persian Period.* Winona Lake, Ind.: Eisenbrauns, 2006.

Sacchi, Paolo. *The History of the Second Temple Period.* Sheffield: Sheffield Academic, 2000.

Weinberg, Joel P. *The Citizen-Temple Community.* Sheffield: Sheffield Academic, 1992.

Hellenistic Dominion

Bickermann, Elias J. *The Jews in the Greek Age.* Cambridge: Harvard University Press, 1988.

Davies, Philip R., and John H. Halligan, eds. *Second Temple Studies 3: Studies in Politics, Class and Material Culture.* Sheffield: Sheffield Academic, 2002.

Goodman, Martin, ed. *Jews in the Graeco-Roman World.* Oxford: Clarendon / New York: Oxford University Press, 1998.

Green, Peter. *Alexander to Actium: The Historical Evolution of the Hellenistic Age.* Berkeley: University of California Press, 1990.

Hengel, Martin. *Judaism and Hellenism: Studies in Their Encounter in Palestine during the Early Hellenistic Period.* 2 vols. Philadelphia: Fortress Press, 1974.

Holbl, Gunther. *A History of the Ptolemaic Empire.* London: Routledge, 2001.

Levine, Lee I. *Judaism and Hellenism in Antiquity.* Seattle: University of Washington Press, 1998.

Momigliano, Arnaldo. *Essays on Ancient and Modern Judaism*, Part 1. Chicago: University of Chicago Press, 1987.

Tcherikover, Victor. *Hellenistic Civilization and the Jews.* New York: Jewish Publication Society of America, 1961.

Maccabean and Hasmonean Periods

Anderson, Robert T. "Samaritans." *ABD* 5:940–47.

Bar-Kochva, Bezalel. *Judas Maccabaeus: The Jewish Struggle Against the Seleucids.* Cambridge: Cambridge University Press, 1989.

Coggins, Richard J. *Samaritans and Jews.* Atlanta: John Knox, 1975.

Grabbe, Lester L. "Hasmoneans." *NIDB* 2:740–48.

Harrington, Daniel J. *The Maccabean Revolt: Anatomy of a Biblical Revolution.* Wilmington, Del.: M. Glazier, 1988.

Rajak, Tessa. "Hasmonean Dynasty." *ABD* 3:67–76.

Rappaport, Uriel. "Maccabean Revolt." *ABD* 4:433–39.

Zeitlin, Solomon. *The Rise and Fall of the Judaean State: A Political, Social and Religious History of the Second Commonwealth, Vol. 1: 332-37 B.C.E.* Philadelphia: Jewish Publication Society of America, 1962.

Chapter 11: Traditions of Colonial Israel: Completing the Law and the Prophets

Barrera, Julio C. "The Origins of the Tripartite Old Testament Canon." In *The Canon Debate*, ed. Lee Martin McDonald and James A. Sanders, 128–45. Peabody, Mass.: Hendrickson, 2002.

Barton, John. *Oracles of God: Perceptions of Ancient Prophecy in Israel After the Exile.* New York: Oxford University Press, 1986.

Blenkinsopp, Joseph. *Prophecy and Canon: A Contribution to the Study of Jewish Origins.* Notre Dame, Ind.: Notre Dame University Press, 1977.

———. *Sage, Priest, Prophet: Religious and Intellectual Leadership in Ancient Israel.* Louisville: Westminster John Knox, 1995.

Clements, Ronald E. *Old Testament Theology: A Fresh Approach*, chapters 5 and 6. Atlanta: John Knox, 1978.

Crüsemann, Frank. *The Torah: Theology and Social History of Old Testament Law*, chapter 8. Minneapolis: Fortress Press, 1996.

Grabbe, Lester L., and Alice Ogden Bellis, eds. *The Priests in the Prophets: The Portrayal of Priests, Prophets and Other Religious Specialists in the Latter Prophets.* London: T & T Clark, 2004.

Morgan, Donn F. *Between Text and Community: The "Writings" in Canonical Interpretation.* Minneapolis: Fortress Press, 1990.

The Priestly Writer

Coote, Robert C., and David Robert Ord. *In the Beginning: Creation and the Priestly History.* Minneapolis: Fortress Press, 1991.

Haran, Menahem. *Temple and Temple-Service in Ancient Israel.* Winona Lake, Ind.: Eisenbrauns, 1985.

Knoh, Israel. *The Sanctuary of Silence: The Priestly Torah and the Holiness School.* Minneapolis: Fortress Press, 1995.

Milgrom, Jacob. "Holy, Holiness, OT." *NIDB* 2:846–58.

——— . "Priestly ("P") Source." *ABD* 5:454–61.

Olyan, Saul M. *Rites and Ranks: Hierarchy in Biblical Representations of Cult.* Princeton: Princeton University Press, 2000.

Ezekiel

Cook, Stephen L., and Corrine L. Patton, eds. *Ezekiel's Hierarchical World: Wrestling with a Tiered Reality.* Atlanta: Society of Biblical Literature, 2004.

Davis Ellen F. *Swallowing the Scroll: Textuality and the Dynamics of Discourse in Ezekiel's Prophecy.* Sheffield: Almond, 1989.

Halperin, David J. *Seeking Ezekiel: Text and Psychology.* University Park: Pennsylvania State University Press, 1993.

Hals, Ronald. *Ezekiel.* Grand Rapids: Eerdmans, 1989.

Kaminsky, Joel S. *Corporate Responsibility in the Hebrew Bible.* Sheffield: Sheffield Academic, 1995.

Lapsley, Jacqueline E. *Can These Bones Live? The Problem of the Moral Self in the Book of Ezekiel.* New York: de Gruyter, 2000.

Mein, Andrew. *Ezekiel and the Ethics of Exile.* New York: Oxford University Press, 2001.

Odell, Margaret S. "Ezekiel, Book of." *NIDB* 2:387–96.

Robson, James. *Word and Spirit in Ezekiel.* New York: T & T Clark, 2006.

Isaiah of the Exile (Deutero-Isaiah)

Adams, Jim W. *The Performative Nature and Function of Isaiah 40-55.* New York: T & T Clark, 2006.

Clifford, Richard J. *Fair Spoken and Persuading: An Interpretation of Second Isaiah.* New York: Paulist, 1984.

Gottwald, Norman K. *All the Kingdoms of the Earth: Israelite Prophecy and International Relations in the Ancient Near East,* 330–50. Reprint. Minneapolis: Fortress Press, 2007 [1964].

——— . "Social Class and Ideology in Isaiah 40-55: An Eagletonian Reading." *Semeia* 59 (1992): 35–57.

Janowski, Bernd, and Peter Stuhlmachr, eds. *The Suffering Servant: Isaiah 53 in Jewish and Christian Sources.* Grand Rapids: Eerdmans, 2004.

Seitz, Christopher R. *Zion's Final Destiny: The Development of the Book of Isaiah: A Reassessment of Isaiah 36-39.* Minneapolis: Fortress Press, 1991.

Willey, Patricia Tull. *Remember the Former Things: The Recollection of Previous Texts in Second Isaiah.* Atlanta: Scholars Press, 1997.

Wilson, Andrew. *The Nations in Deutero-Isaiah: A Study on Composition and Structure.* Lewiston, N.Y.: Mellen, 1986.

Whybray, R. Norman. *Thanksgiving for a Liberated Prophet: An Interpretation of Isaiah 53.* Sheffield: JSOT Press, 1978.

Williamson, H. G. M. *The Book Called Isaiah: Deutero-Isaiah's Role in Composition and Redaction.* Oxford: Clarendon, 1994.

Haggai and Zechariah 1–8

Boda, Mark J. H., "Haggai, Book of." *NIDB* 2:715–18.

Curtis, Byron G., *Up the Steep and Stony Road: The Book of Zechariah in Social Location Trajectory Analysis.* Atlanta: Society of Biblical Literature, 2006.

Kessler, John. *The Book of Haggai: Prophecy and Society in Early Persian Yehud.* Leiden: Brill, 2002.

Rose, Wolter H. *Zemah and Zerubbabel: Messianic Expectations in the Early Postexilic Period.* Sheffield: Sheffield Academic, 2000.

Stuhlmueller, Caroll. *Rebuilding with Hope: A Commentary on the Books of Haggai and Zechariah.* Grand Rapids: Eerdmans, 1988.

Sykes, Seth. *Time and Space in Haggai-Zechariah 1-8: A Bakhtinian Analysis of a Prophetic Chronicle.* New York: Peter Lang, 2002.

Tollington, Janet E. *Tradition and Innovation in Haggai and Zechariah 1-8.* Sheffield: JSOT Press, 1993.

Isaiah 56–66 (Trito-Isaiah)

Baer, David A. *When We All Go Home: Translation and Theology in LXX Isaiah 56-66.* Sheffield: Sheffield Academic, 2001.

Emmerson, Grace I. *Isaiah 56-66.* Sheffield: JSOT Press, 1992.

Smith, Paul A. *Rhetoric and Redaction in Trito-Isaiah: The Structure, Growth, and Authorship of Isaiah 56-66.* Leiden: Brill, 1995.

Malachi

Glazier-McDonald, Beth. *Malachi: The Divine Messenger.* Atlanta: Scholars, 1987.

O'Brien, Julia M. *Priest and Levite in Malachi.* Atlanta: Scholars, 1990.

Redditt, Paul L. "Malachi, Book of." *NIDB* 3:772–76.

Weyde, Karl William. *Prophecy and Teaching: Prophetic Authority, Form Problems, and the Use of Traditions in the Book of Malachi.* Berlin: de Gruyter, 2000.

Obadiah and Joel

Ackroyd, Peter. "Obadiah, Book of." *ABD* 5:2–4.

McQueen, Larry R. *Joel and the Spirit: The Cry of a Prophetic Hermeneutic.* Sheffield: Sheffield Academic, 1995.

Nogalski, James D. "Joel, Book of." *NIDB* 3:339–43.

Simkins, Ronald. *Yahweh's Activity in History and Nature in the Book of Joel.* Lewiston, N.Y.: Mellen, 1991.

Strazicich, John. *Joel's Use of Scripture and Scripture's Use of Joel: Appropriation and Resignification in Second Temple Judaism and Christianity.* Leiden: Brill, 2007.

Chapter 12: Traditions of Colonial Israel: The Writings
1–2 Chronicles

Japhet, Sara. *The Ideology of the Book of Chronicles and Its Place in Biblical Thought.* New York: Peter Lang, 1989.

Kalimi, Isaac. *An Ancient Israelite Historian: Studies in the Chronicler, His Time, Place and Writing.* Assen: Van Gorcum, 2005.

———. *The Reshaping of Ancient Israelite History in Chronicles.* Winona Lake, Ind.: Eisenbrauns, 2005.

Klein, Ralph A. "Chronicles, Book of, 1-2." *ABD* 1:992–1002.

Knoppers, Gary N. "Chronicles, First and Second Books of." *NIDB* 1:622–31.

Throntveit, M. A. *When Kings Speak: Royal Speech and Royal Prayer in Chronicles.* Atlanta: Scholars, 1987.

Ezra–Nehemiah

Eskenazi, Tamara C. *In An Age of Prose: A Literary Approach to Ezra-Nehemiah.* Atlanta: Scholars, 1988.

Gottwald, Norman K. "The Expropriated and the Expropriators in Nehemiah." *Concepts of Class in Ancient Israel*, ed. Mark R. Sneed, 1–19. Atlanta: Scholars, 1999.

Hoglund, Kenneth G. *Achaemenid Imperial Administration in Syria-Palestine and the Missions of Ezra and Nehemiah.* Atlanta: Scholars, 1992.

Klein, Ralph W. "Ezra and Nehemiah, Books of." *NIDB* 2:398–404.

Talmon, Shemaryahu. "Ezra and Nehemiah (Books and Men)." *IDBSup.* 317–28.

What Is Biblical Poetry?

Alter, Robert. *The Art of Biblical Poetry.* New York: Basic, 1985.

Berlin, Adele. *The Dynamics of Biblical Parallelism.* Bloomington: University of Indiana Press, 1985.

———. "Parallelism." *ADB* 5:155–62.

Gottwald, Norman K. "Poetry, Hebrew." *IDB* 3:829–38.

Kugel, James L. *The Idea of Biblical Poetry: Parallelism and Its History.* New Haven: Yale University Press, 1981.

Psalms

Brueggemann, Walter. *The Message of the Psalms: A Theological Commentary.* Minneapolis: Augsburg Publishing House, 1984.

Gerstenberger, Erhard S. *Psalms, with an Introduction to Cultic Poetry.* 2 vols. Grand Rapids: Eerdmans, 1988, 2001.

Gunkel, Hermann. *An Introduction to the Psalms: The Genres of the Religious Lyric of Israel.* Macon, Ga.: Mercer University Press, 1998.

Limburg, James. "Psalms, Book of." *ABD* 5:522–36.

Mowinckel, Sigmund. *The Psalms in Israel's Worship.* 2 vols. Nashville: Abingdon, 1962.

Nasuti, Harry P. *Defining the Sacred Songs: Genre, Tradition and the Post-Critical Interpretation of the Psalms.* Sheffield: Sheffield Academic, 1999.

Pleins, J. David. *The Psalms: Songs of Tragedy, Hope, and Justice.* Maryknoll, N.Y.: Orbis, 1993.

Wilson, Gerald H. *The Editing of the Hebrew Psalter.* Chico, Calif.: Scholars, 1985.

Lamentations

Dobbs-Allsopp, F. W. *Weep, O Daughter of Zion: A Study of the City-Lament Genre in the Hebrew Bible.* Rome: Pontifical Biblical Institute, 1993.

Gottwald, Norman K. "Lamentations." In *The HarperCollins Bible Commentary*, 577–82. San Francisco: HarperSanFrancisco, 2000.

Hillers, Delbert. "Lamentations, Book of." *ABD* 4:137–41.

Lee, Nancy C. *The Singers of Lamentations: Cities Under Siege, from Ur to Jerusalem to Sarajevo.* Leiden: Brill, 2002.

Linafelt, Tod. *Surviving Lamentations: Catastrophe, Lament, and Protest in the Afterlife of a Biblical Book.* Chicago: University of Chicago Press, 2000.

Song of Songs

Exum, J. Cheryl. *Song of Songs: A Commentary.* Louisville: Westminster John Knox, 2005.

Murphy, Roland E. "Song of Songs, Book of." *ABD* 6:150–55.

Walsh, Carey Ellen. *Exquisite Desire: Religion, the Erotic, and the Song of Songs.* Minneapolis: Fortress Press, 2000.

Ruth

Fewell, Dana, and David M. Gunn. *Compromising Redemption: Relating Characters in the Book of Ruth.* Louisville: Westminster John Knox, 1990.

Sasson, Jack M. *Ruth: A New Translation with a Philological Commentary and a Formalist-Folklorist Interpretation.* Baltimore: Johns Hopkins University Press, 1979.

Trible, Phyllis. "Ruth, Book of." *ABD* 5:842–47.

Jonah

Craig, Kenneth M., Jr. *A Poetics of Jonah: Art in the Service of Ideology.* Columbia: University of South Carolina Press, 1993.

Marcus, David. *From Balaam to Jonah: Anti-Prophetic Satire in the Hebrew Bible.* Atlanta: Scholars, 1995.

Sherwood, Yvonne. *A Biblical Text and Its Afterlives: The Survival of Jonah in Western Culture.* Cambridge: Cambridge University Press, 2000.

Trible, Phyllis. *Rhetorical Criticism: Context, Method, and the Book of Jonah.* Minneapolis: Fortress Press, 1994.

Esther

Beal, Timothy K. *The Book of Hiding: Gender, Ethnicity, Annihilation, and Esther.* London: Routledge, 1997.

Clines, David J. A. *The Esther Scroll: The Story of the Story.* Sheffield: JSOT Press, 1984.

Day, Linda. "Esther, Book of." *NIDB* 2:317–20.

Fox, Michael V. *Character and Ideology in the Book of Esther.* Columbia: University of South Carolina Press, 1991.

What Is Wisdom?

Bergant, Dianne. *Israel's Wisdom Literature: A Liberation-Critical Reading.* Minneapolis: Fortress Press, 1997.

Ceresko, Anthony R. *Introduction to Old Testament Wisdom: A Spirituality for Liberation.* Maryknoll, N.Y.: Orbis, 1999.

Crenshaw, James L. *Old Testament Wisdom: An Introduction.* Rev. ed. Louisville: Westminster John Knox, 1998.

Murphy, Roland E. "Wisdom in the Old Testament."*ABD* 6:920–31.

Perdue, Leo G. *Wisdom and Creation: A Theology of Wisdom Literature.* Nashville: Abingdon, 1994.

Proverbs

Camp, Claudia V. *Wisdom and the Feminine in the Book of Proverbs.* Decatur, Ga.: Almond, 1985.

Lang, Bernhard. *Wisdom and the Book of Proverbs: A Hebrew Goddess Redefined.* New York: Pilgrim, 1986.

Miles, Johnny E. *Wise King—Royal Fool: Semiotics, Satire and Proverbs 1-9.* London: T & T Clark, 2004.

Sandoval, Timothy J. *The Discourse of Wealth and Poverty in the Book of Proverbs.* Leiden: Brill, 2006.

Washington, Harold C. *Wealth and Poverty in the Instruction of Amenemope and the Hebrew Proverbs.* Atlanta: Scholars, 1994.

Whybray, R. Norman. *The Book of Proverbs: A Survey of Modern Study*. Leiden: Brill, 1995.

———. *The Composition of the Book of Proverbs*. Sheffield: JSOT Press, 1994.

Yoder, Christine Elisabeth. *Wisdom as a Woman of Substance: A Socioeconomic Reading of Proverbs 1-9 and 31:10-31*. Berlin: de Gruyter, 2001.

Job

Brown, William P. *The Ethos of the Cosmos: The Genesis of Moral Imagination in the Bible*. Grand Rapids: Eerdmans, 1999.

Good, Edwin M. *In Turns of Tempest: A Reading of Job*. Stanford: Stanford University Press, 1990.

Gutiérrez, Gustavo. *On Job: God-Talk and the Suffering of the Innocent*. Maryknoll, N.Y.: Orbis, 1987.

Hofman, Yair. *A Blemished Perfection: The Book of Job in Context*. Sheffield: Sheffield Academic, 1996.

Jantzen, J. Gerald. *Job*. Atlanta: John Knox, 1985.

Newsom, Carol A. *The Book of Job: A Contest of Moral Imaginations*. Oxford: Oxford University Press, 2003.

Penchansky, David. *The Betrayal of God: Ideological Conflict in Job*. Louisville: Westminster John Knox, 1990.

Perdue, Leo G. *Wisdom in Revolt: Metaphorical Theology in the Book of Job*. Sheffield: Almond, 1991.

Zukerman, Bruce. *Job the Silent: A Study in Historical Counterpoint*. New York: Oxford University Press, 1991.

Ecclesiastes

Fox, Michael V. *A Time to Tear Down and a Time to Build Up: A Rereading of Ecclesiastes*. Grand Rapids: Eerdmans, 1999.

Gianto, Augustinus, "Ecclesiastes, Book of." *NIDB* 2:178–85.

Koh, Yee-Von. *Royal Autobiography in the Book of Qoheleth*. Berlin: de Gruyter, 2006.

Leithart, Peter J. *Solomon Among the Postmoderns*. Grand Rapids: Brazos, 2007.

Ogden, Graham S. *Qoheleth*. 2nd ed. Sheffield: Sheffield Phoenix, 2007.

Salyer, Gary. *Vain Rhetoric: Private Insight and Public Debate in Ecclesiastes*. Sheffield: Sheffield Academic, 2001.

Schoors, Anton, ed. *The Preacher Sought to Find Pleasing Word: A Study of the Language of Qoheleth*. Leuven: Peeters, 1992.

———. *Qoheleth in the Context of Wisdom*. Leuven: Leuven University Press, 1998.

What Is Apocalyptic?

Carey, Greg, and L. Gregory Bloomquist, eds. *Vision and Persuasion: Rhetorical Dimensions of Apocalyptic Discourse*. St. Louis: Chalice, 1999.

Collins, John J. *The Apocalyptic Imagination: An Introduction to Jewish Apocalyptic Literature*. 2nd ed. Grand Rapids: Eerdmans, 1998.

———, ed. *The Encyclopedia of Apocalypticism*. 3 vols. New York: Continuum, 1998.

Hanson, Paul D. *The Dawn of Apocalyptic: The Historical and Sociological Roots of Jewish Apocalyptic Eschatology*. Rev. ed. Philadelphia: Fortress Press, 1979.

Hanson, Paul D., Lloyd R. Bailey Sr., and Victor P. Furnish, eds. *Old Testament Apocalyptic*. Nashville: Abingdon, 1987.

Hellholm, David, ed. *Apocalypticism in the Mediterranean World and the Near East*. Tübingen: Mohr, 1989.

Sacchi, Paolo. *Jewish Apocalyptic and Its History*. Sheffield: Sheffield Academic, 1990.

Isaiah 24–27

Bosman, Hendrick Jan, and Harm van Grol, eds. *Studies in Isaiah 24-27: The Isaiah Workshop*. Leiden: Brill, 2000.

Hibbard, James Todd. *Intertexuality in Isaiah 24-27: The Reuse and Evocation of Earlier Texts and Traditions*. Tübingen: Mohr Siebeck, 2006.

Johnson, Dan G. *From Chaos to Restoration: An Integrative Reading of Isaiah 24-27*. Sheffield: JSOT Press, 1988.

Millar, William. "Isaiah 24-27 (Little Apocalypse)." *ABD* 3:488–90.

Polaski, Donald C. *Authorizing an End: The Isaiah Apocalypse and Intertextuality*. Boston: Brill, 2001.

Zechariah 9–14

Boda, Mark J., and Michael H. Floyd, eds. *Bringing Out the Treasure: Inner Biblical Exegesis in Zechariah 9-14*. Sheffield: Sheffield Academic, 2003.

Person Raymond F. *Second Zechariah and the Deuteronomic School*. Sheffield: JSOT Press.

Petersen, David. "Isaiah 9-14." *ADB* 6:165–68.

Tuckett, Christopher, ed. *The Book of Zechariah and Its Influence*. Burlingont, Vt.: Ashgate, 2003.

Daniel

Collins, John H., and Peter W. Flint, eds. *The Book of Daniel: Composition and Reception*. 2 vols. Leiden: Brill, 2001.

Collins, John J. *Daniel, with an Introduction to Jewish Apocalyptic Literature*. Grand Rapids: Eerdmans, 1984.

Froehlich, Ida. "Time and Times and Half a Time": *Historical Consciousness in the Jewish Literature of the Persian and Hellenistic Eras*. Sheffield: Sheffield Academic, 1996.

Niskanen, Paul. *The Human and the Divine in History: Herodotus and the Book of Daniel*. London: T & T Clark, 2004.

Russell, David S. *Daniel, an Active Volcano: Reflections on the Book of Daniel*. Louisville: Westminster John Knox, 1989.

Towner, W. Sibley. "Daniel, Book of." *NIDB* 2:15–23.

van der Woude, A. S. *The Book of Daniel: In the Light of New Findings*. Leuven: Leuven University Press and Peeters, 1993.

Wills, Lawrence M. *The Jew in the Court of a Foreign King: Ancient Jewish Court Legends*. Minneapolis: Fortress Press, 1990.

Conclusion: The Interplay of Text, Concept, and Setting in the Hebrew Bible

Bach, Alice. *Women in the Hebrew Bible: A Reader*. New York: Routledge, 1999.

Barton, John. *Understanding Old Testament Ethics: Approaches and Explorations*. Louisville: Westminster John Knox, 2003.

Boer, Roland. *Marxist Criticism of the Bible*. London: T & T Clark, 2003.

Boff, Clodovis, and George V. Pixley. *The Bible, the Church, and the Poor*. Maryknoll, N.Y.: Orbis, 1989.

Brueggemann, Walter. *Theology of the Old Testament: Testimony, Dispute, Advocacy*. Minneapolis: Fortress Press, 1997.

Carroll, Robert P. *The Bible As a Problem for Christianity*. Philadelphia: Trinity Press International, 1991.

Childs, Brevard S. *Old Testament in Canonical Contexts.* Philidelphia: Fortress Press, 1986.

Clines, David J. A. *Interested Parties: The Ideology of Writers and Readers of the Hebrew Bible.* Sheffield: Sheffield Academic, 1995.

Cosgrove, Charles H. *Appealing to Scripture in Moral Discourse: Five Hermeneutical Rules.* Grand Rapids: Eerdmans, 2002.

Domeris, William Robert. *Touching the Heart of God: The Social Construction of Poverty among Biblical Peasants.* London: T & T Clark, 2007.

Eagleton, Terry. *Criticism and Ideology: A Study in Marxist Literary Theory.* New ed. London: Verso, 2006.

——— . *Ideology. An Introduction.* London: Verso, 1991.

Frye, Northrop. *The Great Code: The Bible and Literature.* New York: Harcourt Brace Jovanovich, 1982.

Gilkey, Langdon B. *Naming the Whirlwind: The Renewal of God-Language.* Indianapolis: Bobbs-Merrill, 1969.

——— . *Reaping the Whirlwind: A Christian Interpretation of History.* New York: Seabury, 1976.

Girard, René. *Violence and the Sacred.* Baltimore: Johns Hopkins University Press, 1977.

Gnuse, Robert K. *The Old Testament and Process Theology.* St. Louis: Chalice, 2000.

Gottwald, Norman K. *The Hebrew Bible In Its Social World and In Ours.* Atlanta: Scholars, 1992.

Gottwald, Norman K., and Richard A. Horsley, eds. *The Bible and Liberation: Political and Social Hermeneutics.* Maryknoll, N.Y.: Orbis, 1993.

Jameson, Frederic. *The Political Unconscious: Narrative as a Socially Symbolic Act.* Ithaca: Cornell University Press, 1981.

Kugel, James L. *The Bible As It Was.* Cambridge: Harvard University Press, 1997.

——— . *How to Read the Bible: A Guide to Scripture, Then and Now.* New York: Free Press, 2007.

Levenson, Jon D. *The Hebrew Bible, the Old Testament, and Historical Criticism: Jews and Christians in Biblical Studies.* Louisville: Westminster John Knox, 1993.

——— . *Sinai and Zion: An Entry Into the Jewish Bible.* Minneapolis: Winston, 1985.

Niebuhr, H. Richard. *Christ and Culture.* Expanded ed. San Francisco: HarperSanFrancisco, 2001.

——— . *Radical Monotheism and the Western Tradition.* Louisville: Westminster John Knox, 1993.

——— . *The Responsible Self: An Essay in Christian Moral Philosophy.* Louisville: Westminster John Knox, 1999.

Patte, Daniel. *Ethics of Biblical Interpretation: A Reevaluation.* Louisville: Westminster John Knox, 1995.

Penchansky, David. *What Rough Beast? Images of God in the Hebrew Bible.* Louisville: Westminster John Knox, 1999.

Prior, Michael. *The Bible and Colonialism: A Moral Critique.* Sheffield: Sheffield Academic, 1997.

Smith, William Cantwell. *What Is Scripture? A Comparative Approach.* Minneapolis: Fortress Press, 1993.

Tillich, Paul. *The Socialist Decision.* New York: Harper & Row, 1977.

West, Gerald. *Biblical Hermeneutics of Liberation: Modes of Reading the Bible in the South African Context.* 2nd ed. Maryknoll, N.Y.: Orbis, 1995.

Yerushalmi, Yosef Hayim. *Zakhor: Jewish History and Jewish Memory.* 3nd ed. Seattle: University of Washington Press, 1996.

Young, Jeremy. *The Violence of God and the War on Terror.* New York: Seabury, 2008.

Introductions to the Hebrew Bible (since 1985)

Anderson, Bernhard W. *Understanding the Old Testament.* 4th ed. Englewood Cliffs, N.J.: Prentice-Hall, 1986.

Ceresko, Anthony R. *Introduction to the Old Testament: A Liberation Perspective.* Rev. ed. Maryknoll, N.Y.: Orbis, 2001.

Collins, John J. *Introduction to the Hebrew Bible.* Minneapolis: Fortress Press, 2004.

Coogan, Michael. *The Old Testament: A Historical and Literary Introduction to the Hebrew Scriptures.* New York: Oxford University Press, 2006.

Flanders, Henry J., Robert W. Crapps, and David A. Smith. *People of the Covenant: An Introduction to the Hebrew Bible.* 4th ed. New York: Oxford University Press, 1996.

Harris, Stephen L., and Robert L. Platzner. *The Old Testament: An Introduction to the Hebrew Bible.* Boston: McGraw-Hill, 2003.

Kugel, James L. *How to Read the Bible: A Guide to Scripture, Then and Now.* New York: Free Press, 2007.

LaSor, William S., David A. Hubbard, and Frederick W. Bush. *Old Testament Survey: The Message, Form and Background of the Old Testament.* Rev. ed. Grand Rapids: Eerdmans, 1996.

Mendenhall, George E. *Ancient Israel's Faith and History: An Introduction to the Bible in Context.* Ed. Gary A. Herion. Louisville: Westminster John Knox, 2001.

Rendtorff, Rolf. *The Old Testament: An Introduction.* Philadelphia: Fortress Press, 1986.

Reference Works

The Anchor Bible Dictionary. Ed. David N. Freedman. 6 vols. New York: Doubleday, 1992.

Danker, Frederick W. *Multipurpose Tools for Bible Study.* 5th ed. Minneapolis: Fortress Press, 2003.

Dictionary of Biblical Interpretation. Ed. John H. Hayes. 2 vols. Nashville: Abingdon, 1999.

Encyclopaedia Judaica. Ed. Fred Skolnik. 22 vols. 2nd ed. Detroit: Macmillan Reference / Jerusalem: Keter Publishing House, 2007.

The Encyclopedia of Apocalypticism. Ed. John J. Collins. 3 vols. New York: Continuum, 1998.

Encyclopedia of the Dead Sea Scrolls. Ed. Lawrence H. Schiffman and John C. Vanderkam. 2 vols. New York: Oxford University Press, 2000.

New International Dictionary of Old Testament Theology and Exegesis. Ed. Willem A. VanGemeren. 5 vols. Grand Rapids: Zondervan, 1997.

The New Interpreter's Bible. Ed. Leander E. Keck et al. 12 vols. Nashville: Abingdon, 1994.

The New Encyclopedia of Archaeological Excavations in the Holy Land. Ed. Ephraim Stern. 4 vols. Jerusalem: Israel Exploration Society and Carta / New York: Simon and Schuster, 1992.

The New Interpreter's Dictionary of the Bible. Ed. Katharine Doob Sakenfeld. Nashville: Abingdon Press, 2006–.

The Oxford Encyclopedia of Archaeology in the Near East. Ed. Eric M. Meyers. 5 vols. New York: Oxford University Press, 1997.

Soulen, Richard N., and R. Kendall Soulen. *Handbook of Biblical Criticism.* 3rd ed. Louisville: Westminster John Knox, 2001.

Theological Dictionary of the Old Testament. Ed. G. Johannes Botterweck and Helmer Ringgren. 15 vols. Grand Rapids: Eerdmans, 1977–2006.

Methodology in Hebrew Bible Studies

Barrera, Julio Trebolle. *The Jewish Bible and the Christian Bible: An Introduction to the History of the Bible.* Leiden: Brill / Grand Rapids: Eerdmans, 1998.

Barton, John. *Reading the Old Testament: Method in Biblical Study.* Rev. ed. Louisville: Westminster John Knox, 1996.

Bible and Culture Collective. *The Postmodern Bible.* New Haven: Yale University Press, 1995.

Clines, David J. A. "Methods in Old Testament Study." In *On the Way to the Postmodern: Old Testament Essays, 1967–1998,* 1:23–45. Sheffield: Sheffield Academic Press, 1998.

Keegan, Terence J. *Interpreting the Bible: A Popular Introduction to Biblical Hermeneutics.* New York: Paulist, 1985.

Kugel, James L. *How to Read the Bible: A Guide to Scripture, Then and Now.* New York: Free Press, 2007.

McKenzie, Steven L., and Stephen R. Haynes, eds. *To Each Its Own Meaning: An Introduction to Biblical Criticisms and Their Applications.* Rev. ed. Louisville: Westminster John Knox, 1999.

Morgan, Robert, with John Barton. *Biblical Interpretation.* Oxford Bible Series. Oxford: Oxford University Press, 1988.

Patte, Daniel. *The Religious Dimensions of Biblical Texts: Greimas's Structural Semiotics and Biblical Exegesis.* Atlanta: Scholars Press, 1990.

Segovia, Fernando F., and Stephen D. Moore, eds. *Postcolonial Biblical Criticism: Interdisciplinary Intersections.* London: T & T Clark, 2005.

Yee, Gale A., ed. *Judges and Method: New Approaches in Biblical Studies.* 2nd ed. Minneapolis: Fortress Press, 2007.

The Hebrew Bible and Literary Criticism

Adam, A. K. M. *Handbook of Postmodern Biblical Interpretation.* St. Louis: Chalice, 2000.

———. *What Is Postmodern Biblical Criticism?* Minneapolis: Fortress Press, 1995.

Buss, Martin J. *Biblical Form Criticism in Context.* Sheffield: Sheffield Academic, 1999.

Davies, Phlip R. *Scribes and Schools: The Canonization of the Hebrew Scriptures.* Louisville: Westminster John Knox, 1998.

Dundes, Alan. *Holy Writ as Oral Lit: The Bible as Folklore.* Lanham, Md.: Rowman and Littlefield, 1999.

Exum, J. Cheryl, and David J. A. Clines, eds. *The New Literary Criticism and the Hebrew Bible.* Sheffield: Sheffield Academic, 1993.

Fox, Everett. "English Versions." In *Encyclopaedia Judaica*, 3:611–27. Detroit: Macmillan Reference USA / Jerusalem: Keter Publishing House, 2007.

Gottwald, Norman K. "Social Matrix and Canonical Shape." In *The Hebrew Bible in Its Social World and in Ours*, 177–92. Atlanta: Scholars, 1993.

Green, Barbara. *Mikhail Bakhtin and Biblical Scholarship: An Introduction.* Atlanta: Society of Biblical Literature, 2000.

Hens-Piazza, Gina. *The New Historicism.* Guides to Biblical Scholarship. Minneapolis: Fortress Press, 2002.

Jobling, David, Tina Pippin, and Ronald Schleifer, eds. *The Postmodern Bible Reader.* Oxford: Blackwell, 2001.

McKnight, Edgar V., ed. *Postmodern Uses of the Bible: The Emergence of Reader-Oriented Criticism.* Nashville: Abingdon, 1988.

Metzger, Bruce M. *The Bible in Translation: Ancient and Modern Versions.* Grand Rapids: Baker Academic, 2001.

Patte, Daniel. *The Religious Dimensions of Biblical Texts: Greimas's Structural Semiotics and Biblical Exegesis.* Atlanta: Scholars, 1990.

Sanders, James A. *From Sacred Story to Sacred Text: Canon as Paradigm.* Philadelphia: Fortress Press, 1987.

Schniedewind, William M. *How the Bible Became a Book: The Textualization of Ancient Israel.* New York: Cambridge University Press, 2004.

Sweeney, Marvin A., and Ehud Ben-Zvi, eds. *The Changing Face of Form Criticism for the Twenty-First Century.* Grand Rapids: Eerdmans, 2003.

Tov, Emmanuel. *Textual Criticism of the Hebrew Bible.* Rev. ed. Minneapolis: Fortress Press, 2002.

Trible, Phyllis. *Rhetorical Criticism: Context, Method, and the Book of Jonah.* Minneapolis: Fortress Press, 1994.

The Hebrew Bible and Historical Criticism

Ahlström, Gösta W. *The History of Ancient Palestine from the Paleolithic Period to Alexander's Conquest.* Sheffield: JSOT Press, 1993.

Albertz, Rainer. *Israel in Exile: The History and Literature of the 6th Century B.C.E.* Atlanta: Society of Biblical Literature, 2003.

Appleby, Joyce et al., eds. *Knowledge and Postmodernism in Historical Perspective.* New York: Routledge, 1996.

Banks, Diane. *Writing the History of Israel.* London: T & T Clark, 2006.

Brettler, Marc Zvi. *The Creation of History in Ancient Israel.* London: Routledge, 1995.

Cohen, Shaye J. D. *The Beginnings of Jewishness: Boundaries, Varieties, Uncertainties.* Berkeley: University of California Press, 1999.

Coote, Robert B. *Early Israel: A New Horizon.* Minneapolis: Fortress Press, 1990.

Davies, Philip R. *In Search of "Ancient Israel."* Sheffield: JSOT Press, 1992.

——— . *The Origins of Biblical Israel.* London: T & T Clark, 2007.

Finkelstein, Israel, and Amihai Mazar. *The Quest for the Historical Israel: Debating Archeology and the History of Early Israel.* Ed. Brian B. Schmidt. Atlanta: Society of Biblical Literature, 2007.

Grabbe, Lester L. *Ancient Israel: What Do We Know and How Do We Know It?* London: T & T Clark, 2007.

———, ed. *Can a "History of Israel" Be Written?* Sheffield: Sheffield Academic Press, 1997.

Halpern, Baruch. *The First Historians: The Hebrew Bible and History.* San Francisco: Harper & Row, 1988.

Hayes. John H., and J. Maxwell Miller. *A History of Ancient Israel and Judah.* 2nd ed. Louisville: Westminster John Knox, 2006.

Isserlin, B. S. J. *The Israelites.* New York: Thames and Hudson, 1998.

Kofoed, Jens Bruun. *Text and History: Historiography and the Study of the Biblical Text.* Winona Lake, Ind.: Eisenbrauns, 2005.

Lemche, Niels P. *The Israelites in History and Tradition.* Louisville: Westminster John Knox, 1998.

———. *Prelude to Israel's Past: Background and Beginnings of Israelite History and Identity.* Peabody, Mass.: Hendrickson, 1998.

Liverani, Mario. *Israel's History and the History of Israel.* London: Equinox, 2005.

Pixley, Jorge. *Biblical Israel: A People's History.* Minneapolis: Fortress Press, 1992.

Soggin, J. Alberto. *An Introduction to the History of Israel and Judah.* 2nd rev. ed. London: SCM, 1993.

Van Seters, John. *In Search of History: Historiography in the Ancient World and the Origins of Biblical History.* New Haven: Yale University Press, 1983.

White, Hayden. *Metahistory: The Historical Imagination in Nineteenth-Century Europe.* Baltimore: Johns Hopkins University Press, 1973.

———. *Tropics of Discourse: Essays in Cultural Criticism.* Baltimore: Johns Hopkins University Press, 1990.

Whitelam, Keith W. *The Invention of Ancient Israel and the Silencing of Palestinian History.* London: Routledge, 1996.

Society, Economy, and Politics in the Hebrew Bible

Alt, Albrecht. *Essays on Old Testament History and Religion*, 133–259. Oxford: Basil Blackwell, 1966 [1925–51].

Bendix, Reinhard. *Kings or People: Power and the Mandate to Rule.* Berkeley: University of California Press, 1978.

Berman, Joshua. *Biblical Revolutions: The Transformation of Social and Political Thought in the Ancient Near East.* New York: Oxford University Press, 2008.

Biale, David. *Power and Powerlessness in Jewish History.* New York: Schocken Books, 1986.

Carter, Charles E. *The Emergence of Yehud in the Persian Period: A Social and Demographic Study.* Sheffield: Sheffield Academic, 1999.

Carter, Charles E., and Carol L. Meyers, eds. *Community, Identity, and Ideology. Social Science Approaches to the Hebrew Bible.* Winona Lake, Ind.: Eisenbrauns, 1996.

Chalcraft, David J., ed. *Social-Scientific Old Testament Criticism: A Sheffield Reader.* Sheffield: Sheffield Academic, 1997.

Chaney, Marvin L. "Ancient Palestinian Peasant Movements and the Formation of Premonarchic Israel." In *Palestine in Transition: The Emergence of Ancient Israel,* eds. D. N. Freedman and D. F. Graf, 39–90. Sheffield: Almond, 1983.

———. "Debt Easement in Israelite History and Tradition." In *The Bible and the Politics of Exegesis: Essays in Honor of Norman K. Gottwald on His Sixty-Fifth Birthday,* eds. David Jobling et al., 127–39. Cleveland: Pilgrim, 1991.

———. "Models Matter: Political Economy and Micah 6:9-15." In *Ancient Israel: The Old Testament in Its Social Context,* ed. Philip F. Esler, 145–60. Minneapolis: Fortress Press, 2006.

———. "Systemic Study of the Israelite Monarchy." *Semeia* 37 (1986): 53–76.

Cook, Stephen L. *The Social Roots of Biblical Yahwism.* Atlanta: Society of Biblical Literature, 2004.

Coote, Robert B., ed. *Elijah and Elisha in Socioliterary Perspective.* Atlanta: Scholars, 1992.

———. "Israel, Social and Economic Development of." In *NIDB* 3:138–43.

Coote, Robert B., and Keith W. Whitelam. *The Emergence of Early Israel in Historical Perspective.* Sheffield: Almond, 1987.

Davies, Philip R., and John H. Halligan, eds. *Second Temple Studies 3: Studies in Politics, Class and Material Culture.* Sheffield: Sheffield Academic, 2002.

Dearman, J. Andrew. *Property Rights in the Eighth-Century Prophets.* Atlanta: Scholars, 1988.

Deist, Ferdinand E. *The Material Culture of the Bible: An Introduction.* Sheffield: Sheffield Academic, 2000.

Domeris, William Robert. *Touching the Heart of God: The Social Construction of Poverty among Biblical Peasants.* London: T & T Clark, 2007.

Esler, Philip F., ed. *Ancient Israel: The Old Testament in Its Social Context.* Minneapolis: Fortress Press, 2006.

Fager, Jeffrey A. *Land Tenure and the Biblical Jubilee: Uncovering Hebrew Ethics through the Sociology of Knowledge.* Sheffield: Sheffield Academic, 1993.

Flanagan, James W. *David's Social Drama: A Hologram of Israel's Iron Age.* Sheffield: Almond, 1988.

Fox, Nili Sacher. *In the Service of the King: Officialdom in Ancient Israel and Judah.* Cincinnati: Hebrew Union College Press, 2000.

Frick, Frank S. *The Formation of the State in Ancient Israel.* Sheffield: Almond, 1985.

———. "Social Science Methods and Theories of Significance for the Study of the Israelite Monarchy." *Semeia* 37 (1986): 9–52.

Gottwald, Norman K. "Government, OT." In *NIDB* 2:644–54.

———. *The Hebrew Bible in Its Social World and in Ours.* Atlanta: Scholars, 1993.

———. "A Hypothesis about Social Class in Monarchic Israel in the Light of Contemporary Studies of Social Class and Social Stratification." In *The Hebrew Bible in Its Social World and in Ours,* 139–64. Atlanta: Scholars, 1993.

———. "Israel, Origins of." In *NIDB* 3:132–38.

———. *The Politics of Ancient Israel.* Louisville: Westminster John Knox, 2001.

———. "The Puzzling Politics of Ancient Israel." In *Reading from Right to Left: Essays on the Hebrew Bible in Honour of David J. A. Clines,* ed. J. Cheryl Exum and H. G. M. Williamson, 196–204. Sheffield: Sheffield Academic Press, 2003.

———. "Social Class as an Analytic and Hermeneutical Category in Biblical Studies." *Journal of Biblical Literature* 112 (1993): 3–20.

———. *The Tribes of Yahweh: A Sociology of the Religion of Liberated Israel, 1250-1050 B.C.E.* Twentieth anniversary edition with new preface. Sheffield: Sheffield Academic, 1999.

Gottwald, Norman K., and Richard A. Horsley, eds. *The Bible and Liberation: Political and Social Hermeneutics.* Rev. ed. Maryknoll, N.Y.: Orbis, 1993.

Hamilton, Jeffries M. *Social Justice and Deuteronomy: The Case of Deuteronomy 15.* Atlanta: Scholars, 1992.

Hamilton, Mark W. *The Body Royal: The Social Poetics of Kingship in Ancient Israel.* Leiden: Brill, 2005.

Holladay, John S., Jr. "The Kingdoms of Israel and Judah: Political and Economic Centralization in the Iron IIA-B (ca 1000–750 B.C.E.)." In *The Archaeology of Society in the Holy Land,* ed. Thomas E. Levy, 368–98. New York: Facts on File, 1995.

Hopkins, David C. *The Highlands of Canaan: Agricultural life in the Early Iron Age.* Decatur, Ga.: Almond, 1985.

———. "Life in Ancient Palestine." In *NIB* 1:213–27.

Hutton, Rodney R. *Charisma and Authority in Israelite Society.* Minneapolis: Fortress Press, 1994.

Kessler, Rainer. *The Social History of Ancient Israel: An Introduction.* Minneapolis: Fortress Press, 2008.

King, Philip J., and Lawrence E. Stager. *Life in Biblical Israel.* Louisville: Westminster John Knox, 2001.

Lowery, Richard. *The Reforming Kings: Cult and Society in First Temple Judah.* Sheffield: JSOT Press, 1991.

McNutt, Paula M. *Reconstructing the Society of Ancient Israel.* Louisville: Wesminster John Knox, 1999.

Nakanose, Shigeyuki. *Josiah's Passover: Sociology and the Liberating Bible.* Maryknoll: Orbis, 1993.

Premnath, Devadasan. *Eighth Century Prophets: A Social Analysis.* St. Louis: Chalice, 2003.

Sharkansky, Ira. *Ancient and Modern Israel: An Exploration of Political Parallels.* Albany: State University of New York Press, 1991.

———. *Israel and Its Bible: A Political Analysis.* New York: Garland, 1996.

Sneed, Mark R., ed. *Concepts of Class in Ancient Israel.* Atlanta: Scholars, 1999.

Stevens, Marty E. *Temples, Tithes, and Taxes.* Peabody, Mass.: Hendrickson, 2006.

Strong, John T., and Steven S. Tuell, eds. *Constituting the Community: Studies on the Polity of Ancient Israel in Honor of S. Dean McBride Jr.* Winona Lake, Ind.: Eisenbrauns, 2005.

Walsh, Jerome. *The Mighty from Their Thrones; Power in the Biblical Tradition.* Philadelphia: Fortress Press, 1987.

Walzer, Michael. *Exodus and Revolution.* New York: Basic, 1984.

Weisman, Ze'ev. *Political Satire in the Bible.* Atlanta: Scholars, 1998.

Wilson, Robert. *Prophecy and Society in Ancient Israel.* Philadelphia: Fortress Press, 1980.

Religion in the Hebrew Bible

Ackerman, Susan. *Under Every Green Tree: Popular Religion in Sixth-Century Judah.* Atlanta: Scholars, 1992.

Albertz, Rainer. *A History of Israelite Religion in the Old Testament Period.* 2 vols. Louisville: Westminster John Knox, 1994.

———. "Israelite Religion, History of." In *NIDB* 3:145–61.

Anderson, Gary A. *Sacrifices and Offerings in Ancient Israel: Studies in their Social and Political Importance.* Atlanta: Scholars, 1987.

Anderson, Gary A., and Saul M. Olyan, eds. *Priesthood and Cult in Ancient Israel.* Sheffield: Sheffield Academic, 1991.

Barton, John. *Understanding Old Testament Ethics: Approaches and Explorations.* Louisville: Westminster John Knox, 2003.

Bird, Phyllis A. "The Place of Women in the Israelite Cultus." In *Ancient Israelite Religion,* ed. P. Miller et al., 397–419. Philadelphia: Fortress Press, 1987.

Blenkinsopp, Joseph. *Sage, Priest, Prophet: Religious and Intellectual Leadership in Ancient Israel.* Louisville: Westminster John Knox, 1995.

Bloch-Smith, Elizabeth. *Judahite Burial Practices and Beliefs about the Dead.* Sheffield: JTOS Press, 1992.

Burch, Bruce C. "Ethics in the OT." In *NIDB* 2:338–48.

Coogan, Michael D. "Canaanite Origins and Lineage: Reflections on the Religion of Ancient Israel." In *Ancient Israelite Religion,* eds. P. Miller et al., 115–26. Philadelphia: Fortress Press, 1987.

Cryer, Frederick H. *Divination in Ancient Israel and Its Near Eastern Environment.* Sheffield: JSOT Press, 1994.

Day, John, ed. *Temple and Worship in Biblical Israel.* London: T & T Clark, 2005.

————. *Yahweh and the Gods and Goddesses of Canaan.* Sheffield: Sheffield Academic, 2000.

Dearman, J. Andrew. *Religion and Culture in Ancient Israel.* Peabody, Mass.: Hendirckson, 1992.

de Moor, Johannes C. *The Rise of Yahwism: The Roots of Israelite Monotheism.* Leuven: Leuven University Press/Peeters, 1990.

Dever, William G. "The Contribution of Archaeology to the Study of Canaanite and Early Israelite Religion." In *Ancient Israelite Religion,* ed. P. Miller et al., 209–47. Philadelphia: Fortress Press, 1987.

Edelman, Diana V., ed. *The Triumph of Elohim: From Yahwisms to Judaisms.* Grand Rapids: Eerdmans, 1995.

Eilberg-Schwartz, Howard. *The Savage in Judaism: An Anthropology of Israelite Religion and Ancient Judaism.* Bloomington: Indiana University Press, 1990.

Gnuse, Robert K. *No Other Gods: Emergent Monotheism in Israel.* Sheffield: Sheffield Academic, 1997.

Gottwald, Norman K., and Richard A. Horsley, eds. *The Bible and Liberation: Political and Social Hermeneutics.* Maryknoll, N.Y.: Orbis, 1993.

Grabbe, Lester L. *Priests, Prophets, Diviners, Sages: A Socio-Historical Study of Religious Specialists in Ancient Israel.* Valley Forge, Pa.: Trinity Press International, 1995.

Graham, M. Patrick, Rick R. Marrs, and Steven L. McKenzie, eds. *Worship and the Hebrew Bible: Essays in Honor of John T. Willis.* Sheffield: Sheffield Academic, 1999.

Hadley, Judith M. *The Cult of Asherah in Ancient Israel and Judah: Evidence for a Hebrew Goddess.* Cambridge: Cambridge University Press, 2000.

Hendel, Ronald S. "The Social Origins of the Aniconic Tradition in Ancient Israel." *Catholic Biblical Quarterly* 50 (1988): 365–82.

Hillers, Delbert R. *Covenant: The History of a Biblical Idea.* Baltimore: Johns Hopkins University Press, 1969.

Houston, Walter. *Purity and Monotheism: Clean and Unclean Animals in Biblical Law.* Sheffield: JSOT Press, 1993.

Keel, Othmar, and Christoph Uehlinger. *Gods, Goddesses, and Images of God in Ancient Israel.* Minneapolis: Fortress Press, 1998.

Kennedy, James M. "The Social Background of Early Israel's Rejection of Cultic Imagery: A Proposal." *Biblical Theology Bulletin* 17 (1987): 138–44.

Lang, Bernhard. *Monotheism and the Prophetic Minority.* Sheffield: JSOT Press, 1983.

Lewis, Theodore J. *Cults of the Dead in Ancient Israel and Judah.* Atlanta: Scholars, 1989.

Meyers, Carol L. "Temple, Jerusalem." In *ABD* 6:350–69.

Millar, William R. *Priesthood in Ancient Israel.* St. Louis: Chalice, 2001.

Miller, Patrick D. *The Divine Warrior in Early Israel.* Cambridge: Harvard University Press, 1973.

————. *The Religion of Ancient Israel.* Louisville: Westminster John Knox, 2000.

————. *They Cried to the Lord: The Form and Theology of Biblical Prayer.* Minneapolis: Fortress Press, 1994.

Mowinckel, Sigmund. *The Psalms in Israel's Worship*. Oxford: Blackwell, 1962 / Sheffield: JSOT Press, 1992.

Niditch, Susan. *Ancient Israelite Religion*. New York: Oxford University Press, 1997.

Olyan, Saul M. *Asherah and the Cult of Yahweh in Israel*. Atlanta: Scholars, 1988.

Rehm, Merlin D. "Levites and Priests." In *ABD* 4:297–310.

Rendtorff, Rolf. *The Covenant Formula: An Exegetical and Theological Investigation*. Edinburgh: T & T Clark, 1998.

Smith, Mark S. *The Early History of God: Yahweh and the Other Deities in Ancient Israel*. 2nd ed. Grand Rapids: Eerdmans, 2002.

———. *The Memoirs of God: History, Memory, and the Experience of the Divine in Ancient Israel*. Minneapolis: Fortress Press, 2004.

Toews, Wesley I. *Monarchy and Religious Institution in Israel under Jeroboam*. Atlanta: Scholars, 1993.

Vanderkam, James C. "Feasts and Fasts." In *NIDB* 2:443–47.

Zevit, Ziony. *The Religions of Ancient Israel: A Synthesis of Parallactic Approaches*. New York: Continuum, 2001.

Theology and Ideology in the Old Testament

Adorno, Theodor W. *Kierkegaard: Construction of the Aesthetic*. Minneapolis: University of Minnesota Press, 1989.

Boer, Roland. *Marxist Criticism of the Bible*. London: T & T Clark, 2003.

Brueggemann, Walter. *Theology of the Old Testament: Testimony, Dispute, Advocacy*. Minneapolis: Fortress Press, 1997.

Carroll, Robert P. *The Bible as a Problem for Christianity*. Philadelphia: Trinity Press International, 1991.

Childs, Brevard S. *Biblical Theology of the Old and New Testaments*. Minneapolis: Fortress Press, 1992.

Clements, Ronald E. *Old Testament Theology: A Fresh Approach*. Louisville: Westminster John Knox, 1979.

Clines, David J. A. *Interested Parties: The Ideology of Writers and Readers of the Hebrew Bible*. Sheffield: Sheffield Academic, 1995.

Cosgrove, Charles H. *Appealing to Scripture in Moral Discourse: Five Hermeneutical Rules*. Grand Rapids: Eerdmans, 2002.

Delaney, Carol. *Abraham on Trial: The Social Legacy of Biblical Myth*. Princeton: Princeton University Press, 1998.

Diamond, James S. *Homeland or Holy Land? The "Canaanite" Critique of Israel*. Bloomington: Indiana University Press, 1986.

Eagleton, Terry. *Criticism and Ideology: A Study in Marxist Literary Theory*. London: Verso, 1991. Rpt. with new introduction, 2006.

———. *Ideology: An Introduction*. London: Verso, 1991.

Gerstenberger, Erhard. *Theologies in the Old Testament*. Minneapolis: Fortress Press, 2002.

Girard, René. *Violence and the Sacred*. Baltimore: Johns Hopkins University Press, 1977.

Gnuse, Robert K. *The Old Testament and Process Theology*. St. Louis: Chalice, 2000.

Gottwald, Norman K. "Ideology and Ideologies in Israelite Prophecy." In *Prophets and Paradigms: Essays in Honor of Gene M. Tucker*, 136–49. Sheffield: Sheffield Academic, 1966.

———. "Rhetorical, Historical, and Ontological Counterpoints in Doing Old Testament Theology." In *God in the Fray: A Tribute to Walter Brueggemann*, eds. Tod Linafelt and Timothy K. Beal, 11–23. Minneapolis: Fortress Press, 1998.

Habel, Norman C. *The Land Is Mine: Six Biblical Land Ideologies.* Overtures to Biblical Theology. Minneapolis: Fortress Press, 1995.

Houston, Walter J. *Contending for Justice: Ideologies and Theologies of Social Justice in the Old Testament.* London: T & T Clark, 2006.

Jameson, Frederic. *The Political Unconscious: Narrative as a Socially Symbolic Act.* Ithaca: Cornell University Press, 1981.

Jobling, David. "Deconstruction and the Political Analysis of Biblical Texts: A Jamesonian Reading of Psalm 72." *Semeia* 59 (1992): 95–127.

———. *1 Samuel.* Collegeville, Minn.: Liturgical, 1998.

Kugel, James L. *How to Read the Bible: A Guide to Scripture, Then and Now.* New York: Free Press, 2007.

Levenson, Jon D. *Creation and the Persistence of Evil: The Jewish Drama of Divine Omnipotence.* Princeton: Princeton University Press, 1994.

———. *The Death and Resurrection of the Beloved Son: The Transformation of Child Sacrifice in Judaism and Christianity.* New Haven: Yale University Press, 1993.

Oden, Robert A., Jr. *The Bible Without Theology: The Theological Tradition and Alternatives to It.* San Francisco: Harper & Row, 1987.

Penchansky, David. *The Betrayal of God: Ideological Conflict in Job.* Louisville: Westminster John Knox, 1990.

———. *What Rough Beast? Images of God in the Hebrew Bible.* Louisville: Westminster John Knox, 1999.

Pleins, J. David, *The Social Visions of the Hebrew Bible: A Theological Introduction.* Louisville: Westminster John Knox, 2001.

Prior, Michael P., *The Bible and Colonialism: A Moral Critique.* Sheffield; Sheffield Academic, 1997.

Segovia, Fernando F., *Decolonizing Biblical Studies: A View from the Margins.* Maryknoll, N.Y.: Orbis, 2000.

Segovia, Fernando F., and Mary Ann Tolbert, eds. *Teaching the Bible: The Discourses and Politics of Biblical Pedagogy.* Maryknoll, N.Y.: Orbis, 1998.

Soulen, R. Kendall *The God of Israel and Christian Theology.* Minneapolis: Fortress Press, 1996.

Thompson, John B. *Ideology and Modern Culture: Critical Social Theory in the Era of Mass Communication.* Stanford: Stanford University Press, 1990.

Tillich, Paul. *Biblical Religion and the Search for Ultimate Reality.* Chicago: Chicago University Press, 1955.

———. *The Socialist Decision.* New York: Harper & Row, 1977.

Young, Jeremy. *The Violence of God and the War on Terror.* New York: Seabury, 2008.

Zizek, Slavoj, ed. *Mapping Ideology.* New York: Verso, 1994.

The Hebrew Bible and Feminist Criticism

Anderson, Cheryl B. *Women, Ideology, and Violence: Critical Theory and the Construction of Gender in the Book of the Covenant and the Deuteronomic Law.* London: T & T Clark, 2004.

Bach, Alice, ed. *The Pleasure of Her Text: Feminist Readings of Biblical and Historical Texts.* Philadelphia: Trinity Press International, 1990.

———. *Women in the Hebrew Bible: A Reader.* New York: Routledge, 1999.

Bal, Mieke. *Lethal Love: Feminist Literary Readings of Biblical Love Stories.* Bloomington: Indiana University Press, 1987.

———. *Murder and Difference: Gender, Genre, and Scholarship on Sisera's Death.* Bloomington: Indiana University Press, 1988.

Bird, Phyllis A. *Missing Persons and Mistaken Identities: Women and Gender in Ancient Israel.* Overtures to Biblical Theology. Minneapolis: Fortress Press, 1997.

Brenner, Athalya, ed. *A Feminist Companion to Esther, Judith, and Susanna.* London: T & T Clark, 2004.

———, ed. *A Feminist Companion to the Latter Prophets.* Sheffield: Sheffield Academic, 1995.

———. *The Intercourse of Knowledge: On Gendered Sex and Desire in the Hebrew Bible.* Leiden: Brill, 1997.

Camp, Claudia. *Wise, Strange, and Holy: The Strange Woman and the Making of the Bible.* Sheffield: Sheffield Academic, 2000.

Collins, Adela Yarbro, ed. *Feminist Perspectives on Biblical Scholarship.* Chico, Calif.: Scholars, 1985.

Day, Peggy L., ed. *Gender and Difference in Ancient Israel.* Minneapolis: Fortress Press, 1989.

Delaney, Carol. *Abraham on Trial: The Social Legacy of a Biblical Myth.* Princeton: Princeton University Press, 1998.

Dube, Musa W. *Postcolonial Feminist Interpretation of the Bible.* St. Louis: Chalice, 2000.

Eilberg-Schwartz, Howard. *God's Phallus and Other Problems for Men and Monotheism.* Boston: Beacon, 1994.

Exum, J. Cheryl. "The Ethics of Biblical Violence Against Women." In *The Second Sheffield Colloquium,* 248–71. Sheffield: Sheffield Academic, 1995.

———. *Plotted, Shot, and Painted: Cultural Representations of Biblical Wisdom.* Sheffield: Sheffield Academic, 1996.

Frymer-Kensky, Tikva. *In the Wake of the Goddesses: Women, Culture, and the Biblical Transformation of Pagan Myth.* New York: Free Press, 1992.

Handelman, Susan A. *The Slayers of Moses: The Emergence of Rabbinic Interpretation in Modern Literary Theory.* Albany: State University of New York Press, 1982.

King, Ursula, ed. *Feminist Theology from the Third World.* Maryknoll, N.Y.: Orbis / London: SPCK, 1994.

Meyers, Carol. *Discovering Eve: Ancient Israelite Women in Context.* New York: Oxford University Press, 1988.

Ortner, Sherry B. and Harriet Whitehead, eds. *Sexual Meanings: The Cultural Construction of Gender and Sexuality.* New York: Cambridge University Press, 1981.

Plaskow, Judith. *Standing Again at Sinai: Judaism from a Feminist Perspective.* San Francisco: Harper & Row, 1990.

Russell, Letty M., ed. *Feminist Interpretation of the Bible.* Philadelphia: Westminster, 1985.

Russell, Letty M., and J. Shannon Clarkson, eds. *Dictionary of Feminist Theologies.* Louisville: Westminster John Knox, 1996.

Terrien, Samuel L. *Till the Heart Sings: A Biblical Theology of Manhood and Womanhood.* New ed. Grand Rapids: Eerdmans / Dearborn: Dove, 2004.

Trible, Phyllis. *God and the Rhetoric of Sexuality.* Overtures to Biblical Theology. Philadelphia: Fortress Press, 1978.

———. *Texts of Terror: Literary-Feminist Readings of Biblical Narratives.* Overtures to Biblical Theology. Philadelphia: Fortress Press, 1984.

Yee. Gale A. *Poor Banished Children of Eve: Women as Evil in the Hebrew Bible.* Minneapolis: Fortress Press, 2003.